ALEXIS WRIGHT

Tracker

STORIES OF
TRACKER TILMOUTH

GIRAMONDO

FIRST PUBLISHED IN 2017
FROM THE WRITING & SOCIETY RESEARCH CENTRE
AT THE UNIVERSITY OF WESTERN SYDNEY
BY THE GIRAMONDO PUBLISHING COMPANY
PO BOX 752
ARTARMON NSW 1570 AUSTRALIA
WWW.GIRAMONDOPUBLISHING.COM

© ALEXIS WRIGHT 2017

DESIGNED BY HARRY WILLIAMSON
TYPESET BY ANDREW DAVIES
IN 11/15 PT GARAMOND 3

PRINTED AND BOUND BY LIGARE BOOK PRINTERS
DISTRIBUTED IN AUSTRALIA BY NEWSOUTH BOOKS

A CATALOGUE RECORD FOR THIS
BOOK IS AVAILABLE FROM THE
NATIONAL LIBRARY OF AUSTRALIA

ISBN: 978-1-925336-33-7 (PBK)

ALL RIGHTS RESERVED.
NO PART OF THIS PUBLICATION MAY BE
REPRODUCED, STORED IN A RETRIEVAL
SYSTEM OR TRANSMITTED IN ANY FORM OR
BY ANY MEANS ELECTRONIC, MECHANICAL,
PHOTOCOPYING OR OTHERWISE WITHOUT THE
PRIOR PERMISSION OF THE PUBLISHER.

9 8 7 6 5 4

PRAISE FOR TRACKER:

'A magnificent work of collaborative storytelling.' THE AGE

'A unique, majestic biography. It is one man's story told by many voices, almost operatic in scale…the book sings with insight and Tracker's unique humour.' STELLA PRIZE CITATION

'Wright builds, as much as anyone is able to in writing, a detailed portrait of a complex man, whose vision "to sculpt land, country and people into a brilliant future on a grand scale" is inevitably accompanied by an irrepressible humour and suspicion of authority.' THE GUARDIAN

'Tilmouth was a man who worked through conversation and yarn more than with paper and pen, and this is a book about the place of the story in Indigenous culture and politics as much as it is about Tracker himself.' THE MONTHLY

'[Wright] enacts the complex relationship between self and community that a Western biography could not…There is a cumulative power in the repetitions, backtrackings and digressions the formula necessitates: a sinuous, elegant accommodation of selves. It is a book as epical in form and ambition as the life it describes.' THE AUSTRALIAN

'Wright's brace of ineffable, awkward, uncanny novels will be unravelled and enjoyed by readers when other contemporary fiction is forgotten. *Tracker*, a book performed by a folk ensemble rather than a solo virtuoso, adds to her enduring non-fiction oeuvre that captures the unique ground-level realpolitik of Aboriginal Australia.' AUSTRALIAN BOOK REVIEW

'Alexis Wright is one of the most important voices in our literary landscape…This is a landmark work – epic in its scope and empathy.' READINGS

ALSO BY ALEXIS WRIGHT

PLAINS OF PROMISE
TAKE POWER (AS EDITOR)
GROG WAR
CROIRE EN L'INCROYABLE
LE PACTE DU SERPENT ARC-EN-CIEL
CARPENTARIA
THE SWAN BOOK

FOR THE TILMOUTH FAMILY

CONTENTS

Introduction 1

PROLOGUE
The Warlpiri Invasion of Europe 19

I. TRYING TO GET THE STORY STRAIGHT
Have Scone, Will Travel 29
They Had Nowhere to Put Us 57
He Worked The Crowd, You Know 65
Mad Enough to Try Anything 96

II. BECOMING DANGEROUS
The Troika 115
It's a Scientific Endeavour 136
Chief Was the Chief 143
I Know It All Backwards 161
You'll Never Get Rid of Me, I'm Like a Virus 181
Off to the Next Idea Already 191
Arise Ye Aborigine, I Recognise Thee 214

III. THE INSPIRATIONAL THINKER
Look! I Don't Like Your Donkey 239
Dare to Dream 257
I Am Counted as a Pet Nigger 275
The Human Sewer Rat 293

IV. THE VISION SPLENDID
A Bit of Heaven 343
Fiddling While Rome Burns 356
The Argument Is, We Are Excluded from the Argument 379
The Only Protection You Can Afford 398
Big Name, No Blankets 416
The Space That No One Really Wanted 450
We Are Going to Make This Map 465
My Agenda Is to Set Up a Food Factory 476
The Deal Is to Do a Deal 503

V. THE UNRELIABLE WITNESS
You're Supposed to Kill It Before You Cook It 517
Big Chief, Little Laptop 534
Hello Natives, How Are You? 542
Feeding Cream to Pigs 555
The Greatest Footballer That Ever Played 567
Travelling with the Ancients 576

List of People, Places and Organisations 583
Contributor Biographies 609
Acknowledgements 617

LIST OF ACRONYMS

ABA Aboriginals Benefit Account
ACF Australian Conservation Foundation
ACTU Australian Council of Trade Unions
ADC Aboriginal Development Commission
ALP Australian Labor Party
AMSANT Aboriginal Medical Services Alliance Northern Territory
APG Aboriginal Provisional Government
ATSIC Aboriginal and Torres Strait Islander Commission
CAAMA Central Australia Aboriginal Media Association
CAAPA Central Australian Aboriginal Pastoralist Association
CAAPU Central Australia Aboriginal Pastoral Unit
CAEPR Centre for Aboriginal Economic Policy Research
CANCA Combined Aboriginal Nations of Central Australia
CAO Combined Aboriginal Organisations of Central Australia
CDEP Community Development Employment Program
CFMEU Construction, Forestry, Mining and Energy Union
CLC Central Land Council
CLP Country Liberal Party
CRA Conzinc Riotinto of Australia Limited (now Rio Tinto)
DAA Department of Aboriginal Affairs

EBA Enterprise Bargaining Agreement
ERA Energy Resources of Australia Ltd
GMAAAC Granites Mine Affected Areas Aboriginal Corporation
IAD Institute for Aboriginal Development
IBA Indigenous Business Australia
ILC Indigenous Land Corporation
ILUA Indigenous Land Use Agreement
IPA Indigenous Protected Area
JCALM Joint Council on Aboriginal Land and Mining
KLC Kimberley Land Council
NAIDOC National Aboriginal and Islander Day Observance Committee
NAILSMA North Australian Indigenous Land and Sea Management Alliance
NARU North Australia Research Unit
NITV National Indigenous Television
NLC Northern Land Council
NTER Northern Territory National Emergency Response ('the Intervention')
PUP Palmer United Party
SIHIP Strategic Indigenous Housing and Infrastructure Program
TO Traditional owner

Introduction

Alexis Wright

How do you tell an impossible story, one that is almost too big to contain in a single book? A hunter of words might pace around the countryside in an endless quest like Nabokov with his butterfly net to get closer to the real thing, but writers of stories know that some distances are too great and might never be crossed, and will remain a mystery if the rare thing does not want to be caught, does not want to give up all of its secrets.

In all honesty, an Aboriginal writer would admit to being hard-pressed to understand all the nuances and depths of differences, or what is really in the heart of another countryman's or countrywoman's song, the deep inner spirit of their traditional country, and its full significance in our world. You cannot. Too much has happened. Too much about this country is never resolved, and this is also what has shaped us. And we learn to guard what we know too much.

The big question for us now is what our era represents. What kind of people are we? We are becoming more complicated. Were we ever more individualistic in spirit than we are today, even though we remain strongly connected traditionally, culturally, socially, economically, or by colour, identity, race politics, or by any of the characteristics observed when others look at us, and on our behalf, either to separate us, or to define us as one people? This is a country where you always hear that Aboriginal people are like this, or like that – but were we ever one homogenous mass, with exactly the same thoughts, the same ideas, goals, ambitions? What are the border lines? Where are the transgression points precisely?

Only the holders of these inner truths will know what is truly on their minds. This is why it will always be difficult to capture, with any great deal of confidence, the full human complexities of the contemporary Aboriginal world – our hearth, and our heart, of where we are at in our contentious time – where the survival of our culture continues to be challenged, and we deal with each and every challenge.

In 2015, on the sad occasion of Tracker Tilmouth's memorial in Alice Springs, he was described by his good friend, the Central Australian Aboriginal economist Owen Cole, as the champion of the have-nots. Tracker would not have called himself a saint, nor would he have believed that he was God's gift to humankind, but he was regarded as one of the most influential and selfless Aboriginal visionaries of his time. He was an Eastern Arrernte man who was born in 1954. He was the sixth child in a family of eight children who were removed from their father Roy Tilmouth and family in Alice Springs after their mother, Betty, died in the late 1950s. Tracker was about four years of age. His five older brothers and sister – the Nayda children of his mother's first marriage, whom the authorities deemed were 'lighter skinned' – were sent south, and into institutional care for so-called half-caste Aboriginal children in Adelaide.

The 'dark ones' – Tracker and his two younger brothers, William aged three and Patrick who was a baby – were sent north, to Croker Island, a thousand kilometres away from Central Australia. The official reason for creating so much distance was so the families of the children would never have any influence over their upbringing. Tracker and his two younger brothers would spend the next decade growing up on Croker Island, *and did not know that our older brothers and sister existed*.[1] They were adults when they were eventually reunited with their siblings on the Nayda side of the family. This system, where government authorities had enormous power to remove Aboriginal children from their families and to place them in missions, state-run reserves or foster care, was part of the unsuccessful policy of assimilation that had operated across Australia for many decades.

Whatever happened to Tracker in life, he never saw himself as anyone's victim, nor would he allow anyone to treat him as a victim.

---

1. Interview with Tracker Tilmouth, *Guestroom*, ABC Radio Darwin, 30 April 2010.

He became a force to be reckoned with. Everything about him was epical. His mind was shaped through the influence of books, observation, and dreaming of what lay beyond his stolen-generation childhood on the Croker Island Mission. When he was a young man living back in Central Australia, his mind was shaped by powerful Aboriginal men and women of his father's generation, such as Bess Liddle and the late Arthur and Milton Liddle, and through the deep cultural knowledge and influence of senior law men, the feared red ochre men of the Western Desert traditional domain who joked and laughed with Tracker as he drove with them around their country.

Many say that Tracker was bigger than life, and when he died from heart and cancer complications in 2015 at the age of 62, he left a chasm in the hearts of many people. In his life, he had made space for himself in the world of those who enjoyed the highest influence in Australia, as he did in the lives of the many Aboriginal people who knew him in their towns and communities, or living out in the bush across the country. With a great sense of fun, he challenged people with his endless wit and intellect. He made himself understandable in any situation. While speaking to eight hundred traditional landowners from across remote lands in Central Australia at the Kalkaringi Aboriginal Constitutional Convention in 1998, he told them: *I have got a sore arse from being kicked in the arse in Canberra from them mob telling me we get too much in the Territory*. He knew how to find people and to bombard them with ideas of how to develop an Aboriginal economy. The ideas were often huge, and necessary he thought, to create real Aboriginal economic self-sufficiency to safeguard the future of Aboriginal culture and homelands, or in other words, give true meaning to what he called *the enjoyment of land rights*.

Through Tracker's working life, many Aboriginal people, and others associated with them, sought his help and advice, and trusted him. He always made himself available to them. There would not be many people in this country who would have had the capacity, willingness or energy to go where he travelled in his lifetime, or equal the pace of his travelling, or the breadth of his thinking and ideas, which he spread around the country through his many different connections.

Most would say that there was nothing conventional about Tracker.

He created stories wherever he went. He was among the most extraordinary contemporary story-makers in the Aboriginal world. He was the story. The stories about what he said or did are legendary. Some are about Tracker with his number-whatever-it-was Akubra on his head, speaking to some government minister in Canberra on his mobile loudly enough so everyone could hear, while walking unannounced into a crowded meeting room – big or small it did not matter – taking over the proceedings, and requesting someone make him a cup of tea. He did this all the time. He would stay long enough, interrupting whatever they were talking about, while fearlessly dishing out his humour and criticism, and shocking into silence anyone who tried to remind him it was not his meeting. Continuing on, he would drive home to them a situation happening in the Aboriginal world that he thought they were responsible for, but had failed to see, or to comprehend what needed to be done about it. He would tell them how to attend to this situation, list a number of government threats that would affect their ineptitude, and finish by saying they ought to admit failure and immediately resign from their jobs. He called this *rattling the chains*. Others tell stories of his shocking irreverence. For instance, while the members of the national Aboriginal leadership were meeting together to talk seriously about the complex legal implications of native title after the *Mabo* decision, Tracker told them that native title was just a donkey. It was not the big black stallion that everyone thought it was.

    Tracker was a deadly serious man, but he had an innate way of knowing how to get to his audience through his sense of fun, and his seeing the absolute ridiculousness of what Aboriginal people were forced to deal with. The force he worked to springs from the modern world of Aboriginal people, which is epical in its ability to make stories happen, and to tell the stories of what has happened. This practice for story-making and story-keeping, with its roots in traditional culture, was the main dancing ground for Tracker. The entire country was his ceremonial ground for creating prospects and ideas. The word *epical* perfectly describes Tracker because he was like a constantly travelling traditional song man who conjured up exceptional times, and these times became embedded in the minds of the people who knew him. He was memorable, and people remembered him through the stories they kept telling about him, of something he had done, or something outrageous he had said, or other crazy situations, and just as much for his ideas and dreams.

Always at the centre of what was happening, Tracker epitomised Aboriginal thinking at some of this country's highest levels of political manoeuvring, for land rights, native title, and economic development. Tracker always looked at the bigger economic picture, larger than the actual reality for Aboriginal people, which he frequently called *the vision splendid*. He immersed himself in it, engaging with all the battles caused by the effects of government policy on Aboriginal culture. An extraordinary reader of the times, he spared no one from hearing his verdict on them, be it those from his own communities, politicians, business people or professional academics, whether they wanted to hear exactly what he thought of them or not. He never held back even for a moment about what he thought, if the people he was engaging with were not up to scratch from his point of view. An Aboriginal statesman he might have been, but he was a leader who could cut to the chase in any company, no trouble at all.

Tracker fought a long hard battle with cancer. He never gave up for a second. He continued working in every available moment as soon as he was well enough after each round of treatment, however badly it had affected him. He was up as soon as he could, and travelling and caring for country and people, or otherwise, if he was too ill, he was travelling through his imagination, creating new ideas for the people who needed him. Tracker sought knowledge and gathered strong thinkers around him. When he gave them a job to do, it was always urgent, like raising millions of dollars for an important project. He had an inquiring mind that was global in its interests. There were many occasions when he was downright shocking, but he was always full-on honest, and with his wit he got the message through, as much from his ability and confidence as a storyteller and story-maker as from being a natural show-off. He was attractive to people wherever he went, be it on a Qantas flight, in a city café or bush camp. He showered practically everyone who came into contact with him with endless rolling ideas that were beyond comparison, and by having enormous fun with them. He loved the scene, and the scene loved him. An unofficial statesman for his people, he spent practically all of his working life, twenty-four seven, constructing visions of Aboriginal economic and cultural independence. Tracker understood perfectly that Aboriginal culture had been shaped by sharp economists over tens of thousands of years.

You can jump in a truck, do a three-kilometre trip thirty times a day for twelve hours, two weeks on and two weeks off. I don't care how many Slim Dusty or Charlie Pride tapes you have listened to, if you aren't an axe-murderer or social misfit you will go home with your soul destroyed. This was how Tracker described the narrow choices for economic opportunity being forced on Aboriginal people, such as having jobs as haul-truck drivers in a mine but not more challenging or managerial positions. Or when talking about then Prime Minister Julia Gillard: *Probably the last time she saw a real Aborigine was when she was licking a postage stamp.* Or in his famous quote about ALP preselection for a federal Northern Territory Senate seat: *Labor likes pet niggers, and I'm counted as a pet nigger. I'm allowed to mow the lawns, but I'm not allowed up on the verandah.*

Tracker had a rare ability to see beyond the present situation. He had one of the finest intelligences among Aboriginal leaders of his generation, and at times a total irreverence which spared nothing, and nobody. He was legendary for his sharp wit in an Aboriginal world which is well known for its sense of humour. Yet Tracker was an enigma, and he was very difficult to understand. Many thought he was bigger than life, that his impact was overwhelming, that Tracker was too much. He was outside of this world. He was another kind. All would agree though, that his life was lived through some of the most challenging events of our time, as Aboriginal people faced the legacies of injustices on an enormous scale, from the ongoing dispossession of land and property rights, to the struggle against intergenerational oppression, injustice and inequality, with inadequate and dwindling resources, to the damaging legacies of the stolen generations, the enormous land rights battles in the Northern Territory – each fought bitterly for years by the Northern Territory Government and others – to the hard work involved against the ongoing attempts to erode the Aboriginal land rights legislation, to finding the money to buy pastoral properties and return them to Aboriginal land before the sunset clause over claiming land rights took effect. Then there was the development of the native title legislation, and the work required to prove native title cases and negotiate agreements over land use, while also dealing with a long list of confronting social justice issues, and the ongoing fight for the recognition of the rights of Aboriginal people, and the enormous hurdles that Tracker was trying to jump over to build a strong Aboriginal economy for the future.

He was both loved and hated. He could leave people reeling in bitterness over something he had called them, but whatever way the emotional scales leant, he had the knack of making you want more of what he was giving. He was fun. Not many people have such a gift, the confidence or the ability to create so much fullness of life in those around him, or to leave so much emptiness in one's spirit from his absence. He was one of the few brilliant statesmanlike leaders we have had – one who stayed close to his own people, and who really had the capacity to push back the boundaries for much of the action that shapes how we think and have thought about our times.

There was nothing normal about him, and other peoples' ideas of normal would never have cut ice with the Aboriginal leaders who knew him, or in their thinking of how to describe someone like him, or in their politics and philosophies about the way our stories are told. A Western-style biography would never do for Tracker. It would not have been a wise move for any biographer, or the correct way to attempt to remember somebody like Tracker, who tried with just about every breath he drew to manufacture enormous change. His life was lived with the aim of achieving something greater, to sculpt land, country and people into a brilliant future on a grand scale. A statesman for dreams that were much bigger and better than the realities he saw around him, and in himself.

It would have been a difficult undertaking to retrace Tracker's footsteps up and down the country, or along those rough roads he had taken into the heart of this land or, by necessity, to write selectively about what would become a narrowly analysed life no matter how good the skills of the biographer. These would have been inappropriate ways to represent this life force whose legacy remains in the lives of so many diverse people, all with their unique stories about Tracker. Who knows the many who remain strangers to each other, the memories that he left in the hearts and minds of people all over the place? There is no trail of sugar to lead you through the forest. Nor a long piece of string, thousands and thousands of kilometres in length, to mark the paths of his continuous travelling and work. Nor would a biography do for someone who said he was like a virus that could spread everywhere and never be gotten rid of, or like a chameleon that could change into whatever anyone wanted him to be. He could eat the second-guessers and spit them out for breakfast through a single comment that would leave you flabbergasted for days after. You couldn't match him. He left you for dead, and he knew enough about almost everything.

I once thought I might tell Tracker something that he would not know about, something peculiar about the little-known Attacus moth, which is usually found in only one or two small areas in the Top End, and only ever seen for a couple of hours from around two in the morning as it clumsily flies short distances in its brief lifespan, not to eat but to try to find a mate. But Tracker already had an encyclopaedic knowledge of this moth, and said rather dully that it was good for catching fish, and he and the Aboriginal mob in the Top End had been using it as bait for years.

How did Tracker use his own stories to do what he did? Through humour and intelligence and his powers of persuasion, he was able to shape a story – the right or straight story – for those he was representing. He created stories that would have the greatest impact in political or economic bargaining forums. Sometimes he was driven by boredom or irreverence to regain the focus of others who were lagging behind his thinking, but mostly, he did whatever he did while having the maximum amount of fun. He seemed to have had an acute sense of vulnerability, that life was precious.

You could spend a lot of time with Tracker and never really get down into seeing the real thing of who he was. The reason for this may be because he was working with the urgency of utter chaos in which the Aboriginal world is placed. Many say that his thinking was too advanced for his time, but he stayed close to his country and people, and dedicated much of his life to the question of how to build an Aboriginal economy, based on the traditional knowledge of cultural economies and survival. What he wanted to do was to create the groundwork for implementing a visionary roadmap – the way to fight a deadly serious war. He always called it a war. The future for Aboriginal people in this country was the war.

Tracker never left behind a trail of paperwork about his ideas. The only papers he left strewn over the country were other peoples' newspapers and documents. Some of his ideas have been squirrelled away inside other peoples' research and recommendations and under their ownership. There are no spreadsheets of his stuck to walls with Blu-Tack. No printouts of what he called *el grande plano* filed away in archives. No mud maps of *the vision splendid* hidden in notebooks, or manifestos he authored, or books, or scholarly papers where he had analysed in his own hand his ideas for building an Aboriginal economy.

Tracker hated being tied to an office desk, or sitting around hour after hour to belt out his latest ideas and theories on a computer. He preferred to walk the talk, to be with people, to be where he could talk directly to them. Distance was never an obstacle. Vehicles! Qantas! Single-engine aircraft. Rough roads. The rougher the better. He travelled constantly to communicate his latest ideas in person.

His left hand was almost glued to his mobile phone – the contemporary equivalent, perhaps, of throwing a spear over the greatest distance with the least physical exertion, speaking straight to the battlefield from the lounge chair or *the chaise lounge*, as he often referred to what he was sitting on, or talking to someone important long distance while standing around in a backyard with friends, or in a café with an audience he had created of complete strangers overhearing the conversation and jokes he was making with a minister or member of parliament. The time of day did not matter to him, there was no escaping Tracker if he wanted to talk to you about an urgent matter, even a prime minister could be called by Tracker in the dead of night. He had everyone's phone number, or if he didn't, he knew how to get it.

The greatest part of his life was spent working for his own people, whether he was out in a desert community, or negotiating a native title agreement for a massive resource project with powerful people in the big end of town, or wearing out the carpet to lobby politicians in Parliament House. He knew full well his mob either couldn't, didn't want to, or wouldn't read. They worked in the oral tradition of making story-memories as the method of achieving outcomes.

One thing Tracker realised more than most others was that controlling or working a crowd, no matter how big or small, to achieve outcomes, was about the way you used your voice to create the story. This was key, and the weapon to be constantly sharpened, and used to full advantage in the attack – for attacking before being attacked. The oral storytelling tradition was more in line with how Tracker wanted to communicate, rather than producing a piece of writing to email to somebody, or plonking it in front of someone and saying, read this! What was the point? How would you know that they had actually read it properly, could read it, or had comprehended the message enough to do something about it? It was better to speak face to face, to look into the eye of the listener, to make sure they understood what to do.

There is no one else I know who loved the idea of having an audience hanging on their every word so much, either for the fun of it, or for something deadly serious, and who thought one always had to have fun no matter what, and who enjoyed people being spellbound by his irreverent wit. Always knowledgeable about the importance of how to be heard, he was a masterful orator with highly refined skills in the art of influence, using stories to transmit very complex issues, which were always locally tuned to capture the recognition and understanding of his audience. The written word would never be totally sufficient, would never do in a world where people speak to each other to be understood. The story, told verbally and with verve, is still as important for the future of Aboriginal peoples as it was in traditional times.

It was not that Tracker did not like to read or seek knowledge through reading, even if he created no paperwork. Tracker read quickly, comprehended content on a breathtaking catalogue of interests, and had a photographic memory for the written word in the same way that he observed people, and read the country. It was just that he preferred to be with people – to have and to create dialogue, and through oral communication to share stories that offer ways of understanding and remembering. In using storytelling as communication, he was able to engage even the most important listener – Tracker liked nothing better than pointing towards the future, and showing the way. He kept memories alive by recalling stories time and again that people liked to hear him tell, such as how some of the most important senior traditional men would diverge from the official discussions at Central Land Council meetings held out in the bush, to talk about themselves. One story he told was of Mr W. Rubuntja who, while chairing such a meeting, turned to an old senior man, Mr M. Wagu, and asked how he was going. Mr Wagu apparently said, *I have been riding a donkey for miles and miles, back in the old days.* The chairman then asked in front of the full Council meeting, *How's your ass then?* Old Mr Wagu replied, *I have a good arse, but thank you very much for asking.*

Tracker should have had a personal secretary taking down all of his ideas and patenting them, but he gave them away freely in conversations, with the action plans for projects that were on an enormous scale, or small community projects to create income from commercial activities. All of these ideas depended on the understanding of people from government, professional workers and developers; and mostly, his thinking was more advanced than theirs, and they would not have the willingness, or ability, or resources, to put plans they had not thought of themselves into action, with the paperwork they required.

Some of these ideas can be seen in the opportunities he created for thousands of Aboriginal people. But the full legacy of his work and thinking lives with the people who heard his stories, experienced his wit, or worked with him. He always left the details for others, those who listened to him, and in the work they did with him. You could say that his visionary ideas will be missed by Aboriginal people, but much of his work still lives in the minds of some of the best thinkers in the country. Tracker's legacy is in this archive, his filing cabinet, the minds of other people. The road maps or blueprints of the vision splendid, *el grande plano*, are spread among people of all walks of life around the country – the politicians and political thinkers, economists, resource and land developers, media representatives, Aboriginal communities and their leaders, and the everyday people who were Tracker's mates. Some of this rich tapestry of knowledge has been drawn from the vaults of these other peoples' minds, and told in this book.

I have always thought that all stories are important, but stories only come to life and stay alive when they are being imagined and remembered, and then in the telling, how they are retold to make sure they are being heard. The problem with creating this book was the question of how you would write a story about someone who challenged all expectations? Tracker used to say, *I want you to write something for me, Wrighty*. But how could you do the imagining on behalf of someone who was impossible to keep up with, who could never be contained, who never wanted to sit still long enough to go through the details time and again, as a writer would need to do to get the story right. Instead, he expected you to know exactly what was going on in his head, and to drop whatever you were doing, and get his stuff done at once! He was never going to sit around long enough to let other people define him, or to allow himself to be compartmentalised in somebody else's smaller orbit of thoughts.

Wrighty, I just want to bookend this. Let others tell the story. Let them say what they want.

This was how Tracker envisioned this book, which he wanted to call *The Unreliable Witness*. He was simply saying what our mob say time and again, *Let people have a say. Let them tell their own stories. Let people speak for themselves*. This is a reasonable response to a lifetime of confronting the legacy of our stories being told and misrepresented by others, as has been happening since the arrival of the First Fleet. Tracker made stories happen in reality. For him, stories were for changing reality at whatever level it took to make something happen. These were not stories that could make people live happily ever after, they were stories to make peoples' lives better by making a difference, and along the way, to create amazing memories.

The stories in Tracker are told from many points of view, including Tracker's own, when he was well enough to do so and found space in the last years of his busy working life. The book helps to explain some of his ideas and his significance as a leader of his times. There are many voices in these pages. The contributors were all chosen by Tracker. He wanted them to tell their parts in the story. They include his two younger brothers William and Patrick. Patrick sadly passed away in 2016 from cancer. The book also includes many of Tracker's oldest friends and closest colleagues.

Sometimes it is the little stories that people tell that are the most potent, and when fragments of remembered stories are placed together, they combine to create a truer and fuller portrait than a single story on its own. Yet this is not what we generally teach one another, or practise in our story-making and our literary endeavours. We like to create our own versions of the story. The author or the biographer interprets and selects, decides what will be told to the best of his or her ability, and writes on behalf of the subject. But the biography can only offer a fraction, the fractional stories, snapshots, flavour or sense of the whole, and relies more on what is unsaid sometimes, than said. *Tracker* attempts to follow an Aboriginal tradition of storytelling practice for crossing landscapes and boundaries, giving many voices a part in the story. This blessing of stories and voices was very much Tracker Tilmouth's way of creating stories for others to expand and make use of in creating *the vision splendid.*

Tracker once threatened to roll the car he was driving and kill both of us, and our co-worker Forrest Holder, during a five- to six-hour argument that he and I were having on a road trip from Camooweal to Tennant Creek late at night. Forrest was in the back seat trying to be a referee and peacemaker. We were travelling in a low-roofed vehicle made more claustrophobic by the darkness, and Tracker and I were arguing about the value of having principles, whether we should always maintain the high moral ground, or leave our principles at the door while doing business in the world we lived and worked in, that did not respect Aboriginal interests. I suppose this argument which was going nowhere was just testing who could last the distance of each story, to stay awake on the long boring drive back to the Northern Territory from Mount Isa. The only break in the argument was when Tracker saw a large taipan snake on the road. He hit the brakes, and wanted Forrest to go out and catch it, while he shone the car lights on the thick, waist-high grass on the side of the road where the snake was heading. Forrest declined to follow it. We had nowhere to put the snake anyhow. Tracker wanted to take the snake home to Alice Springs to give to his young daughter Cathryn as a pet.

Earlier that day, Tracker had spent many hours arguing with Aboriginal ex-ringers turned ATSIC regional councillors in Mount Isa, trying to convince them to support the purchase of a pastoral property – the country of the local traditional owners who had asked Tracker to help them acquire this land. That long argument was about how Tracker – a Central Australian Aboriginal – was muscling his way into Queensland to count the cattle, to establish the value of the property, and how would he know the difference between what were cows and what were bulls? Tracker had ended up in sheer frustration, hours later, after explaining the same things again and again, telling them he would shine a torch up the bum of each bullock as it went through the drafting race, and that was how he would know the difference. End of argument.

There were other great memories. Tracker telling me he was at home on the sea and at home in the desert while I was turning green with seasickness in a small boat off Mornington Island; hearing traditional landowners in the Gulf of Carpentaria saying they were already *scientify* and did not need him to tell them about the scientific and technical details of the extraction process of the Century zinc deposit; or the fun of watching him and Owen Cole having an argument; or listening to his hilarious stories about Geneva; or walking down the mall in Darwin with Tracker and listening to him discuss economic ideas and plans with people he ran into along the way, and where I later counted about twenty-one ideas he was working on with all these different people. This included methods for the extraction of gold nuggets in an area of the Northern Territory, growing cotton with water from the Century mine, extracting lime for cement in mines across the Northern Territory, buying for Aboriginal people some of the Northern Territory cattle stations whose owners were suffering from the Indonesian downturn in the live cattle export trade, his idea of how to supply gas for generating power for industry in remote locations, rare-earth mining, red mud extraction, sulphur, supplying the skins of commercially grown crocodiles to the high-end fashion designers of Paris, the old growth forests intellectual property rights test case, working with the Kalkadoon, Crims-R-Us rehabilitation of Aboriginal prisoners, giant prawn farming, fattening cattle, and much more.

At least for now, the real significance of Tracker's story belongs to the future, but the reader may come closer to understanding this visionary Aboriginal leader through the stories of many of those that he gathered around him throughout his life. And this is what Aboriginal people understand, that it takes the voices of many to tell the stories of country, the story lines. This is because stories are powerful and must be handled carefully, as when they are sung by many men and women from their parts of the long song travelling over country. Each should speak for themselves, and for the whole to form the consensus, or complete story. This is how it goes for our responsibility to country, ourselves, and for our times, as the carriers of all time.

Tracker the phenomenal life force with great intelligence, quick recall, plenty of vision operating on multiple fronts, had a precise insight into whatever political or commercial states of play were happening in the Aboriginal world across Australia. He had it all in his mind, and being anywhere near Tracker in action was like James Joyce once saying, of *Finnegans Wake*, this was *going to take them a hundred years to figure out.*

Prologue

The Warlpiri Invasion of Europe

Tracker Tilmouth

The best story is the Warlpiri invasion of Europe when we went to the UN. I went to the United Nations originally and I said this is all wonderful, but it is really a talkfest where the Australian government gets up and tells the world how good they treat the blacks. When you compare that to Africa or South America, we are way out in front in terms of money, and spending, and treatment. They, the Australian government, kept doing this. I said to [Michael] Dodson, *We've got to out-think this process.* I said, *We need to bring a bit of culture.*

So I said, *I am going to bring dot painters and all that so they can paint in the UN.* When you go to the UN no one is allowed to bring anything political because no state is to be upset or whatever. So we brought it all. We got all the Warlpiris lined up, old Rastus, old Roy, old Topsy, all them mob, they are all finished now, and Frankie [Jakamarra] Nelson. And got on the plane. First we go to Alice Springs. Someone asked them: *Where are you mob going?*

We're going to Chin-ni-pa.

They had them little football bags full of a couple of shirts. So we had to go down and get them cases and clothes from Sainties [Saint Vincent de Paul], and we loaded them all up and got them attired properly, Harry Nelson and everybody else. Anyway, they got on the plane to go to Darwin and that was fucking freaky for them, to be going on this big plane in Darwin to go to Singapore.

I did not really tell them where they were going. No. They thought we were going just over there. It would have been wasted showing them a globe and saying, *You are actually going to go around here.*

Where's that? And what's that?

I declined to inform them, wasting my time and theirs, in

understanding exactly *where I am taking you*. Just turn up. So the Tennant Creek mob rang me and said they wanted to know where Geneva is? I said, *Don't tell em*.

Anyway we loaded them all on the plane in Darwin and Harry Nelson was on the plane and he knew how to order a beer, and they said, *When you are on Qantas you actually don't pay for the beer.* So that was wonderful and the next minute the woman, waitress, air hostess, was carting grog down to the Warlps who decided to bring out the boomerangs and there was loud singing of love, then of country, then unfettered crying for Yuendumu, all in Warlpiri, and the grog kept flowing.

Then the air hostess said to me, *Can you tell your people not to make too much noise.* I said, *They're not my people let's get that straight, and if you keep giving them grog the noise will get louder.* And the worse thing was there was green *pituri* [bush tobacco] marks in every basin.

So we get off there [in Singapore] and we get to the hotel and we are sitting back at the hotel, and old Rastus and I were having a cup of tea in the garden. We had no room service. I said, *No room service*, to the hotel people because of the drunks. Anyway, Harry Nelson had worked out that all he had to do was go off to a bar somewhere. Right! So Rastus and I was sitting there and the next minute we heard this *yak-hi-*ing, this singing and waving to us. Here is Harry, going past in a rickshaw, one of the little things, with a brand new fake Rolex on his arm and hanging out of it, and waving to us. I said to Rastus, *Oh! Shit, we'll lose him in the traffic.* Anyway Rastus said, *Oh! No. They'll eat him.* I said, *What do you mean?*

Payback. We ate a couple of them. This old bloke from the Tanami remembered the gold rush days, and probably heard stories about eating Chinamen.

Anyway we got Harry Nelson back into the plane for the flight to Paris, and we get to the Charles De Gaulle Airport in France. That was alright, I got everyone across that. Get to Geneva next, yeah no worries. I am buggered by then, absolutely buggered, jet-lagged, I couldn't sleep because I was worrying about losing these Warlpiris in mid-flight. Anyway as we were getting into the hotel they came knocking on my door, *Tracker*. Oh! Yes! I had brought all the art equipment, all the rolls of canvas and all the paints and everything else, I had a box full of it.

I gave it all to them, *Wonderful, do you want to do some painting?* Off they went and it must have been a couple of hours and I was sleeping away and then I hear *bang, bang*, on the door. The manager, *Monsieur.*

Yes.

You must leave.

Why?

They are an-e-MALS. This little French bloke.

I said, *What's your problem? You know? That's a bit rough.*

He said, *Monsieur, we inspect.* I went over there and opened the room and what they had done is they had painted, and when they did the yellow background they painted it on the carpet so there was a yellow square when they lifted off the canvas from the floor. And then there was a red square and a black square, and a red and a brown square all over this carpet. He wanted them thrown out.

While he was carrying on like a pork chop, Frankie Nelson brings out this folder and here he is, [a photo of him as] artist in residence at the Georges Pompidou Centre, with the French premier, shaking his hand. This bloke just about went down on one knee. He had met van Gogh in life. So he went down on his knees to pay homage to Frankie Nelson, and then out of the blue, out came this dot painting of Geneva, do not ask me how, but this little dot painting which they said: *This is Geneva.* The bloke was nearly crying.

So that was all well and good, and the next day I went to the UN, and for two days I did not check on them. The next day I went to the UN and came back and as I was getting into the lift, in came this bloke with the hors d'oeuvres, and another bloke with the champagne in flutes and everything else, and they got off at the same floor as me. Well! Someone is having a party. They went past, *Excusez-moi,* and went off and I followed them, and they went to Harry Nelson's room and I opened the door and here was the manager of the hotel with Harry Nelson selling dot paintings to Japanese and German tourists, no French francs, only Swiss francs, Deutsche marks and American dollars. They had made twenty-five thousand dollars for the day. That was what they had made.

So, wonderful idea. Then they went down to paint in the UN as the guest of Madame Diaz, the Special Rapporteur on Indigenous Rights. The guards wanted them to move along and she went out and said,

Non, non, non. Please, they are my guests. They had this big Milky Way Dreaming that Frankie Nelson painted for the UN and gave it to her. Beautiful big canvas. Absolutely.

Previously, on our first trip to Geneva, we were all living in a little dog box and I went for a run as I was pretty fit in those days, and I went for a run along Lake Geneva and running along there this Israeli girl came running past me, and then she had spun around and chased me back. She thought I was Palestinian or Israeli or something like that. I said, *No, I'm Aboriginal.* Anyway, her name was Sarah and she was very friendly and so the next day she said, *I'll show you Geneva.* I thought just a normal motor car will turn up. She turned up with one of those convertible BMWs and we were flying around Geneva. She was chauffeuring me around. Her uncle and her father owned the hotels along Lake Geneva, Jewish mob, and they were all full of Arabs. She said, *Where are you mob staying?* I said, *We're in this little hotel with a limited amount of room.* She said, *No, we can do better than that, you can have my uncle's chateau for the time you're in Geneva.* So twenty minutes walking from the UN there is this massive villa, four stories high with swimming pool, grounds and everything else. We called it the Aboriginal Embassy and Mick Dodson was the ambassador.

We got to the UN and Mick had allocated tasks to all sorts of people, he gave Dickie Bedford the cultural attaché title, and he said, *Dickie you know how to speak French? Yeah.* So we pulled up alongside a car with this mob in and Mick said, *Talk French to them.* Dickie said, *Yoplait or my play.* This is Dickie Bedford. There were these lunatics in the car. We went to the UN and Dick Bedford said, *We've got a problem.*

What's that?

Who's going to clean the house and do the dishes? So I went to all the missions, the German, the French, the Irish, everything else, and said to all the young interns there, *Where are you living? Oh! We live in the YMCA,* or whatever, for the period of time they were there. *Forget that, come and live with us. Free board and you can look after the dishes and do the cleaning sort of thing.*

So we had all these young sheilas and we invited Robert Tickner, [Daryl] Melham and Pat Turner to a barbecue at the villa, the Aboriginal Embassy. We had all these young girls in bikinis swimming and carrying on and Melham turned up and he said, *This is not fair.* The Central Land Council had the top level, Coxy [Barbara Cox] and me and everybody else. We opened up all the big windows, beautiful cool breeze at night, magnificent, and the Social Justice Commissioner had theirs, then the Northern Land Council, and way down the bottom was the Kimberleys – because they did not amount to much. Anyway I told the missus but she does not believe it is true. So we did that for about four years straight, lived in this villa, every time we went to Geneva.

So the Warlpiris turned up there the next year when I took them. There was the first year we went, and then the next year when they came with us, and old Frankie Nelson was dot painting and full of good cheer, he fell into his painting twice, and he had dots all over his forehead and we had to extract him from the painting. Talk about body of work. So with all the tape around him and everything else, and pulling it out of his hair while they were still dotting away there, and a little porcupine walked past him and [Mick] Dodson reckoned, *He's not concentrating, Track.*

Dodson in all of his glory was there, oh mate, I tell you. We went to this function at the New Zealand Mission and the Maori women were singing beautiful songs and we were all there. I was sitting there, New Zealand ambassador here, Tickner next to him and Mick Dodson next to Tickner, who nearly fainted because of what was being said in our conversation. Then I said, *Mick, we've got to think, we are going to go and look at Dachau because we need to understand what happened and how close it is to us,* and so forth and so on. Anyway. So we are driving in from Switzerland into Germany. Dodson was flaked out in the back, lying back, head out like that, snoring away there. We go through three tunnels, the autobahn tunnels and everything else. So when you go in there the lights are on and when you come out it is sunlight, and so forth. Driving along, about a hundred and eighty kilometres an hour, and he said, *Traaacks, Traaacks.*

What?

Pull over, we're lost.

I said, *What do you mean we're lost?*

We've been travelling for three days. What had happened was, he woke up in daylight, woke up when it was dark, woke up in the tunnels.

So anyway, Don Som [Mick Dodson], Monsieur Don Som gets to Munich and that night he wanted to go down the pub. So I thought I better go with him. The sheila dropped us off and she went off to see her mother or whatever. Me and Dodson were in the hotel. I walked downstairs and he was playing darts. We were playing them for a beer and they were beating us, and he started goose-stepping to the bar.

He said, *Tracks, they lost.*

No, they're killing us, Mick.

No, they lost.

No, we've been paying for their beers.

No, they lost the war.

I had known him since I was a young fella, years ago. His wife used to ring me to make sure I looked after him. Not for the first time, the Mr Pickwick Hotel in the middle of Geneva would ring me up because I would give them my number – to go and pick him up because they had been trying to throw him out, and he was wanting to fight them.

Frankie Nelson and Mick were out, and I said, *I'm not picking you blokes up, go and get a cab.* I went back [to the hotel], I had Coxy and everybody else, and you had to do your work, you couldn't just be over there fucking around. So next minute, I am half asleep: *Traaacks,* you could hear this voice, *Traaacks.*

What?

Come down here.

I went down, and there is this little French taxi driver started shaping up to me. He said, *Monsieur we fight.* I said, *No, I don't want to fight.* What had happened is that Mick had no money and Frankie Nelson had decided to pay the taxi driver in Australian dollars. The French taxi driver said, *That is rub-bish,* and threw it on the floor. Frankie Nelson took offence, *How dare you disgrace Her Majesty's currency, put your dukes up,* and Dodson is shadowboxing on the side. So I paid him and told him to fuck off and I had these two idiots looking at me. Oh mate, I tell you. Don Som. Crow in jam tins. The boots and skinny legs. Every time I see him, *You got them big boots?* He tries to shrug me off by calling me Leigh instead of Tracker, he says, *Hi Leigh*, and I say, *Fuck off Dodson.* I tell him, *I've got enough to put you away.*

And then we took the Warlpiris. We took them to Tromso in Norway to meet with the Sami. We were lining up for a feed and they were in front of me and eating the meat and spitting it out.

They said, *Tracker.*

I said, *Yeah, what? Why are you spitting the meat out?*

No Tracker, Tracker they don't use salt with their corned beef.

It's not fucking corned beef, it's reindeer.

What! The little thing that Santa Claus flies around with?

I said, *Yeah one of them.*

Oh! We didn't know that.

Then daylight. I said, *Now you mob, this is summer so there is no darkness. At twelve o'clock it's still light. The sun does not go down.*

Aaah! Tracker, we own the Dreaming, we own the story, we aren't little kids. We don't need you.

So I said, *Righto, you mob all come back at twelve o'clock tonight.*

Yeah we'll be here, we know that story backwards. We are kurtungurlu/ kwertengerle for that one – like this.[2]

So I came back to the hotel and I pulled the curtains across the windows so that it was all dark and I said, *Righto what time?*

Jakamarra checked his watch and said, *Twelve o'clock, yeah.*

So night-time?

Yeah, night-time.

Right, open the window, and pulled them [the curtains] back. *Hey, it's daylight.*

I told you the sun doesn't go down.

Oh! That's good, we can stay at the pub all day, and off they went. *Don't tell us, we are not little kids.*

I said, *How do you tell the taxi driver which hotel you're in?* They said, *Oh! I don't know.* I said, Come downstairs, and I am thinking, what is

---

2. *Kurtungurlu* or *kwertengerle* is a Warlpiri term used to describe people who have the responsibility to make sure that ceremonies are carried out correctly, usually in their mother's traditional country.

the Warlpiri word for polar bear because they had a big stuffed bear in the foyer when you walk in, big, huge bear, and the closest I could get in Warlpiri was big white dog. So Harry Nelson, he came back and said, *We had really good taxi driver.* Yes, why? *I just said you look for them pig pear.* Drunks.

I got crook coming back [from Geneva]. I do not know what I ate and I was really sick in Bangkok. So we got out of there, got on the plane and got to Darwin airport and I am in a wheelchair being wheeled off, with Gerry Hand, the minister, and Clarky [Geoff Clark] and Josie Crawshaw mob decide one last attempt at sovereignty and jumped the fence, so off they race across the airstrip and I am in a wheelchair. Gerry Hand said, *I hope you're not running,* and I said, *I can't.* I said, *Take me to the fucking hospital.* Anyway, Clarky and Michael [Mansell] mob jumped the fence and they got arrested, made the news [and were saying], *Oh! We need to be locked up {as political prisoners}.* Gerry Hand said, *Don't waste my time, piss off. I am the minister.* He knew them all.

So I turn up at Darwin Hospital and Rossy's sister Sally and Shieldsy [Bernadette Shield] came in to see me. I am lying back there and there was a little Indian doctor looking at me, and they said, *Oh don't worry about him, he's got AIDS.* They reckoned, *He has got AIDS, definitely got AIDS.* So the little Indian doctor took off and came back with a mask and sprayed all around the room. I said, *You didn't believe those idiots, did you?* He said, *You never know.* So Mrs T. flew up then and said, *What's wrong with you?* I said, *I'm nearly dead.*

Yeah but I didn't need to come up and see you.

Anyway so that was the end of my overseas trips but, oh what a joke, an absolute joke, the Warlpiri, they were classic, absolutely classic.

Where is that Geneva?

Over here.

That's not far. Other side. It is very, very hard to teach Aboriginal people about geography, especially when Yuendumu is the centre of the world as we know it. Anyway that is enough. That is the joking side.

1.

Trying To Get The Story Straight

Have Scone, Will Travel

Tracker Tilmouth

My political education began at a very young age when Lois Bartram, the house mother of our cottage on Croker Island Mission, read stories to the boys under her care, and because we showed an interest, she read to my brother William and me the book about South Africa, *Cry, the Beloved Country,* written by Alan Paton.

I shall do this, not because I am noble or unselfish, but because life slips away, and because I need for the rest of my journey a star that will not play false to me, a compass that will not lie.[3]

I went to Croker when I was three or four years old with my younger brothers – William who was about two years old, and Patrick who was about eighteen months. We were first sent to the Retta Dixon Children's Home on Bagot Road in Darwin for about six months to a year after we were taken by the Welfare Department from our home in Alice Springs, and then we went to Croker Island or Minjilang as it is called now. The process for Aboriginal children who had been taken to Croker Island was that you were stuck in dormitories or cottages with a cottage mother, and there were twelve boys in our cottage.

When you had Lois being politically astute like she was, the political process was very, very clear.

Lois had a very acute understanding of the politics of the world that we did not have. No one was exposed to it. We did not have newspapers

---

3. Alan Paton, *Cry, the Beloved Country* (Jonathan Cape, London, 1948), p.131. The protagonist is Stephen Kumalo, a black Anglican priest from a rural Natal town, who is searching for his son Absalom in the city of Johannesburg.

or radio or anything like that. I think the first cool drink I ever had was when I went back to Darwin, the first soft drink, the first lollies, the first bit of chocolate, and I was twelve at the time, or thirteen.

We were in a bad situation but there were people worse off than you were, and she made sure that was a part of our message – so that was alright, I was told that since I was a kid. It was sort of ingrained from when you were young of how to see things in terms of personal gain versus the greater good. We had Lois teaching us that and mind you, the church at that time was different to what it is today. It was a Methodist church and they were into that sort of philosophy, but today the Uniting Church is a gathering of old fogies. The glory days have gone, and if they do not become evangelical or something like that then you would probably close the doors on them.

At the end of the day, her teachings were based on what she understood her religious background was, and you can see that when you read the Bible, or the Koran, or any of those great books, because you can see there are these same philosophies behind it. It was like the *Life of Brian*, it could have been anyone, but it wasn't, and so when you go through that process and you read it, then it is not hard for you to understand the difference between self gain or self political gain, and the sharing of benefits with the community – the political community – and the political gains for the community. This kind of thinking was even more in focus when I was working for [Central Australian Aboriginal] Congress in the 1970s, the Aboriginal health service in Alice Springs, on the drunks pick-up bus. There was me and Johnny Liddle who had the job to pick up the drunks, clean them, wash them, feed them, and take them home. The spin dryer we used to call it. We ran the bus service, and it was that level of helping our own mob, and growing fruit and vegetables at Little Sisters, before the establishment of Tangentyere Council in 1979. I was working for the Department of Aboriginal Affairs after I had worked for Congress, and Johnny was working for Congress.

The other thing that Lois did for the children she looked after on Croker Island, was that we never had social distractions and destruction. We never suffered like some people from Croker by hitting the grog, and who were taking the overall experience of being taken away from their families and put into a mission a lot heavier than we did. We were a pretty sane lot when you think about what a lot of people went through.

Lois Bartram

I went to Croker in 1956, and Bruce [Tracker] came in 1957. I was twenty-five when I went to Croker. It seems young now but I did not feel particularly young then. I had done general nursing training and mid and infant welfare, and when I did infant welfare we had to read a book by John Bowlby which was called *Maternal Care and Mental Health*.[4] He knew what he was talking about. His work was about the effect on children when they are denied maternal care right from birth, but also then over the years too, and it was really disturbing. It explains a lot of things I think, as to how people get into trouble in later life and so on. And it really hit me as to what dire effects it can have. That affected me greatly and I knew then exactly what I wanted to do. I wanted to go into childcare for children who for some reason could not stay in their own families. I came from a very stable and large extended family and really appreciated that.

My family and my grandparents on both sides lived in Nullawil which is north of Wycheproof in north-western Victoria, and were farmers in the area. My mother's parents were original selectors, and Dad's parents came over to Nullawil in 1907, which was about fifteen years after Nullawil was originally selected. I had been very involved locally: we went to school locally, and to high school in Wycheproof. We were very involved in the local church, Methodist and partly Presbyterian, and all the local sport and everything. Then I went to Melbourne to do my training.

I should also say that at that time [of going to Croker Island] there

---

4. John Bowlby, *Maternal Care and Mental Health* (World Health Organisation, Geneva, 1951). Bowlby's book demonstrated the devastating effects on children of maternal deprivation – effects that ripple through the generations where neglected children can become neglectful parents. Bowlby (1907–1990) was a British psychologist, psychiatrist, and psychoanalyst interested in child development and known for his pioneering work in attachment theory.

was no talk of a Stolen Generation.⁵ Not just the term but the fact, and I was completely ignorant of the fact that Aboriginal children were compulsorily taken from their mothers' care or their parents' care even, and put into institutions. It was a government law but the churches cooperated, partly because I have since learnt that most of the government-run institutions were a complete disaster.

The Alice Springs one was not, from what I heard, but some of the others were. The one at Pine Creek I think had a terrible reputation.

Eventually I was told I could go to Croker to relieve as a nurse when the nurse was on holidays, but that would only be for three or four months. However, when I got there, I relieved for four months and the other nurse came back, then she got sick and left after about the same amount of time – maybe six months, and thereafter, I was the nurse as well as a cottage mother.

Well! As I say I went to Croker Island in 1956 and Bruce came in 1957. Bruce and William to me, and Patrick to the house across the road. That was no big deal because there were no fences between the houses, only a dusty road in between, and one vehicle at that stage on the island. So the kids played on the road and they saw each other every day. And Bruce's two cousins [the Cassidys] were with me at the time, whom he knew.

We had heard at the beginning of the year that these three brothers were coming but then they didn't come. I suppose it was about May, and I cannot really remember exactly as I was not told why, but that they were just held up in Darwin. I learnt years later when I met the boys' Aunty Doreen that she and her husband had gone to court to gain custody of the three boys, which was an amazing thing for an Aboriginal couple to do in Alice Springs of all places at that time.

The law that said children could be removed had just been changed. It had been repealed so that they could no longer be removed but the same bureaucrats were still in power, and they got around it by charging

---

5. The Stolen Generations, or Stolen Children, were Aboriginal and Torres Strait Islander children who were removed from their families by Australian federal and state government agencies, often to be put into church missions. These removals occurred approximately between 1909 and 1969, and in some places the practice went on into the 1970s.

the kids with being neglected. Doreen and her husband fought this, and said they were not neglected. In court, Doreen told me, the magistrate agreed, but he said they might be in the future when you have your own children, so it is better they go now. They got away with it. Anyway, they came. Bruce was four, William was three and, I think this is right, Patrick was two.

There were three of them and they had each other, and that has been their saving all along. And they were not separated. At one stage there was a threat that Bruce was going to be sent to Sydney, to the institution there along with another boy of his own age on Croker, and I applied actually for the seven to take south. I had taken them south already on holidays with me once. And I was told ahead which was a bit unusual, usually we were told and that was it.

Brown paper parcels, that's what they are, one of the other cottage mothers said to me one day: *They think our kids are brown paper parcels and they push them around everywhere.* And to us they were our kids. Anyway, I did actually get permission to take the Tilmouths, but only the Tilmouths, which meant I had to leave the others and I could not walk out on the others, so I turned it down.

Patrick and William Tilmouth

Patrick: Sister Bartram was a good lady. And a tiny lady, she was only tiny. She put the fear of God into all of us.

William: I think the saying that Tracker used all the time, *chopping wood for practice*, came from that, because you would be sent out to the wood heap to chop the wood, but the wood was already chopped. A lot of it was already chopped so you would chop some more. And so the term chopping wood for practice came from there. She did have control [of the twelve boys in Victory Cottage]. She would bite her tongue and everyone would bolt because that was a sign that she was not pleased.

Patrick: Don't mess with her; *don't mess with me.*

William: Mind you she was a really brilliant, brilliant woman; she was the only medical person on the island. So she was not only dealing with the sick and issuing medication, fixing peoples' wounds and boils, or sores and also skin rashes. She was also the coroner and midwife. She did everything, from go to whoa, whatever medical. If someone had died in the camp she was the one who dealt with it. If a woman gave birth she was the one who dealt with it. She was just an amazing, amazing, amazing woman. On top of that she had twelve kids to look after.

Patrick: We used to have homemade ice cream and all the good stuff. Lois tried making bacon.

William: She tried to make bacon out of wild boar. She got close, too. She made ginger beer. I mean you never got a cool drink in your life on the mission unless you found boxes of cool drinks that were left over from some mining company that had gone through. Exploration mob, they would leave all their stuff, too much to take back so they would leave it all piled up underneath a tree and if you stumbled across it, you would find these rusty cans that had Coke or Fanta or something in it. She was just an amazing, amazing woman. When she had left the mission, we had also all left the mission. She got pushed out because she did not fit the bill as a cottage parent, and she went off to Laos. She used to write to me in gaol, and talk about how during the war, how scarce food was, and how people had nothing to eat. She was doing everything over there in those villages in Laos, for women giving birth and treating war wounds, she was basically it. Unrecognised spirit. Unrecognised Australian. She was a really good role model and staunch as anything. She lived her life in honesty. She was a very sincere, honest person. Righteous. But she could see the wrongs of the world and she could see that us kids were heading down that road quickly. She tried to prepare us in some way to combat some of the things we were about to face. The real world.

Lois Bartram

Bruce was not a difficult child. He was not angelic, but I had far more difficult children than him in the household. The fact that those three had each other I am sure helped them all. He was reasonably cooperative and he was bright, and he was a happy boy. He joined in. You never ever heard kids on Croker saying, *I'm bored*. They always found something to do.

In many ways Croker Island was a beautiful place. In my first letter home I said Croker is lovely, but it is really not a good idea to try and bring up children to fit into a community that they have no knowledge of, which was what was happening. They were staying there until they were eighteen, and actually there were some married couples there, some couples who had married and stayed but that was no longer encouraged. It had been originally, but when they turned eighteen they were choofed back into Darwin which was a far from ideal place for either the girls or the boys.

I had furlough every three years for four months, and on my second furlough I knew that I could get free airfares for the children under some government scheme that was encouraging the kids to have some experience outside the north. I got that and took them home to my parent's farm at Nullawil from December to March, where I had already had them home on holidays. They went to the local school and William says Bruce caused the first race riot in Nullawil's history.

They were used to playing some sports on Croker. They had footballs I think, and certainly one of their teachers had them playing hockey which they played with great gusto, but they had not played cricket. It was summer so they went to Nullawil school. Bruce went into bat and he got bowled out first ball. He was not going out because he thought he had only just got there. He refused to give up the bat. And William told me this story actually later, they did not tell me at the time. They, all the Croker kids, ganged up with Bruce and all the other kids of course were on the other side and knew they had right on their side. Anyway it was settled and I presume Bruce did give up his bat, I do not really know.

William Tilmouth

I went to school down there [in Nullawil]. First there were seven of us who went down there, and we walked through Melbourne, and stayed at some hotel and the newspaper boy on the corner was singing seven little nigger boys all in a row.

We nearly had a fight on the corner of Little Collins Street with this newspaper boy calling us seven little nigger boys.

We got down to Nullawil in Victoria, and we were playing cricket one day. You could hear the chaos happening and us boys got up and half of them were playing cricket, Tracker and Jamesy's Wauchope mob, and not knowing what cricket was. Cricket was totally fucking alien to me.

I went up to the cricket pitch and there was Tracker wanting to fight everyone. He just could not help himself. And the problem was that Tracker was out. He was bowled out but not according to Tracker, and he was saying, *No, no, I am not out. You're not going to take this fucking bat off me. You're going to wear this bat.* He started a big hoo-haa on the cricket pitch and so Eddie Horrell, James Wauchope and Kenny Wauchope, and me and Tony and Terry Cassidy, we all moved in for a defensive role for the Croker boys. We were going to strike a blow for Croker. It was a stand-off, a Mexican stand-off with all the non-Aboriginal guys that were there. The Croker Island boys were unknown in terms of their ability to fight, no one knew.

But anyway, the principal had a big assembly that afternoon and talked about *racism* in his school. So Tracker started the first race riot in outback Nullawil.

Nullawil was just a few houses and a silo, a couple of big silos. That was all there was. So it ended up in a fight, all because Tracker had refused to be out, even though he did not know that he was out. We had not seen cricket. I mean just to show how ignorant we were of the world, I was given a tennis racquet and a pocket knife for Christmas and I could not make common sense out of it. I got the pocket knife and cut all the strings out of the tennis racquet, not realising that that was the wrong thing to do.

Lois Bartram

For a short time I had sixteen children in the cottage. When I moved in there were only about two or three of the actual oldest boys there, but I suppose four older boys from the next cottage were moved in so that I had about seven of these older boys, the youngest of whom was twelve and the oldest eighteen. Then I got first of all two brothers, and then Terry and Tony [Cassidy], who were Bruce's cousins, so there were six younger ones. But before the older ones were leaving, more younger ones were moved in and that is when I had sixteen but that was only for a brief time, a few weeks. Twelve was the usual number.

The boys were not too bad really. Sometimes there were problems. The climate was helpful, because they could spend a lot of time outside, and the older boys particularly did that. The cottages, I might add, had concrete floors, unlined asbestos walls – but then it was not unusual, and the dangers were not known – no ceiling and a corrugated iron roof and inside they were partitioned, there were not separate rooms. The kitchen and bathroom were separate at the back, but the bedrooms were just partitions with curtains on the doorways, except for my room which had a door. There were three bedrooms, plus mine. But at times I had a younger child, and the youngest child would sleep in my room quite often.

Tracker was quite good at his schoolwork. We had a government school and usually very good teachers. He was a loveable little boy, and William and Patrick too. William particularly was the kind of child that most people warmed to. He had curly black hair. He was quite dark and had dark eyes and a very winning smile. Bruce was fairer and older and more dependable probably, but cooperative. Look, there was not room for the kids to do much. Also I was much stricter with them than I would be now but part of that was, it was policy, not written-down policy, but what actually happened: that if they misbehaved too badly, then they would be moved.

Because of this fear that they would be moved I was very strict and I regret that now, but it is a bit late, you cannot go back. I used corporal punishment more than I would have. One of the other cottage mothers when I got there, whom I respected, she said to me, *You've got a wooden spoon, see that you use it when necessary*. I did not use it every day but I regret now that I used it at all.

This saved my life, my bacon: we used to go camping twice a year in the school holidays and I loved those times. We went camping and we did not have tents or anything, we slept on the ground. We took mosquito nets quite often because there were a lot of mozzies, but the kids could just run wild for a few days. Those days were never long enough for me.

They had ponies when they were older but when they were little we went to the beach. And they used to go pig hunting on the ponies when they were older. How one of them was not killed I do not know. There were these kids, all from about ten upwards and they went out on their ponies with knives, like scout's knives, and they killed wild pigs. Actually when they were young I suppose they did not kill too many, it was the older ones. One of the other cottages had a dog they used to take with them and they gave the dog a medal once when they came back because he saved one of the boys. They went looking for the wild pigs and stirred them up and one of the boars charged this kid who ran for a tree. The others were all up the tree and he slipped and fell. The boar would have got him but the dog fastened on to it and Vincent got up and climbed the tree. Oh! Great stories they had when they came home. They said the dog, and I cannot for the life of me say his name, deserved a medal.

I did read a lot to the boys. I read them *Winnie the Pooh* and I tried to get books that had brown people in them, and I did have a few, and I had records. I belonged to the World Record Club and I made a point of buying some gospel singers, such as Marion Williams who was a really good gospel singer and she was black. Because the rooms were only partitions, they were not very private at all and sound carried very well. I would put them to bed and after they went to bed, I would let them talk for perhaps five minutes and then I would go around and kiss them goodnight and say go to sleep now.

But then I would put on a record and that meant that I could not hear if they were talking, and they did not talk for long. I am sure it helped them go to sleep. I did have lots of different ones. I know with one of the boys his favourite was *HMAS Pinafore*. And the kids could pick which story I read. I tried to read to them individually so that each one had a story with me in my bedroom on their own so that we had a bit of time when it was just them and me, but sometimes, I did not have time for that and it would be to all of them together.

I did read to them about black American civil rights people when they were a bit older. I would have told them stories about black Americans. We used to have prayers, this was part of the routine, you had to have prayers at breakfast, communal prayers, and it was usually a Bible reading and a prayer and that was it. The Lord's Prayer. But as they got older they were more restless during the Bible reading, and so I read them, *Cry, the Beloved Country* by Alan Paton. It is about a South African black man and it is a really good story, but it is actually an adult story. William has spoken to me about that a few times as that story stayed with him apparently, far more than what a Bible reading would have.

Patrick and William Tilmouth

Patrick: In the Tilmouths, I am the youngest, William the second youngest, Tracker, then on the Nayda side with our older siblings: Harold Nayda, Kenny Nayda, then Margaret Nayda but she became Margaret Hampton, then Ian Nayda, and Lesley John Nayda being the eldest.

Us three, we stuck together [through life and we] would hear from each other every couple of weeks at least.

William: We belonged to each other. It was really apparent with the elder brothers and sister, Les and Margaret and all them, because their skin was fairer they were sent south, and the dark ones were sent north. They were told to *forget about them, you have got to stop worrying about your younger brothers*. And they had to fight the fact that they knew they were Aboriginal but on appearances they weren't. There were a lot of Aboriginal people who doubted their Aboriginality. There were a lot of people who tormented them, teased them and said, *You're not black*, and all this, until such time as I came out of gaol and I was introduced to everyone as their brother and people started saying, *Oh! Shit, he is black, Les is black,* or, *Harry is black*, or whatever. It really was a case of these five that went south had to fight the double whammy, one, to find their way back home and two, they had to fight for their identity every step of the way. Whereas the colour of our skin made us who we are.

People knew, and also the name Tilmouth was synonymous with the central Australian region. So there was this, *Oh! Tilmouth, you're Alice Springs blokes.* So you always had that identity.

Patrick: It is a big name. Like Smith in England.

William: Yeah! It is a big name. Everyone knew. We were like Ching in China. Tilmouths in Central Australia is fairly well known and so people would identify where we came from. We did not have the same problems that the elder ones had.

When Mum passed away, and in those days – welfare was just sitting like vultures on the fence sweating to take kids away. When Mum passed away, I do not know what she passed from or what was the problem, welfare swooped and Aunty Doreen actually tried to take us and I sat down and had really long talks with Aunty Doreen about it. Doreen McCoy, Doreen was married to Freddie McCoy, and Freddie was a taxi driver and they already had two children.

I think Doreen and Dad tried to go to court – and I am yet to explore whether there are court records – for us to be put in her care, but I think they told her that she already had two children and life was going to be hard enough without growing up another three. So welfare decided what was best suited, and decided to send us to Croker Island, which they did. We went to the Retta Dixon, and Retta Dixon was nothing but a drafting yard where they sent you out to the four points of the compass, and we managed to get sent to Croker Island, and there we managed to stay together. But the moment we hit Croker Island we were separated. Patrick went into Sea View Cottage and Tracker and I went into Victory. They had Illawara, they had Deloraine, they had Reynella, they had Malila, Sea View and Victory, so they just split you up into whatever cottage. Patrick went to Sea View because I think there were a lot of other younger lads there as well. Whereas, I stayed with Tracker in Victory with Sister Bartram, and later she got Patrick in with us.

Patrick: In Sea View we had Harold Furber, and we used to tease him. Then I went across the road and lived with these mob in Victory.

Harold was a cheeky bloke too. I was a really skinny fella, but yeah, I lived across the road from them originally.

William: And one of the things about Sister Bartram, and I believe I am reading it right, she recognised that kids were being split up all over the place and being fostered out and taken. A very smart woman and deliberately, I think she took us to Nullawil so that we became familiar with her parents, who I believe were going to foster us if it ever came to us being taken away, or split up, or fostered out. So I think she was also part and parcel of our identity too. One, she was the only mother we ever knew. Two, she was trying to politicise us, I mean in her own way, she played gospel music and black negro spiritual music and there was also reading books, like on South Africa, *Cry, the Beloved Country*, and all that sort of stuff, about the minister Stephen Kumalo, whose son had gone to Johannesburg.

Patrick: She used to read out of books every day, there was no TV. We would sit around and she would read.

William: Tracker used to read a bit too because he was the only one who could read.

Patrick: That is right. He was smart.

William: He was a good reader and she used to make him read to the kids. He used to read bedtime stories to the kids.

Patrick: He taught us about photosynthesis and that. He tried to explain that to us. That was above us and we had no idea. He was always too smart for us.

William: Seriously, one night we were all going to run away from the mission, we hated the mission. We wanted to go. We packed up our swags. We had it all hidden. Sister Bartram did not know what was going on, and we were all heading out, me and Eddie Horrell and the other kids in the cottage, and Eric Roberts and everything. We were going to get the horses and we were going to ride off into the west and not come back. A bright night it was, at midnight, you could clearly see your shadows underneath the tamarind tree and everything, it was crystal clear and you could hear the curlews in the background – how they whistled – and we were heading out. Slowly we snuck out and then Tracker comes out. He says, *Where are you blokes going?*

We're running away. He said, *Running away where?* We said, *We're going to run away.* He said, *You've got to realise this is an island.* And then he pulled out this bloody dictionary and it was not until after that we realised it was a Bible, and he said, *Look! Here*, and he flipped a few pages, then he said, *See that, the Lord said thou shalt not run away.* So we fucking unpacked our swags and went back to bed. He bluffed us. I remember that very clearly, *The Lord said thou shalt not run away.* None of us could read so we took him by his word, so we just unpacked our swags and put our clothes back and all got back into bed. We were about eight or nine, somewhere around there, seven or eight. As fucking naïve as the day is long. Just out of the blue he did that.

He was just smug in his own fucking self. You could see the smugness on him. But he said, *I'll tell you first it's an island.* He had this way about him. He had that ability to give you the directive in what you were thinking and it made sense. You would prop your head up and think.

Tracker Tilmouth

Peter Hansen and all these blokes were standing there, and were all going to run away, and my first idea was to say to them, *Which brilliant person thought this up because you are on a fucking island?* That was the first thing that flowed through my mind, but I thought that would not be telling them anything, because if they had not worked that out they should not be here. Anyway, I did not say you are on an island because it occurred to me that if I told them that, that would not have had any effect, and I thought how am I going to do this? I knew none of them could read so I grabbed the Bible and I said, *Righto.* I was about seven or eight at the time.

I got the Bible and I said, *You blokes all go to church,* and they all said, *Yes, we all go to church.* I said, *This is one of the rules of the Ten*

Commandments, thou shalt not run away. I had them stuffed because if I had told them don't run away, they would have done it. I told them this is not me you are arguing with, you are arguing with the Bible. They all went back to bed. No one ran away. Oh! Yes! They would have been in big trouble. The island was fifteen miles long and about five miles wide, not a very big place to hide. No one really tried to run away, not with the brains trust from the elder boys. They asked me for counsel which I gave them. For free. And the best of the New Testament that said *thou shalt not run away*, but none of them could read, not properly anyway.

The mission wanted to make a movie and they did an audition. I stood out as the main actor, as I could quote Shakespeare and Christ knows what else. So they said righto, and they made a movie about sly-grog running on Croker. This was an ad to stop grog coming on the missions and I was the main offender for the advertisement. I saw the smugglers and I jumped on my little horse and galloped back to the mission and informed the mission and all that sort of stuff. I got attacked by the smugglers who threw me in the water, and everything else. It was a good movie. I was nine at the time. It was an ad against grog and it was played a lot, at every movie night, over and over.

William and Patrick Tilmouth

William: But you know what, they made a movie there on Croker Island, the superintendent, Jack Goodluck. Tracker was the main actor. He put his hand up to act. It was about this kid who rode his horse and came across these grog smugglers, and he walked up to the little boat that had pulled up on the beach and he was looking in it and saw all these bottles of beer – all empty but it looked like the bottles were full of beer, then when he got discovered, he got thrown in the water and that was a really good script. The choreography needed some assistance and so did the camerawork but we used to watch this film every Friday. Every month we had a film on Croker Island but if the film did not arrive from Darwin, we had to watch the same old same olds. Tracker's story would be told and everyone laughed and giggled at the appropriate times.

The mission got rid of it in the end, they got rid of it because Sister Bartram enquired, and apparently the new superintendent said it was racist and actually destroyed the film. But you would see Tracker come tearing out of the scrub on this horse and gallop up behind the old tractor and trailer where the camera was sitting and the horse would be just heading off into the scrub, bolted. It shied away from the tractor, and there was Tracker holding on. Oh! Jesus Christ.

Another time on Croker Island he pulled up, this was in the first paddock there, and he was on this horse called Sugar Bush and he pulled up and said, *Jump on the back, jump on the back*. This horse, she was a quarter horse and very, very frisky, jumped around a lot, and could gallop like the wind. And he was sitting there with his shorts on, those big bloomers that they used to give us mission kids, and I asked him, *You can ride?* He said, *Yeah! I can ride. I'm a good rider.* So I jumped on the back and you hear *click, click*, and you do not do that with Sugar Bush. He was gone at the drop of a hat. Me and him tearing through the scrub flat chat up towards the stock gate and where there was all the erosion off the road, flat chat and eventually a branch comes along and me and Tracker were sitting in the dirt there, and Sugar Bush was gone. *You fucking told me you could ride you bastard,* and fighting in the mud.

Tracker Tilmouth

No, I was never spoilt. I was with the scones. You have got to quickly learn what your situation is and act accordingly to benefit yourself. Forget the masses they can look after themselves – feed them cake, but make sure you do not give away too many scones.

There is a photo of me, Emily has got of me, at school. There is Henry Yamirr and Andrew Yamirr at the bottom end of the steps at the school. We were all sitting on the steps reading and they were sitting there. Then there was the two – Jack Goodluck's boys, and somebody else, Mr Hocking's boy and me in the middle. I was sitting with the white people. I said to Mrs T, *Doesn't that photo show you everything?* It says it all. I very quickly worked out what the situation was. Where food was. Scones. Remember scones. Have scone, will travel.

Peter Hansen and Tracker Tilmouth

Peter: Tree of Knowledge. Sometimes we would be up there smoking you know, and the smoke would go right up over onto the side of the hill and anybody walking past could not smell it because we would get a sea breeze and the leaves used to make a lot of noise. Sometimes the lights would go on and it was, *Oh! Shit! We did not see that.*

This particular night Morris Scott and I went up the Tree of Knowledge to have our smoke and we see the lights go off while we are out there. Anyway it's a bright moonlit night, and we were wondering, *Who turned that off?* Boom! Boom! Boom!

Anyway someone comes up, and another one goes there and they meet at the eight o'clock bell – just there. Next thing they embrace. What's going on here? What's going on here, we reckoned. We saw them. Then they go from there up to the recreation room. There was a double bed there and after twenty minutes or half an hour while we are still up the tree they come out, have a hug and kiss, and then they part company, and they don't even know we saw them, and this happened more than once. And we were supposed to be taught Christian values and we see all this. Are you serious? It is a wonder we are still sane. But anyway, that is only some of the stories. I have got heaps I could tell you.

Tracker: Remember all of those ponies Bob Reynolds stole off us? Pick your best horse and I will take them to Darwin and look after them for you. When we got there he had sold the lot. Yeah! That old ookey [pony].

Peter Hansen

There was a time when we were out there, where there was this first group of children, one of the girls there, anyway she has been gone a long time, and the builder there got friendly with her you know, and he decided he wanted to adopt her, and the missionary said, *Yeah! Look! We are not here to adopt children, we're here to look after kids, adoption is simply out of the question.* So we thought gee, he was falling in love with this teenage girl. Anyway next thing – she is pregnant.

Listen now! So they went to the TO [traditional landowner], old Dick – he is Aboriginal and *mullaga* [Top End name for white people] – said, *Dick. When she comes back from Darwin you're going to marry her.* He said, *No, bunyi {friend}. I've got nothing to do with her.* He said, *I didn't even go near her.* The superintendent said, *Be quiet, when she comes back you will marry her.* She goes to Darwin, has the child and she comes back minus the child. The child was born white, absolutely white. They sent him through to Garden Point, Melville Island. That was a child that Europeans said was fairly normal. It happened. Nothing said. All these things I am telling you. It never came out. It never ever came out. And the older girls would not have said, *You've got to take the church to court,* but said, *Oh no, they've been so lovely.* I said, *Listen here you're not taking the people to court, you're taking the church for not making sure this sort of thing didn't happen.* But you cannot get through to them so I will just tell you my story. There was lots of this. There were boys in the cottage missing their girlfriends after lights out, and they have seen the farmer come in and go into the net over there visiting that girl – and Ronny Roberts froze and you know what, and black pudding there couldn't move. And Ron said, *I couldn't see* – they had the army net and you could not see in even if you shone in a torch, very hard to see in. Anyway he walked back out. And he does not know that these boys saw him come and go. True story. Tree of Knowledge. Even a house was a house of knowledge.

Lois Bartram

About from the time of my arrival, there was talk of us moving to Darwin one day, and that was an idea that had come up, that we were too isolated, and I agreed with that, although I loved Croker. But always, when it was talked about, it became more than just an idea, it became yes, we are going to move one day, but the cottage families will be kept together.

The idea was that houses would be built in separate suburbs in Darwin but we would still all be the same, and there was Croker Island night at the local church in Nightcliff which had been started up and had been going for a few years, and was a very good idea I thought. Every Friday night they could meet at the local church and it was just a social evening and it meant that all the ex-Crokerites got together and they supported each other.

In 1965 I had sort of worked out that there were definite plans made for us to move to Darwin but the houses had to be built, and then the time that we were to move was getting further away because it was taking longer to build the houses than had been anticipated. But Jack [Goodluck] went to Darwin and he came back, and he had found temporary accommodation. We would all be living together and I forget what the previous use of the premises were, but we would still keep our cottage, our cottage family identity.

The kids had always been told this, that when we go to Darwin you are still part of this family. But then, we had a change of superintendents and it was a drastic change. For three years with Jack we had had a man who had more modern ideas of childcare, and he treated the local Aboriginal people with respect. But his replacement was the other extreme. And it was not a very happy situation at all. Anyway, at last in January 1968 we moved to Darwin, and our cottage went to Clarke Crescent, and there we were told that Bruce and another lad who had been with me twelve months longer than Bruce had, they would only stay with us for three weeks and then they would be moved to another cottage in Stuart Park. We were in Rapid Creek [ten kilometres away], and there was to be no connection between the two cottages. That was to be their family.

The superintendent got onto the local church and got them to close down those Croker Island nights because he wanted the children to make friends with their neighbours and schools and not stick together, which was extremely short-sighted of him I think. Of course they needed each other. They were an extended family. The kids objected and I objected. I went to the chairman who was living in Darwin but no, *what the superintendent says goes,* and that was to be it.

In the meantime, while we were there in the first three weeks, Bruce had been in high school. The army had visited the school and well, you can imagine what it was like. Bruce had shown interest to join the army, and at that stage the army was taking kids at fifteen and signing them on for seven years and that could not be broken. In the newspapers there were letters and articles from distressed parents who could not get their boys out although they were having what amounted to a nervous breakdown because they had signed on for seven years and therefore, they stayed for seven years. This was during the Vietnam War. Now I was and still am very anti-war and I was certainly very against our involvement in Vietnam, and I had visions of Bruce being sent off to Vietnam as well. He would not have been sent at fifteen but he would have been sent at eighteen. I did talk to him about it, I made no secret of the fact to anyone, and anyone who knew me at all knew that I was against our involvement in Vietnam. One day the superintendent came to see me, and he said Bruce seems to be wavering in his, I forget his wording, in his ideas of joining the army. *I want you to do all you can to persuade him to stick to his original idea.* And I, probably very unwisely, said, *I will do all in my power to convince him not to join the army.*

It was very, very difficult when the kids went to Darwin I might add, and a lot of them got into trouble in one way or another.

Tracker got into trouble too, but not so spectacularly as most of them. I do not know if he was ever in gaol, but I said something to Patrick one day, and he said something about being up before the beak and I said, *Patrick, were you?* He said, *Oh! Many a time*, and he just laughed it off. But as far as I know Patrick was never in gaol. And not all our kids ended up in gaol, but they would get pulled up, Aboriginal people or part-Aboriginals would get pulled up for doing things whereas other people, it would be only a minor thing. They would be charged and it would go on their record.

You can ask Bruce about his ideas of what it was like on Croker, but I would say he had a fairly happy childhood apart from the trauma of being separated from the family he knew and I would not underestimate what that was, the cost of that.

I did love them dearly and I was very, very pleased, better not tell Bruce this, you can I suppose, it does not matter, he said to me one day that they were lucky to have gone to Croker. I questioned that and he said, *If we had to be taken then Croker was the best place.* Bruce might not have said that, it might have been Harold [Furber], *The best place to go.* But Bruce said, *We were fed, we were educated.* I queried as to how well, they did have a good grounding in primary school, but high school was a disaster for nearly all of them. And Bruce said, *And we were loved*. I said, *Wow! I'm glad you knew that.* I do not know about being proud of the way these boys turned out, but I am very pleased, very happy. They have done extraordinarily well to start off at such a disadvantage. Their mother died to start with, and then being removed and removed a thousand miles away, but that was done deliberately and the ones from Alice were sent north, and the ones from further north were sent south to St Mary's in Alice. The idea was to disconnect them completely from their families when they were here.

I do not like to say this but it is true, the original philosophy if I may say that, was that they had been rescued from the blacks' camp, they were better than that, and they were taught to look down on Aboriginal people. And I noticed that amongst my older boys, quite often I had to pull them up about talking disrespectfully about Aboriginal people. Originally, when the mission on Croker was first started the Aboriginal people living there were forcibly removed: they had to go. Now I think they all had roots on the mainland anyway, but they were forcibly driven off. Then they gradually came back and under Jack [Goodluck] quite a lot of them had, so that we had more than a hundred there I think by the time the kids left. Quite a big community. But the housing was appalling.

Peter Hansen

Some of the boys brought up in the mission on Croker Island ended up drinking a lot – whether they wanted to fit in or what, but I think there were some boys there where it would not have mattered what happened to them, they were going to end up going to the pub. Then there was the other half who were trying to figure out how we are going to survive because there was no halfway house once you left the mission and the island. I was there for the whole twelve years or more, whatever it was, and I had never left the island.

What happened to me in the beginning was that they [the mission authorities] told us the island belonged to us and that when we grow up we can get married, and have children, and build houses. And they did. They started building houses. Some of the boys and girls got married there and then they [the mission] took the lease out on Murgenella, which is situated two hundred and fifty kilometres east-north-east of Darwin. If the families got too big, then we could move across there. So that was going really well. I think too well. I did not know what happened but two or three years down the track they came back and said, *You're all going to Gawler in South Australia.*

We said, *Where's Gawler?* They said South Australia. And we did not know what was going on until we got to the archives here years and years later, and found out why. But as kids we thought we will be able to go to the shop just down the road there with a penny, and we can buy chocolates and everything. We did not care about leaving, because what mattered was that we were all going together. Anyway, I do not know why but after another two or three years, they decided we were not going. They came back and said, *When you turn eighteen you have got to leave the island.* And some of them said, *We do not want to leave the island, this is all we knew, we grew up here, it is ours.* They said, *Look if you don't leave the island, we will get the police to remove you.* Seriously. So we were to be dragged out of there, and you were going to be dragged off if you did not actually leave.

Lois was still there then and I think the worst feeling of my life was when they said *you have got to go to Darwin.* It was pretty much the end of the world for me because I had never been to Darwin, I had never been anywhere outside of the community when I was sent to Croker Isand, and it was only a little joint. To me, Darwin looked like New York. You might have eight or ten houses in the mission on Croker Island, but Jesus, in Darwin there might have only been a thousand houses, but it looked like New York to me.

The mission managed to have a church hostel in Darwin. It was an apprentices' hostel. They had just bought it, and I went straight into that, and otherwise, I would not have had any occupation. And then they found a job for me but I may as well not have had a job because I was living in one end of Darwin, and going to work at the other end, at the airport which was five miles away and that was a lot of mileage, back in those days. And no transport. We had to get a lift from somebody at work, or catch a bus, and we did not know anything about that. We were bush kids. If they had taken some from the city and said, *Look, come out here and do this*, they would not be able to do what we were doing.

When I came to Darwin in April 1960 I was seventeen, in fact I had turned seventeen that year, but I was still sixteen when they told me. When I was out there [Croker Island] they changed my date of birth, and decided that I should be two years older. But I am still working on the same birth certificate that I had in the very beginning. When I came in I was sixteen, and they were trying to tell the people in Darwin that I was eighteen and I wasn't. I was a little kid.

The stories I could tell you from that island. I got nothing back. No papers or anything. When I went to the church hostel in Darwin, they asked me whether I wanted to pay some money towards the church in those little envelopes. They gave me fifty-two envelopes and I threw them in the bin. That is the only time I saw them, I never saw them again. We got no assistance. You have got the Catholics still over there, but the Croker Island missionaries just disappeared. You never see any of them, except Lois Bartram comes up and visits. She is the only one.

What was Lois like? She was really nice, I liked her. Sometimes she had to be stern, but we accepted that. We accepted whatever she gave us because we liked her. If we had done something wrong, okay, no worries. And it shows, she visits every year and I promised to go down and see her and I am going to go down.

Out of all the missionaries she was the only one that really sticks out. When she said she was going to do something, she did it. And we did not know she was going to come back and visit us. I mean once maybe, but not every year. She might miss a year, but definitely she will visit us the following year. She has been doing it since a reasonably young age. She is one of those genuinely likeable people and she followed us all the way through life. I said to her one day, Lois – she is a nice woman, and maybe I should not have asked her, but I said: *How come you're not married?* She said, *Nobody would have me.* I thought, *Why did I ask?*

But Tracker came out there years after I did because I was only little when I was sent there. Anyway Lois really looked after him. I do not know what he reckoned about Lois, but I think she has done a really good job. She had all the time in the world for the little kids, more so, because the other boys in the cottage like myself, we were sort of grown up. She was taking them down to the beach, down to the water to go swimming, and she would take something for them to eat, swim there all afternoon and then bring them all the way back again. Today people are flat out giving you the time of day, but she did it way back then.

In Darwin, a few of the kids were sent to Essington House way down at Myilly Point, and I was at the Flinders Hostel which was a five minute walk away. Tracker was in Essington House. It was like a reform dormitory. I lost track of them because I was only in Darwin for five years then I headed bush and stayed bush, so I sort of lost track of Tracker. I had more to do with them when I was on the island. With the age difference, they were just too small to follow us around. They were looked after and Lois had them pretty much all the time. We were busy riding our ponies and going hunting. We did not want Tracker tagging along.

We had horses out there, and we all learnt to ride for the simple fact that if you did not learn to ride and you wanted to go from point A to point B, you had to walk with the dog or whatever in the heat with no shoes, so we learnt to ride so that we could go from here to there in a quarter of the time. The mission kept horses in paddocks and we all had our own horses. We just went out and picked our own horses. The older boys handed their horses down to us growing up, but I got horses that used to buck with the older boys and they did not want them, so they said, *Do you want them*, and I said, *Yeah I'll take it*. I was desperate for horses, hunting, and riding. I got them quiet enough and I would ride them all day. Even then I used to like horses. I used to bake bread and I would work half a day Saturday and finish about one o'clock, and then I would get my horse and I would have to go riding. We knew everybody's footprint out there, except the younger kids but everybody else I just knew, and when I saw their footprint I knew where they were going. I would just ride and I knew where they would be.

Patrick and William Tilmouth

Patrick: I was protected by these two [William and Tracker]. I was a baby and life did not worry me that much. I did not see the sort of sorry things they saw, I did not even look…

William: There were times when the three of us – I remember very clearly, we would sit down and cry uncontrollably because there was just this vacuum left in our lives. We did not really know what we were crying for, or how to express ourselves, but I think Tracker felt it more acutely than I did with him being older, he would have known a lot more. I had vague, very vague memories of Mum, whereas Patrick has none. There is just this vacuum of yearning I suppose, not having anyone to recognise, or to fall back on.

Very much left in limbo. An emotional limbo at that, and there was no bottom to it. You could not go up to your father and say this is my dad, or this is my mum, you have nothing, you have nothing to substantiate your reality and your emotions. We did meet Dad years and years later on one of those trips down to Victoria, when Patrick went to South Australia, and I went to Nullawil. The aeroplane landed at Alice Springs airport and a welfare lady came up to us and she said, *Are you the Tilmouth brothers?* I said, *Yeah*, and this bloke here [Patrick] spewed his guts out on the tarmac from air-sickness.

As the plane had been taxiing in, before we got off the plane, we had noticed this very large gentleman standing out the front, an Aboriginal guy, very large stomach and he had white overalls on. Me and Patrick were thinking, *Oh look at that bloke*, he is a big bloke and we were poking fun at him and not realising it was our father. But when we got off the plane the welfare lady said, *Are you the Tilmouth brothers?* We said, *Yeah*. And she said, *Oh! Your father is over there*, and she pointed to the very same person who we had been looking at. And it was Dad. We really did not know what to think. I mean, *God*, and we went and sat down with him and he was extremely proud of us.

I sat on one side and Patrick sat on the other and every man, or woman, or child who walked passed that he knew, he introduced us, *This is my son, this is my son, this is Willie, and this is Patrick*. He asked us what we wanted. I think I wanted a bowie knife and all those things, not realising that it was illegal to have those things in those days. It was not until we were halfway flying to Adelaide that Patrick and I realised who the hell that was.

We had jumped back on that plane and we were flying to Adelaide, then he and I started crying, because it dawned on us that this was the father that we missed. That was the father that we had spent all that time at Croker Island yearning for and not knowing who we were, and yearning for him. He was a big man in those days, and he still was a big man. And it dawned on us on the flight. Hang on. Because no one told us we were going to meet our father. If we had known we would probably have been more prepared for it. It got dropped on us as soon as we got off the plane, those old DC-3s with propellers droning along through the air, and this bloke spewed his stomach up on the tarmac because he was air sick. We had been sitting there for long, long hours. I think they allowed smoking on the planes in those days, all up in First Class puffing away. Fucking people smoking cigarettes all over the place. People thought lighting up pipes was distinguished. Eight hours. It even landed at Leigh Creek [in South Australia]. Oodnadatta, then Adelaide. Focker Friendship.

Tracker Tilmouth

I do not know what it is but my wife reckons I have a form of autism or deficit syndrome, one of the two. She reckons I am a mental case, which is probably correct, but I always sort of saw things differently to a lot of people. When I see something, I see it totally different and I have the ability to do the analysis outside of the debate, then come in at the right time and say, *Aren't you talking about this or aren't you talking about that, why don't you consider this and why don't you consider that?* I do not know what it is but I have always had an innate ability to read the play.

I was just a normal sort of a kid. I thought I was normal, and everyone else thought I was a bit different. Some of them liked me. I got on well with the traditional landowners, Mary, Daisy, and Andrew, and old Mick Yarmirr's mob. I got on really well with all of them.

We were not imposed upon, we did not have the righteousness of who you are and who you were not, or had that imposed on you. Lois allowed you to find your own way to a certain extent, without bending too many of the rules. And was a lot freer in that discussion, than what you would normally enjoy. So Croker Island and Victory Cottage was a good place for us. We liked it.

With the Stolen Generation thing, people were sad about their parents, yes they were and still are, but we grew up well. We got taught well. You have only got to take the Croker Island mob by themselves and see who is working, who's not, who is doing this and who is doing that. They are doing well but at the end of the day, you can also pick the ones that could not handle it in other cottages. I think Lois understood all of that, so she was a lot gentler to us than other cottage mothers.

She wasn't strict. She made out she was strict.

I had no fear, and I have no fear now. I suppose it came from Croker Island. There were good people at Croker. There were people like Peter Hansen, Emily Deveron. Big Peter, brilliant horseman. I felt totally, utterly safe. Crocodiles were there, and people would get rid of the crocodiles, they would not muck around. They would eat the crocodile as food, the mission mob. No, I felt well protected. Mary Yarmirr mob [traditional landowners for the area]. I am still classified [as family], and get hugged to death up there by the Yarmirr mob.

Sometimes when you go to the emotional side [of being taken from your family and put on a mission], it can get hectic because you are dealing with people's souls, you are dealing with people's spirits, you are dealing with people's emotions. I might be able to wear something, but somebody else might not be able to handle it. Lois took us and she tried to make it a happy place. I was only a kid. Retta Dixon, we saw that. Croker Island was a different argument. Croker Island was an argument where you decided that it was a happy place and you had to make it a happy place, because there was nowhere else to go. And people like me who got harder, we got a different feeling on life, because nothing was given. You had to learn a process, you had to earn a position. If you did not work that out very quickly in life, when they let you out of Croker you died. You died from grog, you died from drugs, you died from domestic violence. When you look at the fifty or thirty kids that I would have grown up with, they have all gone, except for about four or five of us and they include my cousins and my brothers. Out of Victory Cottage they are the Cassidy boys, Willie, Patrick and myself. The rest are gone. Grog mostly. Elizabeth Mosley, people like that. People out of Tennant Creek, Mick and Pat Bourke. From Alice Springs. They had a really hard life. A terrible life. There is a report which talks about what the mission was trying to do which would be good in a court case because it shows the true intent of the government.

It is a shocking agenda isn't it? Because you know, you get ten victories but you lose a hundred. After I left Croker Island I could have gone anywhere. I am very thankful I had very good advice at the right time for some fluke, and that there were people like [Bob] Beadman, [Neville] Jones, Arthur Liddle, Alfie Liddle, Bessie Liddle, Geraldine Liddle, Peter Hansen, people like that. It could have gone either way.

They Had Nowhere to Put Us

Patrick and William Tilmouth

Patrick: Then Tracker went to Essington House in Darwin for high school while we were still at Croker. He used to come back for holidays. Then we all moved to Darwin when they closed Croker Island down.

William: In 1967 when Aboriginal people got the right to vote.

Patrick: We were shipped out. We were put in homes in Darwin. And then Tracker was a couple of years older than me, so when you are a teenager and older you are knocking around with different groups. He did not have much to do with us when we went to Darwin. He was still our brother. I would have been about twelve or thirteen.

William: There is about a year difference each way.

Patrick: I am a couple of years younger than Tracker. We are all about a year apart.

William: We decided to go to the football one Saturday morning and so Patrick and I caught the bus into town to Gardens Oval and we thought we will be right, Tracker was working at the abattoir then and we would get Tracker to give us bus fares home. He was there alright, but he had all his circles of friends. Me and this bloke decided to hitchhike home. We were walking along up the hill towards the Darwin High School when Tracker comes past, just him and Milton Liddle in the car and he waved and kept going. There was no way to turn around. But he was in his own group. So me and this bloke was left walking. I got into a fight in the Parap Hotel that night, I was that angry. Not in the hotel,

I wasn't drinking, just to drive people for a fight who had followed us and started punching trees, and so I started punching him, a Croker Island bloke who wanted to fight. Me and him always fought.

Lloyd Bray

We were in Darwin in 1965. Well! I was there in 1964. We were in the boys home there, Essington House at Myilly Point and Tracker was at Croker. They come over from Croker, him and Harry Furber in 1965. They were the little boys and we were the senior boys, and it was the first time I met him since he was sent away from Alice when he was more or less a baby.

We knew the Tilmouth family, and when they came to the home there in Darwin in 1965, they were very frightened little boys amongst all the big boys but we told them who we were, and how we were related to them. I think they were more secure then, more happy with being with family. I think he was around about eleven, ten, something like that. That was a young age.

They knew nobody, and when they came to Darwin they found there was a big mob of Alice Springs boys in that home. They were all related to Tracker and Harry Furber. Anyway, they started going to school from there. I think they went to the Darwin High School and that later on. But he got involved with us blokes. We did things together and went to football. I remember Tracker used to carry my football boots to the Garden No. 1 Oval where we used to play. When he first came there he was a bit shy, wary and scared of the big blokes, but after being with us boys from Alice, you could see him changing, being the jokeful bloke, always playing jokes. He used to crack jokes, play jokes on blokes, and you could not get wild with him because he made you laugh and all that. He just had a knack for it.

Tracker Tilmouth

I was at Essington House for two years to go to high school after I left Croker Island mission. Because there was no other accommodation available, Harold Furber and I were put into the boy's reformatory near the hospital in Darwin. Then I went over to Carpentaria College near Nightcliff in Darwin with two other boys from Croker Island, Peter Deveron and Harry Furber. When I was at Essington House I was a caddy for Doug Hall who was the superintendent. He and Mick Ivory, a big bloke and whoever else was there.

Anyway, Peter, Furber and myself did grade seven on Croker Island quicker than anybody else. The mission could not send us out to cattle stations or wherever else to work as they did with everyone else, because we were too young. We were only twelve or thirteen, and we were already past grade seven, and no one did it as quick as us because we had a good schoolteacher. We just cleaned them up and we all got good marks. They said: *Oh! You can't {go to work}, you better go to high school.* So we were the first mob ever to go to high school from Croker. We also had Maurie Ryan there, the smartest man alive – he will tell you. You had to finish everything at school, or you stayed back to do it.

We had good teachers. We had really good teachers then for some unknown reason, and a teacher who took an interest in us. I think we skipped grade six, the three of us, because we were that far in front. Peter Deveron is a smart bloke, and still is, and Harry Furber is smart if you could stop him being stupid. We jumped a grade and went straight into grade seven and after that, what do you do? You couldn't go to work, we were too young for that so they had to send us to high school. They had nowhere to keep us [when we were sent to Darwin], so they put us in a reformatory with all the thieves, and then we got transferred to Carpentaria when they finished building Carpentaria College, which is now the Greek college.

Tracker Tilmouth

I fell for a foolhardy trick with Puggy Hunter. Puggy Hunter had decided that while he was not incarcerated physically, he was incarcerated in spirit.

So he decided to run away with Harry Furber and me because we wanted to go to Wyndham [in Western Australia].

We got to Berrimah and Arnold Hunter, which is his name, was in charge of victualling, supply of food thereof – one tomato sandwich for a road trip of thousands of kilometres which he ate by the time he got passed Noonamah, by himself.

So I declined at Adelaide River to join them.

That was the end of the breakout, and Harry Furber would not go anywhere without me.

Shocking was old Pug, Arnold Peanut I used to call him.

Tracker Tilmouth

Willie by that time had ended up in Yatala [gaol in South Australia] after assaulting and doing some damage to a policeman. He gave him a hiding. So he went to Yatala and he looked after Maxie Stuart. He was Maxie Stuart's hit man in the gaol. Willie was a big bloke and he was brutal too. He was hard as nails. You wouldn't think that he is the same bloke now.

Anyway, Patrick was adopted by the Greeks. He was the only Aboriginal painter who could speak Greek. He worked for the Stiliano mob at Roper River [Ngukurr]. They had the shop and did painting and tiling service and all that other stuff. He worked for them. He was adopted by them. Anyway, so I was in Woolworths one day and old Geraldine Liddle and old Alfie Liddle saw me and Geraldine said, *You're a Tilmouth eh?*

Yeah.

Your father is Roy.

Yeah.

Ah! Where are you living? Old Alfie said.

I said, *I'm down the beach.* He said, *No, no, you come over to Blake Street.* So I went and camped there with Harry Furber. Harry Furber, Johnnie Tye, and Trevor Reid. Not Palmer Reid but the other cheeky bugger who died a long time ago, big Trevor, Trevor Reid. We all used to live at number one, Blake Street. And the Ludwigs used to be down the road on Gardens Hill, and that is how I know Wendy [Ludwig] mob. This is why I know Ursula [Raymond] mob, because old Geraldine mob was a relation to Raymond mob, Ursula Raymond and all that mob. Geraldine's sister had married one of the Raymonds [old families of Darwin]. There was Geraldine and Damian was her brother, Damian Liddle they used to call him. But he had no name. Old Geraldine and Freddy Servelis, Geraldine Servelis. So we would play football for Buffaloes and old Alfie was coach of St Marys. Johnnie Tye was absolutely brilliant and I used to carry his boots down to the oval. So when Johnnie Tye was a slaughterman, I got a job at William Angliss out at Berrimah. He would go and get me drunk when I was about fourteen. So I was at the Darwin Hotel hitting the piss with a bloke called Rodney Keelan, and another young fellow called David Ross who was that drunk he got thrown out by bouncers so he started pulling out the palm trees in the cool spot, in the middle of the green room. The David Ross we know today. The nice quiet one. And then he was lying crying and spewing on the Darwin oval, the original one up at the cenotaph, where they have the ANZAC marches and all that, and which used to be the oval. So there you go.

I would have been older, about sixteen or seventeen. Then when I was seventeen, I went down to Angas Downs because I was helping to relieve people of their jewels, by breaking and entering. Johnny Ah Kit was helping me through these louvres on this upstairs house and I was standing on his hands because I was skinny as hell and I could get through the louvres, and so I got in there and opened the door. I did not turn on any lights. We had a comrade called Charlie Lawrie. He was with us breaking and entering, him and Willie Stokes. Anyway, we got in there and we were looking at these photos, pictures of Dawn Lawrie, Delia Lawrie, Charlie Lawrie and I said, *This looks like your mob*. You know, it was dark. He said, *Yeah it's our house, I've got a key but no one asked me*. Here I was hanging on my guts on a glass louvre. Puggy Hunter tried to join us but he could not get through the louvres. *I've got a key but no one asked me*. He was robbing his own house. It should have clicked because the dog was very friendly, jumping around and patting it. I was standing on Ah Kit, he was holding me up and I was trying to get through the fly wire sideways, through the louvres. I wanted to kill him.

So her Majesty's government, or her Majesty's judiciary, decided that I should take a holiday down at Angas Downs – down to Alice Springs. Old Alf had fronted [to court] and said he came from Alice

Springs, and *my brother will take him to work at Angas Downs*. This was when I first went to Angas Downs.

The skin head. I had a skin head. I was as skinny as all hell and that is when I started at Angas Downs. Oh God, what a laugh.

Vincent Forrester

You know with first memories, some things stand out, and one morning there was a lot of crying, and then these kids who I knew had disappeared. As you start growing up your memories become clearer, I have always remembered this old man Uncle Roy Tilmouth who was a great friend of my mum, old Anita Kruger, old Eva Copp, old Marie Liddle, old Ethel Maloney, Emily Hayes, and all those old girls in The Gap in Alice Springs, these beautiful, beautiful old women. Old Uncle Roy used to come around, and you would ask questions, and he would say his wife had died and his children were taken away.

Then in 1965, these kids from Croker Island came and stayed in Alice Springs at old Kelly Hargreaves place. Harold Furber, Tracker, and I think there was another kid. It was around the Aileron bush picnic weekend, so these kids were allowed to come with us up to Aileron to the rodeo, about a hundred and sixty kilometres north of Alice Springs. The old blokes we went with decided to grab quite a few cartons of Southwark longneck beers, and they let us kids drive. So a kid going too fast slid off onto some gravel with Tracker and Harold sitting up in the back and Tracker fell off. He got scarred on his eyebrows and his knees.

These are some of the things you remember as a child. Tracker had to go back to Alice Springs Hospital for about a week. So I knew him from my childhood memories and it must have been something that clicked there, knowing old Uncle Roy really closely, and then I did not see him again for a few years.

You know when you are a young boy you think you are a big man and you leave home, and I took freedom. I left Alice Springs. When I got to Darwin I had to go and live with an uncle called Alf Liddle in Blake Street near Coles store, Gardens Hill, Darwin. When I got there I had to go to church twice every Sunday. Down the road the first mob

I met were at a home called Croker Island Home in Westralia Street, in the suburb of Stuart Park in Darwin. And Tracker mob was there. Those young fellas when they started to reach puberty off on the island, they started sending them into Darwin – for transition, to be assimilated into the society in Darwin. So Tracker was going to Darwin High School with Peter Deveron and Harold Furber, and in his class were blokes like Gunner Christophersen, Puggy Hunter and all that mob. Tracker was the smallest kid in class, but the smartest kid.

He had a really sharp mind with the wit to go with it and topping the bloody class at school, but he was challenging. Tracker always had that bit of a challenge with authority and pushed things to the limit. Anyway, then Tracker left school, and he and I got a job at the Angliss Meat Works in Berrimah. We were first working for a quid. It was like being an apprentice, and you started work at five o'clock in the morning and finished at five o'clock at night, for eighteen dollars a week or some ridiculous thing.

We would go to work early morning before the sun came up, catch the bus and get out to the meat works and start first thing, into it, and then after work we would hitchhike home, back into Stuart Park from Berrimah. But every day, guaranteed, we would get a lift. One day this bloke rocked up there in a dark-red station wagon full of kids – him and his wife. Tracker was there. *Hi, hello Bruce.* This is before we started calling him Tracker, *Hello Bruce, hello. Who's your friend there?*

Oh! My name is Vincent.

My name is Bobby Randall.

Before I went up to Darwin, Mum said you have got an uncle up there whose name is Bobby Randall. He was taken on a camel a long time ago. *One half-caste boy,* they took him north. So I said to Bobby Randall, *My mum said I've got to say hello to you. My mum said you were taken on a camel from Angas Downs.* That sort of went bang: it hit me between the eyes.

In those days there was a lot of sport involved in people's socialising in Darwin, and a lot of the football sides were made up of the Stolen Generation people. They all played for the Buffaloes, St Mary's, Nightcliff. So Darwin was an interesting town. They were not relations but they were relations, all that Stolen Generation who got together.

While working with Tracker, he would get into anything and push everything to the limit, the bastard. One day at the abattoir, one of my jobs was to push the cattle up the race until they got slaughtered, and you use an electric jabber, to jab the cows. This bloke was having a piss against the iron and Tracker got him with the jabber, and of course that bloke turned around and give Tracker a fucking slapping. I had come around the corner and there was Tracker getting a slapping. I was bigger than Tracker so I said, *Here, pick on your own size.* This bloke was about ten feet tall I reckon. He gave me a flogging and I wore a black eye for Tracker, the bastard, for doing that. This bloke punched the shit out of me. But Tracker now, sticking up for Tracker, and anyway, *Tracker look what you done,* I said. He just said, *I didn't get the black eye, you did.* That bloody Tracker.

Old Uncle Alf and Aunty Geraldine [Liddle] were Stolen Generation too. They came from [a mission on] Melville Island, but all the same, they were Stolen Generation – not your family, but they were your family. Uncle Alf and Aunty Gerry knew old Roy Tilmouth, and took Tracker under their wing, because when you got a job while you were living in a Croker Island home in Darwin, you wanted to get out of that home. So the umbilical cord of the mission was cut and Bruce went over to Uncle Alf and Aunty Geraldine's.

Essington House where Tracker was first sent to from Croker Island was a reform school, where if you pinched a bit of chewing gum they would fucking send you away. The Stolen Generation was really hardcore intervention in all of our lives. So when Tracker got a job he started getting his independence.

Anyway Tracker came down to Angas Downs, in 1970 at Christmas time. Uncle Alf and Aunty Gerry took him with their children out to Angas Downs for a holiday. Then he asked old Arthur to give him a job and Tracker was like, *No.* Tracker was the skinny, snotty-nosed little boy. Hmmm! What could you do? Oh! Well, so he got a job with us and he was Aunty Bess' driver. Ha! Ha! *Feed him up a bit old Arthur, feed him up a bit,* and us boys would be getting desert oak logs, and they would take Tracks out for a couple of hours and no, *Take him back, take him back,* building him up slowly, slowly, slowly.

He Worked The Crowd, You Know

Tracker Tilmouth

Do not sweat the small stuff, and do not chop wood for practice. On Croker, all the punishment we had was to go and chop wood, wood that was already chopped.

I was put in Essington House, a home for boys at Myilly Point in Darwin so I could go to high school, and because the mission had no other place to put me. I was there for about two years and then I went to Carpentaria College in Darwin for about a year and a half. After that I worked around, and I was in and out of what they called foster homes.

I was famous for being taken to school in Darwin in a paddy wagon and all this other stuff. The reason I was a mongrel was I was way out in front of everybody. We pushed the police van with the policeman in it. We could have walked away and left him, he was too fat to run. We were silly pushing a police van to start it. Anyway, that is another story for another time.

I kept going to all the different foster homes and different homes and that, and then Geraldine and Alfie Liddle decided to look after me, and I went down to Central Australia. I was in a bit of trouble, just misbehaving more than anything else. Just breaking and entering, kid stuff. Nothing spectacular. Alfie decided to take me on a trip to Angas Downs. I was living with him in a foster home. Alfie ran a foster home, him and Geraldine Liddle. So they took me down to Angas Downs and I met old Arthur and everybody else. Everyone was happy that I was out there, including the judge and everybody else. So I stayed out there. He got permission for me to stay at Angas Downs to work but I was not allowed in the township because I was in some trouble in those days. I went to Angas Downs for about four or five years, whatever it was, and I was not allowed into town. Three years I stayed out bush. I did not go into town, not even for Christmas.

The relationship originally with Johnny and Vincent and everybody else was pretty hairy for me because I was a stranger. They knew each other well and except for Timmy, they took a lot of pleasure in Vincent giving me a touch up every now and then, in the yards, or kicking me, or whatever.[6] He was just like any other young bloke out of Alice Springs. He did not know which way he was going, and he was finding himself like everybody else was I suppose. Nothing spectacular or anything else. And that was alright, you grow up tough, big deal. So I had a fairly hectic first couple of years there. To escape that, Bess used to take me out hunting with her. I was Bess' driver and I'd go hunting and we would dig witchettys and goannas and everything else and talk language.

I was about seventeen. I nearly tried to commit suicide, I was that messed up because I did not know whether I was accepted in with the Liddles, or what I was doing there. I had spent all my life in Arnhem Land. The first couple of years were fairly full-on for me, and Bess allowed me to escape. Bess was, I think, concerned about how messed up I was as a kid. I was totally messed up. So, for a bit of entertainment they [the other boys] used to have Vinnie go the knuckle on me every now and then. He was one year older than me and bigger, stronger. I do not know what it was, I did not think I was a threat to anyone, but anyway. I could do things good because I always learnt off Snowy Lander, as Snowy Lander's offsider. I did everything Snowy did, and Snowy was very good at what he did. So it was a hectic first couple of years. And you can do that, you can grow up anywhere. You have got to fight your way through, and you have got to be accepted for who you are. I think I did that quite well because I could ride a horse, I could do just as good as anybody else in anything. Snowy Lander made sure I learnt all that.

Snowy Lander at the end of the day ended up looking after me more than anybody else. And so I treat him as a big brother. When

---

6. Johnny Liddle, Vincent Forrester and Tim (Snowy) Lander all worked with Tracker on Angas Downs, and were about the same age as he was.

I got into trouble, old Bess would take me away and we would go getting *mingkulpa* or *pituri* [bush tobacco] up in Kings Canyon and up at Wallace Rockhole. There was no one out there, there were no roads, no anything and me and old Bess and old Maggie Armstrong, we used to drive around in this poxy old Land Rover doing all this sort of stuff. I was picking *pituri*, I knew how to mix *pituri*, around all the boxwood swamps to get the bark, how to cook the bark to mix with the *pituri*, because you had to have certain bark otherwise the *pituri* is poisonous to you, and you had to do it properly.

The old girl made sure you did it properly because she did not want to kill her mob. So we did all that and old Bess taught me language. We were not allowed to talk English. She taught Timmy Lander language as well. So we ended up like that, doing that part of Angas Downs.

Tracker Tilmouth

Yes, Lois spoiled me, and Arthur Liddle and Bess spoiled me, [and their son] Johnny Liddle was very upset. You see, old Arthur and my old man grew up together in the Bungalow [government institution for Aboriginal children removed from their parents]. He was in the Bungalow with my old man, and when they were twelve old Harry Tilmouth [Tracker's grandfather] took them out and employed them at Alcoota and Mount Riddock.

There is a post at New Bore in the old stockyard there, I think it is burnt now, but Tommy Webb showed me when I was at Utopia and my old man's and Arthur Liddle's initials are carved in the post. They did it when they were twelve and thirteen years old. So when old Arthur Liddle saw me he was really overcome because my old man was a good mate of his. He treated me better than he treated his sons. Old Bess absolutely loved me. I would not have to work. All I had to do was drive around the countryside digging *tjala* [honey ant] and picking *pituri*.

A hard life making damper and scones. Cups of tea. They would be all out working and I would be sitting under the tree eating scones. So you have got this picture of scones all through my life. Old Bess, they treated me really well.

He was a good sounding board, old Arthur. You could talk to him and he and I would go for drives. I would do all the bore runs with him as his offsider, go around and check all the bores.

I camped by myself normally. I was outside. Me and Snowy would pull our beds out in the moonlight at night-time. I kept to myself to a certain extent. I got to be really good mates with Johnny Liddle. He was a good bloke Johnny. But, the rest, I sort of kept closer to Snowy Lander more than anybody else.

Anyway, Old Arthur was a good bloke, he meant well. A thorough gentleman, he was a thorough gentleman to everybody. That was the reason he got done over, he was just too nice a bloke. I think he favoured his older son Lawrie more than he favoured Johnny. Firstborn and all that I suppose. Johnny was a bit of a ratbag. Johnny was the third child but he suffered the second-child syndrome. Complete mongrel Johnny Liddle, complete mongrel. He would do anything for you, Liddle would do anything for you but madness goes with it.

John Liddle

Uncle Alf was the one that brought him down from Darwin, Uncle Alf Liddle. He was doing the same sort of thing up in Darwin where he was looking after kids because he got sent to, I forget which island it was, Croker Island or one of those. He was one of the original people that got sent from Alice Springs. And he never came back to Alice Springs to live, he stayed in Darwin. So somehow or other, I do not know how, Uncle Alf got to know Tracker and he was living with him. Uncle Alf and his family used to come down every Christmas for holidays so we were sort of expecting them: it was Christmas soon; all the Darwin mob will be down soon and we can mix with our cousins and all that.

They brought this bloody cheeky, skinny little mongrel of a kid and it was Tracker. I think we all wanted to kill him straight away. We were out mustering and I think my dad said to his brother Alf, *What are you going to do with this young bloke?* and Alf said, *Well! I might leave him here and you mob can have him.* My old man said, *Oh! If he wants to stay he can stay.* So he went and asked him and Tracker said, *Yeah! I'll stay.* He just sort of fitted in with us.

I think he enjoyed it and he was the centre of attention and that sort of stuff, so he just stayed with us for years. We could not get rid of the bastard. I think my mum and dad actually treated him more like their family than any of their own family to tell you the truth, because he was such a skinny little bugger, and I think they felt like he could not find out who his family was. He was a little bastard of a kid. One of those kids that annoyed everyone and got in everyone's way.

Everyone wanted to kill him, but he was like Dennis the Menace. He was a kid who was always in your face, doing this and doing that, asking questions, that sort of stuff. My dad had a weird sense of humour too so they got on really well. My mum used to mother him more than anyone else, so he got special treatment, even though he says that she would tap him on the shoulder with a stick and say, *You behave yourself.* Which she used to do, but he got away with everything so he was pretty spoilt by my mum.

He worked the crowd, you know. So he knew how, he knew that from that age, and I reckon even when he was twelve or thirteen or something like that. Skinny little bugger. Then he just stayed with us and he blended in with everyone and pretty soon he was king of the world sort of thing.

Lawrie Liddle

Well! It goes back to our fathers actually, who were both a part of the Bungalow and taken away from their parents. Tracker's Dad and my Dad [Arthur Liddle] were at the Bungalow at the same time. And of course from the Bungalow they went to Jay Creek up until their school days finished, and both of them were put back into the workforce, which was the requirement in those days, where you had to be employed, sort of like an apprenticeship.

I think Tracker's father went back to Alcoota and my dad went out to Undoolya. So the two fathers knew one another well and later on when I was a little kid, they lived in The Gap [on the south side of Alice Springs] and we did too, and we knew one another from a long way back. Tracker was a long way younger than I am but I knew him as a kid, and then he was taken away as part of the Stolen Generation, and Tracker and his two brothers were sent up north to one of the islands, Croker Island.

He was away until he was a young teenager, probably twelve or thirteen, and in those days we were living and working on a property called Angas Downs. So Tracker was brought to us by a welfare officer to try and find him a job to be away from town because Tracker being what he was, there was less temptation in the scrub to be naughty.

Naughty! Gosh. He was sort of like another kind. When he turned up he would have been about twelve or thirteen or a bit older, with a welfare officer who asked my old man whether there would be a possie [position] out there for him. Tracker gets out of this old Land Rover and he would have weighed about six stone, no hair, pair of baggy shorts, no shoes, no hat and a runny nose. Took one look at him, and you know you were meant to be fairly fit to work on a station, and we said we did not think he can do the job. So the welfare officer took him down to Curtin Springs which was next door about thirty-five to forty mile away.

There was no possie there for him either, so the welfare officer took him over to Tempe Downs which was another neighbouring place to us, and there was no work, there was nothing there. The welfare officer took him around a bit to Mount Ebenezer and still nothing. So the very next day the welfare officer turns up again with Tracker, *We can't find a place*. Anyway, my mum [Bessie Liddle] was not too far away listening to the conversation and it was all, *I don't know, you might have to try us again next year*. Mum piped up and says, *Stop here,* and so that was how he got to be with us.

Tim (Snowy) Lander

Back in the 60s and 70s of course life was a lot simpler than it is now and the Liddles were just good family people, just had family values. Money was not everything. I mean they lived on Angas Downs all their lives and just scratched a living out of the drought, and the good times, and the bad times. They sort of had no value of money, but just the value of family I think. With Old Arthur, us boys could never do any wrong. If we went into town and got into trouble he would stick up for us like he was our father. It was pretty innocent in them days. We did not really get in trouble, we just did what normal boys do, go drinking and stuff like that when we was kids, but we never did it in front of him I can tell you.

He would not approve and we respected him. Lawrie would not even smoke cigarettes until he was twenty-five in front of his father, and we all smoked cigarettes when we were fourteen or fifteen. He was just a really respectful old gentleman, old Arthur, and he never lost his temper with us kids or anything. He taught us the values of being a family. And also at that time at Angas Downs, there were probably about fifty or sixty Aboriginal people camped there just in humpies and that, before the community started up, and that was part of Angas Downs life too then.

We were fencing and yard-building, and the stock work was all horse in those days. We used to break in our own horses, the brumbies, I suppose they called them brumbies, but they were just horses that had gone wild on the place. We all had our own horses that we broke in ourselves. Sometimes we went and caught them. We used to wheel them in with an old Land Rover if we could not catch them. But it was all good fun. A few tourists used to come through and we would intermingle with them sometimes. We had a little bit of a shop at Angas Downs, plus Aboriginal people were just getting into that art situation then, and people used to come in looking to buy carvings, not so much paintings but mainly the carvings in those days, with the burn marks on them, clap-sticks, lizards and stuff like that. We met a few people from other parts of the country and even other parts of the world, and Bruce just seemed to get on with everyone. He was one of the characters at Angas Downs and he always had a smile on his face. Sometimes you could not shut him up. We used to grab him by the left ear and twist it like a volume knob on the radio and go, *Click, there Bruce, stop talking.*

He used to take it all in his stride though. It would not shut him up for long. On top of that, even though he left school when he was pretty young he was a really smart bloke, no doubt about that. He was a really intelligent kid. The things that we had been doing for a few years he would pick it up in no time. Also, getting on with people – and that too, because he did not have that shyness about him like a lot of kids.

We all grew up together as brothers. We used to have our little tiffs and that but nothing serious. We used to tell him to shut up when he talked too much and all that. He had come straight off Croker Island and talked about bloody mud crabs and fishing boats and stuff when he came there. He did not take long to learn our ways. But he fitted in no worries.

We used to doll ourselves up to the nines in clothes. That was one of our things. Spend all our money on clothes so we could go to the late night at the Stewart Arms or somewhere in Alice Springs. That was the local disco in those days, the only one, and that was where all the girls used to congregate. I don't think it was only Bruce, but I know he used to fall in love every time he'd go to town with a different girl, before he grew up of course, when we were all teenagers.

He bought a car. I do not know how he got that. He bought a car, a Valiant ute and it was a good car, better than any of the cars we ever had, and he lent it to his brother one night, that was Patrick, and I think he run into a tree or something. That sort of put the mockers on it for Bruce. He was really down in the dumps about it, so he didn't worry about driving that car again. A couple of months after that we said, *What are you doing with the car, Bruce?* He just gave it to me and Lawrie to use. We fixed it up, we put a mudguard and bonnet on it, we did it ourselves and brought it out to Angas Downs. He never ever asked for it back or anything.

He used to be a bit frightened at night. I think he was there on his own once because in the old days we had lots, not lots of guns, but we had a shotgun and a few other guns at the station which you normally have for snakes and that. So he went to bed this night with a shot-gun next to him. We had a few scrawny old chooks at the time and the dingoes must have been bad, and when the dingoes were bad the chooks used to come inside the house in a panic. And he woke up in the middle of the night and this chook was sitting on the end of his bed. It was one of them old beds with the end on it, and the chook was sitting about a metre up above his foot on the end of the bed. He just reached down and got the shotgun and shot it. He thought it was someone standing there. Lucky it was not someone standing there.

Tracker Tilmouth

When I was at Angas Downs, I also had an uncle there called Johnny Stewart, who was absolutely, totally mad. Anyway, we were building the stockyards at Wallara, fixing them up and putting in the loading ramp and everything else, and across the road was the Wallara pub. Snowy Lander who was also at Angas Downs got on with the waitresses, so we went over there for a couple of beers one night and he stayed and got drunk and came back horrors. We were all laying back in our swags and Snowy comes along and goes in the tucker wagon and pulls out the toilet paper and torch. He struggles out there into the witchetty bushes. You could see him, he did not go too far. He started to choke a brownie. So Johnny Stewart grabbed a long handled shovel, crept up and pinched his shit. Have you ever seen a drunk looking for his turd, while wiping his arse? You shine down to see that you do not step in it and there is nothing there. He looked under his boots. He was looking in his trousers, looking around the bush, shining up in the trees and for days he was absolutely fucked, he could not work out where his turd was. Every time we saw him we just cried. You wonder why I am mad.

John Liddle

I agree that some of his cheekiness came from Croker Island, because the first time I saw him I wanted to punch him in the head, and I think we wanted to punch each other in the head for years afterwards. He was a cheeky little bastard. Well! He always was though. I would not say that Willie or Patrick or even old Roy his father were not built like that, but Tracker had that habit of annoying people. And you wanted to punch him in the head sometimes. What used to give me the shits with him was that he would say something stupid and if I was there he would say, *Isn't that right Liddle?* Include me for his sort of backup. I would not know whether to say yes or no because either way, I am in the shit. *I've got John Liddle here.* Oh fuck, do not do that for God's sake. A bastard, there was no doubt about it.

We did a lot of silly things, him and I. It is a wonder we never got killed, especially in cars. He had this thing, I don't know what the cause of it was, but he used to sleepwalk. At Angas Downs we put up a big building with a roof right over the top but hardly any walls, then my old man brought out a truckload of bricks, and put all the bricks up, to close in the outside verandahs, all the boys used to be on one side, and everyone else used to camp on the other side. In the middle was the dining room, kitchen and that sort of stuff. The living area I suppose. So Tracker got into this state where he jumped up and wanted to punch things in his sleep. The walls had just been put up so everyone said *let's get behind the walls*, new windows and that sort of stuff, but he got up and punched the new line of bricks. Knocked a bit of it down.

I do not know where this came from but it might have been something from his childhood. He never talked about that. But another time when we were out doing this fencing job in Angas Downs all the young blokes, about five or six of us, went out in this truck. It got late in the afternoon and we had our swags, so we said we will just camp on the back of the truck, the big long tray of the truck, the five or six of us. I think he was second from the end of the truck. I was sort of over here, at the front of the truck. I reckoned it would have been about two or three o'clock in the morning and something made me wake up. I looked and I saw Tracker get up and he just looked around like that, then he walked along the edge of the tray of the truck, which is only about that wide. Walked right along the edge and got to the corner, round like that, round like that, right around. I woke one of the other blokes, might have been Vincent, Lawrie, or Tim, I woke them up and said *look at this*. He just walked right around us like that, right around the edge like a tightrope walker and he got back to his swag, got back in it and started snoring. And the next morning we told him but he did not believe it. We all saw it. The truck was that high off the ground and the part that he walked on would be just that wide on the side of the truck.

It would be hard enough to do that in the daytime, when you are awake. But he just walked right to the corner like that, and just went swoosh, then got back into his swag, and started snoring. Amazing. So that really pointed out to me that he was mad and I have told everyone since. But apart from that when we used to live in Mum's house around the corner, he smashed windows in his sleep, and punched into us and all this sort of stuff. Because the boy's room is about half the size of this, and one bed here, and one bed there sort of thing. He would wake up and start punching into you in your sleep. He did not know he was doing it. Or punched the wall. I do not know how Kathy [Tracker's wife] got on, poor bugger. She would have got a few punches in the head in her sleep.

Tracker Tilmouth

I wanted to hang myself in the engine shed. I was there by myself. I was three months by myself, living by myself. Well! It rained and the place was full of grass and water and everyone went into town and left me there. They just left me there. I looked after the place for three months by myself. I do not know why they had left me – Vinnie [Vincent Forrester] had left and gone into the army but this was before.

I went mad. Then I got a religious experience. Well! I was going to kill myself and I thought, put the rope around my neck. I thought the rope would break. It was only a blue-grey old thing and I would have done myself more damage and probably died a slow and miserable death. And so I got off that, I could not even hang myself. So I sat down and I thought about it all and I did not know where to go. I picked up Psalm 23 in the Bible, because the old preacher Pastor Kaleski [from Areyonga] left a Bible. We never read it, never said anything about it. So, opened it up. It said, *I will lay a table for you in the face of your enemies.*

I thought, *Fuck, that is a pretty heavy saying that is.* What do you mean you will lay a table for me in the face of my enemies? Do you want to know how many enemies I have? You do not know where I am going. You do not know who I am. How are you going to lay a table for me?

Then I got a feeling and I just said, *It is going to be up.* You are going to be different. You are different to a certain extent. And I kept that thought with me all of my life. So when I have problems now I just say, *You have done more than lay a table, you have laid a feast for me.* I have had the best go at anything ever, and I have had the smoothest run than most people ever, than anyone else I can remember. I have done things that people only dream of doing. It all started when I wanted to commit suicide at Angas Downs.

Yes, I have always got this feeling at the back that I have got someone watching me. Even with the current problems I get, so what? Big deal. Move on. That's it. This is the way I go out and do things. *Shouldn't you be in bed* or *shouldn't you be doing this?* No, I am doing that. *Are you? Oh! Right.* That was the saying in the Psalm that hooked me. There is a similar saying in the Koran. There is a similar saying in the Koran to Psalm 23. The Koran mirrors the Bible. I talked to the imam in Alice Springs. He told me it is the same because I went to Israel and I was confused about what I saw in Israel, the patriarchs. You had Abraham, and you had Sarah, and you had the Christians, and you had the Jews, and you had Islam, all from the same bloke Abraham. You know the people of the book, I saw all that and you try and get the answer.

Getting back to that day when I wanted to hang myself, I then walked down to Three Mile Dam with a .22 rifle and shot two rabbits for my supper. Everything was right. I came back and did not light the generator even though it was wintertime and cold. I did not need lights, so I made a fire outside and cooked them over the fire bucket, made a rabbit stew. A young fella. Sat there all night, looking at the stars, laying back in the swag by myself. Did that for about three months, two months, or whatever it was.

I had a radio. Listened to the Rolling Stones on the record player which ran on batteries. You put the batteries in the oven to heat up to make sure they were charged, and put them in the record player. Heat will charge batteries. I was very good. I never tried to commit suicide again. It was not worth it, but so what? I was not lonely.

Yes, so that was Angas Downs. Happy place for some, lovely place for others. Everyone wants to go back there. I would not mind going back there. But it is not my country. I am the Stolen Generation, I have got no country.

John Liddle

When Tracker first came back here [Alice Springs] none of his Tilmouth family knew who he was, although they knew he existed because he was living with us [at Angas Downs]. Mum and Dad used to look after heaps of kids, like wards of the state and all that sort of stuff, it became sort of fashionable. I do not think they got paid to do it, they just wanted to give the kids a home.

In exchange for a home they had to do work like the rest of us kids. No one had any money to talk about so we just lived the same, shared sheets, bed, clothes and all that sort of stuff. But when Tracker came back to Central Australia it took a while for him. I think the older generation knew who his family was, but he was feeling a bit nervous about going around to see them. I think I actually took him around to meet his father.

I will never forget this, and other people might dispute it, but I remember taking him around there. *His old father* he used to call him. He gave him this nickname *Strawberry* for some reason. He was a big old bloke, bit like Tracker's shape. I will never forget him standing at the stove cooking some meat, like most of them old blokes they like to have a drink and he was standing up, around at Tippy Miller's mother and father's place cooking this steak, and I knocked on the door and they said, *Come in.* I said, *We are looking for old Roy Tilmouth.* I did not know him properly, but I knew who he was. *And I have got this bloke here.* Someone said, *Who?* I think Tippy and those other mob were there and Marilyn and her sister, about five or six people were in the house and they said, *Who are you?* I said, *I've got this bloke here, I think he is Roy's son. Ah! Yeah! Well! He wanted to come around and meet you mob.* And the old bloke was standing up there cooking at the stove. He said, *Yeah! I think you're one of mine.*

No! No sentimentality, but you know that was how people were brought up, and it was normal behaviour. Now you would look and think, *oh shit it was tough.* What I always told Tracker was that he was mad, but I tell it to his face. I put that down to where he got his madness from, to that sort of disruption in his life. He got taken away from his family. He did not know who his family were. He knew, but he could have walked past them in the street, and I think at that stage some of his family did not want to know him. I do not know why. I reckon they would dispute that now because they all loved him like the rest of us, but that was the way it was.

I was quite surprised really that a relationship developed between Tracker and his dad. Like I said, we shared everything, cars and clothes and money and all this sort of stuff. We never had much, but he used to always go around and see him and give him a few dollars and have a laugh. He got to know those Tippy Miller mob and they sort of accepted him after a while. They introduced him to this or that one. It just went down the line and they finally worked out where he was in the family. We were driving cars so we would have been sixteen or seventeen. He was a skinny little bastard and I think he was only thirteen, fourteen or fifteen when he came out to Angas Downs.

Tracker Tilmouth

The old man [Roy Tilmouth] was a joker. A big bastard but he was a joker. He could not stop, you could never get a straight answer, he was always laughing and joking. He was a little bit like David Ross's dad. They grew up in the same time and knew each other well. A lot of men of that generation were like that and had a tough life, really tough, and they were tough men.

My old man was famous for when Nugget Morton and him ran through the big trenches and Nugget Morton always wanted to beat my old man in a footrace, and the old man tripped and fell. Morton beat him to the shovel, only one shovel left and said, *Oh! I won*, and the old sergeant said, *You sure did*. He knew what old Roy was about. Roy fell over so he would not have to do any work. And Morton had to pick up the shovel. His famous one is about a pub in Adelaide River during the bombing of Darwin. He was in the bar there and a little short-arsed white bloke was getting smart and said to the old man, *Hey! Tally, how about you pick a few of the stars* – you know, in the night sky – *pick a few stars and bring them down a bit.* The old man punched him in the head and said, *How about you pick a few of them out of that.* Boff! I do not have any other stories about him but old Arthur Liddle had a few stories about him in the old days.

Patrick and William Tilmouth

William: He had the same approach and the same humour as Dad. Dad had that. When I first met Dad, he said, *Oh come around here, we were going to play cards,* and he had the same tone of voice and all, as Tracker. Tracker had the same tone of voice as him. And I am sitting behind him and he was playing cards and he said, *What are you doing boy?* I said, *What do you mean?* He said, *What are you doing watching me play cards for? There's a lot of young fillies out there,* he reckoned. And all the girls were in the kitchen cooking for all the card players, and here I was sitting behind Dad watching him play cards. He thought I would be best suited to be out there introducing myself to all the young fillies. He had the same sort of bite in his humour. And they looked alike. Some of the same characteristics that the old man had, Tracker had. We all have them in a way.

We came back [to Alice Springs after leaving Croker Island] in the middle of winter and I had Darwin attire, T-shirt and a pair of jeans and thongs and you do not walk around Alice Springs in the middle of winter with that sort of garb on. But anyway we got there, it was six or seven o'clock at night and we got down the Mall and Richard Day was one of the guys I hitchhiked with and he said, *Hey, that's Terry Tilmouth over there.* And sure enough there was Mirrors, we called him Mirrors. He looked in a mirror whenever he could. And so they sung out to him and Terry came over and Richard said, *This is Willie,* and introduced me to him and I said, *Where's Tracker?* He said he was in the Stuart Arms [Hotel], so Terry went and got him. Tracker came out and says, *Oh! How ya going bro?* So all this, and he was surrounded by girls. He had the blonde hair. Green eyes, bow legs. Flares.

He had just come in from the bush [Angas Downs] you know. So he took me up home to see the old man and as we walked in I stopped and stayed in the old laundry part. The laundry was nothing but just an old laundry wash type. But I could see through the louvres the old man sitting down, him and Aunty Tilly, and the old man had his packet of Country Life and his bottle of Southwark and they were playing patience. And Tracker walked in, *Guess who's here, guess who's here?* And you could see the old man spin around, *Who, who, Tracker, who?* And Tracker said: *Oh! The prodigal son has returned,* and the old man says, *Who's that? Young Bill, Willie's out here.* Dad said, *Bring him in. Bring him in.* I thought, *Tracker, you have to fucking say that.*

My reputation preceded me because of him too, you know. I was getting into trouble, but I was getting into trouble because I mean, any kid that had gone through the life that we had would be angry too. Any kid. I did commit crimes, but my crimes were so pathetic and trivial, and were more crimes of poverty than anything because you know, you had to eat and you walked past restaurants where all these whitefellas sat down to huge steaks and dined out and you could smell the food cooking, and there was no way in the world you could get in there. So you started working out ways and means of accumulating some sort of wealth in order to get a feed. And whether it was by hook or by crook you took your chances. No one gave us a home when we left the mission. No one said this is your home, *come home*.

There was no homecoming when we came back [to Alice Springs] either. Tracker probably had the best introduction into the family than we had because he was boisterous, he moved his way in with people. He was new. Patrick and I were coming behind and really nobody took any notice of us. So we were not welcomed wholeheartedly. The prison system was prepared to take me so that was the only accommodation I had. And it served its purpose because I did have a place to go to, I did have a place where I could afford three meals a day and that sort of shit. At the end it was not ideal but I was already caught up in the prison system. The judges threw the book at me, that was all.

Patrick: I came back to Alice Springs looking for my brothers. I went to Darwin and then I came back. And by that time Willie had been locked up and Tracker was at the station [Angas Downs]. The difference between Willie and Tracker was they used to fight. Tracker was not a nice fella when he was a young fella, he was a cheeky bastard.

William: We were too close. From Croker even since we were little kids you would try and follow Tracker, and he was a hard act to follow. Sometimes you were the brunt of his jokes. Tracker reckoned that I was the fat kid who got to the cookie jar. I thought I would come back [to Alice Springs] and play football and I thought, because I had played a few games with Adelaide Nungas in Adelaide, I would have a game just to keep fit. So I went over to play B Grade and Tracker was the coach.

I was training away and come Saturday we all went out on the oval and I had the Pioneer guernsey on because the old man was a Pioneer bloke. Tracker was a Pioneer bloke, and this bloke [Patrick] was always South. I wanted to honour the old man a bit so I put on the guernsey. At quarter time, I had been running my guts out, it was a hot day and at quarter time we had come off and we were all sitting around having refreshments, and Tracker reckons, *You.* I looked at him and said, *What?* He said, *Can you stop fucking running like a gorilla.* I was that deflated I never put on a Pioneer guernsey again. I mean what more can you say?

Patrick: No, we would have a good laugh when we are together, us three. We all teased.

William: We talked shit didn't we?

Patrick: We would go and visit Lesley John [Nayda] at the old timers' centre and it was just one big laugh.

William: Yes, but poor Lesley John.

Patrick: Yes, but we were laughing in our own laugh, it had nothing to do with them.

William: This is one side that is sad. Les never ever really came back and when he did come back he was too sick to do anything. I mean his identity and how to deal with it and all that, there is a vacuum in his life now. You cannot fill it no more, because we do not really know where we come from, apart from the Tilmouth family. We could claim by Warlpiri, we could claim by Anmatyerre, everyone claims you.

Patrick: People just look at you and even though they do not know what your name is in the Tanami, they just claim you, and they say: *Where is that Tracker?*

William: Yes they all want to claim you. They all knew Tracker, and this was half of it. You cannot hide. You cannot hide. Yes, they all loved him. I know he was going through hard times but he was a fighter, always been a fighter.

Patrick: He was positive. He broke your heart but he was very positive. He would come here and get you all fired up, and you get all bouncy and bubbly again, and then he would fuck off. He just left you all confused. Ah! Tracker! What was this? Most of the time, he calls me Bones, although I am not bones anymore.

William: And you did not realise until afterwards that he was taking the fucking mickey out of you. He had no right doing that. But that was how he was. It was a defence mechanism for him too. He would get you first before you even thought of getting him. And as I say, he lived outside of himself, he had a very personal side that he kept to himself, and it was his sanctuary. I tell you what, you had to get through this whole charade of jokes, humour, and he could see you coming a mile off. Come in spinner, and he had you. Whereas, I am more reserved, I live inside of myself, I mean this place [William's home] is a padded cell. You give me this and I will never leave, I will never abscond. So it is the way it was.

Patrick: There is going to be no cell extraction here.

William: So this is it. The whole problem with assimilation is there is no smooth path back home and you end up asking, *Who am I, who the fuck am I? Where do I fit in this world? Who am I? Where do I belong?* These questions are continuously [being asked], and even to this day we feel we do not belong.

Tracker Tilmouth

Getting back to Alice and getting back to Central Australia, it was extremely difficult finding out where you belonged. It was difficult because you did not know where you came from. Simple as that. People look at me and say, *Righto, he can speak the language, he has been able to do this, he knows this and knows that*, but that has been a long, long journey. And that journey, like every other journey, never starts off on the right foot.

It is hard getting back to where you fit in the scheme of things as well as acceptance. Alice Springs was a wild place to say the least, it still is. The conflict between urban and non-urban, bush, whitefellas, blackfellas, is extremely fraught.

Croker was paradise in comparison. Getting back to Alice was very difficult but getting accepted in Alice was even more difficult because you had certain elders who [needed to accept you], and you sort of floated between living down The Gap, being part of the Gappies and playing footy, all that sort of stuff but very difficult to work out who you were and what you were, and a lot of people I befriended had not been able to recognise their own grandfathers or grandparents, or even their relatives who were probably in the creek looking at them.

There was a stigma attached, which was the softer version of Darwin – *I am a blackfella but not that black.* So you had this situation where you kept running into this area of acknowledgement, you had to acknowledge who your family was, but you did not mix with your family so to speak, and that became a lot clearer when I joined the Department of Aboriginal Affairs with Gordon Williams and people like that, because all of a sudden you were part of the process and meeting Gordon and blokes, who really assisted you in being accepted as an Aboriginal person within Central Australia, by Aboriginals, not by whitefellas, but by Aboriginal people, saying that was somebody, he belongs to that mob and so forth and so on. That took a long time, it took a very long time. I was assisted in that by Milton Liddle, Roy Dubois, Tony Petrick, and some of these other people, but it was a very long journey. A lot of people do not make it. Brothers of mine still do not make it, like Les and Harry, my sister and so forth and so on.

The arguments for Aboriginal recognition by Aboriginal people is that when you leave a place and come back to that place and say, *Righto, my mob is this or my mob is that,* or *I have been told this, this is what I know or understand,* then you always have the scrutiny of somebody else saying, *Well! Hang on a minute, this is that, that is this,* and it all came to this with land claims and the Land Council.

You had this argument of ownership and misunderstanding of ownership by Aboriginal people who were not culturally *au fait* with where they stood, and you had this argument time and time again, of people saying, *I am a traditional landowner, what are my rights?* This happened with all the land claims that I have been involved with.

I think there has been great difficulty in understanding, a lot of angst and emotion and so forth with the land claims. Their journey was similar to my journey, finding out how you were taken away, whether you were moved to Alice Springs, or to the Bungalow, or whether you were moved to Darwin or Minjilang [Croker Island] or wherever, it did not matter where, the journey was the same of coming back, and a lot of people do not come back. They would rather forget.

The people in the southern states that I know of decided that it was just too hard, they would rather be who they are and stay where they are. They would be Aboriginal people in name only rather than culture, and we are getting this difficulty to a certain extent, about what are we saying is Aboriginal, what are we identifying as? Each argument for each person is a different one, about how much do you grasp the idea of Aboriginality? How much do you live within a society that is willing to recognise that bit of Aboriginality?

In Alice Springs there is a concentration of that issue. Yes, we are all Aboriginal. Yes, we understand that, but are we more Aboriginal than that Aboriginal – and on and on it goes. So you have this argument time and time again with what being Aboriginal means, going out to bush camps and so forth, saying you want to understand your country and finding it difficult because language and cultural norms are not there. So Aboriginal society itself, it is not a different society, it is a vast society of transition if you like, from traditional Aboriginal life to the urban Aboriginal life.

I have seen it time and time again in New South Wales and everywhere else, where they were forced into transition, Aboriginal society along the river banks, to camping areas, to communities, to being concentrated and losing country because of that, and it is no different to American Indians or any other indigenous groups. The journey as a young bloke that I inadvertently went on was really about who you are. You cannot be anybody else. There was no other road for you. Your fate was already mapped. There is no *that door opens and that door closes*. Yes, you can make detours and do all sorts of things, but at the end of the day the main thing is, *Righto! Am I Aboriginal, or how much of an Aboriginal am I?* Do I take the trappings of a middle class, non-Indigenous person? How do I marry that within my mind with where I came from? That argument sits on my mind on a daily basis. You have got that, and that is just me. Imagine the turmoil of other people and what is going through their minds at the same time.

Who is Aboriginal? Can a real Aboriginal stand up? This is Tony Abbott's mantra. This is why he wants to go to Gove all the time, where they are really Aboriginals out there. And the Aboriginals standing around the fringe camps may not be real Aboriginals. *In fact he is creating a story about who is an Aboriginal.* He is doing it on purpose, and it is good luck by default that Michael Long and these other blokes are saying, *Hang on a minute, it is all of us.* Longie is still saying *it is all of us,* and he is using recognition [the movement for constitutional recognition], and to a certain extent it is a vehicle for saying *it is all of us* whether it is the best thing on offer, or just what happens to come along at the time. He is a pretty smart thinker old Longie, and he has got this argument that recognition is the vehicle that brings everyone together.

We have not got anything straight. We have been trying to get our story straight.

Tracker Tilmouth

When I was out there at Angas Downs, Arthur Liddle had a calming effect on me because he explained things in great detail about what he thought were the issues of the day, and a bit of politics, but mostly about yourself, where you came from. He knew my old man, knew my family backwards. He talked about my old man, and talked about working and everything else, and gave great guidance on how you should behave and what is the norm and everything else. This was also backed up by his wife, old Bess.

Bess took me out hunting and gathering. I knew how to dig honey ants. I knew how to dig witchetty grubs. I knew how to get lizards and we went out to Tempe Downs, and I knew how to pick bush raisins – *kampurarpa*, which is berries. I knew all of the language. I knew how to pick *pituri*, which is wild bush tobacco. I used to come back with the Land Rover chock-a-block with it. It looked like a hay bale of it.

And then later we would go and get all the bark from the boxwood tree, coolibah tree in the swamp, and they would use that to mix with the ashes. There was Bess and old Maggie Armstrong and all the old people.

There were other blokes, but I think Arthur Liddle could see they were not interested in learning about culture and language. If you had most of the Angas Downs blokes lined up and we spoke Luritja, me and Johnny Liddle would leave them for dead, because we used to talk Luritja absolutely fluently. My best mates talked Luritja, and Lawrie Liddle too, but more so me and Johnny and Timmy Lander. We learnt Pitjantjatjara as well because the old blokes [senior law men] came through.

Bess wanted to make sure that I understood culture and country, and talked the language, and understood where I stood within any Aboriginal society. I went off to work at Ayers Rock where I did garage work, fixing up vehicles, and then I ended up as an outstation community advisor for the Department of Aboriginal Affairs at Docker River.

They could see I knew language and I knew culturally the right place to be and where, and what for. I have still got that. So I got taught a lot about my Aboriginality by Bess and Arthur. Arthur taught me how to speak a little bit of Arrernte. Bess made sure I could talk fluent Pitjantjatjara, Yankunytjatjara, and Luritja. My job when I ended up at Docker River was working for the Department of Aboriginal Affairs with Gordon Williams, who was my boss.

One of my jobs was to actually drive the [Western Desert Aboriginal law] businessmen around the countryside. We called them *tjilkata*. They were the red ochre blokes and I drove them from Docker River to Areyonga, and from Areyonga to Papunya, with a government Bedford truck, four-wheel drive truck. Carting all the old people like Lesley, Harry Brumby, Tjutjuna, Windlass, the whole lot.

They all saw me, including Andy Kenyon and other staff of the Central Land Council, as part of those old important law men, and it came very clear at one incident at the Central Land Council when some of these old men demanded money off the traditional landowners for Mereenie Gas, and Mr Breaden [former chairman of the CLC], and Ben Clyne and those blokes were there. Mr Ross came over all flustered and said, *I've got a group of red ochre men in the conference room.* They were trying to get some money out of Breaden and Ben. *Do you know Pitjantjatjara?* I said, *Yeah.* So I walked in there and these old men say,

Our grandson, how are you? Where have you been? We haven't seen you for a long time. Big hugs all around from these extremely fierce-looking bosses of the business. I explained to them that there was no money but they eventually had their way. Ben and Bruce gave them some money for food and tucker, and fuel. There were no royalties to be had. Mr Ross will tell you how these blokes from the bush, when they first saw me, they could not believe it: *Our son where have you been, our grandson.*

They remembered that I took them around in Docker River when I was community advisor in the 1970s, before Mount Liebig was established, and before Kintore was established. My job at Docker River was to actually run rations near Well 13 on the Canning Stock Route. They were bush Aborigines. They used to walk around, and they would say, We *will light a spinifex fire, and you can follow us by this fire.* They would say, *You look for the fire, we'll be lighting it, and we'll tell you where we are.*

We would drop them off and they would walk around the bush up there. In a fortnight's time we would go back and look for them and they would light a fire the day we were supposed to be coming there, and you would see the fire, and you would just drive across the country with an old Holden ute – a government ute, full of rations, and drop it off for them, flour, sugar, tea, bully beef, everything like that.

We followed the tracks back. It was me and Gordon Williams, and we did not need a four-wheel drive. We did it without a four-wheel drive most of the time, in the old Holden ute. So at Docker River, I was outstation community advisor with Gordon Williams, and then I went back into Alice and I was working around Congress [health service] and Aboriginal Legal Aid. I worked for Congress, then I worked for Legal Aid, and then I went back to the Department of Aboriginal Affairs. I worked for them for years, the Department of Aboriginal Affairs, and I ended up community advisor at Mimili at one stage, Ernabella, and Amata, so I could talk Pitjantjatjara.

There was Gordon Williams, Dougie Turner, and Andrew Wilson working for the Department of Aboriginal Affairs. Bob Beadman was my boss, and I also worked with Neville Jones, Richard Priest and all of those people [senior government bureaucrats]. I went from Congress first when I come into Alice because I did not want to stay out at Docker River, so I came into Congress and worked on the drunks pick-up bus. Then I joined the Department again, and I did Mimili and those places, and afterwards, I was sent as community advisor to Utopia, the traditional home of the Alyawarre and Anmatyerre people two hundred and fifty kilometres north-west of Alice Springs, and that was how I met a bloke called Toly Sawenko in my early days.

When I went to Utopia in that eastern country, my mentor for that area was Milton Liddle, because I came from that country but I could not speak Anmatyerre and Alyawarre or anything like that. So he was my mentor and interpreter, on more than one occasion, and he would come with me. Me and him drove around, and he told me about my old man, he told me about the country, and who were my relations at Utopia. And we camped at Goofy Bore on Mount Skinner Station more than one occasion, and out at Three Bores at Utopia, and at Ampilatwatye, Ammaroo, right around Lake Nash, Harts Range, Mount Swan, Number Five Bore, all those places. Milton Liddle took a lot of time teaching me who I was and I liked Liddle because he was a very smart man. He was Arthur Liddle's younger brother and he just passed on knowledge. He must have thought I wanted to learn. Well! I wanted to learn. I was hungry for knowledge.

I stayed with old Katie and Roy Potter. Katie Potter was my old man's aunty, and it was just a tin shed they lived in at Goofy Bore. So instead of camping in the community we used to camp there and she would cook for us. We would bring out a bit of meat and bread and some rations and we left it with them. That was Goofy Bore, which is on the edge of Utopia near the Sandover River, beautiful country. There is nothing there now. The old tin shed has gone. Old Tom Williams used to be there. It was just desert mulga, big gum trees, beautiful big red ironwoods and bloodwoods, big, big trees like that and good water.

One of the best things about Goofy Bore is that I would go out there with Milton Liddle and Roy Dubois – people would turn up, and old Milton could handle any political debate you wanted. I learnt just by listening to old Milt, how he talked, him and Roy Potter, where they would be exchanging stories. Milt Liddle and Roy Dubois would hold forth with old Katie and Roy Potter, with a young bloke like me just sitting there listening. I was only a young fella. Old Milt had so many stories that I could not stop laughing at some of them, but he had a very serious side to him, old Milt. He was pretty strong on Aboriginal rights, very strong. He talked about it, who did what and how and why, and he knew the country backwards.

He was really a forward thinker, because he helped set up Congress, he helped set up Aboriginal Legal Aid, all of these organisations. He was always in the background, and you could have a discussion with Milton. He would work you hard, nothing wrong with that. Many a day when I was working for the government, I would be out cutting wood for him up at Bond Springs. He was famous for his kangaroo pasties. He used to make these pasties out of kangaroo meat which were beautiful. We used to have that for lunch up at Bond Springs, chopping wood.

My mob showed me where my country was, right through to Aileron and Ti Tree, Adelaide Bore and Alcoota, Wake River and Bushy Park, and then Harts Range mob who are my cousins. We used to go gem fossicking at Harts Range, where we had a project to sell gems to Hong Kong, which paid for our Toyota and the wages and everything. I set that up with the Department of Aboriginal Affairs. We bought our own Toyota, bought our own metal detectors and our own gem-making machine, everything – the cutting machines, and we cut gems from Harts Range. We did all that.

What sort of man was Milton Liddle? He was a hard man with his own family. He was a strict disciplinarian, but if you could sit down and talk to him, he had all the jokes – up at the woodheap, up where the Pine Hills Football Club shed is located in Alice Springs. He was supplying wood to all the houses in Alice Springs, and on weekends I would go and help him cut wood. Myself and little Nicky Liddle helped him cut wood. He would sit down and tell you jokes and tell you all sorts of things, but when you got him out bush you could not beat him. He knew the bush. He knew everything about the bush, especially that eastern side, around Utopia, up Ampilatwatye, and elsewhere. He had been around, and it was the same with Roy Dubois. We always went with Roy Dubois, so I had these two old blokes driving around with me in a government Land Rover. We would go everywhere and meet this person, meet that person, do that, do this, camp here, camp there. They would tell stories at night. You could not beat it. So Milton

Liddle has played a huge role in the way I thought – he and Arthur. They used to call me Roy, never Tracker or Bruce, they called me Roy after my old man, *Hey Roy*.

My father was related to them. He was a good bloke, just different. We did not keep in touch that often. I was doing my own thing. I was out bush a lot because I never had many town jobs, and when I did come in to play football I worked for Terry Lee. Terry Lee came into Alice and lived down The Gap with us, and he was a mate of my old man and my uncles. I could always get a job with Terry Lee in the butcher shop, or in the abattoir, the Alice Springs abattoir. I could use a butcher knife pretty well. Me and George Somers always got a job. George Somers was related to my mother's mob, or his wife was, through the Wades and those families. So I always had a job with those people. But Milton and Arthur were the main educators. Arthur had more politics than Milton, because Arthur was a lot straighter than Milton. Milton would laugh and joke whereas the old bloke wouldn't. When Arthur talked to you there was no joking, it was straight up and down. You took it on. What to do about everything – the politics of the day, and all sorts of discussions. He and I would drive out from Angas Downs and do the bore run, just me and him, and he would be talking all the way, about this and about that.

It wasn't really straight-out politics but what he thought of the day, about Indigenous and non-Indigenous issues. How it should be thought of and so forth. So with my grounding in Aboriginal affairs, I was very lucky. I had some good teachers.

When it came to running the Central Land Council, well first of all I went to university, and when I came back I was three feet in front of everybody because I had experience as the only director of the Central Land Council to actually have lived on an Aboriginal community and run it as a community advisor, and not just one, but three or four communities, and my experience in Aboriginal affairs, from west, east and south, down at Docker, down in the Pitjantjatjara Lands, but also up around Papunya, Yuendumu, and Lajamanu. So I had very good exposure to how communities worked, and who made the decisions and how they were made, and how you went about getting a decision made by the Council. You had to do your own lobbying, your own work in the system. Yuendumu was a classic. Papunya was the same. I had a lot of uncles at Papunya. And that was what old Arthur would say to me. He would say, *You're in Alice and people, old people, are sitting on the side of the footpath and you always got to say hello to them, because nine times out of ten they will be related to you – they will be looking at you. You've always got to be respectful.*

Bess would tell you off if you did not say hello to somebody. She would say: *Hey boy, come here*, and she would say, *This is your aunty*, or who this is, *This is your uncle.* Call you boy, she would say, *Hey boy.*

I came from a wild background and the old bloke Arthur Liddle, he tamed me down. He made me think. *Don't be such an idiot.* He made me dangerous, in how to use the brain.

John Liddle

He got to know all the big men. There used to be a lot of Aboriginal people coming through Angas Downs, proper people from the bush. They were just settling in places like Docker River and Papunya and places like that as new settlements. So Tracker went from Angas Downs to Docker River to work with his mate, Dave Simpson. He is a white bloke who took him from Angas Downs, first to Ayers Rock when it was known as Ayers Rock, then from there to Docker River, because it was Dave Simpson who actually helped set up Docker River as a settlement. Tracker got to know all those old blokes because they were sort of like our family anyway. He knew all those old elders you know like old Nosepeg [Tjupurrula] and old people like that, those famous old blokes. They used to come to us with their broken-down old cars, or on a camel, or something like that. We actually saw people, the last of the walkabout mob. They were walking, not driving in cars. He got to know all those mob. He learnt some of the language and they sort of claimed him also. He would be teasing them and they would be teasing him. All those heavies, the big ceremonial blokes, he used to drive them around.

So Tracker worked with all those old fellows and the old women. He knew all those mob. Knew their family and who is this one, and where they fit in, I cannot remember them, but he knew which one is which and who is their family. And those old blokes sort of adopted him. And he was one of the Liddles, that is our family, he is our family. So he had seen a lot of things other people would not have because of that.

He learnt a lot from Dad and that helped to shape the person he became and like I said, my dad had a dry sense of humour, but a mad sense of humour and he used to tease, like all those old Liddles, Uncle Milton, Uncle Harold, they all had this funny sense of humour. They would be teasing young blokes all the time to make them shape up. You cannot do that sort of thing any more, but back in those times that was how you got young blokes to learn how to work and pay attention.

When long hair first came in, Tracker always wanted to be better than everyone else. He would have the first set of flares that came in. And he wanted to get the prettiest girls. So the old uncles, my dad and his brother Milton, I think they were very proud of what all these young blokes were doing, getting up to mischief and those sorts of things but they had to tell us, *You guys ought to behave yourself, you've got family responsibilities. We have to live in this town.* The town is small and all this sort of stuff. So we would get all these lectures, *come home early*, and do this and do that, *you have got to work*. One of the things that these old blokes taught us was the work ethic. You have got to get up early, wash your face, get the gravy out of your eyes, so that you get out there and you are ready for work.

And that was what they taught him. It was normal behaviour, there were not any easy times, it was all work. We used to have lots of fun, muck around and tease each other with work place rivalry sort of thing. Try and outdo each other. You had to make your own fun then. It was good clean fun but you had to do your work at the same time. You might come to town every now and again and get on the grog and fall in love, but while you were out on the job you worked, and back in those times if you went on the dole it was like a shame job. So no one went on the dole. You had to go and find a job and there were not many jobs, it was all hard jobs that blokes could do, unskilled jobs. Well! They were skilled back in those days but nowadays you might call them unskilled. So you had to do the best you could with whatever you had.

Like I said, we had to share everything, clothes, sleep in the same bed. You tell people that now and they cannot believe that sort of concept, sleeping head to toe. Someone pissed the bed or they have smelly feet then you had to put up with it. And not many blankets in wintertime while sleeping on those old cyclone bunks, old ex-army bunks that were just made out of a bit of wire and some pipe. But you just had to do it, there was not anything else.

Whenever you talked to Tracker, you had to have an argument with him, or he had an argument with you. He told you his view on the world and then he would tell you a silly story. And what he always did with me was he would tell these stories where he was the main character, but he would put me in there instead of him. *That was Liddle,* he would say. *Isn't that right Liddle?* Oh! Yes. He told such a convincing story it was not worth me saying no it wasn't me, everyone believed what he told them, *No that wasn't me, that was Liddle,* doing all these silly things, but it was him. He continued to do this all the time.

All the stupid things, and they were stupid things that we were doing, bloody misbehaving, but it was never him that instigated it, or was the main actor in it, it was always me. I was a little bit back to front but not as much as he made out. But whenever we went somewhere he would still tell those stories, and he always put me up the front in the story. I used to try and argue against it but I knew I could not compete against his story, so I just let it go.

That was Liddle, that was Liddle. And they would all look at me and think you stupid bastard, why did you do all that sort of stuff. *No it was Liddle*, and pointing at me. So I decided to give up in the end because you were up against a much larger force trying to compete with him. You could not beat him, you just had to agree with him and let him go.

Like I said, my mother had sort of sheltered him a bit from the real world. He was her pet, so he got away with a lot of things. She stuck up for him and gave him the easy jobs, so he did alright. He knew how to milk that sort of reaction from people. He used to put his hand up but in a subtle way, and she would say, *Oh! Yeah! You can come and drive us.* They used to go hunting for *pituri*. They would go for days and come back with a car load. And some of the leaves were about that big, like normal tobacco, domesticated tobacco. They would take big chaff bags. And because he was young and silly the old girl would send him up the hills where it used to grow in caves. He would be the main carrier of all that sort of stuff. He got to know a lot of those senior women like that. They knew who he was and they would boss him around, but I think he enjoyed that. He would be the driver and all of those old girls would jump on the back. So he would be there fetching the water and lighting the fire, and climbing the hills and that sort of stuff.

They would be away for days and would have gone one hundred and fifty miles sometimes from Angas Downs up to near Kings Canyon there, where you would go in the middle of nowhere, and up all those winding valleys and climb up on top of the hills. Some of the stalks of tobacco would be as thick as that – you would have to chop it, and it has got big leaves, like palm leaves they were that big. So they would bring back ten or twenty bags, big chaff bags full. Might be more. Then you have to dry it, take the stalks off. But the smell is enough to make you go bonkers. That nicotine, it is a tobacco smell. Oh! God! It was terrible, but those old girls could not live without it. He used to say he fell for that job, but I think he volunteered in a sneaky whisper, *I'll go with you. When you're going let me know, I'll go.* Getting away from the real work.

And he used to tease all the old girls, have them giggling and then they would be teasing him. It was how he was, you know, he knew how to work the room. He knew how to get people to lean his way. A very convincing sort of bloke, and he was always an ideas man. He had all these schemes about everything. I don't know the story but I know there was a dog that died. He would have thought, *Geez! How am I going to get out of this,* because he was always trying to get out of things. He most likely killed it. Starved it or something. Too busy to feed it. Because he would drift off a lot you know. You could be talking to him and he would go somewhere, I do not know where. And you say, *click click* [clicking fingers] – bloody silly bugger. That would be him. He was always passing the blame onto other people.

William Tilmouth

I remember old Sandra Armstrong telling me the story about when Arthur Liddle came into town and left Tracker out there [on Angas

Downs} and the old dog, Arthur's old favourite dog passed away. Somehow it died and I do not know whether it died from a snake bite or just a natural death, but when it passed away, Tracker did not know what to do.

He thought he was going to be in a lot of trouble so he decided not to bury the dog and put the dog in the freezer. And old Sandra Armstrong, an old Aboriginal woman from the Imanpa community, went to get some meat and there was this fucking dog, on the floor, in amongst the meat. And that was because he was worried that he would get scolded for allowing the dog to die suddenly, and he was not going to bury it because the evidence would be buried then. He put it in the freezer.

Mad Enough to Try Anything

Vincent Forrester

Oh! Righto! Tracks, we were yarding up these cattle, so yarding the mob with young micky. Young micky are about two-year-old cattle, horns and everything, and you have got to yard them. You have got to teach the animals to go in the yard, so we chased this bloody young micky trying to get him in the yard. He would not go in the yard. So! Hmm! Hmm! We were on a horse, and we knocked this bloody micky over on the ground, collared him and twisted his tail and kept him on the ground.

Righto! So we have got the tail, and Tracker's in front of this young micky, *Come on come this way, come this way,* and he is walking back towards the creek. We let that bloody micky's tail go, and Tracker was trying to run backwards, and the micky was horning Tracker in the guts. He was running backwards and he fell over and bloody young micky is on top of him. Ah! No! Tracker. Me and Lawrie Liddle was hanging with the bloody micky. It livened him up. *Get out of the way Bruce we're trying to put him in the bloody yard.* Whoa! Whoa! The fucking bull has got hold of him. There would be safety issues, health and safety issues now if you ever done that. He was good with animals, that bugger. Old horses would know him. He would spoil the bloody horses, working horses.

Tracker could always ride because on Croker Island they had this little team of ponies. So he had a bit of a touch for horses, and breaking in horses, and he was pretty good. He knew what he was doing with a horse and all that type of thing, shit yes, bloody oath he did.

One day he got this beautiful little filly, this creamy filly, and he broke it in, and you know how every time a cowboy goes into town and falls in love, and then by the time the romance is starting you have got to go out bush again, so nothing happened. Anyway, he named it Dianne. He trained horses really well, and he was training her really well.

The little mare could spin on a sixpence and take off like a V8 supercharged motor car, tiny little thing, so he was going to teach her how to be a show horse. He puts a log down on the ground and he walked the little mare over it and then he put some sand, made it a little bit higher and no worries. A little bit higher, oh! Yeah! No worries: the little mare stepping over. Then he decided to get the four-gallon drums – empty ones, and he goes up to the four-gallon drums with a stick across this little mare. Bumped that bloody log and made a noise. And old Tracks was *shhhhooo*, he was Saltbush Bill style, up in his saddle. Off he sails into the air and there was this German tourist there, *click, click*. *I don't know whether I got it, can you do that again?* Tracks turned around and said, *You can fucking stick it, are you smart or something?* He was showing off in front of this young German chick with her camera there. *I am going to show you mob how I am going to break in my horse.* Oh! I laughed. We would have to go out bush for three months or so, and in the bush you make your own fun, but you would have a chance to have a bit of release.

Tim (Snowy) Lander

I think he learnt to ride horses from being with us at Angas Downs with me and Lawrie, and old Arthur was a really good horseman in his day. He actually taught us to break in a horse, old Arthur did, and to be slow about it and be patient, and all that sort of stuff. But one of the things when Bruce was young, he never ever smoked in his life. He never smoked cigarettes and we all did. In those days we used to carry matches and one day, I think it was me, I got on Bruce's horse because there was no other horse there and he said, *Oh! You can ride my horse today.* And I got on this bloody horse, it was only young, he had only broken it in a couple of months back, and I rattled these matches to light a cigarette and it had never heard matches before. It bloody chucked me to the shithouse only because it got a fright from the matches. It never ever threw Bruce off.

Tourists used to come through and we ended up getting really friendly with one particular tour bus that came through only two or three times a year. They camped at Angas Downs with us. It was a good little event for us to look forward to. We would go over to the camp fire, and some of the people used to have a little bit of a singalong, and they would all welcome us to their little camp fire.

Anyway the camels were about but not in the numbers they are now. We were out mustering somewhere once and a camel walked into the camp and we actually caught it. We put a rope around it and led it home. We had a few horses which we called plant horses, for when you were out mustering and you would have a dozen horses or so, and I think we just put it in with the plant horses and drove it home on horseback, hunted it with the horses. Or someone led it. Bruce led it half the way I think with a rope because somehow, it just followed him. It was about twelve or fifteen miles back to the station. A day's ride. It was a real novelty to us to have this camel and we quietened it down no trouble at all. We called it Jude. Well! That camel never left then. We had a little sort of night paddock there. We grew fond of it so we put it in there because we did not want it to go. Just like a pet. So we ended up taking it back to the homestead and the next time that tour bus came, *Oh! A camel,* and everyone went apeshit over this camel. It was before any of these camel farms started in Alice Springs or anything. And anyway, so then we went out specifically and caught a couple more and in the end we had half a dozen camels at Angas Downs, just pets they were. We did not know how to break them in, but we quietened them down and tried to break them in like a horse and that sort of thing.

Then old Arthur knew a bit about camels and he made some saddles up for us. We ended up putting nose pegs in them because his old dad used to use camels, so he showed us what to do with that. These camels ended up quite a novelty with us. Of course Bruce claimed he was part Afghan which he was, and he reckoned he was the Camel Man.[7]

---

7. Tracker took great pride in his Afghan as well as his Aboriginal inheritance. He relished having a special affinity with camels, and being related to the history of Afghan cameleers in the Northern Territory.

Vincent Forrester

I think Alice Springs centenary was in 1972 when we took the camels into Alice Springs. Lawrie [Liddle], Timmy [Lander], Tracker and me, and these camels that only knew how to buck loose in the Todd River. This was the first Camel Cup where they had to run down Todd River from where the bridge is, down through the causeway near where you go across to the Olive Pink Reserve, and then they let them run wild, so there were mad camels going everywhere.

Tracker, the bugger was really good with the animals and he had this camel called Freddy and the bloody thing would gallop. So the first year we got done in the Camel Cup, but a couple of years later, after Tracker had mucked around with this bloody camel and put a bit of time and effort in, the bloody camel could gallop. So he was king of the Camel Cup there for a while, old Tracks. But Tracker had this thing with animals, for horses and camels, because the animal knows if you are a bastard sort of person and will not do what you want it to do.

Anyway, Tracker started getting a bit of meat on him so when it came to horse work, he was allowed to live in the stock camp with us during the cold times. We all had birthdays in the bush in the stock camp because it was mustering season, and at that time there were no fences or paddocks, it was called open range. The only paddock would be for the horses. The night paddock. When you were mustering you would put them in half a square mile or something so they could get food overnight, surrounded by barbed wire, and that became the horse paddock. Everyone had their own horse to look after, groom him and feed him, but then you would have the horse tailer if you were going to go a long way, might be twenty or thirty miles, although the old horses would take you where you were going, the horse tailer had a special job in the camp.

The horse tailer looked after the horses. So after we had worked the horses all day long, each man has to put the hobble on the horse, brush him down, check his back and all that, check everything and look after the animal. Then they were hobbled in this big paddock so they could feed on the grass – whatever grass was around – but you would also have to give them a good feed of chaff and oats. You were working the animal so chaff and oats were on the back of the trailer, because there might be a dozen horses and you have got to keep up their energy and feed them. And so after looking after the horses, we would go to sleep.

Then early morning: *Hey Vincent, Vincent, the horses are gone. I forgot to close the gate.* So the old horses had a great feed thank you very much *and we are off home,* so they took off in the middle of the night. Tracks must have got up about three o'clock in the morning and, *Shit I've forgotten…* and he went and looked and there were no horses there. So shit, in them days you had to be gone before daylight, breakfast and gone.

Oh! Shit the old man is coming you blokes, we've got no excuse.

Bruce, here's a bridle. What am I going to do with that? Tracks said, *I'll go and find them.*

The sun was starting to break just before dawn, and Bruce is off to go and look for these horses. So then, old Arthur rocks up about half past seven in the morning, *What are you boys doing in the bloody camp? You should have been gone hours ago. What happened?*

We said, *Well the old horses got out.* They were heading back towards home. *I seen the young fella walking with a bridle in his hands.* Arthur had just drove past him, and he knew what was going on, he had seen Bruce running about three miles behind the horses, and he just kept going. Anyway, Bruce comes back to the stock camp about ten o'clock, a big smile on his face, with these horses and of course, we now give him the mickey. *You are a real good Tracker, hey,* old Arthur said. And that was where he got his name Tracker. We laughed, and we are still laughing about it today.

Tracker Tilmouth

I learnt to ride camels and I won the Alice Springs Camel Cup three times. I could sit on anything in my young days. I was mad enough to sit on anything too. I rode horses at Croker bareback, and this was where I learnt to ride when I was about six or seven – and I could ride anything. On Croker Island we rode horses, we mucked around, we mustered cattle. We did everything you do when you are kids, such as riding horses in the sea and swimming, and hunting. We did not have any crocodiles in those days because they were shot out. We could not do it now on Croker.

So riding with a saddle on Angas Downs was pretty easy but I was not as good a rider as Timmy Lander or Lawrie Liddle who also worked on the property. Lawrie Liddle could ride anything. Johnny Liddle was mad enough to try anything.

Camels were there naturally at Angas Downs. I trained them. I had this camel that could run faster than a horse. No joke, we used to call him Frederick Heinz. I just thought of a name. This big black camel bull called Frederick Heinz. I used to give him two cans of beer before the race and he could beat anything. He would take off like a horse. He left old Noel Fullerton and Brandy and everyone else in the dust. I won three Camel Cups with him. Noel Fullerton would train his camels for years and years to try and beat me, and all I did was sit on a camel and give him a can of beer and he would leave everything standing.

We had pet camels at Angas Downs. Frederick Heinz camped between the house and the toilet, so in the middle of the night when you were going out to the toilet, you would trip over this huge camel that was going *boob, boob, boob,* blowing bubbles at you. But oh! He was a pet. I would walk to the sandhills out near the homestead – the big paddock where they were, and he would come bolting over the top of the sandhills to try and kill you, like a bull camel would normally. He would come and try and squash you on the ground. That is what they do and you'd have to climb a tree. He would come galloping up and he would see me and stop. I could get him down. I would tap him on the knee and he would come down and I could ride him. I would ride him with a stick, I did not have to put a nose peg on him or anything. I was not frightened of him. No, no. I knew him backwards. Big bull bluff and blunder. Big bastard though. But go, Jesus could he go. Catch a horse full strap. I rode him for years. Three Camel Cups. There are photos of me riding camels – this camel motoring along.

You could run alongside of them and spring up, grab them by the hump and swing up. Oh! No. It was not really risky. You just hit the dust, or sometimes they buck a bit but you would be right. I did not mind falling down, did not mind getting up, or that sort of stuff. You just took them on. Yes. I was mad. I could ride anything. When I was young, I could run alongside a mob of camels, climb up on them while they bucked, and jump off again. There was a picture of me running with the camels. I ran seven kilometres one day chasing camels, just riding and mucking around. I was fit and skinny and could ride anything. I had nothing better to do.

Do not just sit there and look at it, work out what it is, and get on with it. That has been my motto. I get bored very quickly just sitting down and talking, I just have to do things, I have got to go. The hardest part in my opinion is when I was sick, you sit there and you cannot move. I cannot have that. I have got to get up and move. Even after massive operations which I have had, I would be up in two days. People at the hospital were screaming, *What are you doing out of bed?* I would say that I feel good. *That's good, walk around. Get up and go out.* If the devil is coming to get me, he is going to have to be fast on his feet because I will be moving.

Doug Turner

I remember when Tracker used to ride the camels and he said to me, *Do you want to come and help in the Camel Cup?* I said, *Yeah! I'll come and help you, what do you want me to do?* He said, *You hold onto the camel by the nose with this rope and make him run when they blow the whistle or the horn to start the race.* So I am standing there hanging onto this bloody camel, and there were all these other camels lined up beside him and you could not see daylight between them, and Tracker said to me, *When they say go you've got to start running with this camel and you've got to get back behind the camel and get out, get off the racecourse, otherwise you'll get bowled over with the camels.*

I said to him, *You rotten dirty…*and all the names under the sun. I said, *How the fuck am I going to get out of here?* I looked at these camels and they kick in any direction, and they spit and they bite. And they are cantankerous, and they will run, or they will sit and get up and run again, and sit again, and sometimes, they will turn around and come back the opposite direction, and if you are in their way, they will bowl you straight over. I said to him, *I can't even see daylight between you and this bloody camel here.* He said, *You'll be right, you'll be right.* That was all he said, *You will be right*. So I was interested in starting the camel and getting off the track. I was looking for the nearest gap between the camels to get out to jump the fence and get off the track, as well as keep an eye on him to see where he was in the race.

I was too interested in the race and I forgot about getting out off the track. I was looking at the camels and seeing who was racing, and who was out in front, and what camels were coming back towards me, and what ones were behind me. I just had this intricate vision of where everything was at, and it was grand and I was thinking I am safe, I can still stay here on the track. I was looking at – *Oh, go you bastard, go go,* trying to urge him around the track so he could win the cup.

He made it to the finishing line. About ten camels, that cantankerous, some will run, depends on the rider, and of course Tracker was as mad as a cut snake and he would get on anything and ride, so he rode the camel in the race. That was my introduction to the Camel Cup. Before then we were training camels out south of Alice, running them from the open paddock down to where all the other camels were, so we were training them on about a kilometre run and we were out in open country. We took them about a mile up the paddock, out through the scrub sort of thing, but they could see all the other camels down the other end, and he would make them run, run down to where I was hanging on to the other camels and waiting for the riders to come down towards where we were. Of course, he kept the bloody camels in full bore heading straight towards you, and they were nearly on you and *holy shit*, I had to get out of the way because he wasn't stopping. Yes. That was the training session before we went to the Camel Cup. Because when a bunch of camels come running, the camels that you are hanging onto, they all get stirred up as well.

Well! Someone was looking after us. Nothing happened, and we all had a good time and walked out of there.

But whatever you do, the thing was to never ever go spotlighting for rabbits at night with Tracker. He was mad, absolutely mad. Do not give him the car. Do not let him drive the car while you are on the back without looking where you are going, when you are spotlighting looking for rabbits or kangaroo or something because he goes – he has got the wheel while you are on the back with a gun in your hand, hanging on for dear life, and he will be doing doughnuts. He has done that. Of course when he stopped, Johnny Liddle jumped off and walked up to the door of the car and ripped it open and said, *Get out here you black bastard.* He was going to punch the shit out of him. Well the old man, he was on the back of that bloody Toyota. Tracker was, *Oh! I was just having fun.*

Yeah! That was fun you stupid bastard. You can print every word I say.

Patrick and William Tilmouth

Patrick: I remember when I was young he would come in from the station [Angas Downs] and you would remember when Tracker was in town, he and Lawrie Liddle mob. Party! There would be a big party. Come in, have a big party, and then they would go out a week later and we would not see them again for six months.

William: He had this black Torana, really hotted up. It would fly like anything. Once, we were coming down the Mall when the Mall was a two-way street, and there was this yellow Torana behind him and I did not know he was signalling to the yellow Torana for a drag. I am sitting there quietly as a passenger not realising what was going on, but as soon as he hits the top of the Mall he just squalled it straight out, hit the causeway, straight across where the pizza thing is, and we were airborne when we hit Undoolya Road. And Undoolya Road did not have roundabouts, nothing, it was just straight, and that yellow Torana had sat right up behind us and then Tracker just flattened it and we hit the grid at the end of Undoolya way before the yellow one but, Oh! Crazy. *Don't do that again bro,* but he could drive. Damn good driver.

Patrick: He could drive along like that while he was having a feed. Out in the country flat out and he is eating chicken and whatever, anything. *T-R-A-C-K-E-R, what are you doing?* Woooooo! This bloke here nearly had an accident with him. On the sandhill, he was eating chicken, and the thing was going up a sandhill, *Hey Tracker,* he said, *Ah! This is only a sandhill,* and he pulled it back.

William: Tracker was aggressive and he did not like losing. He was competitive to the extreme. Very competitive.

Patrick: I played for the opposition [AFL team in Alice Springs] and he would chase me around and punch me.

William: You did not take a mark in front of him because he was behind you swinging. You kept running. You take the mark and you keep running because he was behind you, trying to take your head off. He never liked being beaten. Very competitive. He was a brilliant footballer. He had a raking left foot, a magic left foot.

He had a speed about him too. And he could really get distance with his left foot. He was very naturally talented. I know that he had a serious accident once when he was playing. I was not there, but I think they were playing Federals and he was playing for Pioneers. He was going for the ball and instead of his team supporting him and protecting him, the Westies or Federal bloke got through and crashed straight into him and caved his temple in. He ended up having no temple bone on the side of his head. They pulled it out because he nearly died in hospital. Then he started playing again and wore this super-thin headgear which could not protect him from anything. He was cheekier than ever. He did not lose that.

I went and watched a game once where they were playing Westies and he started a fight up in the forward flank there, and all the Westies guys came running over including the water boy. And next thing the water boy was flat out on his back with the water all over him. Tracker drove him. He would have a go. He was not scared.

Patrick: A smart-arse, Tracker. Quick. Very quick. We all talked the same language. We were very much on par with our humour. I mean he was extremely funny. We would go out together when Tracker came to Alice Springs. He would say, *Let's go for tea*, but he would forget his wallet. Me, I am just a painter and I do not make money, and he reckoned, *You have got a few dishes to wash in the restaurant*, especially in those Asian restaurants where you've got to get past the ninja mob you know, and table six is a long way away from the door.

I do not know where the humour comes from. We cannot deal with the other mob, the Nayda side of the family. They are different. They are dry. We were always like that. We learnt to laugh in adversity, and when things were really down you looked at the funny side, or you would think of funny thoughts and start communicating, and before you knew it you were a lot happier than you were when you were not laughing. I think that had been a defence mechanism of ours for a long time.

William: I saw him in a meeting once with government bureaucrats and he had taken off his shirt. He wanted to fight them right there and then in the conference room. I do not know who it was, but it was ADC [Aboriginal Development Commission] days. I said, *Fucking hell Tracker, calm down you know*, and he was saying: *I'll fight em.*

Patrick: One Federal woman was mouthing off at him when he was playing footy – one white woman, so he ran over to the fence and said to her, *Hey you*, he said, *How about me and you go halves in a coloured kid?* Cheeky bloke.

William: You have got to be careful there. I mean Kathy, she is one strong woman I think to put up with Tracker. She must have really loved the guy because I tell you what, she was staunch. She was his backbone. I mean through his hard times now, if she was not there…

Patrick: You could tell when she was not there.

William: He went to water.

Patrick: He was depressed.

William: Down. But when she was there she put him back on the right keel.

Patrick: Cathryn {Tracker's daughter} has cooked tea tonight, he would say, and he was all bubbly again.

William: He was a good one too for making you do work. He was building this chookyard around his place in Alice Springs when he lived there in this little cul-de-sac thing. He got me over there one day, and me and him were sitting there and he said, *I've got this chookyard to plan out.* I said, *Okay then.*

Patrick: He got us to do a lot of that.

William: So him and I went out there and he had all these pine logs and everything, chicken wire, sheets of metal and all that, and he and me paced it out and squared it off. *Yes okay, a post goes there, a post goes there, a post goes there. Yes righto? Right how many posts? Yeah! We're right, we've got enough posts there. Righto.* I used a crowbar and he used a shovel. So I got the crowbar and we started digging out this hole and it was hard rock, I mean it was hard soil. So I am going round in circles, chipping away at the edges making the hole the right size and going deeper and deeper, and I got down to about a foot and – *no Tracker*, he went inside. He said, *I've got to go inside*, and I looked up and I could just see a glimpse of the bull bar on his vehicle and he was slowly pulling out of the drive – that was the bull bar moving. So I walked around there and said, *Where are you going?* He said, *I'm going to see Colesy* [Owen Cole]. Yes. *You're fucking leaving me here doing this fucking work.*

Patrick: He left us like that another time too. I was mowing the lawn and I was painting the floor of the little basketball thing out the back, and Tracker was gone, he had to go and see someone.

William: It was Colesy, it was always Colesy.

Patrick: Kathy would come out, and it was a stinking hot day, and she brought big jugs of cordial out, and he just left us. He did that all the time.

William: I tell you I was sweating there with that crowbar. It was like clay that ground, it was hard. The crowbar was bouncing back at me. He was off to see Colesy. I don't think he ever finished that chookyard.

Remember the cubbyhouse he built Mandy? He put that much steel in it, he had to get a crane to lift it out. He was welding here and welding there, welding this and welding that. It was heavy as anything. Mind you it was heavy steel too. I looked up to the bloke I tell you.

Tracker Tilmouth

When I was a young fella at Angas Downs we had drought times. We could not get employed so the old bloke [Arthur Liddle] sent me off to work for Dave Simpson at the Ayers Rock Garage. The Ayers Rock Garage was on the east side of the Rock, Uluru, where the pubs were, Ayers Rock Hotel and everything else, the Red Centre Resort and all that sort of stuff. Anyway, we were in the garage and I was learning how to be a mechanic, how to weld, and everything else off old Dave Simpson. He had all these vintage cars and all that. Anyway the bloody hippies turned up. This bloke set up a dome in the middle of the camping ground. Him and his missus. He had two young sheilas living with him. He would not wash. He would drive around in this old Land Rover and he had this big carpet snake in a glass cage at the back of the Land Rover.

Anyway he came in at night to fix his Land Rover and I am there trying to weld up the springs and everything else. He broke the springs. Land Rovers were always breaking the front spring. Anyway, I am there fixing it up and Simmo was supposed to be fixing the spring, and suddenly Simmo had hit him with the oxytorch on, and he had all of these dreadlocks. A couple of dreadlocks got burnt up. You could smell the fire.

The community had the shits with him because he would not wash and he would not do anything, and they tried to kick him out. Ian Cawood was there, the head ranger, and so they went out there and inspected his camp and it was all clean and everything else, so they could not kick him out. Then one night, one of the publicans saw him have a shit out in the middle of the camping ground, not in the toilet. They rang the police at Kulgera. So daring Dean Symons, and old Tjuki Tjukanku Pumpjack, who was his black tracker, came screeching down the highway from Kulgera with lights blazing, blue lights going, and you know when you get the old cowboy movies, the Lone Ranger turns up and everyone is cheering and he goes into the pub and everyone shouts him a beer? They shouted old Dan the beer, and of course Tjuki was not allowed in the pub, he had to get his out the window. The next morning Tjuki had to track him, track this bloke where he had the shit. And not only that, dig the shit up and put it in a plastic big as Exhibit A. Well! They could use this as evidence to kick the bloke out of the park.

Anyway, before that, before they could kick him out, this bloke came to see Simmo. Simmo was out the back where he used to live with old Windless, old Captain Number One, Harry Brumby and everybody else [senior traditional landowners]. They were out the back behind my caravan. I was living there too. I knew them before when I went to Docker River.

Anyway, this bloke wanted to get into the culture so he wanted Windless and Captain Number One to feel him – Right! and they could not stop laughing. They were telling me in language *this bloke is fucking mad and he won't wash, he stinks*, and all this in language was going on. He said, *Not only me, but my two wives*. Right! And they said to Simmo, old Dave Simpson, *We'll give you the tjuma* [information] – you know, all the string and stuff from all the ceremony. *You wear it and put a blanket over you so they can't see you – you whitefella, and you can go and touch them, and the young fella, you take him with you*. So I said to him, *Righto, tomorrow you might get a visit*. Oh! True.

So anyway, Simmo put on this didgeridoo music on the tape recorder out in the bush. Ambience. And Simmo scared the shit out of me because he had this feather foot, the full regalia that he had got from Windless because he was a real murderer. *I am a murderer.* He used to introduce himself, *I'm the murderer,* like that, old Tjamu see, he would tell me, *I'm a murderer*. Anyway, so Simmo got all this regalia and turned up under the blanket and it scared the shit out of me because I did not see him coming. I heard all this *rumm, rumm* – didgeridoo music and everything else, and this woman took all her clothes off and lay there on the ground. Simmo had to kneel down and start touching her, pressing here and pressing there like a *ngangkari* [traditional healer]. The other woman was there and she was saying, *Can you touch me too like this?* I am trying to keep a straight face and thought if they took the blanket off him they would see that there is a white bloke underneath. Because the old blokes reckon, *No! No! If we touch them we'll get sick, they're mad them people.*

So Simmo did this and I have never stopped laughing ever since. That was Ayers Rock. Then I went from there back to Angas Downs and then DAA [Department of Aboriginal Affairs] turned up. Neville Jones broke down on the road. I went and fixed his motor car up and towed his vehicle back to Ayers Rock. This was when he said, *Do you want a job?* I said, *Where?* He said, Docker River. I said, *Yeah, no worries.* I know all the mob. Speak Pitjantjatjara.

When Gough Whitlam came in and there was no more conscription Vinnie got upset and joined the army. Everyone was coming out [of the army] and he was going in. So they sent him over to Townsville, Puckapunyal, or wherever it was, and he came back madder than when he went in.

Vinnie decided to teach us how to fight. He had come back from the army and he could do jujitsu and everything like this with them skinny legs and big riding boots, swaying his arms around. Anyway Johnny Cottrell, who was a jujitsu exponent, he had a black belt and everything, and Vinnie for some unknown reason got caught up with these bouncers [at a nightclub in Alice Springs], and in the middle of the dance floor this bouncer swung Vinnie. Vinnie was shaping up to them and doing all that sort of stuff and this bloke just grabbed him and swung him around and put a nelson lock on the back of his head, and squeezed the shit out of him.

Vincent is out in the middle of the dance floor going, *haa, haa,* so Johnny Cottrell jumped up and grabbed the bouncer in the same headlock. He squeezed the bouncer, and he squeezed Vinnie. So these three blokes were in the middle of the dance floor squeezing each other. So much for teaching us how to fight. Me and Johnny Liddle were sitting out there crying [with laughter].

He came back from the army with all the skills in unarmed combat. Recite. Recite the recipe. What is a recite? I said, *What are you fucking talking about, recipe.* I did not know what happened in the army anyway. So we had to sit him down and ask him what happened in the army. I said to Liddle, *Lucky they didn't give him any written orders to advance, he'd be fucked.* Vinnie got all flustered one day and said, *I need to write a letter to the Queen.* I said, *Oh yeah. Can you even write?*

Yeah. Why don't you write it?

Yeah, I said, *Righto. To whom shall we address this to? Dear Liz*, I said, *How's your corgis?* Johnny Liddle read the letter and he reckoned, *You're a fucking idiot.* I said, *I was being dictated to, I am merely the scribe.*

What did he want to say to the Queen? I don't know, about something.

Sovereignty, that's right. That is right it was about — sovereignty. *Dear Liz, how's the corgis?* I was writing, following instructions. Even her husband does not call her Liz. But your hands were tied. Always. You were just doing the best you could. Then Vinnie decided that while we were all in town, we had come in at night [from Angas Downs], so he woke us up at about five o'clock in the morning, *Get up, get up, get up.* What the fuck for, fire, accident, what happened? *It's daylight savings.* Yes. We know that. *The banks are open daylight.*

So we made a story up that you could go to the bank and, *Do you want bacon and toast with your withdrawal? How do you like your eggs?* You know the bank manager is cooking breakfast for you, a cup of coffee to go with it. He fucking believed it. It is fucking madness I tell you. Johnny Liddle was mad as well, he was madder.

He tied Vinnie, was it him, it might have been Chutty Campbell, no, no Vinnie, no, no Chutty Campbell, tied the curtains to him at the pizza shop when he was in the horrors…Vinnie and Chutty Campbell. *Come on, we're going now.* They got up and walked out and all the curtains came down. I was then in a double yacka. I jumped the counter with a butcher knife and Colesy was holding a seat fighting Vinnie off like gladiators, and Donny Campbell ran around the back and turned off all the gas so the ovens went off. And then Vinnie was sword fighting, he would go – *Touché. Touché. Touché – Stav.* We used to call him Stav, Stavros the Greek. We just made it up. This is what I would say to Liddle, *Guess who I saw? Stavros.* He knew straight away who I was talking about. Touché. Oh laugh.

Vinnie was fucking mad I tell you. And Johnny Liddle was worse, absolutely worse. Johnny Liddle had this weird idea that he would cut up a new pair of jeans and sew the sides up with copper wire, down the side, and bend the sunglasses so that one eye pokes out, and the other one is up here, and he is looking at you with one glass.

What for? Don't know. He was stoned most of the time. He went to his sister's wedding with one of those sunglasses. He sat there grinning and the old man said, *Make sure that idiot isn't in the wedding photos.* He was a complete nut, Liddle. Oh! Yes! We had so much fun we could not stop laughing. We laughed all day. And then we had these little motorbikes like little miniature bikes and a little three-wheeler when we were living at 14 Dallingall in Alice Springs, and we set up this track through the house with little jumps over the ledge. Old Bess [Liddle] came over and saw there were three idiots, *rrrrow*, around and around, in and out the house, chasing each other around on motorbikes. She was trying to hit us with a stick. She was waiting there with a *kutra*. It was amazing.

We went to the Henley on Todd, you know, where they used to have the little bridge running across a bit of water and Richard Lake wanted to commit suicide. He wanted to jump off the bridge and drown in the water. The water was that deep [shallow] and he kept falling off the bridge. He is dead now. We were absolutely fucking mad. We would do all sorts of things. And this is all without scones. Non-scone period. Angas Downs stuffed me up. Look it was so crazy.

2.

Becoming Dangerous

The Troika

Tracker Tilmouth

I always was the chief. I thought of everything and told people what to do. And that was the way I grew up in the mission, of understanding non-Indigenous people, and trying to work out what they were thinking long before they said it. I had the ability at school to do that. I could finish my schoolwork as the teachers were writing it up on the board. I knew exactly what they were going to say next for some unknown reason. I learnt to read very young because books interested me, and books still interest me, I read a lot. I watch the news on television, I read everything, even my kids reckon, *Oh! Boring!* but it is not, it loads your mind, and especially with the discipline of university, where you get the discipline with homework and study, and then you come back with the ideas. Too often Aboriginal people have gone to universities and they have got tickets for turning up rather than doing the work.

The Troika: Rossy, Colesy and I decided we were going to the real universities, and we were going to stay there and get a proper ticket, but the other thing we said was that we would return to the community. We would not work for the government. And that is what we did. That is why Alice Springs, in terms of intelligence and ability and boost, got its economic platform. The Aboriginal community had David Ross, Owen Cole and me and that is what we quietly call each other, the Troika, because even today, there is nothing that Rossy does without me knowing about it, or Colesy knowing about it, and commenting. And that has always been the way that we have held things together. You cannot split the three no matter how much lobbying you do because the other two will definitely talk to the third and vice versa, and that has been a very good team for many years. I learnt this ability to try and work out what they were saying early in the piece.

Owen Cole

He once said to me, *Colesy, I can be anything you want me to be – an Arab one day, a Jew the next. I am the chameleon.* What he was saying in his usual cryptic manner was, to really understand and appreciate people from all walks of life you must be able to walk in their shoes and see things from their eyes – and you must work with them in finding a solution.

When we were talking about this book Tracker said to me, *Make sure you tell the truth.* I said, *How can I tell the truth when I am talking about you Tracker?* I knew him all my life – which is sixty years, as we were both about the same age. I have known his family more so than Tracker, and Tracker when he was young would have known me through my family and our extended family. His father used to come and sit down at our place [in Alice Springs] and the kids were there when they were really young, and of course Tracker was taken away and sent to Croker Island, and then we lost track of one another for quite a few years.

I knew some of the family and his extended family, his aunty Tilly, and we just knew one another from the fact that we all mixed whenever the occasion arose. I had known him pretty well all his life. They moved to the east side of Alice Springs, whereas we were living down at The Gap but that was where they came from originally, and I like to think we all claim the same sort of connections.

When he came back to Central Australia, I remember going to the football in Alice Springs after I had come back from Adelaide where I was studying. I was about thirty I suppose, and I had not played football for five years and they said, *Have a game.*

So I went there and there was this loud-mouthed footballer there telling me I ran like I had a crankshaft up my arse. *Why don't you run properly, Colesy?* I had to turn around and say, *Who's that big-lipped bloke? That cheeky fella?* And they said, *That's Tracker.* I had not seen him for years but he was just as abusive as always. So we were just like long-lost friends and it was as though we had never parted.

And then I went and worked with the Aboriginal Development Commission and Tracker was working with the DAA right next door.

Then we worked together when they abolished or closed DAA. Tracker came across to ADC and we worked out in the western communities in Central Australia. We were going out to Aboriginal communities and delivering housing programs, and also some economic development programs, and that was always Tracker's special interest to try and get economic development happening on Aboriginal land.

Later on he went and worked with the Central Land Council, but even when we were working with the ADC and I ended up as regional manager we started pushing to acquire Aboriginal land, and we identified the groups, Eastern Arrernte people and the Luritja people.[8] They had missed out on land rights, because most of their traditional land could not be claimed under the Land Rights Act.

I tried to purchase pastoral property, so we were doing this with the ADC and Tracker was equally interested in the pastoral side of things because he worked out at Angas Downs with the Liddles and those types of people. He had that background with Vincent Forrester [then the Northern Territory chairman of the National Aboriginal Conference, the peak Aboriginal political organisation in the 1980s]. So he pushed it, which was a little bit different because when he was working for the DAA, the Department did not recognise the need for economic projects and Tracker was saying, *Well! You need to get people involved,* and he always pushed it from day one.

He never changed his tack really. He was the one who said it was all well and good looking at the traditional law and custom side of things, but you needed to get people thinking about being able to use their land, the same way that other non-Aboriginal people can use it for economic development and generate wealth, which in turn could be used to build up and support traditional law and custom. He believed this came hand in glove. I remember when he was working at the Central Land Council and the native title legislation was being negotiated, Tracker called me in and said we have got to tell these people [Aboriginal leaders, academics, lawyers and politicians], that

---

8. Eastern and Central Arrernte includes Harts Range (Atitjere), Bonya (Uthipe Atherre), Santa Teresa (Ltyentye Apurte), Amoonguna (Imengkwerne) and Alice Springs (Mparntwe). Luritja is spoken east of the Pitjantjatjara lands from Oodnadatta in SA through to Finke (Aputula).

it is equally an economic development argument as well. It is not just legal rights because Mabo was quite restricted with the rights the High Court found in the Mabo case.

Basically Tracker was saying, *Look! We should see the right for Aboriginal people to access the land, and to use it for economic development to generate wealth,* and to be quite honest we got thrown out of the meetings because it was all about: *This is what the Mabo decision was and we will work within those parameters.* Tracker was saying, *Stuff the parameters, this is a political argument, let's really push, we want to access the land and develop it and use it to create wealth.* That was not favourably looked upon at that time, which is quite surprising because it has become a bit more fashionable now. But Tracker was pushing that argument from before the legislation was enacted.

His argument was about the population of those Aboriginal communities coming into towns like Alice Springs and the problems that brings. Tracker's argument was that we needed to get these people actively involved, particularly in the pastoral industry because they had a long history of doing that. So let's set up these pastoral properties and run them properly so these people can continue to work there, and give them a reason and means to stay on the land. Build up the infrastructure, and give people the means to sustain themselves out there on their traditional lands. That was not the fashionable view then. It was all about the welfare-oriented perspective and Tracker always challenged that. As it proved, he was absolutely right. We have seen a lot of those communities which were not given the opportunity to develop wealth and employment opportunities depopulated and they are living in Alice Springs, a large number of them. I just look back and say, Tracker was absolutely right.

David Ross

That was a political act. It took all these acts of politics to get that taught, something along those lines Tracker would say. *Going to the toilet is a political act.* That was one of his favourites. He used that for years.

I had known Tracker since we were teenagers. I first met Tracker here in Alice, and saw him in Darwin a couple of times but most of the time, he was elsewhere as a teenager and he ended up at Angas Downs. So then he used to come in to Alice Springs from Angas Downs. He was part of the workforce and he was tear-arsing around. He was living at Ayers Rock at one stage and it must have been around 1974 or 1975 that we were working over in Van Senden Avenue in Alice Springs, around that area, where it was all new housing west and south from the old cemetery on Memorial Drive, and all through that area with the building of new houses. I was laying bricks and he was working for Terry Smith and his father putting on roofs. He and Lawrie Liddle were roofies, putting the roofs on all the new houses.

That was a real hoot as you would have these bastards singing out and yelling out, cracking jokes. Tracker always did that, always up for a giggle and a laugh. That was probably our later teenage years as young blokes, but he was a few years older than me. I am probably about the same age as his brother Patrick. Patrick and I went to school together at Nightcliff High School in 1970.

Welfare decided back in them days, when Tracker and them were taken away as young'uns. My mum died in 1964, and it was left to our grandmother and older brothers and sisters [to look after me]. As I got older Welfare threw me into St Phillips, in 1968 and 1969. Then once you got to a certain age they wanted to send you away. That was their policy. I had a bit of a history of going walkabout, going home and seeing the family when it suited me rather than when it suited them. Anyway, they decided that they were going to send me off to Adelaide or Melbourne or somewhere, because that is what they did. And I said, *Well! You can send me wherever you like but I won't be staying. I'll be coming home.*

An older brother was living in Darwin, so they talked to him about me going up there, and that was why I ended up in Darwin. To cut a long story short, that was where it all happened, and that was how I knew Patrick. I never met Willie until much, much later. I met Tracker first, and then met Patrick, and then got to know Tracker over the years through work and what not, bit by bit. I laid bricks for ten years or more after I left school and then I came to work at the Central Land Council, and around about that time Tracker was working for the Department of Aboriginal Affairs, in the late 70s. He was at DAA and he went on to the Aboriginal Development Commission. He and Colesy were there and I forget the exact year, but it was down at Ayers Rock where they had the big Central Australian Aboriginal Pastoralists meeting.

We had the big thing down there, it was a big meeting with lots of people and the meeting finished late on the Friday and we were going back Saturday morning. We never took much notice and the second tank on the Toyota did not have a fuel gauge on it. It was a new car and it did not have a fuel gauge. We were just outside Orange Creek and realised we had run out of diesel. We switched over to the reserve tank and some bastard had milked it on us down at Ayers Rock the night before, because we had filled up both tanks. I know, I had filled them up. We could not make it home. So the memory of the meeting down there around these other issues sort of sticks in my head. We ran out of diesel and we were stuck on the road. You remember these things because all you want to do is get home on a Saturday night, after a week of meetings. That was a big impact on CAAPU [Central Australia Aboriginal Pastoral Unit], and Aboriginal people throughout Central Australia, and we got some support and some funding.

Owen Cole

We were involved in setting up a Central Australian Aboriginal Cattlemen's Association in the 1980s. I remember the ground-breaking conference at Mutitjulu, where they actually said, *We need to get together and form this Cattlemen's Association, and let's harness our collective strengths and make sure we are represented in the industry.* So we worked on that and once again, Tracker was a pioneer, and a lot of people just sort of looked at him and said, *Whoop! Whoop! What are you doing?* Meaning to say, *Hang on. This is the equivalent of the Northern Territory Cattlemen's Association, they are our enemies, why are we trying to emulate our detractors?* But Tracker was a visionary, and that is the only way I would look at him. He was way out there and a lot of people did not really appreciate it, including Aboriginal people, did not appreciate what he was trying to do.

I have often thought about what had nurtured the way he looked at the world. He was a visionary. He had seen the vision splendid. Whereas us people tend to look from a very narrow perspective, Tracker had seen endless opportunities. And he would just build on them and I do not know how he did this. I have thought about it, and I have had these discussions with David Ross, and some of his ideas were too far out there and were probably not going to work, but you need those type of people who could tease out all these opportunities, and Tracker was one of those blokes. I think this was probably a result of his background where he was taken away from his family and he had to come back, and to develop the wherewithal to survive and to grow, and so forth. He lost connection to a great degree, and the rest of his family as well, and he had to come back. He became very independent. He knew that he had to survive and to survive, he needed to be creative and strong and be out there. That was him all over. And then he would come up with gems. He would just toss them, these endless ideas about something, and all of a sudden there would be an absolute gem and everyone would say, *Let's grab it and run with it*. But none of us would have thought of it.

He would tire you sometimes. I mean he was a real intellect but not in a sort of academic sense. It was his creativity of looking at things differently. It was just the way he thought. He was out there and he looked at things, looked at a particular subject, and he saw it differently. He always had the entrepreneurial flair, and that gets back to the fact that you've got to survive, and you've got to survive in any shape or form. He was able to mix with anyone, the paupers, the queens and kings, the politicians. He just had that personality. He had no shame whatsoever, whereas most Aboriginal people would be a little bit circumspect I suppose. He would walk up to anyone and talk to them, engage in conversation, and throw ideas around. Walk into any meeting and take it over.

His philosophy was identify what the issue is, work out the solution and if there were any barriers, either knock them, or work out a way to undermine them so that they fell over. So that was his technique, and he did it. For example, when he was working as the director of the Central Land Council when David Ross went and studied in Adelaide, there were still a lot of Aboriginal groups that did not have land, and David Ross had started a land acquisition program. Tracker had just came back from Roseworthy College where he had completed his applied science degree or whatever it was, and he said, *We've got to get this land back and what we need to do is put in a system. We've got to do it better than anyone else.* There was a lot of money there, but a lot of the Aboriginal groups did not know how to access that money. So Tracker said, *Let's set up a system, an acquisition system and property development system.*[9] So he could do that, and my job was to come in and just pull together the application and it was a formula type of thing, where if you needed to get anthropological things, where do you get it from and so forth, and Tracker would set up the framework, the computer framework. He just got the system working, and he and I worked together, and I think in one year we ended up purchasing about six pastoral properties, which was unheard of in those days, and it was like a production line really. We said, *Right! This is the property, bang.* But he ran into a lot of resistance.

A lot of people did not want to sell to Aboriginal people, so Tracker said, *We'll just set up a system where we get these smart lawyers to set up companies and we will buy it later on. The company will purchase the pastoral property, and we will purchase the company and they will not know that it is an Aboriginal purchaser.* So that was one thing. But he also ran into a lot of problems in the Land Council. Some of the lawyers did not agree with that philosophy of pushing the economic development side of things, so Tracker and I just ran straight over the top of them if they did not want to do the agreements.

I would sit down with Tracker and we would draft the agreements and say, *Here it is. You people have got until tomorrow to approve this and it needs to come from you,* so of course they would be hastily running around trying to make it more legally binding and correct. So he forced that change, the ideology of some of the people who worked there who thought we should be concentrating on the cultural side of things, and Tracker said once again, *Let's get access to land, let's try to get enterprise development there.* And we needed to have those things going simultaneously. So he just pushed it through and eventually they had

---

9. The Land Council wanted to acquire land for land claims for Aboriginal groups that would miss out on land rights after the 'sunset clause' came into effect on 5 June 1997. The sunset clause was an amendment to the *Aboriginal Land Rights (Northern Territory) Act 1976* that prevented any further land claims being made under the act, especially over pastoral land that had been purchased and claimed by Aboriginal people under the act.

to kowtow, had to comply with what the director wanted to know and they got involved, but they were hesitant. If the need was there, Tracker would run over the top of people.

A lot of the land we were purchasing really was unsuitable as pastoral properties, so we tried to pick the ones that would be sustainable and to make sure we accessed funds to develop those properties the way they should be developed. Properly! And my background was working in a government department at one time, where I learnt how to play the games as good as anyone else, and I knew the economic side of things, of pulling the figures together and what they needed, which we could serve up collectively. Tracker was the agricultural genius or so he thought, and he actually set up a system with Barney Foran from the CSIRO. It was pretty complicated and I did not know one end of a cow from the other to be quite honest, which Tracker kept on reminding me was the case, but once the model was there, I could input the data and get any sort of information out of it.

The ILC [Indigenous Land Corporation] had never come across anything as sophisticated. They tried to attack it, and of course they couldn't, because they were used to using simple spreadsheets and this was really complex with climatic conditions and fertility rates et cetera, which Tracker and the CSIRO people had developed. So we had to educate half the bureaucracy on how to interpret the stuff.

Anyway we just kicked down [the barriers]. We knew how to play the politics, and Tracker was excellent at playing the politics. I knew how to do the economic stuff because that is my background, and we both knew the community side of things, how to get out there and talk to the right people, and we had worked at doing this for a long time by then, having been involved for ten or fifteen years out in those communities. And it was always an eventful experience working with Tracker because you never knew what was going to turn up. And it was good fun working with him.

Then you had Rossy [David Ross] who was the director of the Central Land Council and Tracker was his deputy prior to Rossy going and after Rossy came back, and they just complemented one another. You know Rossy was a straightlaced director, and Tracker was the far-out one, and Rossy would bring him in, and collectively they would mesh their ideas and they worked well together. But you needed people like Tracker, otherwise you were just going to settle for the status quo.

He was never about settling for less or the status quo somehow. So we worked on the Central Land Council, we worked on the Cattlemen's Association, we worked on pastoral properties, all the acquisitions, and we worked on the purchase of Mistake Creek which is one of the best pastoral properties and Aboriginal-owned pastoral properties in Australia I would suggest, and it is still going strong after all these years.

What else did we do? Oh! Look we worked on setting up new stores [on communities] and that sort of thing. We knew how government policies worked, and we knew how to use those policies and programs to get things done. And we introduced flexibility that was not intended within those program guidelines to get things done. I think it was because of that sort of attitude, that we have ended up with things like the Yeperenye Shopping Centre in Alice Springs, as well as Imparja Television, because if you tried to set those up today with the bureaucracy that is supposed to be setting up economic development nowadays, you would not get any of that. Aboriginal people would just run into barriers.

And of course Tracker had this amazing relationship with Kumantjayi [Charlie] Perkins. He was sort of Kumantjayi Perkins' protégé I suppose in a lot of respects, and he would use Tracker for all the cultural side of things when he came into Alice Springs. Tracker would make sure that he would talk to the right people and Tracker learnt a lot from him as well. So those two had a lifelong relationship, sometimes a little hostile but full of respect, and we all had that sort of relationship I suppose. We loved one another, but we also hated one another at various times.

His favourite term that he coined for me was *big-lip Luritja*. He said that every time I had a few beers my lips used to drop, and so with my Luritja backround, he called me that if he wanted to be insulting. I regarded it as a term of endearment more than an insult, and whenever he was feeling down I would ring him up and say, *Ring me up and have an argument with the big-lipped Luritja*. That helped. So he was great.

I mean he could be frustrating at times but when you take everything into consideration, he was just a champion in my opinion.

Doug Turner

Tracker came back to Central Australia from Croker Island [Mission], and he was part of the Stolen Generation. He always said that he learnt how to sail with a bark canoe, but I do not know how true that is because he was always making up stories.

What was he like? He was mad. But I think that was the best way to be because even in your madness you can achieve a lot of stuff. It breaks down barriers and opens up doors. He had a big heart, and he gave his time and energy to a lot of people and his expertise which was short on the ground I suppose, but he always says that he knew everything and did everything. That was how mad he was.

He would get up and go. He had a lot of people that he knew, and friends, and he was willing to have a go about what was right for the community, for the Aboriginal community in the local Alice area basically. He knew people out bush. He could speak the language, especially Pitjantjatjara, Yankunytjatjara, and maybe a little bit of Luritja, but I am not a hundred per cent sure on that. He had that sort of understanding about people and because of his madness in that era where there was a lot of racism still around, you had to brace yourself for that racism and get over it so that you could get on with life and achieve things. He got on well with different people, whitefellas and blackfellas and stuff like that, Aboriginal fellas when I say blackfellas – this is how we spoke, we spoke like this within the Alice Springs Aboriginal community.

I think if you were a local Aboriginal person in Alice Springs during that time you sort of grew up with the mainstream community, the white community, and people were aware of your background and you fitted in basically. But coming from the outside, people would look at Alice in a different light and say there was racism in the town because of the experience of half-caste Aboriginal people and full-blood Aboriginal people, there was that social difference, between traditional lifestyle coming from the bush, and the other which was sort of semi-traditional – and between European and Aboriginal society, they conducted themselves in a different way so to speak.

I would not say because they were more civilised or anything like that, that is probably what a lot of white people saw basically, but because there was a lot of social issues with pastoralists and that stuff in Alice Springs, and I think to some degree that still exists today. The Aboriginal community in Alice is very outspoken and wanted to see change and a better community with better infrastructure and all those sorts of things, and that is what the local Aboriginal community put in place. We had to break down a lot of barriers and stand up for our community. When I say our community, the Aboriginal community in the Territory. Because the Territory was a territory, it was not a state, it came under the jurisdiction of Canberra, and a lot of funds came out of Canberra to go into Alice Springs to develop different programs, town camps and all that sort of stuff. So we put a lot of time and energy while working with the Department of Aboriginal Affairs, as members of the local Aboriginal community, into trying to improve the lifestyle for Aboriginal people in Central Australia.

There were a lot of town camps around Alice, and I am going back now twenty-five years, because we were involved in going out bush and working with Aboriginal communities on grants and aids. We set up programs in a lot of remote communities, but some of the programs around Alice were to help clean up the town camps, because the level of rubbish and the dogs were an issue.

If you could not get a grant program to help do this sort of stuff you had go out of your way and do these things out of your pocket, and you would go and talk to the camp communities around town, where you provided a service, and help clean up. We got involved in actually cleaning up a lot of rubbish around some of these camps and all that support came through ourselves, outside the services of government, even though we were working within government, because the government was very slow to get things done.

So we provided services to communities, and around the town camps out of our pocket and out of our spare time, to help move things along and get things done. We would beg and borrow machinery to go help clean up yards. That was a big thing that Tracker got involved with in those early years. This was before Tangentyere Council got off the ground, and I think that was probably one of the reasons why Tangentyere actually started, to provide this community service into the town camp areas around Alice.

He was not only a good communicator, but he would put the time and energy into different business companies in Alice, white business companies, and he built up a reputation with the people and it was my understanding that he put a lot of energy into these businesses for nothing. He grew up with white families who owned businesses in Alice, so they saw a local Aboriginal person trying to do things for the community, out of the goodness of his heart on a voluntary basis, so some of them got behind him and helped him.

Not only that, he was part of a stronger network of Aboriginal people, get-up-and-go Aboriginal people, who were needed to try and bring about a change of attitude within Alice, the mainstream business community of Alice where they were members of the Chamber of Commerce. Those were the sort of games I saw that Tracker was playing, with other strong Aboriginal members in the community to bring about a positive change for Aboriginal people in Alice Springs, for Aboriginal artists, the businesses, the abattoir, to get mainstream local business support.

Dave Murray

I lived in Alice Springs at the time and I had a mobile abattoir which I was operating at a place called Amoonguna, an Aboriginal community about twelve kilometres out of Alice Springs. And at that time Tracker was a liaison officer with ADC and he came to see me about whether we were able to join forces to supply meat to the Aboriginal communities and instigate a vertical integrated program to utilise the finances that were coming into the communities, to utilise them rather than just having them going back into white organisations I guess. And that is where our relationship started.

We met several times with an accountant who worked for Howarth and Howarth, and we did have several discussions to see whether it was appropriate and how it could evolve. It did evolve and we were working together for the next three or four years at least. During this time he formed the Aboriginal Cattlemen's Association. The ADC funded a big meeting down at Ayers Rock which Tracker coordinated, where each community that had land was invited to participate. And out of that meeting came the formulation of the Central Aboriginal Cattlemen's Association.

I guess in setting up any organisation there are problems to sort through and sort out, but Tracker was the main instigator in sorting through those things, bringing people together and making sure everybody understood their roles, and that they had adequate input into what they wanted to see come out of it. The main thing that came out of it was the fact that each week the main commodity through the stores seemed to be meat, the main sales seemed to be meat. A lot of Aboriginal communities were breeding and raising cattle, but these cattle were being sourced off through the local whitefella markets. It seemed feasible that if the markets could be established, if you could capitalise on these markets and the cattle that they were breeding could be turned around and be resourced back through the communities, there would be a bigger piece of the pie. And I believe that was instigated by Tracker and he was the one who pushed the boundaries for that. It was a great idea actually and very feasible and very workable.

He was unique in that he was very well read, and he had a photographic memory. I proved this time and time again, when he would call me up and say, *I have got a meeting going on, blah, blah, blah, Murray, and I might need you over here at such and such. I will pick you up at such and such time,* he might say, 2.30 sort of thing, and we might drive for fifteen or twenty minutes to get to the meeting. During that period of time he would ask a series of questions and he would really have a discussion with me, driving from point A to point B, and I would think that he was not really taking much notice of what I was saying, but having been a party to listening in at the meeting, I know he would almost quote you verbatim what you had just discussed. After a while it was evident that he had this photographic memory with his ability to retain information and bring it out at the appropriate times. It is quite a unique ability to have. Then afterwards, he would not only remember what was being said, but he would have deciphered the lot. He had an uncanny ability to do that. The biggest attribute of the guy was his absolute honesty. This was why people could not pin him down, because of his ability to absorb information, and because he was absolutely sure and honest with his dealings.

Basically what happened to his idea of an Aboriginal Cattlemen's Association in Central Australia was too many people with too many hands in the pie. I believe that there was a certain amount of funding through the Aboriginal Development Corporation to get this up, but their requirement to release funds was that they needed a feasibility study. Most of the finances that were made available were eaten up with feasibility studies unfortunately, and then when the time came to instigate the programs and put them into actual being, it was the lawyers, accountants and people doing the feasibility studies who were the ones that got funded first and foremost, and the project itself just sort of fell by the wayside. Very disappointing. Tracker worked very hard with myself to liaison through the abattoirs, and we believed that we could still get it up and running provided that we had the support of the local Aboriginal community stores. If we could get the stores on side then it was still feasible. And so we went down that track for a couple of years funding it through the operation of a butcher shop, and with the instigation of a training program for Aboriginal slaughtermen. A very hard slog, when you did not actually have the support of some of the organisations that should have been backing it.

I believe Tracker actually was a competent slaughterman, so he did understand the cuts of meat. He did understand the facts of finance, and could see the amount of finance that was actually going into the stores on a weekly basis. He could see the correlation between these things, and he had invited me a couple of times to do some musters on Aboriginal communities with him to see what stock was available on their land. As he sussed that sort of thing out he could see that sometimes the cattle that were provided, or the finance that was provided to put cattle on some of the properties, ended up on adjoining whitefella stations, and there was a trade-off that happened sometimes with the whitefellas. They would do a muster and they would take cattle in lieu of their input to the muster, but unfortunately, lots of times the cattle that they actually took far exceeded the amount that those cattle should have bought even in a normal sale situation. Tracker was very much aware of that, and he brought it to the forefront, which put him out on a limb. He was out on a limb as far as the whitefellas were concerned, and the whitefellas Cattlemen's Association, and then he was at loggerheads with some of the members of the Aboriginal Cattlemen's Association because there was this double standard play going on.

Because sometimes you have got a handout, and you can see the handout, and that handout is tangible, so you will take the handout. You do not see the long term or bigger picture. And basically, if you have a dozen people, a dozen different groups if you like, and say the benefit would benefit eight of them, what are the other four going to get? They see a piece of the pie does not turn up on time, then you have this dissension happening. So he had a very hard row to hoe, but the idea and concepts were very much on track and inline and very feasible.

The Aboriginal Cattlemen's Association was absolutely part of a broader picture and vision that Tracker had because of his knowledge of the land. Because of his Aboriginality. Because of his background in having been a slaughterman and having worked on communities. And understanding the store situation and the finances going into them. He had a very strategic role to play. He was a qualified stock inspector, and I believe probably one of the few Aboriginal stock inspectors of his time. With his knowledge of the finances and what was going on in stores, he was very strategically placed.

Even today, his ideas would still be workable. See, he developed what we called a vertical integrated program, where the same dollar value stayed within the marginal groups. They would have gotten to the point where they would not have been relying on government handouts, or bureaucrats playing politics.

That was the way it was. He did have an understanding of the land and breaking in horses and stuff like that. In that whole sector, he had let's say a handle on what was really going on, but unfortunately, he could not get the powerbrokers to follow through. It happened time and time again.

Patrick and William Tilmouth

Patrick: Tracker was at the head of everything. They talk about Tangentyere [Council] and all this shit, but I cleaned Freddy Fry's block up when it was a dump at Little Sisters [town camp], when there was nothing there. I had got away from painting and Tracker said, *Come on you're gonna drive this tractor.* So I went to Geoffrey Liddle to get a tractor, and Geoffrey Liddle gave us a backhoe and we cleared that block. I cleared it, not Tracker, he was gone. I was operating that tractor.

William: I think he was the first community development officer with Congress when Neville Perkins was the first director. I remember when Tracker got me to paint the clinic.

Patrick: Yes I had to do the floor, tile the floor and I knew nothing about tiling. He had me doing the floors and everything like I knew how to do it. He just said, *Oh! Bones will do that.* For nothing mind you, I never got paid for it. I did a lot of work for him just for nothing.

William: Johnny [Liddle] was one of their first bus drivers.

Patrick: Tracker got him the job, didn't he?

William: Tracker was a bus driver for Congress. The bloke was a visionary, no doubt about that. He is an ideas man.

Patrick: He had more vision than anyone I have seen. Thought outside the square all the time. We used to say that he was twenty years ahead but it is true. A lot of people gave him a hard time for thinking outside the square too: that he was not the full quid. But when it all comes to fruition sooner or later, everyone else takes the credit for it. I used to think, *Tracker, that was your idea.* I remember, I was there. But this person and that person…

William: I have a thing about people who just out of their own ego claimed to have started this and started that.

Patrick: Like CAAMA. That was Johnny Macumba. I do not care what anyone else says.

William: Yes, but it all came from the need of the most disadvantaged, poor people who had a need and, like Congress, it was not started by anybody, it was started by the people who needed a health clinic. The need was there, Legal Aid, the need was there. Even with Tangentyere Council, the need for housing was there, the need for land was there, and it all came from those people who had nothing. And for those poor people in those days in Alice Springs, it was a real rough and tough town. It was crazy town. People lived anywhere, any old how. Old Freddy Fry and that block he had down there it came from nothing, it was just a little humpy. So Tracker was a forerunner in a lot of things. He definitely was.

Patrick: And he was always thinking of ideas, *I want to do this and I want to do that*. We would say, *Tracker pull up now. Grab Kathy and just go around the country. You have been around the world that many times*. He had been everywhere. He knew everything.

Gordon Williams

I knew Tracker's brother Willie back in 1975, and then in 1977 I actually started mucking around with Tracker. In 1978, Tracker got a job at the DAA [Department of Aboriginal Affairs] and he was my project officer. At that time we travelled extensively throughout Central Australia, Alice Springs, Areyonga, Mutitjulu, Docker River. We spent a lot of time in the field and our main area of work was contacting communities and outstations to check requirements regarding housing, water, et cetera.

Later, in 1979, I was sent out to Docker River, and Tracker came out to stay with me for a month to gain some more experience in the bush, working with traditional people, although he had already worked with a lot of traditional Aborigines, but out there it was completely different because you were in one spot. We spent a lot of time in the field again because Tracker always had ideas of enterprise. We drove around the country, up to a place called Tjukurla checking on camel numbers, checking the sites for an outstation, and we were using a Holden ute and Tracker just could not get over how a Holden ute could travel that back country in those days. He did most of the driving, I was just the passenger and he did most of the talking.

When Tracker was out there with me he learnt about administration and how to look after a community the way the government required. He always had ideas, even back then which surprised me. He talked about camels and harvesting camels and all this stuff. After about a month, he was sent back to town as a project officer and I was still out there.

In 1981, I was staying at this Aboriginal hostel in Alice Springs at 7 Lindsay Avenue with a few other males. Tracker had no place to stay so I said to him, *Okay, mate, look there's a room at the hostel but you'll have to share one side of the room and I'll have the other.* So Tracker moved in and I said *if you bring a woman home, we will make a partition.* I will even camp in the lounge. So after a couple of months Tracker brought his future wife there. So from then on I virtually camped in the lounge. Every weekend a few others and myself, we would go out hunting and we would bring back a kangaroo which is very unsightly, and leave it in the kitchen. Kathy would get up and cook breakfast for all of us, and she was appalled at the idea of a kangaroo sitting up there, so she would ask Tracker to put it somewhere, out of sight. We actually stayed there for quite a long time.

Then I was transferred away and Tracker still worked out of town until 1980, and we were both seconded to the Aboriginal Development Commission, and during that time Tracker was the project officer. He got involved with an abattoir at Amoonguna. Dave Murray actually ran it, and again Tracker wanted to do this and do that, expand it, and then we travelled extensively again with the Aboriginal Development Commission throughout the southern area of the Northern Territory. Tracker loved hunting, he would let others do the shooting, but he always knew what to do, everything like that.

One thing with Tracker, he was always into enterprises. *Let's do this, let's do that*, and at ADC and DAA it was the same thing, he was always looking at doing something and it was always to do with the land, cattle, horses, abattoir, pet meat, anything like that he was interested in. He got support, and the ADC met every six weeks to look at projects, and some projects got up. A lot did not, because it was up to the whim of the commissioners which projects they supported. This frustrated Tracker a bit. Later on Tracker kept saying, *You know, I need to learn how to write properly. I can speak.* I said, *Boy can you ever.* He reckoned, *My writing's not too good.* So Owen Cole and Jerry Tilmouth said, *Why don't you go back to school. No,* he said, *That's easy for you guys to talk.* They said, *No, you should.* So between him and Douglas Turner, they decided to go to the Rural [Roseworthy] College in Adelaide.

So off they went and I never seen Tracker for about three or four years, and then when I did he reckons, *Well! Bro, I've got letters behind my name.* That was the first thing he said. I said, *Well! Good on you.* I reckoned, *I've got letters too. It is Williams and it is hyperactive.* So he started showing me how to type and he did not get far, but still. He started blaming the typewriter. Anyway, he was still the same Tracker. One thing I must say for Tracker was that he never ever forgot his friends, because when he was down living in his car it was his friends that pulled him into gear and actually looked after him. When I say friends, I mean people like myself, the Liddles, Willy Bray, Owen Cole, Jerry Tilmouth, a lot of us, we all supported him.

We liked him a lot and he had a lot of character. He always had some scheme in his head. After those years I lost track of him, he caught up with me in Katherine. He was the director of the Central Land Council and so he said, *Hey, come on, do you want a job there?* I said, *Yeah! I'll think about it.* I was on holidays at the time. So he offered me the job, and I took the job, and he was the same Tracker. He always would say to myself and a few of the other mates, Lawrie Liddle, Stevie Ellis and that, he would just say, *Okay, come here,* and he would start talking again about enterprises, all this stuff, about his prawn farm that he was going to establish. He was still heavily involved in the rural side, even as a director of the Land Council. He would be up and down to Mistake Creek, and looked at all the cattle stations around Alice. At meetings he would always use terminology of, *Well! This fence, that fence,* and all of his analogies would be rural virtually. He would always say – *this land* – put the cattle in here, and then you do this and do that but everything he spoke about revolved around cattle, horses. He would always have some idea of how you could make money out of cattle and stuff like that.

Dave Murray

One of the things I remember very clearly was that we actually funded a Japanese delegation. We were in the process of wanting to get meat into Japan through the abattoir situation, and we were working with a broker from Sydney and he brought up four or five Japanese people with an interpreter and a business manager, an export broker. So we had this delegation, and they came out to the meatworks and wanted to see some cattle slaughtered. The next day they came to see the meat getting boned out, and wanted to know how we would do it in an appropriate way.

They wanted some photographs and this Japanese guy in his enthusiasm handed this camera to Tracker. He extended his hand with this thing saying *you take picture, you take picture* or something or other, and Tracker put his hand out initially but pulled it back and he said, *You take your own fucking pictures.* He said, *You fellas invented it, it's not our invention. You fellas invented it, you take your own fucking pictures.* The broker from Sydney's looked, and was like, *What in the heck is going on?* It was a fairly delicate situation if you like. We were trying to sell thousands of dollars worth of product through these fellas, and everyone was tiptoeing around them like you would not believe and Tracker turns around and says, *You invented the fucking thing, you take your own fucking pictures.* That was just the way he was. He was just so down to earth. And you could not take offence at it because it was always true.

It's a Scientific Endeavour

Tracker Tilmouth

[One day] I went around to Amata and it is Dog Dreaming in Amata, and you have got to be very careful.

I could not go around shooting the dogs. We had three hundred and fifty cows and calves in the paddock, and when we came back there were about three hundred and forty cows and no calves, and very large and very contented camp dogs.

We could not shoot them because they banned you from shooting dogs there because of the Dreaming, Dog Dreaming.

So I went and got a leg of beef, I got the bone, doused it in purple lolly – 1080 [poison] – and anything else that was going.

Where the spare wheel was on the Toyota I took it off, and I tied the bone underneath where the spare wheel was, and I drove into Amata and parked near the shop. Anyway, I was talking to Pat D'Arango and her husband [who were working at the Craft Centre at Uluru].

Out come the camp dogs and all had a nibble, a bit of a piss on the wheel and all strolled off and flopped.

There were dead dogs for fucking miles.

The whole community did not have one dog left and the ceremonies went for months because someone had cursed their dogs.

I would have massacred five hundred dogs and pups.

They all had a nibble.

They walked along, had a bit of a chew, pissed on the front wheel, and strolled off. *Boomp.*

I murdered a mob of dogs there. They still have not worked it out today.

They had to restart the ceremonies early, all *tjilkata* turning up from Pipalyatjara and everything to see who had done wrong. The great dog massacre.

Tracker Tilmouth

Anyway we had these petrol sniffers at Docker River. They were just starting to sniff petrol then. They brought in a store manager for a brand new store which was built up on stilts, but the petrol sniffers kept breaking in [from underneath the building] so they wired up all around the bottom of the store and they put these German shepherd dogs in there to guard it. Every night they would open a trap door and the dogs would come up and stay in the store. They were savage dogs, really savage, and everyone was really frightened of them, and even the old blokes said that, *Those kids are going to get killed.*

Anyway, the petrol sniffers took a while to work it out. So what they did one night, they pulled a sheet of iron off the roof and they lowered in this old camp dog on heat with a rope. These two prized guard dog German shepherds were killing each other trying to mate with the old camp dog. One of them got knotted and the other one was nearly dead, and the petrol sniffers helped themselves to the shop. Gordon Williams reckoned, *Well! That's the end of that.* That was Docker River.

Then Chris Marshall and Richard Priest invented CDEP [Community Development Emplyment Program] and everyone had to do CDEP, and Jonesy rings me up, Gordon was on holidays, Jonesy rings me up and says, *Have you got a CDEP program?*

Yeah I've got em.

He said, *Where are you?*

I said, *I've got em all along the Western Australia border.*

What for?

I said, *They've all got a tin of white paint and a brush.*

He said, *What for?*

I said, *I've got them moving east and numbering the ant hills.*

Jonesy reckons, *We've got to relieve you, you've lost it.* They were all in sequence. I said to Jonesy, *I need a numeracy course to teach them how to count before I start.* I said, *It's a scientific endeavour.*

He said, *How do you know where the Western Australian border is?* I said, *I'm still trying to work that out.* I said, *I've been over to Giles {in Western Australia} and asked them for a map.*

Yes, my job was to go and chase Nosepeg Tjupurrula around the scrub before Kintore and Kiwirkurra were around. We had a radio which was used with an old coat hanger with a wire that you put out on the trees. I would do it in a Holden ute with a drum of fuel, and water and rations. I would go in and out of the sandhills, in places you would not go anywhere without a four-wheel drive, that was why we knew where all the springs were. I had old Windless and old Leslie with me and they knew where every spring was all the way up to Mount Winter [in the Great Sandy Desert] through the back road. Mount Winter is a magnificent spot. All through that country and old Nosepeg, he would light fires and he said, *Watch my fire*. They knew where he was, them old blokes would say, *That fire over there would be the start of him. That's where they are, over there.* So we would go and see him.

Anyway we dropped a ration off and one day, I seen about four young blokes when we were driving along and old Leslie said, *No, no, you're not allowed to pick them up.* I said, *Why?* He said, *Give em ration.* He said, *They're naughty boys. They weren't properly done in ceremonies and so we put them in gaol. That's our gaol.* One old bloke looking after them in the bush, in the scrub so they would not die. But they were not allowed back into the community. That was their gaol. I could not believe it. They had the whole system worked out. They were camping separate to the main mob, but naked people everywhere, naked, with no clothes on.

I seen a skeleton in the sandhill from the other side of the clay pan and that must have been from Maralinga. It must have been that the water had got poisoned, contaminated or something. *Dead people.* This is what the old bloke said. He said, *That's from that bomb.* Old Lesley. The wind came that way and it went right across, right through Docker River. It took all the fallout from the nuclear tests. Anyway, so that is from my background. This is why I knew them some years later when some of these men turned up in the conference room at the Central Land Council to get old Ben [Clyne], Breaden and Yatala [Max Stuart, executive members of the Land Council]. This was because Nahasson Ungawaka from Duck Dreaming near Finke [a *tjilkata* – important traditional law man in the Western Desert], had given them a promise on royalty monies. They all came around, and Rossy [director, CLC] came and asked me, *You know Pitjantjatjara? Yeah. You know these old blokes?* I walked in there and they all said, *Oh grandson.* Anyway, *Oh! That's our grandson. Hello my grandson* — like that, all these old Pitjantjatjara mob. Then I had to explain to them that this bloke is telling them bullshit, that royalty had nothing to do with it, that was Mereenie Gas, and he was trying to get all the *tjilkata* to come across and put pressure. Promising them money. Six years later he died, they killed him. Rossy will tell you [and at the time Mr Clyne, Mr Breaden, and Mr Stuart helped the *tjilkata* men with food and fuel to travel back home]. But that is my connection with the Pitjantjatjara mob.

And then I went down to Mimili [in South Australia]. I always took Windless with me so when I went down to Mimili, Windless moved down there too. We had these poxy old Land Rovers. Dougie Turner and another bloke turned up as workers for the department, and because they had been to the Aboriginal Task Force they were made our bosses, they had qualifications and we had none. They gave the other bloke the Pit [Pitjantjatjara] Lands to look after. So I had to drive him down and introduce him. First of all I wanted to drive the Land Rover and he said, *No, I'll drive officer.* He was all formal — he was a nut. Anyway he reversed the Land Rover out and took out all the front and side mirrors, a real good start. So we got the side mirrors fixed up and off we went down to Amata in the afternoon. It is night-time when we get to Kulgera and all these black cattle are on the road, all the Aberdeen Angus black cattle. I said to him, *You want to slow down.* I said, *There's a lot of cattle here. Oh! I know how to drive,* he said. I said, *Switch your high beam off and just have it on low so the cattle can see you and get off the road. No, high beam,* he said. He had high beam on and then he is driving along and the big bull comes straight through the front window and it made the whole Land Rover look like a Ferrari.

You are telling me, it is a wonder we were not killed. Anyway, he got out and the fan was on the radiator, bent over. So to stop the fan making noise he cut the fan belt, rather than pull the radiator off, so the engine blew up. We were only about ten kilometres out of Kulgera so we got a lift and stayed there overnight, and the DAA sent a recovery vehicle down and picked us all up. So we got back and got into another Land Rover. I said, *I will drive.* We got to Mimili and I am sitting there with the community advisor going through all the funding and everything else, and he is there listening in. Anyway in comes Andy Dargo and Andy said, *Can you give us a push, start us off?* This bloke said, *I'll do that, I'll do that, you stay here, Tilly.* Right! So he went out and I am listening through the window. Next thing, *ruuuum – baaang, ruuuum – baaang*. And I am looking out at this old Leyland truck, and you could hear the banging and a move forward, another rev up and bang and move forward, going past the window and all the people sitting on this old Leyland truck. He was ramming the bull bar of the Land Rover straight up the arse of the truck. Wrecked the Land Rover. And the recovery vehicle turned up again for Land Rover number two.

The Incident Report had this question: *What gear were you in?* And he answered: Jeans, tee shirt, and thongs.

Beadman [then director of the DAA in Alice Springs] wanted to kill him. Anyway he went back to Docker River relieving Gordon [Williams], and he came out to Mimili, because he was supposed to come out and check up on us. He drove this Holden ute from Ayers Rock, and at that time the Ayers Rock road was all dirt, all the way from Alice, where from the Stuart Highway it was all dirt. Anyway, he got a puncture on the other side of Shaw Creek towards Docker River. So he spends four hours putting the jack between the spare tyre and the body trying to jack off the spare wheel, because he had not worked out that you pull the tail plate down and you put the crank handle in and crank it down. No, he jacked it off.

I was in Alice and coaching Pioneers Football Club, you know the B Grade. He came on, kept wanting to come on the ground and Colesy [Owen Cole] said, You've got to give him a run: *Give-him-a-run*. Like that. Anyway I said, *Where will we put him?* Colesy said, *Put him in the centre.* I said, *Righto*. So we put him on and they attacked down on him and he dodged this bloke and bounced the ball around that bloke, and handballed over the top and picked it up and ran like a scalded cat straight through the middle of the goals. Wrong way. He got confused dodging people. The crowd sang out, *Take him off*. And I said, *There's the crowd Colesy. The people have spoken.*

He was a nut, that bloke. When they had the Aboriginal Pastoral meeting at Ayers Rock in early 1980s, when Vinnie [Vincent Forrester] made a big speech about the Korean meat market, me and Colesy were departmental officers. Colesy had fifty thousand dollars in cash in a bag [to cover the expenses for the delegates travelling across Central Australia to attend this large meeting]. A briefcase and we were looking after it. We were camping and the nut said, *Why don't you blokes share my tent?* He did not know how to put the tent up anyway so we helped him. Colesy and I were arguing as we always do, *Look lips, put it like this. Don't call me lips.* Right! *Luritja lips.* Anyway we get in the tent and we are all cosy, as it is winter now and everything else, and we had one of those lanterns with the mantle – a gas lantern that you turn off and on. He tried to turn it off and a flame shot up. So me and Colesy were still in our swags, and punching each other trying to get out the door, trying to escape, forget the money. We just left the money. Let's get out of here. Colesy had one of them swags, a flash one where you zip up the side and he was not able to pull the zip down, so he was crawling in the swag across the ground. We saved the money. We had to pay everyone the next day. The tent got burnt: a brand new tent, DAA tent. Oh! Colesy will tell you. What a bloke.

Owen Cole

During the Aboriginal Cattlemen's Association Conference down at Mutitjulu we were paying sitting fees, so we invited all the people to come along for the conference, and we set up this tent, and that was the treasury. A bloke from the department was in there, and we had this little till which had probably twenty thousand dollars as payment for all these people over four days.

He decided that it was cold so he put the gas stove in the tent. Unfortunately, he turned it up too high and the bloody tent caught on fire so he was running around screaming and Tracker was saying, *Stuff you, just bring the money out. Don't let the money get burnt.*

Tracker Tilmouth

Gordon wanted to teach this bloke shooting, and I had to drive. So Gordon! He is a really good bushman, and you cannot beat him in the bush. Anyway, Gordon said, *Righto! This is a rifle,* blah blah blah, *this is a scope. Now Tilly, drive over to the rabbit hole.* Righto! *There are a couple of rabbits sitting up there.* And the bloke sights up a rabbit. He puts the barrel of the gun straight past me, like this. I just froze. The edge of the barrel is there and he is up there looking through the scope. Now Gordon said, *Can you see a rabbit?*

Yeah I can see a rabbit.

Right, put the cross hairs on him – Yeah! And now gently squeeze the trigger. Yeah! Righto. I am just holding the steering wheel and I am holding my breadth. Bang! Fucking glass went everywhere because the end of the barrel was against the rear vision mirror and the scope went across the top. You could see the animal but the barrel was two inches down and blew the rear vision mirror to pieces. I am feeling and looking for holes in me. Gordon said, *No! No! We'll have to do this differently.*

Anyway we go along and we saw these kangaroos and this bloke got so excited. I said, *Gordon you've got to sit in the middle, put him on the outside.* Anyway he got so excited. Gordon said, *There's kangaroos over there. Now grab the gun.* He got so excited he pulled the trigger in the Toyota, there is a hole in the roof. Richard Priest [another former DAA employee] was driving along one day and could not work out where the little tiny light was coming from. It was a fucking hole in the roof. Anyway Gordon shot this kangaroo, shot it in the leg from long distance. *Go over and finish it off.* He thought this nut would load the gun and go and pop it. No. He did not go over there and pop it. He went over with Gordon's brand new rifle and he went like this to hit it on the head and it jumped, and he hit the ground and broke the rifle in half. Gordon was looking for an axe. Oh mate, a laugh a minute I tell you.

Chief Was the Chief

John Liddle

I remember that time when he was working for DAA and he had this big Alsatian dog. He used to take it everywhere and he used to insist that it goes and sniffs women in the crutch. He would stand back and smile at people. Fucking bastard. Now anyone else would feel ashamed for doing that but not him, he just thought it was the right thing to do, not the wrong thing to do. And I have been with him everywhere and he did the same thing, no matter who it is, just walk straight in, as he had gate-crashed Congress staff meetings [where I was the director], and he had gone in and taken over the meeting. There might be a hundred people sitting there, and he would sort of slink in and all of a sudden he had [taken over the meeting], and people looked at him and would think, *Who the fuck is this bloke? He is not one of us.* Next minute he was up there talking and telling people to do this and do that. Then create all the confusion. And off he goes. And they all walk around saying, *Who the hell was that?* That bastard.

He continuously rang me up and I would ring him up, *Oh! Well what about this,* this scheme to get rich, this scheme to change the world. That bloody Centrefarm stuff [to develop horticulture on Aboriginal land in Central Australia], he and I were sort of talking about that for years, not that scheme specifically, but something broadly which I reckon he had sort of tweaked into what turned out as Centrefarm. We were talking about farms, and he was responsible for sending me to Israel for three and a half months back in the early 70s.

I did not even know where Israel was. I was straight from red sandhills out there [on Angas Downs] and he said, *Do you want to go overseas?* I said, *Yeah! I do, where?* He said, *I don't know.* I said, *I'm going.* He said, *Don't worry, I'll come with you.* I said, *That's alright, be like a holiday*. Holiday alright. And he did come with me, but he came about two months after I got there. He was only there for one week. So I was left over there for three and a half months. He said, *I'll get you a trip*. And I said, *No worries, I'll go*. Because I had thought, *Oh! Alice Springs is not for me, it is too small. I want to learn things and see different things and go overseas*. So, *Bloody oath, I'll go*. He said do not worry about anything, money, people will look after you. Alright. We landed in Tel Aviv, me and Johnny Kelly. Me and him went. And Tracker came. He brought some blokes, about five or six of them came after us.

We landed at Tel Aviv airport, two blokes from the bush. The furthest we had been before was maybe to Adelaide or something like that. So that was a great adventure. We landed at Tel Aviv airport and soldiers come on to the plane to search you before you actually get off, with little machine guns. And here were these two blokes from the bush, shitting ourselves. We did not know what the hell was going to happen. Anyway we get off and we got sent to a rural college I suppose you might call it, and it had something to do with cooperatives and trade unionism because that was going to be the push for Aboriginal people, to establish cooperatives and learn how to work with one another, bulk buying and all this sort of stuff.

Then I suddenly woke up that he was not on the plane with us, and somehow or other, I worked out how to ring from there to Alice Springs and I rung up Charlie Perkins. He was sort of helping me. He was the one who got the fares for us, because we had free tickets from somewhere, although I do not know where. I said, *Where's this Bruce Tilmouth, is he coming over to thing?* Charlie said, *Oh! Yeah! Might be another month or so*. I said, *What!* He told us he was going to be there, he was going to be here with us, and there would be three or four of us, not only two.

Anyway we had to go to daily classes and lectures and all this sort of stuff, so we are going every day, and sort of getting used to it. Could not get used to the food, and trying to learn the language. So after about a couple of months Tracker and these other mob started to turn up and said, *We're here, where are you?* We said, *We're downstairs*. Anyway we go downstairs to where we were living. I think it was three or four storeys like a big motel, and we went down there and he had got these blokes with him. Anyway they were not going to stay with us. They did a quick study tour, and we saw them for maybe two days for a couple of weeks, and then he said, *Oh! We're going back now bro.*

I said, *What!*

We're going back now.

I said, *I thought you were going to stop here.*

Nah, nah, I've got to go back.

So another couple of months later we were still there, but he had gone. He had gone home.

He had caught me out a lot of times that bastard, I tell you, with those schemes like that. He had some great ideas and he would look around for a sucker, *Ah, Liddle there, I'll get him to do it.* So I fall for him all the time, I do not know why, I should have learnt the first twenty times. But he is responsible for me working at Congress I reckon, and working in Aboriginal health, so I have got to thank him for something I suppose, but he had hounded me ever since with all of those harebrained schemes, and I have had a few too that I had handed him over the years.

Vincent Forrester

I went in the army after working at Angas Downs, and when I came back, we had this bloke wandering around causing trouble, converting us into communists so they said, *black power*, and his name was Charlie Perkins. He come back to Alice [in the 1970s] and started off the Central Australian Aboriginal Congress medical service and Central Australian Aboriginal Legal Aid. We were workers, Tracker was at Congress, and then Neville Perkins and Janet Layton mob came.

This was the early days of the Aboriginal political movement with Charlie's leadership in Central Australia. He could ring up Gough Whitlam and get a hundred thousand dollars of government money to buy the drunks' farm with land previously owned by the Italians in Alice Springs. So Tracker and us, we worked together, and his first job was a bit like a welfare officer. In those days no one was on a pension, no child endowment, and no dole. Our job was to go out into the camps and take 44-gallon drums [of water] to the mob sitting down at the town camps, the old-timers' camp, Little Sisters, over at Morris Soak, and those ironwood trees that would become Truckies Camp. But every time you took water the fucking dogs would be getting a drink of water instead of the people. And they were mangy, mangy dogs. So our job was to shoot the dogs and when people died take the body in a coffin back to their traditional country and bury them in their country. Everybody had their little areas of work to do.

An interesting thing was that we did a survey amongst ourselves, of who died young, who died old, and which communities they came from, and taking people back. There were some startling statistics, and we knew who died from grog abuse and all this type of thing. A lot of our peers at that time started dying from alcohol abuse – all the boys, and the most frequently visited place was the first alcohol-free zone of Hermannsburg. This was where we started carting all the bodies back to, because they all came out to Alice Springs and got on the piss. The eighty miles did not stop them. Santa Teresa was another place, but Hermannsburg was the worst.

This was the genocidal stuff of the early 70s that took place in relation to grog. It started kicking in actively about 1967 to 75, and was wiping out a whole bloody generation. When they got citizenship right, everybody got on the piss, flagon-sherry half gallon, that one there. You could get five bob for an unbroken flagon by taking it back to Underdowns [tavern]. Get five bob, a cab was a shilling and sixpence.

I think Tracks went to the Department of Aboriginal Affairs then and he went out with Gordon Williams at Docker River. He was at Docker River for quite a while. So he had his apprenticeship in the bush. Then he went to ADC, the Aboriginal Development Commission. He was setting up a Central Australian Aboriginal Cattlemen's Association, and he worked with a bloke called Dr Stuey Phillpot who used to work at the Institute for Aboriginal Development, and Tracker considered himself a cattleman. When the eradication of brucellosis had wiped a lot of the cattle herd in the Northern Territory, Tracker and Stuey Phillpot were playing with a pet project at a place called Amata in South Australia. Those mission settlement whitefellas had bought up a good breed of cattle at Amata. There was a lot of natural water so the cattle got wild, but they were really, really well-bred cattle. Stuey Phillpot, Arthur Liddle, Tracker and old uncle Alec Kruger, and I think old Ray MacDonald was there too with old Minnie Stewart. They worked around this whole area of the cattle industry, trying to restructure the industry in Central Australia.

The only blackfellas that had land rights at the time were people on Schedule 1 lands.[10] We knew what we were trying to get back eventually, and we tried to address that question by putting in strategies to buy back land for people living on stations because at that time, there was only a couple of stations [owned by Aboriginal people]. One had been bought by the then Aboriginal Land Fund Commission and that was Utopia, and also Willowra. A lot of these people, traditional landowners on the cattle stations, had nothing. So we put in a sound strategy with policies attached to it and outcomes. Land rights did not give us all the land, we had to buy some of it, including Muckaty where the government was going to build a nuclear waste dump. That was not given to us, that was bought by sound strategies, by creative accounting by the ABTA [Aboriginals Benefit Trust Account] with royalties from mining.

The ABTA did not do anything for about five years. They kept the money in the bank, and then they bought back all the stations that we managed to purchase because we saw on the horizon what was going to happen when they eradicated all the cattle because of brucellosis and tuberculosis. The pastoralists had to get rid of all the cattle on their properties and they had little compensation. But, they also had to put in good fencing, and if you had a fence you controlled the herd. We saw that, *Hey! They're not going to be able to have money.* So that was a critical time to buy back that land, because the pastoralists were all going broke.

The Commonwealth Government was in favour of it, and so was Clive Holding mob [former Labor Minister for Aboriginal Affairs]. We had a good rapport with the Commonwealth Government, even though we did not agree with everything. At least that government

---

10. The *Aboriginal Land Rights (Northern Territory) Act 1976* provided for a number of areas of land that were formerly gazetted by government as Aboriginal reserves. These reserves became Schedule 1 lands attached to the Land Rights Act when the legislation came in to being, in effect directly handing these lands over to Aboriginal people with freehold title, not needing a land claim.

gave us something with Clive, and he gave us freedom to purchase the stations as minister. That was a sound decision and well researched, and from there we looked at broader economic policies, with Tracker going to Roseworthy Agricultural College, Colesy going to Adelaide University, and Rossy going down to university too. Three blokes went down south to university so that they could manage some of the work that had been developed in Central Australia.

I remember trying to sell this idea of buying the stations with sound principles behind it, but we had to sell the idea to the Aboriginal Development Commission and so we went to Canberra. We wanted a deal, and we had backup from old Nugget Coombs, and the government was quite interested. Alice Springs was a pretty dynamic go-ahead place because we had gathered the intelligentsia of the movement. Alexis Wright, Marcia Langton, Pat Dodson – the movers and shakers of the movement at that time. We coordinated the Federation of Land Councils where there was a sharpening of the minds with the Peter Yus of the world involved, and we would get together and debate issues and strategies.

The strategies of buying the cattle stations in the Territory came out of the meeting of minds and discussion of landless people, the people who land rights forgot. They were the people living in the towns and on the cattle stations. We were successful. The government were encouraging it to a certain extent, and if we had kept on we would have bought up the whole Northern Territory, and they could not have that. So the government put a sunset clause in the Northern Territory Land Rights Act. We were too successful, and there was one little hole in that Land Rights Act that we went through, so they closed it off.

But it showed the importance of collective thought, and how this came through the Combined Aboriginal Organisations in Alice Springs, and the likes of the Federation of Land Councils. We commissioned an economic report on the Black dollar with economists Greg Crough, Bill Pritchard, and Richie Howitt.[11] Rossy had come back after going to university, and Tracker came back and so did Owen Cole, and with all

---

11. Greg Crough, Richie Howitt and Bill Pritchard, *Aboriginal Economic Development in Central Australia: A Report for the Combined Aboriginal Organisations of Alice Springs*, IAD, Alice Springs, 1989.

those old people like Wenten Rubuntja that were in the leadership roles at the land councils, it was an exciting time in the development of the movement, and of course Tracker was at the forefront of it.

Senior Aboriginal people gave us another education. That was my spiritual education, my spiritual nurturing. It comes from the elders, from each tribe, and being able to get to a forum like the Central Land Council because the first Land Council was made up of all these old men, corroboree men, ceremonial men. You had old Wenten, old Tyamiwa, old Nosepeg, old Johnny Lynch, old Trigger Derrick, Joseph Mantjakura, these were the ceremonial men.

The whitefella education is good to have, it is essential, but the guts of us, and I cannot stress the importance of this, is that we must always have our cultural practices at the forefront, of how we are going to protect our cultural legacy. Those are some of the biggest questions to ask in forums where we can make our own decisions. It is important that we get the younger ones to carry on, to educate them on what we have done, because I go along to the meetings of the Central Land Council and we are talking about the things we were talking about twenty-five bloody years ago. Those young people say, *Oh! This is new to us.* Hang on a minute, their fathers and grandfathers have already discussed these matters and put in place policies and strategies, and now that they have gone, we have to go and re-educate a whole new generation of decision-makers and policy implementers. This is something I am really concerned about.

Owen Cole

Tracker was great mates with my father, Willy Cole, and he would often visit and sit down with Dad. He often bribed Dad with fresh station meat to back his claim that he was a better footballer than me. Dad was easily bribed and usually agreed with Tracks.

It was our parents who used to mix with one another, and we would just run around and play together before he and his two brothers were taken to Croker Island. With those green eyes, you could not miss him. I am sure he would have been the same when he was a kid. His father, old Roy, had a similar type of personality, he was a real storyteller and a real jokester. I always say he got it from his father. He used to love doing exactly what Tracker did, where he went and visited people on a weekend, he would go and visit six people and sit down and have a cup of tea with them. That was exactly what his father was like.

Tracker was real close to my dad, and Dad was a good mate of his father. So Tracker would always make the journey down to Alice Springs and see my father who is eighty-six [in 2013]. We purchased all those pastoral properties and I never got one piece of meat from any of those properties. Tracker would be dropping sides of beef off to Dad, and I said to him, *What about me?* He said, *Stuff you. I am looking after the old fellow.*

He loved all the older blokes and I am a bit like that too. He loved the stories. Listening to the stories. I will spend hours with old people listening to the stories, and Tracker he loved doing that. It could be old Jack Cook up at Mistake Creek, and I remember sitting down there with him and Tracker was cross-examining him on his life, *Where did you go, where did you go from there, and how did you come back to Mistake Creek?* Tracker would get all these stories out, and of course he had a mind like a steel trap. He virtually had a photographic memory, where he could digest a piece of information and have it there forever, whereas I would probably retain fifty per cent of the story. He just got it.

When he was doing his degree down at Roseworthy, where most people would delete most of the stuff, he could throw it up at you word for word basically. The only thing he could not do was economics, and he would rock up to Adelaide University, where we used to go to the Aboriginal Task Force on a Thursday, and say, *How are you going cuz?* I would sit down with him and Dougie Turner. They were doing their first year and they rocked up there saying, *Oh! Let's go and have a beer.* So we go down and have this beer, and he said, *Anyway, we have to do this economics essay.* I said, *No worries, come around on the weekend. No,* he says, *It has got to be done now. We have to hand it in tomorrow morning.* And then you had to sit down and help him do this economics degree.

He could organise all the people he had to, to get something done. That was the secret of Tracker. If he ever needed anything, he would just harness, or if he ever needed a bit of assistance, or he needed a few ideas, he knew where to get it.

He had contacts all over Australia who could be the Jewish, the Arabs, Lebanese, the Greeks up in Darwin if he had projects up there. He would go, *Owen, I have got this idea. You mob own that property up in Darwin?*

Yes, we do.

Then he said, *Right next door is Danila Dilba {Aboriginal health service}, and they need new headquarters. What would you say if you mob develop a new medical centre for them, completely state of the art, knock down the old building and*...I said to him, *We never thought of that possibility Tracker. Well that is a possibility.* He said, *Well! I have a mate there, a bloke called*...you know, Costas or whatever it is. Nothing happened on that occasion, but he was far out. Who would have thought, *Why don't we build something like a mini hospital for Danila Dilba?* He would.

Tracker Tilmouth

I remember when we set up Tangentyere Council in 1979, and I remember when we set up Congress, where I worked with Trevor Cutter who was the first doctor recruited by Congress in 1975. We established the first market garden down at Little Sisters which is a town camp in Alice Springs – a bit of fruit, vegetables, tomatoes and everything else. I used the Amoonguna tractor to use the plough, and everything it had, and I took it all down to the Little Sisters and started a market garden with all the drunks. All the vegetables grew well. We gave them to the town campers, and put up tents and shelters for them. We made sure they had firewood. And the Jim Downing Memorial Toilets: the Reverend Jim Downing from the Uniting Church was at IAD and they built the toilets down at the Little Sisters. We had all the drunks working on the vegie garden, and John Liddle and I went and got goats from Harts Range–Atitjere and brought them in and slaughtered them and gave them to the campers, and then we would keep a couple back and make stews for the drunks, or we used kangaroos and rabbits as well. Congress had that role in those days and we were kept busy, but they will not let you do it now.

I went out to Utopia with the Department of Aboriginal Affairs in the early days with Rod Horner and my job was to take over as project officer for Utopia, Ammaroo, Harts Range and those other eastern communities on pastoral leases. We were negotiating living areas, one square kilometre of land to put houses on pastoral leases. That was my first job out there. Talking to pastoralists and talking to communities about where they wanted to live and how much water they needed, houses and so forth, through the Department of Aboriginal Affairs. And at the same time establishing health and education services in the region under a bloke called Toly Sawenko. He was a schoolteacher who had just started at Utopia and had built a little shack on the side of the Sandover River [where he lived]. I camped there a few times over the years, and with Toby McLeay and all these other blokes who were health-service people, they all lived there, in and around that country at Three Bores. Three Bores is the main community centre where you have got your store, you have got your fuel, and you have got everything else.

We sat down with the government on a few occasions about how we provided health services, how we provided education services and so forth. We decided to follow their education model, where we had schoolteachers in each of the outstations, or teacher's aides, on health services. So when you had a clinic at Utopia, it was not that big a clinic, and it had a lot of health workers who were located in remote communities or in remote outstations. Over time the health services were pretty good compared to Papunya and elsewhere. But it looks like these health statistics have now deteriorated because of lack of infrastructure, water, housing and so forth. So Utopia was a hard-learnt exercise for me because we had all sorts of programs to run. I negotiated the living area for Atitjere which is Harts Range and for Mount Swan, Number Five Bore, Alcoota, Woodgreen, MacDonald Downs – all in the eastern Alyawarre region of Central Australia. I did most of that work and I lived in the back neck of the woods there. Most of the Aboriginal people in the area were living at Mount Riddock, and then we moved across to Harts Range near the police station. There has never been a land claim. It was a special purpose lease, called a community living area. It is still a community living area. The only bit of Aboriginal land in the area is Utopia with Alcoota and Lake Drouin, and Atula. The rest are all pastoral leases with living areas.

The pastoralists were quite good because they all knew my grandfather, old Harry Tilmouth, an old whitefella. They also knew my father well, they knew who I was and I got on with them, especially with the Webbs at Mount Riddock and Huckitta. Those days were very good days because we were able to negotiate some good areas of land to live in, not big enough some of them, but we pushed the envelope when we could.

I did that for a couple of months or years or whatever it was, and lived at my own place of residence which was at Goofy Bore on Mount Skinner with old Katie Potter and Roy Potter. I used to work there but most of the time it was just bush work, driving around. I established a gemstone fossicking project out at Harts Range because of the amount of gemstones there. So the community was paying for its own vehicle, fuel and wages and selling gemstones to Hong Kong through Mr Cummings. The store, the service station and all that were established. Harts Range became a little bit of an economic activity on the Plenty Highway.

Utopia was pretty straightforward because it allowed me to interact with my mob, people I was actually related to by blood, with old Tony Petrick, old Paddy Webb, all those blokes now passed. They were extremely strong people. They introduced me when I used to come back into Alice, and they were all related to Wenten Rubuntja and were his mates. The Chief [Wenten Rubuntja] and me were very close because we had the same linkages.

That is it, *I am your government.* That is what he used to say.

So those early days were the formation of what I thought of as Aboriginal affairs, and you could do the Aboriginal affairs work if you wanted to and not bother with the next step, or you could think of *how do we improve the situation?* I always had this argument on how we improve the situation, to such an extent that when Bob Beadman was my boss we had a big argument on the highway about how things should happen, and that is why I pissed off to university. Bob wanted the Utopia health service to be like any other health service, with a centralised clinic and school. But people were not going to drive twenty kilometres a day to bring their kids to school. It was just not going to happen. We managed to keep him away from developing his normal operational model, which he conceded in the end did not work.

Working with Utopia, and with Papunya and Yuendumu with the Department of Aboriginal Affairs, was pretty full-on. Anyhow I was able to connect with a lot of people out there. I was out at Haasts Bluff, and Papunya especially. Even now I go back there and I am welcome to go back any time.

Tracker Tilmouth

Old Rubuntja? When I went to Land Council, Chief was the chief. I knew Wenten because I was introduced to Wenten by my old man, and also I met through my old man Tony Petrick who was a senior traditional landowner from the Harts Range region in Central Australia, and former executive member of the Central Land Council. I also met Toby Paul and Mr Paddy Webb who were both Eastern Arrernte senior traditional landowners from the Alcoota–Huckitta–Harts Range region of Central Australia, and other people like that. They were my old man's relations, and Wenten was close to my old man. So Chief, his idea of politics was different to the average person, and his ideas on methodologies and getting things done was different. He knew how to use the system, he taught me a lot about how to talk to the good boys and good girls, as he used to call Aboriginal people.

Old Chief, he had a different way of dealing with people. He was very good at putting people down in public through his little jokes and all that sort of stuff. In a public debate he would put people down by calling them good boys or good girls, and by saying: *I'm your government, I'm your president.*

We went through all of that with Wenten, arguments with him about how he dealt with people, even though he was not chairman all the time, and where he would declare the current chairman a gibbering idiot or nut in his own language. He did not know how to talk to white people and there would be comments like that coming from the floor in the big meetings. It was funny, it was absolutely funny, because the way he would say it everyone would laugh. And the chair, the only bloke that would be out there would be [Bruce] Breaden, and Breaden would be so embarrassed he did not know which way to look, or what to say, or whatever.

So anyway that was how it all went with the Chief. Tony Petrick was very good at the Land Council as well, as was Breaden. I grew up with Breaden so I knew him. He used to be at Tempe Downs and Angas Downs, and he is Bessie Liddle's brother. So we knew Breaden. He used to call me a son, and that was all fairly easy for the Land Council in those days when I was the acting director, and then director, because you could do things. You had a very good executive with old blokes and old women that knew what had to be done, and knew they had to be strong to do it.

I do not know about the executive of the Central Land Council today. It is made up of younger people doing things. I suppose with the same agenda but it is a bit tougher now because you are more politically attuned to the wishes of the government of the day, whereas in those days we went on regardless of the position of the government. We were a bit more militant.

The old people on the executive in those earlier days were a lot stronger, like Mr Zimran from Kintore and elsewhere. There were blokes like that who could get up and tell them what they thought. Old Dick Leichleitner – old lightning [senior member of the Haasts Bluff Aboriginal Land Trust], Rexy Granites [senior Warlpiri traditional owner] to a certain extent, Harry Nelson [senior Warlpiri traditional owner], Mick Wagu [senior Luritja law man] and people like that who knew how to say things and when to say it. We do not get that anymore nowadays. I could not say some of the things that they would say, I couldn't, it would be rude, especially Wenten's commentary on the way back from a meeting, you would be absolutely red. The Chief always nailed it. It is a difficult one to go there [to talk about these times].

Mick Wagu was someone you learnt a lot from. Mick Wagu was a senior traditional Luritja law boss from Mbunghara near Papunya, but my real boss was a relation of my grandfather Mick Boolard from Alcoota, and this was Wenten Rubuntja, from your father's father you would say.

The greatest philosopher and storyteller we ever had was Wenten Rubuntja. He could tell stories like you have never heard but it all had meanings if you listened to him. He would tell stories that would bring tears to your eyes. Him and old Breaden to a certain extent, but certainly nothing like Wenten though.

Wenten would get up and philosophise in three different Aboriginal languages, plus English for the uneducated. He used to say, *I will talk in English for those people who aren't educated.* If you could not understand the language then you were not educated. So the Chief had it all. And he could sit there and he could just spell it out, step it out, and the stories to go with it. What are you talking about? This, this and this. It comes from traditional leaders, Aboriginal leaders, because nothing is written down. It is all based on *tjuringa* and Dreaming tracks, and everything else on the songlines.

This all came to the Central Land Council. Yes, very much so, and you were only as good as a director if your bloke at the head was philosophising, having strategies based on Aboriginal concepts. If he has no idea of Aboriginal concepts, just because you are black does not mean you are Aboriginal. Unfortunately, that is when the shit hits the fan, because by osmosis you are supposed to be able to move within the Aboriginal community, and if you have not bothered to learn who you are and what you are and so forth…it goes too hard on the argument about young blokes going out and being initiated and having no language skills. Unless you understand exactly what they are talking about and how they are talking about it in that framework and that concept, unless you have had that experience it is extremely difficult.

I was well looked after by Wenten and all my grannies and that [all the people who fall into the classificatory skin name of his grandparents' generation], and also by my adopted grannies down at Docker River. They looked after me very well, and then down Amata, and down the Pit [Pitjantjatjara] Lands and I could travel within circles. You know I had Harry Tjutjuna, Leslie Muntantji, Windless, Harry Brumby, old Mick, Barney Donald who is Vincent's grandfather, the whole lot.

Gordon Williams will tell you that they taught me. We spent a lot of time out bush with them and you learnt it all. When it all came to pass [while I was deputy director at the Central Land Council] we had arguments with people at Hermannsburg, and they turned up in the Alice Springs office of the Land Council and had brought all the business people with them who saw me sitting there, and the old men said, *Hey, my grandson how are you?* That was the end of the argument. *No! We'll stay with him.* All those sorts of things were built on that framework and if you do not have that, it is very difficult even in the Top End. I can get around in the Top End because I have Ronald Lami Lami, Victor Cooper, Sammy Cooper, Henry and Andrew Yamirr and all these blokes I grew up with and went to school with on the mission. They see me in the Top End and they say straight away, *Oh! He's Minjilang* [Croker Island] Or, *Galiwin'ku* [Elcho Island], or anywhere else for that matter.

When it came to finishing university and going to run the Land Council, I knew most of the people, I knew most of the bush mob. I had already been a community adviser out at Papunya, Docker River, Kintore before it became developed, all sorts of places, Yuendumu and so forth and so on. I was out at Utopia for a little bit. So Angas Downs allowed me to develop all those connections and a big part of knowing who I was, and Mr Breaden and those blokes made sure that everyone knew who I was. Breaden would make sure, call me Sonny Boy in front of everybody, just to say *that is my son*. Old Bess taught me a hell of a lot of responsibility and a hell of a lot of relationships in the bush. Today she is a very senior person, very senior person amongst the Aboriginal cultural scene, very senior. There are ceremonies that cannot go on without her, so she is way up there.

She knows the whole lot. Two woman's story, the Devil Dreaming, chasing the Seven Sisters. She knows all those songs, as she is the main person. So for her to teach me stuff going along as a young fella was good. Then I had old Maxi Armstrong. I had Dave Longway. I had Esky Armstrong. I could talk language to them, I could mix with them. I was a bit more removed from being a station bloke, I was sort of in between the station blokes and the blacks if you like, to a certain extent. I could mix with them and I could talk language to them. So Docker River was easy. Warburton was easy for me. It was not hard. There were good blokes in the Department [of Aboriginal Affairs] who understood if they wanted to know something, ask the bloke on the ground. There were people like [Bob] Beadman and Neville Jones. They were all before their time. Jonesy had economic programs running that people would just weep if they ever thought of it now. The same with Beadman. They were progressives, and they knew all about Aboriginal self-sufficiency, self-determination, doing things for themselves. The trouble is that government policies never respected that and Beadman, being a bureaucrat, went on to do other things. You survive.

Bob Beadman

I went to Alice Springs as regional director of the Department of Aboriginal Affairs in the middle of 1980, and Tracker was already employed in the Department in a middle-ranking, field-officer type position. I think I knew him before that, but in that regional director role I came to work fairly close with him over the next four-odd years.

The way the office was structured, we had the region split into four area offices, and each area officer had some field office capacity. They were generally Aboriginal blokes that improved the go-between between remote communities and the non-Aboriginal people in the Department. Tracker was in that sort of capacity. He had an excellent range of contacts around the bush and was well known, good family connections, knew the lay of the land well, knew the bush well, and I consequently travelled fairly extensively with him, particularly in the north-east sector out of Alice Springs. I saw the way he operated on the ground as well as in the office and the way he interacted with people, his peers and the bush.

He had excellent relationships with people, but probably he was too involved. I thought that he had difficulty standing back and getting the broader perspective of what was going on. He had an amazing ability to grasp the complexity of issues but tended to undermine himself by frivolity, ridiculing issues to the point that it got to the most celebrated moment, of my once telling him under a mulga tree on Bushy Park Station, on returning from Utopia, that he was a pain in the bloody arse. I told him that one of these days he will feel passionate about an issue and desperate to be heard, and will find that the audience have already written him off as superficial and a joker.

He took great exception to that, and he was threatening to give me one in the mouth. I suggested he think carefully about whether he was good enough for the task. Old Milton Liddle was with us, we had taken him out there to do some interpreting. Milton was watching all this in horror, and Tracker's response was to walk around kicking at sticks and kicking at the fire, and he cooled down a little bit. That issue blew over but ten years on probably, sitting in Canberra, I got a phone call one day. I picked the voice immediately, and he said, *Do you know why I'm ringing you?* I said, *Obviously through past connections to say g'day.* He said, *No, no, why am I ringing you?* After a while I said, *You tell me.* He said, *I'm ringing you to thank you. You remember one day you abused me under a tree on Bushy Park Station?* I said, *Yes, very well.* He said, *You caused me to hold a mirror up to myself and make some decisions about what I was going to do in the future.* Tracker's recollection of it was that I had said to him, *Why don't you go and get a bloody education*, and his response was, *You pay.* We had slightly different recollections of what happened under that tree on Bushy Park Station but whatever it was, it resulted in that phone call from him to me probably around 1991 or 1992, I forget the year. *I'm ringing you to thank you. Tomorrow I graduate as a Bachelor of Agricultural Science and it's a consequence of you forcing me to have a look at myself and do something about it.* I think the clearer truth of it is that I was the motivator probably, the catalyst that caused all that to fall into place. I was absolutely chuffed by that phone call from him all of those years ago, acknowledging that I might have played a part in him turning his life around.

You had to pull them up occasionally, and remind them that they were professional public servants and that they had a profile to protect. The boys would play if you gave them enough rope, so sometimes you had to pull them up and say *hang on a minute*. But there were always issues there that produced the humour and kept people amused. One of the boys was an absolute shocker on motor vehicles for example, and at one stage of the game I said that he was not to be given the keys of any departmental vehicle ever again, and some wag in the office pulled up the old Commonwealth General Orders and found a provision there where you could pay somebody a bicycle allowance. So Tracker delighted in things like that. *The bloke's grounded, instead we'll pay him a bicycle allowance.*

But he was always one of the brighter blokes. He was operating at that field-officer level but he could always contextualise the issues better than most, complex issues too. He could see a way through, and see what the end objective was. I think that is lacking these days. People seem to process a piece of paper in their inner vacuum, and they do not contextualise what has gone before, or what the end effects are. They have lost the ability to analyse cause and effect. He could grasp exceptionally complex issues. I have listened to him out there on the verandah many times talking about carbon tax and how you might utilise the vast expanses of Arnhem Land as carbon entrapment schemes on a commercial basis. I cannot quite think through all that, and how it is going to work, because it is more money for nothing, and I think probably the greatest destroyer of remote communities is money for nothing. He had many balls in the air, and he managed to catch most of them before they hit the ground.

There was one other suggestion I made to Tracker early on and that was you have got to work with the government of the day, whoever is in office, irrespective of your political persuasions or theirs. You have got to put any partisan policy approach behind you and deal with the government of the day. It was something he did successfully.

I Know It All Backwards

David Ross

In 1985 I decided that I needed some education, formal stuff, because I had been putting up with the likes of Paul Everingham [Northern Territory Chief Minister] and others saying, *Oh! You blackfellas don't know nothing. You rely on whites all the time to do everything in the organisations and always have to have these whitefellas do everything for you.* I decided that I needed some more education and understanding of finance and things of that nature. CLC at that time was running its management based on Nugget Coombs who did a review back around 1982 or 1983, and he had come up with a model of participatory executive and members, and everything was based on a committee-type thing that ran the organisation. It just was not happening. We had a chair who was not really engaged in the organisation, who just went walkabout and was not really engaged in the organisation. I was secretary to the Council and found myself making decisions that had to be made. It was just the way it was.

So myself and Bruce Donald, who at the time was a lawyer with the CLC, went to Darwin and spoke to Jack Ah Kit. Jack at the time was director at the Northern Land Council and we figured out how managements worked. So I think it was around July or August 1985 we put to the Council at a meeting in Amoonguna that we needed to implement a new system of management and we needed to have a director and delegations. Bruce and I talked to the Council and the chair said, *Well! If that's the case I'm out of here.* The Council said, *Yeah! That's pretty much what we're going to agree to do.* The Council had had enough of his running around, just not doing the job and taking huge pay and all the rest of it. So he walked out of the Council meeting that day and we implemented the position of director and, at the same time, I was also applying to go to university.

By the end of October–November, we advertised the job and Patrick Dodson was the successful applicant. I went off to university in Adelaide to do a business management course so that I could understand what I needed to know about money, and to have a better understanding of budgeting, and how to do all those sorts of things. I did not know that I would get down there and Colesy was at Adelaide Uni next door, and I ran into him. *Jesus!* He was doing a degree in accounting and he said, *Tracker is out at Roseworthy Agricultural College.* I said, *Bloody hell.* I did not know these blokes were there. As time goes on we were sitting one day having a yarn and I said to Tracker, *So you're going to uni, what are you doing?* He said, *I'm doing a science degree.* I said, *What's it about?* He said, *It's all about land management and this and that.* I said, *Hmm, okay.* I said, *The Land Council would be interested in what you are doing, what are you going to do with it?* He said, *I don't know but I'll go…* I said, *The Land Council is going to need people like you with these sorts of skills, so you need to think about what the Land Council is doing.* He said, *Oh! Yeah, alright.* That was sort of the discussion that we had, and it went on from there.

Anyway, I was not doing a degree, I was only doing an associate diploma course which was for two years of my time from 1986 and 1987. I came back to work and they anointed me and gave me a job as assistant director I think at the time, that was the terminology that was used. It was in early 1988, and then Patrick Dodson decided in 1989 that he was packing up and going back to Broome and the job would be advertised. I said to Tracker, *You should put in for this job.* He applied for the director's job, but the trouble was he was not ready and was not keen to take on the job. He was not finished school and the Council executive at the time said to me, *You're going to have to step up to the plate.* I said, *I'd prefer not to. I prefer to do what I'm doing.* Basically their response was, *We sent you to school for two years, you either take on the job or go find another job.* That is what happened. *And Tracker can have the other job when he is finished.* I had to be the bearer of the bad news to Tracker and he was happy with that and so that is how it all came about. I am not sure exactly when, but I think he finished in 1989 and started work in 1990 at CLC in early January.

It was very funny because Tracker turned up very well dressed, good pants, and – oh! flash shoes. I said to him, *Where are you going?* He said, *I'm coming to work.* I am sure Kathy [Tracker's wife] must have said to him, *You get dressed properly.* Anyway he comes in and we are all walking around in jeans and working boots, as you do at the CLC. Anyway, it took him all of a few days and he was back to normal like the rest of us. I don't think I had ever seen Tracker that well dressed again. That was pretty much where it all started and I suppose we have done a lot of things since then.

I remember these different things at different times, of trying to acquire land, and scheming in different ways, and bringing people in who had different skills to help. I think the acquisitions of pastoral land was the first job I gave to Tracker. There was money in ABA [Aboriginals Benefit Account] and we had minister's approval to buy some land, and so Mistake Creek was up for grabs, and Loves Creek. I think they were [both for sale] at that time. I gave him the job to put it all together and we dragged Colesy in at one stage to help us with Mistake Creek. They both had a few trips up there and all sorts of stories came out of that. I heard from old Jacko Cook, who was one of the main TOs [traditional landowners] from up there that at one stage there was a gun involved. They loved to argue and fight, them two.

At the end of the day the properties were acquired and we purchased Mistake Creek from Gary Dann who was known as one of the best wheelers and dealers in the cattle business. A man who started life as a butcher and ended up owning quite a number of properties, and not only had his own butchery but had his own abattoirs and all the rest of it. Tracker was open to beating these people at their own game, and I think we ended up with possibly a thousand or fifteen hundred head or more cattle than what we actually paid for. You don't do those sort of things without having a bit of smarts about you. I think Gary offered to help us acquire Loves Creek from the owner at the time who just refused point blank to sell to blackfellas. We had to use two or three other people in a roundabout way to actually make the acquisitions.

We got what we wanted, and I think Gary pointed out to the owner at the time: *Well! These blokes will end up with it one way or another, so if you deal with them up-front then you will pay less in commissions.* The bloke did not want to and he ended up paying a lot out in commissions. Well! That is the way it works. That is life, that is the way it goes. Tracks had a lot to do with those acquisitions, and I think James Nugent

[CLC lawyer] and Colesy all played their parts. The overall strategies, in terms of making sure the stock was there and all the rest of it, that was all down to Tracker and his ways of doing things.

The next acquisitions came when Bobby Tickner [Robert Tickner, former Minister for Aboriginal Affairs] offered me a job as a part-time ATSIC commissioner. I said, *Yes, no worries.* It was a way of getting in the door and we were able to acquire some money through there and buy some more property. Alcoota was up for grabs and that was a whole different ball game. When it was first raised that old Tom Webb [then owner of the Alcoota pastoral property] wanted to talk to us, he dared not come anywhere near the CLC office because of the rednecks. He was so afraid of the rednecks and being seen to be talking to the Land Council. So we met with Tom in the car park down the back of the creek behind the old Woolworths in Alice Springs. Oh! Yes, it is a true story. This is true. When Woolies used to be in the Mall in Todd Street and we ended up down the back, in the car park near the creek. That would seem to me to be a much more public place, but that was where Tom felt a bit more comfortable about talking to me and Tracker about acquiring the property. Charles Perkins had raised the issue with him, about if he wanted to sell then Aboriginal people should get a chance. So that was why he was talking to us. And that is where we started that process. Tracker took pretty much control of that process.

My job was always to go and get the money. That was always my job, to get the money. Tracker's job was to make it all work and then drag whoever he needed into that process. It got very personal with Tracker and one Mr Turner, at that time.[12] Tracker was abused inside out when it then became public that we were going to buy this property

---

12. After eleven years of dispute, the Northern Territory Court of Appeal on 26 August 2003 dismissed a claim made by the Alcoota Aboriginal Corporation – which was made up of Arthur Turner, the station proprietor, and a traditional owner – that the purchase of the station by the Central Land Council on behalf of the traditional owners was illegal. Mr Turner declared that consent had not been sought, and challenged the acquisition in court with financial backing of the former CLP government. The court's decision finally freed up the official land claim process to return this land to Aboriginal title under the Aboriginal Land Rights Act. The process was finalised with the handing back of title to the Alyawarre and the Anmatyerre peoples as the traditional owners of the land under the Alcoota land claim No. 146, in July 2012.

for the traditional owners. Mr Turner, who was living there, was not necessarily a traditional owner, but part of the relationships, and family, and married in and whatnot.

So there was a lot of personal stuff there, but we got through it. There was a time when Tracker and David Avery [principal lawyer at the Central Land Council] actually came in the office and said to me one day, *Let's use the money to buy something else.* I remember saying to them, *Get out of this door and you go and make this thing work. It's not about us. It's not about how hard it is. It's about acquiring this land for the people.* I probably did not say it so nicely to him, but things happened. We led people to believe that that was what we were going to do and that was what we did. But it was one of the most difficult acquisitions we ever did. Mr Turner really personalised it with Tracker, he really personalised it.

This all began in 1993 or 1994, while dealing with native title and trying to put the act together, all at the same time. I cannot remember who the chief minister of the Northern Territory was at the time, I mean they have had so many chief ministers. It could have been Marshall Perron. Turner had a very close relationship with this CLP government, and they were on the phone to him every other day. He was a favourite son, running their line while all this was taking place. There were all sorts of other things going on at the time within the CLC, which was just its normal business. This was just acquiring land. This was six million dollars we are talking about, and it was a lot of money. It was a great property, really good cattle, good infrastructure. So paying good money for a good return. There was a lot of personal stuff involved and Tracker pretty much wore a lot of that. He is listed as a traditional owner in the claim, with his brothers. So he was heavily involved in the whole thing. Life is life and it is pretty rough. It took a long time and we got through it all. I think Tracks is very proud of what finally happened but it was a long-winded process. A lot of problems come with it.

Tracker Tilmouth

At the end of the day you can say, *Righto! We just paid five million dollars for a cattle station that my family owned for forty thousand years.* We had to pay five million to get it back. We did not get it back because the government still owns it, still runs it, and if it comes across [as land returned to the traditional landowners] it would be run by the Land Council anyway, which is the government. I do not want to enter into a false pretence of land ownership. So do not invite me. I said the insult to injury is the five million dollars that we had to pay because someone stole it off us in the first place. We have land rights today from Gough Whitlam, and we paid millions of dollars for land that we already owned.

All the court cases! All those poor people out there who had to go and bare their souls in front of judges who knew nothing about them. And today, still know nothing about them. So I declined the offer [to go to the official handback of Alcoota to the traditional owners]. I was glad they missed me out. They actually missed out inviting me. The Central Land Council forgot to put me on the list and I bought the property as director. Rossy and Avery left me off the list.

I thought it would be good to get an invite at least. They gave Willie an invite. He went. He does not share my understanding of the process. Never got an invite and I bought the place. Rossy mob went. They only got put down because Willie put their name down [on the claimants list] for old Don Ross. Nothing against that. Ask Nugent. Ask Rossy. Did Tracker ever get an invite to go to Alcoota? It is run by the government. The Indigenous Land Corporation runs it. The traditional landowners are on the board. There is one white bloke on the board from Ti Tree. I did not want to run cattle.

I know all the stories. Got it all. Mount Bleechmore and all that country, New Well, Rabbits Rock, I named all the sacred sites. Drove all over that country with Petrick Mob and the Tilmouth mob, old Kenny, Walter Dixon, all them blokes, old Dave Ross. I know it all backwards. That is it. Right down to the border and Loves Creek because I knew all about it.

William Tilmouth

Tracker was really good in a scrap as a driver. I remember one time when we went out to the land claim, this was the Alcoota land claim and that is our traditional country, our father's country. And there was a move to put Alcoota under the Anmatjere Council which was run by another family member, and that family member was listening to the Country Liberal Party who were totally against Aboriginal land claims and Tracker and I went out there.[13] Tracker was the director of the Central Land Council and really he should not have gone out, it was a direct conflict of interest.

But we went out there and to this meeting, and the meeting started turning violent because this guy who is family of ours, started getting aggressive because people were listening to Tracker, and people were listening to me. They could see the sense of what we were saying. We were saying that we are not Anmatyerre, we are Eastern Arrernte and that is a fact, that is the truth, we are not Anmatyerre and so why should we be under Anmatjere Council, we are Eastern Arrernte mob. And our Alcoota is right on the boundary of three different groups, Alyawarre, Anmatyerre and Eastern Arrernte – but it is on the Eastern Arrernte side.

So that debate was going on and this guy wanted to [fight], he had boomerangs and everything, and he was jumping around. It was a rainy day, so I said, *Come on Tracker, we'll go down to the station,* so we jumped into the Toyota and we drove off. The car, the Toyota was just spinning and sliding in the mud, and that bloke had a Toyota too and he followed us. And I said, *Here, pull over Tracker, we've got to deal with this.* So we pulled up and I jumped out, and Tracker jumped out his side and we started to walk over to his Toyota and the guy jumped back in and drove back to the community. So we followed him back. And there he was jumping around with boomerangs and everything for Tracker. And Tracker was wild but he had to contain himself. He was fuming. He was really angry and you could see it. He really wanted to do something about it right or wrong.

This was twenty-five years ago when the land claim was first being negotiated. Tom Webb [then owner of Alcoota Pastoral Lease] said to the traditional owners, *You might want this, if you want it say yes and I will get ATSIC to buy it for you*, and they said yes. So all of a sudden Alcoota was coming under the Aboriginal Land Rights Act.

---

13. Anmatjere is another way of spelling Anmatyerre.

Tom Webb could not see the value of that, but Tom Webb got paid out handsomely in the end. He has passed away now, but he was very familiar with the people, he knew the people, he could even speak the language, so Tom was not alien to the people, but the Country Cattlemen's Association did not like him for it. He said stuff them, if these old people want it, they can have it, they need to have it back and I am going to give them first option.

Anyway we left the meeting and you could see Tracker was fuming and it was very quiet driving back. The roads were all wet and on some of those outback roads they put gypsum on and when the gypsum gets wet it is like soap. Tracker was starting to fly along, then all of a sudden a big corner came and we lost it and – Ah! Straight through the scrub at full speed, he did not slow down. *Ah! Go on. Give it to em bruz. Give it to them.* I had nothing else to say. I knew he was going to tear his way out of it and I tell you what, he controlled that vehicle at full speed and missed a few trees. Just full speed, he was just full concentration and that Toyota was going sideways and everything, and we come back onto the road and he just held it and kept going, but by Jesus, I turned white.

You could see that driving skill come out of him. All of a sudden he had to be serious and when he got serious, by Jesus, we were lucky to be alive, but it was his skill that got us out. Because as we came off the side of the road, it was all wet, it was really soaked and boggy and he did not slow down one iota, just whacked it back.

David Ross

One of the other really personalised attacks that he had is probably not on public record but I am going to tell you this. I think it was when I was a part-time ATSIC commissioner and also the full time CLC director and we tried to acquire Angas Downs from the Liddle family, and they had a lot of debt. ATSIC had approved the purchase, the figure I cannot remember but within ATSIC and government authorities, they always give you ten per cent up or down the market price.

Tracker had been talking with the family and doing the deals, and Lorraine Liddle [a lawyer, and daughter of Arthur and Bess Liddle] had somehow been acting as a legal person for the family, and we were having a Land Council meeting up at Mistake Creek and I got a phone call, Lorraine wanted to talk to the chairman, Mr Breaden, who was her uncle, a brother to her mother. Tracker had grown up with them at Angas Downs after he had come back from Darwin.

So he was very much part of the family. It really took a toll on Tracker at that time, quite a heavy toll. It was very much personalised, and it was like he was outcast from the family. It was not nice to see all this. That was one of the sad parts about people not understanding the business that they are dealing with. And when you have got someone from the other end who has very good knowledge of these things, very good knowledge of cattle, negotiating these sorts of things, it was a terrible thing to see. We see all the other sides of Tracker, but I have seen this side that a lot of people do not know about.

It was because people do not understand, we could not pay any more money. The price was set, it was market value, you have valuations done and ATSIC will go ten per cent higher or lower, that was it. And as I say, we had to hold up the Land Council meeting for a number of hours because she insisted that the chairman ring her directly. So the old bloke, old Breaden, drives all the way up there to Mistake Creek homestead to ring her up. This was days before we had satellite phones and all this, you had to go and use the landline. So he went there to talk to her. It was not going to make any difference, but we held up the Council meeting for three or four hours while all this took place. And it was all personalised and pointed back to Tracker, because he had grown up with that family and was very much a part of that family structure. It knocked him around. He would not admit to it, but I know it knocked the shit out of him for a long time.

They would not sell us the property. They ended up selling it to the Imanpa community somehow, who got some money, and as far as I know they still have control of that property. We were still in the time limit to run a land claim on it, and it could have been Aboriginal freehold. That is the sorry part about the whole thing. The money was there and the moment we could have purchased it, the old people would have had some money in the bank. But the longer it went, the higher their debt, and they ended up with very little in the bank. That is life. That is the way it goes. We did everything we possibly could to give those old people as much as we could in terms of the valuation.

These are some of the downsides as I say, that a lot of people do not know and have never seen and probably never heard of.

Steve Ellis and Lawrie Liddle

Steve: I did not really meet Tracker until I came to work with the Central Land Council. I knew who he was when he was playing football and I can remember a few things about him and his old Land Rover. He would pull up and start talking about Angas Downs, remembering his training there for five years. But I did not really get to meet Tracker until I worked for the Land Council. He was assistant director then.

The biggest thing that I reckon started with Tracker and me was the purchase of Mistake Creek. Colesy and Tracker were going up there to talk to the owner, then all of a sudden they said, *Why don't you come with us too.* We flew up there and had a look around the place and I did not even know what was going on. And then all of a sudden, yes, they were negotiating with Gary Dann to buy the place. So that was my first big thing. There have been other pastoral properties later on, but that was my first big thing. And of course Tracker and I had to go back the following year once they had worked out the deal and did the bangtail muster.

One thing I will give Tracker, you could not take away his knowledge of the cattle game. He knew the ins and outs of the cattle game, not only the ground stuff, I am talking all the stuff that goes with it. People could find it surprising because coming from the Land Council, what would he know? But he was across the board with the whole lot. The whole cattle industry, everything. And that was part of the reason why Mistake Creek is running so successfully. Because of the way he and Colesy set it up to start with, it was just set up right – no problems, so it would not fall down, even though the Land Council do not have much to do with it now.

Lawrie: Yes, this came from working at Angas Downs with my father, he also went across to Mount Ebenezer, and in those days they used to have a motel as well so you did motel work and you did pastoral work.

You got to know how business works through dealing with tourism and government operators every day, and road workers. It was a fairly varied cross-section of the way the world works.

He was sort of like the green-eyed boy with my parents. I do not know why, but it was his personality and he was pretty easy to like.

Not long after, I came to the Land Council, when the regionalisation plan was being put into place to have regional offices of the CLC in the scrub. Tracker put a lot of work into making sure that plan worked. The other thing was what to do with the start-up of the CLC pastoral unit, which was dealing with pastoral concerns in the bush with the traditional owners. Tracker put a lot of time and effort into that.

Steve: I do not know if I should say this but maybe it is time that he heard it. Tracker said to me once the Land Rights Act is coming to an end, we have got all this land, now we have got to go and do something with the land. Not so much to try and get more, we have got to do stuff with the land that we have now. And then he turned around and left. I can understand why he left but as soon as he left I think it went backwards.

I was a little bit pissed off but when I think about it I can understand he wanted to get things done for himself. In a lot of ways I was sort of pissed off and thinking, *He has got this up to this stage and now*, as far as I could see it, *he is letting it all down*. You could see after he left that he had been the driving force behind it, and it was going to go down, and in my opinion it has. Whether that is right or wrong I do not know. I know he really tried to get things going on the Aboriginal-owned pastoral leases because Mistake Creek and Alcoota were a success. He wanted them to feed off those other two places, and to build themselves up from there.

Lawrie: When they started off CAAPA, Central Australian Aboriginal Pastoralist Association, apart from one person all of the directors were people from these newly acquired properties, namely Mistake Creek, Alcoota, Loves Creek, Ti Tree, and Mount Allan, Mount Wedge and all of those places, and Tracker actually started a meatworks processing plant at Amoonguna. Vertical integration is what he wanted.

Steve: Tracker had a lot of good ideas but it was not easy for him. I think if he had a little bit more support a lot of these things would be working right now. They would be a lot better than what they are right now.

One of Tracker's strategies that I remember was when we were both in the regional office out at Atula at a Council meeting, and the Native Title Act was just coming in, and he was trying to explain what was happening to the Council. You have to draw pictures which is the easiest way to get information across, so he just drew a line and said this [side of the fence] is the white people and mining companies, and [on the other side of the line is] the Aboriginal Land Rights Act and Aboriginal land. At the moment under the Land Rights Act, he said, there is one gate in that fence, and it is a big fence with one gate so everybody has got to come down [to the gate] and the CLC sits there like a big cheeky dog. Then he explained that under the new Native Title Act there are gates everywhere in the fence where they have busted holes, so they can come in anywhere and the law itself is like a spider, it has got all these legs and the government pulls a leg off, and pulls another leg off, and in the end you have got this spider with no legs so he cannot do anything.

You could see these people, the delegates [from remote areas all over Central Australia] actually pick up on what he was saying. It was not just saying, *Under the Native Title Act this is what will happen and under the Land Rights Act this is what happens.* It just goes over their heads. By doing things like that, they could understand. I asked him how he thought at a meeting. He said, *I just look at the people and I think how they are dressed, if they have got hats on, if they have got jeans, so I try and use something that they will relate to when I am trying to explain something to them.* I said to him that was really smart, because I had heard a lot of lawyers and people talking at these meetings and they have not got a clue how to talk to those people. Lawrie and I were just sitting down and giggling to ourselves about this spider with the legs going off in every direction. He communicated by telling a story that could get them to understand what he was trying to say.

Lawrie: I suppose this way of communicating by telling a story goes back before modern technology had come up into that part of the country such as TV, commercial radio, and all the other stuff that goes along with it. You were lucky if there was one telephone in the street. So you had to be pretty good at yarn-spinning, otherwise life would be pretty boring, so you have always got your own little collection of yarns you like to tell. In the bush, the mail delivery was, if you were lucky, once every two weeks by air. We barely had any radio reception, no commercial radio, nothing, I think that did not come until the 1970s. The reception did not last for long, it was only a couple of hours and after that just static. So you had to be able to tell a yarn or lie pretty well. During the workday you would always find something amusing that you could build on later at night to make it worse, or make it better.

Steve: I think Tracker was trying to make all these places work, so the traditional owners could make a little bit of money off them and live on the land and do what they really wanted to do. Ninety per cent of them were people that came from the pastoral industry, so they could have employment and do their own thing. You are not going to be the next Kidman or anything like that, but just have enough and, if they had small killer herds, they could sell them to the abattoir if it had gone ahead. And for a fair price. And then you were not shipping, because you were only selling a small number, and there would be no freight costs of shipping into town. It would have taken different steps, and when the cattle were sold it would generate the money to be able to pay back people to buy the cattle the following year. And also to help them breed their herd and get up to scratch like other pastoral properties, having good bulls and things like that. I think that was Tracker's long-range plan, from hearing him talk about different things at different times. But the problem was, he just did not have enough support. Not so much with us, we were going to support him, but higher-ups and from government.

Lawrie: Even with the meatworks at Amoonguna there were all sorts of barriers, with the Department of Health and quarantine, and cleanliness and hygiene. It just got harder, and harder, and harder, so in the finish they said *leave it*.

Steve: Later on he was going to try and set up an abattoir in a central place where you would get the contracts from the stores. You would kill the animals there and farm them out to all the community stores. The trouble with meat, a lot of the meat is rubbish. I think he had thought about all this earlier on, but it was a long-range plan.

After I went over to Calton Hills I had only been back a couple of months [in Alice Springs], and at the old greenhouse [Land Council office] down there at Hartley Street, he said to me, *Oh! You've got to catch a plane tomorrow, you're going to Mount Isa.* I just said, *Yeah.* There was nothing planned or anything, but he said, *You've got to be there tomorrow, by the weekend.* So what do you do, you go. But it was good, and I made a mate of that old [Kalkadoon traditional landowner] bloke there, and he turned out to be a good friend of mine, and the Dunns [former owners], they were good people. But if it was not for Tracker I would not have got to meet them.

Lawrie: Even at times when we went over to the Gulf of Carpentaria for that mining meeting, that was spur of the moment. He said, *We're leaving tomorrow.* He said, *Make sure you've got enough clothes to last two or three days because I'm not sure when we'll be back.* So five or six of us jump on this charter and went to Lawn Hills, and there was a major mining meeting with the mob that wanted to mine the land. We spent a couple of days there arguing, and wheeling and dealing with the mining companies and the traditional owners. And from there we come back to Alice Springs. He said, *Go home and have a shower because you're going to Canberra.* Same day.

When we went down to Canberra, Tracker said to this young fella, *Hey! I need you to take my staff up through the building, Parliament House, take them for a tour.* This young fella said, *I don't work for this Tracker. He thinks he's my boss.* And out of that little trip you've got Laurie Brereton and Nick Bolkus, and we took them through the Tanami, and up through Darwin to Mistake Creek. He had been on them for a long time to come up and have a look. That was all part of another scheme that Laurie told me about. *Tracker wanted me to come and do this for a long time.* It was all about pastoralism on Aboriginal land.

It was about business with Tracker. In another time, in another place, he probably would have been a top businessman, because once people got past, *That's Tracker!*, and actually listened to what he had to say, you forgot about his joking. He carried on but after a while it clicked that this bloke is terribly, terribly smart. You actually listened to what he had to say.

Steve: One funny story that I can remember which happened only a couple of years ago at a Central Land Council meeting at Tennant [Creek], and Tracker rang me from down at the BP service station there, so I went down and picked him up and when we came back out of the council meeting, it was lunch time. And you know Ned Hargraves [Warlpiri traditional landowner from Yuendumu], how he has got a limp? So Tracker walks up to get a feed and Ned looks back and did not recognise him. He walks up there and being Tracker, he called out, *Ned Hargraves, I'll fight you any time you like.* Old Ned took a step back. I am sure that gammy leg straightened up and then he looked around and said, *Tracker you, you mongrel.* All he had heard was his name and *fight you anytime you like*, and it sort of shocked him.

He livened people up. Well! Him and old Max Stuart were a good combination during the Land Council meetings when things were starting to get slow, and old Max would get up and he was chairman, and he would say to Tracker, *Oh! Son, we're going to go and look for a new mummy for you tonight.* And just when things were getting slow them two would start and wake people up, they were good.

Lawrie: I remember the story about Tracker saying he had a letter from NASA asking Land Council delegates to volunteer to be sent into orbit. He said, *You know what, I will just show you how much attention these people pay to me at these meetings.* So Tracker is talking and he says, *We have a new program coming up and I want some volunteers, who wants to go into orbit?* One old bloke puts his hand up and he says, *I want to go into orbit. I'll go.* Tracker says, *See what I mean.* Lovely old bloke too. *Yeah! Into orbit.* He asked, *You're going to turn into a spaceman?*

Tracker Tilmouth

With Loves Creek it was pretty straightforward. We [the Central Land Council] had offered to buy Loves Creek and every time we went in there to make a price, the price kept going up. Loves Creek was a good place to get some of the Santa Teresa people back onto their country, like the Ryder families and the Bloomfields, and what we did was to end up with a bidding process. One was Danny Schwartz out of Melbourne, and Ross Ainsworth out of Darwin, with both bidding against each other, and they took the price higher than expected and the property agent said, *We're getting prices from one bloke in Darwin who wants to buy it, and another bloke in Melbourne who wants to buy it.* And I said, *Oh! Yeah…* And so they priced it higher and outbid the Central Land Council. They said, *We are going to go with one of these blokes out of Melbourne or Darwin, this is the bid.* I said, *Oh! We can't match that.* And then there was a hiccup in the pastoral industry, on live export or something like that, and so Ainsworth dropped his price, and Danny Schwartz dropped his price, and they kept dropping their prices until it was below the Central Land Council price. So we went in there and bought it. We organised it that way. We got Loves Creek for a good figure, because we knew the minute we put our hand up that the price would go through the roof, so we organised that through the Aboriginals Benefit Account and the Central Land Council. There were no other deals done like that that I know of. Mistake Creek was straightforward. They were in financial trouble.

Owen Cole

One of the biggest arguments I had with Tracker was at Atula Station. We had purchased that pastoral lease and then it was a question of what happened to it before the sunset clause in the Land Rights Act prevented it being put through the land claim process. And Tracker mob from the Land Council rocked up at a meeting and Sandy Taylor, an Aboriginal lady, had got there beforehand and the meeting had started at nine o'clock. He had rocked up at about ten o'clock, as they were camped further away or something, and she had convinced the mob there to put the station under Northern Territory legislation. So I said, *Tracker you can't blame her, she's only doing her job, and if you people had got up early like you should have and got there at the right time…* You can just imagine he wanted to kill me, so we are sitting down at Mistake Creek at old Jack Cook's place actually, and Tracker was abusing me, *You are nothing but a blah blah blah.* I said, *Look you got done over by a female, an Aboriginal one at that. She beat all your lawyers.* I was really shit-stirring. Next minute he jumped up and he said, *I'm gonna shoot you, you bastard.* So he grabbed a gun – he had his stock inspector's licence and he comes out with a gun. So I said, *Go on, fire away. Go right ahead, do your damage.* He smiles, puts the gun down and says, *You're nothing but a big-lipped bastard.*

So him and I used to have a fight and the next time was in the Gulf of Carpentaria, and we were up there talking about training and employment and enterprise development. We are in the back of the car and we were arguing and of course all these Carpentarian mob had never expected something like this. We were supposed to be working together and there was this big bloody argument. Next minute, *Go on!* You are throwing punches. They were saying, *You mob are bloody mad.* I said, *This is par for the course. This is the sort of relationship we have. Go on hook me, I will hook you.* So. *Okay, good.* We had a lot of arguments.

I remember when we purchased Mistake Creek and you had to be careful with the bangtail muster with the cattle. This was one of the times when we could not get the legal section to quickly draw up the agreement to organise the muster. So I drew up the agreement and tossed it to them and they fixed it up quickly. I said to Tracker, *You've got to sign these papers every day, do the count, ear tags, the whole works and you've got to put it on this form and get both parties to sign it.* So, *Yeah no worries, that's good bro.*

So I shooed off, and I was only up there for a couple of days and he was doing the muster which went about five or six weeks or something, and anyhow, I come back and I said, *Where are those tally sheets,* and he said, *I've got it here.* And he opens up his diary and he has it all written in pencil, see. I said, *That's not worth the paper you use to wipe your arse with.* I mean if we got into a legal battle or a legal fight what were we going to do, *show your handwritten notes.* So him and I were shaping up to one another. *I spent all that time organising this thing, making sure it was legally watertight and you go and do that.* He went, *Oh! Yeah, dickhead, you wouldn't know what you're talking about. You don't know one end of the bullock from the other.* Which is true. But anyhow, I remember that.

We were supposed to have so many cattle, say there were fifteen thousand, and we done the bangtail muster, and from one paddock alone there was a photo that Tracker had where the cattle were strung out from next to the road to beyond the horizon. They got something like fifteen thousand from one paddock. No one had ever mustered it before. So that was the only time when Aboriginal people actually ended up with a hell of a lot more cattle than what we actually purchased.

That was one of Tracker's little triumphs upon acquiring the property with fifteen thousand cattle that no one had ever mustered before. Before that I can remember he said, *We've got to get down to that country, to the southern country.* I said, *Okay.* So we hopped into the Toyota and were driving along next to the place up there – Kununurra – and when it rains it pours. There were all these little gullies, ten metres wide by ten metres deep, and Tracker goes, *We've got to get across it.* I said, *I'm not driving.*

He said, *Well! You walk and I'll do it.* Tracker was mad enough, and he goes down and he comes up while I was running, and he would go to the next one and he would go down it again. No wonder they never mustered it properly because it was almost impossible to muster. I basically ran the whole southern boundary with Tracker driving, and every now and then you would get two hundred metres and jump in the car and go to the next one. That was the type of bloke he was. No one else would have driven the Toyota down those gullies. That was the paddock where he picked up all those cattle. Anyone would have said, *Nah! Let's use a helicopter or fly over it,* but not Tracker.

He drove the whole boundary, and saw how many cattle were still in the gullies that had not been branded and so forth, and he said, *When we purchase this property, first thing I'm going to do is go out there and do a thorough muster of that paddock.*

I can remember driving along the road there and the next minute I saw this helicopter come up beside me. There was the pilot with his hands up, and there was Tracker controlling the helicopter. He was flying this friggin' helicopter. Of course he did not know how to, but he had seen the pilot and said *anyone can do this.*

James Nugent

I had some interesting experiences flying around the country and Tracker used to enjoy that. I remember going to a meeting in

Burketown and coming away with Tracker in the right seat, and a very large fish strapped into the back seat. A big fish, it completely occupied a seat in the back of the plane. I think he must have got it from Mornington Island.

I remember coming back once, again it might have been in a little twin, and of course Tracker was saying, *Tell everybody I can fly Nuge,* and that was always good fun. We were coming back across the Tanami and I had decided that I would use the fuel in the tip tanks until they were almost exhausted before changing to the main fuel tanks, and of course Tracker and I got talking and at some point one of the engines started surging and then cut out, and Tracker went from calm and just chatting about things to, *Jesus Christ Nugent what are we going to do?*

It's alright, hang on. I changed fuel tanks and got the engine going again. Tracker was quiet for about the next twenty minutes which I don't think I have ever heard in my life. I was guilty, but I had a slight grin on my face. Then we got back on the ground and he proceeded to tell everyone how I had nearly killed him in the plane.

One time he wanted to land the plane, but as soon as Owen had said, *Righto! Tracker that's enough, now just hand it back,* Tracker of course would not let it go. He was sort of looking over his shoulder going, *Look! Look Colesy! I'm going to land the plane, here I go.* He got reasonably far along the way and Colesy said, *Nugent! You just take it over.* But Tracker would not let go. He just had to keep ribbing Colesy about it, it was too good a joke for Tracker.

Owen Cole

Another time we went out to Ikuntji where there was a smart-arse community advisor, and Tracker and I were there to meet with the Council. We were standing up there waiting for about thirty minutes and we said, *Have you spoken to the chairperson, we need to talk to him and some of the Council members,* and he turned around and said something along the lines, *Why don't you shiny-arses get back to Alice Springs and do something productive,* or something like this. Anyhow, I said, *What did you just say?* He repeated what he had just said, so I jumped the counter and I grabbed his hair, and I said, *You ever say that again I am going to shove your head up your bum and knock your front teeth out.* Tracker was standing there and we go outside, and he said, *Totally unprofessional, Owen.* I said, *I felt like thumping the bloke talking to us like that.* Tracker said, *You don't go and do that type of thing.*

Anyhow about a month later we were there again with Neil Bell, who was the parliamentarian for MacDonnell Ranges region, and Tracker was having this discussion with the same bloke and he was being sarcastic and rude to Tracker. So next minute, I saw Tracker drop his left shoulder and whack, and he knocked this bloke. And Neil Bell, he was trying to be the perfect gentleman and he tried to stop Tracker by saying, *Come on, come on,* and I said to him, *Tracker, I thought you said this was totally unprofessional behaviour*, and he said, *Shut your mouth or I will give you one.* Different circumstances, same action. Whack.

You know we used to be a pretty volatile sort of bunch and we wore our hearts on our sleeve, and sometimes, we did not put up with fools that well, and there were a lot of fools out there on those communities. Some funny stories I tell you.

You'll Never Get Rid of Me, I'm Like a Virus

Julie-Anne Stoll

I got a job at the CLC – due to start on the 12th of March 1990, and I was moving my whole life to Alice Springs so I came a week early. Steve, my partner, was coming up a month later. I was in this tiny little CLC flat and I was sorting out my life. I think that I had only been there a day or two when I got a knock on the door and it was Tracker Tilmouth. I introduced myself. I had met him at the interview, and he says, *You want to come out bush next week?* I think I had arrived on the Saturday and it was the Sunday, and he was there. He said, *I'll go bush with you just to see what it's like before you start at the CLC.* I jumped in this motor car with him the next day and drove out to Laramba and this was for the sacking of a council employee. It was a big meeting and this was my introduction to the CLC. I had Tracker yakking and yakking, and driving out to this meeting with traditional landowners who were really, really angry with the situation. I am at the back of this room thinking *what have I let myself in for?* There was this so-called boss who was quite mad by all accounts and all these traditional owners who were really angry, and I was new and had really bad hay fever that day.

Anyway, that was all done and dusted and we were driving back, doing the whole circuit from Laramba. I was the one who had to get out and open all of the gates. Tracker was telling all these stories. The next thing, we stopped and he had this black case which he pulls out, and he says, *Want to see what I've got?* Sure. He pulls out this Magnum handgun and I thought what do you use that for? *Oh! You know, if you hit a cow you've got to shoot it.* I asked him whether that was standard CLC issue. Of course it wasn't but that was the start of a very interesting relationship with Tracker over the years.

There are many, many stories and he had been an absolute delight to work with. He called me Stolly through my whole working career at the Land Council. Nobody else called me that. We had a lot of robust exchanges, and apart from the occasional humiliation in public, he was a good mate.

You want to hear another funny story? It was the day I nearly left the CLC when I had been to Kalkaringi for a mining meeting and there was a funeral, so the meeting was postponed, not cancelled, people wanted to do the meeting, but they did not want to do it until the following Monday. So I made the call of staying up there instead of driving back twelve hundred kilometres, and then doing it all again two days later. I did not get approval, I just made the decision to do it and when I got back after the meeting, I got into the biggest trouble. Tracker was supposed to discipline me but it was pretty funny. He just yelled and carried on. He was smiling the whole time.

I guess Tracker instituted a lot of the land management and the land information system at the Council – back with old Monty [Soilleux], who was diabolical to work with. We were able to record things and take much more of a holistic approach to land management. We produce all of our maps, we work with shape files, we can produce all of our own information, and then upload it into maps. It is not only about sacred sites, it is also about areas of biodiversity and other significant areas. The system is very advanced. He had that vision in the early days to get something good. It cost a lot of money and was complicated but it has held us in good stead. We have better capacity than a lot of the mining companies to get good information.

He did have great vision. When I first came to the CLC we did not even have our own individual computers. So there has been massive changes and he instituted that change really quickly, he saw that vision.

Ellen Stubbens

Tracker and I were cousins and his father was my godfather. I remember Tracker as a young fellow, playing football and also the first camel race and I think he won that race. He spent a lot of time with old Noel Fullerton and he was pretty close to him.

I did not know much of Tracker until he started working at the Central Land Council. He was really good as a boss but sometimes it was hard to nail him down, to have a conversation with him. You would have to talk to him when he was on the road. I worked in the field section of the Land Council and we all had a good relationship with Tracker. One time when we were down at Finke having a Council meeting, he said he was going to cook rabbit. I thought, Oh! Yeah, this will be alright. Here is what happened – the next thing he was pouring cans of Coke in it. Some people really enjoyed it, but I could not believe he was there cooking this rabbit stew type thing with Coke. I thought he might have been a bit mad or something.

It was pretty full-on at the Land Council meetings. We had to leave about two or three days before, depending where the meeting was going to be, and set up the kitchen. The kitchen was just like a big tent. We had to erect the tent, unload the truck, stoves, tubs of food for the meetings. On Monday members of the Land Council would have to travel there from across Central Australia, meet for Tuesday and Wednesday, and we would have to provide meals for up to one hundred and fifty, or two hundred people in the middle of nowhere. Oh yes, it was really hot in some places, or really cold. We would have to set up the kitchen, prepare meals for Monday night when people arrived. We used to have to cook up three very large pots of whatever, for example stews, and sometimes Barb Cox and Steve Lake used to put the roast in the ground to cook and it was really lovely.

We would have to cook three meals a day, and for afternoon tea we would just hand fruit and stuff, and for morning tea we would put out biscuits. It was a bit of a hassle when it came to making tea for everyone but in the end, they got a big large pot, like an urn, to sit on a gas burner to constantly have hot water for everyone coming up with their billy cans and making their own pots of tea in that. And Tracker would be the centre of it all, teasing the staff and carrying on. Never lost for words Tracker, the stuff that would come out of his mouth! He would stir everybody up and then you would get all your stories.

It used to be long days when you were out in the bush. You would have to get up about five in the morning to have breakfast ready by 7.30, 8 am, because then, they would start the meeting about 8.30

or 9 am. You would no sooner finish one meal and clean that up, and you would have to start all over again. It had to keep going and going, and going. By the time you went to bed: Well! We used to all sit around and talk and all the delegates used to be there playing cards. It was really fun because some of the delegates used to get into groups, maybe three or four groups, you know, sitting down and playing cards until all hours. There was a generator on the back of a truck, or sometimes they used to have someone there just holding up a torch so they could see while they were playing cards.

It was pretty hard for the fieldies [field officers] too, because they had to go to all the communities, pick up the delegates and get them all to the one place. Sometimes they used to arrive late with their delegates and they would be buggered, and having to get up in the morning and help prepare breakfast. It was really long, really, really, long days for those blokes. We got ourselves into a routine of what had to be done and we just got in there and did it. I am not sure how long I worked at the Land Council, it was probably only for about six or seven years.

One time we had to go to Utopia where the Land Council had a meeting and the truck got bogged. It tipped and that was really hard for the fieldies too because even Bookie [Mr Bookie of the Eastern Plenty Region, a former chairman of the Central Land Council], he reckoned the only way we were going to get this truck out was to cut down the trees. They ended up cutting down gum trees and shoving the logs under the wheels of the truck, and then they had about three or four Toyotas towing it, to get it out of the mud. That happened in the afternoon on our way out there so we were all stuck. There were three of us trying to sleep in one troop carrier. Me, Barbara [Cox] and Kathy Booth, all in one troop carrier. So we were stuck there that night, and we had to camp there with the truck. That was a hard slog, that.

And the way those blokes used to unload that truck, it was just like a conveyor belt, throwing boxes at each other. It was shocking. Terrible. Not only the vegetables and fresh food, but all the canned stuff, sugar and milk and tea, spaghetti, everything. This was how it was to unload it, and get it into the kitchen. Really hard work. There was Laurie Presley who used to be on the truck, and before that I think it was

Laurie Clarke who is now deceased. He used to be the truck driver there for a while as well. Lawrie Liddle used to drive the truck. And Steve Ellis. Kathy Booth took over field work after I left the Land Council in 1999. They used to have the full Council meetings four times a year, at different sites. One time we had to go to Lajamanu, and it was fifty-four degrees Celsius. It was that hot at night you could not sleep, and then it would try to rain and you would roll in your swag, and then jump in the car to get out of the rain. I could not believe it being that hot. It was shocking.

The Kalkaringi Convention [the Combined Aboriginal Nations of Central Australia Constitutional Convention held in 1997] was huge. That was like cooking for about seven or eight hundred people. Eight hundred and fifty I think we fed one day. It was hot up there. Not only that, the Kalkaringi Council mob dug the toilets, dug the holes and put the forty-fours [gallon drums] down, and then we had to run the mesh to partition them all off, the toilets. So that took forever.

Then there was the big meeting for the Coniston Massacre. They had a meeting and Remembrance Day where there was this large rock where they put the plaque. That was a pretty big event. There were about three hundred people there and we cooked for them. And there were those women's meetings too which were big events. Barb fell off the truck at the Tennant Creek Women's meeting. She was pretty sore for a while.

Toly Sawenko

I arrived in the Northern Territory in 1975 as a schoolteacher. I was going to teach at a remote outstation west of Papunya, but the school did not continue there for various reasons, so after a year or so at Papunya I ended up teaching out in the north-east part of Central Australia at a place called Utopia. Now I had not met Tracker during those early years in Central Australia and my first clear memory of meeting him was at Utopia when I had left school teaching in about 1977, and become the Aboriginal health service administrator for the Urapuntja Aboriginal Health Service, based in Utopia and serving the communities in that region.

I guess Tracker at that stage in the late 70s had moved from a role where he was working with Pitjantjatjara Yankunytjatjara people in the south-west corner of the Territory and South Australia, and was working for the Department of Aboriginal Affairs as a field liaison officer in the Eastern Region of Central Australia. Part of that was within Harts Range, and areas along the Plenty Highway, but also extended out to where I was living and working at Utopia. So that was where I first have a clear memory of meeting him and I think he knew of me and I knew vaguely of him, just through mutual friends, but he arrived at Utopia there one day, in a white Holden utility and in the back he had some goat meat and a goat skin. He joined us that evening and proceeded to cook the goat which I think he got from Harts Range where the community there had some goats that he was helping them to raise and breed, and use for milk and meat. So he put on a bit of goat for us and also left the skin and I think his idea was that we would use the skin for a kind of bush chair, but we never got around to figuring out how to tan and treat the hide to make it work for that. That was the first meeting.

Tracker was very confident in getting around the bush communities, and you could see that he really really enjoyed travelling around Central Australia and working with the Aboriginal communities, and he was very much a confident and happy-go-lucky sort of person. Lots of jokes and he was good company. I think he was interested in meeting the people working on Utopia because he had not directly dealt with that community. He would call in every now and again, sometimes just stay for a cup of tea, conversation, sometimes camp overnight and head off the next morning. These were occasional meetings and I did not really get to know him better and spend more time with him until later on, when I was working with the Central Land Council and he was involved there as deputy director and then as director. That was the next phase of my working with and developing a friendship, a relationship with Tracker, by working with him and for him, and also getting to know him as a person, and his family.

The relationship I had with Tracker and the relationship he came to have with my family, and now my family with his family, just developed and grew over time. The things that we all enjoyed about each other's company was the warmth and the sense of humour. In the workplace and in politics, a sense of humour has its place and purpose. As we got to know Tracker better and more personally, we all really enjoyed lots of good times together because there was a sort of uplifting spirit about the relationship. We were all working hard and had our problems and issues, and we all knew how to enjoy each other's company. Tracker always enjoyed the *comedy of incompetence* as I call it. Nothing amused Tracker more than reflecting on dealing with people who just didn't get it, who were so politically prejudiced or biased, or just ignorant, that it was amusing. It was not just despairing, he actually got a lot of amusement out of it.

He had favourite sayings when you asked him about a meeting he had gone to with a bureaucrat or politician who needed to be aware of some issue. He would come away and I would say, *What was that like Tracker? What was that person like?* He would say, *Thick as pig shit on a cold day.* That sort of thing. Oxygen thieving. He called some people oxygen thieves. That was one of his favourites. There was a vein of his humour where he did not suffer fools gladly, but he was not vindictive or nasty to them, it was just farcical and amusing that someone could be so incompetent in what they were supposed to do. He loved that sort of humour, from Monty Python and *Blackadder*, particularly *Blackadder* and Baldrick where the joke was of a well-meaning person with an incredibly dumb idea, like Baldrick saying, *I have a cunning plan.* What is the cunning plan? It turns out to be hopeless and stupid. He saw great humour in that because in a way he identified with a lot of people who were trying to do something valuable but just didn't get it.

He had his own methods and standards and was obviously a very insightful and intelligent person but like I say, ignorance did not appeal to him. It amused him and I think that is a strong feature about people in the Aboriginal political movement anyway. They are used to not being understood or even acknowledged, or respected, but rather than just feel bad about it, people turn that into humour and it is a sort of humour that can be used as a shield to protect you from the consequences of being badly treated, but it is also kind of a refuge, it prevents you from being depressed and angry about what is going on in the world.

It also creates a bond between people. So the people who get your joke about how bad things may be, or how ignorant some of the people you have to work with are, it bonds you to them, you share a common perspective. It makes you feel stronger rather than just totally frustrated.

I remember during my time at the Land Council there was to be an orientation for new staff and Tracker was the director then, and quite often there was a certain type of person, this was a non-Aboriginal person, as there were lots of positions at the Land Council that could not be filled by Aboriginal people because we did not have enough applicants, and there were also technical experts that needed to be hired. So there was always a component of non-Aboriginal staff in the Land Council and certain kinds of people always applied for these jobs. People who were very conscious of trying to do the right thing by Aboriginal people and very socially progressive, and there for social justice, and it felt like their mission in life was to overcome the wrongs that Aboriginal people were suffering.

Anyway Tracker was well aware of this and I remember one occasion where we were having an orientation session, probably a dozen of these young staff and they are all bright-eyed and very keen and well motivated and hanging off Tracker's every word. I got up and made a little explanatory statement about the work I was doing, just telling them about the different parts of the Land Council and what it did. Tracker got up and they all looked awestruck and were looking at him as the great Aboriginal oracle and his speech went along the lines of, *Well! You've come to work for us here at the Land Council and that's what we want you to do, we want you to work for us but we don't want you to die for us because we're not worth it.* They did not quite know what to make of all that. People did not know whether to laugh or look at each other but that was him saying we do not want a bunch of devotees who believe that we are all perfect. It was all about the work, but it was also all about being realistic, and about having your feet on the ground, and not everything is right just because an Aboriginal person says it is so. And that was Tracker's irreverence. He did not want people to go around and worship him because he knew his own strengths and limitations, he did not want anyone to have an idealised picture of him. He was not the sort of person who would allow himself to be idealised. In fact he could shock you just as much as anything else with something that he did or said.

When he was the director of the Land Council, he was always talking to people at Council meetings and community meetings about important issues of the day. These were things like various government attempts to weaken and damage and eliminate the Land Rights Act and all the rights that people had that went with it. He was there during the period when native title was a big issue and when the Mabo judgement had been passed and so on.

I worked on the Reeves Review with him, organising community meetings.[14] The name of the game was being able to work in that situation where you were dealing with people for whom English is a second language. You are dealing with people who had a particular history and circumstances in communities, and you had to discuss a particular issue of importance to them but find a way of communicating it and explaining it so that it related to the real world of people. And I still remember the meeting where Tracker was talking about the Native Title Act and he wanted to ask the question about what benefits might flow to people from the Native Title Act. Whether it was a really important achievement or whether there were serious limitations about it. His way of explaining that was to relate it in a very direct way and say to people at the meeting, *Well! We're talking about the Native Title Act, is it a stallion or is it a donkey?* Immediately the discussion and debate hit home. People could see that they were being asked to look at something carefully, that it might look like something else but be of much lesser value. So he was always good at translating things in those sorts of terms. He would always have an analogy or an idea to make things understood, particularly by the bush communities that the Land Council served. But that was just part of his repertoire of communication skills. He knew how to deal with particular audiences, whether he was talking to scientists about land management or politicians about the employment policies or mining companies about how they operated. He was skilful enough to know what ideas resonated with them.

---

14. The Reeves Review of the Aboriginal Land Rights (Northern Territory) Act 1976 was undertaken by John Reeves QC in 1997–98.

He was a realist, always a realist and not someone who allowed himself to get bogged down in rhetoric and empty gestures, always very down to earth, really cutting to the basic essence of things. He knew how to do that with whatever group he was talking to. So that is about storytelling, but it was also about understanding your audience and understanding who you are dealing with and the world that they inhabit, and the values they have.

I think one of the very early Tracker quotes that he used to use a lot was *chopping wood for practice*. It was a way of saying you were doing something, not for a real purpose, but just to occupy yourself, and it was not going to lead to anything good. I do not think he invented them all himself, but he knew which ones he liked to use, like *if intelligence was electricity, we'd all be in a dark room.*

I think Tracker had a realistic idea of himself and he also understood to some extent, what kind of driven person he was. So when he came to visit our family, and he would do that regularly, he was probably thinking *I do not want to wear out my welcome here but I do like coming around and having cups of tea and chats with my friends.* His way of defusing any sort of wearing-out of his welcome was to just take it, full on, and say, *Well! You know, once I connect with your family, you'll never get rid of me. I'm like a virus.* That defused the whole issue of how often he was coming around. But virtually we became his second family there [in Alice Springs] and that was fine.

Off to the Next Idea Already

Ian Manning
___

Tracker got onto us, the National Institute of Economics and Industry Research, through union networks, because we have done a bit of work for the union movement. This was when Tracker was pretty new as director [of the CLC] and he was moving on mining agreements, particularly employment generation as part of that. And so I came up to join him and several others, and we went as far as Yuendumu for the ride. Then we went on and called in on the mine manager at the Granites mine, where we were all well received and shown around the joint and talked about what they did, the conditions of employment, what the fly-in, fly-out people do. Then went onto the Tanami itself. Had a look at the Tanami mine – Zapopan, which was just closed, and it was beginning to collapse.

And then we went south to where new exploration was taking place, and I think that was where another mining agreement was developed. We met the geologist in charge and talked to her. And then we also visited a drill rig where they were in a spot of bother because they had lost the drill bit down the hole. So we left them to their bother.

At Lajamanu we held another meeting with the senior men, again the same sort of discussion, and some of them had actually worked on the original Tanami mine, and they were quite in favour of a bit more mining work. And there was some talk that we would be flying back, but I think by then Tracker had worked out that I did not throw up when in a troopy, so he drove us the whole way back. It says something for his sharp eyes that, when we were barrelling along the Tanami road, he brought us to a sudden stop and backed up so that we could get out and say hello to a thorny dragon three inches long.

Now that was my introduction to the CLC. I had previously worked in the Territory for the Welfare Bureau. The reason that

I started there was that way back about 1988 or so, I did a job for the Association of Local Government Grant Commissions on methodology, and in the course of that, I dutifully trundled around all of the grant commissions, including the one in Darwin. They were sufficiently impressed with a southerner who was willing to come to Darwin to talk to them that they then put me on the job to do a review of their grant distribution methodology.

Anyway, that is how I first started working in the Territory, and I do not know whether Tracker knew that I had that background or not, anyway he did not care because he said he liked turncoats, people that worked for the other side and shifted.

I do not know if it went as Tracker originally thought, but at various times in 1994 I came up to Alice and my job was to background or just to add a little bit of weight to negotiations with the various parties. Tracker was at that stage trying to develop joint ventures or partnership arrangements between Aboriginal groups and not only the mining industry, but the suppliers to mining.

So Forrest and I went to discuss [Aboriginal employment] with various businesses around Alice, and we also talked to Roche Brothers in Melbourne. Tracker came down for that and it gradually shaped up into a program of writing Aboriginal employment into the mining agreements and also backing that up with training and so forth. My job was basically, I think, to give Tracker a bit of confidence, somebody from an office down south who thought that what was happening was reasonable. As he said, we've seen good mines and we've seen bad mines, and the more he was in the job the more he saw a mixture of good and bad mines. Basically the mining industry has the habit of crying poor, and spending a few billions to cry poor. So it has to have somebody who would actually say, *Well! Don't believe them as a mob,* even though individual mines may be pretty marginal, the industry as a whole is thoroughly profitable and raking it off. The association was really quite successful. We did have, of course, some marvellous evenings in Alice, especially with some of the blokes who spend their lives as miners in remote locations. They tend to be characters and they certainly accumulate stories, and when you had a bloke called Stan Padgett [then from Tanami mine] and Tracker trading stories!

I got the impression that Tracker building relationships and being able to sit around and tell stories was how the CLC was managed at the time. When difficult decisions had to be made, they would end up going in a troopy somewhere telling stories over a campfire of an evening. That way a lot of the personal relationships were cemented, but also difficult issues got aired in a non-threatening way. It was a very different style of business management from what the textbooks recommend but it worked. He did tell me that as a result of all these negotiations the ladies of Lajamanu art centre now have forty-tonne coolamons, according to the tonnage of rock you can put in the truck. That was how he summed it up. That was Tracker. And of course all of these things were put in place so that traditional responsibilities could be attended to without disrupting the workforce. That was quite a complex thing.

The storytelling style of management in the CLC was remarkably effective, particularly when you compared it to the Northern Land Council, and a lot more practical and down-to-earth approach, and respected the traditional owners. We got the impression there was possibly a different genesis, where the NLC was pretty bureaucratic and it was a mixture of bureaucracy and people from down south who had fairly fixed ideas on how to assist the Aboriginal cause, and was far worse at the grassroots level. They had a different kind of society to deal with. The groupings in Central Australia were a bit smaller and so personal-name basis was much easier to work with than where you had very complex traditional ownership patterns like they did up the Top End. So it was not entirely the NLC's fault, but they certainly did have less resources at ground level, and they did not have anybody like Rodger Barnes [former mining manager, CLC], who was a geologist who was really on top of the game, and it ended up that the CLC knew more about the mineral resources of the Centre than anybody else. They had accumulated data and they interpreted it. The Northern Territory Department of Mines was supposed to do it, but were not as good at it. The CLC was fairly good at its pastoral resources too, and Tracker used to talk a lot about Mistake Creek and cattle, and even camels as I recall.

I became fairly unnecessary at the end when the mining agreements took a life of their own so I think the last time I was involved in any of that would have been sometime in 1995. I also did a bit on various reports when Tracker got interested in what the ABTA was doing or not, and so I had a look through their finances. Tracker was one of the early ones to realise that royalty-type flows and Toyota money and so on were all very nice, but you do not get the kind of guaranteed income flowing, and you do not get the kind of self-respect and so on too that comes from employment.

The last lot of work I did with Tracker was in September 1999 when I went to Darwin, and Tracker was there. That was when Tracker was working with the Gundjeihmi Corporation and Yvonne Margarula [senior Mirarr woman], and so in October, I went to Gundjeihmi with Matt Fagan [legal adviser]. We had this talk about the Buff Farm.[15] There was a fifty-something pot-bellied bloke, an old Territory stockman, supervising the Buff Farm from a shed somewhere hidden away in Kakadu, down one of those tracks without a signpost. He had an Aboriginal housekeeper. He was reputedly still a pretty good shot with a gun when it came to magpie geese, and we had discussions about that, and whether it would be possible to shift the Buff Farm into Arnhem Land because it was financially a hopeless proposition in Kakadu, it just did not turn up enough product to make its keep, so Gundjeihmi was actually subsidising it. It was getting on to that period when the Ranger mine people were still salivating about Jabiluka, and Gundjeihmi held the title not to the Jabiluka deposit, which was approved, but to the haul road, and the whole thing was not a proposition without the haul road. So it was a question of whether any sort of deal could be done and also whether Gundjeihmi could actually get a better part of the tourism industry around there. So for example we had a look at the Kakadu airport, which unfortunately was on a laterite surface and the runway was not long enough for a 737 to land.

So we hummed and haa'd a bit because, fairly obviously, Kakadu becomes a more saleable destination if you do not have to do that three- or four-hour drive from Darwin. I was there in October and Forrest was there too, and Jacqui Katona. Tracker, Jacqui Katona, I and a few of the locals went to one of those billabongs to fish and Jacqui tried hand lines. I proved that I was not much good with a rod

---

15. Kakadu Buffalo farm was created in 1988 to provide free bush meat to traditional owners.

and I do not think Tracker was all that much better. He was treating it as an opportunity to talk to people, and I think he was sussing Jacqui Katona out, could you really trust this girl from the south. And I presume that he decided he could.

I was up there again in March 2000 and Conway Bush was a young bloke who was to some extent under Tracker's tutelage at that stage. He was of pretty fully tribal descent but he was western-educated. Tracker was trying to see if he could be fitted into the network. The traditional owners insisted that since we failed to catch a fish at the billabong in October we could not leave their Territory without a barra, so Conway supervised my catching of a barra.

He put a net in and caught the little fish that were in the gutters by the road, used them to bait a hook then just chucked it in to the Nourlangie Creek from the road bridge.

We had the TO's permission. Then the following night, Tracker and I went to the same place and fished the same way, and Tracker caught a black bream and a file snake.

We hauled in the file snake and killed it up on the back of the ute and presented it to Yvonne Margarula's mob, as bush tucker. The following day we were out on the road and Tracker spied a long-neck turtle so we caught that too, and to maintain the equity among the various people in Jabiru, that got presented to the Christophersons [traditional landowners of the area] who put it in their washbasin and said, *Mum will like it.* Once again, Tracker was trying to take advantage of circumstances and put together consortiums that might get a business going, but I think he was fairly up against the NLC at that stage and who knows what else.

Tracker just seemed to be saying, *I got all these people here and basically jobs would be good for them.* I think he was trying to achieve plain basic jobs. Of course to get the best deal he could. I do not think he was particularly good at the fine print, and certainly day-to-day administration, but he was very good at strategy level. And not only that, but putting together consortiums of fairly unlikely people sometimes. He did not allow ideology to stand in the way. He could see the crap merchants fairly quickly. He got on well with anybody, those in the mining industry who were genuine and willing to negotiate.

He had a pretty good understanding. He used to say he did not have a vegie degree, he had a genuine higher education did Tracker. He had a dream that, one day, there would be an Aboriginal university which would take Aboriginal languages seriously and would reassess Western learning in an Aboriginal way.

Mistake Creek was technologically backward in some ways because a lot of the blokes there liked riding horses, but on the other hand when it came to GPS-based land management, which Tracker had implemented at the CLC, it was right at the forefront. And that was not a bad combination. It meant that the traditional owners actually saw the country when they rode around on their horses. The country was better managed than the average Northern Territory property.

James Nugent

I met Tracker when I first came to the Land Council as a young lawyer in 1990. I was a callow and ignorant young fellow from Melbourne. So it was quite a revelation to be at the Central Land Council and to meet someone larger than life, as Tracker was. At the time people were talking about Mr [David] Ross, who was then the new director, saying, *Well! He's no Pat Dodson*, and he was very different and created that role in his own image. Tracker was in the newly created role of assistant director and had quite a different function, or created quite a different role for himself in that space. It took a while for me to work out what was going on.

We were working in the last decade of the possibility of land rights claims, as there was a sunset clause in the Land Rights Act. Most of the vacant crown land had been claimed, and the strategy was to try and acquire pastoral leases so that they could become Aboriginal land.

And of course that land under pastoral leases was the much better, much more productive land in the Northern Territory, and the idea was that, within the last seven years of land rights claims, to try and get as much good land back for the traditional owners.

Tracker had a very deep and abiding love of all things beef. He had a variety of big views at the time on pastoral management, how Aboriginal cattle properties could work together to be much more productive, and like the big cattle companies basically, to spread the risk and to try and have a real economic base. That was always one of Tracker's themes, that without an economic base, the land was only a very small part of it. And really, in order to change their lives for the better, traditional owners needed the edge to be able to create that economy, and to have that opportunity. And so during that period there was a lot of work done by Tracker and by Rossy.

Certainly when Rossy moved away to be an ATSIC commissioner, and then chair of the Indigenous Land Corporation, Tracker was instrumental in seeking out finance and funds to acquire those interests in land so they could be claimed under the Land Rights Act. I was thinking particularly of Mistake Creek which was one of the first properties I was involved with when I got to the Land Council, and Rossy, Owen Cole and Tracker were all instrumental in that negotiation and purchase. I was at Mistake Creek last week, and it is just magnificent. It is one of the best-managed properties in the region.

Since the property was bought it has never received any further funding from government. It has funded itself, and it has completely refurbished all of the facilities up there, the homestead, the director's quarters, the workshops. They have put in a training facility and they actively train schools and other young people in cattle management. It has an Aboriginal board of directors, an Aboriginal manager and his wife who are tremendous. They have got a wall full of ribbons from the Kununurra shows, where their cattle are regularly best in show. And it is a magnificent place. One of the great things about it and one of the good reasons it has been so successful is that there was a lot of work put into early governance with the directors, it was not just the purchase.

It was Tracker who got Jim Downing and Stuart Phillpot involved in carrying out some training, doing the money-story training with Jack Cook [senior traditional owner] and the other directors. It is something that really has held them in good stead. I think in a lot of ways it did not get done to the same extent on each of the other purchases, some places were much more marginal, where it was not the best use of that land to have it under cattle, but on Mistake Creek, Tracker did a lot of work, and he used to regularly go up there. That early work really did pay off. I think it is by far and away the best-managed property, Aboriginal-owned property in Central Australia, in our region.

He was sort of unique in that, in a wonderfully Australian way, Tracker was a larrikin. He was someone who was brash and boisterous, and he had such a quick and cutting wit but it was very engaging, and very disarming I think for a lot of people in his negotiations. He could completely disarm people because he would be self-deprecating, but he would be very humorous and that ability to cut through and disarm people puts them at ease and once they were disarmed, then he could go in and surgically carry out what he needed to do, which often was just getting his idea implanted so that people could go away and start working on it.

There was a lot of staff at the time when Tracker was director of the Land Council who found him very difficult to work with, but Tracker was a very intelligent character. He was insightful and strategic but for whatever reason, if people were not on board with the strategy he could be challenging – I do know there were a lot of senior staff who found it difficult to deal with Tracker. He was obviously someone of vision and intelligence and I did not have the same difficulties working with him that other lawyers did. Partly, I think it was that Tracker would have an idea of the vision, and then would expect the underlings to go off and do something about it without further ado.

Sometimes in the doing of things you realised that there were other obstacles, and maybe they needed to be massaged or dealt with by those in authority, and Tracker was off to the next idea already. He was not so much worried about those problems, as he was with his next idea and the next vision and expected that those under him would implement the vision. Just on that, Tracker was a great networker. He was networker par excellence, and would constantly be ringing around keeping in touch with people, touching base, getting the gossip. I guess it was quite exhausting for people on the other end of that to be tapped, but to be in that network of Tracker's was to be involved intimately with whatever was going on in his mind at the time.

Ross Ainsworth

I first met Tracker when I was a government vet, the new government vet in Alice Springs, and I was sent to Angas Downs to do a job there with testing some cattle, for the Liddle family. Arthur Liddle had this stock camp and we were testing cattle at the Mount Ebenezer roadhouse. So I met him there with a stock camp mob, and we had an interesting couple of days working there. We just sort of connected and I found him to be a fascinating fellow, very funny and clever and astute, and he would come to Alice Springs now and again, and I would see him occasionally.

Over the years we continued to keep in touch. I started an Aboriginal camp-dog treatment program in 1984 and I know he gave me some support there, but most of the activity was around Katherine which was where I was based in those days. I do not think there was a great deal of direct contact until I left Tipperary [Station], where I had been working in 1991, and started doing some consulting work. He was working at the Central Land Council and became involved in the land acquisition and land management for pastoral properties. We really hooked up together again when I assisted him initially with the purchase of pastoral properties.

We had quite a lot of involvement with preparing the approaches to buy those properties. But the main project that we got involved in just after I left Tipperary, was the development, or the re-organisation of Mistake Creek.

Tracker had arranged through the Central Land Council for the purchase of this property, and he drove that from the beginning. Then I was heavily involved in the management as it got started, and they had a few difficulties with the owners and finance and one thing and another, so he got me involved there. Then the really significant thing that we did together, the thing that I am most proud of, and it was really a team effort in that somehow or other I had talked to a few people, and we gave this training thing a go, where we got the old Anglican minister bloke, Reverend Jim Downing, involved.

Jim was retired back in Darwin but still active, assisting people where he could. Then we got Stuart Phillpot who is an economist, and he was working at Canberra at the time. Basically, what we got them to do as a team and it was a group of us, is that we set up a project, got some money out of an Aboriginal funding group in Darwin, and we put together a training package where they literally trained the traditional owners, the key traditional owners who were on the board of Mistake Creek, about the management of the property.

It went back to scratch, constitutional law, commercial law, criminal law, and how the parliament worked, and how all these things worked, and they were just amazed. They suddenly got it. Then Stuart Phillpot had invented a board game that was like Monopoly but instead, it was cattle stations, where you roll the dice and you go into drought, or you roll the dice and you have lots of weaners, or you roll the dice and you run out of fuel or something, so you had all the vagaries of running a cattle station by sitting around playing a board game.

These guys literally went out there, the two of them, sat down in the bush, and went out to various sites around the station, for two weeks at one point, and I think another week or two not long after. The message got through, and the senior TO said he wished someone had explained this to him before because now *I understand what it's about*. We developed the board which did not really function so we paid people, just like you pay the board of BHP where they do not turn up there for nothing. *We paid the board to come to board meetings, and got them organised with the capacity to get there, whether it was cars or buses.*

We just facilitated it. Suddenly the whole thing started to work. We were also lucky at the same time to get a really good new manager in Stephen Craig who had the combination of being very smart, but also a very sensitive sort of guy, and a hard worker. He drove the place with the cooperation and goodwill of the owners and primarily the senior traditional owners, who explained it to everyone else what had to happen and what was not allowed to happen. All of a sudden people stopped pinching killers, they stopped taking the fuel, they stopped breaking the cars, and everything just started to work. The station then was the most, and probably still is, the most successful totally Aboriginal-run cattle station in Australia.

And then as a result of that I left. I said, *Well you don't need me anymore*. So they just ran it through the CLC. The Land Council provided ongoing accounting services and legal stuff as they do, and they just got on with business. It was so successful that it did not need constant outside input. I think they got people from time to time but apart from that, it was just a great project and it was a real team effort and Tracker was at the head of the team, drawing in all the resources because of his enormous network. He knew people. Otherwise, I would never have met old Jim Downing. I would have never come across a person like him. I am not a religious person and he had lived in the bush all his life, and I had never been out to where his country is, so it was a wonderful situation where Tracker was able to gouge the sun out of different places and it just worked. That was the great thing, the main thing we did together and we can still claim it was a great thing and we're still very proud of it, and we were just very good friends.

Geoffrey Bagshaw

I had known about Tracker for some time because my father had worked for the ADC in Alice Springs, and had quite a bit to do with Tracker, and in fact I can remember years later when Tracker was in Adelaide, of his wanting to visit my father. I think it was a bit of a mutual admiration society between my father and him.

So I had heard of him and known of him probably before I actually met him, but I recollect that when I did actually meet him it was through the Central Land Council, and I think at that time he was probably the deputy to David Ross. And subsequently Rossy came down to Adelaide to do some study and that was when Tracker took over the director's role and I had a bit to do with him there.

Probably the most important thing was a project to do with sacred objects that were in European museums, and this, I might add, is still ongoing. The view is to assess collections of Central Australian sacred objects in Europe, notably Germany because of the missionaries in places like Hermannsburg were German. I went over to Europe, I think it was early 1993, and visited a number of European museums.

I got information about the provenance of objects and brought this information back to Australia, to the Central Land Council, and for one reason or another it was not too long thereafter that Tracker more or less left the Central Land Council and nothing really became of the project for quite some time.

In recent times it has been revived, but I remember very clearly, and I think it was one Saturday morning in late 1992, Tracker, David

Ross, David Avery and myself were sitting around at Avery's place and just talking about this particular issue and it was really Tracker who provided the impetus and actual suggestion to say yes, let's do something about this, actually go over there. I was going there in any case, but the CLC said once you are over there we will pay you to go to various places – Frankfurt, Leipzig in former East Germany, Switzerland, France, and so on to have a look at collections. I really think that without his enthusiasm for the project, and concern more generally for the repatriation of sacra from overseas, that it would never have happened.

This is more Rossy's idea but I do think it was shared by Tracker, that these objects in effect represent the title deeds to traditional land, and whereas whitefellas have their bits of paper and so forth, Aboriginal people have their sacra and apart from their intrinsic value as sacred objects, they also have political value as title deeds to the country.

Perhaps it wrongly surprised me, but I always thought Tracker could come across as somewhat superficial, oriented to the business, or the contemporary economics of Aboriginal Australia, so to be as clearly interested in and committed to a project which really goes to the heart of Aboriginal traditional belief came as a welcome surprise to me.

He had had such a long life in Aboriginal politics in particular, that without such a commitment and clear view I do not think he could have achieved what he did, or lasted as long as he had frankly. Many people would say Tracker was jocular and jovial and so on, and in fact David Ross said to me something I have never forgotten about himself and Tracker, he said, *Nobody knows when Tracker is being serious, and nobody knows when I'm joking.* That sums up their characters extremely well.

I was always surprised at Tracker. He would crop up everywhere. I was doing native title work in North Queensland around Doomadgee for the Waanyi native title claim, and Tracker was involved in giving operational advice to the Carpentaria Land Council. I was in Yirrkala in the late 1990s doing work and I bumped into him, I think it was at Gove Airport and I said, *What are you doing here?* He was involved in some sort of discussions there. It was probably an economic project, and he seemed to have a finger in a lot of pies of that kind. Those pies have a common ingredient and that is the rights and interests of Aboriginal people. As far as Aboriginal Australia is concerned, he had a pretty wide, maybe even a continental perspective on what was happening which is fairly unusual I think, as people tend to be focused on their own values.

I think he was very well positioned, David Ross as well, but Tracker too in that closed Aboriginal world, where often the people perceive the enemy as each other, the only people that are worth getting angry with are your family and there is lots of division and so forth, particularly in traditional communities. I think Tracker had always been aware of that and had tried to negotiate a course that allows people to still have their traditional social dimensions, while at the same time not letting that necessarily stand in the way of economic ventures. I think an important thing was that Tracker was very rounded in the Northern Territory, it was his home, they were his relations and so on, so he was not some sort of amorphous, or a better term, unconnected Aboriginal bureaucrat from somewhere. He had this deep connection to Central Australia which I think informed all aspects of his approach.

Murrandoo Yanner

I met Tracker in October 1994 roughly. Actually I met him earlier [about 1993] in Alice Springs before native title and the NAILSMA Alliance of the Kimberley, Cape York, Carpentaria and Northern Land Councils which used to be called JCALM. We all went to Alice Springs. My wife Rachel and I went with Mungubadijarri [my oldest son] who was then a little baby. And Tracker was there. He was a bit more withdrawn than later when I knew him. He did not leap out at me. He certainly looked after me. I had come home to Burketown when Dad died and I had a one-staff land council, and we had to build to get things going.[16] I was on a Wik tour that had been organised by one of the whitefellas, Galarrwuy [Yunupingu]'s offsider Shaun Williams or someone, and they took me to Cape York, northern and central

---

16. Murrandoo Yanner is referring to his father Phillip Yanner, an important Aboriginal leader from the Gulf of Carpentaria, who had set up the Carpentaria Land Council and ran it singlehandedly from his home in Burketown, often traveling vast distances to represent the interests of traditional landowners in the area against powerful mining and government interests. Murrandoo returned to Burketown in 1991 to run the Council when his father died.

Australia. In Central Australia, Tracker made sure that I got looked after and shown around all the different things that were happening at the Council, of how to build a land council, and what you might do as a coordinator or CEO.

But I think it was later in October 1994, because the Queensland Land Act had come in 1991, and the Queensland Government were meant to gazette the national park out here for claim and hadn't. We took two hundred people into Lawn Hills National Park for two or three weeks, moved in at midnight from Doomadgee and from everywhere else.[17]

Impressed by what we were doing at that stage, Alexis Wright told Tracker, *You have got to get over and help this mob, they have got no resources, they have got this young bloke*, and stuff.[18] Tracks came our way and brought the might and experience of the Central Land Council and its resources. We did not pay for anything. He brought it all, and all for free, and put a lot of muscle and experience behind us, and he really gave us a bit of ground, got us moving in the Century debate in the boardroom, rather than just the sort of crazy stuff we were doing.[19]

He helped us maximise on our direct action and put it to use, a double-edged strategy I guess, in the boardroom and out in the streets, or the park. He really opened it up. I was mesmerised, just fascinated by

---

17. The Queensland Government had failed to incorporate Waanyi traditional landowners in the management of the Lawn Hills–Boodjamulla National Park, so the Carpentaria Land Council organised an extended protest and sit-in at Lawn Hill Gorge.
18. Alexis Wright was employed at that time by the Central Land Council, with Waanyi connections in the Gulf.
19. The Century mine debate concerned the development of a large open-cut zinc, lead and silver mine in close proximity to the important cultural heritage of the Waanyi people and the pristine environment of the Lawn Hills National Park. Aboriginal nations in the region were concerned that they would be strongly affected, culturally, socially and economically, by the development of the mine, its pipeline to the coast, and shipment of slurry in the waters of the Gulf of Carpentaria. The development of the mine took place without a proper process of negotiation with the native title holders in the Gulf of Carpentaria regions that would be affected by its development. After protracted protests, including barricading rivers and preventing Queensland government politicians from landing in the Aboriginal township of Doomadgee, a groundbreaking agreement was reached though the support of Tracker Tilmouth. The agreement was signed in 1997, and the mine created was the biggest zinc mine in the world. It closed in January 2016.

him. I think to this day what always impressed me was his confidence. There was nothing the bloke did not know or could not answer. It was not bullshit. You can tell a bullshitter from a real person.

He was just supremely confident even when he knew nothing, his confidence would carry him, and next to my father, he was my greatest inspiration in life among men. On one of his very first trips out to the Gulf, he came to sit down and talk it all out with me, what we needed to do, and to make sure I was on board, that he was not going to be wasting his time. We had dinner at Mum's and she cooked a big cabbage stew, the famous Gulf cabbage stew to welcome Tracks.

We were sitting at our table and he looked up at the wall and there was an old photo of an army blitz with about sixty little Murri kids on it, all little brown kids, or white-looking kids, and Tracker said to my mum, *What are you bloody doing with my photo?* Mum said: *That's not your photo, it's my bloody photo*. He said, *Well! What are you doing with it?* She said, *Well! I'm in that photo*. He said, *No you're not, I'm in there*. And then they both pointed to each other on the truck. *That's me and that's me,* and then: *Oh!* They remembered each other, strangely, from little kids. *Oh! You were that kid,* it was amazing.

When I was taught for Aboriginal law – when I went through, you interpret signs and things like that you know, and I always thought: *I am on the right track*. It was a really strange quirk of fate back then but that is the whitefella way of expressing it. For me, it was a sign things are going the right way. We had obviously created a bit of kerfuffle, we were doing every mad thing we could to have a go at the company. Then with Tracks, we went down to Brisbane where there was a big economic summit in 1996. There were all these mining companies, Murris, and government mob in Queensland at this economic summit thing in Brisbane, and Tracker said, *There's bloody Paul Wand here. He's deputy chair of CRA {Conzinc Riotinto of Australia} so why don't we do this and that?* I said, *Oh! Yeah*.

We bailed him up at this big conference and sat down, him and me and Paul Wand. He was only known to me publicly through the newspaper. I had never met him and he had never met me, but we had obviously said a lot of bad things about each other – and each other's interests. Tracker was a greaser, smooth as, had cruised in and got Wand to sit down, and he had told me not to talk too much so I did not stuff it up. He was like, *Watch the show brother, come for the ride.*

And it was amazing. He had this incredible mind, and he pulled out a little notepad from his pocket and it had about four bloody things written on it: employment, training, properties, boom, boom, a few little squiggles underneath. He said, *Here's the beginning of an agreement. Boom! Boom! No worries. I reckon about one hundred and ninety mil.* Gee! I thought, *How could you take anyone seriously with a scrap of paper*, but that was actually the beginning of the agreement. And from that little notepad, it was not even A4 size, it grew from that.

Out of his pocket and out of his head, and it literally grew from that. These were the first major things put in the agreement. Somehow he impressed Wand. I thought, *Geez! He could have come prepared with a bloody slide graph show or something*, but he got Wand by the hook and Wand said, *Alright, I'll send this bloke Ian Williams to meet with you and sit down, and do the thing.* And Tracks said, *Yeah don't worry, this young fella he'll do this, if youse are playing ball, we'll play ball.* It started to happen from there. Even ATSIC, who had nothing to do with us until then, started to jump on board because Wand told them, not because Tracker or I told them, because Wand told the bloody Minister [for Aboriginal Affairs].

They thought if Yanner mob did not sit down quiet in the Gulf, [John] Howard is going to go and amend the Native Title Act, and then when we did sit down quietly, the idiots they did not learn: *Don't trust the whitefellas*, because he went and amended it anyway. So they screwed us over nothing. But with ATSIC at that stage, because Wand said to whoever it was, *Don't worry, give them some money, they're playing ball*, the Carpentaria Land Council got a heap of resources and things grew.

Ian Williams was a famous character in Australia back then, the new general manager of Century at that stage, because he had just broken the back at Hamersley Iron with the first major fly-in and fly-out versus local employees battle in Australia. The unions had taken on a massive battle about privatised contracts and Enterprise Bargaining Agreements versus everyone having to be unionised, and he basically broke the backs of the Australian unions, worker's unions, at Hamersley Iron. He was the jewel in the crown for the right-wing resource industry.

And they [CRA] sent him out because of the trouble here in the

Gulf of Carpentaria, and he was meant to sort us all out, but we ran amok on him and said, *Why is there a Sunday for eight years*, and did a far better job than the white unions were able to do against him I think. But anyway, we were down at the Mungabai [Aboriginal Housing Association] office in Burketown and Tracker said, *Look! Bloody Wayne Goss ain't gonna gazette the national park, even though he promised they would in his negotiations we've been having with them and the company said they supported it.*

I said, *Shit*. Williams mob was sitting down here at Mungabai, and I was meant to be at the meeting and I said to Tracks, *There's no government mob there, we can't hammer them today about the national park*. He said, *If you want the park gazetted get Williams to do it*. He said, *I'll show you how mining companies can run state or federal governments.*

I was very young then, nineteen, twenty or twenty-one, and I did not know too much. I said, *Oh! Yeah*. He said, *You do this* – I will explain what I did, I went down to where he had this meeting happening with the mining company – *and about halfway through you ask Williams, when I give you this, pull my ear or cough or something, and you say to Williams, 'Oh! What's happening with Lawn Hills National Park?'*

So we go through hours of negotiations and I hear him suddenly cough, bloody when I least expected it – it was in something interesting I wanted to listen to, so I go, *Ian, by the way, what happened with Lawn Hills National Park? Do you know if Goss has gazetted it yet?* There was a big silence, and things were going so well and Williams did not want to tell me, and then he said, *Actually he made a decision not to*. And Tracker, I was still trying to get him to play bad cop but he had me play it, and when Williams tells me that, I jump up and I bang the table. Tracker made me do all this, *and bang the table*. He had said: *Make it bloody genuine or they won't believe you. They have seen a lot of blokes put acts on.* So I bang the table and say, *Fucking ridiculous, you can't trust you bastards. I told you Tracker, you can't trust these bastards.* I go outside and Tracker told me the next part later. I jump in my car and do big figure eights and spinning gravel, and off I go swearing. Ian Williams shits himself and the mob too because everything was going so great, and he says, *Oh! Well! Shit what are we going to do?* Tracker says, *This is what you do.* State parliament was sitting that day and he says, *Ring Gossy now, get him out of parliament for a second.* Boom, boom, boom.

And bugger me, there is a historical fact. If you go to the transcript or Hansard whatever of the state parliament, you will see it was gazetted that afternoon, late afternoon, that day. That very day Goss got pulled out of parliament, got spoken to on the phone from Burketown by Ian Williams, and went straight back into parliament and gazetted it after publicly saying he wouldn't. And I was blown away, not just the fact that it was done, but the fact that they really do run the state government at times, and that his mad trick worked.

I thought I would just look like a nutcase. But of course when Williams went, *Oh! What are we going to do?* Tracks just stepped in with the solution and calmed everyone, and sells the whole thing. And that has been like *Starsky and Hutch*, good cop, bad cop. He played that strategy a lot, and it was effective. More recently with Arman, the gas mob [developing a gas field in the Gulf of Carpentaria], I had been getting him to play it a bit, and I had been telling him, *It's your turn now, it's been twenty bloody years or so.*

Forrest Holder

I know Tracker from when I started at the Land Council in February 1992. I was engaged originally as a research officer, but I was made a policy officer very shortly after that.

The main thing I worked on with Tracker was the development of the Land Council's approach to mining agreements. When I first started I browsed around and had a look at various things, poked my nose into places and was surprised when I came across the mining agreements because they just were not delivering what the traditional owners could get. The Land Rights Act gave the traditional owners monopoly rights over their land and they were not extracting monopoly rents. The agreements had been done way below what could have been achieved. I do not know for certain, but I think that was because when the Council started doing these agreements it did not bring in any specialist negotiators, it just looked up to the mining staff and the legal staff to come up with the agreement.

Not long after that I spoke to Rossy and Tracker [then director and deputy director] about it, and I said these agreements need to be improved and they said, *Well! Alright, the next agreement that comes up, you can negotiate it.* It was for the Tanami joint venture which was Otter Gold and Billington, and that ratcheted up what could be achieved under the Land Rights Act. Shortly afterwards, the Century zinc mine came up under negotiations on native title, and those negotiations were stalled and the Queensland Government got Tracker in. I really do not know why, I do not think I was ever told. But it was probably through Martin Ferguson and Tracker's relationship with him, and Ferguson's relationship with the Queensland Labor government.

We went up and made the first informal but formal contact between the Carpentaria Land Council and Central Land Council and we got our instructions from Murrandoo Yanner and I was parachuted into a meeting introduced by Tracker and told just to deliver my blurb which I did. It incorporated the same elements of the Tanami Agreement. It was just me explaining to them how to structure the operative elements of a mining agreement in relation to employment and education and career pathway outcomes, and access to contracting. That is all I did. I explained to them that it was in place already in Central Australia at the Central Desert Joint Venture. It worked there, and I gave them examples of how it worked and I walked out. Tracker did the hard yards, but I was never present at any of those meetings.

All I did was bring to bear my knowledge as an economist and as a miner, it was not any big deal, but the big battle was Tracker overcoming the organic inertia inside the Land Council and taking the risk to try and take things further. And once he had seen that, then he took it into the native title arena through the Century zinc negotiation. And that then redefined what was achievable under native title, and set the benchmark for native title agreements. In fact the silent partner within that Central Desert Joint Venture picked up the operative elements of the agreement from the Land Rights Act, and incorporated it into their Western Australian tenements, even though they had no requirement to do so.

Tracker always had the capacity to see an economic vision and then he would get someone else to work for it. He did not interfere with your work and when you needed his support he usually gave it. He ran into intense opposition from a lot of Land Council staff because they lacked the vision that was required to work for Aboriginal people. I thought far too many of the staff, and not denying that they had good intentions, but the road to hell is paved with good intentions, they had a bureaucratic mentality. Far too many of the lawyers looked at the Land Rights Act as if the Land Rights Act was a set of railroad tracks and Land Council staff were the engine for the rail cars on the tracks. They did not deviate and stuck to a narrow definition of the Land Rights Act. It was a very artificially tight and narrow interpretation of the act because I think it made their jobs easy and they felt confident – I never had conversations with them but my guess is that it made their lives easy so they did not have to use imagination, and they did not have to worry about getting hauled up in the political process by people in Canberra jumping up and down saying the Land Council is too radical, or this or the other. They did not see that their job was to further the aims, the political, social, economic and cultural aims and aspirations of the Aboriginal people that they worked for. But Tracker did.

Some actively attempted to undermine Tracker. When I came in to do the mining agreement senior staff were in and out of Rossy's office with steam coming out of their ears that the directorate [the policy section in the Central Land Council] would put me, *a newie*, into their hallowed turf. This had nothing to do with me, it was the way they reacted to Tracker. That was how they saw him, as a threat I think, a threat to their comfort. And they did not have the wit or imagination to realise that the Land Rights Act was the one and only mechanism in Australia at the time to mediate the engagement between the non-violent processes of the colonisation of Australia and the Aboriginal people of the land. They did not see it in that context. They had not decolonised their minds. Of course Tracker had because he was a political animal.

Tracker was a good bloke. What Tracker needed was a team of about ten people walking around behind him and picking the ideas up and making them come into fruition. The things that he could have achieved by using us as his tools were limited because he had limited tools.

His strategies were to use the people he was going to use as his tools, or the people that he saw were going to be political players, and give them a leg up. But then he kind of let things go. He went on to something else. He kept your back covered most of the time. He would either initiate something out of his own head, or he would encourage you with something that you thought was something that was in his head, that he wanted done, and then he would give you the freedom to get it done and he would give you the support to get it done. He did not suffer fools well. He would either squash them with a quick remark or he would just walk away, and leave them. He did not go much in the way of stand-up battles. I do not think I ever saw Tracker in an argument. Tracker and I for example had lots of discussions which might have amounted to arguments where we would discuss the tos and fros and whys and wherefores on a particular point. Like the time we were coming across the Barkly Highway and we were discussing mining agreements and principles.

My view was that when it comes to negotiating an agreement, whether it was with the government or mining companies, principle gets up and leaves the table and says: *I recognise I am not needed here, I will come back when you want me.* But when it came to having a row with someone who was circumventing him like Wayne Pash or Darryl Pearce [employees in the policy directorate of the CLC], or Rodger Barnes or Julie-Anne Stoll [mining section], or David Avery [head of the legal section], he never had a row with them. He would just be rude and sulky with a very quick comment, or he would walk away from them. That is my memory. I am not saying this as a criticism, it was just how he dealt with things. He had other ways of getting things done.

You had his support for the [Northern Territory Aboriginal Constitutional Convention] *Today, We Talk About Tomorrow,* which was a precursor to the One United Voice and CANCA [Combined Aboriginal Nations of Central Australia], and brought in First Nations people from the United States, Canada and New Zealand, and Michael Mansell from Tasmania, a really high-powered event that again the likes of David Avery and others were saying, *What are we doing this for? What are we doing CANCA for? It's got nothing to do with Land Council.* But Tracker could see that it did. I do not know how else to put it, I am not political on these things, but the extent to which the Land Council was an agent in delivering to Aboriginal people what they wanted in relation to their hopes and their aspirations, politically and economically and culturally and socially, a lot of that got done by Tracker and by Rossy backing Tracker, and in direct opposition to some of the staff.

One of his favourite sayings was that you keep your friends close but you keep your enemies closer. I used to get no end of frustration with Tracker's willingness to put up with the likes of those staff that were backstabbing him. He should have just sacked them. But he worked according to that principle. He was a man who I had great undying affection for. I would have done just about anything for Tracker. In the course of doing it I put up with more from him than I would have put up with from anybody else. I put up with a lot of shit from others on his behalf that I ordinarily would not have put up with. I want to make the point that he and Rossy could inspire in those who mattered unconditional loyalty and affection. There are others, people I worked with underground and others, but they are very few and far between.

Tracker was pretty good picking people to support him. He knew people everywhere but also kept his relationships. I remember when the relationship between the Croker Island's Minjilang mob and the Northern Land Council was not that hot. They had the relationship with Tracker, even though he was not from there but he had grown up at the mission, so they got him to look at an economic development plan for them. They were keen to get something happening so Tracker sent me up there to do preliminary work on aquaculture on the place. When was that? That was like 1994 or 1995, twenty-five years after Tracker had left the place, and rather than going through their own Northern Land Council they got Tracker to do it, and he did. He said, *Yeah, righto!* And he cut through the jurisdictional boundaries, and cut through the crap and the Land Council saying: *You can't do that Tracker, where are we going to get the money from?*

Aboriginal people out on the communities loved him. They trusted him. There was no doubt about it. It was more than just that though, there was a genuine affection that they had for him. They trusted him. That is an essential element, but it does not describe the relationship, it is just a component of it. He made you feel happy. If you did not work for him he made you happy. If you worked for him he could make you very frustrated. I could not keep up with Tracker. It was impossible to get all the things done that he wanted done. As much as I would have loved to I just couldn't. He was a hard man to work for because he put too much on your plate all the time.

Arise Ye Aborigine, I Recognise Thee

Sean Bowden

In the late 90s Tracker and I had started to work a bit together, and I had the benefit of knowing him better, and seeing his human side as well, and his humour, and his larrikinism. I always remember the first time I saw this was at the Yeperenye Shopping Centre [in Alice Springs] when I was not even sure that he knew who I was, or where I existed in the world. I was just a young lawyer and he was an important political player and I admired him.

We were coming through Yeperenye, me and my little family, Denise and the two boys, and my young son Conor was famous for doing knee slides on the tiles in the Yeperenye Centre. He would run up to people and his greeting would be to slide into them on his knees. He did one of these knee slides and Tracker was in the vicinity, and he yelled out something about that being a typical Bowden, and control that Bowden child or something like that, he yelled out to Denise. I don't think he had ever met Denise. He yelled out, *Mrs Bowden, control that child.* It was hysterical. And Conor looked up and we said, *That's Tracker Tilmouth, Conor.* He went, *Oh! Tracker Tilmouth.* Tracker said, *Who are you?* He answered his own question and said something to him like, *You're Mike Bowden's grandson.*

And then he just walked off and I did not think at the time, but little incidents like that reminded me, and taught me that Aboriginal people in the Northern Territory see everything, and they see everyone. They put you in your place, in that they understand where you come from, or they want to know where you come from. And then they want to link that somehow. They put you in a spot within their world, which makes it all understandable and comprehensible, and maybe Tracker was doing that, not just to me but to my family. It was my first lesson of how good an observer he was and how subtle his intuition of what was going on around him, and who was who around him.

By that time I had heard some classic Tracker stories and I would come to know that as a young fella he was known as Bruce and people used to use that against him, *There's Brucie Tilmouth*. I always thought it was terrific that the man had been able to be called Bruce, and was now called Tracker. I thought that was awesome. I thought that the name Tracker was appropriate. Later on I learnt that his real name was Leigh, and occasionally when I was angry with him or deadly serious with him, I called him Leigh just to remind him that I knew enough about him as well, and his past, and that he should not try to be too cheeky with me, or take too many liberties.

A bit later on after I'd got to know him better, I was on a plane next to him coming from somewhere, and he talked about how he was leaving the CLC, it was killing him. He got very serious, as Tracker can, deadly serious, and said it would kill him, and he was going to leave and he was going to go up to Darwin and run a prawn farm. He had started doing work at Jabiru [on the campaign to stop the Jabiluka uranium mine], as an advisor to Jacqui Katona and Yvonne Margarula. He wanted to make a new life for himself and that was part of it. You will see that he throws lures out all around him, trying to hook something into the future.

He would ring up, usually before Christmas, and say, *Well! Mrs T and I, we've made the decision, we're going to Burketown*. I think that was one. I said, *Oh! Really, Burketown, Tracker? Yeah! We're going to Burketown. We've got a farm picked out and we're going to farm barramundi* – or a cattle station in the Gulf. That was maybe a few years ago, the last one was Geraldton. They had picked out a block and a farm at Geraldton and they were going. I just took it with a grain of salt.

So I somehow got involved with the Jabiluka issues in late 1998, and this was probably my big break in terms of wanting to be a real lawyer as well. I knew the managing director of the mining company that ran the Ranger uranium mine and owned the Jabiluka deposit, Malcolm Broomhead. One of those classic Australian stories I guess, where I knew him through my family. When I was at university I used to babysit his kids. He came to Alice Springs, and he dropped in to see Mum and Dad, and they said Malcolm is coming over. He was married to a cousin of my mum's. He was talking to Mum and Dad about this terrible predicament he found himself in with the Jabiluka uranium mine, and that he had inherited from Pancontinental issues that they never really understood. They had got things wrong and made some fundamental mistakes in the mid-90s, including legal mistakes, an absolute clanger of a legal mistake. If they hadn't made that mistake they probably would have the Jabiluka deposit now.

The mistake was not to gain Yvonne Margarula's consent to the road. This was before Malcolm's time but the company was so arrogant and so convinced of their control over her and her family – her father – that when they did a deal, it might have been the late 80s or early 90s, to secure Ranger, they forgot the road. They did not do an access agreement for the road. The traditional landowners were advised by Brett Midena, senior lawyer at the Northern Land Council, who was very clever, and it was probably one of Brett's major achievements as a lawyer, that he was able to withstand this very powerful mining company who at the time ruled the Northern Territory, and to quietly go about preserving the rights the traditional owners had as best he could. He preserved this one right that was to give consent to a road between the Ranger deposit and the Jabiluka deposit.

So when it came time to mine the Jabiluka deposit the mining company did not have a road. They had the deposit, they were mining it, they were hitting it, hitting this incline, and they did not have a road. That was what produced the Jabiluka conflict.

Tracker went up there to assist Jacqui but also, in classic Tracker style, to be a double agent, to also be the person to talk to the other side. He was talking to me about it a little bit, because I was working for Charlie Perkins. So Malcolm Broomhead turned up at my parents' house. So somehow, I got over there and spoke to Malcolm. Maybe he called me. And it went from there.

By that time the mining company had pulled the noose so tight they were choking themselves, they were just too brutal, too awful. They caused Yvonne and Jacqui to be incarcerated for trespass on their own land. It was the craziest thing. The mining companies had still not learnt their lesson in those days. They were still pretty awful. Their plan was just to roll right on over her, and encircle her. I said to Malcolm something like, *If I am going to do this, I would love to do it, but I need some help. I need some help from Owen Cole.*

I went to Owen and I said, *Listen! I've got this opportunity of going to do some work for this big mining company on this horribly contentious issue, and I'm sort of exhilarated but terrified, and will you be my partner and we'll do it together? We'll write a report for them. We'll go down and have a look.* Owen said, *Yeah I'll do that.* It was very good of Owen. We were going to get paid for it of course, as part of doing it.

So we got calls from the company and we got engaged and off we went, and Tracker was there. This was my first real, dynamic interaction with Tracker. It was quite awesome actually to watch him in action. Not that he got everyone frightened, but he was using all his contacts, and he had incredible contacts in politics. His political contacts were just incredible. I always felt that Tracker was underused and underestimated.

So we did this brouhaha around Jabiluka and it went on for a couple of years. By the time I was doing this sort of work and hanging out with people like Tracker Tilmouth and the like, the other legal partners I had in Alice Springs did not understand what I was doing. I said, *Look, I will keep what I am doing and give me a year, and I will be on my own.* And that is what we did. I ended up by 2000 as Sean Bowden and Associates, legal consultants, and I moved with my family to Darwin, which was not just where my wife wanted to be because she is a Katherine girl, but it was also where Tracker Tilmouth and his family were now living.

Tracker became one of my most important and valued colleagues, and at Jabiru even though he was working on the other side, we were working for the same thing and we were rebuilding relationships that had been badly damaged. Our task was to get a proper offer on the table. I could spend an hour just talking about the ins and outs of negotiating that deal and the secret meetings, which were false secret meetings, they were not secret at all, they were just these concocted environments that Tracker put together as a way of making the mining company executives sweat, and bringing them out of their comfort zone.

For instance, there was a late-night meeting at the Parap Apartments where, and I am sure he walked us all in and around the front part just to disorientate us, as if it was a game which it was, where we met with Jacqui and others, and talked through things. It was a good meeting, and he was actually able to create an environment where people could talk to each other for the first time in a decade probably. I was privileged to watch that, to see how he did it and it gave me that access to him, so that I learnt how mining companies thought, and how he thought. And we created the deal which he in his own inimical way called the WGO, the World's Greatest Offer, and it was. It was a great offer. In the years that followed uranium prices went from seven dollars a pound to something like a hundred dollars a pound, maybe a hundred and thirty dollars even at some point over that period. So it was a great offer.

Yvonne did not accept the offer. A number of things happened. North Ltd, the company that owned Ranger and Jabiluka, was taken over by the great multinational Rio Tinto. Just as we were getting somewhere that stopped everything. And suddenly Tracker was absent, he was forced out or something, and Jacqui disappeared as well. I really do not know why, but there might have been other things going on. All this stuff takes a toll on you. I think Jacqui was exhausted and ill, and I think she thought, *Well! I've done my bit now, I've done my bit.*

Jacqui Katona

I met Tracker in the 1990s. I became aware of him working with the Central Land Council and participating in national meetings where he was talking about strategies and negotiating outcomes in terms of native title and things like that. But the first time I sat down to really talk to him about anything in a professional sense was when I was working for the Stolen Generations in the Northern Territory.

We were preparing the High Court case to challenge constitutional issues relating to the removal of children, and we were doing a lot of organising amongst people who had been removed from their families and who knew quite a few people who had been institutionalised in Alice Springs, or were removed from Alice Springs and institutionalised in the Top End and had returned to Alice Springs. Some of those people were seeking repatriation to country and finding links with their family, and in doing that, they had worked with the Central Land Council.

We wanted to secure the support of the Council in the overall objectives of the Stolen Generations. Tracker was not able to make it to the *Going Home* conference that was held in 1994, so I went down to Alice Springs to talk to him in his capacity as director of the Council.

Tracker was not serious at all at that meeting. He had a cattle prod. I walked into his office and just close to the door on the right hand side, I noticed a cattle prod. He told me to sit in the visitor's chair, Olga Havnen [senior policy officer] and Furbes [Harold Furber, deputy director] were there, and as he came in to sit down at the desk he picked up the cattle prod and just casually turned it on, and we started the meeting. Every so often he would move the cattle prod around as if he was inclined to do some prodding with the electrical sparks, and frankly I was not going to be intimidated so I did not move, and I saw it definitely as a tactic on his part to try and unsettle the discussion.

He was not really sure what I was there to advocate because, himself being a person removed, he was adamant that he supported every other person that was removed to return to their country and things were working well, and almost, *why was this discussion necessary?* He was not aggravated, but he didn't really see the importance of sitting down and talking about things like that. I think the cattle prod was one of his ways of testing what I was on about, and the issue. I found that that was an ongoing theme with Tracker. He would, especially when he met people for the first time, use language or behaviours which were designed to unsettle or embarrass people, and I think that was his way of breaking the ice. That was Tracker's ice-breakers, to embarrass himself and everybody else at the meetings and see how they reacted. He was definitely testing people.

The Central Land Council gave an undertaking to facilitate a group in Alice Springs to move forward with the Stolen Generation stuff, but I knew him personally through Greg Crough [economist] and Christine Christopherson [traditional landowner in Arnhem Land] as well, because he used to work with Greg quite regularly and I would bump into him at their place. But very soon after working with the Stolen Generations I moved back out to my family's country at Jabiru and started working for my family, to prevent the expansion of uranium mining in the area. We already had one operating uranium mine and the company wanted to open up another one. My family was opposed to that so they asked me to come out and help.

We kicked off a campaign that was really about getting traditional owners' rights asserted in the administrative regime with numerous competing Commonwealth and Territory organisations. The situation with [Aboriginal] land ownership in the Northern Territory is that the Northern Land Council will advocate for those who have title to land in the northern part of the Territory, and the Central Land Council will advocate for those who have title to their land in the other parts of the Northern Territory.

They are all governed by the one act and there are precedents about how decisions have been taken with negotiations each Land Council has undertaken, and there are quite differing histories and approaches to how politics will be exercised. We were finding significant difficulty gaining the cooperation of the Northern Land Council, and simply because they operated under the same act, and there are constant threats to the operation of the Aboriginal Land Rights Act, we thought it wise to keep Tracker informed as Central Land Council director, of the likely consequences of the lack of cooperation from the Northern Land Council, because one of the strongest parts of the Land Rights Act, or the most important part, is Section 23 and the consultation process, where the Land Council gains instructions from traditional owners through a proper process of consultation, that then forms consent or opposition to a development going ahead.

The Northern Land Council was refusing to accept the instructions of traditional owners in our case. The Northern Land Council expressed no difficulty with opposing traditional owners, and fortunately Tracker could see that there were problems for the Aboriginal Land Rights Act if the Councils started to sacrifice their constituency.

So it was important to us, and whether the mine would have been uranium or tin or copper really did not matter. The issue for my family was having their say over their land. They were given title to the land, they believed themselves to be primary owners, and they wanted to manage and control the activity on their land. Having Tracker's insights into the broader political picture was very helpful, because the only other parts of society that were prepared to assist were environmental groups and some social justice groups.

Basically, the environmentalists had a similar objective in terms of them wanting to prevent the pollution or contamination of the environment and of course, we wanted to prevent the contamination of our people. So it was convenient to form an alliance, but the fundamental issue for us was really one about Aboriginal rights.

Tracker's advice became quite important in the scheme of things. We could manage a media campaign, lobbying, taking on different organisations and the mining company, advocating internationally through the World Heritage Committee, securing a native title claim and those sorts of things, but we were not really able to work effectively with players in the federal parliament and that really was where Tracker opened the doors.

Which I would not have done. I would have remained a stone-thrower in the wilderness, but being able to explain your position – how you saw it being lived out, and how you saw it benefitting more than just the local Aboriginal people, but the ideas around Aboriginal land ownership – I had no faith that they had the capacity to understand that. Tracker said that national politicians did and I was surprised, but I never would have attempted it without him.

I think there was certainly an approach taken when he was at the CLC to lobby national politicians intensively, and to make them fully aware of the situation of Aboriginal people, and why Aboriginal people sought to control their land and to undertake economic development.

But Tracker would always say you have got to be able to deliver. There has got to be something that you can bring to the table because you cannot have people just feeling sorry for you and expecting that their generosity is going to meet your needs. Which I agreed with. One of the things that he spoke clearly about, especially when it came to Jabiru and the work for our organisation, was the post-mining economy.

This was a very new idea conceptually in the late 1990s, that anybody would think of a post-mining economy. It allowed us to have better engagement with agencies on the ground, and a capacity to make meaningful change where we were. There were lots of barriers to that in terms of the beliefs of the traditional owners because in the area of

Jabiru they had mining royalties and they had invested in local tourism infrastructure where they owned two hotels, and they had been ripped off successively by executive officers that had come in and walked out with their pockets full of money.

They did not trust a business model or a commercial model, so there was a lot of work that needed to be done to build people's trust, that a commercial model could meet their needs. But we had to undertake an investigation of what were the likely other economic drivers in the region, and could we capture those. How do we harness them? How would we enhance them? And have access to a reasonable quality of life beyond mining, rather than the only alternative being mining income?

And that was revolutionary at the time. I mean nobody was talking about that type of development, that type of analysis of land tenure and looking at what facilities needed to be improved. Tracker was able to attract resources so that we could undertake a scoping in terms of how the [mining] township of Jabiru could be redeveloped. What stock would be too old because the township had been in place since the 1980s? It was just about going on twenty years. You had service blocks but a lot of the housing stock was quite dilapidated because they did not spend a lot of money building houses for miners. We needed to look at what was possible in terms of creating tourism hubs within Kakadu National Park, and the potential for trading tourists between those hubs as economic units. We would not have got advice like that anywhere, but Tracker's ability to harness the resources that exist, and to have a creative look at how economic development can take place was a real advantage for us.

There was a lot of pressure brought to bear on traditional owners about how too much change was not in anybody's interest. I think they felt that they were being left behind a bit and there was a lot of conservative resistance. That came from people who have had an interest in mining being the successful, the only economic driver in the area. Those people were in the Northern Territory government, and they were part of the mining companies, people who wanted the status quo maintained.

I think entrepreneurs, venture capitalists, people who want to see new ways of doing things will work towards or will articulate ideas, and people might be quite comfortable with it in non-Aboriginal scenarios, but as soon as it has an application in an Aboriginal community, there are unrealistic views or fears about the impact on Aboriginal people. So in a way, once you put an idea that moves towards some kind of progress, people see that or will characterise it as being something that is inherently or of itself, negative to Aboriginal people. When in a lot of ways, it liberates Aboriginal people.

It initially started because of the financial money trail, where it was in the Northern Territory government's interest to keep mining happening in the Northern Territory, but it was also in the interest of the Northern Land Council to secure mining because they receive partial income from it. In fact, with every [mining] agreement in the Northern Territory, only one third of the funds is received by the local Aboriginal people who have agreed to the mining going ahead. The other two thirds of the money is distributed between other communities and the operating land councils. So revenue raising is a real issue for the administrative infrastructure, and they do not want to think of any alternatives, or think how development has to adapt to new economic circumstances. They are quite happy to keep the same old, same old going. And they certainly cannot conceptualise Aboriginal people as economic leaders. In fact, it appears that they will do everything that they can to make sure it does not happen.

It would have been made easier if the Northern Territory and the Commonwealth came to the table. That was why we put the native title claim over Jabiru, so that we would have an opportunity to engage with the Commonwealth, engage with the Northern Territory Government, and through the processes of mediation at least get a clear picture as to how traditional owners saw this moving ahead, and how the Commonwealth and the NT Government were to be partners in this move. The Commonwealth Government flatly refused on the basis that they would only contemplate Jabiru being returned to traditional owners if traditional owners agreed to the Jabiluka [uranium mine] going ahead. That was just their position. Totally.

This was the Howard Liberal government. And that position did not change under Labor in the Territory. So the deal was ultimately done with the Northern Territory Government and it really revolved around not very significant outcomes in terms of housing blocks and things like that, but there was an opportunity there to really rethink what were the outcomes of mining for Aboriginal communities.

At the time, the Ranger uranium mine had already been imposed on Aboriginal people. There was also a national park, there were promises about protections from contamination, there was the township, the urban development, the range of services available to miners. Managing all those interests was seen to be the high watermark of Aboriginal agreements really. And after twenty years we had a chance through a social impact study to look at how those impacts had been delivered. It was very clear that we were living out the negative impacts, now how could this be addressed? The Commonwealth Government's view was with another mine. The mining company's view was with another mine. Any other alternatives, to analyse the economy, to find other economic drivers to build on those, was rejected outright. The best we could do was to protect the sacred site underneath the mine and the mining company eventually agreed to a moratorium. But that has not meant that the alternative economy could move forward, and it hasn't.

Tracker worked a lot with analogies and what I have noticed was that people would be a bit cold to ideas, especially if they could not understand them, and he would just beat down people's defences through humour, and through his unsettling behaviour, so that people would just about be prepared to listen to anything else except him carrying on the way that he did. And they did become quite receptive to a different way of looking at things. Tracker brought about a paradigm shift in the people that he was talking about, so that they would become receptive to ideas. He did not just lay the idea out and expect that people were going to consume it, understand it, and then be able to articulate it as well. He knew it takes quite a while for people to understand all the adjacent issues to a particular concept.

He characterised most of the non-Aboriginal economic development as paddocks in Kakadu, of cattle being moved from one paddock to another. He broke it down to peoples' everyday understanding, which gave them more confidence to see themselves in the picture.

Another strategy that Tracker used in his work, because the relationship between our organisation and the Land Council became so broken down, was that his view wasn't, *Oh! Well, that's just too bad and you'll just have to work with the statutory authority that you've got.* His view was that the organisation was capable of administering its responsibilities under the Aboriginal Land Rights Act, which again I would not have even thought was possible, and of going to the federal government, to attract some funding from ATSIC so that we could formally and officially administer our rights under the Aboriginal Land Rights Act. Now that really is an act of independence for Aboriginal organisations not to be under the thumb of government departments, but to be part of the implementation of the statute themselves and to meet the responsibilities that they interpret as part of managing their own land. So there were strategies of political independence that Tracker would take up, and I think that was fundamentally at the heart of his reason for being, if you like.

I think overall what he was about was not having to be reliant on a public servant to determine what you are going to achieve, how you are going to achieve it and when it is right to stop achieving. Tracker certainly demonstrated the ambition for that kind of independence in many, many ways, and usually in everything he had his hand in.

Danny Schwartz

I met Tracker during the time that he was working with Jacqui Katona on Jabiluka. I met Jacqui in Melbourne when we brought her down for an artists' symposium where Indigenous issues were the highlight. Following that, and her meeting with me, she realised that I was a property developer, and she and Tracks came down and we met at the Pratt Foundation's offices and Tracks put to me something that I will never forget. Tracks said, *Danny, we want to do the opposite of what's happening up in the Territory now.* I said, *What's that?* He said, *Well! Today we compound the Aboriginals and let the tourists run free, we want to compound the tourists and let the Aboriginals run free.* So I said to him that was a fantastic concept, and he explained to me what was happening up there and that the plan was to take over Jabiru which is the mining township and create that into a central hub for tourism for the Kakadu area and have the tourists fly in, fly out of there, and take over the town from the mining company Rio Tinto, and manage the town and create a tourist precinct.

We were going to negotiate with Rio who had mentioned that they were interested in selling the land, in divesting the land, and we were going to negotiate with hotels and with tourist operators to take over the town and to make it into one big tourist centre. And to compound tourists is a well-known concept around the world. You put them in big hotels and then you put them in buses and you take them around. The problem was, and the problem still is, that people hop in their cars or caravans and drive around and there is no restriction on where they go.

The whole of Kakadu is open to the public so people come along during ceremonies, they come into townships and they just drive through willy-nilly, and there is no control. And even though there is a gate to get into Kakadu anyone can get in, it is controlled by whitefellas, there is no control over where anyone goes. Whilst we were working on this, there were some great little projects that we carried out. One of the examples was an Aboriginal guy who wanted a fishing licence, and out of all the fishing licences in the area, and I think there were seventeen for the Alligator rivers, all seventeen fishing licences were owned by whitefellas. And we had a blackfella who came to us and said that he had an opportunity, because he had been working with the whitefellas, and they were not catching any fish because they did not know where the fish were.

It had been pot luck as the fish stocks were drying out. They did not know where to go, whereas all the Aboriginal people knew where to go. So one of the guys came up to us and he said, *Listen, I've been working with this guy for years and he's getting old and he's willing to sub-licence me the licence.* And so we financed him to sub-licence that licence and to buy his own boats. He has made a fortune. He has done very, very well. That was one of the first things I did with Tracker. And he was a great young man with a lot of vision and he ended up buying a few boats and although I have not spoken to him for ten to fifteen years, I am sure he is doing well.

It just showed to me how in control all the whitefellas were. So we set out to begin the process of trying to take over Jabiru and I got some architects to work with us. We went up north a whole lot of times and visited Jacqui and Tracker up there, and what Jacqui and Tracker had decided to do first was that we would have to get approval from the Northern Land Council to go ahead, and for that we needed the approval of all the traditional owners in the communities in Kakadu.

What we in fact wanted to do was to close off Kakadu like Arnhem Land, and create a scenario where you could not just drive through willy-nilly, where you had to be controlled where you go, where you travelled, what you saw, the times you went there. We embarked on an exercise to inform the rest of the community what we intended on doing. It was fascinating because between the architects, Tracker and Jacqui, to demonstrate what they actually planned to do, the architects created a sand box which was empty when they would arrive on site in the communities, and they would put some sand from that land inside this big sand box.

The sand box was about a metre by a metre, and with their hands they first drew in the sand the plan of Kakadu. And with the sand, they formed the mountains, the river lines, then they formed what they were intending to do with their hands in the sand to show the communities, and before you knew it you had the whole community sitting around them as they were doing this in the sand box. It was very interactive and it was wonderful.

Jacqui had this incredible system of taking out babushkas, those Russian dolls, where one sits in the next, which sits in the next, and she described to the people the way the government works through these babushkas. The biggest babushka was the Queen. When she opened that babushka, the next babushka had glasses drawn on it and it was John Howard. And then the little babushkas became the people. She showed the communities how they had to deal with the government through these babushkas. We spent hours out there and we really created an impact and explained to them what the desire and the plan was, and the plan was essentially to create Jabiru as the central tourist hub for the Northern Territory. Even more so than Darwin, to try and get people to fly straight into Jabiru, when people were going to Darwin and were driving out.

Why not fly straight into the heartland and become an Aboriginal centre for tourism? From there be driven to Arnhem Land, and from there we would take them down to Katherine and all the Gorge, and from there down to Alice Springs. You could really create an incredible hub. And we were getting closer and I remember Jacqui and Tracker telling me, *You have got to come up and you have got to meet the Northern Land Council*, because we were getting a lot of support from all the communities.

I had not met the people from the Land Council before and I was expecting to go up there and be surrounded with a table of blackfellas. You know, this is the Land Council. And my shock in going up there and in my excitement to meet everybody – I had to meet all the traditional owners, I sat around this table and there was not one blackfella around the entire table. Norman Fry was the head [of the Northern Land Council], and he was like this head on a stick. He was like this one single blackfella who was working in the whole place at the time and everyone else were white women, mostly from Melbourne, mostly do-gooders from Melbourne and gatekeepers as Tracker called them. Missionaries and gatekeepers and do-gooders and people for whom it was much easier to say no than to say yes, because if you say yes you have got to do something. If you say no, nothing can happen.

So they actually said yes to a study that was put together by Access Economics, again another whitefella crew who had no real understanding of what we wanted to do, and a hundred and twenty thousand dollars later, the Northern Land Council commissioned [Deloitte] Access Economics to do this report.

One hundred and twenty thousand dollars later their report indicated there was absolutely no viability in what we were proposing whatsoever. Well! We had had reports upon reports, cash flows, designs, diagrams, interest from tourism parties from around the globe, not just from Australia, and Access Economics came back and said, *Not viable*. And because they said it was not viable, the whole thing fell apart.

In fact it was quite dramatic in many ways. For Jacqui, it created a friction for her in the Mirarr community because she had to do so much travelling during that time, she had already won the moratorium, she had won the timeframe, to do this sort of project. You know she had been overseas, she had won the moratorium, there was going to be ten years of moratorium with no discussion on the mining in Jabiru, and so she went out and she said, *Okay, now it's time to do this sort of work,* which was to work with us to try and create Jabiru into a very special centre for tourism.

Economic development and economic empowerment and all of that, to be in charge, to be on the gates, to be the gatekeeper at the doors of Kakadu, to create an environment within Kakadu that was controlled by the Indigenous communities. And of course Access Economics said, *Unviable, can't be done.* The whole thing fell apart, and as I was saying for Jacqui, she had to go out and spend a lot of time with us travelling around, meeting the people, she came to Melbourne often because the architects had done a tremendous amount of work in trying to remodel the town, and also doing the financial modelling which was really intense, of taking this mining township, taking it over, making sure that it was stable and that it would also grow.

So it was difficult for Jacqui because that was time away, and it created a bit of separation between her and the Mirarr. The Mirarr felt as though she was not there, and because we did not get this through the Northern Land Council, they thought it was all for nothing and it was very disappointing. I spent three of four years doing that project with Jacqui and Tracker and became very close to them of course, and I still count them as closest friends. But that was a time when I got to understand the real lay of the land, the difficulties, the difficulties of empowering the people from a zero base, and letting them understand what the potential was. But once they understood the potential, it was then trying to get it through the gatekeepers, the white gatekeepers in the Councils. It was a real eye-opener for me, but for Tracker and Jacqui it was just par of the course, this was what they were used to.

We took it up with the Northern Land Council but there were very stubborn people in there who felt as though they knew best for the communities, and what was best for the communities was to listen to Access Economics. Norman Fry understood, but he was almost like a figurehead, and he was outvoted. The first time I sat in Norman Fry's office with Tracker, Norman Fry drew a line across Australia with his finger, halfway through, let's say from Townsville on the east, all the way horizontally across to the west, and he said everything above here should be controlled by the Aboriginals. That was what he said, *Everything above this line we should control and we should manage.* But impossible to get through the bureaucracy, and through the people who thought they knew best.

Access Economics did quite an extensive report, although for a hundred and twenty thousand dollars, which I knew they had been paid for it, it was not as extensive as I thought it should have been. But their report was damning, it was damning of what we were asking for, what we were seeking, and it was just illogical because no one had the skills to be able to do what we were saying needed to be done. And of course they were not talking about up-skilling, they did not talk about education, they did not talk about the potential, they just talked about the actual position at that time, at that particular time and to say that it was not viable. It was difficult.

I have also got to say that coinciding with the Access Economics report we actually went back to Rio Tinto. Access Economics did speak to Rio Tinto, and Rio Tinto were smarting from the court-case loss they had from when Jacqui took it overseas, and it is interesting, we felt as though we were very close in negotiating with them to be able to get the township of Jabiru.

As it turned out they came back and said *you give us mining in Jabiluka and we will give you the town.* Of course we had to say no. It came to that. That was the point it came to. But when you hear Marcia Langton getting up and talking about how the mining companies have had to change their tune over the last ten or fifteen years, I do believe that we were instrumental in making them change their tune. When Jacqui started negotiating with them, the moratorium was what made them realise that they could not just do as they liked on Aboriginal land. They needed to negotiate. They needed to understand how to get them on side. Now I am not going to go into the politics of what Marcia was talking about and whether it is right or wrong, but I do know that some of the people who Marcia considers to be her close friends, who work in Rio, were just coming on stream as this was happening, as we were talking about Jabiru. And there is still potential for this to happen today. But again, the people who run the Mirarr, the whitefellas running the Mirarr today, are not big thinkers, they cannot see, they did not have the vision that Tracker had, and that Jacqui has.

That is the problem. Through that relationship that was created between Tracker, Jacqui and I, to redevelop the township of Jabiru, a lot of good has happened, and a lot of projects were initiated, and the relationship is constantly growing. So that was a fine beginning. We felt very demoralised by it coming to naught, but we have felt demoralised by a lot of other things that came to naught during the times that we have known each other too. We have started a lot of projects, not many of them have come to fruition, and you get tarnished by the constant loss, by the loss of success.

Lloyd Bray

In his position as director for Land Council, I am sure Tracker played a big role in Aboriginal affairs. But he had elder blokes, like Charlie Perkins, who was Tracker's uncle, who he would listen to, and older old blokes within the Aboriginal Affairs Department and the National Aboriginal Conference. He would go to Canberra and all over the place to a lot of their meetings, take it all in, he certainly learnt, and he liked learning. That gave him a lot of confidence, so when he became director he knew how to handle the job. He would say things and he would back it up. He was, like I said before, determined.

He told me when they went over to Israel, and they looked at how people lived and how they started the kibbutz, he was amazed at what they had done to all that desert country. He came back and said, *Brother, geez, you look at Israel compared to Central Australia, and it's a lot of desert.* He said, *You know what they did? They turned that into farm land.* I think he had aspirations about doing the same thing here in Central Australia.

Tracker was the bloke who looked into the future, and he tried to do things. He did a lot of good things but then he was blocked. He had that vision for the future. A lot of his people did not like his views – of looking ahead, but I think Tracker was a really good inspiration to a lot of these people, even though he had knockers, there were a lot of people that said he made a lot of changes to the Land Council when he was there.

He knew all about the culture and aspects that go with it. He was told a lot of that by the old blokes. He even said to me that our culture is not as it should be, like years ago, it was very, very strong, and people lived by the law, lived by the culture. But we were told to keep that to ourselves. Tracker had that same upbringing, but I think his goal was get things moving from the time he was there at Land Council and having a vision for the future.

He had the broader vision, from the old ways to the new ways, and he might have been a referee between the past and the present. He knew that he had to protect and look after the old ways to the present day, but he had queries about what was going to happen in the future with the culture. Is it going to be stronger? Is it going to be faded out? He always said that. The culture is getting complicated in some ways, and weak in other areas. Those old blokes he learnt from were big visionaries, and big thinkers too.

Even when we came back from Darwin, we could see the changes. Before I left here when I was a teenager, before I went up to Darwin, I could remember all these old people, they worked for their living on the station and they would come in once every month or so to buy a bit of rations and a bit of clothes, and they would be gone back out bush within a couple of days or so. This would be right up to when Tracker came back to Alice Springs, there were a lot of people still working out bush, and then over the years we have seen a massive change, and we spoke about it a lot of times. We have seen all these young people, where you drive past the Riverside [Hotel] today in Alice Springs and you would just look at it. We were fighting, or being sceptics, about where our culture is going to go, what is going to happen to it. That is the talk even today with most of the old people.

Now we are in our sixties, we can see the change. We can feel the change and it is on the streets every day. So I think when Tracker was looking towards the future, he was seeing what was happening and what was going to happen. I think he might have had some scary [vision], and could foresee something that was going to do harm to Aboriginal people, I do not know. You might have to ask him that.

John Liddle

We talked about catching camels and sending them to the bloody Middle East and how we were going to do it. We did fantastic submissions – but they never went anywhere. We had all these great ideas. We sat up all night doing the figures, and doing the proposals. But then, another idea came along, and we forgot about the one we had been working on and started on the next one, and the next one, and the next one. We have had lots of good ideas, but not many of them worked out. Tracker would always come up to me and say, *You should do this*, and I said, *Yeah! I should, but I can't do it. I've got bills to pay.* So I am very proud that he did something with his life after he left the Land Council. He had all those schemes and I was amazed by the people that he knew.

Bloody Danny Schwartz, he sent him to see me. He said, *I'm sending this Jewish bloke up to see you.* I said, *Who?* He said, *Talk to him about anything.* And Danny Schwartz said, *Oh! Tracker sent me in.* I thought, *Oh! Well! He said talk to him about getting him to build you a new clinic.* So I did. And we are about to restart talking with him. This was about five or ten years ago, something like that. He knew so many people from the bottom of the floor right to the top, he knew them. He had that effect on people.

He was an ideas man, which was what I liked about him. When he was at the Land Council and I was working in Congress we used to bounce good ideas, to try and make things happen in town and some of them worked, some didn't. People are a bit more reserved and constrained nowadays, but he would always find ways to annoy people. I do not think that he meant to annoy them but he did especially when we were young blokes, where you would go out somewhere and he would want to start a fight with the biggest bloke in the bar. We were not there to fight, we were there to chase women, but he wanted to pick on somebody, or go and spill beer on someone or something like that, so before long you were getting in trouble with people. But he always wanted to have the best car, and none of us had any money to buy good cars, we had to make our cars out of junk.

He ended up having some pretty fancy cars, hotted up ones that would fly past us as we rattled along in an old ute. He would shoot past in a hotted-up Torana, with a stupid look on his face and not even looking where he was driving. He would look at you and the road was that way, and he would say, *Come for a ride bruz.* I said, *I don't really want to go for a ride with you,* because he was a terrible driver, he scared the shit out of people because he never looked at the road. He was talking all the time. He was looking at the passenger. So he would have these cars, but he used to get the cars so he could get the pretty girls. The rest of us used to have to walk or bludge a ride off somebody else and we would say, *Give us a ride.* He would say, *Ah! Ah! No, I'm busy, busy, Mmm! Mmm! I have got no fuel,* all this sort of stuff. He had every angle covered. But at the same time we would share everything, cars, money, tucker. That was just the way things were done here. We did not have much and we would help each other.

I remember the time when he got hurt playing football. He got a knock on his head, and he nearly died. He had a blood clot. So they put him in hospital. I was somewhere else and when I came back they said, *Oh! That mad bloke's in hospital.* I said, *What's wrong?* I went up to see him and he was lying there, and they had drilled a hole in his head to release the pressure. I said, *What the hell are you doing in here?* So he said, *I've got to stop here for a few days. I hit my head.* Someone ran into him, hip and shouldered him see, and burst a blood vessel. He nearly died on the football field.

They thought he was dead I think. Anyway they put him in the hospital. So a few days later I said, *Look! You can't get better in the hospital, come on, I'll take you out.* So he escaped from hospital and I took him. We had some old motorbikes at our place and I said, *Come on let's go ride motorbikes.* He had a bandage that thick around his head. He had just had the hole drilled in his head. So here we were roaring around without any helmets on. But he told everyone, *That was my rehab. Liddle put me in rehab,* he said. But I did not realise how serious it was. They actually drilled into his head to take some pressure off. Well! I did not know, we were young. But I just said, *It's not worth laying there in hospital, you're not going to get better there.* I think some of his family found out he was hurt and they came around and tried to get him to go back to hospital. But he refused, he was having too much fun. This could explain why he is a little bit mad.

Murrandoo Yanner

I followed Tracker all around I suppose since 1994, followed him all around Australia. He continued to come out here [Gulf of Carpentaria], but anything we could do on our own we have done out here. We always have. Whenever we hit a rough or tough spot, or we were having trouble, he was the bloke you called and the thing is, he always delivered one hundred per cent. We have never ever had to really go to a backup to this day, even though he was crook at times, and needing medical attention, but I think it was a mutual thing.

I think he still saw a bit of the old struggle here, you know, *comrades*, and people fighting for the real thing and for each other, for the good fight for the good cause, so he went that extra mile for us. I think particularly while he was crook people really appreciated him more than ever, knowing the lengths he went to help us and *who in the hell are us mob?* He had a million mobs he helped around the country, but his own mob probably needed him more than we did at times, Central Australians, but obviously they have got a strong crew of people with Rossy, Furber, Colesy. They are all clever and strong blokes so he had a real team running stuff there.

He was able to free himself up and get over and help us and I think it was mutually beneficial. I think here he had a mob that did not question him, that trusted him integrally and went along with his advice. Maybe even at home sometimes they might question and branch off at things, but here he was a phenomenon in his own right, and over twenty-two years he had more than earned the respect and credibility for us to sit in awe and listen, and take in the fact. It was not that we were mesmerised and there was no magic trick, but the fact is that when we took his advice and followed it to the letter we would always win.

When we were having a big Waanyi meeting at Adels Grove, in the Boodjamulla [Lawn Hills], half of them were talking staunch, *Rah! Rah! Rah! When whitefella comes over we will says it's our land and you can't do things et cetera.* Tracker said, *Listen you mob, you know what the word sovereignty means?* They said, *It means land rights and we own the place yeah, yeah, yeah. Really?* he said. *Sovereignty is what you're sort of talking about, what we had before whitefellas come, the boss of everything, no taxes, no police, you run everything.* He said, *You mob are sort of talking this but you know your problem? If you think you've got sovereignty then don't talk about it, act like it.* And that stuck with them. It had an impact on many of them and fired them up on the day, but it certainly stuck with me to this day and I think it always will. Even though I thought I was hardcore and staunch then, it took me up to a whole new level. *Oh! You can be arrested if you go on Ascot {cattle station}. Trespass or not, stuff it we're going. They can arrest us under some false, illegal, occupiers' law, that's our land and what do we do? Are we going to talk about it over here in a coffee room forever, or are we going to act like it's our land.* And I certainly try to live by that philosophy, but that was the first time I really heard it.

He said, *What are you waiting for? Are you going to kneel down and have the white man tap you on the shoulder with a sword and say, Arise ye Aborigine, I now recognise thee?* That was exactly what he said. And that has also stuck with me. Even though I strongly respect David Trigger and Ricky Martin and those [anthropologists working in the Gulf of Carpentaria} and the industry in general, and they have allowed me to be equal or supervisory to any of them in my role, that thing of what Tracker said has always allowed me the strength to not have professionals try to lead me around by the nose or tell me who I am.

Our elders will tell us that and our families. But yes, *What are you waiting for? You're on your bloody knees wanting some whitefella to tap you on the shoulder and say, Arise ye Aborigine, I recognise thee.*

3.

The Inspirational Thinker

Look! I Don't Like Your Donkey

Michael Mansell

My first memory of meeting Tracker was at a Federation of Land Councils meetings at Basso's Farm, outside Alice Springs way back in the early to mid 1980s. I think Tracker then was from Central Australia in the Northern Territory. The most striking thing about Tracker, apart from his clear green eyes — I thought I was the only Aboriginal with similar blue eyes — was his wit. He had great one-liners, ones that pulled back to a central point the scattery conversations we used to have at the Federation. In the middle of some complicated discussion where the views were as varied as the circumstances of the delegates, Tracker had this ability to make a mockery of some of our pie-in-the-sky views, and kept us level-headed.

From the early days, he came across as being very friendly, very outgoing, a really nice bloke. I had the impression that he had a swathe of knowledge and experience, and was particular about when to use it. He guided the conversation rather than dominated it. He was not a waster of words or time, but contributed intellectually, often through his anecdotes or analogies or one-line jokes. When he put any of us down it was never personal — it was over the views we were expressing. Mostly though, his barbs were reserved for our mortal 'enemy' — the politicians, the miners, the racists. If you wanted a good punchy one-liner for a TV grab, hang around Tracker for five minutes and you'd have it. Looking back on some of the way-out aspirations some of us had in those days, it was fortunate Tracker, with his endless humour and wit, combined with Pat Dodson's leadership in particular, were there to keep us on the straight and narrow.

Tracker obviously had some good grounding in strategies and politics. I don't know whether his background was with the unions or the ALP, or both. But shortly before he died he helped engage Tasmanian Aboriginals with the Tasmanian forestry industry to strike a deal over use of forests. As it turned out, the Tasmanian Greens – not Bob Brown or Peg Putt – killed the prospect.

In those several talks I had with him over forestry – always driven by his experience and knowledge – he would condemn to merry hell the ALP and warn us about what we should get out of any forest deal. It was apparent early that he definitely wasn't trying to whack something over us on behalf of his contacts. Whatever his organisational background and training, he was loyal to Aboriginals first, and enjoyed the thrill of acting as a conduit between us and his many contacts with friends in unions, industry and politics – always with an intention to help his people. He was obviously not compromised in any way with his support from unions and political parties. He once said the Labor Party wanted pet niggers. He was a one-eyed blackfella. A quality one at that, if ever I did see one.

I ran into him during the native title talks with Keating. I soon realised Tracker could condense a whole lot of information much quicker than the rest of us, to summarise it and often put it in a funny form. He did not put himself forward on complex legal issues, instead taking it all in, biding his time for some punchy line that better explained what we lawyers had taken hours to outline. Everybody knows that humour among blackfellas, whether it is in politics or not, goes a long way. We can laugh at ourselves, although we get testy at others making fun of us. Tracker was the one who could pull out blackfella jokes in the midst of a complicated discussion to ease tension. He was very good at that. He often did it in the post-Mabo negotiations.

When we were talking about the forestry dispute down here in Tasmania, he was putting pressure on unions and industry to open talks with us. Ken Jeffrey and Bob Gordon, both of Forestry Tasmania, made contact with me. Later we had informal discussions with industry leaders. There was a real prospect of Aboriginal people getting a source of revenue independent of government from the forest industry. We were expected to endorse the forest products in return, and no doubt an Indigenous endorsement would help Tasmanian forest operators with certification and compliance requirements. We Aboriginal leaders were cautious – would we take money from industry that was destroying forests that held the stories of our past and hope for our future?

Course not, Tracker said, *but if its gunna happen anyway, your people should get something out of it.* We called a state-wide Aboriginal community meeting in Launceston that was well attended by about a hundred people. I told them we could earn up to twelve million per annum from the Commonwealth and industry combined where there was agreement between the environmental movement, industry, Forestry Tasmania and state and Commonwealth governments for logging to occur. The meeting accepted that whichever areas would be logged would not be decisions we Aboriginals could influence. We had no say in that. Approved logging would be decided by government, industry and the environment movement.

Throughout our talks with Forestry Tasmania and the timber industry, we informed the Tasmanian Wilderness Society of our discussions – though not the private details that industry and government expected to be kept private. Despite Bob Brown seeing the Aboriginal predicament of being landless, financially distraught and powerless and therefore needing to make some sort of deal, the Wilderness Society, as it has resisted for more than thirty years, refused to give unqualified support to Aboriginal land rights. Tracker was right – why throw your hat in with people who use you?

We met with Premier Lara Giddings and Deputy Premier Bryan Green in Hobart. Industry and Forestry Tasmania came along but they agreed this was the Aboriginal community's call. Bryan Green was enthusiastic about the potential but not Lara Giddings. At the time, the ALP was in minority government, with the Greens' Nick McKim and Cassy O'Connor holding down two ministries in the Labor–Greens government. It looked like the ALP would not support the initiative to appease the Greens, even though Premier Giddings sacked the two Greens ministers in the lead-up to the 2014 state election.

After the talks with the Premier, the Tasmanian Greens came out with all guns firing, denouncing any deal with Aboriginals, calling us naïve. In the end, industry walked away, the environmentalists agreed to logging, and the ALP backed the agreement. Aboriginals got nothing. The warnings Tracker had given over the phone had rung true.

During the Tasmanian forest talks, Tracker was not just a brother and ally, he was a source of inspiration. I was talking to him one day and he was giving me all these lines and strategies, and he would come up with these great little captions and I would think, *Geez, why didn't I think of that?* I remember once he said, *And of course brother, those trees are ours, we nurtured them, we burnt all the forest that allowed those trees to become forests.* So true, so every time we argued with the Premier and everybody else, bang, I am up with this Tracker revelation. I never mentioned Tracker of course, I claimed it as an idea of my own.

The development of the native title legislation is all a bit of a blur. There were that many meetings to do with the development of the legislation, but I do remember him being at a meeting in the ATSIC boardroom at Woden Plaza, Canberra. It must have been before the so-called A Team of Aboriginal negotiators went to talk to Paul Keating. It was at one of those meetings that, in the midst of a discussion of the economic benefits of native title, Tracker made this declaration that just stunned me – that he was the only Aboriginal economist in the room! Aboriginal lawyers by this time were a dime a dozen. The room was full of us. I had not seen many Aboriginal doctors, and never an Aboriginal economist. I had never heard of there being such a beast. And in the middle of something we were talking about, the financial implications of clause 398 subsection (b) 4 or something, he came out and says, *Well! Here's the costing. And you ought to listen to me. I'm the only Aboriginal economist here.* We all looked at him and I did not know whether the man was bullshitting or telling the truth, but we all accepted his version of events. So that went in with the legislation.

He used to say, *Native title is not the black stallion that everyone thinks it's going to be, it's just a mule.* That was how he puts things. He did not say, *Oh! This is a bloody terrible piece of legislation*, he would put it in a different form. He always had reservations about it and I think he had a bit of Paul Keating in him, in the sense Keating had such a handle on complex matters from which he extracted simple points. Tracker was like that.

In relation to the Mabo High Court decision, Aboriginal Australia had to have a response. We met at Eva Valley in the Northern Territory on the 5th of August, 1993. A delegation was chosen to pass on to the

Keating government the principles the four hundred-plus gathering had come up with. I was one of the delegates.

The national committee meeting said *here is our delegation*, and I was one of those that were chosen. Keating had no choice but to meet that delegation. I was acutely aware of the hostility the Labor government had towards me personally because I had visited Libya in 1987 at the time the Americans were bombing Libya, and in response to accusations I was taking money from terrorists I said, *We take money from the Hawke government which keeps terrorising Aboriginal people, so what's the difference?* What made my relationship with the ALP even worse was that in July 1990, at a Federation of Land Councils meeting at Ja Ja in the Territory, a number of us established the Aboriginal Provisional Government. I was declared *persona non grata* by the Hawke and Keating governments.

At our first meeting post-Mabo with Keating, all the media were there. Keating was shaking our hands, and when he came to me I got the limpest handshake one could ever get, but the cameras started clicking just before he got to me with his limp and frosty gesture and clicked all the way through it. There was Keating caught in the act of welcoming me! I can't recall what Tracker said about it all but I remember it being funny. The next day the media were portraying the handshake as *Mansell has come in from the cold*. I thought it was all exaggerated.

But during all those times when I was talking to Keating, though as far as I know he is not a lawyer, he was able to pull together the meaning and effect of whole portions of the then native title draft bill and say how it was going to affect all these different…*Friggin oath, hasn't this bloke got a handle on it*. When you talked to Tracker at those meetings that was what he did, he was very much like Keating. He could pull something together and tell all the rest of us with our heads down and bums up that we did not really know what we were doing. He could guide you, he would say, *Look here, we will do this*. Very clever at that.

He had a broad perspective. He could see the implications and consequences of any administrative or political action. He was a real political analyst. He was able to pull the whole thing together and tell you what it means. Very undervalued. One of the funny things about Tracker was that he was always there, someone you really wanted to sit down with and hear the views of, but when it comes to examples of what he actually said or did you cannot think of them. You just valued the man's presence. I remember funny stories about [Aboriginal political leaders] Rob Riley, Geoff Clark, and Bob Weatherall because we were together a lot more, but they were more to do with mucking around being idiots. Whereas with Tracker, it was all to do with the purpose for which you were there, and I always wanted to make sure when he was around that I was on the money. I would sometimes throw things into a national discussion to see which way the political winds were blowing, then watch key players like Tracker to see the reaction, because if he did not agree there was something wrong with it.

Noel Pearson was emerging at the time as an obvious man of great talent. Marcia Langton was also there but she impressed me more as a Noel disciple. Rossy [David Ross] was an important player along with the Dodson brothers, and Tracker. ATSIC, the legislated chief advisors to the federal government, had been caught with its pants down on native title and were playing catch-up, especially on detail and implications. Some of the stuff coming out of Western Australia at the time on native title was worrying because they were being advised by Richard Bartlett from Canada or America or somewhere, and I knew it was very conservative advice they were getting.

I had been part of the inner group finding our way through the labyrinth of native title and conservative political pressures on the Keating government. The group consisted of ATSIC, the two land councils in the Northern Territory, the Cape York, Kimberly and NSW land councils, the Victorian Aboriginal Legal Service, South Australian Legal Rights Movement and Tasmanian Aboriginal Centre. Due to developments, I was soon to part company with the group.

The sticking point at the time was validation of invalid grants. States had alienated native title lands since 1975 without due process and compensation for the loss to Aboriginal native title holders. When this was done to white landowners, the states gave them due process and compensation. The High Court ruled in Mabo that, due to the coming in to law of the 1975 Racial Discrimination Act, native title holders were to be treated the same as other landowners on a non-discriminatory basis. Keating wanted to appease the states with validation of these invalid grants.

The trouble for the Aboriginal group was in maintaining faith with the principles that came out of Eva Valley. The meeting of over four hundred had laid down binding principles which included that native title cannot be extinguished by grants of any interest. This clearly was opposite to Keating's validation plan. The national gathering also stated that *no grant of any interest on Aboriginal and Torres Strait Islander Titles can be made without the informed consent of all relevant title holders.* Neither Tracker nor I agreed to abandon the position stated at Eva Valley. We believed the compromise was to leave it to the states to negotiate an arrangement with each invalid grant and the native title holders.

Lois O'Donoghue, the head of ATSIC and widely acknowledged as a reputable Aboriginal leader, had joined in the chorus of Aboriginal criticism of Keating's leaning toward the states on native title legislation. We knew the states wanted to extinguish native title. Reflecting our collective thinking, Lois had publicly criticised Keating, accusing him of betraying us.

Keating was ropeable. In a stroke of genius, he saw a weakness in the Aboriginal group which he exploited to perfection. He declared, *I am not sure whether Indigenous leaders can ever psychologically make the change to decide to come into a process, to be part of it and take the burden of responsibility which goes with it. That is,* Keating finished, *whether they could ever summon the authority of their own community to negotiate for and on their own behalf.* At the ATSIC Tower in Woden, we had to decide whether to hold to the Eva Valley principles, for we had a meeting with him that afternoon. I strongly opposed abandonment. Marcia Langton was chief protagonist, yelling, *Keating says we don't know how to negotiate. We have to show him we can.* It was reminiscent of children having to perform for adults. I burst out laughing thinking it was a joke, but they looked at me like I was mad as if to say, *No, no, we've got to show him, we've got to prove to him we can.* And I thought, *this does not look good.* I pointed out that *we don't negotiate, we just lobby. We must not go cap in hand begging this white man not to do us over.* Anyway, the only reason they wanted me there was to keep the radical blacks on side. It was one thing for the Commonwealth to validate invalid grants by suspending the operation of the Racial Discrimination Act, it was quite another that we agree to it. I could not go that far.

When the group went off to the Keating meeting, I was not among them.

The next time I bumped into Marcia Langton she was talking to the West Australian Aboriginal leaders, really putting the heat on them. At one stage, she held up this document written by Henry Reynolds, if I remember correctly, saying, *I've got this document, it says that these rights that Mansell and these other ones are saying we're entitled to don't apply under native title.* And within about thirty seconds of having to go to a meeting with the Prime Minister, everybody said alright, *Okay, we won't run with that then, we've got to go now.* I was never particularly interested in the views of people like her.

With Tracker, when he spoke you knew that it was genuine. There was no effort to try to dud anyone, no ulterior political motive. He was very different from the rest of them and that was where his value was.

Oh! Christ could he ever stop Marcia in her tracks too. He used to rub her the wrong way. He was terrific on that. He would do it in such a mild way. He was not nasty or anything.

Tracker Tilmouth

The agenda [during the negotiations to develop the native title legislation in 1993] was to deliver to the government. It had nothing to do with Aboriginal people and that was day one on native title. What does the government want? Not what do you want, not how do you want it, nothing like that, so Mansell, Clarky [Geoff Clark], and those blokes and me were pushed out the door. Because I said, well actually Owen Cole said this, at the meeting at the Red Centre, *I don't know where everyone is getting off on this, this has got nothing to do with anything legal, this has got to do with economics. This is about access to mining.* This is a commercial, economic discussion.[20]

We were thrown out, him and I, and told to leave, and we were never invited to another meeting. It had nothing to do with what Keating could deliver to you. It was about what you could deliver to

---

20. Referring to the first national Aboriginal leadership meeting on the ramifications of native title, held at the Red Centre Resort in Alice Springs.

of our constituents because we live on the border. A royal commission. And they cannot touch him [Murrandoo Yanner, Gangalidda leader of the Carpentaria Land Council], he is in Queensland. We do not recognise colonial borders anyway, we did not draw the line on a map. That is how it has all got to pan out. People who have got professorships – Oh! God! Fair go. If you want a war, let's have a war.

You have got to fight it properly. You have got to have a legal basis of why you want to go to war, and secondly, you have got to have the financial and economic resources to go to war. You have got to know your quarry. You have got to know how they think, why they think the way they think and then you have got to work out how to get there. You have got to build your generals, and you have got to build your soldiers. We have a few people that look good on TV, make all the nice statements and I say to my daughters time and time again, if you want to drown yourself, go work in a black organisation. You will not even know what time of day it is.

As I said you have got to build your generals, build your soldiers, you have got to build your troops. We have none of that. We have no debate. There is no debate at the Land Council about politics anymore. We have education, training, we have nice glossies, we have…but yeah hang on, who is making the pie? You cannot have a piece of the pie unless someone makes a pie. You can dream about a pie but you are not going to get fat. It has got to be based on reality. No one can have a feed unless someone actually makes it. You can have all the theories you like and jump up and down, you can have fifty per cent royalties, you can have an Indigenous [political] party, do whatever you like, but what are you basing it on? Goodwill? It has got to be really strong economics, and that is what I am saying to everybody, you have got to work out how to build it.

This is why I am so keen on Centrefarm, or not keen on – why I am now concerned about Centrefarm. Do you really have to dabble in the philosophical debates rather than stick to the purely commercial? I can tell you how to fly the plane but I want a plane, not a fucking bit of calico strapped to a bit of mulga. Unless you can provide the economics for it, you are going to struggle.

Murrandoo Yanner

Tracker acted the fool at times and masked his intelligence with: *Oh! That bloke's bloody silly. I've sat in there listening to him talking for an hour and don't understand a bloody thing he says. He goes off on sidetracks making jokes and this and that.* Clearly then, you are not of an intelligence to understand, or he did those things for a reason and you were the reason, you were one of the wheat from the chaff he wanted to sort and separate, so you did not throw pearls to swine.

One of the first things he said about – you call them Uncle Toms – Aboriginal people who work against their own people and those who were unlawfully oppressing the Land Council by withholding funding legitimately owed to us, to try and cripple us on our defending, or taking up the people's interests against CRA, he said, *Brother, there's people like me and you, and we're field niggers. They're the corn-feds, they live in the house with the master. We're out in the field slaving. We're the real blackfellas. They're the master's pet. Yes master, no master. I'll go sort them out in the field master.* Corn feds he called them.

And there are a few corn-feds around Australia. He was very original. He came up with his own expressions and labels. He was never afraid to call a bloody spade a spade you know, ever. He was fearless in that sense, always fearless even in a hostile environment, but his strategies were too numerous to mention. He used a whole repertoire, such as *catch more flies with honey than vinegar*. He would use the vinegar too, and he would use you, and he would use whatever it took to win the day. I had been with him for twenty-three years and I was always talking to him even when he was not around, and he continued to amaze me. I wished we had a couple more decades ahead of us because I thought he had a hell of a lot more to teach and contribute.

I really hate to imagine what it would have been like without Tracker. We would have lost the Century battle and we would be like those parts of the Kimberley that have changed only recently due to Century. Examples are the Argyle [diamond mine in the Kimberley], and Comalco [mining bauxite in Cape York], which due to the big agreement that we negotiated with Century, they were able to go and renegotiate with the same company – CRA – and get decent agreements, and sometimes, even improve on the Century one.

But it was our Century agreement that broke [the barrier]. It was the first major mining agreement [with Aboriginal landowners] of any substance in this country. Within months Argyle and Comalco were at the table renegotiating with Noelie [Noel Pearson] and with Peter Yu's lot [Kimberley Land Council], and that can be traced to Tracker, whether those buggers want to admit it or not. I suppose you could say in a way, that every single Aboriginal agreement with a mining company since that day is owed to him doing it with [Paul] Wand, and I think they would all be amazed to learn it started with a little notepad scrap of paper.

Andrew Chalk

I had known Tracker for at least twenty years. I first met him during the native title negotiations in 1993 when he was working at the Central Land Council with David Ross, and Tracker was playing the role then that he seemed to have played all his life which was sort of half fly on the wall, half get in there and fix it, and half raconteur who keeps the troops amused when things get dull, as well as many other things in between.

Tracker's role in a lot of the matters that we have been involved with was not necessarily to design the strategy. What he had been really good at was facilitating communication, getting people talking. Sometimes people start with fixed positions and ideas as to what the strategy ought to be, and Tracker's amazing skill was to break the ice and in the most irreverent way getting people to deal with one another as people. And things fall out of that. So he was an unusual marriage broker in a way in that he did not mind conflict, but he had an interesting way in how he handled it. He sort of tosses in a bomb and then walked through the aftermath helping people pick up the pieces, and showing them how things could be put together and reconfigured in a way that they may not have thought of. His ability not to hold grudges and to see the humanity in all of us gave him an ability to break deadlocks, where others would just stay in rigid formation and no result could be achieved.

To tell you the truth I do not know where that ability came from. He had a very difficult upbringing as one of the Stolen Generation himself, and I think he had been on a lifelong quest to understand who he was. But it was also, and I do not say this lightly, I regarded him as a real Falstaff character. He had genuine intelligence, insight and analytical capabilities, and his wit was an overt demonstration of what was going on in his head, but it was that intelligence which was capable of seeing beyond the immediate friction. He spent a lot of time working in very tense, high conflict situations, and he used his humour as a way of disarming people. I think he had been doing it for so long that it had become second nature to him. When I say disarming, people just enter a lot of these negotiations either with inflated perceptions of themselves in the case of prime ministers, or they are fearful and therefore angry and reactive, and he deflated the big heads by mocking himself and giving confidence to those who were lacking it. In the process he created a space where dialogue could happen.

I remember back about 1998, when he was down in Canberra again for the Wik debates and John Howard's Ten Point Plan on native title. Warren Entsch who was the Member for Cape York had made an announcement because the churches had come out supporting the need to protect native title, and that was when the whole debate over pastoral leases and whether native title was extinguished on pastoral leases was going on. So the churches had been very critical of Howard, and you had Tim Fischer [National Party deputy prime minister] promising bucketloads of extinguishment.

So Entsch, in response to the churches' position said, *Well! If the church is going to take that role we should all boycott the churches,* which was a pretty stupid sort of thing to say, particularly for a conservative. We were sitting in the cafeteria [in Parliament House], in fact I was not sitting, Tracker was sitting, I was walking past and I saw Warren Entsch walking past the other way and Tracker called out from across the cafeteria something to the effect of, *Warren, sorry, got your message too late, I went to church on Sunday.*

For everyone who knew Tracker, he did it in such a generous but funny way, taking the piss out of himself but also taking the piss out of Warren Entsch and the whole cafeteria just erupted. It was rare to see Tracker in the middle of things. I do not say that in a negative way, but he did not make himself the main player. He was not a Galarrwuy [Yunipingu]. He was not a Noel [Pearson], or a Michael Mansell.

But he was somebody who had the attention, and I actually think the respect of all of them. It was easy for people to dismiss Tracker as a buffoon, but there was always a lot more to him than that.

Tracker was a bloke who had a very acute sense of social justice. He saw people getting a raw deal, he knew he had skills, and the confidence to use the talents that he had in the way that he was comfortable with. But the driver was an ingrained sense of what is right and wrong. At different times I have shared hotel rooms with him and when I say hotel rooms I mean donga rooms where you sit and chat late into the night, and I once told him that I thought he missed his calling. I told him that I thought he should have been the black Alan Jones of Australia – that talkback radio should have been his forte, although I would not have liked to see the defamation bill. He was an extraordinary communicator and there would be people who have a view about Aboriginal people who in that sort of context, could ring in to give it to him. The thing about Tracker was that he could always give it back, it would never get the better of him in that regard, but he could do it in a way that you ended up laughing with him. That was an amazing skill.

Tracker told so many funny stories but unfortunately I do not have the recollection for them. Most of the time he was talking complete bullshit, and you were there focused on the job and wondering where all this was going, and Tracker's telling another war story.

But he was creative. I worked with him on the James Price Point issue and he sat back and I think that was probably indicative of Tracker. He was often slow to decide where the merits of a situation lay, and rather than just jumping in and taking sides, he would do a bit of scouting and listening to different perspectives before he made up his mind. It took him a while to decide that Joseph Roe was the real deal there and we were acting for Joseph, we were doing a pro bono and it took us a while as well to go into that situation and work out what was going on.[24] We could see that there were injustices happening

---

24. Mr J. Roe, a Goolarabooloo Aboriginal man led, from 2009, the long campaign of Kimberley Aboriginal law bosses against a multi-billion dollar liquid natural gas hub that was to be developed by Woodside, with the support of the Western Australian Government, on their traditional land at James Price Point, north of Broome. Woodside dropped the plans for the project in April 2013 for what it said were commercial reasons.

but whether they were justified in terms of the overall good of the community needed a bit of thinking and balancing and reflection, and Tracker took a while but he decided, *No, this guy is genuine.*

He did his research and decided that things were crook, and maybe one day the story will come out as to just how crook they were. Joseph Roe was a man who had a culture to protect, a storyline to protect, he had sacred responsibilities and deep law responsibilities which he took very seriously. It meant that he was not in a position to compromise no matter what. The Kimberley Land Council epitomised the deal-making generation of Aboriginal leadership and I have no problem at all with the idea that compromise is important and doing deals, but you don't, you can't do deals and cut across the fundamentals. The problem with the Kimberley Land Council is that they were trusted with important powers to protect the interests of the traditional owners and it does not matter how good the monetary deal on the table is, if your instructions are in a different direction, it is not your job to replace what you think is the best outcome with what your instructions are.

They did everything they could to undermine Joseph Roe when for twenty years the same organisation had been holding him up as a person that you need to talk to about these issues. And for good reason. And the more that we looked into it, the deeper was the strength, the responsibility and knowledge and position that Joseph held, and documented in the KLC's own records. In fairness to the Council, since many of the current mob were largely unaware of it, there was just such a history there of the KLC on oath swearing that this is a person who you had to go and see about dealing with this country, he has the law responsibility for it.

And when the second Woodside put a big cheque on the table it all changed, and I just think when the rep [representative] bodies lose their footing, then Aboriginal people are in a lot of trouble. Particularly for something like this, where it was a gas plant they were talking about, you could put it just about anywhere, and it became an ideological position for [Premier] Barnett.

But Tracker's role in it was really to work behind the scenes, talking to people in gas companies, talking to people in the federal government, picking up bits and pieces of information all over the place to try and work out what the alternatives might be. Both of us sat down and tried to work it through: *Could they put it here without disturbing the songline?*

We both worked very hard to try and find a solution that would appease everyone without damaging the cultural heritage. But that was not to be. Tracker was not being paid for any of this, it was just something he felt was important and so much of what he has done has been about trying to create opportunities for people, both economic and to protect their cultural heritage, or to assert their traditional rights. And for a bloke who called everyone *comrade*, he was actually not ideological in that way at all, he was about trying to get good outcomes for people and solve problems. He was not the only one who wanders the country as a travelling fixer but there are not many who do it as well or as often as he did, and their work is never usually recognised or appreciated.

So often just a conversation where one person or another person would link people together, they created opportunities, and then people carry on and forget how it all started, and Tracker had an extraordinary ability to talk to anyone. The powerful, the weak, and to just see them as people. I think he was greatly respected on both sides of politics, but not by everybody by any means. There would be many that just saw him as a buffoon, but I think those who knew him, recognised he had some unique talents.

The thing with Tracker was there was always a story. It is interesting because you run across a lot of people who tell stories but you struggle to see how they are relevant. Tracker was not like that. Obviously there was a sharpness and intelligence that kept the focus. For others who knew him it could be quite frustrating. Rossy was a bloke with a lot of patience, because he has to sit there and hear the stories again and again and again, but he knew where Tracker was coming from, he knew the values that drove him, he knew why he was doing it and in those circumstances it was easy to be patient. Everyone has their skills, and I would not put administration down as being Tracker's skill. He was absolutely the big picture person. His skills were dealing with people. Rossy was much more the focused administrator, but they made a very good pairing.

I did see Shakespeare as having penned Tracker. I saw him as Falstaff, somebody with a very keen mind, who was observing and watching and even manipulating an outcome, engineering an outcome perhaps is a nicer word, while at the same time presenting as a buffoon, but who could say things to people and get away with it because of that mask. We have had a very privileged job, we have met some extraordinary people right across the country and many amazing characters, and many of them have real flaws. When you are talking about the Murrandoos and the Mansells and the Noel Pearsons and the Trackers, it is easy to identify the flaws, but the thing I liked about Tracker and it took me a while to really appreciate it, you saw the genuineness of his mission.

You had to sit there and listen to it, digest it, and go away and think about it. In 1993 [Aboriginal negotiations with the federal government on the Mabo High Court decision] brought together some amazing people. Michael Mansell was another who I have the utmost respect for. There are others who are quick at grabbing the headlines and who are pretty shallow in comparison, but there are endearing features to all of them; and there are people of substance who do get overlooked, and they do not conform to what mainstream Australia would like to see in a blackfella. But there is an intelligence and a compassion in all of them, and people usually cannot see past the exterior to look at what they are really saying.

I wish I could sit here and recite ten thousand one-liners from Tracker, I have just never been able to keep up, let alone write them down. So in that sense I know I have not done him justice.

Dare to Dream

Tracker Tilmouth

Of all the Aboriginal academics and leaders the one who I found was way out ahead of everybody was Mick Dodson. Compared with other lawyers, Mansell and Mick are the two outstanding ones, because the law as far as they were concerned, and as far as I understood, the law is a way of measuring white blokes' intentions.

There is a whole degree of other social agendas that need to be linked in to the legal argument of the day, and Dodson was an absolutely compassionate man. In fact every time you saw him, you could see the burden of the responsibility sitting on him and it did not sit well. But there was no doubting his commitment or his compassion towards Aboriginal people, and the rights of Aboriginal people. There was absolutely no doubt and he would vigorously defend that, even though a lot of people misunderstood what his agenda was towards the Aboriginal people. But if you knew Mick Dodson like I knew him, he was one of the foremost leaders that I have ever had the pleasure of working with.

Even now I might criticise him a bit but that was all for the game as far as Mick was concerned. He did not mind you having a go at him as long as you understood that his integrity and compassion and his ability to defend Aboriginal rights was not impeded. And he fought vigorously to maintain that position. As fighters for Aboriginal rights, you always had Charlie Perkins with his political agendas, you had Michael Mansell with legal agendas, and then you had Mick Dodson with both, political and legal. Dodson lived and breathed this every day of the week and he did so since I first ran into him. As far as I was concerned he was an absolutely brilliant bloke.

I met him years ago before he ran the Northern Land Council. I knew him in Katherine when he lived in Katherine. I knew who he was. You did not really get to know Mick until you worked with him and I worked with him in the UN. I worked with him at Geneva and elsewhere.

We are extremely good friends and he has always been someone that I could count on at any time to give good advice, and he was always brilliant with his advice. Mansell as far as I am concerned is one of the foremost lawyers in Aboriginal society today. He has always had the ability to talk to the common person. Mansell never has airs and graces and yet he is absolutely brilliant on his legal opinion. He does not murder the English language or play to a non-Indigenous audience like some Aboriginal people whose speech is to the white people who think they are absolutely brilliant. They are not worried about what they are saying, they are worried about how they are saying it, and they judge them accordingly. They like that, because they are up there – and can use bigger words than the white blokes can. Whereas Mansell, if he wanted to say something, Mansell would say something in very plain English and straightforward, and it is meant for the Aboriginal community – this is what I am talking about.

And so when you compare Aboriginal leadership – I am biased because I am a Centralian Aboriginal, and the leadership in the north, in the Northern Land Council and in the north in general, has never had the leaders as we have had. And you have got everyone from Wenten Rubuntja, Charlie Perkins, Bruce Breaden, and Rexy Granites and Harry [Jakamarra] Nelson from Yuendumu, both highly educated, prominent Warlpiri activists and traditional landowners, and former executive members of the Central Land Council. Mr Nelson was also a chairman of the Combined Aboriginal Nations of Central Australia. Also, Kumantjayi Zimran from Kintore.[25] Mr Gunner from Utopia. Those sort of blokes. You never get those sort of people in Darwin, or in the North.

The Top End leaders did not have this ability to incorporate young people into the debate so there is no Breaden, Wenten, or Smithy, or any of those old senior men. They would make sure that you understood your role, and they would say: *This is our message, and you take the message.* Right! They would say: *We don't need to debate it, we don't need you to tell*

---

25. Tracker is using the mourning name of Mr Smithy Zimran.

us what you're thinking, we will give you instructions on how you deliver the message and what points you make. They were able to do that quite easily in the Centre. So Rossy and I were only two young blokes and we had our own political agendas, but at the end of the day, the people who called the shots were the senior men in the Central Land Council. That still remains today. In the north though, I cannot for the love of me see any relationship between the senior level of the Land Council, their workers, and the communities they are supposed to be servicing. There is no connection, in fact there is a disconnect.

This is historical because the Northern Land Council was the bureau of the Northern Land Council, where you had an administrative arm that was separate from the Council when it was first formed. Whereas, in the Central Land Council, the Council had direct links to the administration. So they have had that historical process to deal with.

The non-Indigenous community, especially in the north, had this perceived idea: that *when we are talking to Aboriginals, we are talking to the full blacks, and mission blacks. We weren't talking to the urbans, or Stolen Generation, or anyone else for that matter.* They were the half-castes and the coloureds. In fact, a lot of Aboriginal people in Darwin classified themselves as Sri Lankan to get passed. I remember a number of people that I went to school with who turned out to be Larrakia in later life, who were actually classified as Sri Lankans or Malaysians at school and classified themselves as such, and they kept away from Aboriginal communities at school. They were not recognised and did not want to be recognised by the Aboriginal community.

This was the problem with the Larrakia native title claim in my opinion, where there was a duplicity in identification of native title holders, where a lot of the people who did front as native title holders were not, and never did classify themselves as Aboriginal in my day. I remember who they were and they know I remember who they were because I was there. So you had this situation in the Top End that was perpetrated by community advisors and everybody else – that the urban blacks and the coloureds were not real blacks, they were imitation white people. I managed to escape that process because when I came in from Croker Island and went to high school we were classed as *mission blacks*. I was a blackfella from Croker Island – Minjilang. We had a different classification, and a lot of the urban blacks as far as we were concerned, we were not part of their clique. They had this distinct thing that flowed on from the Retta Dixon days, to the Kahlin Compound, and everything else. So you had the continuation of 'coloured' and urban blacks being discriminated against by non-Indigenous community advisers, white people, government services, government agents, and also being discriminated against by full-blood Aboriginals.

They were in no man's land. Then along comes the land councils, the Northern Land Council for example, where there was the [historical] disconnect inside the Aboriginal world of urban blacks versus bush blacks or community blacks, and that was reflected by the chairpersons of the Northern Land Council. There has never been a half-caste, or a coloured person, or a woman of any stature within the Northern Land Council. All the chairpersons of the Northern Land Council came from East Arnhem, or Arnhem Land itself, except for Gerry Blitner who came from Ngukurr, but very few others ever got up to be chairperson.

Arnhem Land is a world of its own. East Arnhem is a fiefdom of its own. West Arnhem to a certain extent, and then you have got the middle, Central Arnhem which is Maningrida, and they have their own processes as well. If there was a breakaway land council in any upcoming debate with the Northern Territory Government and the [Abbott] federal government – the Liberal government – it would not be hard to draw the boundary of the breakaway Land Council. All you have to do is anything south of Pine Creek – Pine Creek south, and Elliott north, and west and east.

This would be the new land council very easily because the political debate in that area would suggest that there is no connection at all with services from the Northern Land Council, or if there are services, it is very limited. There is no real debate and this has been the problem all along. And now we have the situation evolving where the Northern Land Council has to work out how to keep itself together without being split up. Unfortunately, the Northern Territory Land Rights Act is a single act and there is no difference between how it operates in the CLC area or the NLC area. So the CLC by default will also get split up. And it will be all because of the NLC's inability to service its clientele and its constituents. This is the dilemma that Rossy and people like that will face in the future when it comes to the debate in relation to what do we do with the Land Rights Act.

You have got to remember again, and it is going back to the original position [of property rights], the Land Rights Act is a political process, a political act, and has nothing to do with law. The Aboriginal people do not own the land, it is owned by the Commonwealth, and all the titles to the land are held in Canberra, and you cannot rent or lease or do anything with the land without permission of the Minister for Aboriginal Affairs, or the person responsible, which is the Commonwealth. So you hold Aboriginal land freehold in brackets, in trust, and then you have the Commonwealth statutory bodies which are the Central and Northern Land Councils, Anindilyakawa Land Council [covering Groote Eylandt], and the Tiwi Land Council, holding that land in trust for the Aboriginal traditional landowners that administer their land on behalf of the Commonwealth. Their funding comes from consolidated revenue through the Aboriginals Benefit Account to fund their services, so as a Commonwealth statutory body, they have no responsibility as an Aboriginal organisation. Their role and responsibilities are pretty well defined and many a time the management of the Central Land Council tried, and I tried on more than one occasion, to morph it into an Aboriginal organisation. It was very difficult, and I fell foul of some of the lawyers within the Central Land Council by trying to achieve that. This all started with the debate about Aboriginal sovereignty, CANCA, Aboriginal government and everything else, including the Kalkaringi Statement, to try and say that we are not a Commonwealth statutory body, we are there to support Aboriginal self-determination. And that went sideways at a hundred miles an hour because it was too difficult for some of those senior bureaucrats within government, but also, some of the senior bureaucrats within the Central Land Council itself.

They said, *Well! Your role and responsibility is determined by the Land Rights Act, paragraph this, clause whatever.* But! I said, *Yeah that's wonderful, but there's no debate, and there's no discussion about the enjoyment of land rights in the Land Rights Act.* If you take out Part IV which is the mining provisions, there is nothing worth reading in the Land Rights

Act. And so the debate went on and on within the Central Land Council and wore me down, it wore me down, and in the end I thought, *Well! Reap what you sow.*

And this is the process that also happened within the Northern Land Council. The senior bureaucrats of the Northern Land Council decided that they would stick with the rules and the most compliant political process was the appointment every year and every election, of the chairman coming from East Arnhem. Now there is no political militancy or agenda coming out of East Arnhem and there never will be while I am alive, because now they are royalty receivers and they should do very well out of it, but the social indicators suggest that they do not do socially well out of it. And so you have this situation that is going to come to pass in relation to the closure of the Gove aluminium smelter and the source of the royalties. What happens then? Where are the economic programs after thirty years of three million dollars a year? There is nothing to show for it. Nothing to show for it, absolutely zero.

You have these situations evolving – whereas early in the Central Land Council area we said, *Righto! If you get royalties, royalties are a provision for social programs within the community,* and we dissuaded the use of royalties for payment to individuals. We managed to invest on behalf of the Aboriginal community most of their money, that is why Centrecorp was set up, that is why the royalty associations were set up, and this was how Centrefarm got set up.

Let's go back past the royalties for mining and look at the enjoyment of land rights in its purest form. How do you enjoy being out there? What do you do when you are out there? What natural resources have you got to allow you to stay out there? These are the questions that the Central Land Council is dealing with through its community development section, but it may be too little too late, because the Intervention has come and gone, and they [the federal government] are looking for the next victim. The next victim is going to be [from the government asking]: *Well! Who is impeding the individual?* It is going to be the legal services, the social organisations like health services and the land councils that are all urban-based or centralised. So you have this debate that is going to go on and on, and when you go back through it all, go back to where it first started, the leadership within Aboriginal organisations is lacking, is lacking on having a grand plan of where we are in twenty years time, and what we will have achieved. No vision. We have no vision of where we should be.

What we have got is a situation where even the health services – and I found this quite alarming when I was at Congress and I had some medicine for some treatment and I went to pay for it, they said, *No you don't have to pay for it.* I said, *What do you mean I don't have to pay for it? Oh! No, it's free.* I said, *No, I earn* x *amount, I should be able to pay for it.* They said, *No we don't do means tests.* So any Aboriginal person earning a hundred and fifty grand a year, or your wife, your family and everybody else, you are earning quite a lot of money, you do not pay for your medicine. That is up here in [Darwin] at Danila Dilba Medical Service as well. There is no means testing on anyone walking through the door for their ability to pay for the medicine or the service. You wonder why the bill for the health services is going through the roof. You cannot afford that because it is Aboriginal money. If you are earning good money you should pay. If you are not earning good money, or you are unemployed, or you are disadvantaged, or have a disability, or are on a pension, whatever, well and good, get it for free. But if you are earning good money pay for it.

When you get those sorts of examples staring you in the face, you say: *Well! Where is the political agenda, where is it going, if we can do this to our own mob then we have no responsibility to anyone.* We have no clear understanding of our political agenda. We are there for the ride. That has been the problem, there are too many people having too many rides. You get the debate – I can sit down say with the executive of Congress, of which my brother is chair, and you can see the executive when you talk to them how they spruik the same policies and all the acronyms that go with it. But there is no agenda behind it. It is like turning on a tape recorder and you get the ad of Congress. All the right words in all the right places, but when you turn the tape off everything stops. There is no agenda. There is no debate. It is a spruik. They say that and then they get paid, and off they go home. And they say that is an Aboriginal organisation executive meeting.

Alexis Wright: *How are people going to develop a vision?*

Well! You can't. Until we get another Smithy Zimran, or another lot of people out bush trying to lead the dispossessed and the disillusioned out of the urban centres, they are not going to get any more visions. People have run out of visions because the people that supported them and put forward the visions were not supported by the [Aboriginal] organisations.

The [Aboriginal] visions cut across the agendas of the entrenched ideologues, the white people that saw Aboriginal people as a captive audience. The last thing they want to do is have Aboriginal people escape. Escape through the fence and go into the paddock where you can dream the unthinkable dream. They were very worried for Aboriginal people, that democracy would break out, rather than guided democracy which we enjoy at the moment. The guided democracy is still in place. And so Aboriginal people do as they are told, when they are told, by whom they are told because they do not have any control over the finances. Anyone who says to me *Aboriginal self-determination,* I would say you really want to think about that statement before I hear it again. And so, this is why we need the Michael Dodsons and the Michael Mansells of the world, because Michael Dodson was probably one of the hardest thinkers on these issues. And when you get him by himself and you talk to him and understand him like I understand him, then he is worth listening to. And the same with Mansell. Mansell is brilliant. He can tell you straight up what he thinks, but you come back to the mainland, and everyone is bought and sold.

The Kimberley renaissance of Aboriginal activism has disappeared – it has gone sideways. All we have got now is young Wayne Bergmann [then director of the Kimberley Land Council] talking about resource development which is wonderful, but what is the rest of the community going to do? If you do it as an agenda for the community then you have to include the community. If you do it as an agenda for yourself then you are outside with every other white person and you forget your Aboriginality and go for broke. You cannot trade on your Aboriginality and say, *Well I'm this or I am that,* and then go off and expect to drink at the white man's trough, because you are going to get shot one way or another. You are going to get shot by your mob and shot by the white blokes for doing it. This is the problem for these blokes who can be activists but only within a rarified environment. This is the greatest problem we have. We do not have clear lines of demarcation between self-interest and Aboriginal interest and that clouds the issue.

I do things differently. I have no problem in entering an economic debate or discourse with someone who is already in the industry, because our ability to understand the mining industry or resource development industry is pretty limited. I understand what they do, they dig holes and they mine, and they sell the materials overseas. That is the nuts and guts of it. But we do not know the finance exchange rate, we do not know what the spot market does, we do not know what shares do, we do not know what the stock market does in relation to share trading. We have no understanding of that. We do not know about paper profit versus real profit. We cannot understand a balance sheet. We do not know what the words CAPEX or OPEX are. So when we come to mining, we come to a cargo-cult mentality where the Toyota dream is at its best – *If I'm smart I'll get a Toyota out of this*. We fight over the crumbs. The Toyota lasts two or three years at best, and someone rolls it because they are drunk and that is it, the end of our resources, rather than saying, *Wouldn't it be better if we put half the money away to invest, and with the other half, to send the kids to school to get educated in areas of land use and land management that we need, and let's bring them back, let's not send them off to government departments, let's bring them back to the community and let them work here so that we do not need the CDEP bloke to go from CDEP to being the pastoral manager, or the administrator, who had only originally turned up to run an unemployment program.* These are white blokes you would not normally employ anywhere else. But all of a sudden he is an administrator, or a community advisor. He has got this intelligence and all of this advice from osmosis, from reading books.

So we have this argument and I do not know to a certain extent where Noel Pearson is going. I do not think Noel Pearson knows. He is yet to paint the picture. I cannot understand what he writes. I do not have the grasp of the English language even though I have a science background, and if you talk to me about the four laws of thermal dynamics I can debate you. I can talk to you about land, anions and cations and exchange rates, I can talk to you about ionisation of clays, all that sort of stuff, but I cannot understand what Noel Pearson says. I cannot grasp what he is talking about. I have great difficulty understanding what Marcia [Langton] is talking about. It is all academic. I find it difficult to understand any of them. I know Mundine, his debate is pretty limited. His experience would suggest that he has limited exposure as well.

They appeal to the non-Indigenous society by the very nature of them being acceptable. They are not going to let the caffè latte curdle. They eat the right biscuits at the right time and use the right fork for the cheese. Their discourse can be in language that white people find amazing, that Aboriginal people use the English language better than they can. This is why the white people like them, because they know it is cheaper for the white blokes to have a mob of blackfellas discussing points of view without any effect, than actually getting out there and doing what needs to be done. It is too expensive to do what they need to do, so they would rather have a discourse with a mob of Aboriginal intellectuals, then find it comfortable to say that we have had the debate, and when you boil it all down, we do not know what we were talking about, so no one has to do anything.

You cannot have a social structure imposed on an Aboriginal society if they do not own the social structure. It is as simple as that. You can play with all the economics you like, you can pull the rabbits out of hats and do everything else, but unless the Aboriginal people own it and share in it, then it fades, and you fall into the same trap of the accused – just about every white community advisor I have known and worked with, who I have accused of parking jumbo jets on community air strips. It is wonderful, it is magnificent, but no one knows how to fly it, and if you did take off, you were definitely not going to land, you are going to crash and kill everyone in the community. So parking jumbo jets on community airstrips is what I try and avoid.

Murrandoo Yanner

Tracker knew most of the people in the Aboriginal struggle, white and black, famous people, whom I also met through him, and he was quick to point out their flaws but also their strengths. He said to me the first time I ever saw Michael Mansell when we were down at some big native title bill negotiation thing, the original native title bill, or the amendments down in Melbourne, and Mansell got up to talk and he leaned to me and whispered, *You know the problem with Mansell?* He seemed quite fascinating and intelligent, which Michael obviously is for Tracker to pay him this compliment when he said, *His problem is he's twenty years ahead of the rest of us. The things he is speaking about and the way he's looking and he's right, he's talking about sea rights, and we're still looking at land rights and things.*

When I have seen Tracker and Marcia in the same room it was like throwing gunpowder and matches. I respect Marcia, she is a highly intelligent woman. I once saw a photo of her as a beautiful young woman, and obviously it took a lot of balls standing in the Brisbane mall lobbying for land rights in the Joh Bjelke-Petersen days. She was alone lobbying – no one was with her. She had to do it on her own. I think she is highly intelligent but she wastes all that by going with the established authority of the day, or by following Noelie [Noel Pearson]. She is smarter than Noelie, or as smart or more experienced. I have got a lot of respect for the woman but I have got to agree with Tracks that she could and should be contributing more on our side. I do not know where the thing comes from with them, but I have to agree with him that she scowls at the smell of him, let alone the sight you know. She hears his voice on the other side of the door and she would be smiling, and then it is like bang, the trap closes shut.

Absolutely, he would stir her up and I have seen him do that. He did not hold back on anyone, he would call a spade a spade.

Sean Bowden

He also learnt from Charlie Perkins, I have got no doubt. I spent a bit of time with Charlie, not the two of them together a lot because in my time they were in a little bit of conflict because Tracker was the director of the Land Council, and Charlie was trying to do things with the Land Council.

I think with Charlie, they were not his greatest days but he was just an incredible person, with incredible insight and knowledge, and very generous with that knowledge. I missed working with Charlie in his prime but I still got access to and learnt from this incredible person who was responsible for so much for Aboriginal people. But when I worked with him he was still Charlie and I know that without Charlie, Tracker and a lot of those guys would not have got a leg up into the world that they went to. Charlie used imagery brilliantly, and had lots of sayings. I think Tracker picked a few of those up along the way. And, like Charlie, I think his use of humour was an effort to not just become homicidal with rage. He used it well with politicians and again sometimes maybe he overused it, but it was a mechanism and it was the way he was able to walk into Robert Hill's office, for instance, and have the four- or five-star generals vacate the room, as happened on one of our trips to Canberra.

There were so many Tracker quotes that it is difficult to nail them down. It was usually in this incredible narrative, in the incredible and quite unique way he spoke. One was about Trish Crossin who was at the biting end of one of Tracker's best, or worst comments. Trish turned up at Big Bill Neidjie's funeral, wearing a green dress with yellow sleeves. Tracker waited for his moment and said to her probably in a crowd of about fifteen or twenty people, *Have a look at the wheelie bin over there.* Ever since, Trish Crossin has been known in certain circles as 'the wheelie bin', to the point where people would ring up and say, *That bloody wheelie bin.* All because of Tracker.

Marcia Langton was always frustrated by Tracker for things like that. There was a very funny time, I was having a barbecue dinner with Noel Pearson and Marcia and a group of Yolngu people in Arnhem land. We were at a hotel and we pulled the barbecue out, and Noel and I were telling Tracker stories. It was very funny. We had had a hard day's work. *What about Tracker this? What about when he did this? What about when he did that?* Marcia came roaring over in high dudgeon and said, *You two are obsessed with that man.* Noel and I looked at each other and almost at the same time said, *Who's obsessed?*

But the thing is that Marcia, because she is hardcore operator, was reflecting that frustration that some of us had with Tracker, that he did not reach higher planes. Marcia was very fond of Tracker and had great affection for him, but she got frustrated that he was too glib at times, that he made the smart-alec remark at the wrong time, and sometimes at the expense of the wrong person.

Owen Cole

He used to also clash with a lot of the Aboriginal leaders – some of whom he used to call *the intelligentsia,* and I can always remember the time when I bumped into Marcia at the airport, and Marcia said to me, *Your mate.* I said, *Yeah, which mate?* She said, *That Tilmouth bloke, he's a misogynist.* That was the first time I had ever heard the term misogynist and I said, *What do you mean?* She said, *He hates women that bloke,* and she told me that Tracker was interrupting her when she was making a speech at the conference. So I got the lecture of what a misogynist was on Tracker's behalf. That was Marcia, and that was in the Canberra airport, and I popped into the plane and went to Sydney where I bumped into Olga Havnen at the Sydney airport, and Olga came up and called him misogynist as well.

When the occasion arose and he thought it necessary, he would sit down and make little comments while people were making their presentations, and they regarded it as being very abusive and disrespectful, but that was just Tracker. They hated him one minute and loved him the next I suppose. That was a relationship a lot of people had with him. So misogynist! Honestly I did not have a clue what it was, and then to get whacked twice within two hours.

And of course with Pat Turner that was the same. He would interrupt her while she was making speeches, and she used to get the shits with him as well, and then he would go, *Hey! I'm only messing around with you, what ya getting serious for?* They would say, *You just rubbished me during my speech, and made snide remarks while I'm talking, Tracker. You've got no respect.* Of course he would just say, *Oh come on, you're taking yourself too seriously.*

Chris Athanasiou

Tracker was a complex person. He always accused me of over-analysing, so for once I will take his advice and briefly recount some of my experiences with him without trying to work out why he was the way he was.

I went to the Central Land Council in 1994 to work as a native title lawyer. Tracker was the director. Native title was a political issue at that time and this meant that I had a role in native title policy. This involved Tracker and that is how I got to know him. He had a considerable intellect and a quick wit. His ability to quickly grasp a situation, and place himself and his point of view into it, were evident from the outset.

I came to understand that ideas outside the norm were always bubbling to the surface with Tracker. Many people have enjoyed the experience of Tracker enthusiastically running his latest idea by them, usually ending in them being enlisted to help him make it work.

My first real taste of the way Tracker could completely change the feeling in a room was at a parliamentary inquiry into the Stolen Generation in 1995. The inquiry was taking evidence in Alice Springs. Everyone was looking serious, and rightly so. Tracker understood this more than anybody, but it got to the point where you could see that he wanted to break the ice. So he said, *You know, I was probably the only one in the Stolen Generation – when they took me away everyone cheered and when I came back they all cried.* The panel tried to consider what he said in all seriousness, but, of course, people started laughing. He then made a number of points, with the panel hanging on his every word. Mission accomplished. Because I was very new to it all, I looked at him and thought to myself: *I think I'm in for an interesting ride here.*

In 1995–96, some early problems with the Native Title Act drove the then Labor government towards amendments. The National Indigenous Working Group emerged, facilitated by ATSIC. Tracker supported this national response. Early work was done in developing Indigenous Land Use Agreements.

In 1996 the Commonwealth government changed and the High Court handed down the Wik decision. The former government's proposed amendments were put aside and the government came forward with the Ten Point Plan.

At that time, there was also a push from the conservative Territory government to amend the Land Rights Act. The Central Land Council was opposing this. Our fundamental task with native title was to try to keep the native title rights as close to that of the Land Rights Act as we possibly could. It was good for native title holders, and Tracker's concern was that the greater the gap between native title and the Land Rights Act, the more focus there would be on watering down the rights of Aboriginal people under the Land Rights Act.

Tracker was a significant force in the Ten Point Plan debate. People like David Ross, Mick and Pat Dodson, Peter Yu, Marcia Langton, Aden Ridgeway and Noel Pearson were all dominant.

Early on, Tracker had been prepared to trade off native title processes to secure recognition, economic development and heritage protection. Those were the keys to him, and he tried to move the National Indigenous Working Group to that position. He didn't have the time to do so. It was a bridge too far and that was one of his disappointments. The agenda moved to: *what can we salvage from the Native Title Act?* The introduction of Indigenous Land Use Agreements as a viable alternative to agreements under the right to negotiate depended on it.

Tracker was always active behind the scenes. He would be working the room, working the leaders, working the politicians. He used humour to move things along. When a meeting became bogged down, he would size up the situation, find the humour in it, and out would come something incisive, funny and bordering on the absurd. It usually worked. People would stop being precious about a particular detail that didn't matter in the greater scheme of things.

Tracker strongly supported the strategy of engaging on the issues through the Senate processes and this, I believe, was crucial to an outcome that tempered many of the negative changes that the government sought to impose through the Ten Point Plan.

In 1999, after the dust had settled on the Ten Point Plan, the Northern Territory tried to bring in its own native title regime. Native title holders faced having Territory magistrates decide their native title matters – not something that Tracker was at all keen on. The only way it could be stopped was through disallowance in the Senate. Independent Tasmanian Senator Brian Harradine had the balance of power and his support was crucial to the Territory proposal. Senator Robert Hill was brought in by Prime Minister Howard to broker an outcome.

As had happened with the Ten Point Plan, Sydney barristers John McCarthy QC and Dr Jeff Kildea were brought in to advise Senator Harradine. Senator Harradine's time in the Senate was almost over, so Tracker was clear on our approach. Find legitimate fault in what was being put forward and convince Senator Harradine that there wasn't enough time for him to vote on the matter before he departed the Senate. And that is what happened. The reconstituted Senate disallowed the Territory's legislation.

Near the end of that process, we were in Darwin, in [Chief Minister] Denis Burke's office with Senator Hill, a couple of other Territory ministers and bureaucrats and Messrs McCarthy and Kildea. They were berating us for not accepting the Territory's proposal. It got quite heated because they could see it all slipping away. Denis Burke turned to Tracker and said, *Why are you guys doing this?* Tracker's humour and irreverence came to the fore – he looked up and said: *Denis, Denis, Denis, old jungle saying, when crocodile open mouth, don't put head in.* You could see Burke was about to erupt, but he realised it was all over and there was no point. In the end everyone was laughing. That was the end of it.

In a quieter moment I once told him: *You know, Tracker, I reckon the world has missed out on a bloody great stand-up comic because you didn't take to the stage.* I meant it as a compliment, but I was never sure he took it that way. Perhaps he never fully understood what a gift his humour was to those who experienced it.

Murrandoo Yanner

Fred Pascoe was the first proper Aboriginal elected mayor of redneck Carpentaria Shire in Normanton, and in the next election no one even stood against him, black or white. That was unheard of. This was a place where you could not even get a blackfella on council forever. And he is one of Tracker's, as is my brother Bull. They are close, and contributors from the inside of Century – within the corporate system there – fighting from the inside. They were both mentored and tutored by Tracker and I know Fred continued to use him for Delta Downs, the first Aboriginal pastoral lease ever bought in Australia – for advice on that and probably other things. People like him and Bull and others are to contribute a lot more in the coming years as Tracker's ideas continue to take hold, because some of these ideas were so deep it takes a while to understand them. But in this whole region, anyone who is worth half of their weight in sand or salt out here – there are probably ten or twelve of us in the whole region – have all at one stage or another been strongly influenced by him.

He would say, *The struggle does not knock off, so how can you?* If you put your rifle down at the front line and go for a holiday, who's guarding the trench? Because he said the enemy is still going at us relentlessly, you know? So you never knock off. He was tireless. He remained very prominent even when you could see he was fairly crook, at least the treatment he was receiving could knock him off his feet a fair bit and it must have hurt him a lot, and no one would have thought an iota less of him if he took a break, but he pushed himself. He contributed more when he was bloody crook or tired than half these bastards do when they are entering the morning fresh and starting work. He never stopped working, whether it was at a restaurant in a social atmosphere, or at midnight later, he was still working the room, or working people.

The biggest thing he has really left with me, that sticks with me, and that I live by and am nourished by, is that there is no limit to the imagination, and if I can implement that in a negotiating room or in agreements, then anything is possible, there is no rule book. There is no putting me in a box or square yard. And that is from him, he used to say, *Dare to dream, brother, dare to dream.*

There was a time here when blacks were nothing but slaves on properties and dumped, not even allowed back to fish or hunt their own tucker, and shot at by bloody station owners and choppers even up to the mid and late 90s. He used to tell us during Century, *Don't worry.* I would say to him, *You reckon we can really get those properties and that?* [the five large pastoral properties owned by the mining company that were included in a handback arrangement to the traditional owners in the Century Agreement]. He said, *Brother, we'll get em.* He goes, *Hey! Why do you think we won't? You've got to dare to dream. Don't let them limit your imagination.* And even today, whenever I think of doing anything, even a little thing with the Burke Shire, I will look at the bloody extreme, everything and anything, and then during the negotiation I might compromise or trim back but I dream, I dream of having a little sovereignty, a mini-state within the Gulf again one day in the future. There is no limit and that is the real thing that sticks in my head, what he said, *Dare to dream.*

I Am Counted as a Pet Nigger

Labor likes pet niggers, and I'm counted as a pet nigger. I'm allowed to mow the lawns, but I'm not allowed up on the veranda. – Tracker Tilmouth, *Sydney Morning Herald,* 11 November 2000

He was widely tipped to become a Labor senator three years ago, but was opposed by factions in the NT Labor Party. One of those who was reported to have blocked his nomination was Mr Collins. – The Guardian, 14 November 2000

I mean, the bottom line is that in today's Australia the only Aboriginal people treated, to use Tracker's most unfortunate expression, as pet niggers, are people who allow themselves to be treated like that. So, if that's how Tracker feels he's being treated, the ball is in his court. I mean, far be it for me to give gratuitous advice. Tracker is a highly intelligent, articulate, well-educated man with a university degree. And if that's what he thinks garners support, then fine. People I know have a problem with it. I have a problem with it. And I think that's where he should be looking rather than any sort of general suggestion the Labor Party is against Aboriginal people because he finds trouble garnering support for himself. – Bob Collins, *Sydney Morning Herald,* 11 November 2000

Tracker Tilmouth

Gary Gray was the secretary of the party [ALP], the National Secretary, and he wanted me to put my hand up to be a senator in 1998, and I said, *I can't even get past preselection because Bob Collins and those people have control of the ALP executive in the Northern Territory.*

They [the National ALP] worked on that for some time and then they found out that I was correct, that unless you had Warren Snowdon, and everybody else's endorsement [in the Northern Territory ALP], you could not be nominated for the Senate or the House of Reps, or anything else for that matter, even though the Northern Territory was predominantly an Aboriginal seat.

So Gary Gray came back and said, *Well! Let's get the National Executive to intervene,* and so they started the intervention. I was interviewed with Rossy, where we met with the Labor Party aficionados who asked me, and I said, *Yeah I'll stand.* I said that and then all hell broke loose. Some Territory ALP people wanted a dirt fight – I was a misogynist, I had children all over the countryside, I robbed the Aboriginal community of money, I bought a cattle station for myself, on and on this went, run out of Bob Collins' office.

It was made sure that even the non-Indigenous members of [Aboriginal] organisations, their senior staff, would spread stories about me, and this went on and on. I could not believe it. There I was, having run all the Labor bullshit campaigns with my brother William, Owen Cole and everybody else, and we ended up…I said to my wife, *This is too hard. I'm not this person you're supposed to be.*

And I think senior members of staff in the Council also started taking this on – because I had taken them head on, they had also joined the process. They were all part of the Labor Party. They ran a dirt campaign as well recording my every move. So this went on for about three or four months and my wife was very upset, and it upset my family, it upset me. Then I said, *It's really not worth doing, because it's twenty-four hours a day, seven days a week, you have to be on committees, living out of a suitcase, and you've got to be on an aeroplane. I got a bad enough job now. I don't want a worse job.* So I declined the offer in the end. I said, *No, I don't wish to stand because of the campaign run by Bob Collins,* and Trish Crossin became the senator for the Northern Territory from 1998 to 2013. Why were they doing that? They had decided that we Aborigines were not ready to be a part of the political agenda, and that someone like me who had forward thinking political ideas was not acceptable.

I was independent of them. I had independent thought processes – still have. David Ross would have been more acceptable to them and people like that. I am not that type of person. I pride my independence and my ability to speak as an independent long before I would succumb to any party machinery. My best mate out of all this was Laurie Brereton who informed me that those people who were voting for me would not get it through because of the way Bob Collins and everybody else had acted. My nomination would not get through. He said then, *You have got a choice, you can either go through with the nomination and get knocked back, or you can say you are not interested. I'd rather you said you weren't interested.* I was not interested. It was not worth fighting because you had no say.

I could have dealt with all of the accusations but it adds to the mystery, it adds to the ongoing persona that everybody was so interested in. What are you going to do today? Where is he today? In the media, even today, what is he doing today? I had a bigger profile than Charlie Perkins for heaven's sake. And give it all away? Come to the Labor Party and then the Liberals won anyway? It was not going to amount to a hill of beans in Aboriginal affairs, it is the worst portfolio in the world. You were never going to be accepted anyway because you came from an Aboriginal seat.

David Ross

The other side is the human side, what people did not know about. The thing I will tell you about, he might very well have wanted to put a bullet through me too, but that is alright, was when the Labor Party offered to drop Tracker into the Senate seat in the Northern Territory. It was when Bob Collins vacated the seat and they [NT Labor] made a decision to put Trish [Crossin] in there after the National Executive had offered it to Tracker. He was going to meet with them and he rang me and he did not sound too flash, so I said to him, *Do you want me to come with you?* He said, *Yeah*. So I went along with him and it was Gary Gray who said, *Who are you? What are you doing here?* I said this is who I am and I am here to witness what is going on here. I think Gary Gray was the National Secretary. Anyway, Tracker decided not to do it. What his reasons were I do not know but he came around to my house in Burke Street one evening a few days later and said, *I want to talk to you.* It was when I was still smoking and we went outside and sat down, so I could have a cigarette, and I remember it very well because it is the only time he ever brought Cathryn with him, young Cathryn. She was just a little kid then.

He said, *I've decided not to do it.* I said, *Yes, want to talk about it?* He said, *No, not really.* I said, *Okay.* I said to him, *Oh! Well! Must be more skeletons there than what you tell me about.* He said, *Oh! Well! Something like that.* But the night before when we went to talk to these people, I said to him, *Have you talked to Kathy about everything?* I said, *Because these bastards, the Labor Party and media, they'll dig and they'll dig everything. You know you've got a lot of people out there who you've said things to, you've upset different people over the years, whether it's right or wrong, not my concern. But there are people out there who will probably have the shits.* I said, *So have you raised everything with Kathy? Are you fucking hiding anything from her? You make sure you put it all on the table.* Oh! He and me had a screaming match. Oh! Yes. Just to make sure. Making sure that, *Don't you go putting things on the table, or having people raising stuff outside that you haven't already talked to Kathy about. It does not make any difference to me Tracks, I know you. The media will want to dig everything up and people will want to chuck stones and whatnot, are you comfortable that Kathy knows everything? I don't care about the rest of the world, it's you and your wife. It doesn't matter to me or anyone else, it's between you two.* We had a bit of a screaming match between us to make sure that it was all on the table. I kept prodding him to make sure.

Anyway, that was that. I am just telling you these sorts of things because this is what a lot of people do not know. The human side of Tracker, the vulnerable side. Anyway, I did not prod, and I did not push him for whatever it was, he made the choice that he did not want to do it, that he was withdrawing before it became public knowledge or anything. So that is what he did and that is fine. We make decisions, we live with what we do. People have their perceptions about who you are, what you do, how you do things, but they never fully understand that you have all these responsibilities on a day-to-day basis, and still have to put up with all the personal crap that people heap on you. At the end of the day you have got to go home as a father or mother and deal with your family and your kids, and everyone still expects you to be happy and smiley and do your job and deliver to everyone on a day-to-day basis. People do not understand or if they do, they certainly do not appreciate the level of garbage that can come with doing these sorts of jobs. And there is a lot, there is a lot of it. The media, politicians, talkback jocks and everyone else, when it suits them, they have a go and make cheap shots. Yes, you learn to deal with it, but those were very personal attacks that were not necessary. That was what annoyed me so much.

Gerry Hand

I met Tracker back in 1983 or 1984 I think from memory, when I was visiting Alice Springs as part of a parliamentary committee. I was chairman of the Standing Committee on Aboriginal Affairs and we were looking at education. I can clearly picture Tracker swooping into the meeting of the Alice Springs Labor branch I attended with a couple of other people on the committee, this very lively character with a lot to say, and I was quite impressed by him at that time even though he was giving us a bit of a hard time. I was impressed by the fact that he did not seemed to be concerned or worried too much about the questions he asked. He was very forthright and obviously had a great grip on an array of topics.

Tracker was around when we were working on things like the stock routes legislation, the Land Rights Act amendments, the ATSIC discussions, and he was pursuing his cattle policy, trying to create an economic base even in those days.[26] He seemed to me to be ahead of his time if you think about it now, he was trying to grow the cattle industry for Aboriginal people on their land and that was a significant thing. I used to enjoy him telling me about the advances they had made, the ideas that he had in terms of what was achievable. I think it is fair to say that the level of funding that was required over the last twenty years was not forthcoming.

Tracker could be a fairly forthright character and that was one of the things I admired about him, and he did not suffer fools lightly. He was not afraid to say what he thought. I suspect quite a number of people in the Labor Party could not handle that, which was not uncommon in mainstream political parties. It should have been a walk-up start [for Tracker] to get a preselection in the Northern

---

26. Referring to the *Miscellaneous Acts Amendment (Aboriginal Community Living Areas) Act 1989*; the Reeves Review in 1998 of the Aboriginal Land Rights (Northern Territory) Act 1976; and the establishment of the Aboriginal and Torres Strait Islander Commission that operated between 1990 and 2005.

Territory parliamentary process in 1998, but the great tragedy of course was when he did, he did not get the nod for the Senate. Now I know people say he withdrew, but there was obviously a lot of reasons why he did that, which were mainly due to the undermining and the personal attacks he was enduring at the time. He thought, *Well! Bugger it, it is not worth it.* So he withdrew, but I always thought that Tracker would have made an excellent senator and I think he would have advanced the Aboriginal cause a long, long way if he had gone into the Senate.

There were clearly the people around Bob Collins that went out of their way to undermine Tracker. I think they were basically afraid of him or else they all would have got behind him and got him into the Senate but they didn't. They either worked against him or ran dead. And that is from an outsider. I am not a Territorian but God if you looked at it, if you lined him up against other people up there that seem to have had long and illustrious parliamentary careers, both in the Territory parliament and in the Senate, Tracker, I thought, was head and shoulders above the lot of them. I always had a view that some people responsible for Aboriginal affairs just could not handle an Aboriginal person who was vocal and inclined to say what they thought even if they knew you were going to disagree with it.

He had a saying about some people, something about *they won't have you sit on the back porch*…They talk about the Aboriginal people and let them walk around the gardens but they won't let them sit on the back porch. I tell you what, that reflects on what I said earlier about how he was intelligent. He understood his own people. He had a lot of ideas. He was abrasive to a point, and the story about the back porch signifies why Tracker never got into parliament in the Northern Territory, because those people walked around parroting supportive statements and at the same time always seemed to work against an outspoken, articulate, committed person from the Aboriginal community who wants to go forward. And they did the same thing to Alison [Anderson]. Now I do not know whether Tracker and Alison were close but there are similarities in what happened to Alison and what happened to Tracker, and the same non-Indigenous people were involved in her demise and some of those people were involved in Tracker's lack of success in preselection.

Some of them even worked in Aboriginal organisations and at

the same time resented the people they were supposed to be working for. I have seen a lot of that, of non-Indigenous people who worked in Aboriginal organisations who comment at the side when one of their leaders speaks and there was a lot of that, and they were the ones who went after Tracker because he knew them, and he knew what they were. So they feared him with good cause. They realised that he had seen through them, and so they lined up against him but I think he would have been outstanding.

I was devastated when he withdrew, but I understood why he withdrew, and I respected it. He was a legend I think, Tracker was a legend. So I have never forgiven certain people who worked against him. I have always been forthright in saying who I think did that and Collins was the architect of the campaign against Tracker. But I have nothing but admiration for Tracker and as I said, he was talking about issues long before other people even dreamt they existed or were possible, and that is a great tragedy. If he had gone into parliament, he could have educated a few people down there, and maybe things would have advanced a lot quicker.

In terms of getting his message across, Tracker would have a term or a phrase, and if you look at Keating, he always had a term or a phrase to get his message across. It could be very, very sharp and that was the beauty of it. You were never in any doubt as to what Tracker was saying to you and that was a gift. Not everybody is able to encapsulate in a thought, put it into words, keep it pretty short but make sure everybody in the room understands it.

So that very first encounter stuck in my mind when I watched him at the meeting asking questions and I remember walking out and saying, I think to Allen Blanchard who was travelling with me, *Jesus that young bloody Tilmouth is a pretty impressive sort of character.* So thus began the journey I suppose.

Martin Ferguson

One of my greatest disappointments with Tracker was we had him lined up to be a Labor Party senator. I think it might have been for the 1998 election and Kim [Beazley] had agreed to it. There was a filthy, vicious, personal campaign run against him by people who should have known better, including the late Senator Bob Collins. I had to interview Tracker and his wife. We decided he was a probity risk. The campaign run in the Northern Territory by non-Indigenous people, two of whom were Labor Party members of parliament and one ex-Labor senator, was unforgiveable, because in my opinion it was not about Tracker's capacity, it was about how he would have challenged them in terms of who knows best about Indigenous issues.

My comment about Collins is on the record. Bob Collins running a campaign to stop Tracker Tilmouth, after having had his opportunity in the Senate for years – a campaign of a very personal nature, and Tracker and his family had nothing to be ashamed of. Subsequent events have raised serious questions, more about Bob Collins than Tracker Tilmouth.[27] And Tracker would have been the first Indigenous senator. Beazley as the leader wanted it and in the end, Tracker and his wife made the decision to pull out of the preselection, because the girls were still young, and the campaign showed that certain people would continue in a very public and vicious way. So they made a decision for their family and the Labor Party was the loser.

They went around and lobbied people who were in the non-Indigenous majority to stop Tracker. They did not mind using the Indigenous community for their own election in the Northern Territory seats and in the Commonwealth Parliament because in those communities they have got over ninety per cent of the vote, but when it came to have someone in the Senate – the first ever Indigenous person – *No, no, we can not have them in the Senate, but we expect them to go out and organise the community votes for our re-election.*

Tracker has been good to a lot of people. He has done the job of a senator.

A lot of people [politicians] have also benefited from his knowledge. He had taken them throughout the Territory, fishing and learning

---

27. In 2007 Bob Collins committed suicide three days before he was scheduled to face court on charges of committing an act of indecency and one count of sexual intercourse with a child. Five of his victims were paid compensation under the *Victims of Crime Assistance Act,* after claims for compensation were accepted by the Northern Territory Government.

things, people like [Laurie] Brereton and [Nick] Bolkus. He put in the hard years and the hard slog but never got his proper recognition from the party.

Sean Bowden

It seemed normal and natural to me that Tracker would be preselected and that he would go on and become a senator in the Northern Territory. I might say some more later about the historical ramifications of him not becoming a senator, but the reason he did not I think is important to his story.

The first is the vilification that fell upon him. My father [Mike Bowden] was the president of the Australian Labor Party Alice Springs branch at the time. He was really shaken by this and we spoke about it, and I remember saying, *Well! That is just ridiculous.* The man is the director of the Central Land Council, and at that time I knew the Central Land Council was a heavily regulated body with audit and evaluation processes. So if he had done anything seriously wrong, it will be dealt with through those channels. This should be totally irrelevant to any sort of preselection. The weight came on Dad and he was incredibly troubled by it and it troubled me that he was troubled. I knew what I was going to do but he was now in two minds and this was played out in the Northern Territory Labor administration, the schism between the Labor Party wanting Aboriginal people and wanting the kudos of what came with it, wanting their votes, and wanting those people who were active within the field who they knew could harness the vote. Tracker Tilmouth was one, and my father was another because he worked at Tangentyere Council, and Geoffrey Shaw [managing director] was there, and Dad and Geoffrey were collaborators at the time, and were good organisers.

This was difficult but here it was, the non-Aboriginal members of the branch had made a decision, that *this was too dangerous, Tracker was uncontrollable, he was unpredictable,* and this might be getting to the heart of what they were really on about. They knew they could not control him. They knew there was a gene in him – a strength in him that was also a weakness, and that was his erraticism, but also his willingness to be erratic. His willingness to say the difficult things, albeit that he did not control his willingness to say those things as well as he should have.

At times he did let his emotions and his erraticism overcome him. I was friendly with Owen Cole, and Owen had also become a great friend to me and as much as I had a mentor, a real mentor, it was Owen. Someone I could confide in and who was able to direct me and pull me up a little bit because I was brash and pig-headed as well, and strong-willed. And Owen had said to me, before I met Tracker the first time, that if they sent Tracker to a team of eminent psychiatrists, drawn from the most eminent universities in Australia or the world, and left them with him for a week, by the end of that week all of those psychiatrists would either be mad, or they would be rewriting their books.

Such was the subtlety and the depth, the distinction of Tracker Tilmouth. I remember Owen said, *Seriously*. I remember laughing and he said, *No I'm deadly serious. This man is very, very complex.* And he was. And the Labor Party were afraid of that complexity but also the drive behind it, in that Tracker has always done the right thing by the mob in the bush. Maybe he did make the right decision in the end not to go into politics. It was an awful thing they did to him. I know the personal toll it had on him, the hurt, the fact that he had to sit down with his wife and talk about things. They did not just dredge up contemporary things. The past, and very personal matters from his past were dredged up.

At the time I knew Tracker he was the director of the Land Council. I had been around his family, and I knew he was a good man. I knew he was the right candidate, and now we know about the person who was vacating the seat and what he was capable of. We know that Bob Collins was capable of evil acts against the most disadvantaged and helpless people in the community, and that had been talked about in those days as well. I heard those things as a young lawyer, yet they were never used against Collins. Yet skerricks were taken from Tracker Tilmouth's life and used against him, which was not that mystifying if you assume that all the institutions of the Northern Territory are stacked against Aboriginal people and do not like Aboriginal people who are strong and power players. Tracker was seen as a power player and he showed that in 1998 when he opposed statehood for the Northern Territory, where it was in part his activism and charisma and focus that caused the Northern Territory to vote against statehood.

For instance, there was the famous Kalkaringi event where the campaign against statehood began, and I remember my view at the time was *why can't we have statehood?*[28] Why can't we find a way? But Tracker had the better view. Not only did he know better, he went and found the people he needed to find. He got the non-Aboriginal players in Alice Springs. He got them, and he had them raise concerns which was enough for fair-minded and sensible-thinking people in the Northern Territory to say, this is a bridge too far.

A coalition of the Aboriginal voices with the very conservative voice of old Territorians was unheard of. And to come back to Tracker, this period taught me a few really critical lessons which I have carried with me, and I hope I have been able to learn from, and use properly. One was about politics, the play of politics, that the Labor Party in particular was never really the friend of Aboriginal people the way it said it was. Certainly, it is a better party than the other side on most things, not all things, on most things.

But it has a fundamental dishonesty at its core that has not yet been resolved. This was proved in the Northern Territory election in 2012, where it took a lot of travesties to get to the point where the bush voted against the Labor Party en masse, in the face of people they knew and a system they trusted, which for people with a lot of change and uncertainty in their lives was a big decision. I know a lot of people told me, because they know I am a Labor Party supporter, they said, *Sean, this time I'm voting for the CLP.*

---

28. A reference to the work of the Combined Aboriginal Nations of Central Australia (CANCA), which was established by meetings requested by senior traditional men to the Central Land Council when Tracker was the director. CANCA, supported by the Central Land Council, organised the Kalkaringi Convention to discuss Northern Territory statehood and the flawed draft constitution for a state designed by the then chief minister of the Northern Territory, Shane Stone. The convention resulted in the Kalkaringi Statement which called among other measures for the safeguarding of the Aboriginal future in the Territory and the constitutional recognition of Aboriginal self-government. CANCA established a campaign which included other major stakeholders in the Northern Territory to vote against the Territory-wide referendum for statehood, which was subsequently defeated.

The kernel for that was back in 1998 with what they did to Tracker Tilmouth. The question is a very good one, what were their motivations for this? I really do not know other than they wanted to keep control, and they would use anything. People like my father were terrified and stirred up and scandalised by these stories. Someone else was generating these stories. I suspect it was Collins, but it was also others, there would have been others.

The only thing you cannot discount sometimes in some of this, is that Tracker may not have really wanted to be the senator. You can get very worked up over the backstory which is real, but I also wonder sometimes whether he really did want to be a senator because he could have fought it out, and he would have got it, he had the numbers at the Federal Executive. And the Federal Executive had made it clear that they were going to overturn the Northern Territory Branch no matter what their decision, and install Tracker over and above anyone else.

The person [who became the senator] was ultimately Trish Crossin. Bob Collins was the kingmaker. And Warren [Snowdon] also had to be wary of Collins' power and Collins' numbers, and this could be very unfair on Warren, but the point is, no one stood up and defended Tracker as far as I am aware. No one stood up and defended him and said, *This is rotten, stop it. If you are going to bring him down, bring him down on other bases, don't do this.* That is what they did, and I can only imagine the hurt and the pain that he endured going through it. At the same time, I do want to say this, I wish he had muscled on. I am not sure I could have, but selfishly I wish he had, because if he had have been elected a senator in 1998, a whole lot of what we have had to go through politically for the last fifteen years might have been brought forward, and might have been done differently.

But had he continued I guess they would have sought the first chance to knock him off and there would have been an urbane, friendly, soft white person waiting in the wings to take that seat. Because many political aspirants in the Northern Territory come from a very low base.

Had he become a senator, the politics of the Northern Territory and Australia would have been different. He proved his capacity in 1998 when he spearheaded the constitutional opposition to statehood for the Northern Territory.

Tracker Tilmouth

We had always decided that the Northern Territory could not afford to be a state.[29] Imagine the taxes. Imagine the emphasis on resource development being placed on Aboriginal traditional landowners, the pressure. Imagine administration of the Land Rights Act being the responsibility of the Northern Territory Government, how long do you reckon that would last? Five minutes.

So it is not a good thing. It was not meant to be a good thing. It was part of the ongoing agenda of whites who had managed to get up to the Northern Territory, the unemployable from down south. They turned up working with CDEP as a supervisor and ended up as the mechanic, and then all of a sudden they are the community advisor of the community. They were unemployable when they first started off with CDEP. So it was a push by people like that, that made up the bureaucracy of the Northern Territory, the itinerants who really had no place to go and decided to settle in the Northern Territory, and they dreamt this dream of a society that they thought they could build – a bit like New Guinea, like the Solomons, a bit like everywhere else. So the Northern Territory could never be a state, it cannot be a state today, it is broke for heaven's sake.

In 1998 we spearheaded a strategy to beat the statehood agenda of the Northern Territory Government, because at that time it was very much on the agenda, and people were saying it was a *fait accompli* but we turned that around. We had to, because we had to protect the interests of the Aboriginal community we represented. If someone turned up and said, *We have heaps of money, we can do* x, y *and* z *for infrastructure and employment, and deal with all the social issues, and we are going to allocate funding accordingly*, we would have listened, but do not come to us and say you vote for us and we will do this later. Tell us up-front what

---

29. Under the Central Land Council's direction in 1997 Tracker Tilmouth, as its then director, established Aboriginal law forums of senior traditional landowners to discuss the idea of self-determination and pending Northern Territory statehood. The forums, spearheaded by Mr Zimran, a senior and highly respected Pintubi man of the Western Desert region, discussed the kind of future they wanted to work towards for themselves and Aboriginal land in Central Australia.

the *grande plano* is, because we do not trust them, and if we do not trust them we are not going to support statehood in the Northern Territory.

We were not bereft of advice. We had people well-versed in the area of constitutional law. So accordingly, we followed instructions, as we should. If you do not know about it, go find somebody who does and sit down and talk to them, and see if you agree with their position. If you do, follow it.

Tracker Tilmouth

What would you say has been the fate of Aboriginal politicians in the Labor Party or the CLP, in either the Northern Territory Government or the federal government? Exactly. You have got rabble. There is no decent agenda for them joining a political party while they are subject to the rules and responsibilities of that party and I could not do that. If I found an issue that I thought was detrimental to the Aboriginal community I would be saying something. They would expect me to say things. And when you go through the list of Aboriginal candidates or politicians, there are no shining lights. They are just like the former Queensland mounted police, when they were out there under orders to shoot blacks, simple as that. I have no regrets. I went on to bigger and better things and I will continue to do so. I have carried out the role of supporting people at the level that you would expect from a senator. People come to me for advice. If they want me to make a comment I make a comment. I do not need to be endorsed by anybody. My daughters will go into politics no doubt. They will go with our blessing, but they will understand totally what it entails, and there will be no illusions about – do you really want to do this?

With the Labor Party in the NT, the facade of Aboriginal advancement has been pretty strong, even from the early days when Neville Perkins was the Leader of the Opposition, he had a continuous fight with the rednecks for support in relation to the Labor Party in Darwin. It was the last frontier where we as Aboriginal people are part of this force that has to be fought with, for them [non-Indigenous members of Australian political parties] to survive in the Top End. The Labor Party has never been really comfortable with Aboriginal participation both in the electoral sense, and as people who needed looking after.

They always knew better, what is good for us, and to a certain extent today it is still there. So you do not get any of the safe seats that are within the state parliament for Labor, Aboriginal people are available in those electorates, from Bagot, One Mile and so forth, but there are no Aboriginal candidates as such. And in the last federal election [2013] when all the votes were counted, I think you would find that the pro-Nova Peris votes were predominantly white.[30] She was acceptable to the white community. So if we are playing sport, or if we are going to play hockey and run very fast, then we would be a brilliant candidate. If we are talking politics and land rights, and social dividends and economics, unfortunately we are going to be left behind. But that is our role in life. Our role in life is to entertain. In the AFL grand final we have a lot of Aboriginal players, and when the grand final is over, they go back to their communities, and they end up the same way as a lot of Aboriginal players, doing drugs, being locked up, being drunk, being social misfits in their own community.

What they were paid for was their entertainment value. They could run fast, jump the highest, and do amazing things with the football, and that is all white people want to know. They do not want to know if their community is starving, or has housing, or jobs. They do not want to know any of that. That is not part of the agenda.

So when you take institutions like the AFL and you measure it against racist activities, none of those high-profile Aboriginal people other than Adam Goodes has really taken up the debate about Aboriginal communities. None of them. And Adam Goodes should be congratulated for what he has done. If you get this situation evolving where the Labor Party has got the same agenda, then you are only there to make up the numbers and you are owned: *We don't expect you to come*

---

30. Nova Peris was Julia Gillard's 'captain's pick' to replace Trish Crossin as Labor's number one Senate candidate for the Northern Territory in the 2013 federal election. Julia Gillard asked the ALP chiefs to approve the move by overruling local preselection processes and expediting Ms Peris' application for membership of the party, and to replace Senator Crossin following the Country Liberal Party's victory over Labor in the last Territory election. Peris retired from the Senate in 2016.

up with any policies. *We don't expect you to be part of any debate,* and in the last Labor government, we had a number of Aboriginal candidates and Alison [Anderson] was one of them. To her credit, she decided that she was not going to be part of the bullshit, and so when she found out about the housing and the lack of funding for housing, and the real story behind the Intervention, she hit the roof.

She hit the roof and wanted to expose it all and the Labor government had to show her the door. That was the fall-out she had with Labor. Now when you take Aboriginal organisations such as Congress, they have got a weird idea of how Aboriginal people fit within the landscape, and that idea is shared by people that study up in Darwin under the ideas generated by Professor Nugget Coombs who used to be at the Reserve Bank. Charles Darwin University has a statue of him near the Northern Australian Research Institute. He had a weird idea of how Aboriginal people should be as well, that you are no different to any other minority, which might be all right if we got the services other minorities have, and had no more of a claim than any minority. So the land was forcibly taken from you, and to the victors go the spoils. This was his philosophy and for a long time that has been the philosophy of the Labor Party.

When you are a plaything for too long and the Labor Party has been prominent [in doing this], it is good to see the Liberals and everybody else taking an interest in Aboriginal affairs, for whatever reason, because there is a bit of competition now. It is good to see the Country Liberal Party taking an interest in Aboriginal affairs and getting a bit more proactive. They might do it for all the wrong reasons and maybe have the wrong answers, but at least they have an interest, rather than just the Labor Party and the Greens. The Greens have always had a policy that Aboriginal people are a threat to the wilderness, and in the Tasmanian timber deal they left Aboriginal people out of it.

So you have still got this ongoing political debate with the Labor Party and with the current entrenched ideologues within the Labor Party in the Northern Territory. The most embarrassing thing was when Trish Crossin said to me, *Give me one of your daughters and I'll teach her politics.* I said to her, *Sunday morning around our breakfast table there's more politics than you could handle.* I could not imagine Cathryn working for her, because Cathryn was very good with Martin Ferguson, where she stood her ground. She had her own ideas where Aboriginal people fitted, and where the Labor Party fitted and so forth, and she made it known.

The CLP government know where they are going. They know their agenda. The agenda is slash and burn, simple as that. What you are going to get is a close review of the effectiveness of Aboriginal organisations such as land councils, the health services and other organisations which are supposed to be servicing the remote communities. If you do not have a connection with those remote communities you cannot expect to get money on their behalf.

Look! You cannot save idiots. You cannot legislate for foolishness, or madness. Whatever plan they come up with they will run into a brick wall, sixty per cent will be wrong, thirty per cent will be unknown, and the last ten per cent will be good. That is no different to the Labor Party where sixty per cent is rubbish, thirty per cent is unknown because we do not know where they are going, and ten per cent or less under Labor was good. The status quo will not change. It will be the players that change. The people will have new land councils and new organisations that will be developed, and you deserve the government you get. You deserve whatever is brought up against you if you have not done your homework.

Doug Turner

He once told [Joh] Bjelke-Petersen to fuck off back to his own country, get out of Alice Springs, and he tried to run Bjelke-Petersen off the road when he was in his motor car. This was down The Gap. And the police started chasing him. Told Bjelke to get back to his own country. It came on the news that mad Tracker Tilmouth had tried to run Bjelke-Petersen off the road. You have got to be tough like that, that is the only way you can survive and enforce your thoughts and ideas and your dislikes on politicians and on the broader community. Stand up, this is what standing up is all about.

I mean look at Tracker, he was bloody Stolen Generation and separated from his family and his brothers and sisters. So you had to be tough basically to survive, and I am glad he was like that. I only wish there were a lot of other Aboriginal people like him. The younger generation listen to government people in government departments, they are only gatekeepers who are there to make sure the government is on the right track. They do not give a stuff about our communities. They keep pulling us down. For Tracker to be out doing what he was doing with the network and contacts that he had, I thought that was fantastic.

There are a lot of politicians in the Territory he would talk about, and he would get on the radio and rubbish politicians about what they are doing and how they are on the wrong track. He would not be too frightened to get up and say that in public, or put it on TV, or in the newspapers. That was probably why he did not go into politics, he saw the madness of going into politics and he said, I do not want to be that mad.

The Human Sewer Rat

John Liddle

Did he tell you that George Pell story, you know that George Pell, the archbishop or whatever he is, he was walking, and this might be less than ten years ago, he walked through the Sydney airport and he had a bit of an entourage with him. Tracker sees this George Pell coming and says, *How ya going George?*

How are you going Tracker?

He looked around and made sure that everyone was watching, and he said, *I hope you excuse me, I'm not going to kiss your ring this time.* All the workers behind George Pell nearly fainted. *I hope you will pardon me, but I'm not going to kiss your ring this time,* he reckoned, and he looked around and smiled at everyone. That silly bloody smile he had.

William Tilmouth

I remember Phillip Ruddock when I went to Parliament House and Phillip Ruddock said he had seen me. He thought I was Tracker and he came over and said, *Hey you.* I said, *What?* He reckoned, *You, the last time I saw you, you were tearing down the wrong side of the road on the Tanami Highway and I was sitting in the back going as white as a ghost.* I said, *Me? Must be my brother, Tracker.* He looked and he looked again and said, *Yeah it was, sorry.*

And I went outside Parliament House to have a cigarette and one of those white government cars pulled up and I knew it was Bob Katter, because of his white hair and his white cowboy hat. He got out and I am standing up on the side having a cigarette and he comes up and he starts chatting to me, laughing and joking. I did not know this bloke from Adam. There he was, laughing away. I was not responding and he looked at me and said, *You're not Tracker are you?* I said, *No, sorry mate.* This went on for about five minutes. Then I got a few looks from another mate of his – [Bill] Heffernan, *Heff,* Tracks called him: *No, you are not Tracker*…He knew a lot of people, Peter Costello and all of them. It is a small world with him. A small, small world.

John Liddle

Tracker and Bill Heffernan went all over Central Australia together when they were talking about those Centrefarm projects. He knew how to do that sort of stuff, get people [politicians who he took on trips through Central Australia] to understand what is happening up here, host them, and send them out with people and get them to understand what the hell is happening in this area.

And you have got to do that. You have got to sell the product you've got really.

He had no shame. And I think he sat on Bronwyn Bishop's lap in Parliament House somewhere, in her office and gave her a kiss and said, *I'll go you halves in a coloured kid,* or something like that. I said, *Shit, don't tell me that please.*

No, I did, he said. I do not think her staff could believe what happened to her. She is a big old girl. Bronwyn Bishop and one of those other old politician women have been there for years.

I reckon he has some sort of storytelling aspect to his life. Like I said he spent so much of his time with a lot of those older people and listening to them. He was only telling me last time he was here, but I have heard the story a thousand times, that when the mob used to go on business he used to drive those old bosses, old Nosepeg, and all those old kings of culture, and they would have all the stuff, sacred objects, sitting in the truck with him. So he would be driving along in the truck and they would just have them there, in their football bag sort of thing. There are not many people they would let do that, you know, but they trusted him.

He was a very intelligent man, Tracker. He acted silly, but he had a lot of brains. I have ridden on his back a few times and I have said, *Shit, that's a bloody good idea, why didn't I think of it?* But then he just came out with them, and the next time you saw him he had another bloody box of them.

Sean Bowden

He told me these stories about how he knew Bronwyn Bishop who was a very senior player at the time. Back then, Bronwyn Bishop was a potential next prime minister. He knew Bill Heffernan. He knew Robert Hill as well as the range of Labor people, Kim Beazley, Daryl Melham, Martin Ferguson, Gerry Hand, who I came to know as well at the same time. All this stuff links when you fall into a clique and people start to know you. I guess we started to form a loose group and I was the lawyer for that group in different ways.

Tracker knew that he needed a lawyer on some of the things that he wanted to do because he had endless energy, boundless energy to do two sorts of things. One, he was a sort of a flamboyant, frontier-style entrepreneur which never seemed to quite come off, but he spent a lot of his time and energy exploring these things. The other was he genuinely did the right thing, and assisted people who were disadvantaged, or in need of a bit of social justice through good political and legal action.

I think he moved beyond the protest era, and in 1998, he learnt what he could do by co-opting different parties and knocking over statehood [for the Northern Territory]. I started to follow him into these worlds. The first was probably Wadeye.[31] The Commonwealth Government had formed seven or eight trial sites, where the idea was to coordinate government services and operations for the community, and Wadeye was one of them. There was a man down there called Terry Bullemor [then from the Thamarrurr Regional Council] who Tracker knew, and Wadeye was very much out of sight, out of mind in those

---

31. Wadeye, on the western edge of the Daly River Reserve, 420 kilometres south-west of Darwin, was one of the Aboriginal communities selected to be a part of a program agreed to in 2002 by the Coalition of Australian Governments. The trial was a new approach to the delivery of services to Indigenous communities, based on a whole-of-government, cooperative approach to improve social and economic outcomes, with agreements of shared responsibility between the Commonwealth and Territory governments and the Aboriginal communities involved in the trial.

days. It was a mythological place, a scary place. It still is a bit, but it is much more now in the public mainstream thinking.

It was known for having gangs and for being remote and wild. It is remote. It is not wild, but it is remote. But the gangs were building up, they were getting into trouble, and the community was in trouble. The community was horribly neglected. The Catholic Church had a very strong handle over the community and a whole lot of things conspired to bring the social and economic problems to a head. I always suspect that part of this was the generosity of spirit of the people at Wadeye, in that they just accepted what was given to them and did their best with it. That came from the Catholicism and the fact that it was so far away, and the fact the CLP had maintained a jurisdiction over there, the CLP represented that seat. Because it was conservative Catholic, the CLP politicians managed to win the seat but then did not deliver.

And then there was the remoteness, the inability to access the place. No road, very poor air transport, barge once a week, once a fortnight sometimes, no political voice, and a man called Terry Bullemor out there, who is a saint. Tracker rang me up one afternoon while I was doing a lot of work in Queensland on native title matters, and it was very controversial work, involving [Geoff] Clark and Sugar Ray Robinson [then chairperson and deputy chairperson of ATSIC].

Tracker said, *Bowds, we're going to see Bullemor.* I said, *Who's Bullemor?* He said, *Bullemor, you know Bullemor?* I said, *No, I don't know Bullemor.* He said, *I saw him yesterday.* I said, *Okay, we'll go to see Bullemor. Where is Bullemor?*

Wadeye, we're going to Wadeye.

I said, *My goodness, where is Wadeye? I know of Wadeye, I've heard of it. What are we doing?*

He said, *We're going out there to see Bullemor.*
Why?
I saw him and he said to come out, and Dougy Taylor might come too.
Who's Dougy Taylor?
He's a contractor, a mate of mine, and he is working out there.

As it turned out Tracker might have got Dougy Taylor to pay for the charter. This was classic Trackerism. He had bumped into Bullemor who was the CEO of the Wadeye community, he was struggling and under pressure, he had been there seven or eight years, and he had been banging the drum as hard as he could. Now he had finally got the spotlight on him, they were having this coordination trial. He does not know how to do it. He didn't know what to do, and Tracker was there to get involved.

Terry Bullemor operated the most extraordinary office at Wadeye which was an open office. If you can imagine a community of about two and a half thousand people, he had an open office. He had no computers. His computer was at home. He had files everywhere and his office was open. It was in a corner of the building, at the front of the building. Like in the bow of a ship, there was Terry. And so anyone in the community had access to him. It was extraordinary. And they loved him. And he had a good second-in-command. He was not an administrator and he was not very tactical. He knew that. Obviously he had thought, with Tracker, *I can pick Tracker's brains and see what he knows.* So there we went. I got on this charter. I can still remember it very clearly. A sweaty little Cessna with the three of us, Doug Taylor, Tracker and I, and Doug and I did not really know what we were doing there, or what Tracker was doing there, but we went and we had a meeting with the community, a small group of leaders.

It became clear that Wadeye needed a little bit of help. They did need some political help and they did need some legal help. So Tracker said, *Well! This is Bowds.* I said, *Actually my name is Sean Bowden. I'm a lawyer. I grew up a little bit around Alice Springs. I'm now in Darwin. Yes, I'm happy to assist you.* It was always my role to formalise things. Anyway away we went.

Terry suggested, *We would like you guys to formally assist us.* I think Tracker formally assisted for about a year or so. I am not sure really what he was doing day by day. He was just opening doors and things, and I started doing the legal work which was fascinating because we had every departmental secretary from every department in the Commonwealth and the Northern Territory come and see us at one time or another, often in groups. It was exhausting. So I was forever getting on a charter to go down there and meet with these people. We had a coordination trial, and it didn't coordinate, it duplicated, it was like ten times the red tape. Incredible.

We had to kill the red tape that had come about from a trial designed to kill red tape. Wadeye went from thirty-four grants to one hundred and thirty-four because the bureaucrats all came with their little grant, their little fifty grand, or their thirty grand. There were people higher up the chain who they wanted to impress by showing they were actually involved with the trial at Wadeye: *We can give you this. We can do that.* It was driving us crazy. It was driving Bullemor crazy. And Terry, this man Terry Bullemor is an extraordinary human being. He nearly died with his boots on. He was collapsing at meetings. Tracker's friend Bob Beadman arrived one afternoon, having made an appointment, but Terry had forgotten, or it had not been done properly, and people just assumed they could arrive.

So they arrived on a charter and demanded to see Terry. He had two or three other things going on, and Bob Beadman, who is quite forceful, got really cranky and demanded the meeting. Terry walked in and collapsed and they medivaced him out. The next time I saw Bob Beadman I gave him a piece of my mind, which was the best way to talk with Bob, who is a good mate of mine also. So Bullemor collapsed and then he came back, and before he did, he found a piece of paper and he gave it to Tracker and me, and that piece of paper was a letter from 1979 that gave a commitment from the Northern Territory Government to the Commonwealth Government to maintain education spending at Wadeye at the same level as the Commonwealth had spent before self-government in 1978.

Around the same time Terry had a guy called John Taylor working with him. Dr John Taylor is Australia's best demographer, certainly in the Indigenous domain. He is absolutely supreme. He came up with the statistic that said Wadeye was receiving twenty-six cents for every dollar spent on a school other than Wadeye. Wadeye got twenty-six cents in the dollar yet the disadvantage was extreme and the conditions were incredibly difficult. Terry produced this letter and the Taylor Report,[32] and Tracker and I looked at each other and went, *Wow!* Tracker said, *I've been waiting for something like this for twenty years. We've got em, we're away here.* That triggered us to run a human rights case which Tracker

---

32. John Taylor and Owen Stanley, *Opportunity Costs of the Status Quo in the Thamarrurr Region* (Australian National University, Canberra, 2005).

was the instigator of, and which caused fundamental generic change at bush schools, really positive. I would estimate that has probably over a decade added two hundred million dollars into remote schools, because the government had to change their funding formats. They were underfunding the remote schools run by the Catholic Education Office by at least twenty million a year, if you can believe that. And through this action, which was led by a wonderful and decent leader Tobias Nganbe, and through my work with Tracker, it gave me the courage, and others like Tobias Nganbe the courage, to start to talk publicly about this stuff. And to get the result.

At the time Tracker said, *Bowds, we've been waiting for this. We're going to Canberra. We're going to see Billy Heff {Bill Heffernan}.*

I said, *Hang on, hang on, we need to have a strategy first.* That was my role. He said, *Alright*, pardon the politically incorrect language here, but, *We're going to see the Jews.* I said, *My goodness, who are the Jews?*

We're going to see the Castans, we're going to see Melis.

I said, *Oh! Yeah, who's Melis?*

Melissa Castan, Ron Castan's daughter. Ron had passed away in 1998 I think, and Melissa had set up the Ron Castan Centre for Human Rights Law at Monash University. Beautiful person, wonderful person.

And we got the Northern Land Council involved and this took a special art. Getting the NLC involved could not have happened without Tracker. He got the Northern Land Council to pay for the fares, and he got John Sheldon involved. We took it to Norman Fry and to the NLC and said, *Look at this. If this isn't within all of our mandate then nothing is.* I was really fired up about it too. Here it was in black and white, what we all knew: that the system in the Northern Territory, at its core, was rotten. It was so low that it would deprive children of money, of their entitlements to go to school, and then ignore them and lie about it.

So we got on a midnight flight with John Sheldon who was the policy officer of the Northern Land Council, a very good guy, very decent person, a good sense of right and wrong. He said, *Righto! I can do this. This is within my mandate, let's go.* We went down on a midnight flight and we get off in the morning and we catch a taxi into the city. We have breakfast, and Tracker still has not told us where we are going. I do not think he actually knew. But we ended up at Nellie Castan's

Gallery which is in South Yarra, and Melissa came and saw us with Sarah Joseph, the head of the Centre. He still had not really prepped me as to what to say. I knew we were meeting someone, I knew her name was Melis and that she was a Castan but I did not know where. So we got there and Sarah Joseph who is a professor said, *Tell us about it*. I went, *Okay*, and Tracker looked at me, *Go on Bowds*. I should have known my role by then, but I was still learning my role. So I explained the situation. They said *right, let us look at it*. A month later we got a phone call from Melissa who said, *Yes this is real, and we'll try and help you*. I said, *I need some lawyers*. I think I had come away and prepared another document that really laid it out and said, *This is it legally, as best as I can do*. Melissa took that around to some lawyers, to Maurice Blackburn and others, and it was Arnold Bloch Liebler, Peter Seidel at Arnold Bloch Liebler, who picked it up and said *we will do this*.

The others rejected it, I think because most Melbourne lawyers were interested in sexier issues that are more in line with their progressive views, like anti-uranium and anti-environment action. This was a human issue. It was complicated with a community that was complicated, a community that had overtones of violence, and it was already in the newspapers for being a violent place, where the kids did not go to school. We had to make the argument that the reason kids did not go to school *was that there was no school*. The reason there was no school was because the government neglected to provide them with a school.

So we are probably into late 2005 now, and the next trip was to Canberra. John Sheldon went with us to Canberra from Melbourne to see Billy Heff and others. We went to Canberra and we ended up staying with [Daryl] Melham MP. I said, *Where are we going to stay?* We didn't have much money. Tracker said, *We'll stay in this apartment first, and then we'll stay with Melham on the second night,* which was great. I had met Daryl Melham, the federal member for Banks, who was a great friend of Tracker. Daryl had convinced the then Prime Minister Paul Keating to make sure that the original Native Title Act when introduced did not suspend the Racial Discrimination Act but validated certain titles. Daryl was also instrumental in ensuring that the issue of whether a pastoral lease extinguished native title was left to the courts, and not extinguished in 1993 with the original act as many people wanted.

So Daryl was absolutely critical to making sure Aboriginal people got rights over the Australian pastoral estate out of the Mabo decision, something that people forget was not in any way guaranteed at the time. He was a terrific parliamentarian who sacrificed himself for principle and had his career harmed because of that, when he resigned as the Shadow Minister for Indigenous Affairs because [Kim] Beazley supported [Peter] Beattie [then Queensland Premier] on racist and regressive native title laws which were subsequently withdrawn by Beattie because they were wrong and didn't work. Daryl resigned on principle and paid a price. Not that he ever complained, he is a great man, a great politician who knew the difference between right and wrong.

So in politics you can have these periods of victory, or success, but I unfortunately got to watch Daryl go through a period where his career waned, just because he did the right thing by Aboriginal people. The native title legislation that Beattie had brought in to the Queensland Parliament and which Beazley had supported was so offensive it was eventually withdrawn.

Anyway, Tracker says we are going to see Billy Heffernan. And I am saying, *Why? Because he's the guy who can talk to the Prime Minister, that's why.* I said, *But he's Billy Heffernan. He's a right-wing New South Wales Liberal, hard man.* Tracker replies, *He's a great bloke Bowds, you'll love him.* I said, *I can't imagine that I would.* He says, *Don't worry. Billy, he's a great mate of mine.* I am saying to myself, *This is really getting out there.* I could not believe it was true, that Tracker and Billy were great mates.

I found out though through my father that Bill Heffernan was a practical bloke, a straight shooter, because he had come to Tangentyere Council, and funded something Dad wanted funded to do with underprivileged kids in the Alice Springs Town Camps. So we got up to Canberra, went off to breakfast, and this was a huge experience for me. We were going to Parliament House, for me it was the first time, I was going with Tracker Tilmouth to see Bill Heffernan. We have got an issue to prosecute, we were all quite excited.

This was what made Tracker tick. This was what got him out of bed in the morning, doing something real. This was real. And so we go to the Senate entrance. I did not know how to get into Parliament House, but Tracker did. He got someone to book him in. We walk through the Senate entrance, we walk into the corridor, and a head came out of a door a hundred metres down and yelled out, *Tracker*. It was Billy Heffernan. This is a true story. John Sheldon and I, our mouths just dropped open and Tracker goes, *Billy. Wild Billy,* he called out.

It was like being in the Tardis, Parliament House, you do not know where you are once you are in. It goes forever. And down we went to Billy Heffernan's office. I had learnt to play my role by then, and I knew that I was going to have to explain things, and I did. Of course Bill was harder than Melissa and Sarah Joseph, and he wanted to know all sorts of things. Off we went. He said, *Righto! That's good. I'll take it on board and I'll come and see you. I'll come up and have a look myself.* He was good to his word. Then we went off around Parliament House and this was my first experience with the self-described human sewer rat, which Tracker calls himself when he goes in to Parliament House.

Now follow me Bowds, I'm the human sewer rat, I know exactly where I'm going. People who have been in Parliament House for ten years get lost, but Tracker knew his way around Parliament House like you would not believe, and he taught me it was all about the colours on the carpets, and having a basic sense of direction, which you do lose. Off we went. He had a very good sense of direction. In fact, he would still roll me badly in a walk around Parliament House, even though I have probably been there three or four times more than him nowadays. I still get lost even though I am following the carpet. So off we go. We went and saw 'Bronny' as he called her, who was really Bronwyn Bishop. We just walked in, walked into the office and there she was. He yelled out through the entrance to the back office and Bronwyn came over, *Tracker it's so lovely to see you.* They embraced and she rubbed his belly. She said, *My boy, look at that belly.* She rubbed it. He said, *Leave it alone. Leave it alone.*

She said, *You need to lose some weight young man.* He said, *I'm not that young, well okay, I am.* They had this banter and off they went. It was fantastic to watch. I thought, *what a treasure this man is.* Billy Heffernan! And now Bronwyn Bishop, he could go and talk to Bronwyn Bishop, what an asset. Later on I am saying to him, *You're unbelievable, the cheek of doing this.* He said: *Learn it mate, learn it, do it, just do it, I've learnt it.*

You see, Tracker wasn't the guy who did the one meeting, came to Canberra for the one meeting and dressed up, came in and made a hoo-ha about the meeting, and then afterwards put out a press release. Tracker was determined to use his time better. People like Gerry Hand would warn me about the same thing. Tracker would say, *I have as many meetings in a day as I possibly can and then some more. We are going to make use of our time, Bowds. We are going to see everyone we can.* I said, *Do you have appointments?* He just said, *It doesn't matter.*

So off we went and I think by now it was getting close to two o'clock, which was Question Time. I was saying, *Tracker, come and watch Question Time.* I had never been to Parliament House before other than maybe as a tourist once, but not properly. He said, *Yeah! We'll get there.* It was half past one. He said, *Got to see Hilly,* who was Robert Hill, the defence minister, and we had been past his office and he was not there. Tracker said, *Come on, we'll go back to Hilly's. Oh! How?*

Just follow me, I'm the human sewer rat.

Off we went up stairs and we get to Hilly's, and Tracker walked in. You can see through, there was a conference room – in every ministerial office is a conference room, just adjacent behind the secretary. In this instance the door was a little bit open and you could see Robert Hill in there with four-star or five-star generals sitting there, three of them. Tracker yelled out, *Hilly.* The secretary was not there. Tracker walked around, and I must have followed him, which was how I got the view in and he yelled, *Hilly.* Robert Hill looks around and says, *Tracker, how are you mate? Great to see you. Are you here for long?* Tracker says, which was not quite true, *I'm off shortly.* Robert Hill turns to these generals and says, *Gentlemen, will you just give me a moment?* The five-star generals, maybe they were four-star, maybe they were five-star, fully suited up, walked out, and Tracker and I walked in to Robert Hill's conference room twenty minutes before Question Time. It was just amazing. He just did that.

Tracker started to talk to him about other things. He was keeping the contact, letting Robert Hill know that he was around, that he cared, that he had issues to talk about, that he was a player and that he was on a mission. Fantastic. Every Aboriginal leader should learn from the Tracker Tilmouth Handbook. Every single one.

Of course we went and saw all the Labor gang as well, we didn't miss them, but the challenge was to engage the government, the people in power at the time, and that is what we did.

Nowadays when I go to Canberra I still find it very hard to drop in on people but I make the appointments and I make sure we get three or four or five meetings. I take Tobias Nganbe [from Wadeye], and I have taken Galarrwuy [Yunupingu]. When I started to work with Galarrwuy really properly in 2006, 2007 and 2008, I knew what to do because Tracker had taught me, and Galarrwuy in a way did not know what to do, because Galarrwuy hated it in Canberra. He said, *I don't want to go to Canberra. Why? It's a waste of time.* I said, *We're not going to waste your time this time.*

I remember showing Galarrwuy an itinerary I had developed to see people with Tracker helping me at this stage and Galarrwuy said, *Okay, I'll go.* Previously, one time Galarrwuy said, *I'm never going back to Canberra.* I was on that trip in 2003 or 2004 with Tracker when ATSIC was being dismantled, and we all went down in a lobbying effort to see whether anything could come out of the remains. Galarrwuy said at that time, *I'm never coming back to this place. It's a waste of time. I'm never coming back.* I got him back, and I got him back on the Tracker Tilmouth formula, in 2007 and 2008.

So we did the Robert Hill meeting, and then we did the Labor Party in the afternoon. That was much easier because they were in Opposition, and we met Martin Ferguson who subsequently became a great confidante to myself and others, but I inherited that from Tracker. I owe Tracker. He gave that contact to me. *Here you go Sean, this is a good man. You can trust him. He will tell you the truth. He has got a good heart and he will work hard.* Not in those words exactly, but that was really what he meant. He took me to Melham of course, and it was the most outrageous, one of the most outrageous meetings you will ever go to. Daryl is single, he has never married, he lived with his mum at the time. Poor Daryl, I think Tracker had twenty-five humorous variations on that theme for about the first hour of the meeting. In the end Daryl said, *Tracker, you've been belittling me, having jokes at my expense for the last hour, now what the hell are you here for?* At which point we got down to business again, and then we were staying at Daryl's that night.

We did that, and then we went off for dinner somewhere. We were all exhausted by then, had an early dinner, no drinking. No drinking. It was one of the great things about Tracker, no drinking. I drink alcohol and I quite like it. When I was young I probably drank too much at times. I suddenly found, though, how professional and innovative you could be when you were not drinking. Drinking was a bad way to do business, particularly if you were coming in on behalf of Aboriginal people. Then we went off to Daryl's place. Daryl made us a cup of tea in his pyjamas, and we talked some politics, lots of politics actually, then he made our beds for us and tucked us in and got us up in the morning in his pyjamas with another cup of tea. It was a freezing Canberra night, and by the end of it all Tracker was saying, *Melham, why don't you put the heater on in this stinking place. Look at you, you're like a big koala bear, look at ya, look at the koala bear.* We get out of bed in the morning and he says, *Bowds, a koala bear just served me a cup of tea, did you get yours?* One of the incredible things was this constant banter. Sometimes it was infuriating because he would let it contaminate a serious moment, and sometimes he used it too often, and he would use it when he was under pressure as well. When it was pure, when it was just pure humour, he was the funniest, most hysterical person I have ever met.

Sam Miles

Charlie Perkins was the only other person I know of, when you were in a meeting, that had to be the dominant figure. When Tracker was in a meeting, he had to have the attention otherwise he was not comfortable. Two things I remember about him. It was on TV and Dr John Herron [a former Minister for Aboriginal Affairs] had been criticised after he made his speech and there was a bit of booing or carrying on, and Tracker got to the microphone and said to him, *Hey brother, pass the water will you.* And that just changed the whole atmosphere. Herron was relieved because he could smile and pass him the water. Tracker had the focus.

Tracker was also good at times when a whitefella was talking. He would chip in with an analogy or a metaphor to simplify it, to get it on track for them. He was good at that. Sometimes it was funny, and sometimes he would say it right. He was good at getting attention. Once at one of these business type meetings in Darwin, Tracker and I were the only ones who were not serious money people or anything else, and the meeting was about forestry on Aboriginal land. Tracker got a bit bored and said, *Ah! Well youse government, they couldn't find their arses to wipe themselves.* You can imagine he had the attention straight away. What he had was what the Jews call chutzpah. Boldness, forward with ideas whether it was a government minister or whoever. Pushy.

There was one time in DAA, for some reason or another we all went down to Canberra, a lot of us. The rest of us DAA blokes went to Parliament House and were just floundering around, and Tracker was more junior than us and he said, *Hey! I've got a meeting with a minister organised.* He had organised it, and we met this bloke who was the Minister for Aboriginal Affairs in the Malcolm Fraser government, who was the dumbest bastard you have ever seen in your life. But it took Tracker, this junior bugger from DAA in Alice Springs, who had gone there and knew how to work the politics. He just cut right through and did it. The trouble was we went in there and we did not know what we wanted. The minister expected us to say we wanted a hundred thousand for this or that…and of course we did not have anything in mind. That is what I remember of it.

Owen Cole

One of the funniest stories was when the native title legislation was going through. I think it might have been the ILC legislation that was to create the Indigenous Land Corporation, and we went down to Canberra and we were sitting around with the Labor Party blokes – Simon Crean and Martin Ferguson – at a Chinese restaurant at Manuka, and Bronwyn Bishop walked past, so Tracker called her across.

He knew the Coalition was opposed to the native title legislation and he goes [calls] to Bronwyn and says, *Bronwyn*, and I will give you the sanitised version here, *Bronwyn come here.* She goes: *Tracker darling.* He says, *Bronny we want you to support the legislation that's going up tomorrow or the day after.* She goes, *Oh! Tracker, you know I've got to toe the party lines.*

Tracker goes, *Well! Bronny, if you go against party lines to support the legislation, I'll come around to your place and give you a kiss,* or words to that effect. Or, *I'll pash you,* something like that, *Pash on the weekend.* Of course all the Labor Party blokes, Ferguson and Crean they were sliding under the table. David Ross was there and I was there, but he could get away with it. She went off in a bit of a huff. But there she was walking down the stairs and she was smiling at Tracker.

Of course the legislation got through but I do not think it had anything to do with Bronwyn supporting it after that. He would say those type of things and get away with murder occasionally. The rest of us would not even have the gall to try it. I always remember that. Honestly, those Labor politicians actually sliding under the table, trying to get away from Tracker, what he was saying to a fellow parliamentarian.

Of course, that is the sanitised version of it. He would have said something a little bit riper than that.

Geoff Clark

Then we came to the native title debate of 1992, in Canberra. We spent a hell of a lot of time in parliament, lobbying ministers and whatever. I remember one day we were walking down the corridor and Bronwyn Bishop was walking the other way, and Tracker raced up and started dancing with her and joking, and said she looked like a Boston bun walking down the aisle. He made these comments to people, and he did not care what their status was, or where he was. He would be wanting to dance with her, another time he would be doing a bit of a waltz, walk up and do a bit of a waltz with her. Every time we had a meeting Tracker would come in with a joke or two and sort of upset the meeting. It was always very pointed, he would articulate some very pointed opinions, but he would do it in such a manner that people had to laugh, or cry, or try to ignore him.

The worst thing you could ever do was try to ignore Tracker when he had an audience. He would just roll it out and it would be an opportunity for more jokes.

Laurie Brereton

I first met Tracker when I was the member for Kingsford Smith in the House of Representatives, and it was during the period when the government was formulating its response to Mabo [1992]. I am not actually sure how he came to turn up on my doorstep but he introduced himself, and I think he had been around to see a few friends of mine, Bolkus, Melham, and he got into the habit when he was in Canberra of dropping in to see me. That was how it began.

I think at that point I was the parliamentary secretary to the Prime Minister and then a cabinet minister following that. These were more social calls than work, and I was a keen supporter of the push in the Cabinet to get the very best legislative response [to the Mabo decision]. We were fighting a great fight. We had the National Party and the then Opposition marking out the ground, promising bucketloads of extinguishment in the words of the deputy leader, Tim Fischer, and we all know what a difficult period that was, and we all know that what was fashioned was good work at the end of the day as a result of some inspired leadership from the Indigenous community, and the commitment of the government and particularly Prime Minister Keating to get the best outcome. But in terms of being a prime mover, no I was not, I was basically one of those pressing to get a just and appropriate settlement, or response actually.

Tracker was basically briefing me on what was required in his view, and there were many people who did that, but Tracker kept coming back and then it became a friendship, and in the years that followed I made a habit whenever I was in the neighbourhood, whether it be Alice Springs or Darwin, of looking him up and so the friendship blossomed.

I did a few bush trips with him. Probably one of the nicest was a trip that started off in Alice and ended up in Darwin but involved the Tanami Track and communities, Kununurra along the way, and then across the Top End with my two sons who were both schoolboys then. Tracker very generously organised that trip because, he said, *You boys ought to understand us and the land.* He brought along a couple of mates of his and a couple of vehicles, and he took us out and explained the songlines, the Granites [mine], how you take a killer at Mistake Creek, how you get it butchered up, how you swim and not get too worried about freshwater crocodiles, even when all their eyes are looking at the kids at night. It was a great trip. That was the first of a number of expeditions, shorter and longer that I undertook with Tracker.

Tracker never stopped talking about projects. He always had a project. If he did not have one he was looking for one, always driven by ideas and ambition to do things, commercial, cultural, educational. He was full of thoughts.

All of Tracker's projects are difficult. Tracker never had a no-brainer, they have all been challenges. I have never done anything with him commercially, but I have tried to get some of his ideas over the line, whether it be Ti Tree and a great horticultural venture in the centre of Australia growing melons, or trying to export live camels to the Middle East, or trying to make productive again some of the grazing properties of Central Australia that would afford opportunities for Indigenous lads to get some training, some experience and to be the cattle masters again that they had been. Tracker was always dragging an idea or two along. Of course you had to go and look at them, you could not just talk about them.

You had to go and have a look. So in subsequent years we spent quite a number of trips around the MacDonnell Ranges and back up Ti Tree, and up in the Top End looking at his prawn farm [outside of Darwin] and fishing, in Kakadu on the locked gate trails and having a lot of fun, and being cleaned up by mosquito plagues and all sorts of things, but always an experience with Tracker.

I have been up the Gulf of Carpentaria with him. He had an idea of a project involving cattle right at the very top of West Arnhem Land on Murganella Plains which is immediately below the Cobourg Peninsula 350 kilometres east of Darwin. So we tracked around out there and surveyed properties where he thought there was some potential to get an agricultural operation going.

You were laughing or crying most of the time. I mean that was the way it was. He had a view about everything and I would have heard hundreds of funny stories. He was a big-picture character, and he always had a number of building blocks, and was always charging along.

He wanted to help with the feral camel problem and live camels appealed to him. Getting a camel abattoir as part of the business was also important, but live camels were particularly attractive. He wanted to open that market up almost before anyone else had got near it. That was at the early stage before the rest of Australia learnt about the numbers of camels coming into Docker River and other places. Tracker was onto it like a ton of bricks. We would be looking at the logistics of this, and Tracker had some fellow designing a cage that you could put the camels in in order to get them onto the rail line and up to Darwin, and out of the country. He was working through the logistics of how you actually get something with a long neck that gets through the top of the cage on a train safely to the point of export. But in a remote location you can imagine the challenges of rounding up substantial numbers of camels and then getting them into a loading facility and onto the rail to Darwin. All challenging. A spur gas pipeline down to a mine that he was interested in, or having a plan to put properties together with different strategies, both purchased in the market place and leased from traditional owners, and building relations with the TOs in the respective areas that he was interested in.

I met Bluey Pugh who was involved in Tracker's attempt to get into the camel business and, oh yes, we thumped around the roads in the centre of Australia with Bluey and Tracker, hilarious times, camped out or stopping at Tilmouth Wells, and of course the stories of what it is to breed crocodiles and export them, legend again. But that was something I did not get involved in.

We fished once in darkness, and he wanted to show us a particular place at the back of Kakadu with a heap of fish — barramundi and mangrove jacks. We got there about the time the biggest plague of mosquitoes descended, fishing in the dark, and ended up locked in a car with a state cabinet minister and another parliamentary colleague, with more mosquitoes than you could believe in the car with us. It was worse outside. Driven mad. But we got a lot of fish and lived to tell the story, and barbecued much of it in the traditional fashion, un-gutted, and I must say I still prefer my fish gutted but the company was terrific and the experience just wonderful. Freshwater turtles and all the bush tucker that Tracker introduced us to.

Tracker was a funny bugger. I think his ability to make fun of things was a key part of his makeup, and that is why he got on with all of us so well. Tracker had a serious side, but he was always fun. He never stopped and he had a larrikin streak at the same time, but he could be deadly serious about something that he really knew and wanted you to know was important and needed to be done.

He had a rich life in every sense from his childhood through those early years of hardship, and there was a lesson in every one of his stories but they just came so naturally. He studied and became interested in horticulture. He had an international perspective. His work with the Central Land Council and everything that followed on from that. Everything was a story about Tracker's life experience, what he thought would happen next, and *what you might be able to help me with*. And if in doubt he would ring up and say, *What do you think about this?* Absolutely day or night. And if he thought someone was valuable as a potential future leader, he would want you to meet them. He would want to bring them around for a barbecue or whatever to make sure that they were tuned in, and you knew who they were.

Anything anyone ever told him went straight onto the memory stick, bang! He was a very clever fellow.

Bill Heffernan

I think when Tracker was [in the Central Land Council] I got to know him. I had a few meetings with him and obviously did a bit of work with him and it was pretty disappointing in some ways, to go out there and find people that were, shall I say, taking advantage of Indigenous people, in the art world for instance, and in the housing setup there.

Tracker was always a very articulate advocate for the Indigenous mob, or as we call it in a nice way between ourselves the blackfella problems. I think it is not an offensive term where I come from with people that you deal with, because it's like being a good bastard, or a bad bastard. So I got to know and admire Tracker and he got involved in that Centrefarm arrangement in Alice Springs, and then moved up to Darwin, and as I recall him telling me, he was a separated kid and he said the whiter ones in his family went one way and the darker ones went some other way. He finished up being brought up in the lockup in Darwin somewhere. It was an adjunct of the local prison or the bloody police station, I have forgotten how he described it. It was not because he was in any trouble — that was the only place they kept the kids.

This is going back a good few years. He must have been the first Aboriginal graduate from Roseworthy College, with a science degree in resource development. He was brought up as a separated kid who was taken into some sort of orphanage arrangement where the definition of which way you went was the colour of your skin, it was pretty poor, and who would come through all of that as cheerful and self-confident and proactive as Tracker was, always wanting to have a go? He was always working for the cause and he would come down to parliament on a reasonably regular basis as I recall, and he would walk the halls there, and did it all in a very positive way. There were no sour grapes in the way he presented himself.

One of the things that Tracker was keen on was for Indigenous people to have the opportunity to own their own home, instead of living in some sort of government setup where the mob comes along and kicks all the windows in. If you own your own home you take pride in your home and if the glass gets broken you fix it, that sort of thing. He was certainly very keen, which he demonstrated with his own family, on a good education for kids. At the time when we first talked, there were several thousand kids in the Northern Territory that did not have a high school to go to. There are still quite a few in the same situation. I got to know some of the issues.

Tracker was always interested in further development of Northern Australia and obviously the winners, if the government ever gets it right, will be the Indigenous mob because they own the bulk of the land, in one form of title or another. There were some title problems with carbon trading and so on because carbon credits would have gone to the government, instead of the Indigenous people. He was helpful in teaching: where to go to see both sides of the story. I mean it was interesting to go to Uluru and stay in the flash hotel, the resort, and then go around the corner a couple of kilometres to the people living in sheer poverty.

I think we went out on the Finke River [to Aputula] at one stage. We went down the paddock and kicked a football with a few kids, and what they wanted most of all was a pool to be able to swim in. Tracker was always interested in diet, and he would go to a place like that where too many kids ate chips and drank Coca-Cola. He was very keen to have vegetable gardens set up and a hothouse sort of arrangement.

The hothouse might have been twenty yards long and ten yards wide, and it was marvellous the amount of tucker you could grow in that and feed several families just by putting your mind to it. So he was certainly a contributor and wanted to make a better place for our Indigenous people to live. Obviously, part of that is education and being job-ready. I know he was keen on having residential colleges for kids to graduate through the education system, and to be job-ready when they came out the other end. He had lots of ideas in those areas, residential sort of teaching facilities.

We went on a couple of camps and I can remember the first time I ate a raw witchetty grub. He bit the head off and downed it and I went, *Aagh!* Seeing the harvesting of native foods, it was quite an interesting experience. I remember camping at a bore. I know Robert Hill was in the party and we put our swags down to sleep on the ground and one of the Indigenous people came along waving his hand, and said, *No, no, not there*. The story was that there was a well-known local snake that used to go to the dripping tap on the tank between where we were camped and the tank, and we were on its pathway. You could not help but be empathetic to the issues when an advocate such as Tracker was on the job. He was conscious of some of the lurks, and some of the things that could go wrong in Indigenous funding.

I think it would be fair to say about Tracker, that had the opportunity presented itself, he would have represented his people and his country in parliament, if the right sort of circumstances had fallen his way. He was involved in lots of ideas and plans and would have been a bloody solid member of parliament. He was proud of his family and he was articulate. I recall in his early days he was a fairly strong supporter of one side of politics but he did not let that get in the road. He most definitely did not let that get in the way, and he articulated his case in all political climates and atmospheres.

I think we may have gone out to Wadeye with Tracker and saw a police station that was a compound with razor wire around it. I can remember standing out the front of this police station and the policeman came up in his patrol vehicle and got out and shut the gate. I said, *What did you say to your wife when you said you'd been posted here?* I said, *Where are you from?* He was from Darwin or somewhere. *What did your wife say when you got posted here?* thinking there would be an interesting reaction. And he said, *We wanted to come,* which I thought was a bloody good answer. He said there are lots of good things you can do here.

I remember walking down the street and seeing these women lined up and thinking that it was like half time at the footy. They were lined up down the footpath and I said to Tracker, *What are they doing?* He said, *That's the Centrelink phone.* There was this black hole in a wall with a phone in it, and that was the Centrelink office. We did something about that because it was just a phone back to bloody Darwin or somewhere. So as a consequence of complaining about that, they got a Centrelink person on the ground.

Tracker, I suppose, was my mentor in getting my head around the Indigenous perspective on some of the issues, some of the complexities of the communities, and some of the internal politics, and like all things, there is always contest, ideas and personalities. It was quite an interesting time in my life.

Another thing I recall was the dialysis. In whitefella communities, in Sydney or elsewhere, you can go to someone who has got diabetes or needs dialysis and they have their own dialysis unit in their own home, but you go out there, and some people choose not to go into Alice to get their dialysis. They choose to stay home and die. You go along the Todd River and there are people camped along there who have come to town because of health problems, and so to think that whitefellas just take it for granted you can have that at home, these people have to uproot themselves and go hundreds of kilometres into Alice. These are the sort of things that the average person just does not think about.

I was sort of thinking back then, one, I would not mind being a minister for this, but then you may recall that I buggered up a certain speech in parliament and had to resign as the cabinet secretary. Hmmm!

Anyhow there you are. It had nothing to do with Indigenous Affairs, it had a bit to do with a certain judge. So there you are.

You couldn't help but want to help Tracker because he wanted to help everyone else. There was no question about Tracker working like a one-man show in a really hard environment. Coming up to elections he would be on the phone saying, *This is what we ought to do Bill, have you thought about this, have you thought about that?*

David Ross

I will tell you about the time when we first met Robert Tickner. He was a minister [for Aboriginal Affairs]. We were having a Council meeting up at Hatches Creek and we had not met him before – brand spanking new, had just appointed the first three ATSIC commissioners, there was Lowitja [O'Donoghue], Gus Williams and I cannot remember who the other one was. Anyway, we were having a Council meeting at Hatches Creek and, *Oh! The minister wants to come, Yeah! By all means come along, come to the Council meeting.* We get up there the day before the Council meeting and the following day the minister was going to arrive, and somehow this bloke from DAA turns up and says, *We got to put these tents up for the minister. Oh! Yeah! Well we're camping down here.*

Is it safe?

It is safer out bush, nothing is going to get you here.

This is the first time we had ever seen tents at a Council meeting. There is a bloke from DAA turns up and puts up tents for the minister. Oh! Yeah! Putting up another. *Who's that for? Oh! This is for the commissioner, Mr Williams. Oh! Jeez! He gets a tent too.* Another one for this bloke. He had two or three tents being put up. It was all brand new. Later that afternoon, Geoff Clark was there, he was at the time the coordinator for the National Federation of Land Councils. He was a guest at the meeting, he and his wife Trudy as guests of the land council.

At some point Tracker and Clarky decide they were going to get a killer and they come back, and it is dark and they quartered it up and left it hanging in the tree. At some stage the minister had turned up and was in bed. The minister gets up in the morning and there are these quarters of bullocks hanging in the trees, and he wonders what the hell is going on. So Tracker cuts some meat off and he is feeding the minister this beef. I am not sure if he is the first federal minister…who owned the killer we had no idea, but technically it was stolen meat. And here was Tracker sweet-talking this minister about how nice the meat was, and how *you should have some, minister.* Brand spanking new minister. Mr Williams knew exactly what was going on, but he was having a piece too. Geez, here was Clarky and Tracker feeding the minister.

So that was Robert Tickner's first meeting with the CLC, eating – oh lovely meat it was too, geez it was beautiful meat. Them two. Tracker was a butcher so he would have taken Clarky along for the ride. Some of these things are outside the normal day-to-day work, and all the big things that have taken place.

Nick Bolkus

I spent quite a bit of time in the Northern Territory and you could not go to Darwin taking an interest in Aboriginal politics without coming across Tracker one way or another. So we met in Darwin. In the Senate I was on the front bench when I first met him, and I met him through Warren Snowdon MP, and Daryl Melham, former MP for the Labor Party. We kept on catching up with each other in the Territory and in Canberra and it was always a whole raft of issues, from gossip to issues as important as native title we would talk about, and I found Tracker to be a really valuable source of insight into the Aboriginal community, and into the broader community as well.

We stayed pretty close to each other on issues such as heritage and native title. I was delegated the role of taking an interest in the so-called B Team during the Mabo debate. Gareth Evans had the A Team, but I spent a bit of time with Greens senators from WA and their advisory base and support groups, and so on. Having Tracker to bounce ideas off at that time was extremely valuable. I then had carriage of the Wik legislation in the Senate after we lost government in 1996–97 and 98. It was a pretty torrid legal and political debate and Tracker to me was an anchor into the Aboriginal community. He could see through the fraudsters who pretended to represent Aboriginal interests. He could in very colourful language describe who was worth listening to and who was not. He had an enormous store of support from people in the Central Land Council who worked very closely with me, legal advisors as well as people like David Ross, and he was a good store of information on Aboriginal communities from the Cape to north-west Australia.

The thing I found about Tracker was he had a basic instinct that could assess people very quickly, whether they were government ministers or junior lawyers, and my view of those people was very close to his as well. The Wik legislation was the longest debate, through its second reading, in the Senate's history, and there were issues after issues and Tracker's capacity to instinctively understand where Labor should be taking those issues was very valuable. So yes, we developed a good close working relationship, as well as a personal one, over a ten or fifteen years or so.

Quite often in working with him, he would say, *This was the way to go. You will get yourself in trouble if you cut corners here or there or whatever.* He understood that because he would talk to a lot of well-informed people, from lawyers to the Opposition, and when I say Opposition, I mean Liberal and National Party people. As a consequence, his advice on strategy as well as on policy was very valuable. For instance, he could argue with Bill Heffernan by using the sort of language that Bill would use, and he could argue with Gareth Evans on Gareth's language, while playing around as well. No one saw Tracker as being a mug politician, everyone respected him. His capacity to say, in a very endearing way, *You're talking bullshit,* was one of his characteristics.

Tracker was very much the big picture. Big-picture policy directions. It was not just the policy, he was involved in projects in the Territory, whether it was prawn farming or supplying food to Aboriginal communities, where he had the big-picture view. The details sometimes escaped him, but that was quite understandable given the sort of character that he was. He expected people to understand and go with him, but he soon found that they did not quite appreciate things the way he did.

There was one day when we were in Darwin and both Mary and myself were at Ros Paspaley's home for a barbecue and I said invite Tracker, I had not seen him for a long time. So Tracker rolled up, not on his own, and he goes for a walk around the house as if he was casing it and Ros said to him, *What are you doing Tracker?* He said, *Well! When I was a kid, we used to live across the way and I used to get a few dollars out of playing pool and all the Greeks used to bet on me. But I often looked at this house and wondered how I could break in. It wouldn't have been hard.* We all rolled about laughing after that one. He did have that background. He had to make a buck one way or another and when he was a young kid he was playing pool in Greek coffee clubs, while a lot of old Greeks were sitting around gambling away, and putting money on him.

There was always a story, always, for him to take you aside and say, *Bolks, you've got to learn about this,* or *I'm going to tell you this story, something about aunty so and so.* And then of course his background. I still cannot identify which of the number of stories he told me, about his Afghan or Indian or Greek whatever blood, I should believe – probably none. You always thought with Tracker that there was that mischief-making aspect of him, that made him even more enjoyable to be with.

There were trips where we went through the centre of Australia with Tracker, myself, Laurie Brereton and Simon Crean. We went camping one night and we went for a swim. Before we went for a swim, we all had to ask Tracker for an assurance that there were no crocs. Of course he gave us the assurance. We went for a swim. We had the campfire. Woke up the next morning and we were surrounded by crocodile tracks. Oh! Yes. We never trusted his advice on swimming in the Territory. It was somewhere close to the Territory and WA border, across from Yuendumu. The next morning there was some mysterious laughing and chuckling. He did not go swimming with us. That should have been a giveaway at the time. His sense of mischief was more irresponsible than not. He must have done something about those crocodiles, or he might have just walked around making crocodile tracks around our sleeping bags.

There was one night we had him around for dinner at home at Henley Beach. He rolled up about an hour late and: *I can only stay for an hour, I'm being picked up. I don't need you to take me anywhere.* About an hour and a half later, this car arrived which was a remnant of the psychedelic 60s, painted in all sorts of colours, with three women, a couple of blondes and another one. He assured us that they had been students together somewhere in his dim past. He looked old enough to be their grandparent.

I think the good thing about Tracker was he could actually see through people, and see their strengths but also their weaknesses, and I think he identified a few of Noel [Pearson]'s long before other people did. We should have got him into parliament representing the Northern Territory, he would have been good. I have a few sayings that I cannot repeat actually. He left his best sayings for the politicians from the Northern Territory. He had an enormous degree of respect for the Dodson brothers, Rossy, and [Harold] Furber, and a couple of lawyers from the Central Land Council who he was very close to, a young Greek guy, Chris Athanasiou, and James Fitzgerald.

It was really fascinating listening to conversations that they would have together – the three of them. Those guys were technically very, very smart and adept on native title issues, and all issues affecting Indigenous rights whether it was heritage or native title, and Tracker was able to follow intricate points of law and would be able, in a funny way, to monitor the conversation, and then intervene with his perspective of how whatever we were thinking of doing would be met by Indigenous people and others. He was no intellectual slouch.

Michael O'Connor

His stock in trade was telling stories and there was not a well-known politician in this country that he did not know at a national level, and he had a story about nearly all of them.

I got to know Tracker when he turned up at the ALP National Conference, and I will never forget the time he was with Laurie Brereton, and Laurie is a mad fisherman, and he was going fishing up the Top End, and telling Tracker how he had employed people to show him how. And he had got a great bargain and he was going to pay x amount. I remember Tracker just wetting himself laughing and I did not know what he was laughing about. Afterwards he said he had paid like three times the going rate, he was an idiot. And then he told me what happened when Laurie went fishing, funny stories, it was hilarious. But ALP National Conference was where I have been involved with him as well as the ACTU Conferences.

The union, when it does look at doing something in the area of

Indigenous Affairs, we would normally bounce stuff off him informally. He had been like an unofficial consultant to us. If I had a request about doing *x, y* and *z*, and I was not sure what was the most appropriate way to respond, I normally gave him a ring, and he was always up-front and very honest, and fearless about what he said. He was not ducking and weaving about the issue, he was right into it straight away, and that had been very helpful for me and I think for the union as well. And that was the other thing I did not realise when I got to know him, that when he did come to some of the union forums so many people had heard of him – and they had a major amount of respect for him around the trade union movement, especially people who have been involved with working with Indigenous communities. But that time at the ACTU Indigenous Conference, with the Indigenous people he was it, he was the source, it was unbelievable.

He talked to everybody, absolutely right across the board. The person on the plane who was serving you, he made friends with everybody. He was amazing that way. I will never forget this minister from a South American country, when I said to him, *How do you know her?* he said, *I just introduced myself an hour ago.* I said, *What the hell is going on here?*

Daryl Melham

I first met Tracker during the original native title negotiations and debate in 1993, when the Keating government was formulating a response to the native title decision of the High Court. I knew him or got introduced to him through Gerry Hand and Warren Snowdon and people like [Robert] Tickner. I was just a backbencher then, I did not have a lot to do with him but that was my first contact. I was a junior member of the government, although I did play a role in preserving the Racial Discrimination Act 1975 in that debate.[33]

It was after that that I got to know him a little bit more. Indeed when the government lost in 1996 and I became Shadow Minister for Aboriginal Affairs from 1996 to 2000 I had a lot to do with Tracker

---

33. By requiring governments to deal with native title in the same way as other property rights, including the payment of compensation if native title is extinguished or impaired.

amongst other Aboriginal people, seeking his advice and counsel and knowledge of how the show worked, particularly the Central Land Council. I kept in contact with him even after I resigned as Shadow Minister for Aboriginal Affairs.

Tracker had always been a bellwether. The thing about him was that he had no fear and always spoke his mind and that could be off-putting for some people, but for me, I always found him to be quite incisive in some areas, and ahead of the action. I can remember in the debate on native title to do with the Wik amendments, where there was at one stage, amongst Indigenous people, a view about the right to negotiate that would have undermined us, and Tracker brought me along to a meeting, and we managed to convince people that it was their right to negotiate, not the miners or farmers. So very, very bright. Tracker had the capacity to piss people off too with his quick wit, and dry wit, but I think that belies how bright he was, and how creative he could be.

Whenever you are negotiating or when you are representing Indigenous interests particularly in the parliament, you are dealing with a minefield, you are dealing with people who turn on you at any opportunity, so it was always important to have a range of people you could rely on, and also to reassure you – to take you through the minefield. And Tracker – at times tactically we all make mistakes, he was not perfect, he had a propensity in the past to be very quick, and acerbic.

He was an ideas person, and he had a science degree. He was no mug. He could put it out there, but sometimes you needed to have someone else to close the deal, and that was the point. From my position, I always needed people like Tracker around to provide me with the ideas that I could then process, and become their advocate. Tracker famously said to me, *We don't want you to save us, Melham.* I saw myself as an advocate, but I think in that small phrase he captured the whole thing. I did not adopt a missionary approach, and they did not want a missionary approach.

With me most of the battles have always been about protecting native title, protecting the winding back, the undermining of the Racial Discrimination Act. He understood the significance and the potential in all these things. What he was about was to have a place at the table, it was about giving Aboriginal people a seat at the table and then they could negotiate. He understood the importance of the right to negotiate. That was in relation to all matters.

I think the problem was that there were very few allies that we had inside the whole show. So you did not just have to worry about the opposition, you had to worry about the jealousies and rivalries of your own side. There was not a lot of help from people who came from remote areas because they were not necessarily across some of the issues. They might be supportive but they were pests in a sense. People think the Labor Party naturally is a supporter of Aboriginal people and it is not the case. You have really got to get the leader on side.

He would ring up and ask for advice, whatever, and I would say, *No Tracker, you're on the wrong track.* Most of the time he was on the money. It all comes back to roughly the same things, the right of Indigenous people to argue their own cause and to not get done over, because there were all these attempts to keep doing over Aboriginal people. He talked to everyone: he would sit down and sup with the devil if he had to, which was his right, because you have to be at the table.

He was there throughout the whole of the native title debate, and he was there on the Stolen Generation debate, the Apology, and all of those things, and putting a good perspective on it.[34] He played a role with Murrandoo Yanner and with others to settle them down and reassure them when it came to the Century zinc project in the Gulf of Carpentaria. He played a vital background role to seal that deal which was very important for Aboriginal people. If it was not sealed all hell would have broken loose.

He was a character and he might have been a pain in the arse at times, but he was our pain in the arse. I regarded him as a friend, and in politics you have very few friends. He was very supportive of me when I had been down and out with fighting the battles. He never walked away from me. Well! I know he had fallen out with certain people at times, we all do in this game because it is a hard game and sometimes we are hardest on our friends, but I just liked the guy. Firstly, he was

---

34. Prime Minister Kevin Rudd delivered a formal National Apology in parliament to the Stolen Generations on the 13 February 2008.

a character, but I think he was a decent bloke whose heart was in the right place. Not in it for himself.

Murrandoo Yanner

Tracker's connections with federal Labor were extremely beneficial to me personally, politically, and to the cause out here and the battles with Century. This was the one thing I have always found from the first time I ever went with him to Canberra, when we went to see John Faulkner, the sports minister. Daryl Melham was still there, and [Warren] Snowdon. There were three or four government ministers, and we ended up at this little Chinese restaurant late in the evening, but that day we went into parliament, the first time I had ever been in there, and every bastard knew him. From the security guards outside fifty metres away who were all stern-looking while putting everyone through, and they start giggling and I thought, *What's up here?* Soon as they saw him, and it did not matter which door we went in they all knew him, and were calling out to him and joking, *Hey, how you going Tracker?*

It was even more the case when Barnaby Joyce was standing behind us when we went down to Canberra to the Wild Rivers conference two or three years ago.[35] We got Tracker over to the Gulf of Carpentaria to help us when Abbott was trying to push his bill through parliament for to gut the wild rivers, and we were standing up at Joe's Coffee Shop, little Joe, an Italian dude who had the only coffee shop in parliament, who was calling out to Tracker – *What are you having brother?* And he was jumping out and hugging Tracker, and it was that crowded with federal pollies and famous people, but they did not get that treatment.

Tracker introduced him to me and little Joe said, *What are you*

---

35. The *Queensland Wild Rivers Act 2005* was brought in by the Labor government in Queensland to preserve the natural resources of rivers that have all or almost all of their natural values intact. The legislation divided Aboriginal communities in North Queensland, particularly in Cape York, because it would prevent them having an input over the conservation and commercial use of their rivers. The Wild Rivers legislation was repealed by the Campbell Newman Queensland Liberal government in August 2014, and the thirteen rivers in Cape York and in the state's western Channel Country will now be protected under the new Regional Interest Planning Act to prevent inappropriate development from going ahead.

having brother, you never pay for coffee, like this fellow, when you're with him, he never pays for coffee. What stuck with me about that scene, standing behind us was Barnaby Joyce who had to pay for coffee, and his face was all screwed up. Then Tracker would go into these ministers' offices, into Faulkner's office and he knew all the staff. They were all affectionate with him, and while they were in parliament, he would walk into Faulkner's room and put his feet up on his desk, and he would open top-secret files, and the secretary would come and slap him on the hand and say, *You can't do that.* He said, *Oh! It's bullshit, there's nothing in here. It is all gammon.* He was just amazing. They obviously all liked him, but they also took him professionally and seriously, even when he was being a clown sometimes.

A lot of people would get turned off by it because he could be slightly eccentric, but I think the depth of his intelligence was that great. I never knew what my old man meant when he said, *Never let your left hand know what your right hand is doing.* He used to say that a lot when we were kids, but only since I met Tracks I have figured that out. He was obdurate with some of his best ideas, and he would say, *Don't tell any bastard about it. When we've done it and it's all over they can read it and weep. If you tell them beforehand they'll stuff it all up, sabotage it.* I think that is what he meant when he was trying to explain something, when he made jokes or talked silly at times, with people who got turned off, who could not scratch below the surface.

I went with him to the *Bringing Them Home* report, the first ever conference at Darwin, and I was sitting next to him in a room full of people crying out their hearts, literally crying and pouring out their pain, and I do not know if it was his way of hiding whatever happened to him as a kid there, of being taken away and put on Croker with Mum mob, but he sort of embarrassed me and put me on the spot.[36] He said, and I am just sitting there next to him and the room is crowded, and he gets up after about half an hour of all this and he says, *No one bloody took youse away, your parents gave you away and look at you,*

---

36. The *Bringing Them Home* report of the National Inquiry into the Separation of Aboriginal and Torres Strait Islander Children from Their Families, April 1997, was a federal inquiry into the Stolen Generations.

I wouldn't blame them. I thought, *Shit*, and everyone looked daggers at us and we get up and walk out and I am like, *Ooh!* I wanted to be elsewhere, but I think that was just his way of dealing with it. It was very funny in hindsight, but at the time there were a hundred eyes staring at us leaving.

I think a lot of people – Stolen Generation, including my mum and her family, and all her family were the Stolen Generation, and her mum and the oldest brother, it really put us behind, stuffed up mentally a clear majority, not half and half, but seventy or eighty per cent. I think only about twenty per cent are very lucky to come through almost fully intact. There are people who can hold a professional job, but they are a bit of a mess in their heart and mind. Tracker seemed to have the whole package, like nothing ever happened to him. It was just a sign of his strength I guess because a lot did happen, and should have affected him, but it did not show.

Tony McGrady

I suppose there were two episodes between Tracker and myself. The first one was back in the early 1990s when I had just been appointed the Minister for Mines and Energy in the Queensland Government. The Wayne Goss Labor government had established the Carpentaria – Mount Isa Mineral Province and I had carriage of implementing the Province. The whole idea was to get more development particularly in the Gulf of Carpentaria, and one of the large potential mines was the Century mine.

I look back now and one of my best friends is Murrandoo Yanner, however back in those days, he was trouble. You had this new brash young Minister for Mines who thought he could teach some of these blackfellas up in the Gulf a thing or two. Of course Murrandoo and his team had different ideas. Anyway we fought the battle out on the national stage, and it had come to the stage where really there was no way in the world I was going to allow a potential mine employing thousands of people not to go ahead and of course I really believed, as I still do, that the development of the Century mine was going to provide employment and training for the Indigenous people in the Gulf.

Anyway, it almost came to a stalemate and the government brought in Tracker Tilmouth to be the mediator and as a result of his wisdom the mine has been in existence since about 1992. And the funny thing was, at the opening of the mine, the head of the company presented Murrandoo Yanner and Tony McGrady with these accolades because without us two it would never have happened. Of course they really did that tongue in cheek, because if it had not been for Tracker's mediation it may never have got off at the time it did.

Murrandoo Yanner and myself laugh about things now because he was this brash young blackfella who was hell-bent on stopping the development of the mine, and you had this new Minister for Mines who wanted to make an impression and teach one or two people the facts of life. Maybe at that time, maybe, maybe, I was thinking to myself, *Well! I am not going to let this little upstart here stop this mine going ahead.* He was brilliant.

So without being disrespectful, Murrandoo was only a kid at the time, and he was surrounded by similar-type people who really had no practical knowledge of negotiation. They had a dream, they had a vision, but they did not have the ability to transfer those dreams onto an agreement. When you had some of the top bureaucrats and others coming along, they left because they did not have the technique to actually finalise a deal. That was where Tracker came in. He was Indigenous, his wife was a Cloncurry girl, and although they were up in the Gulf, she was perceived as a local girl, and you had people like Martin Ferguson and others involved. I think Martin in those days was probably still in the trade union movement, and was recommending Tracker as a mediator.

That was what he brought to the table, knowledge of people, been there before, could talk the same language to the young gun and, I do not want to be rude, young visionary. Do not forget, in those days when we negotiated the Century deal it was only a very, very short time after the native title legislation had been introduced. People from both sides, from the companies and the Indigenous people, were still searching, and it was even before the Paul Keating Redfern Speech.[37]

---

37. The Redfern Park Speech was made by the Australian Prime Minister Paul Keating on

So we, as the government, had never been involved in native title negotiations before. The Indigenous people hadn't. We were both floundering, but you have somebody like Tracker who was black, who could come in and talk the language of the blackfella, but also the white government people, that was what he brought to the table. I am not being disrespectful but going back to 1992, it was like the blackfellas were blackfellas, and we were whitefellas. Back in those days when the native title legislation really had not started to bite, nobody from either side knew the implications of it. We were searching around in the dark. So when somebody like Tracker came in who obviously had the respect of the company, the Queensland Government, and was gaining the respect of the Indigenous people, that was what he brought to the table.

I think Tracker has seen opportunities with his skills to get a better deal for Indigenous people, but at the same time, if Tracker had been a whitefella he would have succeeded in business. He had all the attributes that are required to run a successful business and I suppose at the end of the day he worked in the Darwin office of one of the big mining companies. He worked for them in a very high position so even if he was not Indigenous I think he would have risen to the top, but because of the special skills and affinity he had with Indigenous people, he was ready-made to do negotiations. He had a brain, and I have seen him demonstrate this in recent times, looking at what happens to the Century mine when the ore body runs out. He had dreams of forestry, quick-growing trees, so his mind was working all of the time. *What do we do with the dam out there? Could we use the water for forestry? Provide jobs for people who used to work at the mine.* That was what he demonstrated to me. It is all very well to deal with what is happening in the present, but you have got to have a vision, you have got to have a dream, and you have got to be looking for what happens at the next stage of this development. I think that was where he shone.

---

10 December 1992. The speech dealt with the challenges faced by Aboriginal Australians.
The speech, written by Keating's speechwriter Don Watson, became famous for the statement:
'We committed the murders. We took the children from their mothers. We practiced discrimination and exclusion. It was our ignorance and our prejudice.'

Bob Katter

We were probably distantly related – not by marriage, because no one ever bothered much to get married in Cloncurry.[38] I first ran across Tracker in Mount Isa and discovered that he had been one of the people heavily involved in the Century mine deal in which he negotiated arguably two hundred million dollars worth of benefits.

Now the benefits that he had negotiated were kidnapped away from the local people, but undoubtedly he still cost the company who had a very, very arrogant attitude to the people of the area, including the people of Mount Isa.

Certainly as a state member or the federal member – if we were not rooting for the First Australian side of the argument up there, we most certainly were encouraging, and the reason for that was the company gave no jobs to the area whatsoever. It was not until Tracker along with Murrandoo Yanner bought into it that he negotiated some jobs, but even then, the contractual arrangements that came down to Indigenous jobs, the mine allocated these Indigenous jobs to a lot of people in Townsville who I most certainly would not consider to be First Australians.

And also in the fly-in and fly-out arrangements with a lot of these people, they might have a great-great-grandmother or something, but I certainly would not put them in the category of being First Australians. That was not Tracker's fault, it was the lawyers' fault that we were all let down so badly, but it was an extraordinary settlement and whilst there are other elements to it, [including the work of] Richie Ahmat and Murrandoo Yanner, it was a most extraordinary settlement. And enormous really to some degree, [by establishing an] insurmountable precedent for the future. It brought home with a vengeance just how capable this bloke was. There was never anything that would have been worth more than twenty million dollars in any project that I had ever heard of, no matter how giant the project. This was a ten-fold increase.

But with this big multinational foreign corporation, they just thought they could walk all over the top of us and Tracker threw

---

38. Tracker's wife Kathy was from Cloncurry.

up a number of legal and strategic barriers. He carefully utilised the state and federal representatives, who were made well aware that the company had no intention of providing a single job to us, thereby provoking the entire population of Mount Isa regardless of background, nobody agreed with that. Really the only jobs we ever got out of it was a few jobs that went to local people of First Australian descent, but we would have been skinned alive if had not been for Tracker.

He mobilised the media, he mobilised trade unions, he mobilised the state members, the ALP member, and the federal member who was a National Party member at that stage. He does not go for outright confrontation like for example Murrandoo Yanner, and he does not go in softly, softly like Richie Ah Matt. He could show ruthless brutality in the negotiations combined with very effective cleverness, some would say deviousness, and really at the end of the day, what was done was quite brilliant.

Tracker was a delightful and attractive character, he was the most charming person and God gave him the good looks to go with it. He would charm the tail off a bloody donkey, Tracker. There are very few people in this country that can ring up a prime minister, and the next prime minister, and the next prime minister, but he had been the go-to man for all of that mining region.

When Tracker negotiated, or Murrandoo or whatever you want to say, the two hundred million dollar deal, the level was raised, and since all governments ended up accepting the arrangement, therefore a new benchmark was created and every single deal was going to be constructed off that benchmark arrangement.

So whilst I would think this was a bad thing for the country as a whole and a very bad thing to happen, and the government should not have allowed it to happen, what they should have done was not stop us from negotiating that deal. What they should have done, the government, was force the company to base the workforce locally, which was the law until the Joh Bjelke-Petersen government fell. Up until then you would have to take the workforce locally. You would not fly in, this was banned.

But having refused point-blank to become involved in any way, shape or form, the idiot Queensland government of the day had left the company to their own provocative stupidity, which Tracker was able to take full advantage of, by not only turning the local First Australian community, but the entire community of north-west Queensland against them. There was not a single person on the side of Century by the time the dust had settled. I think to a large degree the lead singer might have been Murrandoo, but the choirmaster, or at least the person who did the musical arrangement, was in fact Tracker.

When they tried to close the [Northern Territory] land councils down, my own feelings were that they should be closed down, but I listened carefully to what Tracker was saying on that. I said, *Tracker, they are not representative of nor do they represent the people of the area.* I would go to locally elected shire councils because I had set up shire councils in Queensland, community councils they are called actually, which have considerably more power than local government powers. They went much, much further than local government, very extensive powers, for example, they had control of the police force. But they did not have them in the Northern Territory and Tracker said, *We need a shield. If these people on isolated communities did not have the Land Council for a shield* – we were in an isolated community on that day – he said, *The people here, you're telling me they're going to be able to negotiate with mining companies? They'd be run around the mulberry bush forty-eight times.* He said, *It is a shield of protection.* More sophisticated people with capabilities would enable them to negotiate on a level playing field with aggressive representation.

I had better not mention names here but we met once in the Carpentaria Land Council offices in Mount Isa, and Tracker said, *What's going on here?* And I said, *Well! I am backing up {our local bloke against the minister and the department}.*

But you know what's been going on here?

Yes.

Tracker said, *What did you say to the minister?* I said, *He is the head stockman from the Gulf Country, the bloke that been's elected.* Every second word was a very naughty word. He screamed obscenities. You have to have absolute discipline because it is like being on a football field, being on a mustering team you know, because if you are head stockman you tell the owner what to do, the owner does not tell you what to do.

You move into a tight disciplinary regime once you are in the saddle. It is a different world, and of course he had taken that principle back to the Land Council, and Tracker was killing himself laughing at the thought of me trying to explain to a minister in Canberra that this was the way we talked to each other. The minister was saying, *Do you know the horrific things that he's been saying and doing?* Well! I mean the other thing if someone questions you, the head stockman would just go *bang* and down you would go.

But Tracker, the very thought of a confrontation between myself and the minister in Canberra, he nearly died laughing with the thought of trying to explain to a bloke in Canberra how a stockman conducts his regime. That was one of many stories. On another occasion, a bloke was trying to get a mine off the ground. He was a good bloke actually, and I said, *Look, just any problems that you've got, we want this mine to go, we want these jobs – badly.* He was using local blokes in the jobs and so I said, *What do you want me to do?* He said, *Shoot your cousin Tracker Tilmouth.* I nearly died laughing but he was serious. So I said, *Righto! We've got to get this going, what do you want me to do?* He said, *Shoot Tracker Tilmouth. Alright! What's the second thing you want me to do?*

It is hard to separate out the First Australian thing from the bush cattle-ringer thing the way Tracker told stories, but they are inextricably linked – the image of the traditional ringer Australian stockman and the First Australian in the saddle. As Mick Miller used to say, the Australian cattle industry was built on black backs and that was true. Black feet and stirrup irons anyway. First Australians were very good in this industry and still are, but we have not been able to unleash that because if we cannot get the title, we cannot borrow money off the bank, and without the title deed and without the money from the bank we cannot buy any cattle, and so even though we are capable of getting the cattle in and moving them on to the market and looking after them, the water and fences and branding and castrating and everything, whilst we can do all those things, we cannot get the money to buy the cattle because we do not have the title deed. We have got land tenure, but that is not the title deed that banks loan money on. With an inalienability clause there is a comfort there, which I am sure that Tracker fought on.

I think that a lot of what has been accomplished in Australia would not have been accomplished without Tracker Tilmouth and his ability to feel at ease with the prime minister, and feel just as much at ease with some old bush Murri who spent a life in the saddle, camped out bush, and the people that have fallen into the grip of alcoholism and he treats them the same as he would treat one of the bush blokes, or the prime minister. He would treat all of them no different. That is very much a First Australian characteristic, and I think all Australians have got that sense of egalitarianism from the First Australians. I can see that in a person like Andrew Forrest. I can see it in a person like Tracker Tilmouth and in that they were very similar people. That ability has yielded enormous benefits for our people, and not only for our people black, but also for our people white. Put the list together and be one group of people and call them Australians.

Murrandoo Yanner

Some doors would close for us at times because he had obviously ruffled a few feathers, or pissed them off. I know for the Wild River stuff when we took him to help us lobby Jenny Macklin that might have backfired slightly because he said, *How ya going, Genocide Jenny?* You could have heard a pin drop and pistols drawn at twenty paces, and the whole thing went sour pretty quickly.

He said it to her face, bloody oath. And we thought it was a joke between them but obviously it was not, I think she had been dodging him since she got elected and did not go against the Intervention policy. And similarly with [Trish] Crossin, instead of trying to do the decent thing, this federal Labor government stuck with John Howard's Intervention when they had a chance to do the right thing by us and dump it. I think she had been dodging Tracker and this was his first chance to speak to her face to face. I do not think she expected him to turn up with us that day. So she got a bit of a surprise too that he was there, but it was too late by the time she realised.

She was withdrawn into her shell pretty quickly. She still stuck to the meeting with us, but you could see it ruffled her feathers and she knew what it was about, because they had obviously been making public comments on other things during the last year or so when Labor was in Opposition. He was referring to the taking away and further deprivation of hard-won rights in the Territory by the Howard government, and she, when she became the Minister for Aboriginal Affairs in the Labor government, despite saying in Opposition they would not continue it, and would change it, she went ahead with the whole thing and even made more bloody restrictions for us.

So then it was really silly of her to come in and hear him say that, because he had said that publicly in the papers. He just said, *How ya going, Genocide Jenny?* And Marty [lawyer for Carpentaria Land Council] said later, *Did you hear what he said?* Yo!

Martin Ferguson

I had known Tracker since the early 1990s when I became the president of the ACTU. Initially, I knew him through the Indigenous community of the ACTU and then subsequently over many years through a variety of activities, not just in the Northern Territory. All these discussions over many years were about economic opportunities for employment and training in the context of Aboriginal land rights and Indigenous Land Use Agreements. Not focused so much on royalties but more on the capacity to set up businesses, and training and employment for Indigenous people, and Tracker was very good at this.

One of the most important trips I did with him was to the Tanami [Desert] in Central Australia with David Ross, and some of the people from the Central Land Council, where we actually went to the [Newman Tanami Project] mine, camped for a couple of days and then met with the Indigenous community, the traditional owners, and I might say that the management of the company saw in practical terms how when you sit down and work out proper arrangements, they can be of benefit to the investors as well as the local Indigenous communities.

Strangely, this trip happened to be just prior to Keating announcing how he intended to go forward with legislation as a result of the Mabo decision. When we returned to Alice Springs I did a media conference and it was not planned, it just happened to be on the day or evening of Keating moving on legislative proposals.

They were already working on the Tanami mining agreement, just like they were working on agreements around Darwin, the Alice Springs railway, and right across the Territory, as both the Northern and Central Land Council had been for years, part of the leadership with the country in terms of how you work with business and get returns, and not just of a royalty nature. But they were also working, not just in terms of mining agreements, but to clean up the community stores, to get the grog out of some of the communities, to get improvements in nutrition, proper fruit and vegetables, and decent meat. I can remember discussions about whether or not we could grow grapes and oranges in Central Australia and eventually, Tracker developed Centrefarm. There was already a community farm in Alice Springs for Aboriginal people with alcohol problems to dry them out, which was growing fruit and vegetables.

I think it was in January 2008 in Melbourne, where there were discussions [between the Labor government and members of the Aboriginal leadership about the lease of Aboriginal land for the construction of homes]. If I remember correctly they put a proposal on the table to short-circuit negotiations and came up with forty-year leases, because the life of a home in these communities is about forty years because of the nature of the climate. So rather than fighting about ninety-nine year leases [which the government wanted], it was, *Let's get on with the job and do a forty-year deal and get the houses built.* So they always had an idea about how to get the outcomes to suit the people they represented, and bring government business with them.

Tracker also worked at different times on his concerns about nutrition on Aboriginal communities, for instance, trying to think through seafood and prawn farms. He had lots of ideas, and worked with a whole heap of different communities over the years, testing ideas. He was always on the phone to me or my staff. They all knew him. He was a frequent visitor to Canberra and my office, and other minister's offices, the shadow minister's offices, and ministers on the other side too. He used to go and see Heffernan fairly often. He knew how to get in the door.

He would just hound you, and pester you. At times you would have to try and pin him down to determine the practical outcomes, because he would have a lot of ideas, and some you would have to try and work out how you would actually implement them. Which as you know, we have not always succeeded in doing.

There were frustrations on both sides – the government trying to make programs flexible, and give flexibility in different communities. It did not come easy. It was all about trying something new, something different. I think sometimes the flexibility in some of the government departments could have been made easier for Tracker. You've got to take a few risks whilst not exposing taxpayers. And I think from time to time there were people in Indigenous departments and offices who thought they knew better than Indigenous people.

Some of the strategies Tracker used in his work was getting the coalitions together, business people, union representatives, government people, Indigenous leaders, getting leadership of the party into meetings. I can recall a discussion in Alice Springs one weekend at Warren [Snowdon]'s house, and in the back room out there, Tracker had a whole assembly of some of the key Indigenous leaders in Australia talking to Kim Beazley about social disadvantage and what had to be done.

He never stopped. But he also got respect because he was hard-working. He knew how to conduct himself, he had a good turn of phrase, good sense of humour, but also, he was very disciplined in that he was not on the grog, or things like that. He brought a sense of decency to the task.

For him this was not a job, this was a commitment. Clearly he had responsibilities, three daughters whom he and his wife gave good opportunities to in life, all educated and doing well. But whatever work he did it was not just about his responsibilities for his family, he had a lifetime commitment to try and do something.

At times it was not easy. I can remember the Apology to the Stolen Generations. He was invited, but this was one of the first times I saw him emotional and he could not go, and he could not sit through it. He came down to Canberra a couple of days beforehand and gave me a collage of photos of him and his brothers in the community where they were sent. I was looking at it the other day when I was cleaning out the office, looking at the different photos of Tracker and the way the kids were looked after, well dressed et cetera. He always had the cheeky look on his face compared to the others. Though he was taken from his parents, he was not bitter about it. But still very emotional. He broke down in his own way and said, *I can't come to the speech. There are too many memories. But I just wanted you to see this.* And he had got it together and brought it down for me. I kept it in my office as a minister and when I resigned I kept it and now I hand them over to you, because I know how much that meant to him, to show me the background. He brought it all the way down from Darwin to bring to me.

But to be fair to him, he did not carry a sense of guilt about what occurred. There is an Anglican nun in [Northern Victoria] whom he still treats with absolute reverence, who looked after him and his brothers. She is referred to as an aunt by his daughters, and whenever they are in town they are expected to go and see her. He saw them [the mission at Croker Island] as giving him a start in life that he might not have got, which ended up in him going to university and getting an education, which did not happen to a lot of his mates.

I consider ourselves lucky at times to be in some of those meetings of the national Aboriginal leadership and I remember one in my office. Often you do not see the Indigenous leadership work it out amongst themselves but I was lucky enough to be in a discussion once with David Ross, the Dodson brothers and Tracker in my office in Canberra, and going hammer and tongs at one another as they argued about what had to be the position to put to the government and the Opposition. I was lucky enough to be a participant in that meeting which is a rare event. They normally sort it out amongst themselves and come to see you with the outcome but this was a ding-dong bloody argument I can tell you, because they knew they had to sort it out and they trusted me to be in the meeting. They are all tough operatives. No one wanted to give in.

They were all forceful negotiators. Considered. Tracker always had a lot to say because he was so bright, and liked to dominate. They had different styles, but Tracker was always out there and the others were holding him back saying, *have you thought about this?* Then all of a sudden David Ross, who would sit quietly, would speak and everyone would listen. As I said, you had an interesting collection of people, especially the Dodsons [Patrick and Michael], Tracker, Peter Yu, David

Ross. Tracker was the one who had the analysis, and would throw it like a dead cat on the table and force the discussion.

If it was not for people like Tracker and David Ross and the Dodsons and others, we would not be where we are today in terms of the resources sector, and having to come to terms with the fact that native title is a fact of life. We went through all the legal processes and the High Court with the original Mabo decision, and Keating as the prime minister was working it through. It is one thing to achieve a legal outcome, but there is another even bigger challenge to achieve an acceptance on the ground that this is the new way of doing things. The conservatives were saying this is going to be the end of Australia, with Tim Fischer sitting on a TV program holding up a map of Sydney, a map of Sydney Harbour and everything else.

It was the leadership of people like Tracker which meant that they [Aboriginal leadership] had actually sat down with the mining industry and negotiated, very quickly, a series of practical agreements and were sending a big message, *We really want investment. We are not just interested in handouts, we actually want an economic benefit.* When I think back to those meetings, the debates with all of them, sometimes in my room in Canberra, you would not know those emotive days from the reality of today.

Those discussions were pretty instrumental in reinforcing my view that we should butt out. It was not work for the dole, it was a system of, you front up to responsibility and bring a sense of discipline and order back into the communities. It was their understanding of their communities which really taught me and a lot of the union members to actually front up to the fact, the gentrified area from which some of those people came from was entirely different to the reality of remote communities.

Tracker always had a colourful phrase for different situations, sending a message to people, that too many of you still think we are different. He would do an interview and refer to the nigger on the verandah type thing, which was, *I am telling you in a tongue-in-cheek way about how you still perceive us.* He always had those smart-arse one-liners which were also serious messages. I found that you could take him to Brisbane, to a meeting with a major mining company, where he could sit down and be on equal footing, but even then in a very serious discussion you would shake your head sometimes with the one-liners that would come out, and think, *Christ Almighty, where is this going to lead us?*

I can remember meetings with Yanner and Tracker – the old and the new bulls. Yanner having a lot of respect for Tracker and them feeding off one another: who was the smartest in the room and could give the most cheek. Tracker was a very good person for the young people to learn from. He had been around so long, he could do business on an equal footing, but you could also go bush with him, and he was at home with his community, which is not easy. He never forgot where he had come from.

He worked across the political divide. He would go to Canberra including the media gallery, and go up and chit-chat Laura Tingle of the *Financial Review*, and go and give Bill Heffernan a bit of cheek whilst also trying to work out from Bill what was achievable from a conservative side of politics, to go into different Labor Party offices. He could work the political divide but he had also seen the green movement for what they are, opportunists with no real concern for the Indigenous communities. Used them up and abused them if they do not toe the line.

He would go into a meeting knowing what he wanted, but he also knew that life is the art of compromise. He had objectives in his mind, which were always about the people he represented. He had a good business head and from what I have seen, business knew that they could deal with him. They knew he wanted development, but he had to correctly represent the people he represented. And the deal would get done and he would honour it and police it. And that has been for everything from oranges to grapes, oil and gas, and at one stage prawn farms in terms of nutrients and exports for the communities. He always had an idea. His mind never stopped. He did not seem to sleep. He knew the country like the back of his hand, and he would text and phone all hours of the bloody day. He worked the phone. Some people had a love-hate relationship with him too, because Tracks was Tracks. They loved him but also hated him at times. I had been with him out bush, driven around communities and towns, and I remembered the way he was received. They knew him and he knew them. They saw him as one of them.

I stayed in contact with Tracker because it was a question of respect. You knew he was not about himself. He was trying to do something to help others. When I first went to the Territory in 1977, half my union executive on the North Australian Worker's Union was made up of Indigenous people. I knew the Ah Matts, the Coles, the Clarks and now we have lost a generation. Tracks was a bit younger than those people and he was lucky that he got an education, but he used it to try and overcome social disadvantage. He was worried about – not just his own children, he was worried about the community at large. You were always going to try and help him because he was trying to do something, trying to get outcomes. That was why if he rang, I would try and help him. I thought the world of him.

Croker Island – Tracker knew how to read
well from a young age
Lois Bartram Collection

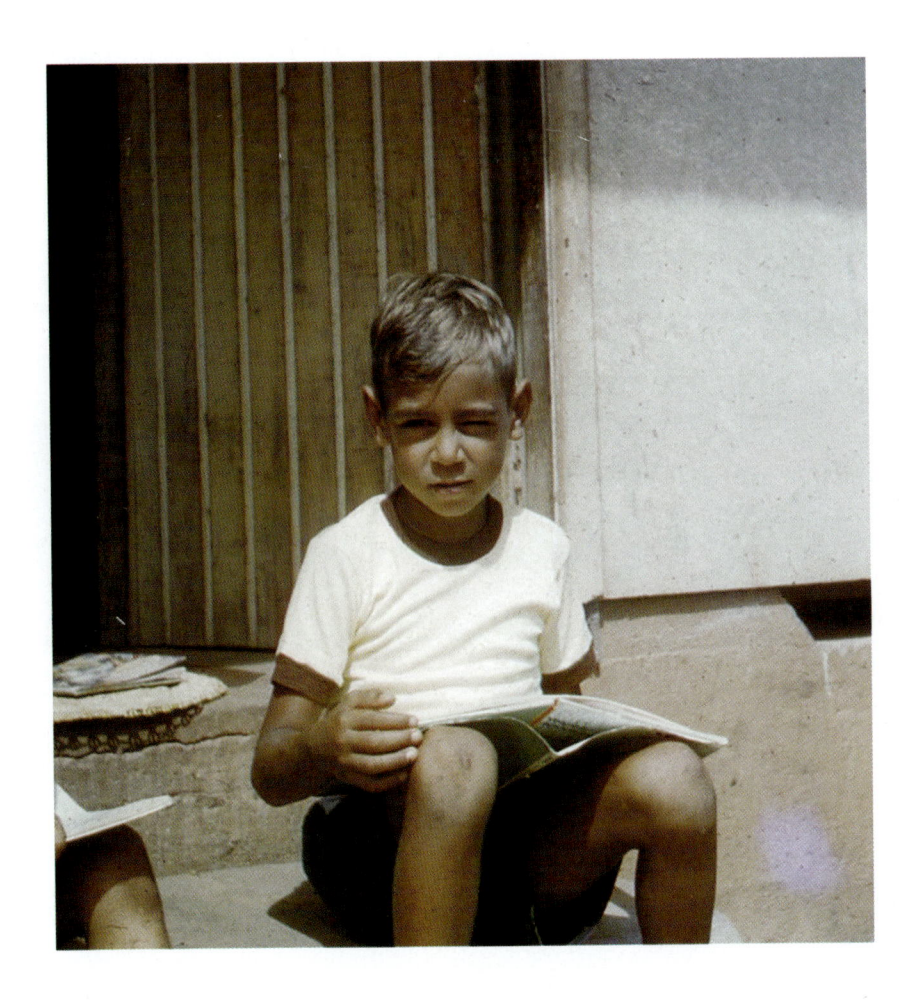

BELOW
Tracker's mother Betty on the right
William Tilmouth Collection

RIGHT
Tracker's father, Roy Tilmouth
William Tilmouth Collection

BELOW
William, Patrick and Tracker on Croker Island
Lois Bartram Collection

BOTTOM
Lois Bartram with the twelve boys of Victory Cottage
Tracker is first from the left, front row
Lois Bartram Collection

BELOW
Victory Cottage
Lois Bartram Collection

BOTTOM
Tracker catching a fish on Croker Island
Lois Bartram Collection

Tracker rode Timor ponies on Croker Island
from a young age
Lois Bartram Collection

BELOW
Tracker collecting quandongs
while working at Angas Downs
Tilmouth Family Collection

BOTTOM
Tracker, Johnny Liddle, Lawrie Liddle
and Tim Lander at Angas Downs
Maggie Urban

Tracker riding in the Camel Cup race
in Alice Springs
Tilmouth Family Collection

Tracker with Charles Perkins and
Doug Turner
CLC Archive

BELOW
Tracker and Greg Crough,
Northern Territory Aboriginal Constitutional
Convention, Tennant Creek, 1993
CLC Archive

BOTTOM
Tracker joking with Bob Hawke
CLC Archive

BELOW
Tracker at a CLC meeting about feral donkeys and camels. Gordon Williams and Jack Cook are on the right *CLC Archive*

BOTTOM
Tracker with Robert Tickner and Billy Baker at the Warlpampa, Warlpiri, Mudbura and Warumungu handback of traditional land, 1995 *CLC Archive*

BELOW
Tracker, Mick Dodson and John Patterson
at the United Nations, Geneva
CLC Archive

BOTTOM
Tracker (as deputy director, CLC) and
David Ross (director, CLC)
CLC Archive

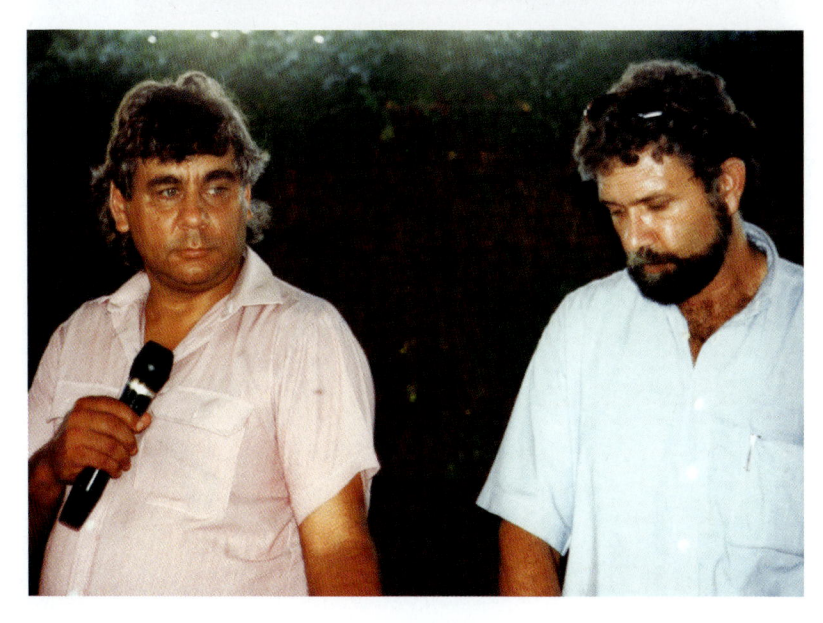

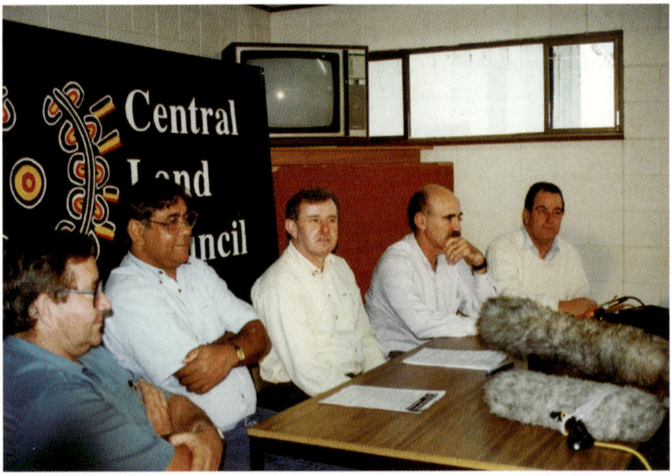
Central

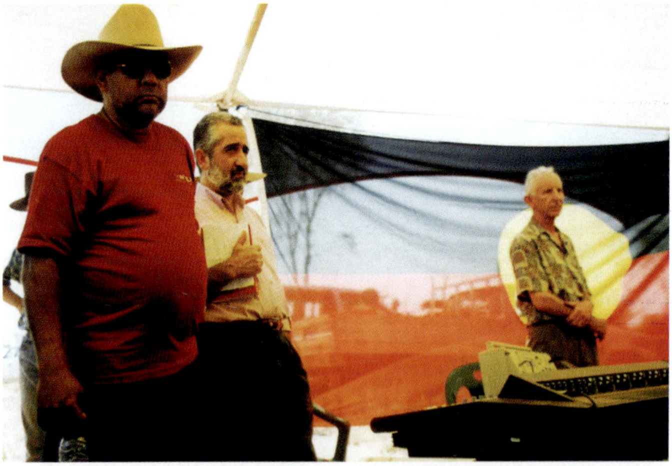

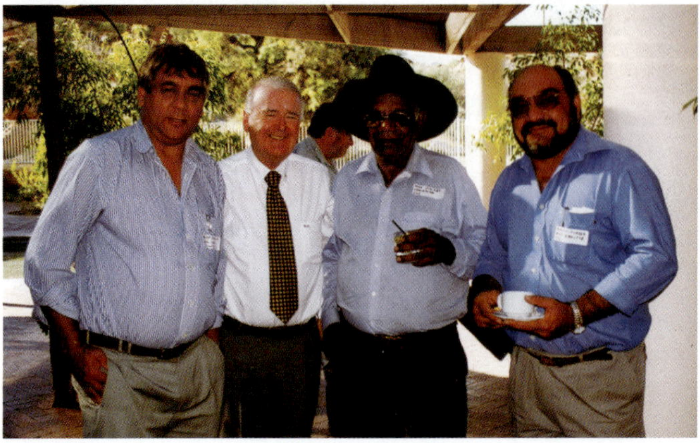

OPPOSITE TOP
Tanami mine manager Stan Paget,
Tracker, Simon Crean and
Warren Snowdon at the launch of
the Tanami Employment Strategy
in 1995 *CLC Archive*

OPPOSITE CENTRE
Tracker with Nick Bolkus
and Brian Harradine at the
Kalkaringi Convention *CLC Archive*

OPPOSITE BOTTOM
Tracker with Governor General
William Deane, CLC chairman
Max Stuart, and CLC deputy
director Harry Furber, 1998
CLC Archive

ABOVE
Tracker with Bill Heffernan and
Robert Hill in Central Australia
CLC Archive

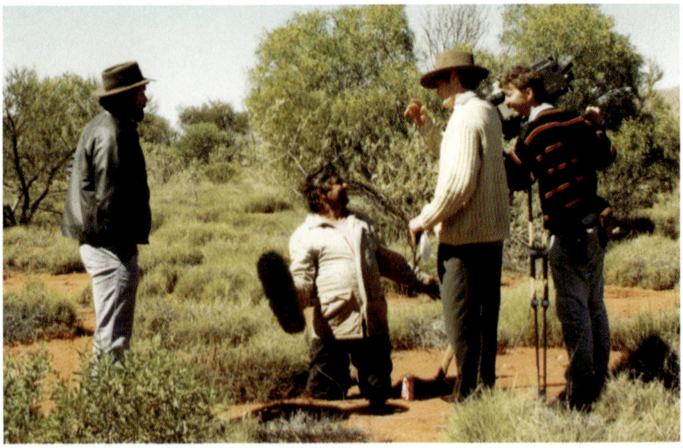

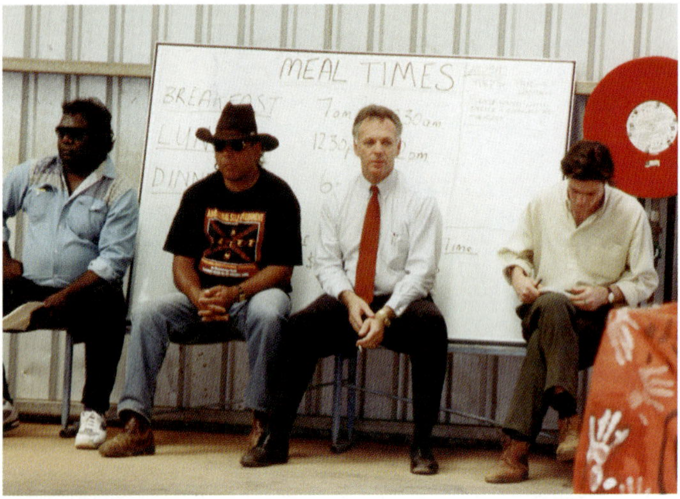
MEAL TIMES

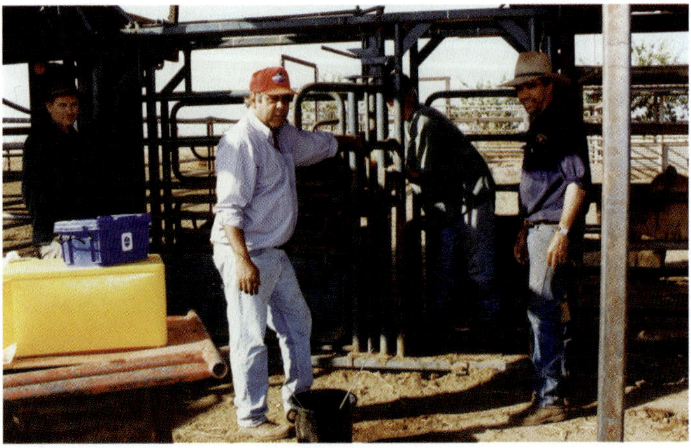

OPPOSITE TOP
David Ross and Tracker working with
CLC Media *CLC Archive*

OPPOSITE CENTRE
Galarrwuy Yunupingu, Tracker and Steve Hatton
at the Northern Territory Aboriginal Constitutional
Convention, Tennant Creek, 1993 *CLC Archive*

OPPOSITE BOTTOM
Forrest Holder (Central Land Council), Tracker,
Ross Ainsworth (consultant vet), and Steve Craig
(manager, Mistake Creek pastoral property) *CLC Archive*

Tracker with Wenten Rubuntja, chairman
of the CLC, and Mr Long, in Canberra,
Central Land Council days
CLC Archive

NT News

YOUR VOICE IN THE TERRITORY

FRIDAY, MARCH 13, 2015

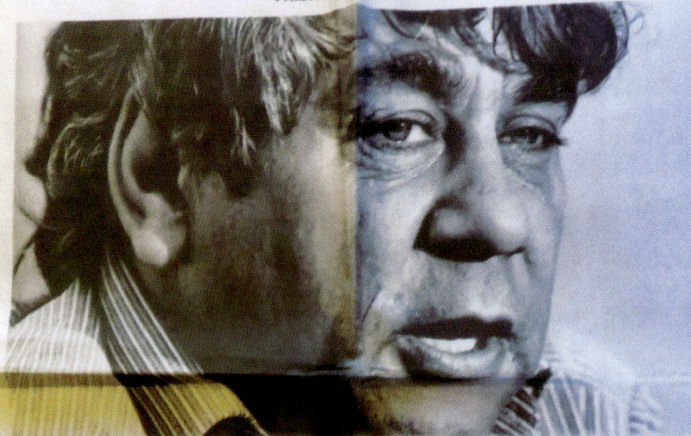

TERRITORY FAREWELLS 'TRACKER'

JUST FOOTY: NTFL GRAND FINAL SPECIAL

4.

The Vision Splendid

A Bit of Heaven

Doug Turner

Tracker was just full of ideas. My understanding of Tracker is that he was a visionary. He saw things that could happen, and he went over it in his head – about how to link things together, to make things work, what support he needed, how to get that support, and what he needed to do as an individual to stimulate those developments. He became a member of the Australian Labor Party and that connection grew and helped support community things in the territory, like the Central Australian Aboriginal Pastoralist Association. In 2014 he was involved with running his own business, looking at things with the mining industry, helping local communities develop their own mining companies and setting up economic initiatives for communities across different parts of Australia, not only the Territory but other areas within Australia as well. And then he links in other mainstream businesses like white community businesses in the mining industry, to help that grow. These are mainstream white communities whom he has helped over the years for them to grow, so he is asking for favours from them now to help Aboriginal communities grow and become independent in their own enterprise operations.

He was always looking for expertise to help his visions grow. He would bring in expertise from outside Alice Springs and from South Australia or from other states, people who knew how to write and understood the whitefellas' world basically, and how to pull things together and make things happen and write submissions for him. I mean he could write submissions for himself and he could do financial statements but he was only one bloke, you cannot achieve everything because the task is just too big. He needed to get people with the skills so that he could make things happen.

INFRASTRUCTURE REQUIREMENTS TO DEVELOP AGRICULTURAL INDUSTRY IN CENTRAL AUSTRALIA

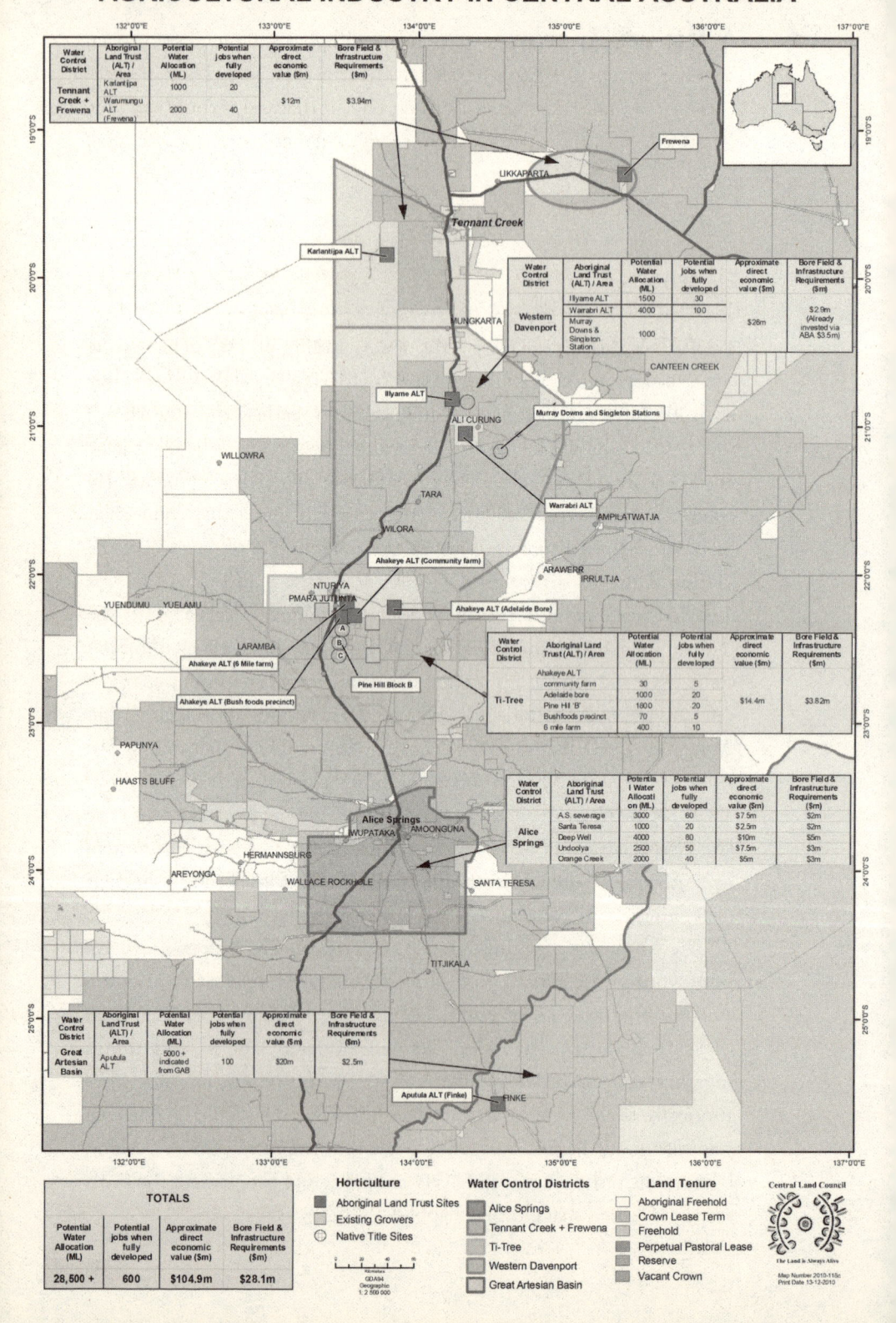

Water Control District	Aboriginal Land Trust (ALT) / Area	Potential Water Allocation (ML)	Potential jobs when fully developed	Approximate direct economic value ($m)	Bore Field & Infrastructure Requirements ($m)
Tennant Creek + Frewena	Karlantipa ALT	1000	20	$12m	$3.94m
	Warumungu ALT (Frewena)	2000	40		

Water Control District	Aboriginal Land Trust (ALT) / Area	Potential Water Allocation (ML)	Potential jobs when fully developed	Approximate direct economic value ($m)	Bore Field & Infrastructure Requirements ($m)
Western Davenport	Ilyame ALT	1500	30	$26m	$2.9m (Already invested via ABA $3.5m)
	Warrabri ALT	4000	100		
	Murray Downs & Singleton Station	1000			

Water Control District	Aboriginal Land Trust (ALT) / Area	Potential Water Allocation (ML)	Potential jobs when fully developed	Approximate direct economic value ($m)	Bore Field & Infrastructure Requirements ($m)
Ti-Tree	Ahakeye ALT community farm	30	5	$14.4m	$3.82m
	Adelaide bore	1000	20		
	Pine Hil 'B'	1800	20		
	Bushfoods precinct	70	5		
	6 mile farm	400	10		

Water Control District	Aboriginal Land Trust (ALT) / Area	Potential Water Allocation (ML)	Potential jobs when fully developed	Approximate direct economic value ($m)	Bore Field & Infrastructure Requirements ($m)
Alice Springs	A.S. sewerage	3000	60	$7.5m	$2m
	Santa Teresa	1000	20	$2.5m	$2m
	Deep Well	4000	80	$10m	$5m
	Undoolya	2500	50	$7.5m	$3m
	Orange Creek	2000	40	$5m	$3m

Water Control District	Aboriginal Land Trust (ALT) / Area	Potential Water Allocation (ML)	Potential jobs when fully developed	Approximate direct economic value ($m)	Bore Field & Infrastructure Requirements ($m)
Great Artesian Basin	Aputula ALT	5000 + indicated from GAB	100	$20m	$2.5m

TOTALS

Potential Water Allocation (ML)	Potential jobs when fully developed	Approximate direct economic value ($m)	Bore Field & Infrastructure Requirements ($m)
28,500 +	600	$104.9m	$28.1m

Horticulture: Aboriginal Land Trust Sites; Existing Growers; Native Title Sites

Water Control Districts: Alice Springs; Tennant Creek + Frewena; Ti-Tree; Western Davenport; Great Artesian Basin

Land Tenure: Aboriginal Freehold; Crown Lease Term; Freehold; Perpetual Pastoral Lease; Reserve; Vacant Crown

Central Land Council — The Land is Always Alive

Map Number 2010-115c
Print Date 13-12-2010

Life is short, and there are so many things you want to see happen without trying to burn yourself out. We used to always say, if those creeks could talk, if those rocks could talk, if those trees could talk, the amount of things that we went over and talked about.

Tracker Tilmouth

[*Speaking at the Northern Territory Food Conference, November 2014*]
Look you have got to bear with me as I am getting old. Can we have those two maps young fella, and slides? I want to show you a bit of heaven. You white blokes drive past it every day. Righto! The first map over there is about one hundred and twenty kilometres north of Tennant Creek, and estimates at this stage would suggest that it has a bit more potential with the gas, the railway, and the Stuart Highway going through the middle of it.

The water potential once developed will be twice Ord River Stage 2 and it is sitting on the Stuart Highway. The other map is the employment potential of Ali Curung, Ti Tree, and the economics of that area of land if we were to take a conventional view of it. The biggest question is, the Indonesians [delegates to the conference] sort of told you in the nicest and kindest way that we really don't want to deal with you.

Right! They were straight up, they were talking about soya beans, they were talking about a whole range of stuff, and they asked, *Can you supply our products systems, can you supply our chains, and if you can, how can you do it for us rather than us doing it.* We are in the same boat. The Aboriginal community has decided that, against the attacks on the Land Rights Act, attacks on native title, we really need a segregated economy. An economy where we can develop our own systems of trade, our own systems of production, our own methods of production, and a whole range of other social and cultural needs that at the moment are not being dealt with as we go forward on a conventional system of development.

So we have an economic and commercial paradigm that we have to deal with. The Indonesians asked the question, *Where did all these {Aboriginal} people go, did they go back to the towns, did they go back to their communities?* Ours went to gaol. We have a gaol out here [in Darwin] called the Fish Trap. There are four hundred people out there, so we have them all stacked up, and we have the internal cultural and social problems to deal with, but that does not mean that we drop the ball and put aside development opportunities that come up.

We want to tell people that when you come and see us about resource development, when you come and see us about economic development, there is a cultural and social fabric that you need to be concerned about. There is a delivery of the social dividend if you like, that has to be done at some stage so that people actually enjoy land rights, they do not just want to get the title for a fifty- or ninety-year lease. You hear it all the time, *Why? Because you are doing nothing with it.* How do you know that we are not doing anything with it?

So we go through this rigmarole of investment and counter-investment, and without any real long-term strategic process. We end up with a shit sandwich, and jumbo jets parked on community airstrips which is a wonderful thing, because a jumbo jet on a community airstrip looks wonderful, but no one knows how to fly it. The pilot walks away and you are gone. We have been through this process time and time again. The agronomists, the economics people, and everybody else we had pegged to come over and help us, some idiot sent them to Manus Island, and so we have to do our own thinking for ourselves now.

At the end of the day, we have to create programs that allow Aboriginal people to live on our land, to develop our land, on a sustainable basis. Not to develop it for the sake of developing – we can do that, we have got Ian Baker [Northern Territory Farmers Association] running around, and he will tell you sell the sausage, not the sizzle. Right! I agree with Bakes, we have got programs that we can do. They were talking about soya beans today. We know where to grow soya beans. We know the prices of soya beans. We know the prices on sugar. We know what Ord River can or cannot do. We know what marine clays look like. We know the anion and cation exchange rates of marine clays. Or what type of vegetables or what type of production you can get out of those clays.

So we have been there and done that. I also spent a long time in Israel in a kibbutz. We need a long-term strategic process but where is the point of doing this on an ad hoc basis, where we have both the federal government and the state running around saying, *Oh! You are not doing anything with your land, we need ninety-nine year leases, we want this, we want that?*

You have a look at the project we have got up there, we have the railway, we have the gas pipeline, we have the Stuart Highway, and we have more water under that land than Ord River Stage 2. So the potential is there. Once we have identified the opportunity and the potential, we can develop the processes that allow us to go forward. But we do not see anything from the government – both sides of politics – we have not heard a word from any government that allows us to go forward, to say to Aboriginal people, *Yes, we do have a plan. Yes, it is a sustainable plan but these are the constraints to that plan.* This is where my argument is. I am sorry that I am hard and fast and rough and everything else, but you do not know me any other way.

So at the end of the day that is what I want to talk to you about. I have been working for some time at this. We have got projects. Yes. You can take a pick at Ali Curung, at Ti Tree, at Willowra, they are there. The numbers are there. The soils and the waters are there. The electricity has to be there. The gas has to be there. This is the infrastructure that requires government input. We do not hear anything from the government about infrastructure going in to Ti Tree. These are the long-term arguments that we are interested in. Thank you.

Tracker Tilmouth

My interest in building an Aboriginal economy began years ago. The reason is that you cannot go to the debate on a treaty if you cannot contribute. A treaty is an economic exchange between two peoples. It is both legal and economic, but it is mostly economic, followed by legal precedent. So you have the argument that your protection of your land is the contribution you make to the economy of the country. It is as simple as that.

How do you measure the contribution in economic terms? Do you measure it in biodiversity? Do you measure it in species retention? Do you measure it in land management? Do you measure it in terms of commercial development, like mining and pastoralism, cropping, whatever? How do you measure it? How does each bit of that pie contribute to your position in an economic debate? What weapons do you bring to the table to allow you to debate the issue in relation to biodiversity? What is the value of biodiversity to your people? The social fabric, the cultural fabric, the economic processes that were part of your Aboriginal society? How do those things contribute? Because that is what you are going to trade with.

You are going to give something because they are not going to give you a treaty for free. Economics plays a huge role in our ability to negotiate a treaty.

How did I develop my thinking about this? You have to get the baseline data and that was what Irrmarne was all about, getting baseline data, setting up a process.[39] The Irrmarne process was about mapping Aboriginal land use and its systems, but from an Aboriginal point of view. That is where the idea of having participation and a management plan evolved. I invented this participation process because we had these idiots running around and saying we can do this and that, and we said, *No, where are the rocks?* I told them, *You show us what the country does and when it does it.* I invented all that. Then you had all sorts of blokes like the ones who used to run the pastoral section in the CLC saying, *I picked it up.* Oh! Wow! Every success has many parents.

Irrmarne was the next stage of that, where you could map the data on a computer screen, and map the country, and then discuss, for example, the value of getting goannas in October versus the value of getting goannas in January, or vice versa. When is the best time to get goannas? What is the economic activity of getting goannas? What are the health issues in relation to going out hunting and gathering goannas? How did that affect you and your social wellbeing, and the people who hold a story for that goanna? You are interwoven to such an extent, and that is an economic activity.

How do you quantify and qualify that, to put it into a model to say, if I left that country there, I could trade off this country over here

---

39. Irrmarne, 350 km north-east of Alice Springs on the Sandover Highway, was originally a stock reserve that was re-scheduled as Aboriginal land, and held under the Irrmarne Aboriginal Land Trust. The CLC Land Management Unit undertook extensive work that included analysis of aerial photography, satellite imagery, and vegetation and fauna surveys, to assess the capabilities of the land.

for that, then we can do certain things? Now we got blessed, because the whitefellas went and picked all the good country for cattle. This has an impact on the good country, and on the bad country that we ended up with. We ended up with spinifex plains and rocky hummocks, and mining and everything else. But we ended up with all the water. All the water tables are under Aboriginal freehold, not under the pastoral leases. So the pastoralists wanted access to our land to grow crops. They want access to our land to grow food.

The idea of a segregated economy is a set process. But you have got to let the plane crash before people will learn – you have got to hit the wall, and they have hit the wall. The pastoral leases in the Northern Land Council are just about defunct and have been leased out to the white blokes. The buffalo industry is just about dead. They have got nowhere to go. They have no idea where to go, and I am sitting here in the box seat.

Tracker Tilmouth

The biggest argument has been and always will be the attraction of capital, and when I spoke at the NT Food Conference [in November 2014], I spoke about a segregated economy. That upset a few people but people who knew what I was talking about understood exactly, the segregated economy means that Aboriginal people develop projects that allow them to produce goods for sale, and commodities that allow them then to sell to a wider market.

But unless you segregate that economy at the start then it's very difficult for Aboriginal people to understand exactly what you are talking about, because the pressures of a normal market are upon them, and where people are forced to do certain things that are detrimental to the program in the long term, you end up with a bastardised system of production rather than something that is going to be sustainable. That is the argument for a segregated economy, where you can talk about tax havens, not tax havens as such, but managed investment schemes and a whole range of other stuff that allows taxation to be used and to be written off to a certain extent, offset against the economy of the Northern Territory, especially in remote communities.

You have to build an Aboriginal segregated economy, because unless you have a massive employment program, you will not have the wherewithal to employ everybody, and this becomes the argument: Do you employ everyone? Do you employ half of them? Do you employ a quarter of them? Because each project is going to have a finite resource in terms of employment. Does it take four blokes to dig a hole? Does it take five blokes? Does it take six blokes? Because when you get five or six, or even three blokes digging a hole, you have lost your efficiency. You have lost the efficiency of two digging a hole.

Now where do we go? It is going to get worse because the Abbott government has cut back ranger programs and a lot of other programs as well. You have got no economy. The one economy you have got is a policy [land care] that can't deliver. *You leave the trees there.* Yes, righto. *We're going to pay so much for carbon trading and everything else.* Where is the industry? *There isn't one.* There is no green industry as such.

Alexis Wright: *Can you sketch out from the top of your head an economic plan?*

Ha! You do not have one, and you will not have one, until you recognise that there is a level of productivity that you can glean from any group of people, and unfortunately you have unemployment present in two or three generations. So you are never ever going to get this good work ethic being part and parcel of it. You have got to rebuild an economy, slowly from the ground up. Long term, that is, taking the long term view. It is going to take real thinking and commitment. But at the moment people are not thinking that way. They are looking for a five-minute grab on TV, and they are getting awards for turning up. Recognition, reconciliation, you name it. Or sovereignty! There is no debate, no real debate, about where the Aboriginal community is going to in the first place. Even if we did get along, we still do not have a plan.

Alexis Wright: *Have you got a vision?*

No I don't, not right at the moment. I have got a bit of a dream, but it is a nightmare.

Tracker Tilmouth

My main argument is that you cannot go to the table with a begging bowl. If you are going to exercise your rights, and your rights are enshrined in the ownership of land, your rights are also enshrined in the economic power that you bring to the table. You cannot negotiate from a point of, *Please be kind to me, I am a coon.* That goes nowhere. The only time you negotiate is when you say, *Righto! If you don't listen to me it's going to cost you.* And it is going to cost you a lot more than you thought. It is delaying your project, it is delaying your resource development, it is delaying everything.

So you go back to the table and say, I want to exercise my rights, my sovereign rights. You have not surrendered. There is no one who has received your declaration of surrender. The argument for land rights, especially in the Northern Territory, is that Aboriginal people can exercise their economic rights. It is not the land rights so much, they achieved a lot in that, now it is the economics of it. Everyone is afraid of this, of what does economics mean? Community development is a form of economic development but no one is game to take it on. This is where it sits.

You have got to have Aboriginal people considering this for themselves rather than being left out of the economic process, and being an integral part of the economic process, because the Northern Territory Government's money is based on the formula that Aboriginal people are hard to service, they live in remote areas, so they get extra money but what they do with that money is spend it on a lot more bureaucrats, they do not spend it where it should be spent. The argument is really to remove CDEP, start developing real economic programs and regional authorities that are able to handle the economic pressures.

The non-Indigenous part of the Aboriginal community is against that because these people have a social agenda that Aboriginal people are living museums. Or they believe that through your poverty you remain pure. This has been the Labor Party's mantra and the CDEP mantra for some time under the social workers. I train Aboriginal people to recognise that the social and economic fabric of the Aboriginal communities is currently based on service delivery, based on services, and therefore it is a cost, they are unable to earn against those services. My aim is to try and turn that around so that everything you see is economic. Everything you do and say, whether you buy a bottle of beer or you get a loaf of bread, it costs you money, there is a cost involved, you are not part of the process, you are a recipient, you are a grant in aid.

The Gulf is a classic example of having to rethink the strategy and with people like Fred Pascoe, Murrandoo, Vernon [Yanner], and blokes like that who can see the argument, it is a matter of just quietly moving that argument very close to them so they get a good look at it.

Freddie Pascoe is way out in front of everybody. He is a thinker. Not only is he a thinker, he gets up and does it. Murrandoo has held back a little bit because he has got to run the Land Council and there are differing political discourses in there, so you can be distracted from the economic agenda. Whereas Fred is the mayor of Normanton in North West Queensland. He runs the Morr Morr Pastoral Company. He understands it, and gets it every day of the week. So you have these types of bloke sitting there and they are not going to have the degrees of the Pearsons of the world, or Langtons, or Dodsons, but they are going to be doing it. Doing it long before these people like that work out how to do it. To me they are neo-colonialists – they have come to colonise the blacks again. As far as I'm concerned they do not have any answers because they have not been around long enough to study the problems. You cannot have a resolution of a problem unless you know the problem and how it affects you. Part of their agenda as far as I can see is that at the end of the day you will get a Basics Card from royalties and if you are not spending it on health, education and welfare…you will not get any money.[40] That was being touted, that was the agenda. Hopefully, I can get to Abbott and people like Andrew Robb and a few others I know, and tell them to kill it. It is bullshit. Based on bullshit.

You have just got to read the book *Beyond Humbug* by [Michael] Dillon and [Neil] Westbury, and all it is to date is that nothing has

---

40. The Basics Card is a device developed by the federal government to quarantine and control the income and spending of Aboriginal people dependent on social welfare payments.

worked, they have been in charge for thirty or thirty-five years that I know of, and nothing has worked.[41] They write books about how it is supposed to work, but it cannot work, because it did not work in the first place. From Maralinga to Maningrida it has not worked. From Oak Valley all the way up to Yirrkala it has not worked. And from Broome, or Port Hedland, across to Yarrabah, it has not worked. Cape York has not worked. There is nothing you can show me today that works, except for the processes of economic development. A welfare-based economy cannot work, it does not work. It is an oxymoron.

Tracker Tilmouth

I have no respect for authority. To a certain extent this has always been a part of my character, whether you are talking to the Chief Minister of the Northern Territory, or whoever, you just talk. You put your point of view and leave it be. I have always had that ability to go and say what I think and let it hang where it may, or fall where it may. I have got myself in a lot of trouble doing that as well as winning a few arguments, so it has been sweet and sour results more than a few times.

The idea has been to get inside places, to walk in, to negotiate, to articulate a position. We are floundering around as a group and saying where is the best way to go. We have a lot of black bureaucrats, and you see this in relation to the recognition debate. All those people that are up in the front representing the community are all ex-bureaucrats, or are paid bureaucrats, they are part of this committee or that committee, they are part of this or that. They are funded. Well! That is not coming from who they think they are. It is not coming from the heart: it is coming from the funding. You forget that you go from reconciliation – we have done that and we cannot keep crossing that bridge – we have to find something else. We want recognition now in the Constitution. It is not even our Constitution. It belongs to the white blokes.

The thing that interests me is that the debate is not a debate that the white blokes are having. As far as they are concerned we are conquered,

---

41. Michael C. Dillon and Neil D. Westbury, *Beyond Humbug: Transforming Government Engagement with Indigenous Australia,* Seaview Press, West Lakes, 2007.

we have got nowhere to go. The best that we are going to get we have got out of native title, because that is what they think. And so we are waiting on issues like the Wild Rivers legislation. Noel Pearson went through that process. We went through that process with the Gulf of Carpentaria and at the end of the day they came back with a worse set of legislation than what was in the Wild Rivers. We all got bailed out. We lost the process. We lost control of the process and you cannot keep doing that. You have to go and find a legislative mechanism. You have to go and find the places that you can win on, and what you cannot win on, what you will lose on. This is part of the negotiation. This is the problem we have. Every time we have a problem we go and buy some bloke from Alaska who has been eating seal meat for the last year. He comes across to teach us how to negotiate. The wonderful people from the Sami in the Arctic, and everybody else.

For example, Rodolfo Vaz de Carvalho, the Brazilian representative at the Northern Australia Food Futures Conference held in Darwin in 2014, said how stupid we are in Australia, and he did it in the nicest way possible. You need a dictator to get this sort of project up [a northern food bowl] – that was his closing message I think. You cannot do it without military support sort of thing. He thought we were in Brazil, where you shoot the peasants.

So you have this debate going on in an Aboriginal community where we never sat down and did an inventory of what we have got, of our resources. And then we have not been able to deal with that as a collective because we are divided. You look across to where the real debate is going to be, to north and south Australia where the mining and cattle industry and everything else is located, that is where the resources are. And the wineries, and the investments and buildings and infrastructure, and the cities. We have not been able to do that successfully. We ended up with Indigenous Business Australia. We ended up with the Indigenous Land Corporation. Really they should be closed down. They should be closed down and people told to go home, we do not need you. They are getting the money of the closed-down ATSIC, being ATSIC by another name. And ATSIC did not work.

You cannot build the sort of economic framework I am talking about inside those types of organisations. This is what I am saying about segregating the economy. You cannot control the debate if you do not control the purse. The purse is the resources that you bring to the table. If you cannot control that you have lost the debate before you walk in the door. This is why there is an inordinate amount of funding for Native Title Representative Bodies, land councils and huge bureaucracies. They are all over-governed, absolutely over-governed. You talk to any organisation and they say, *We've got no money.* Hang on a minute, how much money did you get last year? *We got fifty million to run the Land Council.* Fifty mil! Not to build an Aboriginal economy.

There is no enjoyment of land rights. Enjoyment for land rights is someone out bush saying, *Well! I love being here. This is where I am sustaining myself. This is what I want to do. These are the values I have placed on my country.* Off you go. That is your prerogative, that is your choice. But at the end of the day, if you do not contribute, you get your return on what you invest, and this is the issue. If you want to be out there and do what you need to do, then when it comes to economic and commercial development, you cannot get both mixed up. When it comes to commercial development your income is reflected by your investment. This is the problem, this idea that the Aboriginal sharing-and-caring, the pan-Aboriginality, is not as strong as people would like it to be. And so people who do not have royalties, do not have mining on their land, they are second-rate cousins. You always have that divide. The white blokes can see that divide. That is what they exploit. They are not there to be nice to us. This is the problem we have got.

Fiddling While Rome Burns

Michael O'Connor

The first time I remember Tracker was in Warren Snowdon's office, or running around Parliament House, in the 1990s. You know those people who run around the place and you see them but you actually do not know who they are, you might know the name but you do not talk to them.

So I roughly knew who he was and of course I remember his name being mentioned in dispatches when there was a Senate vacancy in the Northern Territory as well. Around 2004 he rang me up and said he had been talking to Martin Ferguson about trying to do some forestry projects in the Northern Territory, and Martin suggested he give me a ring. He said he had a range of information that would demonstrate there were some good places in the Northern Territory where you could grow plantation forestry, and that could be the foundation for a possible forest industry for some Indigenous communities. He wanted to know whether he could get some advice about forestry, not just about growing trees, but evaluating what you could do to increase the amount of jobs you could create off forestry, for forestry plantations in the Northern Territory.

So I said I was a union official, and that forestry was not really my expertise. I knew a bit about the industry of course, so I said I could easily organise people in forestry and others who I was sure would be more than happy to assist him. The thing that got me, he said he was not interested in that first off, and he basically said to me, if I wanted to help him I had to come up to the Northern Territory to see some of the communities he was talking about.

I was trying to work it out, *Hang on a minute, didn't he ring me looking for a favour,* and next thing you know he had completely swapped it around, because I said I can get you this guy, he is a forestry expert, he used to run several forestries and he said, *No, no mate, you've got it all wrong. You get up here and then we'll work out whether you're allowed to help us.*

And then next you know, I am organising myself to go to Port Keats [Wadeye]. I do not know how he did that. When he was talking to me he said, *Look, unless you know what the communities are going through, if you want to give us assistance you've got to understand something about the problem. You can't just sit down in Melbourne and think you know it all because you're doing something for the blackfellas. Get your arse on a plane and if we think you're alright we might let you help us.* So the next think you know I am on my way to the Northern Territory.

I went to Darwin and he agreed to meet me at seven o'clock somewhere outside a motel and by this stage a big controversy had broken out about the union over allegations about us and Howard in the 2000 election, because there was an allegation that we had received four million dollars. That had all broken over the weekend as I was coming up and he pulled up in a four-wheel drive at the door and said, *Hey brother, if you've got that four million dollars, I'm the fellow to get you a dig tree.*

So I got in the car and off we drove. I cannot remember if Sean Bowden was with me, but Tracker said, *We have to stop off.* He said, *We've got to pick up the interpreter.* I am going, *What do you mean, pick up an interpreter?* He just looked at me and said, *What do you think, they speak English where we're going?* He goes, *You don't know much about your own country, do you?* I just went, *Oh! My God.* Anyway so we picked up Dominic McCormack who is now a partner with Sean in the law firm there and we drove through to Daly River.

Now I had been at Daly River before, I had been there for a week. My brother-in-law lived up there for four or five years. We went through to Daly River, and spent a couple of days there. We had the interpreter and we looked at a couple of places, and they showed me the winds up there. Tracker showed me what was happening in the community and we met some of the people at the school. It was a bit of an eye-opener for me because I had never been to a place like that. I think the community had just gone through a series of violent episodes as well, this was what I was told when I was up there, a couple of the key people and mainly the women basically, had got rid of the pub. They had closed the pub.

I think they burnt it down and chased the manager out of town because they were trying to get it dry, and trying to stop [the violence].

I do not know if it was true but that was what they told me. Tracker had information that there was potential there to do some things, and he was explaining to me that he wanted as much as possible to find some economic activity that was sustainable, that would sustain Indigenous communities particularly in the Northern Territory, but anywhere I think. He was talking about the Northern Territory and he was looking at forestry, and he was looking at stuff to do with crocs as well, and he was really down on a number of initiatives from government where they were not really trying to provide a sustainable economy for Indigenous communities.

He would give an example where people would collect croc eggs say for twenty dollars an egg, but if you have an incubator, with the hatchlings you can get four hundred dollars or something. The incubator would only cost one thousand or two thousand dollars – you could not get money for that, but you could get money for other stuff that was bullshit. He was always looking for those sorts of activities that could be done, and he would give examples of very basic things not happening.

That was the first time when I actually realised what it meant, when I went with him and he explained it to me. I did not realise the provocation of getting different people off different country and into someone else's country, and the tensions and the issues that that caused, until I witnessed it, or was there and having someone like him explain to me, because as I said, I was at Daly River for a week but I never really got that. What he said made a lot of sense. It was, *Hang on, why can we not make people economically sufficient, why can we not make them economically sustainable, why can't we look at these sorts of issues and be practical about creating economic activity which supports people's language and people's culture?* I could not understand why people were not doing this. It did not make much sense why they weren't. I still do not know why they are not.

I do not know how many ideas Tracker came up with during that car trip, of things we could do. He would wear me ragged. I just could not keep up with him. I would say, *Mate you've got to stop plying my head with all these ideas. Just give me one or two things I've got to do cause otherwise I just can't keep up.* He would go a million miles an hour. Every time he would see you he would have an idea. He needed a big bloody infrastructure around him, because there were some great ideas about what could be done, but he was basically just trying to get the logistics for the forestry through. And of course there were a lot of people who were pooh-poohing stuff, who did not know what they were talking about I reckoned.

Tracker's whole forestry thing was based on carbon trading as well, value-adding. Basically, his view was that if you got the right scale you would provide jobs for trained foresters, and you would need trained people to be involved in the management of the forest, a whole range of blue-collar jobs as well as white-collar jobs, or professional jobs. Then there would be the value added, which would be to have people involved in anything from furniture manufacturing to framing, and then the carbon that could deliver an income stream as well. Basically a whole range of jobs, including a whole range of environmental services apart from carbon to make sure you are looking after everything properly.

The other thing I did not realise, and again I was very ignorant of how things worked, Aborigines really only had the right to be consulted and it was not actually a property right, and that mining companies could still do what they wanted. I did not realise that the rights that had been won had a hell of a way to go to call them what most of us would think would be property rights.

Sean Bowden

Tracker never forgot what was required back at home base. The work we were doing at Thamarrurr had been started but was unfinished. This was about the Thamarrurr concept. This was the most important concept at a place like Wadeye, because Thamarrurr is something that means *all together* or *coming together*, coming together for a fight against outsiders is a more literal interpretation that has been given to me. So joining together to confront the outside world might be the contemporary version of it. This had been developed, almost as a last straw, by the leadership of Wadeye who were in twenty-two different clans on one clan's land. They realised they had to come together in a formal way. Previously that one clan had run the town and they realised all the clans had to have a say.

The Diminin clan had to be respected, but the Kulingmirr group had to come together. And so they did and they asked Tracker and myself back to keep helping them with that work. We spent a lot of time working with that concept and with those leaders.

The concept came from the leadership themselves. It came from men like Tobias Nganbe and Leon Melpi who always pay tribute to Tracker Tilmouth. They remembered the work that was done between 2003 and 2007 when he was active with them. And they always paid tribute to him because in later days he would take them to Canberra as well. And then when I was with the Wadeye men in later years, I would always make a point, *I learnt this from Tracker Tilmouth.* They would say, *Sean, how do you know these things? How do you know to do this?* I would say, *I learnt from Tracker Tilmouth.* And Gerry Hand and then Martin Ferguson, and Daryl Melham, and Ah Kit a little bit, and Norman Fry a little bit, and Galarrwuy a lot, but Tracker Tilmouth opened the door for me and for them. That was what he did for many people. He was selfless in his willingness to do it. I was fortunate that I was there, just able to capitalise, it was good for me.

So we started meeting with this Thamarrurr group. Tracker understood it, he understood it was the only way forward, and of course he sold that message far and wide, this was the way to do things and you could not do it otherwise. It also came with a sense at the time, of what we were experiencing up here at Wadeye, that ATSIC had certainly failed, and the [Northern] Land Council system was failing. The Land Council system, at this level, was failing. It was not connected to these groups. It was not connected to these communities. It had no sense, no tactile feel of what was going on.

Tracker and I became the Land Council's informants. We spent half our time going back to the NLC saying, *This is what is happening at Wadeye*, because the NLC had no touch on it. More to the point, the Wadeye people did not want them because they did not know them. We actually reintroduced the Land Council back to Wadeye and there is a history there: the Catholic Church was in a way anti–Land Council, and there had been some adversarial stuff, but that had been dead for fifteen years. To balance things up Tracker came up with a statistic that the NLC had done four hundred lease agreements in North East

Arnhem Land, but had done none in the Wadeye region, and there were more people in the Wadeye region.

So we started agitating for an economic agenda with the Thamarrurr group. Then when Tracker got Richie Howitt [economist] involved, and got the technological and agricultural data and soil sampling, he used that to interest Senator Bill Heffernan. He spoke to people, not just through the prism of the Thamarrurr concept, but the Thamarrurr group as the conduit to an economic development future. And hey: *we need kids educated as well.* So we were able to link the whole argument. Then we started to do it publicly, and I learnt a lot during this period from him and others about the media, and we started to agitate, we started to write things, with me going to the media as the lawyer agitating on behalf of Wadeye.

We started to criticise the Labor government, and they would have been saying to themselves, *Well! We were smart not to let Tracker Tilmouth into politics!* But they were wrong, because if they had had him in politics he would have fixed the problem from the inside. The problem was they had become a closed and insular party, interested only in their own success, in winning the next election in the northern suburbs of Darwin, playing the race card which they did in 2005 with the drunks policy. We nearly had fistfights with other Labor people. We had really vigorous confrontations at places like the Casuarina Shopping Centre [in Darwin] where we would bump into Labor politicians and both of us would say to them, *Oh! Why are you out here, running the drunks policy are you? Telling everyone how Aboriginal people are urinating, defecating and fornicating all over the place.* They would say, *Oh! No we're not!* and we would say, *Yes you are.* We had this double thing going at the time and it was just rabble. We got Chris Burns [Labor minister in the Northern Territory] one day and in the end made him admit that yes, that was what he was saying. We got him in a public domain where he was holding court in Casuarina and challenged him.

But that behaviour has its price because the political machine turns on you, and it starts to run things against you, and I copped a bit but Tracker copped much more, and when I look back on the calibre of his courage, he had a prawn farm he was trying to run, he had a loan from the government. He had a reputation, he had history, and they went for him, they went for him a lot. They never got him. Fortunately in a way it was a Liberal government in Canberra. And in the end we were big and ugly enough to look after ourselves, and we were right, the policy the Northern Territory Labor Party took to the 2005 election about alcohol and drunks was race-based and was a disgraceful thing that would not happen in any other jurisdiction in Australia.

Meanwhile, the Thamarrurr stuff started to build. The NLC then engaged Tracker on a full-time basis to do this sort of work. They realised how important it was. I had started to do some work for the Yunupingus and with Galarrwuy, and Tracker was there with me as well, and in those early days when Galarrwuy was trying to get back on his feet, when he was under all sorts of political fire having just resigned as chairman of the Northern Land Council and being himself a critic of the policies of the then NT Labor government, he was copping it. The administration in the Northern Territory turned on him, calling all sorts of investigations into him which were followed by federal investigations.

The word on the street was that Galarrwuy Yunupingu is finished, Galarrwuy Yunupingu is dead. *The king is dead, long live the king* is what people were saying around the place, and a lot worse. Really awful. I was furious about it because I knew that with all of the people saying that, their careers were made off the back of Galarrwuy Yunupingu.

It was a horrible thing to watch. The Northern Territory Government was on him, and they were working against him. I was acting for Galarrwuy as his lawyer, and I ended up saying to Tracker come on we have got to go over and support Galarrwuy. That was because so many people who you thought would be loyal to Galarrwuy for what he had done for the land rights cause, and the general cause of Aboriginal people, moved away from him, and they all moved away except for Tracker. Tracker got on the plane with me and over we went.

Galarrwuy can look after himself, he is a titan, but he did need support, he did need people to guide him through. I helped him legally and Tracker helped him politically for a time when he was at his weakest. Even his closest friends were saying to us, *I think he's finished, I think he's going to lose it all.* He was under investigation at three levels, from the police, from the Northern Territory Government, from the Commonwealth. The royalties that his clan derived from the Land

Rights Act were under fire, and he was under fire because of that, and it was clear that this was a mechanism just to bring him down and at the same time to weaken the Land Rights Act. Everyone knows that, it is still current, more than ever actually: if you want to get the Land Rights Act you have got to get Galarrwuy. You have got to get his agreement, or you have got to get him out of the way. And back in those days there was a run on the Land Rights Act. Those were tough times and it strikes me that Tracker was not afraid of those times. He had a lot of guts for the fight.

Tracker Tilmouth

If this is a model of success, give me Soweto in its heyday…Give me Soweto any time prior to Nelson Mandela's release or after his release, give me Soweto as a comparison and I'd rather go to Soweto. – Tracker Tilmouth on the clan riot in Wadeye, ABC Radio, 4 May 2006.

There are three classes that I see, of Aboriginals living in Aboriginal society, and one of those is in the bush, where culture and language, law and custom is enshrined, and governs the total operations on remote communities. You can have all the programs you like going in, but unless you understand the cultural and social processes then your programs are not going to go very far. It does not matter how much money you throw at it.

And this came to pass with the Intervention, where the amount of money that went to Aboriginal communities was enormous, but it had no effect on the social wellbeing of the communities. Port Keats [Wadeye] built a hundred houses and there are still eight hundred people between the ages of nineteen and twenty-five or thirty looking for work. There is no CDEP program nor should there be, but there is no prospect of work either.

Why did that happen? Well! It happened because the community built or started to get involved in building the houses, but the benefits flowed to the people who managed the program in Port Keats. They did not flow to Aboriginal individuals, the wages and so forth, even if and when they were available to work.

This is an issue involving the Thamarrurr Development Corporation, the Northern Territory Government and the Commonwealth. At the moment Port Keats still has a massive unemployment rate with no skills, or very little skills.

There was a failure of the Thamarrurr Regional Council to be able to negotiate a proper process, and the leadership of Thamarrurr was proven bereft of any real ideas on where to go. And they never had the experience neither. The management of Thamarrurr took what it could without understanding the full political picture and the processes. And today, now, it is still struggling to be part of anything significant in relation to sustainable economic development.

So you had this sort of program running, but I do not think there is a community that ever had the Intervention turn up and build houses that survived the process, or increased their skills or economy. Or increased skilled workers and skills that could be used elsewhere, or skills that could have remained there today for the next round of housing. That has never been the case. So we ended up with CDEP training programs which were reliant on CDEP funding to employ people. This was after the Intervention. Before, and after the Intervention. So the Intervention made no impact whatsoever.

This was the situation across the board and you only have to go to the social indicators to understand that, the amount of alcohol, the amount of drug use, and the amount of domestic violence, is still the same. In fact it has increased.

You get a flasher house to belt your missus in. That is all you have done. Because you do not have a job, you cannot buy your house, you cannot live in your house, because you do not have any furniture when they give you the house so you are camping on the concrete floor. Or you would rather camp outside anyway and use the house as a shed, or a storage facility for you and your dogs. And that is about it. And then, you run the electricity lines outside and you have your TV sitting outside on the verandah, or out on the lawn, or wherever, and you sit out there, sleep out there, and watch TV out there, rather than sitting in the hot, non-air-conditioned concrete block.

And that is the sum gain of the Intervention. So you look at that, then you look at the urban Aboriginal organisations like the health services, the housing associations, and everybody else. They have no real connection to the bush. In fact they have even less of a connection than before. And I know that AMSANT [Aboriginal Medical Services Alliance Northern Territory] have embarked on the process of developing a regionalisation strategy, but this would mean that the bigger health services would have to share their wealth, share their resources, share their operations with remote communities, and they are very reluctant to do that.

So they go through this process of regionalisation purely as a facade, and they are all very concerned and have all sorts of well-meaning debates, but it is like the UN General Assembly, where everyone goes, *Oh! Woe is me* – about Syria – *but let's not get too close in case we have to do something*. Right! And that is what happens with health services and to a certain extent the service organisations. It is so disconnected that the Central Land Council, in its wisdom, decided to set up another arm called Community Development, which is a very good move because it fills the gap that was left by these so-called service providers, and health service and housing associations, essential services, the legal aid, and everybody else that races out there to support the Aboriginal community. But there is really no real support because the resources are held in Alice Springs, Darwin, Katherine, Nhulunbuy and elsewhere, as part of the centralised service provision.

So there is no connection between the remote communities and the urban Aboriginal operations, really no connection. Right! If you want to connect you have to have ownership, you have to be an agent of change, and that has been rejected on so many occasions by the organisations. The Aboriginal organisations, especially in Darwin and Alice Springs, are deciding to form an advisory team to counter Warren Mundine, Marcia Langton, Noel Pearson, and Abbott's committee, but it is a bit late.[42]

---

42. Tracker mentions the names of Aboriginal people who had strongly supported the Intervention, when it was introduced in 2007, against those who saw the Intervention policies as a backwards step for Aboriginal people. He is also referring to Prime Minister Tony Abbott's Indigenous Advisory Council, established in 2013, which includes a mixture of Aboriginal and non-Aboriginal people, including Warren Mundine as the chairman. After Tracker spoke about service delivery organisations based in towns in the Northern Territory in 2013, the federal

It is like running around with Nero fiddling while Rome burns. And they want to get this connection in the bush, but it is too late, there is no connection. The Aboriginal communities in the bush have never been serviced by these people, never seen these people, and so all of a sudden they are now called on to protect organisations that they have nothing to do with. And this is the position that we find the remote communities in, being asked yet again to do the marches on NAIDOC Day and everything else. So it is the most dispossessed who are being asked to do most of the carrying and the work in relation to protecting the political position of Aboriginal communities.

Then you have this other group that I call the entrenched ideologues, both for and against processes through Aboriginal affairs. They are the blessed academics. They must be right because they have a doctorate behind their name or in front of their name, or professor, and they get a ticket for turning up. When you read a lot of their work, and their papers, you can see that they have a disjointed view of where Aboriginals' survival should or should not be. It all depends who you are talking to because they've split their Aboriginal academics into two camps. One is pro-Labor, and the other one is pro-Liberal. And the pro-Labor people have entered the fray with a mantra – *free of poverty, remain pure.* And the pro-Liberal camp, their mantra is – *social justice can only be delivered through business development.* Now both of them sound good and are entrenched, but both of them are actually counterproductive to long-term Aboriginal economic and social sustainability.

There are the arguments that these people have never been called to task to explain exactly what you mean when you talk about the process of enforced education, therefore enforced assimilation, therefore enforced language loss. This is because you are talking to people who have been devastated by dispossession over a long period of time, who have lost culture and language, and are trying hard to find a long-lost language and culture to give themselves an identity. And you have only to watch the proliferation of the playing of the *yidaki*, which is a

---

government introduced heavy cuts to the budgets of a number of Aboriginal organisations both in urban and non-urban centres in 2015. These measures also followed the 2014 decision by the Western Australian Government to close 150 Aboriginal communities.

didgeridoo. It is all down the east coast now and they make a wonderful noise, but there is no song to go with it. There is a lot of grunt and the wriggling of legs and everything else, but no song. There is no old bloke singing a song that goes with that story. And when you see that, you say is that an adaption and exploitation of didgeridoo playing, or is that a cry for help? This is all we have got. We cannot show you anything else because we have got nothing else to show you. Our culture is in the museum. Our culture is in the books of anthropologists. And we have only been able to get access to our culture because the anthropologists, who have been the beneficiaries of the dispossession, have been able to hide, and keep everything secret and sacred in various guises of manipulation. Aboriginal people are not allowed to get access to that information, so what you see is this cry of: *We want to return to our language, we want to learn our language, want to learn our songs.* That may not involve didgeridoo playing. It is exactly the same for the universal dance of the brolga which you see at nearly every gathering.

These are the issues that you see purely as an observer, when you come from a background like I have, you can see that and say, *Righto! Is this process a legitimate process*, or is it the result or the adaptation of a devastated and dispossessed people who have lost culture, language and everything else, and need to regain that process, and they do it with whatever tools are at their disposal?

The real knowledge is in the universities, real knowledge is in the museums, and it is guarded and guided by some very strong-willed anthropologists, non-Indigenous, I would say. Knowledge is power. And they think that every time there is a land dispute that they have to be involved because no one knows what they know. They went around and swept up the crumbs of Aboriginal knowledge, or remnant Aboriginal knowledge that had been existent with the old people, and they swept the crumbs up and kept them very close to their chest. So the discussions [anthropologists have] of where did you camp, what did you do and everything else, make up – especially in Western Queensland where I have been working – make up for the standing and knowledge of Aboriginal groups. These anthropologists are costing Aboriginal people an absolute fortune to regain the knowledge that they gave to them.

It goes back to the question of native title and the stupid idea that you had to have a continuous connection to land. If you took the arguments that are the background to the existence of the Carpentaria Land Council, the lesson is that if you think you have got native title, act sovereign, do not wait to be blessed. This was the basis of the negotiations for Century mine where Waanyi under current native title legislation could not make the registration test, but the advice that we [the Central Land Council] gave them to give to the mining company was that, *We own the land, we don't care what you say, you prove that we don't and that will take you ten years of delays for your project. In the meantime, we are willing to sit down and negotiate with you on a process that recognises and delivers our sovereignty.* That was on behalf of the Waanyi, and negotiated by the Gangalidda and Garawa leadership of the Carpentaria Land Council, to make sure that the Aboriginal people who did not know who they were had a position that could be defended. And that is why the Century mine agreement was the catalyst [in native title agreements], because we said, *You prove we haven't and in the meantime let's get on and negotiate.* And the mining company saw that, and they went along with that process.

Unfortunately, the big organisations, and these are the land councils in the Northern Territory and the Kimberley Land Council in the west, they stuck to the very letter of native title which excluded a lot of Aboriginal people from participating, and I mean from the Stolen Generation all the way through to urban Aborigines and to some historical Aboriginals that were moved into reserves, they went for the pure examples of native title ownership. They did so without understanding what native title was all about, according to the argument that Keating, the facade that Keating gave on native title, *You enjoy native title at our say-so.*

So you are the traditional landowners of the mine when the mine is finished. And you have a right to negotiate, so you inherit the environmental disaster left by the mining industry if you are not careful. Under native title that is where it stops and starts. The land councils and their lawyers have been absolutely stonewalled because there is no ongoing debate about native title property rights, which was left out on purpose by Keating to placate the mining industry. Now you cannot have native title without the enjoyment of native title, which means the question of property rights.[43] The right to negotiate is a very small piece of the cake. The question is, do you have native title, and if you do have native title, then how do you enjoy it?

Well! You can't enjoy it – there is no enjoyment as such, and that means of their property rights, which is a High Court decision under Wik and Mabo. We are waiting for that to be debated, and the Aboriginal hierarchy has decided that it would upset the latte set, it will curdle their milk, if we were to start debating property rights. Someone will take the cheese and bickies off you if you're not careful. And so they have this reluctance to put forward the debate on native title property rights, while knowing full well that all the agreements in Western Australia done by the magnificent people that work for Rio Tinto really amount to a hill of beans in relation to the total process. Whereas if you had native title property rights, the Aboriginal community would be able to accept from the Western Australian Government state-based royalties regardless of the project. And would not have to negotiate on health, housing and education, and say we will spend our royalties on health, housing and education. No, that is automatically a citizenship right.

How do you tie this failure to recognise native title property rights to the failure of the Intervention on the ground? The Intervention was based on an assumption that the Northern Territory Government at that time was broke and could not supply housing, health and education for remote communities because it was spending its money on the waterfront. Spending its money on Inpex.[44]

It spent millions of dollars fighting land claims over the years. Well exactly, and the Central Land Council has time and time again requested an inquiry into the funding of the Northern Territory Government,

---

43. The argument is that the High Court did not go far enough to recognise that native title is an exclusive property right, to the exclusion of others. The Native Title Act only allows for the right to negotiate over the use of native title land by others, but not to supercede non-Indigenous proprietary rights to develop the land.

44. Tracker is referring to massive waterfront precinct in Darwin combining residential, leisure, business and culture centres. InpexGas Project Darwin is a gas processing plant for the development of the Ichthys gas field near Darwin.

both Labor and Liberal–CLP, on what they spent their money on – both the untied and the tied grants that were identified as Aboriginal money – what they spent their money on and what were the results of their expenditure? Did they put in infrastructure? Did they build roads? Did they build houses? What did they do? And both parties have dodged that question so it is absolutely clear that we have to go and get that question answered through other political means, possibly through the unions and elsewhere. What is the current result of the Intervention, in terms of housing, health and education? And what is the expenditure of both CLP and Labor governments in the Northern Territory in relation to services to Aboriginal communities?

How did the people on the ground respond to the Intervention? Well the issue was then, as you would have noticed, according to the authors of *Little Children are Sacred,* that there was a paedophile on every corner, rivers of grog, the ongoing debate in relation to police and so forth.[45] Now Olga Havnen did a critique of the total process as part of her role with the Northern Territory Government and a lot of people with links to services to Aboriginal communities kyboshed the report.[46]

I find it extremely interesting and telling that the academics and advisors to various governments decided that she had gone too far and asked too many questions. The Intervention, and the results of the Intervention, must rest totally at the foot of the then Chief Minister of the Northern Territory, Claire Martin. Totally at her feet because she knew that here was an ongoing expenditure by the Commonwealth to boost the Territory economy in relation to housing and infrastructure, and she could sail in on that in the next election, and say we have got *x* amount of jobs, employment and everything else, and it is all based on remote communities. The line-up was immense, yet the work ended up going to Leightons and everybody else, the big companies who come out and build houses out bush, while forgetting that most communities

---

45. Rex Wild and Patricia Anderson, *Ampe Akelyernemane Meke Mekarlt ('Little Children Are Sacred'): Report of the Northern Territory Board of Inquiry into the Protection of Aboriginal Children from Sexual Abuse, 2007*, Northern Territory Government, Darwin, 2007.

46. Olga Havnen, *Office of the Northern Territory Coordinator-General for Remote Services Report: June 2011 to August 2012*, Office of the Coordinator-General for Remote Services, Darwin, 2012. Havnen produced the report as Northern Territory Coordinator-General for Remote Services.

have little housing associations with their own skilled workers that could have been doing this work. Because it was the Labor government, the unions went quiet. The CFMEU, of which I am a member, went walkabout on the issue.

It falls at everyone's feet including the land councils. The land councils could have stood up a bit more and said, *Well! You don't have a right to enter Aboriginal land.* Even though they were organisations that flowed from the federal government, the government would have had to completely, compulsorily acquire all rights and interests of that land from the land councils to get out and allow the contractors in. The Northern and Central Land Councils could have said, until there is a forty per cent Aboriginal employment rate, this contractor will not get a permit. They could have done that.

They were totally scared. The bush mob saw the army come in, they saw [the army take] all the medical records of the children, the army went and tested all the children, even though the communities already had medical records in their own health services. The remote health services and the clinics in each community already had records, you only had to inspect the child, and know that child is this, this and this. The army did not find any adverse effects of gonorrhoea, paedophilia, all the target indicators of child abuse. And the rivers of grog, that has not stopped even with more police. So most of the money that came out of the Intervention went to the Northern Territory police for housing for police staff out on remote communities.

The government did not know what they were talking about from the start. And the people in Alice Springs, especially the Anangu Pitjantjatjara Women's Council management, they were on TV saying, *Oh! What a terrible place this is,* and there was vilification of Aboriginal men. So every Aboriginal male since then is identified as a paedophile, and a wife-basher. Automatically now, there is this vilification process, and the depression rates of Aboriginal men because of this public persona of them is quite high. When you go to the men's groups that are run out of Congress in Central Australia, the issues that are being dealt with are ones of depression and lack of role in their community because they now get overtaken by a push from urban white women saying that Aboriginal women should have this role, similar to our role, and Aboriginal society does not allow that. So Aboriginal men have been displaced as decision-makers and heads of families, and so forth. And the service industry has seen this gate open, so when the white Toyota with one person in it turns up – five to each meeting, whether it is Community Aid Abroad, the Fred Hollows Foundation, Oxfam, you name it, they have all been out there, and they all turn up in the white Toyotas, all the single drivers, they go straight to the Women's Centre. The men are saying, *Well! Hang on, aren't you talking to us? Oh! No! No! You are a paedophile.*

There are no community councils anymore.[47] It is all run by administrators. You are getting this process of dysfunction coming from men now that was not there before. This is reflected in imprisonment rates. It has got me beat why the land councils have not picked up this question of property rights, because the argument of land ownership in relation to communities was the invention of a past administration, and that is why there are historical Aboriginals residing in those areas, while there are also a lot of traditional landowners residing in the areas who actually own the country but are not being recognised. They cannot be recognised because the question of service provision by the government is reliant on them getting access to Aboriginal land, and the only way they can do that is through the Northern Territory Land Rights Act. The land councils gave five-year lease arrangements to the Commonwealth – but it is still not their place. The land belongs to someone who has native title and native title property rights. It has got nothing to do with the land councils. They do not own the land. They may administer the land trust, and then have traditional landowners that they represent, but the real property right [and ability to govern the land], which is what we are talking about, is actually owned by the native title holders, whoever they may be.[48]

This is the disconnect that land councils keep falling over, this question about what role has native title got in relation to the Land

---

47. Community councils were disbanded by the Intervention.
48. A land trust is a statutory body under the Aboriginal Land Rights (Northern Territory) Act 1976 that holds the title to land handed back to the traditional Aboriginal owners under the act to hold certain functions.

Rights Act? The answer is very simple, the Land Rights Act is the political process by legislation. This is the Northern Territory Land Rights Act. Native title is a legal decision by the High Court of Australia which supersedes any political process, and requires the property-right argument to be attached to it, which is by a decision or a declaration that we enjoy property rights as has already been discussed in relation to Mabo and Wik. So there is no need to have the legal debate. It is a question of going down to the High Court and exercising your native title property rights.

Murrandoo did that with the crocodile and this was backed up by the High Court decision on fishing rights from the Thursday Islands.[49] They have property rights for fish. And there was the decision for Joe Roe in relation to James Price Point.[50] He has a property right. It is his land, for fuck's sake. It is not somebody else's. He was given that land, or given the story for that land by the traditional landowners. He is the only one who has got the stories left. The people who said they were traditional landowners, they all went and lived in Broome, and Derby, and Port Hedland, and elsewhere. They were not looking after the country. They only turned up when the discussion was in relation to compensation. And then you had a big brawl in Broome on where the money should be spent in Broome.

That all fell through in the end. It had to. It was not based on reality. The mining company walked away, it was a legal issue.

---

49. Tracker is referring to *Yanner v Eaton (1999)* and *Akiba v Commonwealth of Australia (2013)*. In the former, Murrandoo Yanner was successful in arguing that his killing of two crocodiles for food was an exercise of his native title rights and did not require a licence. In the latter, the Torres Strait Islander people won a bid to secure commercial fishing rights under native title in the High Court. The group, whose native title claim was first lodged in 2001, wanted to build an economic base from commercial fishing in the a vast area of sea between Australia and Papua New Guinea. The case was strongly opposed by the Commonwealth and Queensland governments and the fishing industry. While no one contested that the Islanders held native title over the 40,000 square kilometres of sea, they argued that those rights no longer extended to the commercial trade of marine resources. The full bench of the High Court found those commercial rights still exist and had not been extinguished by Commonwealth and state laws.

50. A Western Australian Supreme Court decision, *The Wilderness Society of WA (Inc) v Minister for Environment* (2013), found that the WA environment minister and the WA Environmental Protection Authority had failed to follow valid processes in the assessment and approval of the massive James Price Point (JPP) gas plant.

The economic issue would be: has Joe Roe got the property rights as a traditional landowner, or as an owner of the stories? But the point is that they were not game to take on the legal process because it would ultimately open the doors on property rights.

Tracker Tilmouth

The minute you saw the Intervention in the Northern Territory you thought this is madness, absolute madness. It had taken so long to get people to start [working on] self-determination [which was federal government policy], and to understand what self-determination means, and then as soon as they nearly grasp it, [the government] takes it away from them. The ideas of CANCA – the Combined Aboriginal Nations of Central Australia – was exactly where you needed to be because the next step was not going to be an Intervention. You needed the next step to say, *Righto! You are responsible for who you are, you make your rules and we, as government, will back you.*

These senior Aboriginal people were quite prepared to take that step, and I think even now this right-wing Liberal government might have the same philosophy, *You make your own rules, you look after yourself, and we will back you.* But maybe they don't want to do that for Aboriginal affairs, I do not know. Now that does not mean attack the Land Rights Act, it does not mean anything of the sort, it means taking the services off the states that duplicate [policy, programs, funding], and allowing Aboriginal people to make their own decisions. If you want me to look after myself, give me the rights to look after myself.

Even under Australian government policies of self-determination, self-management was never really happening. It was words. When there is an invasion of land, where there is an invasion of policy, whether it is an invasion of money, you cannot [win]. If there is money coming in, you have to have the resources to be able to handle that money. You either have the economic wherewithal to look after yourself or you rely on others. The minute you rely on somebody else you are gone. You adopt their policies and politics. Then you have no leverage. You are struggling, you are stuck in the mud. So you have to develop a process that will give you the financial and educational and cultural resources to allow you to deal with it. If you do not have that then you better learn how to run very quickly, because they are coming to get you, if they have not already got you.

This is the story in the Gulf, and this is the story in Western Australia.[51] They came in there and went *whack* and they were led by the academics, the black academics who said this is a good thing, mining companies are now our friends, and they preach that philosophy. Mining companies may be our friends but you cannot have friends every day of the week can you? You want a bit of time by yourself.

This is the way Rio Tinto ambushed the blacks, and kept ambushing the blacks. The philosophy is about ambush, nothing else. It dictated to a certain extent the policies and politics of how to interact with Aboriginal communities, especially within Australia. The idea was one of, what is the CIA term, soft, non-confrontation, low-intensity conflict. But they sink you. A history of sinking people, and they are still seen as a friend of the blacks.

So you get these sorts of philosophies that do not allow you to build the fortresses and the bulwark to stop the ongoing encroachment on Aboriginal cultural lands, Aboriginal cultural theories, Aboriginal financial processes, and everything that looks foreign is attacked by both sides. So the Aboriginal people who do not understand land rights attack the Land Rights Act. Aboriginal people who understand land rights attack everything else.

So you have attack, attack, attack. There is no cohesive plan of what we are fighting for, and whom we are fighting with. This is because there have been too many personalities on both sides, big people who want to make statements about all sorts of things and then fail to deliver. I used to smile when people say *I am going to join the public service*

---

51. Tracker is referring to the protracted struggle and negotiations by Waanyi, Mingginda, and the Gkuthaar and Kikatj and other traditional landowners with the mining company Pasminco to develop the Gulf Communities Agreement relating to the Century mine in the Gulf of Carpentaria. The continuing dilemma in this region for Aboriginal people and their leadership is how to successfully negotiate their long-term future in this resource-rich area by securing traditional lands and culture, along with economic security. He is also referring to the Western Australian Government's announcements that they would shut down 150 Aboriginal communities.

to make a change. I know who wins that argument and it is the public service, it is a meat grinder. You are going to come out as a sausage. Go in as a human being and come out as a sausage. So you have this argument that is coming, and it has not stopped coming, and it is that the next boom in the Northern Territory will be gas and oil, and they are going to say, *Righto! What have you got to offer and how do we take it off you?*

Diminished through the Intervention. Totally sat on our arse. Totally sat on our arse because the Intervention was the worst thing that ever happened. Did we get any arguments from the Labor politicians about the Intervention in the Northern Territory? None.

There has to be a royal commission into what happened with the Intervention. There has to be. The first thing we have got to do is to get a good case together and to go back and test native title property rights. I think both land councils are petrified of that because it supersedes the Land Rights Act. Native title property rights goes past the Land Rights Act, to where you actually own the land, not the Commonwealth. Whereas under the Land Rights Act the Commonwealth owns the land under a land trust. So there is an argument there that people are really, really scared of pursuing. That is going to take a lot of thought by people who currently run the land councils on how best to do it. It is going to happen in Queensland and Western Australia long before it happens in the Northern Territory.

Tracker Tilmouth

Compensation is another part of the argument. When we first started talking about native title negotiations after the High Court decision in 1992, Colesy and I sat down as we have degrees in economics, and we asked a question: *Righto! It's like land rights. You can have land rights, but if you cannot enjoy your land rights you might as well not have it – right?* Because if you cannot do anything with it, you might as well go home and be the proud owner of an old shack, and you can go fishing whenever you want, but if you try and do any work on it, you have to get government permission [under the Land Rights Act]. So land rights is a figment of someone's imagination.

When you put native title up against land rights – there is an argument that compensation for the Stolen Generation can be quite easily hung upon, and it is this: the intellectual property of Aboriginal people is not only having native title but having native title property rights, and they have been removed from the enjoyment of those property rights.

You will get more chance of compensation out of the native title property-rights argument than you will out of any other process given by recognition of Aboriginal people in the Constitution, which is the end. These are the games that have been played by the people who have made it in society. They are the ones who are standing up for being recognised in the Constitution of Australia. The Constitution of Australia has got fuck all to do with us.

You have got the property rights given to you since time immemorial which is your Constitution. And then you have got this argument, *well forget your Constitution*, of coming and joining our [Australian] Constitution, when we are the ones that actually stole your land and stole your property. *But we want to recognise you now.* What for? You have got nothing to give me, nothing that I want. The only way we can do this is go back to court and do a native title property-rights argument.

But if you want native title compensation, once you have got native title property rights then automatically there has to be an agreement, a treaty, because every mining company in Australia, every pastoral lease in Australia, every house block in Australia is subject to compensation because they were stolen properties.

These arguments can be mounted through the courts. I have talked to Bret Walker SC. We had dinner one day in Sydney and he said, *I know exactly where you are coming from.* I said, *This is where we want to go, and the first cab off the rank is probably the easiest one, which is old growth forest in Tasmania.* The Tasmanian Government said they own it. I said, *Well hang on a minute, those trees are four hundred years old and you have only been here two hundred years, how the fuck do you own it?*

When you come back to the Stolen Generation, the only time you are going to get a look in for any conversation is when you knock over this native title property-rights issue, but we cannot knock it over until we find some very good cases. We had a win the other day with the

Thursday Islanders with their fishing rights. That the right for all the fish in the sea around Thursday Island under native title is a property right. So the door is already open. The question then is: *Righto, when is there to be an enjoyment of property rights, as well as the dispossession that went with it, and the compensation that goes with that?* There is a whole list of things you hang it off. The minute you get property rights from the High Court, do not worry about the government, the government has nothing to do with it, nothing to do with it, because it's based on British Law, based on the Magna Carta, based on the Privy Council, everything that came out of England. So always remember that when it comes to the question of a republic, you want to be a monarchy because British law keeps your hopes alive. When they become a republic, they will change the Constitution, and wipe you out tomorrow. Whereas the instructions from Queen Victoria was that you shall do an agreement with the natives – that was the instructions.

The Argument Is, We Are Excluded from the Argument

Peter Hansen

All we ask is that they [the government] listen. The first bloke who came out here stole all the land. Let's get down to the nitty-gritty here. We will not be talking about reconciliation here, we are talking about a treaty. There was a song that Yunupingu sang back in the 80s about a treaty. Bob Hawke said, *Yeah! We'll put it on the table.* What table, and what year? Bob Hawke's got one foot in the grave.

The other thing too I am against them saying, *We must educate Aboriginals.* Listen, we have got European intervention, uninvited guests, thieves, the Queen's thieves, it started with Captain Cook.

And you listen! They came around and said the only way to go ahead is education – that Aboriginal people have to get educated. *Listen!* I said to them, *We've had you for two hundred and fifteen years. We've had Aboriginals here for sixty thousand years.* I said, *Hey! They were not sick. They did not have any diabetes.* They did not have anything. I said, *You give me back those two hundred years.* These people are dying, and you cannot find enough dollars in the machines to keep them alive. And I said, *The other thing is, you want them to learn your culture? No. We want them to learn our culture completely before we come over to the white man's culture.*

Our culture lasted sixty thousand years, and this one is only two hundred years. So we do not want to learn their culture until they have learnt ours over there. You come over to this [white man's] culture when you are good and ready. Look at Africa, they have got the blacks from the bush that decided they wanted to go to town and be somebody. Okay! Good on them. The bush blacks who are there. Well! It should happen here too. Aboriginal people who want to go to town and get educated, you go for it, but leave the traditional Aboriginal there and let him do what he has been doing for sixty thousand years. He never had a fridge or anything. They speared a kangaroo and hung it up and that is their fridge. They eat it in a day or two and they are off again hunting. They did not get sick. They were all slim and trim. Not one overweight Aboriginal for sixty thousand years. In less than fifty years they went to people who can hardly walk, they are in wheelchairs, they are dying, throwing away lives. And guess what? The whites know all this but they are not going to change anything – they want them to die like this because they are in the road. Nothing is coming their way, nothing is happening.

Tracker Tilmouth

Anyone who is a student of history will understand that if you do not have an economic framework and a commercial framework, then your political framework does not work either.

And if you do not have those two things then you are on the brink of extinction, you are on the brink of being a historical part of Australian history, rather than operating within a modern concept. Unless you have got the economic processes to back your political agenda, then you become assimilated and you become a footnote at the end of the day as we all become Australian. The biggest gift that the white blokes can give you is that we all become Australians, that we are all equal although some people are more equal than others. That is why the political arguments about funding [budget cuts and the threat of closing down communities and organisations], and the current arguments about the amendments to the Racial Discrimination Act and so forth, are because we did not have the political and economic processes to protect our culture and our traditions.[52] We were not able to contribute to the economy in a meaningful way. In fact, we are seen by many non-Aboriginal people as part of the problem, rather than the solution.

---

52. In 2014, the Abbott government had planned to amend section 18C of the Racial Discrimination Act, which makes it unlawful to offend, insult, humiliate or intimidate on the grounds of race, colour or ethnicity. The changes would have made it unlawful to vilify or intimidate others on similar grounds, but with broad exemptions.

So this is becoming more and more acute and more evident as we look at the economics of Aboriginal activities today, [where] we fall well short of the maintenance, the cultural and political maintenance of our society, because our economic maintenance is not available to support it. We are now forced to go into work [programs], you are now forced to go into education, you are now forced to go into training and whilst that all bodes well long term, that does not reflect the current political processes that Aboriginal people enter into, and the cultural processes that flow from those political processes.

The argument is, we are excluded from the argument. We are excluded all the time because we have never been exposed to the full-blown commercial processes that the African countries were exposed to. They were exposed to commercial vandalism by Europe. We are no different. We are a conquered people and we have got no comeback in relation to how we deal with a sovereign power.

The sovereign power is the occupier of this country, the British. How do we deal with it? How do we deal with it is not from turning inwards, but to expand outwards to take care of our own business. The reason we have been afraid to do that is because we have been told it is white man's business. And so we have been put in the fairytale stories, Jack climbed up the candlestick, all that sort of stuff, Mary had a little lamb. We are stuck in there, *the blackfellas own this country*, in amongst the nursery rhymes. We have got a book on us, of nursery rhymes. We have not been allowed to participate. We are not allowed to participate, not only in what affects us, but what affects our nation.

We are getting this recognition idea now. *Oh! We aren't recognised.* Of course you are not recognised because you are in the what you call those books, you are in the fairytales. You do not recognise fairytales do you? Who are you? You are a fairytale. You used to own the country. They do not have to say it anymore, they know it. And you have not woken up. You are still there bowing and scraping. Patrick [Dodson] wants to go out and hug people and people want to hug Patrick.

I do not want to hug. I want to make sure that when the bank manager sees me down the street, and when he goes to his Rotary Club or to his council meeting, he is not going to make adverse findings against me because I contribute x to his bank. That is what I want.

I want to be able to say you are there because I gave you access. There is a quid pro quo. There is a price on the wellhead in the oil and gas. There is a price on your mining, on your royalties. We have got to have a property-right argument, where we go to statutory royalties. The Commonwealth and state can collect the royalties but they will pay us. We do not need to collect. And they will pay us accordingly and it will pay us to have houses, health and education, not from our royalties, from their royalties as part of the treaty. If you do not like that, do not go mining, we will give it to the Chinese. Let's get a real debate going. Forget Andrew Forrest, and being nice and everything else. He is looking after the blokes who are getting a cup of tea and a sandwich as a fucking act of parliament from it. You help some of the other people. That is the argument you have got. You have got to build that fortress, economic fortress, commercial fortress. If you do not like that get out of the road because you are going to be found wanting very quickly.

I go through a process and look at a problem and then I try and work back to the root cause of the problem. Then I set out to try and resolve that problem. I work it out and I say the first problem we have got is we have been excluded. Why have we been excluded? Because you do not like mining because you are black. Yes, I do not like mining. You do not like gas because you are black. Yes, I cannot see how that affects me, righto. Right! What else can we take off you? You do not like cattle because you like the land. And you like the land so we are going to do an IPA for you, an Indigenous Protected Area.[53] We are going to give those to the Department of Environment and Energy. They now own half your country. You cannot do anything without the department telling you what to do. So you cannot do anything. You are fucked. If you want to own land in Central Australia, make sure you are good mates with those people. Straight up. I will say that in a public meeting if they want me to.

---

53. The Indigenous Protected Areas initiative is a federal program that aims to supports Indigenous communities to manage nominated areas for conservation, and support the integration of Indigenous ecological and cultural knowledge into management practices. Aboriginal land tied up in this government-controlled initiative is dependent on annual federal funding to train and employ Indigenous rangers.

Because everything is locked up with IPAs. You cannot even go and scratch your arse without their approval, so do not tell me you have got land rights. It is a different land rights than what I went to the CLC to get. A different set of land rights, now it is all about hugging everybody and making beanies. So we have all lost the plot. Someone has followed a lunatic – made his own culture – from the Pitjantjatjara lands, followed him off with his fairies. I reckon the rest should go with them. Tangentyere Council, Congress, please leave. Go find somewhere else to go. Don't annoy us, we are building an economy.

Tracker Tilmouth

You want to know what we're reconciling about? It is a distraction, it is there on purpose, to distract you – this group over here from what those people over there are doing. It is the same as the push to have Aboriginal recognition in the Constitution. Where do they go to consult about having the recognition of Aboriginal people included in the Constitution? They go to to East Arnhem Land. Now they call them east-coast corn-feds for a purpose. You put a tie on them, and put a good bit of war paint on them, and they make out they can talk English. They all wear glasses and look down and say [they are] doctor this and doctor that. They have got the worst-run community in the world. Yirrkala has got the highest level of child abuse and everything else than any other community in the Northern Territory. They have got more drunks. Three million dollars a year for the last thirty years and they have got nothing to show for that other than a house. So when you want something done, what do you do? You go to Garma [Festival]. What is Garma? *The nigger's picnic.* And they are trying to get me there to make a statement and every time I am booked I have been sick on purpose – couldn't fly.

They wanted me to talk last time, in 2013. They wanted me to take on Jenny Macklin for them. I said, *Hang on a minute: do I look that fucking stupid? Do I turn up and be an idiot for these wankers?* I said, *No, I'm not going.* And then they turn up with Tony Abbott anyway.

Tracker Tilmouth

We have had football carnivals and Dreamtime at the G, and the Long Walk and everything else.[54] Now we have got this idea that we should be recognised in the Constitution. Now that is all well and good, but the question that I ask and everyone else asks is, *What happens after we have been recognised? Where now brown cow? Where do we go from there?*

And yes, *Can we go anywhere from there?* This is the other question. The situation is that there is no plan. There is a whole range of policies from this new federal government based purely on straight-out economics, but you cannot develop an economic model for Aboriginal people that is alien to the social structure that you are dealing with. The economic model has to be sustainable, but it has also to be culturally sustainable. If people do not know why they are doing something they are not going to do it. No one turns up and digs out weeds for the sake of digging out weeds unless there is an economic return to them. There is no debate about a sustainable economic model. That is what is stopping everybody at the moment. Instead, you have got a hundred-miles-an-hour car that says assimilation: it is called recognition.

You have got to put it into the context of where we are going and why we are doing it, and these are the economic benefits, and these are the cultural benefits, of why you are doing it. Now that does not exclude any industry. Any industry can be part of the process, whether it is mining, horticulture, agriculture, whether it is tourism, retail or carbon trading. At the moment we are spending a lot of money on truancy programs in schools. If people are so in tune with the education system, why are they not sending their kids to school? If they are so in tune with the social systems that are currently running on communities, why are they not turning up for work? They are not. No one is doing anything. You have got a whole range of white blokes racing around to make sure they do the work and then fill out the submissions for

---

54. Dreamtime at the G is an annual Australian Rules football match between Essendon and Richmond recognising the contribution of Aboriginal players to the sport. The Long Walk is a walk prior to the game pioneered in 2004 by former champion Aboriginal AFL footballer Michael Long.

the next year's funding, and to what benefit to the community? None. Just maintaining the status quo.

Now you can go hunting and gathering, you can do that for a while. The income from hunting and gathering has an esoteric value, because people put values on it from their own cultural perspective, and whitefellas do the same thing. If you are protecting a certain species of bird, this is a plus for some of the greener groups but their position is not going to be replaced by you. So you say to these people, *Righto! Why are we protecting this bird? Why are we not doing mining?* And this is where the quandary is within the group. We say, *Righto! We are doing mining because it gives us an economic benefit or financial benefit but is it sustainable?* No it is not. *Is it culturally sustainable?* No, it is totally against anything you culturally understand.

Now if you want to be imitation white blokes and drive around in uniforms and drive trucks and do everything else then off you go, but you have got to understand that what you are doing has nothing to do with Aboriginal culture as such. There is an employment process, yes. There is an economic benefit, yes. There is a short gain, financial gain, but what is the long-term plan, because mines do run out. Nothing is forever. When mines run out of resources, what happens to the environmental aspect of it when you are finished with them? What are you left with? These are the questions you have to factor in, and a lot of Aboriginal people, because of their poverty, are saying, *Let's click now, and think about that later.* Very few people are saying, *Hang on a minute, we have got sacred sites there, we need to protect them. We have got environmental concerns, we need to protect them.* We have got all these other issues about the cash society that we have got to deal with.

We have got a lot of money coming in and this money can be a plus or a minus, but when you are looking at the amount of drugs, grog and everything else, you wonder, *Why do I want to go mining and wipe myself and my community out?* This is the question, a lot of Aboriginal people are sitting down and saying it is not all benefit for us, especially in Western Australia. So you have this debate, and it has to be part of the delivery point with the recognition of Aboriginal people in the Constitution, which I do not think is a good thing because I think the Constitution has got nothing to do with you. It was written without you, and this idea of being recognised by a document, that was drawn up to exclude you, is a bit of a misnomer.

So you have to ask yourself what does the Constitution bring, what is recognition in the Constitution going to bring to the debate? Are we going to be nice to each other? Yes. Are we going to be kinder to each other? Yes. This will happen until there is a dispute over resources. When there is a dispute over resources or resources get scarce, what is the argument then? Who will have the upper hand? Native title property rights, or the government? If you have the High Court versus the government, then you will need to be extremely careful of the modelling, and the modelling too will be extremely difficult, because you really want the model that says we want understanding of Aboriginal ways and processes of production which we do not have, even though we say that we understand them.

If you ask any Aboriginal person, or if you go to any public forums, you will have Aboriginal people saying, *We are doing alright because we understand we are doing alright. We are accepted by the white people so we must be doing alright.* But the question is, if the deal is so good why are you in the situation you are in? Why are all the social indicators where they are? You have to be very careful about how you model the rate and cost of production for goods that have been consumed by the wider society.

Mining is one of those areas. You dig out the iron ore. Why do you want to dig up iron ore? Because you have to sell it to China. What is China doing with it? China is making steel and sending it back in terms of washing machines, cars and everything else, back to Australia. Even the white blokes have not worked it out yet. How the hell do you think the blacks are going to work it out? You wiped out the manufacturing base in Australia. You have wiped out everything, and instead of us selling iron ore we should have been selling steel. So we have these arguments that are difficult within white society, and now we are transposing them into a resource development argument in black society, and that has never been tackled.

We have always had this argument that we will educate people. Yes, you can educate people, and that is wonderful. Every Aboriginal kid should have an education or access to education. The question is how do you get them to school? How do you get them educated? Is education going to bring you better footballers, which is the aim of Clontarf [Foundation]? Will Clontarf use football to bring you better education? Every good footballer I know, the reason why they were good footballers is because they did not go to school, they played footy all day, honing their skills. I think with the exception of Adam Goodes who has thought a lot about all this, the rest of them are pretty dim about this debate.

So you ask the question, what does the model look like? The model is very hard to define and you cannot do that straight off the top because each area is different, although the principles are the same. It has got to be economically sustainable and that means commercial. It has got to be environmentally sustainable and it has got to be culturally sustainable because if you do not have the culture in the back of it, then you do not have a model. When we set up Centrefarm we did that type of modelling, and when we set up the Aboriginal Carbon Fund we used the same modelling. But it is a long history, and it cannot be done overnight, and you do not go and throw the baby out with the bathwater because you want to be recognised in the Constitution. The Constitution is going to be there forever and you do not have to rush that now.

I have thought very hard about the social structures and this is why I am leaning towards a socialist structure. This is why I lean towards the Israeli kibbutz model. It is something you can grab hold of because it deals with social structures as well as cultural norms. It allows you to look at something that other people have done out of necessity, as they had to survive. They had to survive both culturally and economically. They did it with less land, less water, more people. They had to feed each other and they had to make money as well. You look at that and it is the closest thing I can see to the model which I am talking about.

There are too many people out there doing all sorts of things. There is a whole raft of government agencies that have got their silos and their pill boxes and everything else, and are saying, we want to do this, we want to do that, but we do not want you doing it on our patch, because that is worth an income to us. It is our controlling influence.

You can lease out a block of land and have someone come in and commercially develop it and they will do that for a time but at some stage they are going to want to leave and divest themselves of it, and they are going to hand it to an Aboriginal organisation, but how does the Aboriginal organisation pick that project up? You only have to look at the pastoral industry when the government bought the Aboriginal cattle stations. Here is the model, boom. You hit the brick wall every time. Like dropping eggs. There was no sustainable model underneath it.

I try and avoid the urban centres because the urban centre is where you want to be sure that you do not fuck up the invites to the barbecues. You want to be socially acceptable. There is a lot of exercise placed in that area, to be socially acceptable, to be invited to barbecues with the in-crowd, whoever they may be. The arguments in Darwin are a lot more refined than Alice Springs. In Alice Springs you have a cultural clash from day one, and you have people with problems, social problems with alcohol and everything else. You see that every day of the week in the north, but in Darwin this is swept away, it is all hidden. You can go to Casuarina and not be molested over your pork soup, whereas try and do that in Alice and there is an argument. Darwin is a different place to Alice Springs, but Darwin also has its places where you can hide if you want to. It is a place where you can sit and decide which areas of the debate you want to be involved in.

There is nothing much else going on in Darwin. You have employment programs down in Inpex, where you have the Larrakia Nation, but what happens when they finish building Inpex? Darwin is a nice place to be but you do not want to get too serious about Darwin. It is not the place to get serious.

Every year you get political commentators asked to do speeches in parliament and everywhere else, and their stories always are: *We failed and we do not know why we failed in Aboriginal affairs. We fell over and we do not know why we fell over, but we fell over.* It is very costly.

Tracker Tilmouth

I have always had this ability to sit back and work out the situation I am in, and then know how to manoeuvre out of it, or manoeuvre to a better place. It is like the debate in the eastern states at the moment with Aboriginal people, how with the demise of Charlie Perkins in 2000 and the vacuum that left, no one has been able to fill it.

The debate is noise rather than substance, and what we are getting is the people who are trying to be leaders but who do so without authority. You have got to give them a bit of credit because the Dodson brothers, Patrick and Mick to a certain extent, Mick not so much, Patrick has his role, or perceived role of father of reconciliation. That is wonderful for the whites, nothing better than hugging a big bloke that has got a big white beard: *I have been blessed.* There is a lot of blessing going on.

But the debate has been missed. You have only got to look at *Utopia*, John Pilger's 2013 documentary [about Aboriginal Australia] to see how much it has been missed. You are getting people continuously wanting to be blessed, Warren Snowdon wanting to be blessed by the blacks for representing them for twenty-seven years without producing anything. That is a classic, absolute classic. That interview [in *Utopia*] summed up Warren Snowdon's political contributions in about five minutes, there was not much to talk about. You can have good intentions but unless you can deliver, forget it, do not even mention it.

You deliver, but it is extremely hard to quantify what exactly you delivered. Do you measure land rights as a delivery process? Do you quantify the question of access and everything else? Now the significance of the Land Rights Act is based on Part IV, which is the mining section. You take that out of the Land Rights Act and it is not worth reading because there is only a couple of pages left. So you understand where the Land Rights Act was actually going, what Gough Whitlam was thinking. It was access to mining, it brought mining companies to Aboriginal land, without our having a veto.

So you go through this process, and when you look at what has been delivered in land rights, the big question that still lies unanswered is not the acquisition of land rights, but the enjoyment of land rights. How do you enjoy being where you are? Do you enjoy living at Papunya? Do you enjoy living at Yuendumu? Do you enjoy living on a remote community? If so, how do you enjoy it? If you enjoy land rights why are you not back home? Why are you hanging around Alice Springs? Why are you in Tennant Creek? Why are you in Katherine? Why are you in Darwin? So the question is very clearly about the enjoyment of land rights. It is not just land rights, it is a question of sovereignty, it is a question of native title rights, property rights, these questions have not been dealt with. So land rights by itself is a bit over the top, but I have to deal with land rights because that is the field I have worked in.

Warren Snowdon has to live with what he delivered. He has to live with what he has not delivered. When Warren Snowdon leaves politics he will say, well what was that all about? Whereas you have got people like [Daryl] Melham, because he is Lebanese, Melham will live and breathe Aboriginal affairs forever. Melham, you can always have a discussion with Melham about Aboriginal affairs and rights. He is a very good man, Melham. Martin Ferguson is a deliverer. Ferguson will deliver, no matter how it is. If he says something, he will deliver. Laurie Brereton will deliver, because Laurie Brereton will stand by you.

One thing about the politicians that I know, the Labor ones, was that it used to be funny that I would be a mate of Laurie Brereton and he was extreme right, but I am his mate. People could not work out that connection and still can't. But Brereton has a very sharp mind. He knows how to play the political game better than anyone else in terms of factions. He is a very good man but we were on opposite sides of the fence.

Tracker Tilmouth

We will be talking about treaty at the end of the day under a renegotiated process. What we have got to work out is what if someone agrees. We are alright at the moment while everyone is dozing, and saying *fuck off. We can all be heroes.* The minute someone agrees with us we are fucked. We need to understand that we do not have a plan to go to that deals with the mining industry up-front, no more negotiated outcomes, it is all statutory royalties. You do not have to prove your native title, you get a property right and you get a statutory royalty, and fifty per cent of that statutory royalty goes into an investment fund held by the state native title representative body.

You can set up structures but at the end of the day you have to come back to what your economic situation is in relation to remote communities. What have you got? Forget about the welfare. Forget about inherent rights. Forget about unemployment and CDEP, and everything else that has been funding you. You have to come back to the argument about what you have that somebody else wants. The answer is, there is not much. I went through this argument with the Territory Government about resourcing infrastructure for horticulture, and the areas that are going to provide economic benefits should they put the infrastructure in. Now, there is not much outside of Ti Tree and Ali Curung, Willowra, Utopia, and there is not much north of Tennant Creek. There is a bit south of Tennant Creek. There is nothing in Tennant Creek. In the northern region, Elliott is alright, Mataranka and Larrimah are alright. There is nothing at Ngukurr. There's a little bit of potential at Port Keats [Wadeye]. There is really nothing, nothing whatsoever north of that other than the Douglas-Daly and this area is owned by the white blokes, not owned by the blacks. And there is nothing out at Ord River Stage 2 or 3 in Western Australia's Kimberley region. It is buggered. It is being closed. So when you have all these arguments about where the infrastructure should or should not go, the economics of it, then the Aboriginal community has to be really thinking outside the box.

Aboriginal people had better be aware of this – because of the lack of finances the infrastructure has to have a degree of rationality to it. You cannot just put in electricity grids for the sake of it anymore. You have got to have a commercial outlook. So communities that do not have large aquifers, or an industry, or a tourism process, will now probably not be looked after in such a way [as they have previously expected], and will probably go back to diesel and not be a part of the grid. Aboriginal communities will end up with two or three classes of resource development. You are going to have the ones that will be able to survive using horticulture and having investors. You are going to have some who will have mining and not much of it. You have got to remember there are not many mines in the Northern Territory as such.

So when you get this argument about how to fund the infrastructure and the benefit for us, it is a hard lesson that we are about to learn, that it is good to have property rights, but having property rights for the sake of property rights you can end up with an economic burden. It could be a negative, instead of a plus. And this is the essence of the Mount Allans of the world, the Yuendumus of the world, to a certain extent Mount Liebig and Kintore, maybe Papunya, the Haasts Bluffs of the world, being left behind because of the lack of water underneath. Whereas the Larambas, the Willowras, Alkara, Utopia, the Woodgreens, the Ali Curungs and Neutral Junction, these places north and north-west of Alice Springs [which are all Aboriginal communities of hundreds of people or more] have huge potential for economic development, and Mungara south of Tennant Creek and the Karlantijpa and Kalampurllpa north of Tennant Creek. These will have long-term economic outcomes.

And they will be very lucrative because they will have opportunities for jobs and training, employment and everything else. So you are going to end up with a population shift, with for instance Ti Tree becoming a service centre for the horticulture industry. All the fruit packing and all that sort of stuff will be at Ti Tree. So you will not have dislocation, but people chasing jobs within their language region and moving, in this case, from Utopia across to Ti Tree, or across to Six Mile. Or moving from Aileron across to Woodgreen. This kind of movement of people will take place.

Now the hardest thing to emphasise in relation to native title is property rights, because you want the enjoyment of property rights, and there isn't any enjoyment. There isn't any enjoyment other than a cultural enjoyment, which is like outstation development, you can have an outstation but it gets awfully boring watching the sun go down on a whole mob of old motor cars and doing nothing else. It is good for the old blokes, they love it all because they are back with the scrub, but the kids are gone. Kids are all headed to Alice or wherever, Tennant Creek, or Katherine. So the arguments that you must have will be all about what happens after you get property rights.

And this is why the Noel Pearson discussion is extremely interesting. I may not always agree with him but it is still very interesting and he has some good points. What happens to the people who have and the people who have not? This is the argument that the land councils had with mining royalties. Those with royalties received a certain amount of benefits and those without got fuck all. This is still the case today. So these are the long-term arguments that are going to befall the Aboriginal community and probably tear it apart quicker than it did with the American Indians, because their treaties in America are so different to each other. And not only that, one recognises minerals while the other one doesn't. You can do gambling in one, or you have a tax haven in another one, and can therefore run a casino, but in others you can't. And it stops and starts at the fence. This is the argument about some of them, similar to up in Alaska and in the northern parts of Canada, where their arguments were that some people had millions and millions of dollars, and the crew down the road didn't get anything.

This is where the planning has got to be – how do you underwrite the enjoyment of native title property rights when a lot of people are going to miss out? A lot of people are going to be saying, *Well! That was a good exercise. I've got property rights but that's all I got. Now what does that mean in real terms?* And the truth is, fuck all. It does not matter which title you put on it, you can put a land claim title on it, you can put a native title claim on it, you can do a property-right title on it, it does not change the nature of the land that you have [as your traditional country]. It may offer an economic opportunity for the non-Indigenous community, or it may not. You may be able to trade with an external process, the mining industry for instance, or the oil and gas industry. If you do not find oil or gas on your country it's, *Oh! Well! Thanks for the exercise.* That is unfortunately the lot of Aboriginal people in the near future. Some people are going to end up with a lot of money while other people are going to end up with nothing.

This happens right across the Land Rights Act process. You get the Warlpiri in the Tanami, where three out of the five Warlpiri groups get a lot of money [from mining royalties], and the other two Warlpiri groups get nothing. And they are all Warlpiri, but their country is different. The Bootu Creek [manganese mine] exercise is another example where a certain number of clans in the Warumungu tribe get a lot of money while the rest who are also Warumungu do not get anything.

People are trying to re-establish themselves as tribal groups, but you have this discourse happening that splits the community because of the finances. You have to really explain to people that they are going to have a situation where there isn't going to be any money. There will not be any money, and for every cent you make you are going to have to really, really try hard. It is property rights versus native title versus land rights process and you are going to find that like the Waanyi [in the Gulf of Carpentaria] there will be certain groups of Waanyi that are more Waanyi than Waanyi, and certain groups that will benefit. Cook the books. They have lawyers and anthropologists who understand where they are going and *bang*, all of a sudden you have this so-called group of Aboriginal people that were together until the mine turned up, and now they are split more ways than one.

This will happen, this will happen time and time again. This will happen with the gas stuff in the Gulf if it is not done properly. This is happening in Borroloola with the McArthur River mine. It is happening in Gove with the Gove Agreement. That is a classic example. The process rolls on. So having property rights is not going to be your answer, it is going to be part of the answer, it is going to be a tool. It can be used as leverage but there has to be a lot of thought put into what happens if the High Court says, *Yes, you've now got property rights*. What does it mean? That will be the biggest argument.

This is the reason why all of a sudden Michael Mansell has been trying to get pan-Aboriginality in a seventh state [of Australia]. Now I know that the Warlpiri do not like sharing their country. I know the Eastern Arrernte mob don't. I definitely understand that the Kaytetye and the Warumungu do not get on in the best of times. So it is going to be amazing. Anyway.

Tracker Tilmouth

I have read Michael Mansell's idea to create an Aboriginal seventh state. I think his analysis is quite good, but I do not agree with him on the seventh state.[55] I do agree on his assessment of the laws and everything else you are going to have, to have agreements or treaties. You have all of these small groups doing their own thing and it is just madness

---

55. Michael Mansell's book *Treaty and Statehood: Aboriginal Self-determination* (The Federation Press, Leichhardt, 2016) discusses whether democracy, treaty, self-determination or a seventh-state model holds the best solution to issues that remain between Aboriginal peoples and the nation of Australia. He concludes that the seventh state offers the most progressive suggestion. This can be easily implemented through the Australian Constitution, where Chapter VI provides for new states, to which existing states can surrender parts of their territory, without the need for a referendum. Mansell's book explains the model and how it could work, and he believes it will offer real hope for Aboriginal aspirations, preservation of communities, languages and culture.

at the moment, because of the way we put it [the Native Title Act] together, where it cancelled the argument about property rights. The legal position is pretty good [on property rights], but there are no legal mechanics for native title property rights. We want the mechanics of it, to run the court case of *where now brown cow*. What happens then? Do we have a treaty, do we have an idea of what we intend to do, or what we are wanting to do? We will have to deal with all of these sort of arguments.

Winning the court case on the property-right argument is not going to be hard. It is after you win, that you will have to sit down with all of the issues to deal with, which will lead to negotiation, and that can be hard. This is because you have got people who really do not know what they are talking about putting together their weird and wonderful ideas. You have got lawyers and everyone else trying to cut in on the process. It will be a nightmare to say the least.

Anyway, that is what you call a democracy. That is what you call self-determination. That is what you call self-enhancement. That is what you call self-destruction as well. I've seen it happen a few times. So the argument with Mansell at the table is going to be very interesting. Once we have got the rights, where do we go? What do we do? That is the billion-dollar question. I bet you he has not thought about how we will do it. He would have had the legal argument. It is the economic arguments that have to be fairly strong and robust.

It is very important for Mansell and people like that to say this is the framework for what we are talking about. Because you know the arguments about land ownership, it is going to be hard to put it forward on a question on property rights. The next part is how will that be transformed into some kind of documentation, call it a treaty, call it whatever you want. How many agreements do you include? Do you include every group as a block in the Northern Territory or do you include what each state government needs, and they will want someone to sign off. It will be like Waitangi in New Zealand, where some Maori agree with it, and some don't.

I have a little bit of an idea and it is not rocket science. It is about people really. There are those who do not have native title as such, as defined by law at the moment. They do not have continuous occupation and everything else. But their argument is a civil one, so you say, *Righto, you were removed and therefore you are restricted in practising your native title.* Therefore there should be compensation for you, so the Stolen Generation and people like that would have an argument for compensation. They may not get native title property rights but they get compensation, and then that moves the next crew along to those who can prove native title. And what sort of reform should the property rights take in relation to mining and pastoralism and land use in general? These are people who can prove native title under any circumstance. So it can be quite difficult, and then there are other categories as well. That will be the kind of arguments they will have to put forward and what categories people fit into, just like the Maori had to do with the Waitangi Treaty with those that could prove who they were and what they owned, and those who could not.

There will have to be some really tough decisions. If you cannot tell us your country, and you cannot say, *See that over there, that's the Dreaming track,* or this is that, or that, or that. You know, walking along you see this scrub and start looking for spear points, axes or whatever is on the ground, and you say those areas are sacred sites because someone camped there, that is not right. People camped everywhere. You know when you are walking through the scrub, and there is a waterhole or something and you camp there or around there, and then you moved on, that is not a sacred site, it is just a camping area. It all adds to arguments you get over in New South Wales, a bit of Queensland and South Australia, even the Western Australian side too. You have got to have this treaty argument pretty well thrashed out internally by the blacks, not putting it on now, but saying to people, *Look, you can't practise your native title because, through no fault of yours, you were removed, you never went back, your parents never took you back and you lost your language, therefore you lost your songs, you lost your Dreaming, you lost everything.* And it is going to be extremely hard to get all that back because not all of it is documented. And then you cannot practise your native title right. It was not your fault but you were removed and there is a compensatory argument that you can follow up.

They have got no choice even if the High Court rules one way or another on property rights. If you have got property rights, there are criteria on what property rights mean. They [Australian governments] are not going to give you blanket property rights, they will set criteria for it. This is the argument, and that is why Mansell is thinking, where do we go?

The argument on property rights is going to be won easily. But the definition of criteria that follows is the difficult thing to deal with. It will be won easily because it is already stated in the Wik and Mabo High Court decisions. It is already there in the statutory docs. It is a matter of the High Court reading it out. The hardest thing we have got is working out who fits into what categories.

The lawyers we have are not flash, let's be honest, and that is why they say we have not got an argument. We have lawyers that can see a lot of money with native title and the negotiations that flow from it. This property-rights argument takes out the negotiations. You do not have a negotiation anymore, you have just got a property right. That means when anyone mines in your country you get a statutory royalty. And you get the sacred sites protected. You do not have a veto, you have a veto on sacred sites and areas like that, and areas of significance, but you do not have a veto other than that. You end up with the situation where you get a property right which is a bit like the Land Rights Act, where you do not have a veto, but you may have an argument about access and equity, and access gives you the ability to earn royalties.

There is an agreed royalty, an agreement royalty and then there is a statutory royalty. So that is how you do it and how it will probably be done. You do not have any negotiations, or not extensive ones. You are going to get rid of hundreds of native title lawyers that are sitting there and working off the Aboriginal community at the moment. Your statutory royalty would not be a negotiated royalty. Everyone gets the same royalty. It is the same whether it is in Queensland, Northern Territory, South Australia, Victoria or Western Australia or Tassie. What is at stake here is that the Crown owns the minerals. You can take the mineral licence if you want, but you have got to have a big army to do it. That is what my discussion with Mansell would be about. Not about winning the native title argument on property rights, but what you do afterwards.

The Only Protection You Can Afford

Tracker Tilmouth

A hundred and fifty million dollars would give me a bitumen road, in and around Utopia, and an electricity line. And I can employ nine hundred people forever. Or we can keep spending your money at Inpex where you spend three hundred million dollars on that oil and gas thing in Darwin, and employ two hundred and fifty people for twenty years.[56]

That is an example. I can do all your horticulture forever with one hundred and fifty million dollars. And I need infrastructure. This is nine hundred people who would not be on Centrelink. They will be earning a wage. But you have got to close down the Centrelink, you have got to close down that area from issuing Centrelink payments. We can employ, if we did all our horticultural projects on Ali Curung and back to Ti Tree, nine hundred people.

You would do an all-weather road from Ngukurr on the Roper Highway, and a bridge over the Roper River, and then an all-weather road into Gove. The township of Nhulunbuy is the main commercial and service centre of the Peninsula and is eight hundred kilometres from Darwin, and tourists can come in and out of Gove during the wet season if you have an all-access road. In the dry season you can drive back through Bulman and those places, but you would not do that in the wet because there are too many rivers. There is the Liverpool River, there is the Mainoru River, there is everything over there. Cross once at the Roper, and off you go. All-weather road.

---

56. The Inpex project Bayu-Undan is an offshore gas and condensate field in the Joint Petroleum Development Area of the Timor Sea. Gas will travel via a 502 km pipeline from the Bayu-Undan Field to the Darwin LNG plant in the Northern Territory to be converted to LNG and shipped to market.

Tracker Tilmouth

I wanted to say a few things – not about the obtaining of land rights, but in relation to the enjoyment of land rights, and once you establish that enjoyment, the protection of land rights. In the state of Aboriginal society today, the argument is that we can have land rights but the enjoyment of land rights is something else. We rely totally on government subsidies, government funding, whether it's ranger programs, environmental protection, Indigenous Protected Areas, whatever, whatever, whatever, and we rely totally on the goodwill of the Department of Environment rather than arguing that protection of the bush, and protection of areas of cultural significance, is an economic good, because it maintains the cultural fabric of Aboriginal societies. We have decided that that is too hard so we have gone for the easy thing, and we have gone for a doctrine which is, *we will give you any amount of money you like out of the Department of Environment so long as you sign up to Indigenous Protected Areas, and you sign up to a ranger program.* There is no guarantee of funding on the ranger program, and the legislative mechanisms on Indigenous Protected Areas is also subject to the government of the day.

By going back to the argument that there is an economic good in the protection of cultural areas and Aboriginal societies, we will not have the flow of people into urban areas for employment, for entertainment, for services and for everything else. We have to go and source services from a central point rather than, and this goes back to the model that Toly Sawenko, myself and a few others did in relation to the Utopia medical services, where you stay in your place and we come and service you. People are a lot more healthy in and around Utopia and the eastern part of Alice Springs than they are anywhere else because you stay on your outstations and the medical staff go around and see you.[57]

---

57. Tracker is speaking about the Urapuntja Medical Service that services the homelands in the Utopia region of the Northern Territory. Studies have shown that Utopia residents had significantly lower mortality largely due to lower rates of alcohol and related injury, and also significantly lower hospitalisation rates, were less likely to have diabetes, and had a lower average body mass index as reported in 2008 by the Australian Department of Health: R. McDermott, K. O'Dea et al., 'Beneficial Impact of the Homelands Movement on Health Outcomes in Central Australian Aborigines', *Australia and New Zealand Journal of Public Health* 22, 1998, pp. 543–658.

And then you have this argument with the greens, the environmentalists and everybody else saying, *Well! You actually belong to us because we bring our political weight to your cause, so let's forgo the notion of economic development as you see it, and we will make you subservient to our economic philosophies and our politics, and you become part of our movement.* This has been the hardest thing that Aboriginal people have had to shake off, a good example is the arguments with environmentalists in relation to Jabiluka.

And this is the situation when you have a look at Nhulunbuy. There is not a program in Nhulunbuy that can stand up and say, *I'm economically sustainable*, [because these are] totally reliant on the royalties [from mining]. It all looks good but it is all royalty-based and subsidised.

That was one of the reasons that we set up Centrefarm. It was to pick the areas of horticultural sustainability, starting with something very simple. What is horticultural sustainability? How does it manifest itself in relation to Central Australia? When you look at Ali Curung, Ti Tree, Willowra, Utopia, the Finke [Aputula] and those areas, there are large aquifers underneath.[58] The Yuendumu aquifer is no good because it is full of uranium so you have to disregard this as supporting an economic program, it has a different argument altogether. So how do we make those places work in terms of economic development? We have to move away from the green agenda because the last thing they want is for us to be out there using what they see as a natural resource, or a finite natural resource. We say it has been recharged time and time again, with monitoring bores on all the aquifers we use that to say, *Let's produce a saleable commodity to a market.* Once you have done that and you are partly locked in, it is very difficult for governments to come in and take over your assets, or take over your ability to command a process that sustains you.

That is where the arguments with the Northern Land Council sit. I have explained to the Northern Land Council on more than one occasion that the biggest income contributor to the Territory gross domestic product is not the beef industry or the live export industry, the biggest contributor is the mango farmers and the vegetable blokes

---

58. The Great Artesian Basin, for example, is the largest and deepest artesian basin in the world.

out of Katherine and Darwin. They have produced more money for the Northern Territory government than anybody else, and this is shock horror, because we think live-export trade to Indonesia is way up above everything else.

It is catch-up time, or try and catch up time, in places like Mataranka and Larramah where they have good soils and good waters and everything else. They are now starting to be targeted by the Northern Land Council but very slowly, if they are capable of doing it at all. This is not a policy that flows to people easily because there has never been a horticultural land-use debate held by the Northern Land Council with any group anytime, anywhere, any place. We have had the Yirrkala banana plantation, all forty trees, and they provide bananas for the school which is quite good, but there is nothing out in Yugul Mungi, at Ngukurr, and there is bugger all at Port Keats even though there has been a garden there since the Catholic Church has been there. And there is a substantial vegie garden at Daly River, but that is about it. There is nothing, if you go to Peppimenarti, you go to Palumpa, or if you go anywhere else, there is absolutely zero.

So there is no debate by the Northern Land Council or by the land councils on how you protect land from an economic point of view. And the green lobby within the land councils made sure that the debate has been diverted to support their position. So mining is the great target at the moment. We do not have to talk about non-mining issues, we have got our hands full talking about mining issues and royalties. The community is totally distracted from the real issues and has been so for a long time. And when you get this debate about sustainable land rights, you have to remember that, in order to achieve land rights, you should be able to go back and be on your country and enjoy your life, but that is never the case.

You go out there and you have to fight for money for an outstation, you have to fight for money for housing, you have got to fight for money for a road to get there and then once you get there you have to say, *Well! What the fuck do I do next?* The sunsets are beautiful, but you watch one or two of them and if you are not an axe-murderer in three months there is something wrong with you. So this debate has been put it in the too-hard basket by both politicians and by Aboriginal leaders, but you notice they welcomed the debate about truancy, which is an absolute digression.

When you send someone to school, you have to say what do you want to be? *I want to be a CDEP worker. I want to be like my father, I want to wear a good uniform and carry a green garbage bag and paint rocks.* That is it. That is the end of the debate. So children say, *Well! I really don't need to go to school for that.* The parents say, *Well! You don't really need to go to school to be taught how to pick up garbage.* You only need one lesson outside, bend over, grasp rubbish with your hand, put it into a bin. It is very simple. It is not going to take too many lessons to do that. So the debate about truancy and education is a fallacy. It is wonderful to see Aboriginal kids go to school down south, but you know full well that those kids at the end of the day may want to return to their community, and what do they return to? They return to dispossession, alcohol, unemployment, no services, no nothing, and then they head back to the city, and there is a drain from the Aboriginal community of skilled workers. Instead of saying, let's build the economy in the bush and let's train people for that economy.

And it is all coming to a head with the closure of Nhulunbuy [bauxite mine]. It is going to come to a head with the closure of Ranger. It has already come to a head in relation to the Jawoyn situation.[59] It has definitely arrived in relation to Lhere Artepe [Central Arrernte native title representative body], and the Warlpiri royalty process where while they have a lot of money in the bank, their situation as a community has dissipated. It has had more impact on the Warlpiri leaving their land than anything else. They are claiming that Yuendumu is their country, and no it is not, it is Anmatyerre. It's Ngalakurlange. It is not Yuendumu. So they get this argument going and when you look at the financial power of GMAAAC [Granites Mine Affected Areas Aboriginal Corporation] for instance, they have invested in all sorts of areas and, all off Warlpiri land. There has been nothing invested on Warlpiri land. There has been no research done on Warlpiri land, on what an economic program might be. They have had mining, they have had a whole range

---

59. Allegations of misappropriation of funds within the Jawoyn Association Aboriginal Corporation in Katherine were aired by the ABC's *Four Corners* program in October 2013.

of programs where they tried to have employment for mining, but that have failed dismally. And so the end goal for the Warlpiri nation will probably be the rural ghettos of Lajamanu and Yuendumu, which is all off Warlpiri land, adjacent to but off Warlpiri land.

Alexis Wright: *What is the Northern Territory Government doing to develop Aboriginal economic programs? What about the commentators in the media, people like the* Australian's *Nicholas Rothwell, who writes about the Northern Territory, and about Noel Pearson, what he's doing in Cape York – has it had an impact on the Northern Territory?*

They are just commentators. They are commentators for as long as they espouse policies that the government sees as appropriate. This is what I mean by the extreme conservative elements in this society, and that is both Labor and Liberal, who suggest that Aboriginal people should be assimilated at all costs. Jenny Macklin had no idea what she was doing, and she still does not have any idea of what she had done. She was aided and abetted by [Mike] Dillon and [Neil] Westbury and people like that who were really failed departmental officers, and [Bob] Beadman who every year makes a speech on why it [government policy] did not work, not why it should have worked. He is a good bloke, Bob, but he has a different opinion to me. I think he says the government policy was a failure, when you read between the lines, he is saying he was a purveyor of government policy and some of that policy emanated from within his own department but it all failed at the end of the day.

We will always get blamed for it. It is: *We have come to save you and you don't want to be saved, and it's your fault.* It is like bushfire victims. *We are going to evacuate this area from bushfires but if you do not come it is your fault, you die.* That sort of process. That is what happened with Aboriginal people and still happens today. They say: *We dictate the policy, you won't have any input into the policy, but we'll dictate the policy and this is what we think you should be doing. If you don't do it then it's your fault, it's not our fault. We've been there trying to help you.* If you read any commentary this is what it is saying, think about what it is saying, not what it said.

Noel Pearson has decided that he is going to dictate an education rescue plan for remote communities but the trouble is they do not want to be rescued. So we have this argument that is floating between the Aboriginal elite and the academic elite as they call themselves. Intellectuals. And it started off with the Dodson brothers. All of a sudden there was a bloke up there who can grow whiskers longer than anyone else and wear bigger hats than most people. And the philosophies that came from those people was this idea of reconciliation, this idea of being friendly to whites, allowing for people who had a hangup on the policies of the past and felt guilt. Dodson was a mobile wailing wall if you like. A place you could go and forgo all your sins by talking to him. He was a priest and still is a priest, and that is what is happening now with Noel Pearson. If your education system failed he can help you revive it, so long as you adopted his policy and paid him a few bob. And this is how Abbott and everybody else is about dollars, so here, *We have got a policy on assimilation run by the blacks, for the blacks, to assimilate the blacks. We do not have to do anything. All we have to do is throw money at them.*

It is like *Borat*, the movie *Borat*, the running of the Jews, they threw money under the door to keep the Jews away. So you have got this situation being played out with Pearson and everybody else. When you think of how you move the Aboriginal community or your own group as an Aboriginal community into not only living on their own land, but protecting their own land, economic programs are the only protection you can afford. The governments do not recognise anything that will not have a contribution to the economy. This is why you allow mining, because you are contributing to the economy and therefore you are protected. Your ability to say no has been vetoed under the Land Rights Act, and yet there are no veto provisions under the Land Rights Act, there is the informed consent provision so that one or two people who object strongly to it can be outvoted, and that is the way the Land Rights Act is written. So the Northern Territory Land Rights Act is a problem for long-term Aboriginal economic sustainability.

It does not facilitate, in fact it goes to the very opposite of where you want to be, but it gives you a starting point, which is an access question. That is all you get out of it. You have the right to refuse access. And it all depends on the lawyer you have on the day. So you look at that and you say, *How do I move my community, my Aboriginal community, to a position of economic sustainability? How do I move them to a process that allows and develops an education process, and I do not just mean reading and writing, I mean education in terms of life skills and a whole heap of other stuff that you need to survive?*

That is why my brother Willie and I talk quietly to the Israelis about a kibbutz at Pine Hill, on the living area, so we can bring our mob together and we can educate each other on what you need to know to survive, not only your work, work ethics and everything, but how you are contributing to an economy to protect yourself. It is building a fortress and how you do this. *Righto, the closest thing,* I told my mob, *the closest thing I can see to where we need to be is probably a kibbutz-type operation where you have got the whole family group doing certain things and looking after each other, and kids are being looked after and going to school if they need to go to school, people are working, you might not be earning so much money but at least you have got a feed every day. You have got a role.* You develop people's roles and actions that contribute to the community.

This is the discussion we are having behind the scenes in relation to a Pine Hill development. And this is where my problem is with Centrefarm, it is that Centrefarm came over the top and said, *Oh! No! We need a commercial operation.* No, you do not, we do not need a commercial operation. We do not want any more commercial operations that exclude us from participating. You get this when you are trying to develop a model and there is no model because you have dispossession, massive dispossession, dislocation all throughout Central Australia and everywhere else, and how do you model that? How do you bring those pieces together and what does it look like because you are missing a fair chunk of the jigsaw puzzle, and the jigsaw puzzle's base is land rights, not land rights on paper, land rights in the mind: *This is your land, you have not surrendered it.*

That is actually a leap of faith. You have to find a way for people to take it themselves. Yes. You have got to keep saying this to yourself, and the old blokes still have that, when you sit down with Lindsay Bird, Kenny Tilmouth and everybody else, they say, *We want our homelands.*[60]

---

60. Lindsay Bird and Kenny Tilmouth are the traditional Ilkewartn and Ywel Anmatyerre landowners of Pine Hill Station, about 150 km north of Alice Springs, as under the Federal Court native title determination in 2009.

They say *homelands*. They were very clear what they understand as homelands. *We want to develop our homelands, we want to be able to say we own this country.* So we have that as an agenda to run in relation to Pine Hill. This has been the discussion to date.

The further north you go, the impact on the Aboriginal community of land rights in Northern Australia has been massive in comparison to Central Australia. The dislocation, the debate, the division in the north is extreme. We thought we had problems bringing groups together in Central Australia. We have nothing with our problems in comparison to the north, and the Territory Government siezes [on this], and it stands out, when you have got five groups in East Arnhem suing each other. You have the Laynhapuy Homelands, you have Gondarra, you have Yirrkala, you have Rirratjingu, you have Gumatj, and they are all going to court with their lawyers and they have been suing each other for all sorts of things.[61]

The royalty agreement out of Rio [Tinto], the land ownership about Gove, you name it, and on it goes, the misappropriation of funds from Gumatj and a whole range of stuff. And then you get down to Groote Eylandt, it is a bit closer, but there are groups within that that are at each other. You go down to Borroloola, you might as well go to Bosnia. Go to Kakadu. Go to Gascoyne, or go to the Jawoyn [in Katherine]. So it is in this playpen of misrepresentation, dislocation and dispossession, where you have got the Northern Territory government at its best, absolutely slicing and dicing, and they want that type of discourse that is [happening] in Central Australia, à la Alison Anderson and Bess Price as agents of this discourse, because the Territory government needs disruption. It does not need cohesion,

---

61. In January 2015, the Federal Court ruled that the Northern Land Council has the right to determine what percentage of mining royalties it pays to Indigenous clans. The Rirratjingu Aboriginal Corporation challenged the Northern Land Council's distribution of hundreds of millions of dollars in mining royalties from Rio Tinto's Gove bauxite mine and alumina refinery and, according to news reports in 2014, have wanted to break away from the Northern Land Council and form their own land council. The Rirratjingu believed that they should have received half the mining royalties available instead of the majority, approximately 73 per cent, being given to the Gumatj clan, which is Galarrwuy Yunupingu's group in Arnhem Land. See Chapter 2, 'Signing on the Line', in Paul Toohey and Daniel Hartley-Allen, 'When Rights Go Wrong', *News.com.au*, 2014. http://media.news.com.au/nnd/captivate/north-east-arnhem-land/

it needs to disrupt. This is Labor as well as Liberal. And so when you go north, which I have been doing with the northern mob, it is crazy, it is madness. You have on the edge of the Central Land Council region the proposed Muckaty [nuclear] waste dump owned by one group. *Hang on a minute, are you not all Waramungu?* You have got the Bootu Creek mine owned by another group. *Aren't you all Waramungu?*

These are the policies of the Northern Land Council and the Land Rights Act as they interpret it. That is why with the Land Rights Act and the movement, the government does not really need to attack us, because we attack ourselves through the process they have devised for us. The only way through it is not to attack the Land Rights Act publicly, because that is obvious, they are waiting for you to destroy it yourselves. They have the place mined before you walk there. The obvious way to attack the Land Rights Act is the native title process through the High Court, through testing the ability to exercise your property rights.

That is why the Dodsons are wrong about advocating for recognition in the Constitution.[62] It is not our Constitution, it is their Constitution. If you want to be invited to a shit sandwich, off you go. It is not ours, it has nothing to do with us. So we have the stupidity of recognition. What do you recognise? You recognise we own it? If you want to recognise we own it all, give us a treaty. Give us our rights. Give us our property rights. Return the stolen land. Do those sorts of things. Do not talk to us about recognising us because you can do that on a piece of paper, it is not going to mean anything. So you have a dangerous argument coming.

This is why we need strong friends. We really do, and having someone like the CFMEU. It is political power, but it is also financial power, and that is what this government is out to tackle. It is not attacking the CFMEU, it is attacking the hundred and fifty million dollars a week that is being banked by the CFMEU from superannuation with ME Bank and everybody else. They want to get their hands on that

---

62. Patrick Dodson, widely regarded as the father of reconciliation, has been involved in arguing for the recognition of Aboriginal and Torres Strait Islander people in the Australian Constitution.

money. So you get rid of the unions, you get rid of this, you get rid of that, and that is the agenda.

When I came back to Alice Springs, it was me and Rossy [on the Central Land Council], and then Rossy stayed [in South Australia studying] about two years, three years, and then he went off to be a commissioner for ATSIC. So I ran the circus, it was literally the circus, for that long. All the time when it did not conflict with me at night – which it did, it was a total conflict of theories, processes and politics within me – I thought, hang on a minute, didn't Lois Bartram read to you at night, just you and your brother, *Cry, the Beloved Country*, didn't she teach you politics? Did she not say this is the problem you people have got? We were only kids and she sat us down at night-time, everybody else is in bed, and she was the only one with the electric fan and the torch, and she was reading us, *Cry, the Beloved Country*, South Africa, Mandela, all that stuff.

But when you sit on the Land Council and you have this conflict, it is an absolute conflict. So what do you do? Do you protect the Land Rights Act, and thereby the Land Council? Do you take on board what the traditional landowners say? Do you try and meet it in the middle or do you try and bend it? The answer is nine times out of ten you try and bend it, and nine times out of ten it breaks. And you are right back where you started, sitting on your arse, and saying, *Well! What the fuck did I do that for?*

There were people like Wenten Rubuntja, Bruce Breaden, Mick Wagu, on and on the list goes on, the greatest sages of all time. I had the pleasure of sitting at their feet listening to them, even though nine times out of ten they talked about how it is very important for people to stay together, extremely important. The women's business thing [an annual woman's ceremony] came out of their discussions. Wenten Rubuntja suggested that. I was the first bloke of the Central Land Council as director to implement that, to fund all the Toyotas, all the vehicles, all the trucks to pick the women up and say to them, *You go have your ceremonies,* because Wenten said these women are mad because they are not doing their ceremonies, we have to get them to do their ceremonies. He told me off about it. He said that is why they are turning up at the Land Council, they are talking about land but their land is not the issue, they are mad when they talk about land. He said you have to get them to get their ceremonies going so they know where they are. He was being straightforward – the Chief, and that was where that came from. So Coxy [Barbara Cox, former CLC regional co-ordinator] and everybody else, they picked up on it and ran with it, but the original decider was Wenten telling me off because I said to him, *Why don't we set up a women's council?* He said, *No, don't do that, stay within Aboriginal law. We talk about land, and the women talk about ceremonies that they own. Let them do that separately as it always has been. They do it separately. But we have got to look after them.* So the Chief did that and I remember Pat Turner turning up from the Department [of Aboriginal Affairs] to talk to the Land Council about setting up a woman's council within the Land Council. She was held up by senior Central Land Council members from across Central Australia, Dick Leichleitner, Mick Wagu and Breaden and everybody else, who said they were mad, and they should not be talking about land. That night the Chief said to me that you have got to get them to do the ceremonies. He said that is what was missing. *They are too much in the mission...Too many kids to look after and not taking time out to do the ceremonies.* So there you go. That was Mount Wedge where we had that Land Council meeting.

The Pitjantjatjara Land Council were just forming their women's council but they went to the extreme, they replaced the men. That is where the confusion is now to where the men are in relation to Ayers Rock and Docker River, Pipalyatjara, Amata, Ernabella, Fregon, Mimili, Officer Creek. And then the Pitjantjatjara society collapsed, or they went from Yankunytjatjara to Pitjantjatjara, or AP [Anangu Pitjantjatjara]. From Yankunytjatjara first, that is all Yankunytjatjara country. Then you had Preteme down there as well – Southern Arrernte, or what we commonly call Luritja, and then that society collapsed because when the Women's Council was established they brought all their families from Port Augusta into the Pit lands. So the Port Augusta people and everybody else became Pitjantjatjara or Yankunytjatjara.[63]

---

63. According to Johnny Liddle, Preteme is an old language that is not spoken fluently by many people anymore but that his mother, Bessie Liddle, is a speaker and advocate of the language. It is a language of the Western dry river region (including the Finke and Palmer rivers) in

Everything crashed. You call a meeting in the Pit lands now and half of Port Augusta is looking at you. So there is no structure in the APY lands anymore. There is no cultural structure. And Vinnie [Vincent Forrester] is just about the senior traditional landowner of Ayers Rock and Bobby Randall. Juta! There you go. So this is what my mad brain thinks of.

Tracker Tilmouth

You have this situation where Abbott is Pontius Pilate and he gets some Aboriginal people who do the crucifixion. I do not expect anything different, but I would like to think that throughout the debate, there is a discussion about the economic sustainability of remote communities. This has been missing from the debate. Always missing. You are automatically welfare-oriented. If an Aboriginal person walks in the door – they are welfare. They are not economic, they are not commercial, they do not fit into any of those categories. They are unemployed, unemployable, untrained and on welfare, and that is what you are when you walk in the door.

I have got a lot more experience in this area of economic sustainability compared to Marcia or Noel. Mundine talks about business a lot. I would like to see what he has actually done because I would like to put my record against his, Marcia's and Noel's, and let's see who has done what for whom, and for how much. Let us see where the results lie. Forget the debate with the white people. Let's have an Aboriginal debate on the economic sustainability of remote communities and why it should or should not be possible.

My agenda is a lot different to theirs. Mine is based on the assumption that there is an impost. For a start, you cannot have economic development without infrastructure. Infrastructure means electricity, water and good roads. It does not necessarily mean housing. It means jobs for that infrastructure, to maintain it, to build it and do all that is required. So that is the argument that I would pursue.

Central Australia. The language is linked to Luritja, Yankunytjatjara, and Western Arrernte. Many of the language speakers of these languages including Preteme will mix the languages, and several different language words will be found even in one sentence.

The Northern Territory government, under the Northern Territory Self-Government Act, has maintained the status quo. The land rights legislation again is Commonwealth legislation, and again, it is a furphy. Both are furphies. The Northern Territory Self-Government Act means yes, you were given self-government on certain conditions.[64] With Aboriginal land rights you were given land rights under certain conditions. You do not have the rights. This is why we call it – Aboriginal freehold in brackets. You do not have the rights to freehold, you cannot buy, sell or lease without permission from the minister. It is the same thing with the Northern Territory Government where you cannot make laws and legislation without the Minister for Territories signing off on it – if it is deemed that there is not a clash with Commonwealth laws.

The Northern Territory Self-Government Act failed Aboriginal people by its very nature in prison rates, gaols, health standards, housing, employment. How many examples do you want? There have been reports written every year on the ongoing despair of Aboriginal people. There has never been an enquiry into the amount of money that has been spent on Aboriginal people in the Northern Territory and what it has to show for your investment. That was what used to annoy me with Jenny Macklin. All that she said was, *We spent a hundred and fifty million.* Yeah! But what is the result? What have you got to show for it? Do not tell us what you spent, what have you got? If she talks to women in communities who say that she is doing what they want, show me the women. Tell me how you conversed with them because, *Can you speak their language?* The answer is no. *No, I had a white person telling me what they said.* And it is shock horror – it was a white person from Alice Springs! Yes. Even more so, shock horror. Amazing.

Tracker Tilmouth

I will not go to the Garma Festival [in 2014]. I will go and see Galarrwuy Yunupingu some other time. You know after thirty years of

---

64. Self-government was conferred by the Commonwealth on the Northern Territory in the *Northern Territory (Self-Government) Act 1978*.

royalties and whatever, he was struggling to make ends meet there for a while, and then he got the big deal that they signed with Rio Tinto, the big fifteen million a year for the next twenty years or whatever it was. He has basically split with the Rirratjingu who are arguing about their share of the royalties. This is the saddest part about the whole program, where they have never developed anything that stands alone economically. It has always been underwritten by royalties, and that is a complete waste of money. When they go to Garma, they put those up as programs as though they have generated the money themselves, but they were royalty monies, all subsidised, so there is not real economic development out there.

They have gone into mining a bit, but bauxite mining is impossible at this stage, prices are coming back but it is not great. Otherwise they would have Western Cape York if it was any good.[65] Galarrwuy has had advisors over many years, and I do not know if he has got good advice, but there is really nothing you can say for it, the mentality is still the same. The saddest thing is seeing the Rirratjingu and Gumatj arguing over royalties rather than doing like we did, put ours in a bank, and only developing what we need to develop.

They had more advice than we ever had. The Central Land Council started with bugger all, with Centrecorp and everything else, but if we had half the money that these blokes had we would have owned half of the Northern Territory by now. But anyway, that is life. It is a hard one to reconcile, the amount of social problems that you have at Yirrkala or East Arnhem. It is not the flashest place around in terms of social indicators. There are no resources, and you cannot do anything out there. They are trying to harvest buffalo now. Buffalo, for the live export trade.

Tracker Tilmouth

The government is trying to impose a process on Aboriginal communities, and if governments talk loud and long enough about

---

65. Tracker was referring to the Metallica Minerals bauxite mine, near their Urguhart Point heavy mineral sands project in Western Cape York near Weipa in Queensland.

it, the media picks it up and all of a sudden it becomes a media item as well. So people like Tony Jones, who have no experience whatsoever on Aboriginal affairs, only what he has been told, gets this idea that until you have a house with a white picket fence and roses and lawns and everything else, you have not made it in Australia.[66] You know Australia has this idea of house ownership but in the current situation, especially in the Northern Territory and elsewhere, a lot of people will never afford their own house. What is the price of a house out at Port Keats for instance? You are looking at a three-bedroom house, with the lands free, and including the sewage and water and everything else hooked up, it will cost you seven hundred and fifty grand. And this is at Woodapulli outstation in the Port Keats area of the Victoria Daly Shire of the Northern Territory. It is Melbourne inner-city prices.

The real cost of a house to Aboriginal communities without any subsidy is probably about nine hundred thousand dollars. So you are out of the market before you start, and this stupid idea of people owning their own house, and going from a CDEP wage to a big bill of between four hundred thousand to five hundred thousand dollars – talk about intergenerational debt. This is multigenerational debt, never to be owned by the Aboriginal community. Those houses then become the property of the real estate agent or the bank from where they got the loan. So the ninety-nine year lease argument and house-buying argument, and all these other stupid ideas, of buying a house to live in a remote community, it just makes you shudder to think what the economic process was for them to come to that position. They clearly do not understand economics. What is the resale value of it? Once you have paid for a brand new house out at Port Keats, what is the resale value once you have bought it? There is no market, simple as that. There should be a value to it, but the value is only as good as the market price, the floor price. If there is no floor price then you have to artificially inflate the floor price and you do that by subsidy. Therefore instead of paying seven hundred thousand for a new house in Port Keats, you pay three hundred thousand. But it is a subsidised exercise so it has got really nothing to do

---

66. ABC TV *Q&A* program, hosted by Tony Jones and broadcast live from the Garma Festival in Arnhem Land in 2014.

with real economics. That is CDEP economics and that is the problem they have got.

When you listen to Galarrwuy and everybody else talking about land rights, they keep blaming everybody for their position.[67] Time and time again they have had opportunities to expand Gove with subdivisions and a whole range of other things, but they have declined the offer. The reason is that most of the land there, where they want to expand, is Rirratjingu anyway. It is not Gumatj. So you have had this ongoing argument about where does the Aboriginal economy start and stop in the remote communities. The answer is there isn't an economy as such. It is an economy based on a subsidised welfare program and people cannot get their mind past that, even to the extent of food transportation, and a whole range of other stuff.

So when you come to the situation with Gove, you see a lot of money but money that is underwriting programs. You are spending royalties on paying wages rather than reinvesting royalties and getting the wages through economic development. Programs that stand up and are economically viable. So they have gone to a mining company exercise now, calling it the Gumatj Mining Training Centre. Why would you want to train people to mine out at Gove, when there are no more mines? It does not add up. They [Rio Tinto] have got seven years of high grade bauxite left, the rest is rubbish.

It is all over bar the shouting but they go through this facade, signing up new agreements with the blacks, because the minute that they say they are closing the mine, they will have a multi-million dollar bill for rehabilitation. You are getting this perverse argument that the Land Council and the Land Rights Act is stopping them developing. It has got nothing to do with it. They have got all the freedom they like

---

67. In 2014 Galarrwuy Yunupingu, in conjunction with the Garma Festival as the Gumatj chieftain, had written about land rights as sleeping – that it is full of everything yet full of nothing. Land rights sleeps because the system does not give life to the leadership that owns the land. Like the ownership, land rights is a process of claim but not of use. It does not give the land the energy and power it needs to be useful to its owners and to enrich their lives, and it does not unlock the wealth that belongs to the landowners. Galarrwuy Yunupingu, 'Teach Our Young People to Look Up', *The Australian*, 2 August 2014. http://www.theaustralian.com.au/opinion/teach-our-young-people-to-look-up/news-story/e055e6d9d5c51602c0de827ac137560c

and they can have except for selling the land. They can lease the land, there is a ninety-nine year lease. They can do whatever they like. But, at the end of the day, it remains the property of the Commonwealth. It has a lot to do with Commonwealth policies and both the Liberal and the Labor Party are part of it, and they are not going to change the Land Rights Act, it is going to remain the same.

So the argument that Galarrwuy put out, really it was a very sad attempt by Galarrwuy to say, *I'm still the boss and I want to change the Land Rights Act.* Unfortunately, no one recognises his leadership anymore. That is what has happened: the leadership has gone. You grieve for the grave, his brother has taken over, and his brother has decided that his future rests with the Northern Land Council. He does not have the political power that Galarrwuy would have had in his young days to keep the Northern Land Council doing what they need to do.

This was all planned as part of the Garma thing. This is why I really do not like going to Garma because they want you there to say, *Oh! Tracker was there, this is the opinion*, and really that was not my opinion. I was not there, had no role with it and therefore I am not part of the process. It is the same with Rossy. That is the reason Rossy does not want to go. That is the argument that we have got with Garma; yes you will get royalties for ever and a day, but it will not be that much over time, and if you keep paying wages with it you are going to soon run out of money because people will expect to be paid after you have paid them once.

The Gumatj Association has never made any money; they cannot afford anything. There is the Yirrkala School which does not get any money, or hardly gets any money from royalties. So what are you talking about? We go through this bullshit about Garma and cultural appropriateness, and training and teaching and everything else, and where are the school kids? This should be the flashest school in the country. It is paid for by the Northern Territory Government. And people who donate money, are surprised when you tell them this.

Big Name, No Blankets

Tracker Tilmouth

Since the Abbott government's getting into power we have got a few problems. The plans for the Land Rights Act in the Northern Territory and everything else has been in fits, starts and stops, it has been pretty erratic.

It started off with the question of governance: how do you control the process? This was what the Kalkaringi Statement and everything else was all about: *How do you set up the process to control your life and what rights do you have?* Now that was pooh-poohed by some Aboriginal leaders, but it has now come around full circle to where the federal government, the current Abbott government and the imposed processes are telling you that you have to learn to govern yourself.

This is the argument Noel Pearson is running; that you do not need other people to tell you what to do, and that you need to pull yourself up individually by your boot straps. This is what the commentary is. Now the Aboriginal nature, and Aboriginal culture, and Aboriginal communities would suggest that there is a misunderstanding of the right for community title, and for the shared title to become one of individual titles, this is not the Aboriginal process. So there is a fair degree of assimilation being imposed in relation to this. *We want you to be like white people. We want you to own your own house, we want you to be independent and so forth and so on.* Now this is wonderful if you want to live that lifestyle.

It is not just a matter of whether you can afford it, because you can always afford it – it is a matter of where your priorities are. And Aboriginal people are going to say, *Well! How do we economically stay within the context of where we are at?* Are we Aboriginal, or are we assimilated Aboriginals, are we traditional Aboriginals, are we community-based Aboriginals, or are we some in-between definition where we are not Aboriginal at all? The only time we are Aboriginal is when someone says, *Oh! Gee, you look a bit dark*. This is about it. This is the length of our Aboriginality.

And when you get bush communities trying to deal with this there is no model, there is absolutely no culturally based economic model. There is no structure, and the rate of economic development is determined by what the market wants and the economics of it, or how you supply that market, and how you service that market and in return, how you get the benefits and financial returns on that market.

Now that leaves the Aboriginal community very much out by itself because you do not have a model that says the rate of Aboriginal production should be x, and when we come to sell our goods the rate of production is now classified as y, and so we either get over-exploited to a certain extent, or we are over-priced. So our building materials, our building of houses, our service delivery and organisational structures in relation to CDEP and employment programs and so forth, are always over-priced.

We cannot compete. We cannot compete with town-based organisations and Aboriginal organisations, and we cannot compete with non-Aboriginal organisations that supply services. So we end up being part of the program as non-participants. Not participants but observers of economic development, and this all became quite clear in relation to the Intervention with the housing program. Aboriginal people were not employed, Aboriginal organisations were considered secondary to the major organisations like Leightons and so forth who got the major contracts to build houses on Aboriginal communities in the Northern Territory.

It was a problem before the Intervention, but the Intervention brought it all to light. We could not compete in building houses, as simple as that. This is what we were told, therefore the jobs and the construction had to be done by outsiders. There was very little Aboriginal employment, very little Aboriginal participation, and so when you come now to the new model that is been quietly designed and driven through the process with Warren Mundine, Noel Pearson, Marcia Langton and so forth, it is a model that is going to force people into a greater rate of assimilation to be accepted by government, and when you assimilate you take on the nuances, the policies, the politics and the self-development of a non-Indigenous person, and you offload your Aboriginality, or some of it, to a certain extent. And the people who are singing out about this rate of assimilation, they are the people that are stuck within the academic world, and they are living an assimilated lifestyle, and saying that they are Aboriginal, and saying do not come here, this is no good for you, you stay where you are and in the meantime we will carry on, we will be your spokespeople at the end of the day.

And this has happened time and time again, and this is just another piece of the puzzle that will force Aboriginal people into the quandary of – do I remain Aboriginal, and how do I define that in terms of my cultural identify and my cultural process? Or do I assimilate, which is a requirement of this self-governance, this education, and so forth. And education, while education is a tool to be used to allow you to make decisions in an ever-changing world, the argument is still the same at the end of the day when we have this rate of assimilation. The Aboriginal people who come from remote communities in Queensland, they get educated, they go to university, and off they go and they never return. And all of a sudden you get claims for native title and claims for other areas, especially in the Northern Territory, by a lot of people that live in Darwin, Alice Springs and so forth, and they say we are traditional landowners of this and we are traditional landowners of that, and they go out and all of a sudden there is a clash of cultures between the urban Aboriginal – the assimilated Aboriginal people – and the traditional Aboriginal people.

This is the place where Abbott's policies are going to split the Aboriginal community down the middle, and it is his intention to do that because they are always saying, *We want to talk to the real Aborigines.* There is a disconnect between what is actually happening on the ground and what is happening in Darwin or Alice Springs, and this lack of consideration and consultation, and also the lack of understanding of the processes of pan-Aboriginality and individualism, is highlighted when you listen to the upheavals in the Jawoyn Association, the collapse of the trust out at Anindilyakwa, the corruption across the board, where individual Aborigines have decided that they have to adopt the Noel Pearson model at all costs and if that means ripping your own mob off – *Well! Off we go.*

They have misread the Noel Pearson model as well, because Noel Pearson talks about education as a tool and as a weapon to be used to further yourself, but he managed to get caught in the right-wing net and their philosophy of self-determination, meaning self first in determining what you want, rather than what your community needs or needs to be.

And people have a shot at the Land Council because there is nowhere else to go. The Land Council has always been a sounding board for people who are finding it difficult, and for their dissent against government policies of the day. It has always been in that role, and under the current process, all I can see is them closing the door on anyone that has anything bad to say about the Land Council on any issue. That is not a way to operate the Council. You better take on criticism, you can get positive criticism and you can get negative criticism, but at the end of the day you have to deal with it. And deal with it in a professional manner. Now can you deal with the competing interests of the Land Council members versus the Land Council itself – the traditional landowners, can you compete with that? Can you understand that and guide a path through it? The answer is, with great difficulty. And so you have to go and give the power back to the people and that was what happened with the Kalkaringi Statement, it was a re-empowering of people.

I am done talking about it now, I am just saying all this is the result of its [the Kalkaringi Statement's] non-adoption, people could not see the forest for the trees, and that it was the only way that you could develop a process that allowed Aboriginal people a real understanding of what their rights were. The only way you can exercise your rights is to recognise your rights and exercise them, and then act like a sovereign people. And it is being said that we [the Central Land Council] went to a government department-type mentality, so that they are now treating it as a government department with no connections to the remote communities. This is the paradox of the two land councils at the moment. How do you do anything about it now, when the policies of Nigel Scullion to establish regional authorities to govern Aboriginal life will be based on physical boundaries rather than cultural and social boundaries.

So we missed the big bus. We missed the train, the train has left the station on the social processes of self-determination and self-governance, and that is unfortunately the situation that we are now facing and the Labor Party can see that, they can see that we are no threat to anyone. They could impose the Intervention, they could amend the Racial Discrimination Act because we are nothing, we were not even there to complain. We did not complain, we did not even bother to complain.[68] And we accepted it as government policy. So the next lot of Liberals get into federal government and they say, if the Labor Party [while they were in government, 2007–2013] can do that to them, we can do this to them. And they will not complain. Howard's policies will continue. And that is what will happen, time and time again, until [we go back to] this question of who we are as a sovereign people – and if we are a sovereign people, please act like a sovereign people. Do not act like a corn-fed. Do not act like a slave, where you do everything you are told to do. And this is the argument.

The communities understand the process of the Land Rights Act in the first instance. But does the community understand the question of self-governance? Does the community understand any of these processes that will magically bring the money to them? Do they understand the processes that people go through to get those funds? Do they understand what royalties are all about? Do they understand what the mining agreements are all about? The answer is no. There has been no real discussion. A lot of Aboriginal communities think, *I have to receive royalties because I am a traditional landowner and I might spend it on funerals, or motor cars, or grog, or whatever. I want to go to the casino.* And that is it. There is no understanding that you have actually got to think about what you are going to do once the mine closes or whatever happens, *Where now brown cow?*

---

68. Although Australian and international law prohibit discrimination on the grounds of race, the Australian Government legislated in 2007 to override this protection as part of the Northern Territory Intervention, implementing a number of measures that apply only to Aboriginal people living in prescribed areas in the Northern Territory and suspending the operation of the Racial Discrimination Act. This removed any legal protections Aboriginal people in the Northern Territory had against racial discrimination.

With the Aboriginal community it is very simple, if you do not have any money up-front, you have no say whatsoever on what is happening on any part of your land at any given time, there is not a document in Australia with your name on it that says you own the land. There is not one document. The land rights title is owned by the Commonwealth, it is not owned by you. It is a trust, it is held in trust. It is a land trust administered by the Commonwealth and the people who administer it is the land councils who are Commonwealth statutory bodies. So you have no title. There is nothing in your hand or anywhere that can point to you as traditional owners. There is a blessing by the High Court that says you have native title rights and you have property rights, but until you exercise those property rights then you have nothing to talk to about anything. At the end of the day it is the Federal Court who gets up and says, *Rise now, native title holders.*

So when you come back to Kalkaringi, and you look at the opportunity lost, and now it is the opportunity cost, Kalkaringi was the greatest opportunity that we had to develop self-governance. We had these people who gave us advice, *This is where you need to be if you need to govern yourself, or look after yourself, to determine what your future is, this is where you need to be.* Unfortunately, we have been unable to do that. The best thing that I think the Central Land Council can do now is run another Kalkaringi campaign because it is going to be left out on a limb by itself, and it will be a shell of an organisation because of its internal feudings.

This opportunity is still sitting there, and until someone picks it up and runs with it and says we are an Aboriginal community and we want to be self-determining, then bend over because here they come. And you cannot be more brutal with that concept because it is a matter of life and death to Aboriginal communities in Central Australia and in the north. You have chaos at the moment. But you have this argument, the way you do it is plan another conference, and say let's do another Kalkaringi. We will get experts in the area on self-governance, and get it talked about, and then see where that takes us.

Oh! Look! Some people will put their hand up [for an Aboriginal political party], they will fight to get it, but this is alright. You need bad people to carry the day. You need lunatics, you need a radical fringe because you drive through the middle of them. The Charlie Perkins model of community development, he used to say to the government, *You think I'm mad, listen to Mansell and Clarky,* and the government used to listen to Charles – *No we'll listen to you Charlie. Fuck them, they're mad.* And Charlie said, *I told you.* He did the same thing at Redfern. He did it everywhere. So you have this type of argument, and my advice to Rossy would be run another Kalkaringi.

I will say, *You want me to give you advice?* I will say to him straight off, *You just run another Kalkaringi campaign, your chairman will jump on board because he will not be able to help himself. He will think it is his idea and off he will go and you will support him and wow, end of problem, end of program.* And the government will say, *God! Fuck me dead, what have we got here?* They will be very, very reluctant to start looking at splitting up Aboriginal communities. The only thing that Mundine and those blokes can do is wait to be invited, if they get invited at all. And then the direction to Mundine will be, *Well! Mundine do you support Aboriginal self-determination?*

Yes I do.

Well! Shut up.

You have got to run a campaign. I have got the Chief Minister on Monday next week. I am going to build my regional authority at Pine Hill, Alcoota, Wade River, Harts Range, Utopia, Ti Tree – this is my regional authority [north-eastern region of Central Australia]. I will build that because I have authority there.

I have an economic model for it straight away. I have got all the horticultural areas. I can grow citrus out of season, and I will probably need electricity and a bitumen road, and then I have a fully blown regional authority. That will give me at least six hundred jobs. Now I can do that standing on my head. That is a no-brainer, but what happens to the mob next door? Or, the mob before that, and the mob past that?

Tracker Tilmouth

You will end up with regional authorities. The Land Council will become a shell of its former self. This is what is happening today and the government told us at the ABA meeting that this is the way it is going to go. The Minister for Aboriginal Affairs, Nigel Scullion was saying this. I think that they are going to set up regional authorities but seeing is believing as they say.

I do not really know what to think. When you add it all up, the millions and millions of dollars of expenditure on legal issues for Aboriginal people, and you compare that to Queensland [which does not have big land councils], you get more bang for your bucks there because you do not have the big edifices, the big bureaucracy to handle, and with most of them, the money can get out to the community a lot easier.

When it first started it was this mystical beast called the Land Council and as we have gone through it, and people have become a bit more educated and more understanding of the processes, so you get a different argument coming back the other way now. It is a different process, it is an evolving process that over time people are able to look after themselves. And once you get to look after yourselves then the question of Aboriginality disappears, everyone will call themselves something different, and that is the evolution of organisations like the Land Council I suppose. They need to look after themselves, and they are not so interested in looking after everybody else.

We do not have the cultural connections like the Maori or other groups, we are quite spread out and split up. You have got Western Australian blackfellas looking after themselves in Western Australia. You have got Queensland blackfellas looking after Queensland, and so forth. And we ended up following Aboriginal academics and academics in general about where we stand on certain issues. We ended up with *my position...is my position, and it applies to me...in Queensland,* but does not necessarily apply to anybody else in the Northern Territory or vice versa. The Northern Territory's position would be different to Queensland and the governments made sure that this would be the case, that there is no connection between any of us.

So you can deal with Tasmania in one breath and people from Arnhem Land in the next but with a different set of outcomes, or proposed outcomes. This is part of the overall strategy of division that you get, where you do not get the real, or the pan-Aboriginal process. You end up with Aboriginal people trying to get one voice and one process together, but with the whitefellas appointing the leaders of the Aboriginal community by virtue of their participation on various boards, whether it was through Aboriginals Benefit Account, Indigenous Land Corporation, [Aboriginal] Hostels, or whatever it is, and *you are the leaders.*

They are appointed as leaders by being appointed to the boards by the white people. White blokes have blessed them to lead, and so they take on this mantle of leadership without any references to the community they are supposed to be leading. You end up with policies or projects and everything else being outside the control and the debate of the communities, and this has happened time and time again. This is the problem of when you join a non-Indigenous organisation even though it has got an Aboriginal name like Aboriginal Hostels, or Aboriginals Benefit Account, or Aboriginal something or whatever, and you are appointed by the non-Indigenous community [to dispense funds or policy] without really any reference to the Aboriginal community you are supposed to be representing. It is all full of symbolism.

This is the problem that you are getting with a lot of the organisations competing with the Land Council at the moment. You are caught between. There is an old saying that you cannot serve two masters, and you are getting this argument that the Land Rights Act is Commonwealth, and therefore you are a Commonwealth statutory body, so you are responsible to the minister, and off you go and you get your funding according to what your admin books look like, rather than the political and social activity that you have been trying to undertake.

And it is crunch time. It really is crunch time at the zoo now because the governments have got you pegged in a certain area. The Liberals have come in now and they have said, *Right! I know where you're at, you're over there and we know where these sheep are at, and they are over here.* And then the communities are in the middle. The Liberals talk about education, employment and everything else that at the end of the day will be about you getting off your backside and being employed, and thereby adopting a non-Indigenous process of going to work every day, and coming home to a wife, three kids and a car.

So you have got this assimilation process running at a hundred miles an hour, parallel to the dysfunction of Aboriginal communities. And they have to be kept dysfunctional because you do not want any models to evolve from the Aboriginal community, *Well! This is our economic model, this is our social model, this is our governance model.* You do not have that. You will not have a chance to take a breath, because they are going to be on to you very quickly and the main protection you had of balancing by the land councils especially in the Northern Territory, and other organisations in Queensland, was the protection you used to have.

Now this protection is gone because of the advent of the Native Title Act, the rep body [Native Title Representative Body] status, the adoption of land-council models which are non-Indigenous structures, and it is very difficult to understand, for Aboriginal people to understand this. When you are an Aboriginal person, you are responsible to a certain part of your country and your sacred sites, nobody else's, and you have to protect them. What is very hard to understand for a lot of people is that they were [legislated] into this American Indian model of sitting around at councils with great chiefs blessing you and thinking all the best for you, but ignoring your life. You know, group of elders – there is no such thing in Aboriginal society. There is no group of elders as such. There are people responsible for you and your sacred sites, your Dreaming and your culture, and that is it. So you get this process going on and it is going to accelerate on us in the next couple of years, where the assimilation program and Marcia [Langton] and Noel's [Pearson] position is being stepped out.

One side of me says this is a good thing because your argument for survival is that you have to hide in plain sight. And you hide by being assimilated, by having the economic wherewithal to pay for your own lives and being able to do what your independent thought is. You cannot do that when you are on CDEP, or unemployment benefits, or anything else. So you are caught in this quandary as an Aboriginal person where you ask: *Do I go to extreme Aboriginal processes, the full cultural gambit, or do I sit in the middle?* Now do you have a bit of this and a bit of that and balance on a tightrope, and wonder why you keep falling over as an Aboriginal person and this is the grog and everything else?

The escape hatch is a tightrope. Ha! You can see the policies that are being adopted by the federal government will be very much about employment, education, training and so forth, and Aboriginal people will be saying let's adopt some of this purely and simply because we are living in town, we need to be assimilated, we are going to lose our language, going to lose our culture. Which parts of our culture can we afford to lose before we become speakers of creole, and receivers of unemployment benefits through CDEP programs? This is what you have got. This is the agenda that will come out of this [Liberal] government, and it was the agenda that ran with the previous Labor government, and we will not see much change other than an acceleration of the process.

There can be another agenda that is not assimilation. You can have an agenda where you look at being Aboriginal, but you can push the idea for so long and you will get takers, but the minute you leave, everything drops. There is no sustainability in Australia, and in the meantime you do damage to the cultural makeup of the community. That is what will happen over time. You are going to get the old people saying we need to teach Aboriginal people on Aboriginal communities the laws and languages of our culture, but they are going to be very far and few between as these old people die off. The question will be: *Do we need to follow the culture, or do we need to follow the whitefellas?* The pressure is going to be on them to follow the white blokes because they want to be able to survive, and this question of survival is not a question of decisions, you take the best view you can get purely and simply because you live for the next day.

There is this argument about buying your own house on a remote community, but it is in a community you probably do not come from, you were put there by welfare or the missions, and here you are buying a block of land on somebody else's country, and you are paying for a house, so you need a job. The house is not free, and the rent and electricity are not free. So then you have an imposter buying the house – home ownership! Wow! That is wonderful. I do not see the real estate agents flocking to sell Aboriginal housing, not in Papunya, or anywhere else for that matter. They cannot afford it, this must have been a figment of someone's imagination. It is the ultimate deal on assimilation. That if you own a house you are therefore supposedly economically free, culturally free.

Of course this cannot happen when you are living in a community. The Queensland government went through it all when I was at the Gangalidda/Garawa [Aboriginal nations in the Gulf of Carpentaria] meeting and dodging bullets at Doomadgee. Bob Katter had, as the Minister for Aboriginal Affairs under the Joh Bjelke-Petersen government in Queensland, allocated private land in the middle of Doomadgee to certain families, and some people lived there and some had moved on, and they did not even know that they owned their land. Their names were on the books. So when it came to native title they had to go and try to find the people who owned the land. Some people did not even know they owned a house block in Normanton. *Wow! Where are you living now? Townsville. Do you think you will ever go back to Doomadgee? No I don't think so. What happened to the house you owned? Oh! It got pulled down, or they built a new house on top of it. Who did? The council. Didn't they ask you? No, no, we didn't know we owned the land. We didn't even know we owned the house.* So you have got these blocks in the middle of Doomadgee that are privately owned. Some of the traditional landowners own the blocks, some were, and some were not. A lot of them were not.

So! Yes! I am not negative about the process. I am saying it is a difficult choice for Aboriginal people at the end of the process. Right! Do you understand what you are getting into is the question now. Do you understand that you are going to become a worker, and are going to go to work five days a week? A worker on CDEP, because that is the only employment program happening? It is turning around again, we are going back to the future. It cannot work, and it will not work.

Regional authorities will just be another way of packaging the deal, but the deal is still the same. There will be a land-council office but that's all. There will be regional authorities and regional development according to a non-performing economic program that is not based on regional economic processes, but on service delivery, and that is it. No real economic activity will happen. This is what we have got. We have asked for it, the worst thing is, we have asked for it because we have been unable to build the process.

I have still got an economic plan for Aboriginal communities in the Territory, the Northern Territory as a whole, and I will implement that with my group, my family, and we will do that over the next couple of years for sure. I have got to design the model and I am leaning very much towards a kibbutz-type model where everybody works, everybody gets paid, and we all make money and this is how it is done every year. You can see a few bob during the week, but your tucker, housing and education all gets paid for. The kids are fed, go to school in your language and they are taught not only in English, they are taught their language as well, because you want them to know it is important. The more you look at it the more relevant it becomes. You cannot not do it if you want to be an Aboriginal community.

Tracker Tilmouth

My understanding of my family group is Upper Aileron, Alcoota, Bushy Park, and Waite River and Utopia, and when I set up that area, we will be talking about horticulture, and we are going to be talking about cattle. We are going to be talking about organic beef. We are also going to be talking about mining – but mining and electricity supply. We are not talking about just mining, we are thinking about the whole gambit of how we use the land.

We are going to have areas set aside for endangered animals, reintroduction of species, feral animal eradication programs, all that sort of stuff, but we are not going to allow that to dictate the total thing. We want to be able to supply organic beef to the market. We want to be able to supply good fruit and vegetables to the market – to Woolies and Coles.

I worked on the Gibb communities in the western region of Central Australia around Utopia in the 1970s. We called them Gibb communities because there was a report done by [Cecil] Gibb on pastoral leases, and what was the fancy name they gave them? Homogenous De-centralised Units. That was the name of a Gibb community. That was an outstation.

The hardest part was really the Northern Territory Government. The NT Government wanted to stop living areas as such, but the federal government insisted there be living areas, and the pastoralists were quite happy with it because all their labour force came from those communities. I do not think I have ever met a really redneck pastoralist, ever. I have had discussions with all sorts of pastoralists who are a bit gruff and a bit this and a bit that, but once you sat down and had a yarn with them, had a cup of tea, they were nine times out of ten on your side. They were more angry about the government than about the Aboriginal community because they were all their mates. People like Roy Chisholm [former owner of Napperby pastoral property]. Thorough gentleman, Roy Chisholm. Kil Webb, a thorough gentleman, Tommy Webb, thorough gentleman [former owners of Mount Riddock and Alcoota pastoral properties]. The only bloke that was really any problem was a bloke from Ammaroo Station, the young Weir, but at the end of the day he understood where we were coming from.

I do not think I have ever met a really redneck, racist pastoralist. I have had disputes and discussions with people who did not understand my point of view, but when you sat down together, you worked it out. The best bloke out of all of these people, and the bloke who gave me a lot of advice, was old Reg Underwood from Inverway Station, which is up near Kalkaringi, [about] what I was doing with Mistake Creek and everything else. His family owned the southern properties. Thorough gentleman. Very well respected, very smart. I was a stock inspector and I had Dr Ross Ainsworth doing work with me, a veterinary surgeon specialising in the cattle industry in the Northern Territory. Working with the pastoral industry and negotiating living areas was not too hard a deal. The biggest problem was the Northern Territory Government and the public servants within the Northern Territory Government, rather than the Aboriginals and pastoralists themselves. Once we managed to get living areas and people saw that they were going to get real housing and real water and real electricity, and they did not have to live off electricity from the station powerhouse, they would have their own powerhouse, people were happy. The pastoralists were happy. I do not think that has changed much at all.

Well! People wanted living areas purely and simply, and I think the greatest need for the living areas was from the pastoralists because at the end of the day, the pastoralists were worrying about whether Aboriginal people had a living area that they could call their own, where they could grow vegetables or whatever.

Many pastoralists thought that way because these were people out bush who shared the stock camp with them, and then when they went back to their humpy were asking, *Why can't we get a decent house*, all that sort of stuff. So a lot of support came from the pastoralists in that regard, and a lot of the communities said, *We come from this country and we want a living area, we want to be in that place.* Many pastoralists were a bit indifferent. Their antagonism had a lot to do with the people that came along and negotiated stock routes and so forth, and they were Land Council people.[69]

I never had the antagonism they had from the pastoralists, which was probably because they rubbed the pastoralists up the wrong way and did not know how to talk to them. There was always the Central Land Council–pastoralist debate on stock routes. It should never have gone that way, it could have been done quite easily but I came in too late on that debate. I was not there, I was at university when that was happening. But with the living areas, Aboriginal people wanted to be on their country, they had nowhere else to go, that was their country.

There are a lot of properties that have now been purchased by Aboriginal people and converted to Aboriginal freehold. I did most of the purchases with the Central Land Council. Owen Cole and I did most of the submissions. We started doing economic projections of where the pastoral properties should be and we fell foul of the entrenched ideologues of the Council, because we were not allowed to make money out of cattle stations. These were the properties that would be returned to Aboriginal people, so that they could one day

---

69. The two main land councils in the Northern Territory were established in the 1970s. Their work in the early days of land rights claims was to assist traditional landowners to fight their land claims. Many land claims were aggressively contested in the courts by Aboriginal groups, with others including pastoralists and the Northern Territory and federal government not being prepared to relinquish their interest in the land claimed back by Aboriginal people. Under the Hawke government, in 1989 the Miscellaneous Acts Amendment (Aboriginal Community Living Areas) in the Aboriginal Land Rights (Northern Territory) Act 1976 allowed for living areas for traditional Aboriginal landowners to be created on stock routes and stock reserves, which were Crown land (available for land claim) on pastoral land. The pastoral leases were not available for land claims unless they were bought back first, a very expensive process. Pastoralists protested about the stock route claims despite their being over Crown land, as many considered the routes to belong to them.

walk aimlessly across hunting and gathering and maintaining culture. Which is a good thing, there is nothing wrong with that, but someone has got to pay for the fuel, someone has got to pay for the repairs and maintenance, someone has got to pay for the bores.

This argument started off with, *How do you value Aboriginal land?* You had to try to quantify an Indigenous concept of value to a contemporary process and that was quite difficult, and that was what the Deen Mar Research Program was about: how do you say that country over there is worth x culturally, socially, economically, environmentally and so forth? You had those sorts of criteria because people wanted to live there, but how do you sustain them in that landscape, because hunting and gathering would have meant the depletion of firewood and kangaroos from around the community.[70]

Then you get [traditional landowner] people saying my malnutrition is through the roof, my health problems are through the roof because I do not have access to kangaroos anymore, and I have gathered up every bit of wood, and dug up every witchetty bush, and I have done everything else that you can ever do within a ten-kilometre radius of my community. So they race to the ranger program to try and protect the landscape but it is too late, because they did not think about a process of transition.

You are not looking at nomadic people anymore, you are looking at people who have been in remote communities for twenty or thirty years, this is where they live, they do not move around. They might grab a Toyota and go out and get a killer or a kangaroo or whatever, but they are travelling twenty or thirty kilometres. They need diesel, they need tyres, they need vehicles.

I think the biggest issue at the moment is eradication of camels. You roll your eyes and say, *Well! Hang on, why camels?* Why not horses?

---

70. In 1999 Deen Mar, traditional land owned by the Framlingham Aboriginal Trust and located on the South East Coastal Plain of Victoria, became one of the first declared Indigenous Protected Areas. At the time of developing the IPA concept, the Indigenous Protected Areas Sub-Committee, which included Geoff Clark of Framlingham, worked with the Department of Environment when Senator Robert Hill was minister (1996–2001). The sub-committee argued that Aboriginal-owned land should not be excluded from Aboriginal knowledge and values, and for the right of Aboriginal people to use their land to develop economic self-determination.

Why not scrub donkeys? The camels are a big-ticket item for the greenies: we have marauding camels down at Docker River and they found out that the camels had probably been let in by following the pet horses into the water and into the communities. Each community house had a trough at the back of it where they watered the horses, so the camels followed the horses and got a drink of water, and they did this every day. So these marauding camels at Docker River were not really marauding at all, just coming in for water. Instead of shooting the horses, and getting rid of most of them, since they have done more damage environmentally than the soft-padded camels, they decided to shoot all the camels. They spent ten thousand dollars, twenty thousand dollars, forty thousand dollars on each of the shoots and they just left the dead animals lying in the sun. There were no resources. There is nothing wrong with camel meat. They could have quietly harvested them, and the nutrition would have been a factor. None of that happened because the greenies said, *Oh! No! We have got to get rid of the camels.* What is his name, Peter Garrett, the [former] Minister for the Environment, from Midnight Oil? He turned up and gave twenty million to anyone to shoot camels throughout Western Australia and the Northern Territory. *Bang.* They have got absolutely no idea what they are looking at, where they are going, what is happening, who is doing what, and how they expect to survive.

You have this issue of remote communities and how they survive. They have this idea that we will build houses. Wonderful, let's build houses, but let the community build the houses to get the skills, and if it takes ten years to build a hundred houses so be it. Ten houses a year. Is that the strength of the community? Yes. Let them do it because once they build the houses they know how it works and they will look after it. If you keep getting contractors turning up and building houses and handing over keys, it is like parking jumbos on community airstrips, it all looks wonderful but no one knows how to fly one.

They fall into that trap time and time again, instead of sitting back and saying, *Righto, for us to build ten houses, we need plumbers, we need electricians, we need roofers, we need carpenters.* These are four trades looking at you. *We are going to bring the carpenters in, but the rest of the trades are all local Aboriginals.* And build it slowly. Ten houses, twenty houses, continuous. But no, we had this massive Intervention, seven hundred million dollars worth of houses. And communities that never had a house, for example, all of a sudden Woodapulli has got twelve houses. I do not think there are twelve people at Woodapulli.

Tracker Tilmouth

When I was the director of the Central Land Council, I spent a lot of time out bush. You could not just buy cattle stations and have them fall over. You have to allow for the country to come back, to be re-vegetated and everything else. You look at the sustainable carrying capacity in the desert areas, but you have to remember that for every five years, three years in the desert is drought. So you have to factor that in, every three years you are in drought and on drought relief. Now for an Aboriginal cattle station this is pretty hard because the land title is held by the government, you cannot mortgage the title, you cannot get drought relief, and Elders and Dalgety's [agribusinesses] would not loan against the cattle that you had. So your sustainable land-management practices had to be top-notch, and it was a blessing in a way that a lot of the places were not stocked because it would have meant a lot of hardship and and debt for some of the remote communities. On the other side of it though, it was the only long-term form of employment other than housing, health and education and that had been taken over by different organisations.

The hardest thing too, was trying to get a regional economic zone established in these sorts of areas and utilising what is there. Everyone can put their hand up and say we want tourism, we want this, we want that, but if the tourists are not turning up then you have got a problem. Nine times out of ten the only industry that is sustainable out there is the Aboriginal welfare industry, or the cattle industry. Mining was alright, there were exploration programs, but if they did not find anything they soon disappeared. That was the case in a lot of places. We had mining company meetings all over the place but they did not find any minerals, so the projects moved on. You have got to remember the ratio for mining in the Northern Territory is that for every thousand exploration licences there is one mine. This is the average. So you are flogging a dead horse if you are going to rely totally on mining. Real pot luck. But we had Part IV of the Land Rights Act which made a large part of the argument on how you go about accessing land, and it played a large role in giving access to mining companies. But there has not been a mine established on Aboriginal land for a long time because it has that ratio, one in a thousand they are going to find a mine. So Ranger, Gemco, Gove, Tanami, Tennant Creek that is just about it, and Mereenie.

You had to do the agreements. I took Martin Ferguson out there to the Granites [mine] to sit down with [Robert Champion] de Crespigny and go through the mining agreements, and we restructured the mining agreement out there to allow employment and so forth. The debate on employment goes forward. Aboriginal people are seen as anti-mining but a lot of them saw mining not only as an income from the royalties, but also from employment. And when you have an average rate of eighty per cent unemployment in remote communities, any job is a good job.

Alexis Wright: *Those agreements were first of their type that familiarised mining companies with doing business with Aboriginal people?*

Yes. With mining companies, we could have all the philosophical debates, but I do not live out bush, I do not sit in the camp, I am not there in the community, I do not have a humpy, and anything that comes over the horizon is a good thing as far as I am concerned. If it is a mining company so be it, or if it is a pastoral project so be it. And I was not worried about who I upset, whether it was the greens or environmentalists or anyone else for that matter, it was not my call. I was not a greenie, I was not an environmentalist, I was not pro-mining either. My role at Kakadu was surrounded by problems with uranium but at the end of the day the debate was not mine.[71] I could not say, *Oh! Tracker Tilmouth says this*, or *Tracker Tilmouth says that* in relation to mining, because it was not my call, it belonged to somebody else, somebody who was living out bush in a camp and had eighty per cent unemployment rate and if that is where you start from, then the debates about sustainability and economic programs and so forth all disappear.

---

71. Tracker is referring to his advisory role in the late 1990s to the Mirarr people who eventually stopped the establishment of a uranium mine at Jabiluka in the heart of Kakadu.

It is like the Aboriginal debate on the Indigenous Strategic Reserve which is all about holding water in the north. If you allow the current water usage, which is what it is now with the rivers, you may get a drying-out effect over time but you are also getting these peaks where there is a lot more water than expected. Now they have put up an argument that says that we need an Indigenous Strategic Reserve, but when you look at the amount of arable land available in the north for Aboriginal people, it is not very big. Now Ord River Stage 2 or Stage 3 is not worth doing, I would not waste the time. Probably there are very good soils between the east and west plains, some very good soils in around Mataranka and Larrimah but that is not very big, and there is some out at Katherine, and there are some very small bits at Ngukurr, and this the end of the horticultural scenario in the north, north of Elliott, which is bugger all. So to do a strategic reserve for that you are looking at probably eight thousand hectares all up, which is nothing.

The top of Australia is a different argument. You have got some better soils in and around the Gregory [River in the Gulf of Carpentaria]. You have got some better soils in and around Normanton. You have got plenty of water out there, but there are also better soils. Whereas up here the soils have been leeched, and now they are as good as.

[In Central Australia], Utopia has got good soils. Good water. Ti Tree has got very good soils and water, while Willowra has an equal amount, and Ali Curung, Karlantijpa [land trust], and you have got the Finke, and the Finke Basin which is a huge water reserve and soil reserve. This is where the argument is about whether you can develop the north, and it has nothing to do with the north. My mate said it is not a food bowl of the north, it is more like a finger bowl. You know, what you dip your hands in after you have had a feed of crab or something.

Alexis Wright: *You had a lot of really big ideas about horticulture in Central Australia and other places but they have all been really hard to get off the ground. Why is that?*

The argument is that you develop the project now and hold it in care, in trust for whoever is coming through. You cannot go out to remote communities and say, go and get educated, we are going to do this. *Do what? I am going to be a CDEP worker like my father and father before him?* The answer is: *I really do not want to do that.*

Or you say, if you go to school and get educated you could run this farm, and there is some good money in it, but you cannot paint them a picture of a farm if they have not seen one. So you have got to actually operate the farm, and run the farm, and keep the farm going, until such time as there is someone able to come in and say, *I want to do that.* This may take three or four years, or it may take ten years, but you have got to hold the thing, and while it pays for itself and while it pays money – this is the horticulture model at Ali Curung. It pays money to traditional landowners, and there is some interest.

But to bring someone forward now and get the education processes in place! You cannot stand on the rocky ridge and say this country will do *x, y* and *z* when no one can see that except you. This is the idea of the Ali Curung model, which was to get someone in there to put the project together commercially, and hold the fort until such time as a Centrefarm, or an Aboriginal community, or whoever, could take up areas of the land and develop it. You cannot say to somebody *I want you be a Qantas pilot* if you have no plane to show them. What do you want to be when you grow up? This is the first question kids are normally asked when they go to school, what do you want to be when you grow up? *I want to be a doctor. I want to be a nurse. I want to drive a truck.* I want to do this, I want to do that. Ah! That sounds like a good job. Well! On Aboriginal communities there are no jobs like that.

You cannot point to anything that you want, that you think you can do. This is the biggest problem we have got today. It is not whether kids want to go to school, it is what are they going to school for? Parents are saying, *Why do I bother getting my kids to school?* That is the argument. You have actually got to build the program and hope to hell that somebody comes along who is able to pick up the reins. It is no different to any other rural community in New South Wales or Queensland where [the farmer asks his children]: *You want to become a farmer?*

No.
What do you want to be?
I want to be this, that…
Well! You have to go to town.

The white kids leave the old farmer there, and a big agricultural company comes along and buys him out, so they have lost everything. They have lost their connection, lost their whatever.

Whereas in the Aboriginal community you cannot move because you do not own that country over there, it is somebody else's country. For instance, Alice Springs belongs to different people. So it is very difficult to work through economically. It is, when you paint it like that. It is what hits you and there is no easy answer to it.

Tracker Tilmouth

The processes that run the land councils in relation to the enjoyment of land rights have in a way not been dealt with. We have got imposed programs from an extremely active green agenda and this is not only restricted to Central and Northern Land Councils, it is also across most of the land councils, and where we have this idea that Aboriginal people care for the environment and care for the cultural aspects of it, but the question is, *When I go to my outstation, what can I do there, if I can do anything?* Because the cultural paradigm that is put forward by the elders and the old people that want that country is not normally reflected by the intentions of the young, and the middle-aged people who have decided that their lot remains within the bright lights of the local town or city or whatever. So they move off, and this is not uniquely Aboriginal either, this is also in the pastoral industry, the farming industry, and mining as well. So you are getting this rather large emphasis on the Aboriginal community to support the green agenda or the environmental agenda to provide the establishment of corridors, green corridors, that would not normally fly in NSW, Queensland or Victoria, or South Australia for that matter. These programs would probably be set aside by the farmers themselves: *Well! We don't really need to do that, we are doing this and this over there. We are into production, we've got to pay our bills.* It is all loaded onto Aboriginal land where Aboriginal people have to forgo economic development to appease the policy directions of the environmental lobby.

This is the ACF [Australian Conservation Foundation] and some of the more radical green groups, but the question will become larger than life when the Tasmanian timber deal is finalised and the Aboriginal community understands fully what they have inherited, because the position of the greens and the environmentalists in Tasmania means the wilderness without people.[72] Not just the Aboriginal community. They have been excluded from a lot of the real decision-making processes of this agreement, and this is going to come to light sooner rather than later.

It will come to light on economic development especially within the Gulf of Carpentaria when people move away from the mining industry because the mines do close, it is a finite resource, and they try and move to other areas of employment. Now the ranger program in the Gulf is probably one of the better ones, but it is still subsidised to a certain extent by the Commonwealth.[73]

I can see ranger programs dropping off, so we end up with a greater unemployment rate because there is this wonderful idea that we are going to be employed in green industries. There aren't any. This experience was becoming quite clear in relation to the fire-abatement trials in the north where they made two hundred thousand dollars last year on fire abatement in a couple of areas, but they just employed twenty people. Now two hundred grand by twenty people is not much money.

Instead of having pastoral properties and employment or horticultural projects we have ranger programs, and all the green stuff that people in Canberra and the cities in Melbourne and Sydney and Brisbane or elsewhere feel they should have because it has all been depleted in the areas that they live in. So you have bilby enclosures and so forth out bush in remote Aboriginal communities, but this is not funded by a normal

---

72. The Australian Conservation Foundation was set up in the mid-1960s as a national conservation body with a commitment to achieve a healthy environment for all Australians. Since Tracker talked about the Tasmanian timber deal in 2013, the Tasmanian forest industry had endorsed the state government mandate to cancel the Tasmanian Forests Agreement in 2014 with a change of government from the ALP to Liberal.
73. Most land councils operate ranger programs funded by the federal government, with caring for country rangers and activities in formalised structures for the transfer of traditional and scientific knowledge from old to young, as well as training and employment of Aboriginal people living in remote areas in species management, biodiversity surveys, landscape remediation, eradicating weeds and feral animals, beach and ghost net clearance, fire management, cultural support, environmental monitoring, sacred site protection.

process. It is funded by grants from the Commonwealth or the state, and they could disappear at any time the political wind changes instead of being locked in and saying *we put a value on the environment, these are the values*, and it is just like direct action, it is that sort of program. There is no locking in of the process. It is voluntary.

Climate change is here and now, but the arguments that are placed on Aboriginal communities is *don't do anything that will stuff up and knock over the environmental values*. Forget the cultural values. Forget about the survivability of the community in terms of employment and everything else, that has been put aside to a certain extent. That is the long-term argument I think the Aboriginal community has got to understand, that when we enter these programs it is really not our agenda. It has been set up by people from the Commonwealth. It all looks good, but what is the real economic activity?

Murrandoo just said an interesting thing, *Well! You are going to talk about the croc farm, we should capture the crocs and open it as a tourist venture.* I said, *No you can't.* Every crocodile in Queensland is owned by the Queensland government, even when it is dead.

You are prohibited from harvesting crocodiles. You cannot have a crocodile farm in Queensland. The Queensland government owns everything from the egg to when the croc dies. The legislation should be changed is my point exactly. This is an example of finding out that we [Aboriginal people] do not own the crocodiles. You can take the crocodiles for meat, but you cannot sell them. You cannot sell the skins, cannot sell hatchlings, you cannot do anything of that nature. So crocodile farming in Queensland is not on. It deprives those communities of a substantial economic activity on their land. You cannot do this. The fishing is the same, and people in Queensland running croc farms at the moment have all their eggs coming from the Northern Territory. All their hatchlings come from the Northern Territory. They cannot get any animals out of the wild, or eggs out of the wild in Queensland.

They are allowed to farm crocodiles from the Northern Territory but they have a resource centre there looking after them. Now there are crocodiles everywhere in the Cape, more crocodiles than anything else at the moment. So when you go back through this environmental discussion, and you look at what might be the catalyst that provides economic development once mining closes, it is apparent that the environmental groups by default are forcing people to accept mining as the economic process even though it may be adverse to some of their cultural and social beliefs.

I have Yanner coming to Darwin and I am going to sit him down and say, *Look, me and you have got to sort this out before we go much further,* because we need to harvest the rogue crocs for tourists, and we need to breed off them, and we need to be able to sell the eggs and the hatchlings and your staff are very reluctant to do it, because all of a sudden it means that they will be arguing with their environmental mates about harvesting crocodiles. They all want to be Steve Irwin, swimming with the crocs. Go for a swim with the crocs and see how long you last. And we have allowed that to happen to a certain extent. We see protecting the environment as a major issue too. But because of its low rate of return, in terms of financial reward, the government does not share our concerns for the environment, they pay lip service. They do not fund it properly, and the Aboriginal community is then forced to be a training centre for mining jobs.

And that is where the crunch of this issue is starting, in the Gulf of Carpentaria with the closure of Century mine, the closure of Bootu Creek mine near Tennant Creek. Where do you go when the mine closes? What income can you derive from your activity in Kakadu? And the answer is none. You are going to rely on the tourist industry, but the tourist industry is just about dead, and people are not going to share their income with you. The tourist operators are not going to say, *Well! Take half of my money because I am visiting your place,* that is not going to happen. So the economics of it all starts to fall flat on its face.

Two hundred thousand for one ranger group is not worth going home for. The ranger group is twenty employees, so when you go through these programs and look at the analysis of it, and you say what can we do and where can we do it, we get this really clichéd argument that we are the owners of the environment. Yes we are. We are owners of an environment but we were not sedentary, we were nomadic, and moved through the country and took as we needed from it. That stopped. That stopped when the white blokes turned up and said, *Well!*

You can't come across here because I've got a barbed wire fence and I want to run cattle over here, so I don't want you blokes burning the grass. So everything has changed dramatically. The rescue of Aboriginal people was through the establishment of reserves, to move Aboriginal people into a safe area along the riverbank, to keep them away from the evils of grog and white people and interracial marriages, and everything else.

We have got a new way now. *Well! The news out of this is you join the mining industry because we are going to supply you with money and you are going to be able to go home and buy your own house. But I don't live there. I don't come from there. I come from over here. Can I build a house over here?* No, you can't. You buy the house in the reserve that you have been trying for the last four generations to escape from.

And a lot of the Aboriginal people are saying: *Well! That's a reserve.* The traditional landowners, whoever they may be, are about four or five people in the whole community of about a thousand. When we go to most communities the traditional landowner group numbers no more than ten in a community of a thousand people. And the thousand people are there because they were taken there or moved there by welfare and by Native Affairs, or the police, or both. So you are going to buy a house in a country that you do not own. You are going to go and work in a mine to be able to do it. And then if you are a really smart blackfella, we will allow you to move into town and you can buy a house there but you are going to work all your life to pay it off, and it belongs to somebody else's country. Darwin belongs to the Larrakia, and Alice Springs belongs to Lhere Artepe, and Tennant Creek is Waramungu. All that sort of stuff.

So we have this great move of locking up the land in environmental programs, then forcing Aboriginal people to go to the mining industry because there are no jobs in the environment, there is no green industry. And we are going to become social misfits because living and working in a mining camp can be one of the most devastating experiences that a lot of Aboriginal people will ever see. It is bad enough for the whites, this is why they have wet canteens – drown your sorrows because you have just been accepted by the gulag. And we have got some of the Aboriginal leadership – the academic leadership – advocating the total movement of Aboriginal people into mining.

They have not been able to think of anything else, and now we have Andrew Forrest racing around to get fifty thousand Aboriginal people employed in the mining industry. Employed in what? What are you employing for, to dig holes in the ground? How long do we do that for? What is the job satisfaction rate of it because you cannot get white people to turn up? They turn up for a little while and then they go home, and then you go to 457 visas to get Asians to come and do your work because the white blokes cannot handle it. They do not want to be out bush in the hot and the heat digging holes.

I am advocating that the property-right argument on native title be looked at again, and we use that to dictate mining agreements, so the conditions for Aboriginal people going into the mining industry are supported by union processes with Aboriginal people asking unions to go to the negotiating tables, and with the unions ensuring that standards of health and safety are there in the first place. People are going in there and coming out quicker than a mincer. It is an employment mincer. This is why you do not succeed. You cannot get everyone off to work in the mine. This is not Russia. This is Australia, and Aboriginal people decided that there is an income from mining, but working in the mine, *count me out*, and white people have the same argument. They have said we do not mind the income from mining, the taxes and royalties and state-based royalties, but we do not want to do the mining. We do not want to be in the mine. We will leave that for the Asians, the 457 visas. This is the political and economic argument that people have not thought about, the forcing of Aboriginal people into this process, because the doors are locked on horticulture or pastoralism on anything else by the green groups. They have locked the country up. Why don't they lock their own country up in NSW or wherever they come from? No, they cannot get the political power to do it so they pick on the most vulnerable people.

These are the sort of political, financial and economic arguments that have not been thought through. The land councils in the Northern Territory have refused to have this discussion because of the misunderstanding about the enjoyment of land rights. They misunderstand, because a lot of them have never been exposed to

Aboriginal communities as such. They do not understand there is an extremely strong social paradigm of how people act as a community that has not been considered, and it is reflected when someone comes back from the mine. Their money is everybody else's money. And then there is the whole greater extended family. These are arguments that are very difficult to quantify and this is my argument, but Richie Howitt did not like me talking like that. No, he wanted me to be another Marcia type. I said no, I am different and contrary to other people. I have got a different understanding of how politics and economics works because I have seen it in action, and I have seen the policies that drive these processes. And they are racing at a hundred miles an hour to lock up Aboriginal land away from the Aborigines doing anything with it.

Tracker Tilmouth

In 2014, Nigel Scullion and the Prime Minister Tony Abbott went to the Garma Festival. They were talking about regional authorities, but the regional authorities that Scullion was talking about meant an attack on the Land Rights Act, putting the land councils on the side, and that is why we had that Section 28 amendment knocked back in the Senate.[74] Now the blackfellas were not talking about changes to the Land Rights Act under regional authorities, they were talking about government services.

Abbott agreed with them, but Scullion did not know what he was talking about. So Abbott must have appointed Mundine as a bloke who understood what Abbott was talking about, rather than Scullion. And so, Abbott has got two horses in the same race, one is Mundine [as chairman of the Prime Minister's Indigenous Advisory Council] on regional authorities for government services, and the other is Scullion [as Minister for Aboriginal Affairs] on regional authorities to deal with the Land Rights Act, or to nullify the Land Rights Act.

---

74. In 2014 the Abbott federal government intended to change the Aboriginal Land Rights Act by amending Section 28 to allow the Minister for Aboriginal Affairs to directly bypass the land council's power in terms of management of land, such as mining and other developments.

Now Alison [Anderson] very cleverly decided that her lot rested with the Abbott position which is regional authorities for government services, and not with the Northern Territory Government. And this has not dawned on the Northern Territory Government yet: that Abbott wants services to remote communities. He wants Aboriginal people to live according to the same standard that everybody else has. He is going about it in a weird way but this is what his agenda is. Now the Northern Territory Government is the problem. The Northern Territory Government gets a lot of Aboriginal money but it is untied. Here is the Commonwealth saying, *Well! Get out of the road, you're really a hindrance to us.*

What Alison is taking about, when you work it all back, is exactly what Aboriginal people were saying to Abbott at the Garma Festival. The argument is pretty simple. You cannot keep funding Aboriginal affairs in the Northern Territories with untied grants. You have to say, you have got to fund Aboriginal communities with this amount of money that we are giving to Aboriginal communities. There would be a change in lifestyle, a change in a whole range of fortunes, if the amount of money that was allocated was actually spent on Aboriginal people, not on bureaucrats, not on duplication, not on Northern Territory Government programs, but on Commonwealth programs that are well thought out and that allow Aboriginal people to progress.

There would not be a regional authority. It would be the Department of Aboriginal Affairs under the Commonwealth. Simple as that. Get rid of the ILC, get rid of the IBA. Those organisations are public nuisances, they do not perform. Leave the land councils in place to handle the mining stuff, then we would progress.

This is what Alison was on about and this is what Abbott was on about. This is why [John] Howard said the other day that he likes Alison, because he knows exactly what she is talking about.

Rossy agrees with me, and that is why we have got to have a royal commission into funding the Territory Government for Aboriginal affairs – where the money has gone, who spent it, on what? I reckon the taxpayers of Australia would like to know where their money has gone.

Bob Katter

I got friendly with Tracker, arguably as two of a kind, and we hit it off big time together. I suppose it is worth mentioning in the public domain, that when I was on the Aboriginal Affairs Committee that visited settlements in the Northern Territory, a lady called Alison Anderson who I had never seen or heard of before in my life, gave the most fiery, abusive, confrontational address which was in a way quite brilliant, and then she proceeded to burn our report.[75] They had forty or fifty copies and she had this bonfire going. I was standing next to Tracker and that was all we could do, we were all laughing. He said, *Do you like her?* I said, *Like her, I love her. She's fabulous. Where did you get her from?* Tracker just smirked knowingly.

Tracker Tilmouth

We are in limbo land at the moment and political agendas running in the Northern Territory reflect that. This was shown when [Aboriginal] members of parliament [in the Northern Territory Assembly] moved from the Labor Party to the CLP, and then to Palmer United Party.[76] What we are getting is this floating from one party to the next, because we cannot get protection from the Labor Party, we cannot get protection from the Liberal Party, so the next stop is the Palmer United Party. People are looking for protection, economic protection for Aboriginal and remote Aboriginal communities, rather than social and political protection. The real agenda is economic protection because they are talking about infrastructure, they are talking about housing, they are talking about health, they are talking about these

---

75. This protest action was first established in the area by Paddy Uluru who in the 1980s threw the government's plan to only give the traditional owners a perpetual lease of Uluru – instead of a handback and proper title of traditional land – into a fire in a forty-four gallon drum.

76. In a controversial move, on 28 April 2014, three Aboriginal members of the Northern Territory Legislative Assembly defected from the Country Liberal Party government to the Palmer United Party. Alison Anderson represented the electorate of Namatjira and returned from PUP to the CLP in February 2015. Larisa Lee represented the seat of Arnhem and became an Independent in November 2014. Francis Xavier Kurrupuwu returned to the CLP in September 2014.

other issues, and the political protection is not there in any of those mainstream parties.

Aboriginal people do not really understand, or they do not really want to understand, what the rest of the non-Aboriginal society is doing. All they are looking at doing is protecting their society, their language, their culture. This is paramount, but it does not mean that you exclude economic development. What you have to do is incorporate economic development within the political framework and that is not hard if you understand the process. But people like Alison who understand the process are not getting any assurance, and everyone says she is jumping all over the place, she is unreliable. They are saying this because they have no understanding of the Aboriginal paradigm that she works in. They do not understand that she sees the need to protect the economic and political structures of her society, and if you do not protect that first and foremost, then the agenda that you run does not mean anything to anyone. This is how she survives and this is why she is there today, and because she could not get that protection from mainstream parties she has been wooing Palmer United Party to see if they can deliver the protection that is required for Aboriginal economic development.

Alison is trying to get the basic stuff done such as housing, health, infrastructure, roads, electricity and resource development. She knows that if she can supply that, or if the Aboriginal community can receive that, then they can take a deep breath and think of other things. [If] you take white society for instance, the people who think of the environment, and the people who think of other things like refugees and everything else, such as the people from the leafy suburbs of Melbourne and Sydney where there is a social agenda that can be thought about, [this is] because the rest of the societal needs of that group are being met. They have got transportation, they have got electricity, they have got housing, they are well, they are quite wealthy and they can think of other things. These things are all paramount to any society, and white society can think of other things because they are already receiving these social goods.

When you analyse Alison Anderson it stands out every time, and I know her better than anyone else. I know what her agenda is. Her agenda is, *This is Alison, Alison is going to protect Alison,* and at the end of the day the delivery or non-delivery of services to her community is what she will survive or not survive on. There is a famous saying in Papunya [her home community], *big name, no blankets.* You have got a big name but you cannot deliver anything, you cannot produce anything. This is a fairly common and embarrassing position to be in as an Aboriginal person, when you ask people to vote for you because you can deliver things. If you cannot deliver those things then you have got to do one of two things. You can either blame yourself for not delivering, or you blame the party you are in for not delivering.

The Northern Territory Government should never exist, with all due respect to everyone who lives in the Northern Territory. It should never be a state. It cannot support itself. It does not have any manufacturing base. They all talk about the live export trade in the Northern Territory, but the best contributor to the economy of the Northern Territory is actually horticulture, the mango farmers and the fruit and veg farmers from Katherine and Darwin and elsewhere, and that puts more money in the Territory coffers than the live exports combined. The beef industry is not there. The mining industry is starting to slow right down. You have got a whole range of economic paradigms that suggest that unless you get the Aboriginal money, and you get it in such a way that allows you to develop, then the Northern Territory Government receiving Aboriginal money starts to become a toxic process, because you are using money that is supposed to go to Aboriginal communities for other projects.

A lot of people forget that I have known Alison since she was about ten years old. I knew her and her brothers. I was mates with her brothers. I have seen her grow up. We share through one of my aunties the Ilpili sacred site between Papunya and Mount Liebig, so we have cultural connections as well – plus Tilmouth Well. Country says it all, says it all. Now this is through Wenten Rubuntja because the Chief was my old man's first cousin, and the country around Aileron, Napperby and Laramba, and across to Papunya, we know this country backwards, and it ends up at Tilmouth Well at Napperby Creek. So we know where we are, and we know how we are related to Alison's mob. I have never shied away from saying she is my relative, I have always said that. Now you can pick your friends but you cannot pick your relatives. But at the end of the day you have to understand who she is and what she is before you can make comment because it is a complex argument. You can see where she is coming from quite clearly and at the moment I support her. I have got no problems at all understanding what she is about.

It is a hard area [having Aboriginal members of parliament]. Unless you have been exposed to it, to the machinations of political life – you have to remember when you watch people like Laurie Brereton and Martin Ferguson, Ferguson's father was a member of parliament, Ferguson grew up with a silver spoon, him and his brothers. His father was a member of parliament with Neville Wran in NSW, and the Fergusons are from a long dynasty of people in the Labor Party. I do not think any of them had a real job outside of politics, so they have been eating and sleeping and drinking politics since day one. But you take someone from Aboriginal society, even where you bring them in through the Aboriginal organisations and possibly the land councils, you are still going to struggle. You are going to struggle on the concepts, you are going to struggle on the understanding of the minor nuances of political life, and I take my hat off to people like Marion Scrymgour, because Marion was a very good operator and she understood it very clearly. We learnt our politics, our non-Aboriginal politics, from people like Neville Perkins when he was Member for MacDonnell and the Leader of the Opposition in the Northern Territory Government. We learnt a lot off Neville. It is a hard road to hoe.

Unless you have access to and you understand resource development, it is the only road for a lot of Aboriginal people. It is the only road left and as we go along that road we are being attracted to the Dodsons, Marcia [Langton] and everybody else – a whole range of people who I do not really think fully understand what the impact is on non-Indigenous society if it understood what they were talking about. When you compare them to the thoughts of Michael Mansell and people like that, I mean, what Mansell understands is economics. Greg Crough said if you do not understand economics you do not understand politics. Simple as that. That was the first thing he and Richie Howitt would have said to us when we started setting up Centrecorp and everything else in Alice Springs. The two or three mentors that came and visited us were Greg Crough, Richie Howitt and Bill Pritchard. The three of them all came from Sydney University's School of Economics. Greg Crough's a brilliant man in his own right and he taught us to understand economics. If you do not understand economics you cannot understand politics, this was the lesson that he taught us. Richie Howitt pushed that line as well, with a different slant to it. Bill Pritchard was straight up and down. Bill Pritchard was a hard-nosed economist, whereas Richie Howitt dealt with the human geography aspects of economics, but the agendas were nearly the same. This is why people like David Ross, Owen Cole, and me to a certain extent and a few others, switched to a Centralian process of economics as much as possible. That is the agenda that dictates non-Aboriginal society, and non-Aboriginal society the last time I looked, made all the rules for Australia. If that is what is dictating to them, well we better understand what they are talking about, and understand very quickly. Alison has picked up on that, and with all due respect to her, and I might not agree with her totally on all her policies, but she has been consistent, and when you put the personality aside and look at the activity, then it hits you. I am a student of people – always have been, and I never stop learning.

We, as Aboriginal people, at the end of the day because of our current economic situation, cannot afford to pick sides with anyone. We would not be able to stand up in a brawl. Let's be honest. We would be flattened economically within five minutes. So anyone that comes along we hitchhike, we get a lift with a fellow traveller going our way. When they do not go our way, we jump off the cart and walk along the road again. That is all we have been doing. It has not changed. It has not moved. It has not gone anywhere since those days. It is all we can afford at the moment. Our position is economically shot.

The Space That No One Really Wanted

Tracker Tilmouth

This question is a well-known debate. It is a well-known debate for academics. See, Aboriginal society as far as academics are concerned is a historical and *museumesque* society. They forget that cultures in the world survive because they are dynamic and human-based. So when you come to the argument of how do you maintain your culture while you are participating in the wider economy, that is what the real question is, how do you remain a blackfella when you are receiving whitefella benefits – from contracting, employment and everything else?

Well! The argument is pretty simple and faced by every developing nation in the world, in Africa, Asia, and in Australia where Aboriginal society is a developing economy, a developing nation. So we have to tackle our legitimacy, of being able to retain our Aboriginality by also being participants in mining and elsewhere in the economy.

Now when you get these debates going the only way the academics feel comfortable is when everybody is in their right box. They can box you in and say, *Right you represent that, you represent that.* They own the territory, they own the information, and they try to enforce it. I disagree totally with their current position. My position is yes, you can be Aboriginal. Yes, you can maintain your cultural attachments, you can maintain a whole range of things, because Aboriginal land use is about land use, land management and management for the benefit of the community. Mining is no different. Fishing, exploitation, it is no different.

You have to have these demarcation lines between Aboriginality in terms of land management and what the existing economy requires, because the dominant society requires certain goods and services. It has got to be provided in a form that they can read easily or recognise – there are no scary bits about it. You have got to be able to adapt to that process. So when you come home you are Aboriginal, and when you go to work you are white. You have got to have clear demarcation lines. This is what a lot of people cannot work out – why they are blackfellas, when they go home there are ten people in each house and so forth and so on, and sometimes it is a detriment to the worker because he cannot get to sleep, and he has got to be up next morning and go to work.

You cannot escape being Aboriginal. Aboriginal society has to learn whatever pros and cons there are in relation to contracting and employment and everything else, but it is not a great leap over the abyss, and this is where these academics fall down, because they are waiting for the leap over the abyss and no one has jumped. Even though they predicted the jump. So Altman's theories go into the trash bin where they should be, because they are based on the assumption that Aboriginal society would be decimated. He is one of the foremost museum nightwatchmen.

We need a lot more economists and corporate lawyers than we need normal lawyers and anthropologists, because gone are the days of the skull measurers. Everybody in the Northern Territory is listed as a traditional landowner, and since there is no difference for land use clearances or anything else, the role of the anthropologist is diminished, because saying who is a traditional landowner is all they do. It is a bit of divide and rule. Well! That is right.

Tracker Tilmouth

I want to discuss the strategies that seem to be coming in, or not coming in, from the Mundine committee [in December 2013]. To an outside observer, it looks like the [Abbott] government does not have a clue, but even scarier, the Aboriginal organisations do not have a clue either. There has not been an economic reassessment of the Aboriginal situation in Central Australia similar to the report originally done by the social, cultural and environmental geographer and economist, Professor Richie Howitt and Greg Crough. We have had bits and pieces from [Jon] Altman, and a few others, but they were pet projects of Altman's, promoting Altman, CAEPR and people like that rather than the

Aboriginal community.[77] Rather than bringing in outside commercial thinkers, and building a commercial and economic framework for Aboriginal communities, because at the end of the day, the only thing that is going to protect them from the onslaught of Liberal right-wing philosophies, the only thing that is going to protect Aboriginal people, is some form of economic program. Once you are earning money, once you are contributing to the economy, you are less of a target.

People want success, and it is very hard to get success because the government has made sure that the people advising Aboriginal communities have little or no experience themselves in the commercial world. So any programs getting up are very much based on the delivery of the social dividend of employment, rather than on economics. With the amount of money spent on health services, you could build three or four hospitals by now, and have everybody working in the hospital. That has never been the case. Millions and millions of dollars have been spent on Aboriginal health but no one has made any inroads. Health statistics have gone through the roof and there is no real rethink of the Aboriginal economic position in government services.

There is a whole industry of government social services. Yes, exactly. We have been unable, because of the way were are legislated and incorporated, to unshackle ourselves from the welfare process, even to the extent that we have decided as a group, that there are well-meaning whites in government departments that will protect our integrity. We have relied on the Department of Environment, we have relied on the greenies, we have relied on ranger programs, and everything else that is going to protect our way of life, but their agenda is different to our agenda. Their agenda is to protect the environment. Their agenda is wilderness without people. Listen to any of their discussions in relation to Kakadu or national parks, it is just pristine wilderness, which Kakadu is far from being. You get these sorts of debates, but no one has been able to reconstitute the Crough, Howitt, Manning, Pritchard

---

[77]. Jon Altman is the founding director of the Centre for Aboriginal Economic Policy Research (CAEPR) at the Australian National University. CAEPR became influential after a recommendation in a government review of Aboriginal employment and trainng called for an increase in economic policy research in Aboriginal affairs.

type of economic discussion. No one has been able to do a total analysis of the current Aboriginal economic situation and to ask, where do we go from there? What have we done in the past, if it is really good? Is it really bad? Is there need for readjustment?

You need this sort of advice, the type of think tank that would allow you to go forward because at the moment it is stagnating, except for Murrandoo Yanner's position. His position is very clear. He is going to protect his community and their culture and their integrity by taking on the economic and commercial aspects of mining. Right! If you come to the Gulf, you come to a one-stop shop: *We will provide all the services for your mining company, you will do as we tell you, and we will monitor you environmentally, and we will monitor you in terms of social impact, and we also want all your contracts. If we cannot get your contracts we want to be joint venturers with whoever gets the contract.* That is the mantra and he has held that line since day one.

Now this is a very small example but you can compare it to the extremes of the Northern Land Council and Central Land Council in relation to the Land Rights Act. I think the Northern Land Council is leasing out all of its pastoral leases in light of the upbeat market in live exports. Australia will not be able to supply the needs of the Indonesians, Philippines and the Vietnamese. What we have done is this: we have handed out the pastoral leases to people who really are not supportive of Aboriginal people but see the land as an opportunity for them. Instead of doing the work ourselves and having an Aboriginal cattle company for the Northern Land Council, and one for Central Land Council, what we have is leasing out and all sorts of other stuff going on, and we have been the receivers of royalties and payments without any work. We have ended up restating the government's intention about us, which is that we are passive observers to another boom, in the agricultural sector.

So when you add all these things together and ask why we are not protecting ourselves economically from the policies of right-wing governments, and left-wing governments as well, the reason is that we have decided it is a lot easier to do the social programs than it is to do the economic programs. So the Central Land Council has gone out on the community development line, replacing or trying to replace the government. That is not where you want to be. That is one albatross you do not want to put around your neck. Leave that to governments. They have got to have all of the funding responsibility. Leave all that to the people who cannot do anything else. Do not go into community development unless you have a hell of a big pocket. A hell of a deep pocket to be able to write off money left, right and centre on projects that you know are going to fail.

We have seen that time and time again with the Department of Aboriginal Affairs, ATSIC and everything else, and [Bob] Beadman's speeches each year reiterate the problem. Every speech is really: *Why did we fail? Why have we failed?* Rather than, *Where do we go from here?* They can talk very well about how we have failed. Yes. You could write a book on how to fail.

Who has done the analysis on where we have been and what lessons we can learn on how not to do things? We need another process put in place, to get away from the government-sponsored organisations like CAEPR, and the political highway for Aboriginal academics who decide that they do not need to espouse their policies to the unwashed masses – the unrepresented swillers as Keating would call them. They can bounce it off a few nice-meaning white blokes who will all get up and clap and praise, and then they all sit down and you get a doctorate, honorary or otherwise.

Whereas the real issues are what have you delivered to the Aboriginal community as such? What have all your activities within academia actually delivered on the ground that makes sense? The answer is zero in most cases. We have been asked to attend all sorts of forums to listen to these people, and if you read Noel Pearson's column in *The Australian* newspaper every week you would be hard pushed to understand what he is talking about because he has got a language all of his own, and the answer is, at the end of the day, the great gift Noel Pearson has given to the Aboriginal community is truancy officers.

Now we ran a very successful truancy program at Congress when I was at the CLC and my cousin, who has passed away since unfortunately, was in charge of it, and he would go around and threaten the parents by saying, *If your kids aren't out the front every morning I am going to bash youse.* So there would be kids lined up for miles all ready to go to school, all clean, washed, everything. It was most successful, very successful, and he only had to go around once a week and walk into the house and say, *Where's your kids? Why aren't you at school? You idiots.* He was big and ugly enough, I will not mention his name but you can guess who it was, big and ugly enough to scare the shit out of anyone. He used to tell the old blokes who would be shaping up, *Look, sit down or I'll rip your head off and shit in it.* Poor thing. That sort of commentary. He was the truancy officer. The truancy program did not cost millions of dollars either. He was also in charge of the drunks pick-up program. So the drive would be *the spin dry*. Anyway these are the things that did work in the past. Whether you are allowed to do it like this nowadays is another thing.

Greg Crough

I first met Tracker at the launch of our book on Aboriginal economic development in Central Australia.[78] This work was done with the Aboriginal organisations in Central Australia and the book was being launched at the casino in Alice Springs. The organisations invited a real cross-section of the Alice Springs community. There were government people, people from the organisations, business people, and people from communities. It was quite a large gathering and Tracker was one of the people who was speaking to launch the book.

I think this was one of the points he made, which was, *You know, whenever there is any money around, you can guarantee you're going to get big audience.* He made a lot of these comments that a lot of the people that were there to see what this project was about, particularly the business people and the business community were if not completely dependent, very dependent on money being spent by either Aboriginal people themselves or their organisations. Tracker made it pretty clear that he knew why they were there and was saying, *That we, being Aboriginal people, and our organisations have economic power, have a lot of spending, we know a lot of you are dependent on us for jobs and businesses and we are glad you are here. We want to work with you. We want to continue to make sure that everyone understands where Aboriginal people fit in the economy of Central*

---

78. Greg Crough, Richie Howitt and Bill Pritchard, *Aboriginal Economic Development in Central Australia: A Report for the Combined Aboriginal Organisations of Alice Springs*, IAD, Alice Springs, 1989.

Australia. I think that was a message he maintained over the whole period I knew him: *We know why you're here because we have money and we spend money and your businesses are dependent on us, all your jobs are dependent on us, we want a better deal.* And saying that sometimes politely, and sometimes not politely, but the same sort of message.

I worked with him when he was the director of the Central Land Council and in other stages when he was setting up his own business, the prawn farm, other things like that, and also very heavily when the native title legislation was being drafted to make sure that the economic rights of Aboriginal people, or economic benefits that they could get from both land rights and from native title, would be protected. That was the relationship I had with him over the years because I am an economist, and there were not a lot of economists working on Aboriginal issues at the time. Still not. We were always interested in where Aboriginal people fitted into the economy, to demonstrate what they were doing, where businesses and organisations fitted in.

I think Tracker, and the leadership of the Aboriginal organisations in Alice Springs going back twenty-plus years, saw the same thing. They needed to understand how the economy worked and they also needed to demonstrate to other people what their contribution was, and where Aboriginal people fitted in to the economy. He saw that very early on. He showed me a photo of all the Aboriginal kids on Croker Island and there was the white superintendent or whoever it was in the picture, and he said, *Look where I'm standing?* I said, *Where are you standing?* Because I did not exactly know which one of the kids he was. He said, *That's me standing next to the white guy because that's where the power is. That's where the money is. Get close to these people and understand where they work and understand how you can work with them.* He always said that. *I always try to do that, I always wanted to understand the power because I knew that's what they had, understand the economic power and work out how we could benefit as people, use our land rights, use our economic power to improve ourselves.* I think I remember talking to Willie, his brother, about the same sort of thing. They saw where power lay, and you either get close to it and work out how you can benefit from it, or you distance yourself from it.

He was part of the Stolen Generation, but it seemed in some respects he had come through it a lot better than other people had.

In the sense that he was damaged by it, of course, and it affected his whole life, he recognised that. But I think he also realised that he, as a person, he needed to deal with it, overcome it and make his way in life. He was sympathetic to a lot of the Stolen Generation cause but he felt there was another way which, while not denigrating what they were doing, this generation of the Stolen Generation could get ahead by doing what they needed to understand how it [the economy] works.

He always recognised that Central Australia is a very difficult environment in many respects, a very harsh environment. The fact that there are not very many people there and the economy is very limited is not surprising. So I think he always saw that there were not going to be tremendous opportunities for people to do things, but they needed to identify what those opportunities were, and people had land and in some cases there were resources on that land, and not just minerals, but also water resources, and things like growing oranges could work. Even in the Top End it is a very limited economy.

He was very critical of bureaucrats that had been around since pre-1967. They moved from job to job, and there were businessmen that had ripped people off out in the community. I think he used to describe a lot of white people out there as white trash. These people were never going to make it anywhere else in Australia and the Aboriginal community was a community that you could live off, or you could exploit. I am not saying they all were like that, but I think many of them that he saw were. They moved through the bureaucracies of Aboriginal Affairs from its predecessor which I think was Native Affairs, and it had all sorts of incarnations, Department of Aboriginal Affairs and then ATSIC et cetera, and the same people went through the programs. The same people turned up running community stores, and then you would see them in another community. He was very critical of those people. But on the other hand, he had known many of them for a long period of time, and he was reasonably friendly with them because he realised they were in positions of power in many respects.

Part of of Tracker's problem was that he did come across badly in certain circumstances. What he thought was funny and the way he said things often did get people offside. I think that definitely did not help him. It is a little bit like Donald Trump here running for the presidency in the United States. He is a larger-than-life character and he appeals to a certain group, but then certain things he says completely alienates other people. I think Tracker had that tendency quite a bit to alienate people that maybe he wanted to alienate, because he knew where they stood. At times he could have been more careful in what he said. I think some of the comments he would make about women or about other Aboriginal people did not help his cause.

One of the things we talked about a lot was the development of the Native Title Act, and he came to visit us a lot at NARU [North Australia Research Unit] where we had people working who had experience, particularly with Canada and what happened with their land claim negotiations, and how those claims could be used to negotiate broader settlements. That did not just give them what is called native title rights, the right to hunt and fish, as important as those rights are, but the broader issues around governance and economic development and stuff like that. There was a big group in Central Australia that could not benefit from land rights because they were living on cattle stations, and the key thing was that they not have their rights extinguished because they lived on cattle stations. The pastoral leases did not extinguish native title. Otherwise a large group out on the eastern side of the Northern Territory in the [Central] Land Council area would not get anything from native title. Tracker was very strong on that, that we have a once-in-a-lifetime opportunity to negotiate a package that does not take rights away, but gives the maximum opportunities to people to benefit from the native title legislation. I think he was very clear that people needed to be able to benefit economically from this as well. That it not just be a limited set of rights to the land, but that they be able to negotiate with mining companies, or with pastoralists, or with the government, whoever it was, to improve their position.

The issue he saw with the Land Rights Act was that people got land but most of the economic development on the land is when somebody else wants to do something, such as when a mining company wants to come in and explore. He felt that a lot of what the Land Council was doing was reacting. They were reacting to exploration proposals and mining proposals, and no one was really working on helping people to benefit themselves. Because land rights did not do much to improve living conditions.

Richie Howitt

I met Tracker probably in 1988 or 1989 during my postdoc, while doing work for the Central Land Council around the social impact of mining and mining agreements. I was looking at the Tanami [mine], but we really got to know each other when I worked with Greg Crough and Bill Pritchard on the study of the role of the Aboriginal organisations in Alice Springs in the Central Australian economy. That was a piece of work commissioned by the Combined Aboriginal Organisations of Central Australia [CAO] where we worked with students at the Institute for Aboriginal Development to teach a course on political economy. It was really intended to tool up the organisations through their younger employees to take a strategic view of their combined strengths and the opportunities that they created. Tracker was one of the organisational leaders at that stage in CLC, and that really triggered some thinking for him. It was a way of looking at things that shifted his sense of the strengths and opportunities.

I think it was in 1989 that we produced the report which asked, *What can be done now?* Obviously there was a lot of politics in bringing together all of those organisations and those politics changed from time to time, but it was that work that allowed us to say, *Look, collectively the CAO are buying an enormous number of vehicles, an enormous amount of* – We had some companies in Alice Springs who were perhaps ninety per cent dependent on Aboriginal funding for their commercial revenue. We also surveyed all the businesses in town to establish just what sort of reliance they had on Aboriginal funding, and yet we found there were no special deals going on at the Toyota dealership, there were no Aboriginal mechanic apprentices, there were no bulk discounts for paper and things, there was nobody working in retail even though these companies were retailing to Aboriginal people over and over again.

It was that discussion that eventually led to ATSIC funding the purchase of Peter Kittle Toyota [dealership in Alice Springs] and that sort of thing. There were a few people who really shifted their thinking about the value of research and what you might do with it, and how you might have relationships with researchers where Aboriginal organisations defined the terms of reference.

There was also a memorable discussion that I had with David Avery [then principal lawyer of CLC] that Tracker was part of, and I was reviewing some of the Tanami mining agreements, and looking at the social impacts of the Tanami mine and the Granites mine. I had this argument with David Avery where I was saying, *Look these are great agreements,* because there was this one-upmanship with the boys doing deals, where every deal had to be a little bit better than the last one. And I came in and looked at them and said, *Well! One of the problems here is that the Land Council does not have the capacity, neither the Land Council nor the communities has the capacity to monitor compliance with these agreements.*

So you have an agreement that something will happen if it is triggered by a pollution event or a non-compliance event, but there was nobody actually monitoring compliance, nobody monitoring the environmental conditions. All you were relying on was data provided by the mining company, and if the community does not understand what is being monitored then you have not achieved anything, because nobody knows what rights they are trying to secure and protect.

Therefore the paper agreement does not actually achieve what a legal analysis might tell you it achieves. And Avery got really cranky, and said as a lawyer his responsibility was to look after his client's interest and all that. About two weeks later after he had mulled over it, he came back and acknowledged that what I was saying was right, that he was just paid to dot the I's and cross the T's, and I was paid to think, so I'd better bloody well think.

I think that was another one of those arguments that for Tracker probably gave him the ammunition as a bolshy young thinker, it gave him permission to think, to be able to say, *Actually you might be the expert but you are not expert in people's lives. You might listen, but there is more than you're currently listening to.*

It was in that period that Greg Crough went to work as a policy advisor at CLC and worked quite closely with Tracker. One of the things that both Greg and I would say many times over was that it was important for the organisation, and for the leadership, to get diverse advice, not to just keep listening to the same person. Not to get a captive expert that would simply say what you wanted to hear. If you were going to draw from a research foundation, you had to get a bit of diversity into your thinking. One of the things that is a mark of good leadership is that you actually listen to people who are saying things that make you uncomfortable and test that as well, and certainly to test the evidence and advice that you are getting from people who agree with you.

I ended up popping in and out of Tracker's connections at a number of interesting points. There was one job that I did with Tracker around the development of fruit in Central Australia – and even tomatoes. One of the interesting things about Tracker's thinking was his willingness to step outside of the taken-for-granted. You could not rely on Tracker to ever say, *Well! That can't be done.* He was always willing to have a go at thinking things through, and that led him into thinking about grapes and tomatoes in Central Australia.

One of the things that I used to say, if you were sitting down and trying to invent a regional development strategy for a new industry for Central Australia, and you suggested you pull together a few old blokes to paint some doors, everybody would have laughed you out of town. And yet that was part of the genesis of the Central Australian arts movement, and a huge shift in the economic participation of a whole range of communities. Tracker was always able to say, I wonder if oranges, or prawns, or tomatoes, or grapes, are the painting of the doors? Is there a way of thinking outside that square? It was that sort of thinking that allowed Tracker to go in and say, *What about the post-carbon stuff, how do we get to thinking about what we are trying to do? How do we do it better, and do it in a way that actually facilitates people shifting into where the whole economy is trying to move?*

And then there was the second moment and this is the one that led Tracker to try and do a PhD with me, around the economic development element of the Wik Native Title Amendment negotiations. And what we tried to put together there was a proposal for what we referred to as an Aboriginal rural development bank. We went back and said how did the agricultural industry, the mainstream agricultural industry get started? It got given Aboriginal land for free, and then it was given access to government money through the Rural Bank and through government assistance, with the creation of a lot of free capital through grants and so on, and access to appropriately structured loan funds as well. The [Aboriginal] negotiating team [on the Wik amendments to the Native Title Act] actually commissioned some work to develop a strategy, and Tracker was central to that work, and the person that I worked with in framing that. We needed some specific econometric advice on modelling particular sorts of financial structures. We identified a couple of people that we would like to ask for advice including the Centre for Aboriginal Economic Policy Research at the ANU. In the brief that we tendered we asked people not to give gratuitous advice about what they thought should happen. We asked for specific information about econometric analysis, and not for them to frame their report in terms of a trade-off between compensation and native title rights.

I will not actually mention names, but there was an intervention by a senior academic to take over the brief from the person the working party had actually asked to do it, and when the advice came back it included the words *trade-off*, and it gave gratuitous advice about what should be traded off in return for economic compensation. The Aboriginal leadership group, particularly Peter Yu and Tracker, were just ropeable. They insisted that every copy of the advice be destroyed, and they wanted a written guarantee that the electronic files had been destroyed. They refused to pay for the work. It was really interesting because it was such a demonstration of the clarity of their thinking, that there was a link between the political, the strategic and the procedural, and that clarity came from Tracker. It was always couched in his humour and with his personal ability, but there was this absolute commitment not to allow the bullshit to be accepted. And of course that was an event that had echoes for a very long time, for all of us involved.

In a sense, in the 1998 Wik negotiations, that particular proposition went nowhere, like the loss of the social package from the original [Native Title] Act, that never really went anywhere.[79]

---

79. The 1993 Native Title Act, which was part of a response to the Mabo decision, was supposed to be a comprehensive package to address Aboriginal land justice and economic and social disadvantage. The act was to be accompanied by a land fund for land justice to Aboriginal people dispossessed of their land, which became the Indigenous Land Corporation, and a social justice package that was not delivered.

Then there was in the background a whole lot of ongoing negotiations, some of which I guess have resurfaced in some of the contributions and activities of some of the banks, but which have never been formulated into that bigger coherent strategy that we formulated then. Not with that thinking, *Well! We can mobilise collective strength, we can build relationships with major players in the finance sector, in the mining sector, to actually improve conditions.*

There is a group of people I have worked with over the years, that if they asked me to do anything I could not say no. I felt that I was obliged in a deep ethical way to make a contribution or to provide support, and Tracker was certainly one of those people. But my observation was, and I think I said this to him, that anybody who was working on these issues of resource development and environmental management, and Aboriginal participation in those things, *They go and talk to you, they go and interview you, they write down what you say and then they write a PhD about it. Why don't you just do the same and write a PhD?* We talked about how the Macquarie system would allow a PhD by publications, and that all he really had to do was write up what he was doing, to write the case study materials, and develop a few papers out of that instead of everybody else getting their PhDs. He would become a qualified and recognised person out of that. That led him, I think, to make the decision to have a go at doing the PhD. But the health problems, not to mention all the demands of leadership, and working in the industry, and building that post-carbon sort of thinking, meant that he never really got around to it. When the cancer intervened he never really got back to a space where that became a priority for him.

Tracker Tilmouth

My answer to the question about the extent and breadth of my knowledge and how I became the person I am now, working at ways to build an Aboriginal economic independency on a large scale, is that I took up a space that no one really wanted. There were people playing around in it like Darryl Pearce, Wayne Bergmann, and a few other people, but no one really wanted that space because it is difficult.

It is working on the question of how do you generate income? You have got to take the plunge and you have got to get in there and immerse yourself in it, and you do not win every time. I have had as many failures as successes and vice versa, but you get up and have another go, and you look at another project. You look at something else. Nine times out of ten if you do your sums right and you do your thinking right, it will add up, but if it does not add up then move away. You cannot run it by your heart. You have got to run it by your head. If the economics say don't do it, well don't do it. You've got to have an answer to this question every morning, *Is the going up worth the coming down?* You need to say that every morning – *Is the going up worth the coming down?* – because it is a long way down. A long way up too, but it is a long way down as well and you are going to go down sooner or later. You are going to go up a few times, which is good.

You have got to be aware of the process. It is an economic process that you do not control because you are trading in service delivery. You are trading in commodities. You are trading in a whole range of stuff, and if you do not understand that then when you come to trade what you see as your human capital, your intellectual capital, you ask the question, *Is it worth doing?* The question is asked, *What are they paying you?* I say they are not paying me anything. *What?* I said they do not pay me. I said they pay me for travel or whatever, because they have no money. I am not like a lawyer, I do not list a phone call here, fifty cents or whatever, blah, blah.

We Are Going to Make This Map

Tracker Tilmouth

When I went to university, I decided that the new era in relationship to land rights was going to be the enjoyment of land rights and that meant land management. Land management had to be a system that Aboriginal people could understand, and land assessment was the key to it, because you have x amount of hectares or square kilometres of land, and that has to sustain you. So the first thing to do was to sit down with Tim Baldwin, who was the then Minister for Water Resources in the Northern Territory CLP government, and I said to him, I want a water-drilling program to see where the aquifers are so that we can do some horticulture.

He thought it was a brilliant idea, so he gave the Central Land Council six million dollars to do bore-drilling programs on remote communities. So we did all the assessments of water. We were quite successful in locating the bore fields and so we knew that six land trusts could adequately supply water to undertake horticultural pursuits. And so I said, *Righto! Before we go anywhere though we need to do the land assessment*, that means soil types, vegetation types, native bush tucker, and what you use when you are on an outstation to sustain yourself. Which areas do you hunt in? What seasons do you hunt? All this, and document it to have a plan, so that anyone picking up on any piece of Aboriginal land would get away from this crazy idea of standing on a spinifex hill and saying this will do x or y without any scientific backup.

I set this up in the CLC, and I said they could not do this work without the establishment of a geographical information system. So I went and got Siegfried Kempinger who I went to university with at Roseworthy Agriculture College to help set it up. We set it up in such a way that the GIS in the Central Land Council today is probably the most powerful land management tool of any Aboriginal organisation throughout Australia.

That information gave us a list of which areas you could develop under what circumstances without creating a desert. Where there is mining. Where there is tourism. Where there is housing. Where there is health. All that information can be downloaded from the GIS at the Central Land Council and can be used as a community tool to determine the current status of Aboriginal society as we know today, and without doing any more reports, without any Intervention. You could pick up a community and say, right, there are x amount of people, x amount of houses, this is the income for that house, this is the current health status of that house, this is where they shop, this is what they pay for food. It gives you the whole socio-economic picture of a community in five seconds.

That is what is sitting there in the Central Land Council at the moment for Central Australia. You are dealing with information that has a commercial aspect to it, and when you get that sort of database sitting there and you can use it like that, it then becomes dangerous for governments to query your information. If you have got more data and more information than they have got you can dictate the debate.

Lesley Alford

I met Tracker in 1986 when I started studying at Roseworthy Agricultural College. We did a degree in natural resource management. We were called Nat Rats because it was an agricultural college where most of the students were studying agriculture, and we were known as the greenies. I do not know if Tracker called himself a greenie, probably not, but that was how the Nat Rats were looked at by the rest of the college because normally, they were farm fellas, or studying horse husbandry or winemaking and all that sort of stuff. We were basically studying environmental science, but it was called natural resource management.

Tracker had a fairly strong and funny personality and from memory, I do not think there were many Aboriginal students, maybe none, in that college until then. I think sometimes there was racism, some of it was institutional, but I do not remember it being very overt. Tracker used to deal with it in his own way, and he reminded me of it just a few years ago when he was in the media with the Labor Party where he referred to himself as their pet nigger.

I can remember once where he got these whitefellas who were in our course, and they were all good friends of his, to walk up to the lecture theatre like they were the pastoralists, or whitefella role models, and he would carry all their books and come along behind, really like a servant. And he would say, *Come on boy bring our books, we're going into the lecture.* It was in front of a whole lot of agricultural students and that really conservative part of the college and it was just…they did not know what to do. They did not understand it. The people who understood it were probably the ones who were helping him do it. But it was just that dark humour he was really strong with, and as a student he was a fun person to have around. He took the piss out of those conservative agricultural students by being that pet nigger basically, and it was really dark humour, and I just do not know how many people at the time, and probably myself too, realised what he was really doing, that he was making a big statement. But he was doing it in a way that everyone could laugh at it. He was not making people feel really awkward.

When we got to our final year everyone had to pick a big project which was almost like a little thesis, and he asked me if I wanted to be his project partner. He managed to get resources to do an environmental survey of Mimili, which is Pitjantjatjara land in the Everard Ranges. I think it used to be called Everard Park, but now it is Mimili and part of Anangu Pitjantjatara land. For whatever reason they needed an environmental survey done on that piece of land, and so we did that, and that was my introduction to Central Australia, and to Aboriginal Australia basically. We did a few trips. The first trip he took me on we met with all the old men and old ladies and asked for permission, and they showed us around the country.

We worked out how we were going to do the project. He called it the Rocket Wurlie Project because we were using a satellite image as a base image that then had to be interpreted on the ground. He talked to those old men and said, *It's the Rocket Wurlie Project, that satellite up there is taking these photos and we are going to make this map.* And when we did the fieldwork, he got a whole bunch of young Aboriginal students from Port Augusta TAFE who were studying similar sort of stuff to come with us. So there were students from Roseworthy, and the Port Augusta students, and we all camped out for a few weeks and did soil sampling and vegetation surveys, and driving all over the place. It was all really interesting because Tracker had the contacts and was able to get the resources, because we needed cars and a lot of material. We were able to do a really interesting final-year project compared to some people. I remember one fellow, he had to study roadkill that he saw on the way to college every day, boring stuff, how many dead roos and cats were on the roads every morning, to get the statistics.

There were a couple of run-ins with lecturers, you know, you have that, and Tracker had always been a bit of a rebel. I think he acknowledged that himself. He had strife with some of the lecturers and this is where I refer to the institutional racism, because there was this – *Tracker's got to work harder because he's going to be tested harder, because when he goes out into the real world*…A little bit like a woman has to work harder to get through the glass ceiling, they were saying that about him. I remember helping him fight some of those battles where they were trying to mark his projects harder because he was going to be tested harder in the real world than we would be, as privileged white ones. That was interesting.

I would not say that those people did not like him, it was just that they had a background that made them treat him like that. But his fellow students, I am still good friends with a lot of those people, and they all speak really fondly of Tracker. I mean he would do things, such as when we would go on a field trip in a bus for a couple of weeks in Victoria to look at projects, where he would go, *I'm going to cook you a traditional meal tonight.* We would go to his cabin, and he had bought a rabbit and cooked it in Coca-Cola with a packet of French onion soup. We were saying, *What sort of tradition is this?* He would do things like that. A rabbit.

That was probably my main relationship with him and then he asked me if I would be interested in working in Central Australia and he showed me a job that was on offer, which was as a research assistant in the Land Management Unit at Central Land Council. So I applied for that job based on his recommendation, and David Ross came to Adelaide for something else and interviewed me. That was the first time I met Rossy, and I got the job. I do not know if I would even be in the Northern Territory if it had not been for my student relationship with Tracker. We did not have an awful lot to do with each other in Alice Springs. He ended up being the director and he was working on a much different level than me, but we were friends. And Kathy used to always cut my hair. So I knew the family, she was my hairdresser.

I was at Utopia for much of that time and lived at Atnwengerrp just north of Utopia. He was a support to me through those years at CLC too, and a friend, but probably we did not do that much together as such. But I have stayed in contact with the family. I used to babysit those little girls in Gawler when we were at college.

There would be different ideas that came up over the years. He would ring me up out of the blue and say, *I want you to work on growing coffee bush in a plantation to feed the deer farm. Do you want to work on that? I'm going to grow witchetty grubs in sawdust. We're going to make a lot of money out of it. I want you to be the project manager.* Tracker was a big thinker and ideas man. You kind of just had to nod and agree and say yes, until you found out what was really happening. I have not really followed any of those dreams to anything real in our work together, but he did come up with all sorts of harebrained schemes at times.

Rodger Barnes

I was working at the Central Land Council when Tracker arrived from his land management course at Roseworthy Agricultural College, and took over as deputy director. So all my interactions with Tracker have been in the Land Council context, and issues that the Land Council was dealing with.

I guess this was in the early days of the Land Council. Pat Dodson had moved on, Rossy had taken over, and both Rossy and Tracker were sent down south to get qualified, and Tracker had come back. His focus was land management initially, and he was particularly interested in setting up a GIS [geographic information system]. This was at the stage when we had a typing pool, and people were not sitting there looking at computers as their job. So this was a cutting-edge idea, dealing with a body that was focused on legal processes and land claims, and getting land back for Aboriginal people.

It was a bold concept and something really useful which is now fundamental to the CLC's operation in a lot of areas from site clearances to land claims. It is being used for the recent negotiations over community leasing. It is routine to produce maps as part of the exploration process. There is a mapping team and that was something that Tracker was responsible for. It can produce all the features you see on a topographical map, from mountains, rivers, contours, places, railways, roads, all those man-made things, and the topographical features can be overlaid with cadastral land ownership, mining tenements, a whole lot of data. It is something to show traditional owners and it was a very empowering tool because you could produce the maps in large-scale format, or as maps just to look at.

As Tracker got more settled in the position he was particularly interested in mining. One of the outstanding things in mining at that stage was employment, and Aboriginal employment was not happening under the [mining] agreements, particularly at the Granites, and Tracker saw the need for the Land Council to be more proactive in getting Aboriginal people employed in the mines.

Prior to Tracker's involvement, there was a focus on protecting cultural interests, legal rights and the interests of traditional owners, and to ensure everyone understood what was going on, but in terms of benefits received as a result of those agreements, the lack of employment was a feature at that time. It had a lot to do with people not knowing how to go about it and the reticence because of that, reticence because of the fixed ideas about Aboriginal people not wanting jobs, that sort of thing. Tracker broke down a whole lot of those barriers through his work as director of the Land Council, and through his discussions with the mining companies. The mining companies were quite reticent because of those reasons, and it took Tracker being quite forceful and upfront and in their face about Aboriginal employment to actually make some programs happen. And again, his style was to put his faith and trust in people, so he brought in Stracky [Peter Strachan] who had been working at Tangentyere Council in Alice Springs to implement the idea.

Again, this was a new facet for the CLC, which traditionally saw itself as the legal representative of Aboriginal people, and here it was pushing into the zone of an employment agency that involved mining. Tracker brought in people like Ian Manning, because business opportunities were a whole untapped area as well. I think he had Frank Baarda [a Yuendumu contractor] carting gravel out of the Granites mine. Tracker saw a huge deficit in terms of benefits that could be achieved under the mining agreements. He had involvement with the unions and was associated with Labor, and he got Ian Manning to look at the whole setup and come up with ideas. At one point they were playing with the idea of carting fuel from Singapore to Darwin. This was [thinking at] a high level. One of the practical things that happened was that Tracker also grew up with Greg Roche, so he ended up assisting Greg to get the contract on the Granites on the basis of a joint venture with Yuendumu Mining Company, and they were out there for many years doing the back fill and through that time, a number of Aboriginal people were employed.

One of the first things Tracker did was set up the Tanami Steering Committee with people like Stracky, and people from the government he brought in through the employment agency departments, the mining company and the Land Council. It was also a big thing for Tracker to get politicians from Canberra, such as Senator Heffernan and Senator Robert Hill for at least four days looking at the Tanami and meeting Aboriginal people, just laying it out and saying, *This is what is happening and where is the employment?* We were just bumping into the wall. In pushing that whole issue, he went to the top.

Heffernan was from the bush and between Tracker and him, there was actually another side of politics for Tracker. He saw the Howard government coming in, a conservative government was coming in, and he got them out to see what the issues were. He had operated at that level and got experts, operatives, people who had troops on the ground, and he could relate universally to all those people to make things happen.

If you flew to Canberra with Tracker he would know nearly everyone on the route. He would be friends with the taxi driver, know the lady at the Qantas counter and would engage with her, know random people who were sitting in the lounge, who could be politicians or just the plumber doing the job there. He moved across all the boundaries, and it did not matter if they were white people or black people, old people or young people, rich and poor. He knew Tyamiwa [senior traditional owner] if he went to Ayers Rock, he lives in an outstation out west and barely speaks English, like a total bushman, but he was Tracker's friend. He sat across all the boundaries that usually help guide people in their work – like whether they were with us or against us, he just cut across that.

He was very forthright with his ideas, and he was less about discussing them than getting on with it. Laying out a clear strategy with points along the way was probably not his style, and a bureaucracy in particular needs that style. Tracker would like things to happen in his timeframe and in his way, and if setting out things in a planned strategy was a bit slow, you would find he was having things happen along the side and in front, while everyone else was plodding along the path that they wanted him to take. That was quite a tumultuous way to progress these things I guess. With Tracker it was hard to keep up if you were taking a linear, or structured approach. He had big ideas and they were put out there and everyone was expected to drop everything and go that way, irrespective of what they were doing. There are costs around that way of operating.

He really wanted to see Aboriginal people climbing through the echelons of business and economic activity and occupy decision-making positions, while creating opportunities and educational opportunities as well. It was not just the singular *I get a job* sort of thing, he really wanted to see Aboriginal people move and operate and dictate some of the economic activities that affected their lives, and use the opportunities that land rights created to pursue that grand vision of turning land rights into positive economic and social change, so that Aboriginal people could occupy higher levels through the economy.

There were so many Tracker stories in so many contexts. In his rascal-like way he was in a meeting with a mining company which was quite tense because we were pushing the issue of Aboriginal employment, and the miner [the mine's boss] had a bit of froth in the corners of his mouth talking about it, and the staff and everyone were a bit red-faced with Tracker saying, *We've got to make a move, move this along and something has got to happen. Making these excuses is not good enough.* There were many reasons and many barriers being discussed as to why there were not Aboriginal people being employed at the Granites. It ended up closing the meeting because at that point Tracker told the mining company that his principal lawyer was feeling litigious, and he might be on his way down to the court to lodge a subpoena very shortly, if there was no progress or no movement on the issue of Aboriginal employment. It had the desired impact.

Doug Turner

When he moved up to Darwin he was more into enterprise than the social side of things. It was about building enterprise developments for communities in different areas, and helping them through linking them to expertise and open up doors for them in the local area. He did the same work for Aboriginal communities across Australia, and not only in the Northern Territory, to develop their own enterprise and economic independence within their community.

In order to do that, you can bring in a whitefella consultant, or you use Tracker. What Tracker brought to the party was a wealth of experience, he could bring a business opportunity for a local community, and he could link all the resources to that operation in a way that the community would benefit over the long term. He maintained that level of support and expertise in a way that was not putting pressure, or seen as greedy, or seen as whitefellas coming in and trying to take control off blackfellas.

Tracker kept a lot of things close to his chest and in one way I think that was important, because we are our own worst enemy. We see blackfellas doing well and we think, *How the hell is he doing that? What's he doing? He must be pinching money or stealing money from somewhere?* That sort of talking is detrimental basically, because a lot of our community people are not experienced and they are not real knowledgeable about different things. We are becoming more and more knowledgeable, but the level of expertise in our community has been drained because the kids have gone out, and have taken a long time to come back.

The younger generation in the communities today is still growing, and it is good for the younger generation to go out and get an education and come back and work in their own communities and have this connection to the country. But that is all changing as well because of the pressures on our Aboriginal youth today, with mobile phones, iPads and everything else, and they are changing their interests. I mean, my interest as a kid growing up was I wanted to go and see what was over that hill, or I wanted to see what was down this creek. I was interested in country.

Honesty is the best quality, always tell the truth. In any business if you are not honest, I just think that is the worst thing you can be, dishonest. Anything you do you need to be genuine, supportive and honest, and I think Tracker operated this way. Anything he could do for a community anywhere he would go out of his way to try and help that community. He was not only doing this for Aboriginal communities, he was also working with whitefella businesses and helping them as well. People do not see that side of Tracker. A lot of Aboriginal businesses and non-Aboriginal businesses grew from a bobcat, then a tip-truck, to bulldozers and trucks, and a bigger operation. But people do not see that side of things. They looked at Tracker and would say, *Here comes that fucking*, excuse my French, *snake in the grass again. What's he up to now? Trying to rip off some community.* They looked down on him and that is where I say we are our own worst enemy. We have to move on from that attitude within our communities and be a bit more positive about asking the questions, *How do I link the resources? If I don't have the skills where do I go? Who do I see? How do I bring those resources and make that happen in our community?* If you wanted somebody to do that, you would talk to Tracker.

He could get people with financing skills, who have economic backgrounds and could understand the stockmarkets and all that stuff. There are plenty of those fellas in our community today and they are Aboriginal people. We have got Aboriginal people with skills in our community today that we can use, and they are there to help us grow. They also have a cultural understanding and knowledge about culture in their area. That is the sort of stuff Tracker was about. There are a lot of us out there, a lot of Aboriginal people who are doing that same thing because we want our communities to grow. I mean it has got to the stage now where we are actually competing amongst ourselves to make things happen.

We all grew up in the bush basically, and we saw the level of poverty and despair and the past government policies on remote communities, and we knew about the history of pastoralists rounding our mob and shooting them out in the middle of nowhere. We can take you to these places today and the bones are still laying there. That is how communities in Central Australia were set up. Not only in Central Australia, right across Australia. We had this knowledge of brutalities forced upon our communities. So you had to be tough as nails, have thick skin, thick skulls and this hate and love and desire in you to survive. And if anybody said something out of place, you would stand up and say stuff back to them. Tracker's madness gave him sanity.

My Agenda Is to Set Up a Food Factory

Tracker Tilmouth

You have got to have fun or try to enjoy what you do because it is a terrible task going out in the bush and seeing the communities and the conditions that they live in. If you are not affected by that you are really not seeing anything. The distance to health, the distance to good food, transport issues, what is not available in the store, you would wonder why these people are still alive. The meat's off, you get the twice-boiled, oily fish and chips – it has got to be twice-boiled! It is full of oil, and sloppy and greasy, and chicken that should have been thrown out before it got cooked, and lettuces that are non-existent.

Look, that was my agenda and it still is my agenda to set up a food factory where it does not matter if you have diabetes, or heart disease or anything else, you can go into the store and pick up a pack of food that is already cooked, it has been frozen, it has got a green tag on it and that is for diabetes, red tag for heart, yellow tag for something else, and so on and so on. You ask for the green tag, and it costs you about five bucks a meal, and you go home and put it in a billy can of hot water for ten or fifteen minutes, then you have got yourself a little cooked meal with everything in it. That is my agenda to develop one of those food factories.

We have tried to do this with horticulture but we are getting resistance from Centrefarm, and other people who do not see their role as being farmers, but as consultants and so forth, so it has never gone anywhere. But it will go somewhere when I get around to doing this horticultural stuff up at Bootu Creek. I will get around to it. It is one of those agendas that needs to be done, so it does not matter what your disease is, you can go back to your community and know full well that you can get good food that is cooked for you and has a doctor's signature on it, or a doctor saying *this is good for this, this and this*, that it has been made by Congress and the health services on communities.

I have talked to Centrefarm about this. I wanted to do it but no one wanted to do it if you know what I mean. They make you laugh. Everything is all, *Woe is me, and it is a terrible thing, the health service, and I feel so bad.* Ah! Well! What are you doing about it? Oh! Nothing. What are you feeling all uptight about? If they are doing nothing about it then it cannot affect you. So many times I have seen the director of Congress or the director of Danila Dilba with a furrowed brow, or seen the health services, and I have asked, what are you doing about it? Do you want to do something about it? Let the status quo remain. And the argument is yes, you enjoy what you do, but you do it because you can achieve something. If you cannot achieve something then you must get awfully frustrated. A lot of people like to be paid for being frustrated. They do not look at productivity, they look at being paid for being frustrated. There is the gnashing of teeth, the screaming and crying. The degrees of frustration you see are represented in your salary package. Well you look frustrated. It must be terrible. Here is some more money. There are a lot of people who have been paid good money over many decades to be frustrated. They have not done anything but been frustrated.

Danny Schwartz

Tracker did not have one idea a day; he had twenty ideas every day. And the problem with Tracker was that he was not a details man. He was a big thinker and he needed people around him to do the detail.

Tracker was really an engineer – that was his background. When [Gary] Foley went to China and [Michael] Mansell into Libya, Tracker went to Israel. Tracker went and learnt about irrigation and farming practices. He has talked about the Northern Territory being the food bowl of the world for the last twenty years. And he is right. The water is there, the capacity is there, the sunshine is there, and he has been pushing this barrow for twenty-five years. Only now is Tony Abbott talking about this notion, and now that Asia is growing, it is going to happen. There is no doubt it is going to happen and one day someone is going to turn around and go back to this blackfella who had been talking about it for the last twenty-five years and when it should have happened.

The reality is there are a lot of issues. For example, Tracker and I had been talking about setting up a kibbutz up in the Northern Territory for years. The problem is that we did not have a community to set it up. We needed a dedicated community who were desirous to stay on the land and to develop the land and to work the land. There was the analogy of the Israeli immigrants in the 1890s all the way through to the 1940s, they were people who loved the land and loved their community and worked the land and built their community to a position where they were providing for the whole country, this brand new country of Israel.

Today the kibbutzim are not only involved with agriculture, they are also involved with technology, they have factories. There was a time during the 1980s and 90s when it was thought that it was going to be the end of the kibbutz, and in fact they reinvented themselves, and now they do technology and they are producing silicon chips and laptops for the world. The kibbutzim developed agricultural notions of drip irrigation that Tracker worked with in Australia.

There is an obvious correlation between socialism and the way the blackfellas live, in a quasi-socialist environment. You do not produce something for yourself. If you are the boomerang-maker in the community you make boomerangs for everybody, you don't just make them for yourself. It is the same for the kibbutz. So we thought it was a great mix and marriage, but unfortunately, we were unable to find a community to work with to do that.

Tracker was the big visionary. There was no doubt that the Northern Territory has the potential to be the food bowl of the world, but he needed to have the people around him to help him. The ideas that he had for energy provision, agriculture, food, both with meat and agriculture, were incredible ideas but unfortunately for Tracker, he did not have the people around him to handle the detail. He was the big-vision man and he needed detail people. But he was responsible for many success stories, and that one young fella who did the boats, that got the sub-licence for fishing, that was just one example, there are many examples of young fellas who have been inspired by Tracker to follow their dreams and do their own thing. In a sense it is counter-intuitive, in that they are not the socialist community-minded people, they are more the individuals who have gone out and done things for themselves, but Tracker inspired many people, many blackfellas, to go out and do their thing.

Toly Sawenko

It was when I was asked to manage the land-management section of the Central Land Council that I got to know Tracker and worked with him more closely, because he had a very passionate interest in looking at how people could utilise and manage the land for the future, having got back areas of land through the Land Rights Act.

One of his big sayings was the enjoyment of land rights. It was one thing for people to get back significantly large areas of land through land claims or previous reserves being converted into Aboriginal land, or even pastoral properties being purchased and turned into Aboriginal land, but his whole notion was, *Well! The land has to continue to bring benefits to people and offer them a better way of life.* So enjoying the benefits of land rights was something that he worked for always.

Tracker came into the Land Council as deputy director and later as director in a period in the history of the Territory when Aboriginal people who were fortunate enough to gain land, were moving from the phase where it was all about claiming land and land acquisition, to actually owning land and managing it and utilising it for all the benefits that land ownership can bring. When I was working in land management, it was all about developing resources and skills to do land assessment, to assess the economic potential of land. This was something that Tracker understood in detail and it was something that came out of his training at Roseworthy. He had seen all that from the scientific perspective in his training, and he wanted to apply that to land in Central Australia.

The work started out with having scientific analysis and assessment of the capability of land. A lot of the land that Aboriginal people gained under the Land Rights Act was not of high economic value. In some places there was mining activity so there were benefits to be had from mining agreements under the Land Rights Act. Some people acquired pastoral properties through government funding and that land was converted to Aboriginal land. Some people made the transition from being workers on a cattle station to actually owning the cattle station, and then operating it as a cattle resource. So Tracker became very involved in the operation of these Aboriginal owned pastoral properties and he established the Central Australian Aboriginal Pastoralists Association. He was always keen to look at ways that people could manage those pastoral properties profitably, and learn the skills to do with managing them, and there were efforts that the Land Council made to make sure that Aboriginal traditional owners received knowledge and training and advice in how to manage those properties.

He was also very involved in looking at how people could gain lasting benefits from mining agreements, because under the Land Rights Act Aboriginal landowners had some leverage to negotiate agreements with mining companies about how mining activity would be conducted on Aboriginal land. I did not work in the mining area or pastoralism, but I was certainly aware of those things going on in the Land Council. I moved out of land management and worked closely with Tracker on looking at other options for economic development on Aboriginal land. That led to the establishment of Centrefarm which was all about looking at the horticultural potential of Aboriginal land. We were aware that commercial horticultural operators were looking at Central Australia, in fact establishing enterprises there, which demonstrated there were other economic land uses in the Centre apart from pastoralism and mining and the ones that people knew about.

It focused very much on the story that emerged from the table grape industry, around Ti Tree north of Alice Springs, where there were a number of factors which advantaged that sort of business. There was a substantial underground water reserve that could be used to irrigate table crops, and other crops as well. And because of the climatic factors there, table grapes could be grown and ripened early for the market, and then because of that could get a premium price, so it became a very profitable venture and could overcome some of the problems, like being so far from the markets.

Tracker was really the instigator of that idea and with Sam Miles, who was an agronomist and consultant, we worked together for a number of years, pulling together all the relevant information, getting technical information around groundwater and soils, mapping the potential areas for development, and consulting with the landowners in those areas to see if they were supportive of the idea. There was quite a number of years work involved in that, and it also led to our study tour of Israel, which was one of the highlights of the process. It was really all about changing the mindset in the Land Council, but also in the Aboriginal landowners' eyes, and in the eyes of the various government agencies, that there was economic potential to be developed on Aboriginal land, beyond what had already been done before.

One of the important things was to work collaboratively with Northern Territory government departments whose expertise was all about hydrology and underground water basins and yields, and water quality, and all those sorts of things. This technical information was important to demonstrate that these areas of land could be used for irrigation. There was also working with the landowners. I mentioned the trip to Israel, but most of the Aboriginal people who made decisions about what happened on Aboriginal land were the senior people in the community who had grown up in the pastoral industry and maybe had some experience of mining, and their idea was if you are going to do something commercial with the land, that was what it would look like. So there was a story to be told about what commercial horticulture might look like on that land. Part of the the process to change people's mindset was to take five representatives from different land trusts in Central Australia, and show them what a country like Israel had done in terms of horticulture and land use in a desert environment with very few natural advantages, and poor quality water. That was a real eye-opening trip for those landowners. They could actually see the reality of what their land might look like. Tracker had been to Israel before and he knew what it looked like, and what he wanted to achieve there. He wanted the traditional landowners to see that something was possible on their land which they otherwise would not conceive of.

We met Bedouin people in Israel and they had a fairly nomadic existence travelling across the country, subsisting on herding animals, goats and sheep and so on, and knew how to live in the desert environment in that way, but they were also becoming more sedentary, a bit like traditional people in Central Australia living on settlements. So they identified with the Aboriginal group visiting them, but one of the interesting points of conversation was when they came to learn that these five landowners and their families owned areas of land larger than all of Israel. They were perplexed that people could own so much land and yet have so little in terms of resources or wealth, and were not using the land in a directly commercial sort of way.

The Bedouin people could see in Israel what had happened to land there run by the Israelis, where there were all sorts of successful innovations in terms of desert horticulture. The Israelis themselves, the managers and agronomists and commercial horticulturalists that we met, were also somewhat puzzled and almost envious of these Aboriginal landowners who had such large areas of land that was essentially undeveloped in terms of commercial activity, and they came to realise that though the traditional owners had these large resources of land, what they lacked was management expertise and capital to invest. So that was part of the trip, to make people aware, but the rest of the story had to continue back in Australia, and that was in terms of the ingredients you need to make a venture like this succeed, and the land and water was one thing, but what was also needed was a market for the crop, business-management experience, and also investment of money in the project to get it started.

The government support was there at the technical level but the missing part of the equation was the involvement of professional operators who had management experience, and who brought capital to the equation, and were able to work with Aboriginal landowners to set up joint ventures. That was the sort of model that was developed over time for horticulture on Aboriginal land. Tracker was there right through that process and he understood that all those elements were needed to make the project work.

There were difficulties all around because this was groundbreaking work, and particularly in the area of Aboriginal affairs and funding for commercial projects, there was a fair level of scepticism about doing anything new and the risks of failure. A lot of work was done working with organisations like the Aboriginals Benefit Account, which had funding from mining royalty revenues to distribute, and also the Indigenous Land Corporation, which had funds to develop Aboriginal enterprises.

It was hard work convincing people in those organisations that business ventures which had been identified as potentially viable on Aboriginal land should be supported. There was always a lot of resistance and scepticism, and delay. Probably the worst thing was the delay. It was not difficult to find commercial interests that wanted to look at the idea of a joint venture of growing a crop on Aboriginal land and proving that it was economically viable, but it was very difficult to get timely agreement from the Aboriginal side, from the funding bodies that would assist the landowners to put some capital into the project, so that by the time some of those agencies got around to taking it seriously, the business investors had to walk away. They could not just stand there waiting with their money to invest. It was quite frustrating in those early years to pull that story together. Tracker had to be a persuasive advocate of the importance of doing that, and I think it was something he did for his entire life really. He was always looking at economic opportunities for Aboriginal people who had Aboriginal land resources, or even those who didn't, but had some kind of business enterprise that they were aiming to develop.

Part of Tracker's dealings with people was to raise their sights and lift their eyes to something a bit broader than just running a CDEP program, or some kind of make-work program that governments had developed on communities to keep people occupied. This was basically another form of welfarism. He had no time for that, to be bogged down in that world. He wanted to raise people's aspirations to participate in the mainstream economy in a big way. A lot of his communication with landowners was all about getting them to see that, getting them to see that they could do so much more, that they could participate at a much higher and more influential level. Some people in the communities got that very quickly and really jumped to it. Others took a while to change their mindset and their thinking.

When you worked with Tracker, you did not always know what he was thinking. You just kind of went with his energy. He was very much a driven person. He had very strong ideas about what he thought was desirable and important in terms of advancing Aboriginal people's interests in Central Australia, but he would not always sit down and articulate them to you. If you worked with him, that emerged through the work.

He was very much action-focused, and he was also multi-tasking, doing lots of things at the same time. He would be working on potential deals for Aboriginal pastoral businesses to work together and identify market opportunities, and with potential individual projects on individual properties. He would be talking to people at a high level of government and in the political parties about employment and mining agreements, and had such a broad agenda that when you worked with him you did not always know what he was doing, and you did not see the whole picture the way he did. But when you look back on it, the consistent ideas that were driving him are quite clear. It was all about people doing better than just surviving on welfare. It was all about people maximising the opportunities that they had by owning land or having access to land. It was all about real jobs and participating in the real economy.

Tracker did not often talk about his own personal journey and how he came to form the views that he did, but you can see that his development as a person and his working life were very much driven by the idea that he was not going to accept and be defined by disadvantage, and the impact of things that had happened to him through the Stolen Generation policies. He had grown up and worked as a young man at the beginnings of the self-determination era and the land rights era, and he was well aware of the civil rights movement, and the political rights movement in Australia. He fed off that, and what he took out of it was something that would give him strength and confidence as a person, a sense of what he was capable of, and he thought everyone could be capable of that and should not settle for anything less. So while he understood the difficulties of people living in remote communities, he never thought, *Oh! Well! That's all they should ever have, just to live on very limited opportunities.* He always thought there were better opportunities to be had if the people who had influence and power could work to support those ideas.

A lot of the people that I met through my friendship with Tracker, socially or through work, were people who had initiative and went out and did things and set up businesses or ran businesses and saw opportunities and acted on them. Or they were people who had positions of political power and influence and were actually shaping the way things work in the country. He was very much attracted to people who went out and did things. I think he wanted to participate in the political world with people who had the power to make decisions and shape and influence the lives of others, because that was what he wanted to do. He wanted to be influential in improving the lives of people.

There were no class divisions in Tracker's world. He would, if we were walking down Todd Mall or walking down the street in Darwin, stop and talk to numerous people of all backgrounds and persuasions and connections. They might be family and relatives, or just community people who knew him, people that he had known through his childhood. Then it might be a [government] minister or a chief minister walking down the street, it was all the same to him. He had a vast network of people. He did not see any boundaries in terms of how he wanted to engage with what he was doing, whether it was talking to the prime minister or talking to one of the members of his family or his language group.

Working with Tracker and socialising with Tracker was never dull. His sense of humour and his behaviour with people was so full of wit and cheek that you were laughing all the time. He valued that. Sometimes when I was working with him at the Land Council, he would come into my office there and say, *Tol, let's go.* I would have no idea where we were going but we would get in the car – this is during working hours – and you could see that he had been sitting at his office there, doing the administration of running the organisation or whatever other roles he might have had, and he just wanted to get out and mingle with people. I would say, *Where are we going?* He would say, *Oh! Just gonna go down town and rattle a few cages.* His idea of rattling a few cages was to turn up at Congress or Imparja TV, breeze his way in there, say hello to the reception people who he always knew, have a bit of a joke and a laugh with them, and then go in and see somebody like Owen Cole [then manager of Imparja], or Johnny Liddle [then director of Congress] and just chew the fat with them and tease them, make jokes and tell them some juicy bit of gossip, or try and find out some juicy bit of gossip from them. It was just his way of getting into the flow of what was going on, and enjoying that kind of teasing sensibility that he had.

After an hour or two of that he would have done what he wanted to do, which was to break free from the shackles of being a bureaucrat, which some of the roles of his work required him to be, and just be himself, by tuning into what was going on and putting his antenna out there.

He was totally uninhibited when it came to putting an idea out there. When we were on the trip to Israel, the fact that five traditional Central Australian Aboriginal men wearing Akubra hats, with Tracker and myself and Sam Miles and others, were travelling around kibbutzim and farms in Israel, did get media attention. The local TV film crew set up the camera and started interviewing Tracker with the rest of the entourage there, and his first comment on the question of why we were visiting Israel was, *Well! We had our Holocaust as well.* That got people's attention, I can tell you. But he managed to carry it off instead of making it as a sort of totally provocative, disrespectful remark. He used that to draw attention to the way Aboriginal people had been dealt with by history in Australia, to the way they were trying to overcome some of the impacts of that history, and take a step in a new direction. He was totally uninhibited about putting what he regarded as the truth out there and he did that without fear or favour.

Chippy Miller

We were talking one day about some business dealings and Tracker said *Hang on, I'll ring this bloke in Melbourne, he knows all about this company,* so there we were sitting around his mobile phone having it on speaker, and having a discussion with this bloke down in Melbourne. That was the sort of bloke he was, *Hang on and I will ring this bloke and find out for you.* He would go into somebody else's business and tell them what their staff should be doing and everything else. If they were any good he would say, *Look, you should come and work with me.*

Nathan Miller

Originally I met Tracker together with Toly Sawenko. I was working for Netafim, which is an irrigation company, and they came to see if I could help them organise a study tour of Aboriginal landowners to

Israel, which I did. The trip to Israel was undertaken in 2000 and ABC TV made a program about the trip. I was the sales and marketing manager of the company and I think that we were involved together with the Pratt Foundation, and someone had given them my name because I organised a lot of study tours of winemakers and viticulturists at that time to Israel and the United States.

I always had this soft spot for Aboriginal issues and things like that, and Toly and Tracker were different, both of them, to the people that I used to deal with. So I was quite drawn into, let's say, doing more than I usually would do, and then they asked me for some help with the Central Land Council. That was before the establishment of Centrefarm. I travelled to Alice Springs and somehow we became friendly – it was a kind of chemistry. I was interested in Aboriginal culture and Aboriginal life, and Tracker started more and more to see if I could support them from a business point of view.

Every time we met with Tracker it was a new idea. It was not a strategy, it was quite often a crazy idea and, *Let's go for it*. If it did not work we dropped it and that was it. I think Tracker's ideas were much faster than the bureaucracy could accept. A lot were excellent ideas, but did not eventuate. Some did, but at the end of the day a lot of good ideas for one reason or another did not eventuate. The idea on its own was a great idea, but there was a lot of work around it, and a lot of patience was needed for it, a bit too much patience. I mean a good idea can take five years to eventuate. I do not think Tracker could wait five years.

I am not an expert on Tracker's psychology, but Tracker would have a very good idea that would eventuate when other people took it on. He needed other people to take it on and to drive it, and nobody had better charm than Tracker. First of all Tracker could really get you on board with his enthusiasm. Number two: he was an extremely likeable person in a very rough way. The minute you get to meet Tracker you fall in love with him. He might sound or look completely crazy but you would fall in love with him. That was how he would get people to do things with him.

Centrefarm was one of Tracker's ideas that worked. Getting the Aboriginal landowners to understand the potential of the land is not something that you can put a value on in the short term. But the minute people understand that the dirt is not dirt on its own, that dirt is a producing tool, that is very, very important. That was one of the things, through all Tracker's crazy ideas, that managed to rise to the surface, that there is land with potential. That was very important. The minute you got a farmer to invest and start working the land, definitely quite a few things eventuated. I was the matchmaker. I must admit I had a few ideas, because I wanted the Aboriginal community to form their own irrigation company. I wanted to give them accounts from all the major suppliers, things like that. I do not know why it did not happen.

The only thing I can say is that if there would have been an easier way to implement Tracker's ideas, it would not even come to the surface. It was just not in his nature to do it easier, it could not happen. He could also annoy you no end. He could phone you, *I wanted to speak with you.* I say, *Okay*. And it was nothing to tell. Okay, it was nice. And then he would bombard you with another phone call you did not expect, and with information that only in his own mind there was a connection for, but it was very difficult to find the connection. Through his enthusiasm about everything and also his way of giving you information, he needed you to understand in what way it was connected to the objective. He did not explain why it was connected to whatever he wanted. He would give you the information and that was it. But I loved it. For me it was perfect.

I am interested in and love stories. Especially at my age you do not remember everything, but certain things you remember more than others, or you remember and will never forget. While I was in Alice Springs to attend an Aboriginal cultural festival in the 1990s, Tracker's brother [William] spoke to me about the Stolen Generation, and he said to me, *I will never recover from it.* I asked him why. I do not remember the sequence of the conversation, but I know what he said, he said that he would never be able to go completely back to his people because he could not speak the language anymore. He could not communicate with his own people. And that for me was like you punched me in my stomach. He cannot go back to his own people, and it is a free country you can go anywhere, but he could not speak the language. So that was one thing. The other thing was Tracker saying half-jokingly – but if it could have happened he would have jumped on it – that he wanted to be the ambassador to Israel. He said, *I want to be the ambassador to Israel.* I said,

On what grounds? He said, *I've got all the qualifications in the world.* He said, *I'm an Aboriginal, I've got a Muslim background, I'm very pro-Israel, I've got all the qualifications you need to be ambassador to Israel.* I actually thought as funny as it was, it was a good idea. So I took him to meet the Australia–Israel Chamber of Commerce and made a very nice conversation.

He told me about travelling to Israel and that at the time the government gave money to young Aboriginal potential leaders to travel the world to learn, and most of them went to Libya or places like that, and Tracker decided to go to Israel in order to see how a community developed from agriculture. It probably emphasised, more than anything else, his vision. To understand as a young man that what Aboriginal people need is to find a way to support themselves and to develop a community – that is a vision.

I went with him to South Australia, I do not even remember what for, there were so many things that went on that I do not remember now what is connected to what. But I remember going into this Aboriginal office and everyone was in awe, *Look who is here. Look who is here.* I was astonished. I was absolutely astonished. All the women and everyone were saying, *Tracker is here.* It was not a question of impressing me, I was not impressed by it, but it put him in a different light because I knew him, we talked to him, we would be sitting at dinner or lunch and talking shit and whatever, but to see how other people saw him, all of a sudden, responding to him like a rock star, without the screaming and those things, but in a very sort of cultural way, it was really impressive.

Yesterday I spoke with him about politics. He said that he was happy that Rudd came in, that he did not like Julia Gillard. I said to him, *I just can't take Kevin Rudd, I cannot bring myself to vote for him.* I actually would have voted for Julia Gillard. He said no, he did not like her. I said, *Rudd, Kevin Rudd, he doesn't like Israel.* Tracker said he was the one that said sorry to the Aboriginals, and I said, *Yes, and the Aboriginals also don't like Israelis.* He said, *No, we do like Israelis but we also like Palestinians, we like everything, but we do remember that when we had to struggle in the courts and everything, the Jewish community was always behind us, and all the lawyers passed away* – whatever it was he said – *We never forget.* I do not know how serious he was because we were always talking half-jokingly, but I presume he meant it.[80] He said we never forget the Jewish community helping us. And he could throw around a few words in Yiddish and things like that. He kept trying. He never gave up. I think humour was one of his major strengths. If you would get it. It could be crude, it could be stupid, but it was humour. We need it all the time.

Sam Miles

I first met Tracker when I was with Dr Trevor Cutter, the physician that started the Central Australia Aboriginal Congress in 1975. Tracker had come bounding out of the old Baptist church. Trevor Cutter was the fellow who found me and probably found Tracker. He looked for people who he thought could provide solutions to whatever he was doing. After that, we worked together in the Department of Aboriginal Affairs. I remember him there mainly because he wasn't there, he was helping a mate – Dave Simpson, who was building his house and had an antique car business. Tracker used to disappear and people wondered where he was.

He was quite an enthusiastic young bloke when we first met, about eighteen, nineteen or twenty. He was not shy. I remember him getting pissed off once. In those days in the Department of Aboriginal Affairs in Alice Springs, if you were in government you dealt directly with Aboriginal people and the politics was fairly intense. It was not like these days where there is no interaction between government and say a client, where there is always somebody in between. And DAA was a pariah, the government bloody pariah. Anyway, Tracker was in there and Alison [Anderson] was another one in there, but I think she came a little bit later. So he applies for a job and I can remember this one whitefella who was going to be his boss who did not like him at all, in the sense that he was a cheeky young bloke and never turned up and, *Go on, what am I going to do with him,* that kind of thinking. I do not

---

80. Tracker would have been referring in particular to his good friend, Ron Castan AM QC (who died in October 1999), who could always be counted on to play a leading role in supporting Aboriginal people and their rights, and in some of the important legal cases mounted by Aboriginal people, including the Gove land rights case, the Mabo case and *Koowarta v Bjelke-Petersen.*

think there was anything too personal about it. Anyway Tracker did not get the job. You can imagine it would not have suited him, and anybody had every right to think they did not want him working for them, because he would have done his own thing.

Then he was going to try to bring together Aboriginal-owned land with pastoral activity to set up the Central Australian Aboriginal Pastoralist Association. And they had their meetings and Tracker was the manager of that. Then they had the butcher shop on Lindsay Avenue in Alice Springs that they had bought off Terry Lee who, as the vendor, financed it. In other words they did not have to pay cash to get in, and Terry Lee said, *Righto! You've got to pay me back every month,* or whatever. They did not get their cash flow right because we were having to pay. Part of it got funded from ADC wages and we managed ADC. Mike Sheargold was the boss. So we had to pay wages out of that, and they would reimburse it when they got the money. We had it under control then Tracker had to…he had a fairly acerbic wit at times…and Lois O'Donoghue [chairperson of ADC] had it reviewed and found that we were theoretically lending cash, so they closed everything down. That was one thing I learnt about Tracker, you had to be fairly cautious when he got a bee in his bonnet, he was going to have a go. He had serious run-ins with Lois, very serious. Oh the old auditor, did he enjoy himself, he found something to report! So we copped it pretty seriously.

That was when he decided, *Well, I better go off and do something*, and I think he went to uni. He disappeared from the scene for, how many years was he at uni? Four, I reckon.

The other time of course where he and I worked together was setting up Centrefarm. Tracker was sitting on a plane with a bloke and they got chatting and it turned out the fellow, John Burford from South Australia, had a packing shed for citrus. The bloke wanted him to see his navel oranges and Tracker said, *Yeah, we can grow them for you*, you know, the usual Tracker. So the next thing they contracted me to go and look for a spot where they could grow two hundred hectares of citrus. I had to go out and I found that the only place where there was a big groundwater basin was Utopia.

So then we went through this great big thing. There was groundwater, and with citrus, you need a certain amount of water. You have got two hundred hectares – it is a big block, and you have got to find a groundwater basin on Aboriginal land that can sustainably irrigate two hundred hectares. In those days that was quite a big ask.

We had to go out and find the area, get the money to drill the bores and prove it, identify it. Tracker and Toly did the negotiation, discussions with the traditional owners. Then we had to get all the consultants together to do the planning, and we were looking at quite a big project, maybe ten million dollars to get it across. And it was going to be funded, and a bloke called Barry Hansen did a lot of numbers for us. And then another consultant came up from the south, and we did all the feasibilities and the bloke from the south was happy with it.

It went from there. Then we needed the money. It was something like six million dollars to get it set up. I reckon we were trying to get money from ATSIC, ILC and ABA. And all the talk and carry-on, it dragged on and then something happened, and the bloke decided to pull back. I think we were to grow navel oranges, early-season navel oranges. But the Valencia market fell and things went into a bit of a hole. So nothing happened. And the problem was, we had the three different funding bodies involved. None of them could make up their mind. It was too big for all of them, just too technical. There were three bureaucrats there who knew nothing about business. It has not changed I might add.

So out of that, when it collapsed, I think Toly and Tracker together decided we needed to have a strategy for horticulture, and that was when they got me to do the strategy. They had the four pillars. There was a developer, a financier, a lead funding body, agribusiness and training and employment, the four pillars. The first one, the developer, that was Centrefarm, which it was set up to do, to pull the whole package together, to identify the resource, and work with the traditional owners.

That got it all together, and that was how Centrefarm got up. And Toly was the first manager of Centrefarm. Out of that, I recommended that they go to Israel and have a look at the kibbutz idea, and we all went to Israel. There was Tracker and Toly and traditional owners, and a few government people. I said we had to *change the mindset around,* those were the words I used. We needed to go there and it was no good just one or two of us, so Land Council people went, that was Toly, Tracker, two different government departments, I cannot remember which ones. Geoff Kenna [former principal horticulturalist, Department of Primary Industries in Alice Springs] was one, and I think the ABA bloke was another who went to Israel. It was paid for by the Pratt Foundation and Netafim Australia. We had a great time. The Pratt Foundation flew us over and Netafim hosted us.

Centrefarm bumped along the bottom for a while and then about 2005 we got our first round of funding. Tracker was the chair and then he went off and started his prawn farm, and became chair again after that. Toly was manager for a year when Pratt funded it and then the Land Council kept him in the position until the money came.

Of course with Tracker there was any amount of toing and froing with Centrefarm, because he was always calling on us to do something or another. Full of ideas. He was a driving force and I think he got Centrefarm into the Darwin area. We operate under Centrefarm, but it wears a different badge up there, I think it is called Top End Farms. So Centrefarm staff are doing what they started in Central Australia. They are finding the resources, doing the scoping studies on about four different areas. That has been the progression.

It has been a battle because the original strategy for Centrefarm was for it to be the developer, and we needed a lead funding agency. So the concept was, you find the resource, you do the pre-feasibilities, go to the lead funding agency and work together to put together the package. The lead funding agency would find the money. That never happened. The idea when I first did it was that probably ILC would be the funding agency and do all of that. It just never happened. I do not know what the reason was.

From there we did the work on Ti Tree and Ali Curung, and Utopia. We got the water resource at Ali Curung and the money to do that. Jenny Macklin put the funding in for the application to the ABA for the bore field, and Jenny Macklin came down and Allan Cooney [manager for Centrefarm] sat in the car with her to Ti Tree and back, and she had had enough of them and just signed off on four million dollars, three point two million for the bore field. If she did not plunge in, I am pretty sure the bureaucrats would have said it was too big for them.

We have got to develop regional economies, where you develop Aboriginal land as a resource. How do you make sure they have got equity there and it just does not get taken over, that is the difficulty. And trying to package all this government stuff together with the Remote Jobs Community Program, it is just ridiculous, it does not work. You have to combine CDEP with Job Search Australia and that just comes under bloody bureaucracy so I do not want to go there, I would go on all day and get grumpy.

As it is at present, the community councils have been disbanded by the government under the Intervention, and there is a vacuum on the communities now. The shire is there, but the shire is run from Tennant Creek. It is all remote, it is a third tier of government, local government. There is no organisation on a community now where you drive in and say, *Hello, I'm here to talk to this person about this business*, there is nobody like that now. You have got to talk to the shire. That is how the world has changed in the Aboriginal sense. The shire just does the shire's work, it is a local government. It has got nothing to do with the traditional owners. In the DAA days, you would walk straight in and talk to Bob Huey, or Bob Beadman, or John Angel, the minister's delegates. You do not talk to them now – the minister's delegates, you do not even know who they are.

We are right in a new area now. This is what we are trying to figure out, where do we go next? It is institutional architecture, the bureaucracy is all over the place, and there is nobody up there big enough to walk in and say, *Righto! Five year development, twenty million dollars, put all the package together.* There is nobody who can do that. There is a bit of government here, and a bit of government there, there is ABA over there, there is ILC, and it goes on. It is all about jobs, but they do not say how they are going to create them. But at least now, if the traditional owners take the lead, and the land councils, there will be a change in mind about engaging with private enterprise. And Tracker was the start of engaging with industry, bringing them on as partners.

Tracker always maintained his interest in Centrefarm. Whenever he would get a bright idea, he would phone them, and usually Vin [Lange, CEO] would have to write out something for him, and someone would have to make it work. He had an idea for low-security prisoners. Tracker wanted to have Pine Hill B set up as a low-security place. We tried to buy Territory Grapes which is a big grape farm, and we did nothing for three years so we have got some scar tissue there, but we have just signed off and bought the Territory Grape Farm with Kuda, the mob who get the royalties from the Granites mine. There is Kuda with fifty per cent, twenty-five per cent is investors and their own professional managers, and Centrefarm has twenty-five per cent.

Territory Grapes is on Pine Hill and there is accommodation for about a hundred. It is very run-down, but we have got it – ninety-nine per cent sure, but it could still fall over of course. This is where the royalty association could put in one and a half million just like that, without blinking. They have got assets of thirty or forty million. That is how it works and that is an outcome.

We have now got a strategic position in Ti Tree, which is the Anmatyerre area. The problem is that it does not belong to the Anmatyerre mob, but we can develop the other farm that they have under an ILUA [Indigenous Land Use Agreement], the farm area Pine Hill B – it is enough for them to do one hundred hectares which is a decent-sized farm. Because Pine Hill B is close to Territory Grapes, you can grow the stuff and take it to Territory Grapes and pack there, the accommodation is there, and all of that can be worked out. So that is Pine Hill B. Tracker's idea was that we set up Pine Hill B for people who are on DUIs [driving under the influence] who would live and work there on home detention. You could send them there and you would have traditional landowners from the area looking after them.

Now it is a great idea but there are a few gritty areas that have to be worked through. Security. You have got to look after people, who either send themselves there or are sent there by the magistrate. In which case, the magistrate has got to know they are going to be looked after. If they escape you have to go and find them. It will happen, there is no doubt about it, and who is going to do that? Then if they are going to work on the farm, the fellow who walks through the gate has got to be worth twenty-five dollars an hour. And they will need some supervision on the farm, and that is an extra cost.

All of that has got to be worked out. Together with Tracker, we had been trying to get dollars to do a feasibility on it, get the hard numbers so that we can go to the Department of Corrections and they will know that this bloke's in gaol, it is one hundred and eighty bucks a day that it is costing them, but if he was out there, maybe we could do it for one hundred and fifty bucks a day. That is what we have got to get sorted out.

Bob Beadman

We both talked often about schemes like melon farms at Ali Curung and how they utilised backpackers and how, before that, they utilised the mob from Ti Tree, whilst the Ali Curung mob just watched. We talked about how you might overcome that, and we talked about how you might bring the Ti Tree region into greater production. He saw some synergies between the new mine that is going to open near Aileron and the potential for horticulture, by expanding the orchards around Ti Tree and beyond. Apparently the land is there, the water is there, but it lacks power.

He saw an opportunity to piggyback on the power needs of Aileron, to create a grid system that would run power to horticulture schemes and leased land already in Aboriginal ownership, to bring it into production and create jobs. We often talked about the level of Aboriginal incarceration where you have a captured audience already, to use them in some way on employment and training in quasi-economic schemes that could use that labour on Aboriginal land to produce things that could be sold on the open market, and in doing so, you would equip people to be job-ready for when they get out of the prison system. I think the current government is picking up on some of that idea. We have hammered them with documentation from Centrefarm, and some stuff I have helped them write, and some of these schemes happening now on boot camps – youth boot camps – I do not know how much credit we can take, but we will take a bit. It is utilising a negative to try and turn it into a positive. Tracker thought through things like that very, very well.

He fundamentally understood that Aborigines are dirt rich but asset poor. That we have created a mindset through over-generosity of welfare benefits – this is perhaps more me talking than him – that has lowered expectations. There is a mindset out there now that you do not have to work, the government will keep you for life. And it has dumbed down aspirations and expectations. That, unfortunately, then has a terrible effect on demotivating kids from even attending school. They come out at the end of the school system, basically illiterate and not able to compete on the open market for jobs. So then history repeats itself. Tracker saw all of that.

And when he was director of the Central Land Council I remember the effort that he put into schemes to identify water points, or the fencing you would need to supplement natural cartography features, to create enhanced opportunities for cattle production, by using existing land and work force. But he was perhaps ahead of his time because he was not able to motivate the government agencies appropriately to get all that going and likewise, he was not able to motivate the local people who were too reliant on the free money to find a need to get themselves out of that lethargy and into production.

I remember he got himself in some strife once, it might have been Alcoota, in his Central Land Council days, it might have been exasperation about motivating people. I think he told them the next time he came out there he was going to cut a big green stick and get stuck into them. I think there might have been some hand-wringing do-gooder in the audience who was horrified at this pragmatism, and there was some ministerial correspondence firing around at the time.

There was another time, it might have been a combined meeting of ATSIC regional councils here in Darwin, and Tracker had laid down the law about something, and he was met with a hostile response. So in order to introduce a bit of levity to the occasion and get himself off the hook he said, *Oh! Look! There's Bob Beadman over there,* blurting out to the crowd that I taught him everything he knows in order to get himself off the hook.

Allan Cooney

We worked together when I was the CEO or general manager, and Tracker was the chairman, during my time with Centrefarm which was about five and a half years. And we worked very closely together over that time. Those sorts of relationships between CEO and chairman generally go either way. They either become a difficult professional relationship, or they turn into a genuine long-term friendship. We became really good friends as much as we had a very strong professional relationship.

Tracker was a vast font of new ideas all the time. I got to the stage with Tracks that I had to filter his ideas because there were just so many of them. I had this rule of thumb that if he mentioned something to me six times I knew that it was probably something that I needed to focus on. Something that he only mentioned to me once I would say, *Yeah! Mate that's interesting but we've still got the business to do.*

We did a lot of work around economic development in Central Australia, and a lot of it was based on some fundamental principles that Tracker had about the way Aboriginal economic development needs to be developed. A lot of it was by consensus, by actually speaking to the right people, not imposing an external view, but getting an understanding of what people's real ambitions were and then applying those within the legal and commercial context that we had to work in.

One of the key ingredients of that and one of the things that probably sets Centrefarm apart from every other organisation in how it does its work, and certainly is a huge contributing factor to its success, is that we set up a structure that we ultimately called the Centrefarm Business Model, which was a culmination of a whole lot of things that came together at the time, and a whole lot of people's thinking. From my point of view I stand on giants' shoulders because I had Toly Sawenko, and Sam Miles, Tracker and David Ross. People like that who were actually doing a lot of thinking before I got near the place, and what I did was pull all those ideas together.

That business model in its purest sense was to create two separate entities, and those two separate entities deal with two different things. One dealt with Aboriginal law and custom and culture and it became an Aboriginal corporation, and the directors gave direction from there as they worked with the Aboriginal community. That Aboriginal corporation owned a commercial entity, which in the case of Ali Curung was called Ali Curung Horticulture Pty Ltd. And Ali Curung Horticulture did the business on that land. It was the agreement between the two organisations as to how they would work together that made Centrefarm a workable solution.

It was not lip service. We invested a hell of a lot in that relationship, but we do not make a lot of noise about this because we are operating in a commercial world, and people do not see some of the things we do, particularly when we are dealing with cultural issues as being commercially focused. We spend a hell of a lot of time and energy creating a song and dance Dream line, and create the environment for the Aboriginal community at Ali Curung to weave the new Dreaming story about the farm and its development and all that sort of thing into a cultural context that people can actually feel comfortable with.

One of the tools we used was painting. We painted our committee minutes on a large canvas. We would sit down with a canvas, have a meeting and as we did that, we would record the discussions on a canvas. This became a very large canvas, a painting that is now very complex, and is constantly worked on by people during the meetings, and it is the whole Dreaming story to that development.

It starts with western culture, and goes as far back as into Greek mythology. It starts at another level with Aboriginal culture and the Dreaming stories, particularly the Dreaming stories for Ali Curung. Both stories run parallel and then interlink, and the problems and difficulties and all that sort of thing are painted into the story. This is not walked past or ignored. They are now at the other end of that story, painting into the future and where that painting goes in the future. That painting is about two and a half metres wide by about eight or nine metres long now.

It is an important record. We made a conscious decision to do it like this, recording in Aboriginal language rather than keeping it as a black on white printed document that all legal forms take. I was at a meeting one day at Ali Curung and a lawyer stood up and held up a contract and said, *This is your agreement,* and everybody looked at it blankly. They had absolutely no idea what it was about. So next time I went to Ali Curung I took up some drawings and pictures and laid them out on the ground.

I never had any difficulty working with Tracker. Tracker would bustle in with an idea, we would examine it and talk about it. I would put it into some sort of context, and it would either sink or swim based on a few conversations. One of the things Tracker was pretty good at doing was letting something go if it was not going to work. Tracker and I had a great communication so we understood each other pretty well. He did not have that with everybody. We would look at an idea, turn it over in our minds, we would look at it from the perspective of a grand scheme, and then we would start to delve down into some of the practicalities of it. Other times we would take these ideas and walk around with them for a bit. Tracks and I travelled quite a lot, and we spent time in most of the capital cities of Australia trying to track down funding and support for things that we were doing, but he had an astonishing mind.

We probably got on well together because I have a similar way of viewing the world. I see it as endless possibilities and potential, and a lot of things do not work for reasons other than the fact that they are good ideas. You see a lot of this in Indigenous economic development. When I first started at Centrefarm the general attitude of everybody I came across, except for the board, was basically, *This is never going to work. It is never going to happen. You are wasting your time here, mate.* And to a degree that got my back up.

I was determined that I was not leaving until it did work. And we got over those hurdles, but a lot of them were manufactured in people's minds, they were not actually real. They were just things people said could not be done. They said Ali Curung could not be done, and I constantly battled with the bureaucracy and certainly with the Department of Environment, where we had all the agreements and everything in place, and they just would not allow us to go ahead and do what was needed to be done to start the project.

So I got to the stage where I just rang the contractor one day and sent him up there with his bulldozer and told him to do what needed to be done, and I would handle the fallout. I got a red-faced bureaucrat threatening me with gaol and all sorts of things. I hung my head and tugged the forelock, begged forgiveness and said, *Mate, I didn't know, I thought it was all good,* and away we went. They were hell-bent on stopping that project going forward. The only way to deal with it was to bulldoze them out of the way. Then as it turned out I had the support of the chief minister, and I had the support of the minister. I had the support of the heads of the department, but back in the middle-management area, particularly the Department of Environment, they did not want it to happen, and they were determined to stop it.

That was generally what we got, and Tracker and I did a hell of a lot of legwork and we banged on doors in Darwin, Alice Springs and Canberra time after time after time, and what I said to people was, *Okay you think it's a good idea, you think it won't work, but we think it will, so try not to stand in our way while we make it work.*

Some people got that and other people did not. The people that mattered did get it. I got really good support from the guy who was a topographer in the Northern Territory Primary Industries department. There were a couple of people there who really gave me good strong support to the point where they tipped a little bit of money into it, and gave us staff and all sorts of things. That was John Carroll and Matt Darcy and probably without them, it would not have worked. Tracker and I at least had them convinced that we were worth taking a punt on, that they were not going to lose from it and they could gain a lot, which ultimately they did. Unfortunately, Matt Darcy lost his job during that time and the guy that took over from him was very much a naysayer, but we had made enough ground by then not to be knocked off our perch so to speak.

I think there were a number of reasons for the negativity. There is a history of failed projects, and I spent a lot of time looking at those projects and trying to understand why they failed. One of the reasons we turned Centrefarm into a consulting group was because of that. We were not generating enough income to keep going by government grants, so we had to go and make money of our own.

One of the organisations we ended up working for was in Western Australia. They had a failed horticultural project there called Desert Gold and they were famous for the quality of their oranges. People in the old fruit markets in Perth – the older guys – still talk about how the best oranges in the world came from Wiluna. I looked at Wiluna and what happened. It had come down to a personality clash between two people, and that turned into a war that caused the whole project to fail. We set up a structure so that that could not occur again. There was clear division of responsibility and all of those sorts of things.

There was a history of failed projects, and one of the difficulties was to convince people that the way we were going about it was different to what had been done in the past. From the outside looking in it might seem like just another potentially fragile economic development project on the edge of where commercial projects can be developed. One of the things that really sticks in my mind is that, ultimately, the farm developed at Ali Curung was probably the most profitable farm in Australia, getting a sixty per cent return on the assets managed. Most farms in Australia get five per cent. It was a hugely profitable farm.

This guy had gone to the wall, and the only asset he had was the Ali Curung farm, and it was generating so much cash he was actually able to survive bankruptcy, so from a commercial point of view it was a very viable project. I was never in doubt of that. That is the sort of thing that underlined my determination to make it work, because I could see that the fundamental commercial aspects of it were fine, all we had to do was deal with the human complexities of it really, and that was the thing that took the difficulty.

The vision that Charlie Perkins had was an astonishing one and certainly Tracker benefited from that by sheer talent. He took Charlie's vision and made it Tracker's version. I think that is a wonderful legacy that Charlie passed on to those guys, and Tracker benefited greatly from it, but he was also a force of nature himself and made the visions his own, and grew them and increased them and turned them into something else. One of the things that people do not know or forget about Tracker is that he was probably the force behind Desert Knowledge which is a sizeable achievement in Alice Springs. It is now a forty million dollar installation with some of the world's leading desert research. At the end of the day if you follow the story lines back, you will find the start of that story was Tracker, but people forget that. Centrefarm will probably be the same. He is well remembered and honoured in Centrefarm at the moment, but in twenty years time will he be remembered as the driving force, the visionary that gave me the inspiration to do the hard yards? Probably not. Those stories need to be told. He needs to be remembered for the fact that he was visionary enough to plant the idea and fashion me to do the hard yards. He did that for a lot of people, not just me, a lot of people.

The Deal Is to Do a Deal

Ross Ainsworth

Tracker was always a big-picture man and there were not many people who had the vision that he had, and because he was dealing in an area where all the money would need to come from the ILC, or through the decision-making of the CLC, or the NLC, since those places either do not have funds, or have a board of people who do not have vision, or much adventure, or much experience, a lot of the time his ideas just did not get taken up. One of the great things about Tracker was that he did not get too despondent about it, he just went onto the next one.

I think there was no one theme, except that his ideas were often so big that they were too big, too broad, too expansive for most people to get their head around, and they were usually quite complicated, and needed a lot of people to get on board. Most people just are not interested in having to work that hard. They do not have the vision and the drive. They are sitting in their comfortable offices and the last thing they want is a massive project with lots of risks and dangers involved, and lots of management to do, and the risk of having it fall over. I think the biggest disappointment has probably been the ILC. Tracker had some huge ideas about what to do with the land purchasing, not so much land purchasing because there was already a lot of land purchased, but the management of the existing land. The ILC was largely to blame because they seemed very reluctant to do any sort of land management. Because all of these things need to be commercial, at least partially commercial, and most of the people in these Aboriginal bureaucracies are not commercial.

The enjoyment of land rights involved doing things differently. You cannot run a cattle station and then have the community there doing their own thing. It has all got to be one show. That was achieved on Mistake Creek because everyone understood their role and their responsibility on the farm, and we were quite successful in getting money to build houses and a school there. People could see results from playing the game. They did not have to steal killers because they were able to get them cheap through the store. They did not have to steal fuel because they were getting recompense from the company.

There is such a disconnect because it is an unusual situation where a group of three hundred to a thousand people technically own a cattle station, when they actually do not own anything. Nobody can get anything out of it unless the thing is structured to give something back to those people. These are the sort of things that the bureaucrats miss. Yes, the traditional owners own that land. Is it of any value to them? No. They have almost no rights unless it is structured properly. They can walk onto Wave Hill and go traditional hunting and have the ceremonies and all that, they can do that today, where they do not own the place.

But when they own the place, suddenly they go, *Okay we want to be getting something now, this is our place*, and the answer is, *No you don't, piss off*. So they feel as though they got shafted, which they have, but it was not anyone's intention, it was the actual outcome. What extra did they get from going through a land claim and all the bullshit, what now do they have that they did not have before? Zip. So unless you explain what they get now that they did not have before, and how they actually get something personally, physically out of it, they just feel shafted and react accordingly, as I would.

If I suddenly inherited Brunette Downs and went down there and said, *Righto boys, I'm here, what's next? Where do I get my meat? Where's my house? Where's my Toyota? Which house here is mine? Where am I going to stay?* what are they going to say? They're going to say, *No, no, no, piss off. Yes, you are a shareholder, but you get nothing so get lost*. I would not be happy. Tracker tried to address those things, and it needed the resources of something like the ILC with the capacity to put funding to physically manage the place, and to manage the interaction between the owners and the farm. That is the big management thing – that is the one that counts. It just never happened. The ILC and the Aboriginal Trust Fund and all that, they always had some pathetic bureaucratic reason why you may be able to buy the land in the first place, but then you could not access funds to get on with business once you did.

I thought that Tracker should have been stark raving mad considering all the bullshit that he had had to go through but he just got on with it, went to the next project and hopefully made it work and did not get too despondent about it. He was a very mentally resilient character.

The one clear overarching thing was that he was trying to achieve a better result for Aboriginal people without any particular group in mind. He honestly had that goal all the way along. No matter how or what we were talking about, it was not for him to get power, it was not for him to get money, it was not for someone else, it was always for the mob: *How can we get whatever we were trying to achieve* – primarily it was land or funding – *how do we get that land for the mob, and then move on from there.*

Once we got that, how do we not make them feel shafted once they get it? Unfortunately, from what I could tell, after we successfully arranged for the purchase of Carlton Hill they had a lot of internal strife about who owned what, and why they couldn't deal with different family groups who were squabbling about this, that and the other and so it was. I do not know who the winners and losers were, but that was the situation. The bureaucrats took over, and they in their wisdom made certain decisions, and then the mob ended up worse off. They ended up knowing they had their land back, but actually what did they get? One group gets more than the other group, someone has not got their house, where is my Toyota, all that sort of stuff. If you do not handle it well and everyone feels as though they have been screwed, they react accordingly, and that is when you end up with the shit fight that we have seen so often.

Owen Cole

The other thing that I do not think anyone really gave him credit for was with mining on Aboriginal land. He came along and said there was no Indigenous employment, there was no Indigenous enterprise development, no opportunities for it, and he basically said to the mining companies, unless you are prepared to do this, we are not going to renew your agreement, and he made all those employment opportunities possible, because he put the pressure on the mining companies. So they actually put it into the agreement where they said it was not *at their discretion*, it was like, *you will*. It was not *useful to our best endeavours to do this,* it was, *you will do this,* and he just kept the pressure on those big mining companies to do something.

This created a model across Australia. And later on Tracker and myself went over and worked with Carpentaria Land Council where he negotiated their mining agreements, where he was his usual aggressive self, and they got some great agreements out of it. His argument really was to give people the right to get involved in economic development, and if you are a player and can sit at the table, then you can influence what takes place. And that is exactly what he did. He would sit down at the table of Century mine and with those types of people, and he would talk to them as if they were equal. You are talking about managing directors and the like, and a lot of the Carpentaria Land Council had not had that sort of experience until he came along. He showed them that you could be an equal when you are talking about that sort of stuff. He was willing to take on anyone.

Tracker Tilmouth

There are some arguments in there, already sitting down under native title, about the exploitation of native title rights and interests from an Aboriginal perspective. Not taking the letter of the law that the land councils and the representative bodies [of native title holders] are holding onto. The letter of the law means we have a right to negotiate, or we have a right to be consulted and that these are all the rights you have. If you read it that way you might as well go home. If you expand it out, what does it actually mean in relation to a social dividend being delivered? How does that work? Who do the benefits accrue to? Until you have that worked out, the process you have now gives very slim pickings. That is the trouble with the land councils, they stuck directly to the letter of the law and they ended up with terrible agreements.

The MacArthur River Mines Agreements are a fucking nightmare because of the way they have been written. The Bootu Creek Mine

Agreement is shithouse. These agreements do not deliver anything to the community, there is no enforcement of the agreements. They were written by lawyers. They excluded a whole range of stuff that should have been part of it. They have excluded environmental rehabilitation. The destruction of sacred sites.

They do not know how to take advantage of the opportunities. The Bootu Creek mine is going to close in three to four years, and it has been open for ten years and there has been no benefit. There is financial benefit but there is no social benefit. You want financial benefit, go to the pub and watch the drunks in Tennant Creek. You can have a green can [of beer]. Beef and beer for a diet.

There is a huge amount of power in those areas. Financial power, legal power and these people [Aboriginal landowners] really do not know what they have got. They do not understand the process, but we have got people advising them. We have got the blind leading the blind. That is what we have got. That is the argument, how do I enjoy my land rights? How do I enjoy my native title? You don't. Why can't you? Because it is subject to so many rules and regulations. There is a term that they use in economics, minimal use of the utility. Utility means enjoyment or use of in an economic framework. So you have got bugger-all utility.

You have to think about these things on a huge scale, because it is huge. It is as broad and as large as this landscape. You have different groups and different areas, different timeframes, different aspirations. And they will say, *Look for an economic model,* and there isn't one. It is as individual as each group. Someone in the Carpentaria [Land Council region] will think differently to someone at Borroloola, or Borroloola will think differently to someone in Tennant Creek. Tennant Creek will think differently to someone at Pigeon Hole, and on and on you go. Docker River will be thinking entirely differently.

You have to be able to say, *Righto! What do you think about it?* It comes back to the basic processes of enjoyment. Are you really thinking about it because you want me to think about it? Are you telling me what you think you need me to know? Are you saying it just so I can piss off and get out of your hair? That is the question up front. And that is the power of communication. If you do not speak the language, or you do not understand the cultural basis, then it is very difficult to ascertain whether they are telling you what you want to hear, or telling you so you can you piss off, *and leave me alone.*

And that is the trouble with a lot of the leadership in the land councils. Hardly any of them have ever lived on a community for any length of time, or lived out bush. I think I was the only director of the Central Land Council that was a community advisor, and probably the only director that spoke the language, or can speak language. You have to have that relationship. If you do not have that then it is very difficult to understand if this is a real communication, or it's *Tracker you're fucking humbugging me, piss off.*

I present information or a proposition in very simple ideas. You know those maps with fences? You have a hole in the fence. You put it in cattleman's terms, because you are talking to blokes with big hats and big boots. If you are talking about a windmill and a bore, they get you, they know what you are talking about. The Land Rights Act is like a drafting pen, and why have a gate to use when we have so many holes in the fence? The trouble is we left the gates open and we still have the gates open. So you get every lunatic known to man, every idea known to man, out there practising on us.

And I change my approach. I say, I am finding great difficulty in understanding the Aboriginal position in relation to economic development, so I go to the other side to have a look from the other side of the fence, to look at resource assessment from the whitefella perspective. And you are looking at a high-risk venture. You are looking at a multi-million dollar project and at programs that are based on basic commodities. Forget about iron ore. Forget about base metals. This is the gate. Everything comes through the gate. This is how you build it. This is the way I think. For every twenty people, I think I get one person who is able to pick it up, or bits of it, but people find their own way anyway. Water finds its own level, so you have people finding out things and saying this is what I want to do and what I want to be in, not one size fits all. There is a mixture. Every agreement that has happened is a reflection on the community at that point in time.

I find that dealing with business people is pretty straightforward.

There is one thing that gets them every time and that is their greed. You can lay a trap, put money anywhere you like, and it is called access and equity. If you have access to a mining resource or a business person, then it is easy, quite easy, to do an agreement. The deal is to do a deal. You are either successful in doing the deal or you are not. It is a matter of trading off. And those rules are not set by you, they are set by the market, by commercial [interests]. Whether it's commodities, whether it's building houses, whether it's mining, whatever it is, resource development, those things are set by the market. We like to think it is a free market but it isn't: that is access to the resources.

If you do not have access to the resources to exploit your position or push the opportunity, then you go nowhere. This is the problem we have got. We do not have enough people, Aboriginal people, exposed to commercial activity. We were lucky in the Centre because we have David Ross – I call him the *capo dei capi* [the boss of the bosses] – who has built and held the Land Council together, and Owen Cole, and a few other people that were there early in the piece. This was a homegrown process. You go to other areas and you do not have that. You go to Melbourne, you go to Sydney, and there is nothing like it.

We have a lot of Aboriginal people walking around in suits, well-clothed and very articulate and everything else, but they contribute nothing to the economy. There is no return on the investment. We think there is a return on the investment, but I think it is a return on the rate of assimilation rather than investment. *How quick can we become white?* That is the problem. We forget where we came from. It was good the other day when [Noel] Pearson reminded us of where we came from: *Only those who have known discrimination truly know its evil. Only those who have never experienced prejudice can discount the importance of the Racial Discrimination Act.*[81] That is what you need, time and time again, you need someone to ring the bells and say we know what racial discrimination is, the malice, the positive and negative of it. And it was good of him to do it. That is why I have a lot of respect for the bloke. I have always had respect for him. I may not agree with him all the time

---

81. Referring to Noel Pearson's eulogy at the memorial service for Gough Whitlam, Sydney Town Hall, 5 November 2014.

but I have immense respect for him. He says what he says, he does what he does. Not many people get up and say what they think.

I have had a couple of requests from the oil and gas people because oil and gas is our leverage. We cannot afford the argument of fracking and non-fracking. The blacks cannot afford that. This is our leverage point on the treaty because all the new oil and gas finds are going to be where the treaty is. So we need wellhead values. We need production values. We need these things because they are going to be traded off on access and that is going to be our leverage point against federal governments of any ilk. But we are being taken out before we have even started talking about treaty, we have been taken out by the greens. The greens are coming for us. They are coming for us. To take us out of the debate for the blacks on fracking. No you won't. No way in the fucking world will you. We do not want to lose yet again another protest to a mob of greens that are wanting us to be without treaty, without land, without water, without anything.

They want to control it and that is the debate. So I said to [Martin] Ferguson, *Righto! I'm willing to go to war on behalf of the petroleum industry. You give me all the contracts, all the employment contracts on the maintenance programs for all the oil and gas fields.* You are the head of APA [Australia's largest natural gas infrastructure business], boss of British Gas, and on the board of AGL and they are the three biggest companies that I need. They can buy me ten drilling rigs and I will set up an Aboriginal contracting company. So I would say to the local blacks, *Well! there is a job there for you, if you want to stop these blokes getting a job, join us.*

And with blokes like [Murrandoo] Yanner sitting on the board to talk to them, he would be saying this has nothing to do with gas, it has to do with your land rights. It is a leverage point for your land rights. If you want to hand out the Kiran jewels off you go [to the world's largest manufacturer of diamonds]: *Please whitefella, be kind to me when you whip me.* The energy system, the energy debate is a good debate to be in because we need a treaty. We need a treaty so that we can say stop if you do not behave yourself. We can stop your access if you do not behave yourself.

We can do that through the Native Title Act on property rights and it is easy to do. You want to be fucked around, I can fuck you around. I can make sure your boats are not loaded. You want to fuck around, let's fuck around. You want to sit down and do business, let's do business.

That is the leverage point I am at. This is where we have got to be, to position ourselves from a financial and economic point of view, backed by a legal argument, a legal precedent, and the legal precedent is already there. We have been told by leading legal minds that *time immemorial* is there in Mabo and Wik. You do not need to go back to the High Court. All you need to do is read it out loud and the mining industry shits itself. It has been sitting there but nobody wants to pick it up. Yanner will pick it up tomorrow [if he wants to]. What we have got to do is build the economics of it.

Murrandoo Yanner

Recently with this gas mob, Tracker came along and helped us with the agreement. We have a nice agreement and part of the agreement was: *If you bastards want this to flow properly and effectively, and none of you even understand what we have just negotiated,* I told them, *you'll have to keep this bloke on for the next year or two to make sure the stuff flows smoothly and you mob understand, because you are opposite poles to us. Even though Tracks is with us, he can talk your lingo and can show you corporately how you can easily implement this or that, it's not a worry, it's not going to cost you anymore et cetera.* And then they dumped him.

Thinking they could, they even said to me, *Oh! We would rather deal with you direct.* And I said, *Yeah! But hey! You're fucking wasting your time because I'll only go back to him anyway after you've been to me.* But I could not tell them, and they went from buttering him up, *Thanks Tracks,* ringing him constantly with things, to nothing. He tried ringing them a few times and they were all avoiding him and not answering his calls, and a few things happened. One day I pulled up the drills out here [in the Gulf], drill rigs, and I just said, *Fuck it, stop them.* There was an environmental problem, and it also had a bit to do with this stuff. They were not following their agreement.

And suddenly in the middle of the night they were ringing Tracks, dead stop, boom, boom. Boom, boom, and Tracks said, *What are you doing Yanner, what's going on?* First he tried to ring me, but when I stopped the drill rigs I had been on the hop for two or three days around the place, and I just came back and went to sleep. I had just come back driving ten or twelve hours from Cairns or something. And so, *Yanner, the world's gone mad,* because the drill rig costs, out there with fifteen blokes working on it, sixty to a hundred grand a day. And it had stopped.

If I say, *I am getting out of this,* that throws their budget out and investors might walk. So they were shitting themselves, and I have gone to sleep and am out like a log. So Tracker rang Marnie [Carpentaria Land Council legal advisor], and he and Marnie start texting from Western Australia to Alice Springs or Darwin, and Marnie says, *I can't get the bugger, he's asleep,* and she said, *No good trying to wake him up.* Tracks texted her back saying, *My good and graceful Allah is resting. I don't think he hears normal prayers. We might be lucky for midday at the best.*

But I get up at three in the morning and call Tracker back, and he had been ringing me all day, and he said, *What are you doing to them drills?* I said, *Well! I stopped the bastards.* He said, *Alright! Well! They have been onto me now.* I said, *Well! That must be a good novelty, those bastards were dodging you. We'll teach them for doing that to you.* I meant it too, *Teach them a bit of respect, disrespecting you like that.*

Well! I told them that in the first place, *Don't do that because you don't even understand.* I think they had not figured Tracker out after the joking and the things he did. They thought he was a bit of a joker but, *You do not understand that this bloke, anything you tell us or want to do with us will only come back to him anyway. He is the main man with us on this level.* Tracks said, *Well! Don't do that. We might have to leave them for another day, brother.* I said, *Leave them for you, because that will teach them to mess you around.* Because, I said, *Don't you remember you were telling me a week ago these bastards were disrespecting your role? So this is as much for you, you know, to teach them.* He was like, *Alright, alright.* I told him, *Comrade, you've bloody got me burning flags and calling sovereignty, don't go soft on me now.*

He just laughed, and sent me back a couple of laugh texts. Then when it was all fixed and they were eating out of his hand, he rang and said, *Start her up.* So I ring the bloody CEO, or sent him a text at five in the morning. The rig had only been down and out of action about fourteen hours, and I said, *Okay, you can start the drill rig now,* and I went back to sleep. He texted back, *Oh! Thanks*. That was funny. Now we have got them over to the Territory to meet with them. We are setting up a big joint venture with the company and they are playing ball now. I think they realised who or what Tracker was, and not to be taken lightly or cheaply. But they tried the typical old divide and conquer, all that stuff, and tried buttering me up, *you don't need him* type of thing. But I did bloody need him and they could get stuffed.

I loved the bloody lad, I really did. Next to my dad, he was like a father figure to me and a brother, a teacher, and mentor. I could cry sometimes when I think about him. He was a good man.

5.

The Unreliable Witness

You're Supposed to
Kill It Before You Cook It

Alexis Wright

Do you remember that time when I was doing the *Take Power* book, and do you remember Mr Cook?[82] You used to call him *New York, New York*. He was a big boss, wasn't he? I did a session with him at a Land Council meeting, and it was recorded in Warlpiri. The recording took forty minutes and then he said, *Take that tape out*, and he had another tape, his own, and he wanted me to put it in the tape recorder and he said exactly the same thing again, and it took forty minutes. He kept the second tape. He did not want me to send a copy or anything, he wanted to do it there and then. His story was all about where people belonged. He said, *I might leave this on the table somewhere so people can pick it up and listen to it.* It was all about telling some people to get back to their own country.

That is it. Anyway we will see what happens.

Tracker Tilmouth and Peter Hansen

Tracker: Peter, this is what I did, I got them [people contributing to this book] to say what they want. I got people who I knew had an opinion on what I did, or what I did not do, to say what they thought, to involve themselves as well. Their agency in my development if you like. And when I come back later we will say, *Righto! This is what I have learnt off these people.* There are good things, there are bad things. There will be people speaking like [Bob] Beadman and people like that. Beadman taught me how to read tea leaves in a cup when he came to

---

82. Alexis Wright (ed.), *Take Power Like This Old Man Here: An Anthology of Writings Celebrating Twenty Years of Land Rights in Central Australia, 1977–1997* (Jukurrpa Books, Alice Springs, 1998).

talk to me about politics or Aboriginal development because he was in Aboriginal affairs for the last forty-odd years and nothing has worked, and he is still wondering why nothing has worked.

Peter: The people we went to school with on Croker Island were educated. That was the end of the 1950s and probably the 1960s, and they knew exactly what they had achieved. They could go to meetings and when they talked, you would know they were educated. They were taught by Europeans, but today we have still got people saying, *We must educate Aboriginals.* What happened between 1960 and 2013? That is some fifty years ago. We had everything in place in the 1950s and 1960s to educate Aboriginals, why are we still trying to get something in place in 2013? What a load of hogwash.

Tracker: Yes, we had people from the community who were at the top of our class. We had a bloke called the Reverend James Yunupingu who used to come and give us Bible class. James Galarrwuy Yunupingu, the reverend. And then another reverend called Gatjil Djerrkura. They were both reverends. Galarrwuy was taught by the church.

Peter: Another one is the Reverend Dr Djiniyini Gondarra OAM. When you see him on NITV, doesn't he give it to them! We want people like him, like Mansell – we want leaders, outside the fat cats. We do not want the fat cats to tell our story. They are not telling our story, they are telling their story so they can get more money and get fatter.

Doug Turner

Rubber lips to base. He called people different categories, different Aboriginal people from different areas, like mud monkeys or rock apes. Mud monkeys are the South Australians, and the rock apes are the Northern Territorian mobs, Mount Gillen and all that sort of stuff. *You mob are all rock apes up there anyway. Yeah! Well! You're all mud monkeys down there.* And he would call me either, I am not one hundred per cent sure whether I was base, or had rubber lips, because you see some blackfellas looked worse than others you know, and this was just the way that they looked, big nose, big lips, big foreheads. We would stir each other up like that. I said, *Yeah! Well! If I'm rubber lips you must be base.* Because base is more than rubber lips, bigger than bloody rubber lips. Yes, *B-A-S-E,* base, like this is base calling rubber lips. I said, if I am rubber lips you are bloody rubber lips yourself, because base is the foundation of rubber lips basically. Stupid things like that.

Yes, well, telling stories, that is who we are as people basically. We can tell a story from some people say thirty, some people say forty, some people say sixty, some people say eighty, some people say two hundred thousand years. This is what makes us, it is our nature, telling stories. Some of us have got a lot of stories to tell and some of us have a little bit of stories to tell.

Tracker knew his culture. There are a lot of Aboriginals with no culture and they should go back to culture, because culture is their foundation and for them to go back to culture that keeps them in touch with reality and who they are as a person basically. When they do it reinforces their desire for identity and their connection with country and with their culture, not so much with their people, but with their culture.

We shared our culture when we followed the songlines, and you did them ceremonies, and you did them dances on the songlines as you went across country. So we walked everywhere. This was how our population grew in different locations in the country because it is a big open vast land, and Aboriginal populations grew in that area and in that area, and there were more groups, say from the group that left my community, and walked to another part of Australia and practised culture there. That is how the story of *tjukurpa* up that way is similar to the *tjukurpa* in my country. We took that story, that *tjukurpa* from my mob and they practised it up there in say Queensland, or somewhere. We walked this country. This is why that rainbow snake travelled all over Australia. This is how come our culture is obviously similar to a lot of other Aboriginal and Indigenous groups around Australia, around the world.

If people go back to culture it gives them strength and it does affect the way that they tell our stories, because society is at such a fast pace these days, they should have time out to go back to culture, culture is not going and sitting on country, culture is learning about what the story was from this area. Where are the ceremonial sites? Where are the marked trees? Learning about where our fish traps are. Where are the paintings and all that stuff? Where was the mob that just walked in to do ceremonies? Which way did they come? That is going back to culture in a contemporary way. Unless you want to go and follow culture and you sit down with the old fellas in the bush and go the full hog, but even that would give them energy and inspiration. It is having that connection because that is what it does for me. I feel younger when I go back to culture.

I am sixty with many heart attacks, and the triple bypass that I have had, but when I go back to culture, I feel my energy comes back and I can do a lot more. I can run a little bit faster, I can dance a bit more, and I am not suffering with the heart issues after this. But when I go and sit down in the city I am a bit more sluggish, and I slow down a lot. When I am in the bush and culture I get up in the morning and I have got more energy, I just want to walk and do more things.

Yes, because Mamu Kuda, that bloke up there – the God they talk about, he was the one who gave us our culture and all the things in our culture to look after on this planet and the law – *tjukurpa*, and our stories. It was only that man that gave us these gifts and he gave us these gifts on this planet so that we can look after this planet, and we practise those things in our culture. Where do we go? We practise by looking about country and looking after that spirit in that place. We got that gift from that bloke upstairs. So when we go back to that cultural side of things then we can be blessed with little gifts, and those little gifts are to heal somebody with your hands. That is who I am.

They also give you another gift where you can not only heal that person with your hands, you can see the sickness in that person and how far that sickness has gone, and if it's in its early stages, say to that person look we can take that sickness out of you and clean you before that sickness gets the best of you. We can do that today. That is what our culture is about.

Vincent Forrester

The art of oratory is being able to tell a great story, and I suppose it comes from the droving days or when people had no radio, no TV, and your skill at being able to paint a picture by word had to be convincing. We have got to try to get that back, but we do have it in a way through you writing this bloody book, wow, that is a great storytelling method. The oratory of it, spinning a yarn, I love the way that Archie Roach does his songs, it is great storytelling coming through music. But to be able to tell a yarn, that is a different skill, the oratory of being able to talk, and be able to push your thoughts into place to achieve the climax of the story. I was taught that strategy by those old blokes.

I told them one day [as the Northern Territory chairman of the former National Aboriginal Conference], *I've got to talk to the Prime Minister every couple of months, what do you mob want?* They reckoned everything. I went away and thought about this word called *everything*, and it took me a long time to think about it, about three or four weeks, and I still could not work it out. I got them old blokes together again, and I reckoned, *Tjilpa Juta {many old men}, that word everything, that's a big word, where I got to start?* They said, *Oh! We go to the museum.* So we went to the museum, Tracker had done all this secret-sacred stuff, and that was where they wanted to start with all the sacred objects, all the *atyerrenge*, or *tjuringa*, with the Dutch museum, that was the first thing they wanted to do. And so that word, *everything* – Oh! Yes. That was starting from your spirituality. That taught me a lot, in that one strategy those old men had in their mind. They were right because we did go and chase those objects, and while we were chasing the objects, we saw a lot of bad things in that museum too, we saw all the bones of Aboriginal people and the TI [Torres Strait Islander] mob mummified, and all that kind of thing there. So we put the word out from there, that they have a lot of stuffed people in there. Then that started our human remains issues.

But this spirituality that the old people were talking about, we still have not achieved that because of the colonialist system that is in place, and assimilation and whatever you call it. Teaching language at school, maintaining that side of things is not happening. We see a lot of the mistakes being made by our leadership. They are literate in white man way, but they are illiterate in their own way. That is a big problem that we have with some of the current Aboriginal leadership. They say we know, but *wiya malpa {no friend}*, they do not know. They can not hear them old men words in their mind, or the song they sang that night for that story, right? That is another world.

That world is in your thought, in your mind, in your aura. That one! I am not touching you but I can feel you, that sort of stuff and the spirituality of all that, which is all healing, I believe. It is called healing because some of the stories I got from those old men, about when white man was shooting blackfella, how they overcome that and how they overcome their struggles, and passed their struggles on to me. Those old men told the truth because if they said that somebody was shot by the policeman here, you can guarantee it because you can go and see the remains of those people where they were burnt and that sort of stuff. That history is a hidden history that a colonial society would not admit to, but hang on a minute, there was a fucking big war and if you go back and look at the archives of some of the land councils, you will see it. They mentored me through that in my life, in the cultural aspects.

Blackfella got good comedy, blackfella he got a good sense of humour and we have only survived in this world because we can laugh, and we can laugh at ourselves too. Look at Tracker. We can laugh at ourselves but there is some sort of poison that comes out too by telling that story. In some cultures around the world they call it a method of cultural action teaching, teaching by telling yarns about that bully man policeman that has been chasing you, that type of thing. Passing on in humorous ways. I like that style. That's what makes us strong I think.

When I was with Tracker in Geneva he shocked me: *Tracker, you can't speak to fucking white people like that you black bastard. You will get into trouble. No, you watch,* he said, and no worries, he was so outrageous that they loved him. Whereas if it was you or I, they would probably call for the coppers, and they would say, *Hey! Look! Lock this mad bastard up.* He got away with it because of his confidence. Just confidence. He could push boundaries as though a horse would not bite him, or kick him, or the bull would not horn him.

I believe storytelling is a learnt and handed-down skill: the yarn-spinning and storytelling. I have seen masters at work in their oratory, in structuring their stories and the moral of the story, but in a bushman's way. A lot of city people would not understand what I am saying. There are these fantastic one-liners. Blackfella have got the one-liners. You just had to look at Tracker, at how he used his humour and one-liners. We can be pretty mean sometimes. In the bushman's wit, or blackfella wit, we had to have this humour to overcome adversity, but that humour, wit and storytelling has come down through generations, generations and generations through corroboree, *inma*, ceremony and so on. It is all there, where of course you have your theatre, your live acts, and performers within that. There is art, but also, it can be found just sitting around the campfire and telling those stories, and this is a blackfella trait.

There are traditional storytelling elements in the way we have been taught from childhood. For instance, how the Aboriginal economy works. When I was a little boy, I got my first kangaroo when I was about six years old. I took that kangaroo back to the camp and I gave it to my grandfather. First kangaroo. Oh! He made a big fuss that his grandson brought him a kangaroo. I can remember him getting the leaves and putting them down. I can remember the big fuss being made about it. He made a big fire this old man and gutted that kangaroo, really proud of that kangaroo, and he saved all the stuff, cut the tail off, cut the guts and rolled it up in a ball, after the coals burnt down he put it in the fire, the entrails next to the guts, and he cooked that kangaroo. Then he bought it out and started sharing it up. He cut it sitting on the ground, and he cut it in the back, and when he cut this kangaroo it fell to pieces. He gave it to everybody in the camp, a piece of that kangaroo, and everybody got a share of that kangaroo, and that was what taught me what an economy should be about. Their yarn was their way of explaining how to use the land, the animals, and the rules that apply, and it is a good way to tell the story. It is the foundations of what I use.

Geoff Clark

I remember when Tracker and Jakamarra Nelson and I went over to Geneva, and on our way over there we would go through Singapore, and as you walk around Singapore, you walk past these stalls and these blokes come out and try and get you to come in and eat a meal. They would be screaming out, and singing out, and the old Tracks started screaming out, singing back in language at him. This bloke was having a real conversation with him, and we were thinking what the hell is he saying. I do not know what Tracker was saying, but it was hilarious.

People were following us down the street trying to engage, and Tracker being the clown that he was and Jakamarra Nelson, he was very dark and a real traditional-looking fellow, it was quite an occasion I had with Tracker. Anyway, they must have known that Tracker was taking the mickey out of them because I think he ended up getting some salmonella poisoning or something. He got extremely sick, and I know that because me and Jakamarra and Tracker were sharing the same room, and Jakamarra was rubbing him down the traditional way, trying to pull the poison out of Tracker and singing and singing his language. Tracker was lying on the bed, and he was sort of delirious. We got him to the hospital and they gave him penicillin, and he was loaded up with penicillin but during that entire trip Tracker was still very sick. But it did not stop his sense of humour when we got to Geneva.

Me and the old Jakamarra, we would get on the piss at the Pickwick. It is sort of like an English pub, and we would get there and Jakamarra would be painting on the street. So Tracker would take him down all his paints then we would get a taxi down to the mall there and sit around. Jakamarra would be selling paintings for thousands of dollars, people were just absolutely fascinated and he would be singing the language, and playing the clap sticks. Every time Tracker would go and put the hat out, Jakamarra would be singing and I would be playing on the clap sticks, and selling his paintings and telling jokes to people. Tracker would be taking the mickey out of them most of the time even though he was still very sick.

Yes, it was just one circus, every day was a different day. It was like a travelling circus. We would be making jokes and Jakamarra was in a strange town, getting up and down escalators and believing that escalators were going to gobble him up. I think he actually made a painting which Tracker presented to the UN. There is another painting, it might have got auctioned off or something, and I think Paul Coe bought that painting. That was an historic painting. At that stage we were doing some pretty historical stuff on the declaration of indigenous peoples' rights, it was on one of those sessions.

A painting might have been presented to the chair lady. The Indians were doing a smoking ceremony, and Jakamarra did the painting. He certainly had clapsticks and stuff, and we introduced culture to the UN delegation. Since that time it became very popular that Indigenous peoples would bring their own culture, and they would come dressed, and have ceremonies and forming circles, and smoking ceremonies. It was probably a landmark occasion for Indigenous people globally, and those meetings started to get up to six, seven, eight hundred, or a thousand Indigenous people from around the world. Then people would start bringing their food. Inuit were bringing their whales, the whale meat and seal meat. We ate everything from apes in the jungles from South Africa, to whales in the Arctic, to kangaroo from Australia. It was quite a memorial sort of event. Tracker was always the clown of course. He would be holding court. There would be hundreds of Indigenous people sitting around and listening to Tracker's jokes. So a very popular man, and very intelligent in terms of the politics at the time and what we were trying to present.

Jacqui Katona

Tracker was always telling stories. It is hard to separate it as a technique, or to say this set of storytelling achieved these things. It is being able to tell it in a way that is relevant and resourceful for other people, so that other people can make use of it as well. He was very good at this. I do not want to say cultivating or training. It is like placing knowledge in the hands of people that could use it. I have seen him do that with people who have not had an opportunity to get an education. He would draw out the intelligence that those people have which other people would write off and dismiss. He saw them as being valuable, and contributors to something more positive.

And he always took everybody's input very seriously, and he always called for people's input. He would not let people stand to one side and be passive, he wanted everybody to be active in the process. That was gutsy for someone who had been an organisational leader because you can tend to rely on advisors, and seek some safety in a well-crafted, sophisticated statement, but he was not about that, he was about enlivening people whose lives were directly impacted by that sort of change.

He understood a lot about communicating effectively with people. He was an observer of people I believe, from a very young age. He was the type of person who had developed his perception very young and understood human engagement, whereas when you are growing up you are a bit oblivious to human engagement and why someone might be talking to you about a particular issue. But I think Tracker – I think this has got a lot to do with him being removed and institutionalised – had to try to rationalise or make sense of what happened to him and his brothers. He had to have a heightened awareness about the forces around them, and I think that tuned him in for the rest of his life like that. He found a way to actually harness what had happened to him and used it resourcefully.

Humour makes our lives a bit more liveable under the circumstances that most people find themselves in as Aboriginal people in this country, at being disenfranchised and marginalised from the broader society and made to feel like outcasts and illegitimate by those with an illegitimate place. Of course seeking legitimacy requires a great strength internally to assert our visibility in Australia, and the terms on which we want that visibility to take place. So humour is a way of taking the harshness away from the job that we have ahead of us, it plays an extremely important role, not only in terms of helping us think things through, and talking through and building relationships, but it probably protects our health as much as anything else.

Tracker used humour as a tool to try to get things achieved. There were so many times that Tracker made people laugh and shocked them. The story I like the best is the one about the voting booth. I am sure it was in Alice Springs where the CLP insisted on photographing individual voters at the booth and he could see this going on. He was furious because people were being intimidated of course to vote a certain way. He undid his belt and dropped his pants while they were taking the photos and gave them a brown eye. We just roared laughing when we heard that, but there was a very particular outcome that he was seeking, in a situation where we were outnumbered, and outgunned.

He was always saying things that shocked me. There is nothing that stands out, it is mostly everything was shocking. He had a cavalier attitude to most things, even his own illness. If he needed to go for a test – it was to get a torch shone up his arse to see if he had a heart beat. He was a burnt dim sim from radiation therapy. He had a way of characterising different people that he knew as well in a very comical way. He was calling me *Attila the Hen* there for a while. He was irreverent. He used humour all the time, and everybody would wait for him to see what he was going to say first. We used to call it *Trackeresque*, because there was a bit of a riddle to lots of things that he would talk about, as well as a lot of humour, but it kept people thinking about things too.

I think the concerns of Aboriginal people are most appropriate to storytelling, the painful issues, issues that cause people great anxiety, issues that relate to our powerlessness, or our inexperience, or our desire to move away from the status quo. And we use storytelling a lot. It is the most constructive way of communication amongst Aboriginal people because you do not discuss issues in isolation, you discuss issues as part of a continuum, not just with a focus, but an understanding of context as well which gives you a bigger picture.

Our storytelling definitely has a distinctive character. It is more effective for communication between Aboriginal people. I do not hear a lot of Aboriginal leaders using it as Tracker did. A lot of Aboriginal leaders do the non-Aboriginal political speak, to try to capture the media's attention, or to communicate in the media. But I have seen it at Aboriginal protests in 1985, and the protests of 1988, where large groups of Aboriginal people had gotten together and storytelling was at the fore, and there was a requirement that every Aboriginal person be recognised for their right to contribute to the discussions no matter whether it was part of the central idea, or it was peripheral to what was being discussed. There was a respect that was extended to every Aboriginal person attending. It was very supportive and reaffirming to have that ability because we do not have it anywhere else. But storytelling is one of the most important cultural obligations and responsibilities that we have.

It does not happen as much now, because people do not get together much these days. There is more of an emphasis on the individual and the sovereignty of the individual, not the sovereignty of the group and the issue of communal rights. People have acquiesced to native title for example, to schedule their rights and believe that that may be the extent of it, rather than looking at ways to expand on it. I do not know if that is because of the competing economic needs that people have, or their view of how culture changes. I think it is very important for people to have access to storytelling as a fundamental means of communication. It is not linear.

Story in one of its forms is narrative, and the narrative that white Australia accepts now is the narrative of a few Aboriginal people, because the narrative of more than a few seems to be unsettling, or not easily understood. In a lot of ways the scientific framework in which people understand issues rules out anything but a linear representation of issues. So context is ruled out, history is ruled out, an identity is ruled out, and it is becoming less widely known that there is a different world view that we ascribe to. Everybody thinks we are essentially the same as white people, we are just a bit darker and those that can speak English and go to school and get a job have got just as good a chance as any other Australian in succeeding. They do not even acknowledge anymore that our aims may be different, and maybe there are cultural imperatives that we want to meet. Those cultural imperatives are regarded as nothing.

Owen Cole

I can remember at the [Central Australia Aboriginal] Cattlemen's Association [conference at Uluru in the 1990s] where Tracker was talking about setting up this Association and how we would all feed into it, and set up an abattoir to send our cattle through, and how to split up the proceeds. It was pretty complicated. Tracker was trying to explain it and not having that much success and so he gets Harry Nelson, and Harry came along and he used the analogy of when you go out hunting: *That what we do is we all collectively do it and then we all sit down and we split it up* – Dah! Dah! Dah! All of a sudden, from a really complex sort of economic allocation issue, they were all nodding their heads because Harry explained what was really a traditional concept, and mind you, Harry could talk six languages as well so that helped. Tracker would always use cultural concepts to tell stories about how to explain really complex things and if the need arose, he would bring in people like Harry just to get the job done.

I cannot recall him not using stories to be quite honest. So if he was talking about [land] acquisition, say when we purchased Alcoota Station, he would go out there and tell the traditional owners the history of the place, and how *you people are all sitting in your community on the fringes of the pastoral property, and none of youse are sitting at the table, and it is time for you to change that. To do that, you have got to get involved.* That was quite interesting because his family came from out there, and one of his family was a bit of a right-winger if you can believe it, and not really that keen on seeing Aboriginal ownership of their traditional land, and Tracker had to turn that around and he would use a story by saying, *Look! Do you people really want to be sitting on the fringes of your own land and being told you can't do this and you can't do that, or else you can take it over.* He convinced the community that it was the right thing to do. It cost them a lot of money to purchase it, but it happened in the end.

He did get people to stand up and take notice of him, that was for sure. But he did not give a stuff, Tracker. I mean, I went and saw him when there were some negotiations, and they had set up camp in the suburbs of Canberra. They were going to negotiate with the Mining Council of Australia, and Tracker just goes to them, *This bloke Owen, he knows something about economics, none of you people do, and he's coming along.* This was a select group or delegation going up there, and no one dared argue with Tracker. Half of them did not know who in the bloody world I was. So we rocked up at this meeting, it was in Parliament House, and we were sitting across from the chairman of Rio and all that sort of thing, and talking about mining opportunities. That was when Tracker was pushing the point that we have got to get involved in our rights, in mining, and other economic opportunities. But he just broke all the rules. He did not give a shit about the protocol, the politically correct way of doing things. He just did what he thought at the time was the best thing.

I can remember quite a few occasions where he has got up and thrown his one-liners and turned the whole meeting upside down. Rossy used him like a live hand grenade. He was the more quiet and circumspect type of bloke, and he would send Tracker to throw a few hand grenades around the place, and then common sense would prevail after that, but Tracker would go in and whack a few people. Sometimes you wondered whether there was any rationale to the way he did things. I am sure there was, but he always wanted to shake people and get them out of their lethargic mood, and get them thinking far-out-there type of stuff.

I think in just about every project involving Tracker he used storytelling to explain the link to a contemporary issue with something that was relevant to remote community people in particular. His approach to life and the way he did things was completely different to anyone else's. There were no limits with that bloke. When you were dealing with traditional people, Tracker had the ability to sit down and talk on a level so that they could understand complex economic terms. He had the ability to sit down and relate totally with people, where some of them did not have high educational standards, and if he could not do it, he had the tools to get someone who could. He would bring in the right people to talk about it and explain it. He was a different character and we were much better off having him around and realised it. He was audacious, and when you have been pushed back and downtrodden for so long you feel a little bit intimidated, but he was always out there and in your face, and *here I am.* I think people like him really taught other Aboriginal people to get up and stand up for their rights and say, *Right! We want to do this, and we are not going to be intimidated by you.* He was never intimidated by anything. He did not know the meaning of the word. He did not give a stuff who you were, the Prime Minister or the Leader of the Opposition, he would talk straight to you.

Quite often David Ross and myself talked about Tracker, his approach and his totally unconstrained thinking. And of course his ability to put it across, it did not matter whether people liked it or not, he was always pushing, and pushing, and pushing. He always called me in whenever there was any sort of economic issue that was a little bit complex, and it is all good having economic grounding, but you need people who are ground-shakers and deal-makers and that was what he was. A bloke who could come up with the innovative ideas that nobody has even started on. I would just come in and help him really with the mechanics of it. He was an ideas person and he needed someone to do the groundwork and that was where I would come in. I am not anywhere near as creative as Tracker. I would not even start to consider myself that way.

We worked well, when it was Rossy, Tracker and myself. We were all different personalities and with different types of skills, but we got a few things done, bent every rule, not broken it, but we would like to think we bent it, modified it and that got the job done. That was what we liked to think, and down the track when sitting down and reflecting on the stuff we have done, planned land acquisition, economic development, a lot of it was real pioneering stuff.

David Ross

There were all sorts of other things that took place. I do not remember the year where we were in a Thai restaurant in Canberra. There was a big mob of people who must have been involved in native title and ongoing discussions, and that must have been around 1994 or 1995, in this restaurant in Kingston in Canberra. All sitting there having a beer, quite a few people in the place, a big table, a big mob of us, people from everywhere. The next thing you hear this cat crying, everybody could hear this cat screeching and quick as a flash Tracker yelled out, *You're supposed to kill it before you cook it.* Oh! Fuck, I just cried laughing. Geez, he was as quick as a flash, quick as a flash, *You're supposed to kill it before you cook it.* There were people eating. What could they do? He was funny. God it was funny. There were all these people who were not sure whether they should keep eating, or whether they were eating cat or chicken. Oh! God! Look it was one of the funniest things, true.

A few years back we were walking down the street in Canberra – Patrick Dodson, Peter Yu, Mickey Dodson, Tracker, and there might have been a few others. Me and Patrick were walking behind and he said to me, *Does this bloke ever sleep?* I said, *Why?* He said, *Well! He's got all these witty things.* He said, *He's got this wit and he's always got something as quick as a flash.* He said, *Does he dream these things up all night or what? Cause it's just bang, bang, bang.* This was Patrick's way of trying to come to terms with Tracker's wit. I said, *The bastard has been like that ever since I've known him and I've known him a long time.*

There was a downside to it. The sad part about it, Track came up with a lot of good ideas and good discussion, and then he would go and crack a joke at the end of it and everyone would remember the joke, and forget about everything else. I had tried to tell him over the years that when you have done all this work leave it at that. Make the jokes before or something but not while you are doing it, or you are going to lose people.

He had the knack of picking up quickly what people could relate to and what their background might be, and where they have come from, whether it was people from the bush who might have worked in the pastoral industry, or part of the Stolen Generation and how they grew up, or others, toffee-nosed people, so that they could understand the message he was trying to put across to them. Sometimes he could do this with two or three different groups of people all at the one meeting.

The other thing that was extraordinary about Tracker was that he had a photographic memory for things. I have tested him a number of times without telling him. I would give him stuff, *Here have a look at this*, and he would turn around and throw it all back at you. I had watched him do it many times. I watched Tracker sitting and reading and looking at stuff, being crammed full of whatever he needed to be crammed full of, and then he would go and deal with ministers and whoever else. He had that photographic ability or memory, to be crammed full of stuff and then regurgitate it and go *bang, bang, bang.* Most Aboriginal people I know have short-term memories, they have not got that greater long-term memory. This bloke's ability was to just throw it back at you. Be careful what you say to him, he was going to turn around and throw it all back at you.

I have been dragged by him, *Come on, you better come in here and meet these people.*

What for, it's nothing to do with me.

Just come in here.
Jesus.

Anyone. Anywhere. I heard all the aftermath of his travels, all the stories. His version and other people's versions. We travelled around this country quite a bit, extraordinary things, drove around out bush.

Big Chief, Little Laptop

Michael O'Connor

He was the sort of person where, if you were going somewhere and no one knew who you were, and you were with him, you would end up with ten or fifteen people around you pretty quickly. Or, they would want to know who you were in a room of a hundred, if you were tagging along with Tracker. He engaged with people very, very quickly. He had great social skills, I mean – unbelievable.

I went to the UN Climate Change Conference twice with him. He probably would not have known anybody there, but by day two he was dragging me around and introducing me to ministers of other countries, people he had met for the first time and won over. And one of the ways he did that, he told a whole range of stories which were often about his experiences growing up, different experiences, some of which seemed funny but also had very serious points to be made. You knew of him being a bit of a wild youth, getting into a bit of trouble, causing a bit of mischief. He talked about a range of things that were always of interest to me.

He talked about the early days in the Indigenous movement when he was involved as a young man, stories about Charlie Perkins and a whole range of Indigenous people who I have only heard about or read about. So you heard a lot of stories about what it was like then and the pressures they were under, and things they did. Of course I might have met one or two other people, but he was the first Indigenous person I ever met who had been on a kibbutz, and things like that.

Again he spoke with expertise and knowledge about arid farming, dry-land farming and all those sorts of things. He had views about what you could do in the Northern Territory. I saw him in different circumstances talking to people, but the one memory I have that really struck me was when he went to an Indigenous Business Conference and we both gave a discussion, a little talk about what forestry could do for Indigenous communities, and that included the issue of carbon, valuation and jobs, et cetera, and what I remember was the way in which all these young people, mostly young, Indigenous people, gravitated towards him. And they just listened to every word he had to say.

It was really amazing and he talked about how he got to know language and the time he spent with his Uncle and Aunty on the land, and I just sat there watching it. Sometimes when he was telling those stories about learning about his culture you could hear a pin drop amongst young Indigenous people who wished that they had had the opportunity to do that. That was a memory I think I will take to my grave, that really struck me.

His life experiences were amazing. I mean I do not know anybody with his breadth of different types of experiences, which I thought were pretty unique. Another time I remember him clearly was the day of the Apology [to the Stolen Generations]. I happened to be in Canberra more by accident than design that day. I reckon he rang me four or five times, and he refused to go. He refused to go. And he rang me and I know he rang a number of other people who were in Canberra at the time, and he was very, very agitated, I remember that.

I can only surmise the reason why he was agitated, but it was a really emotional day for a lot of people for a lot of reasons. I cannot remember if it was before or just after the day of the Apology but there had been a CFMEU conference, and for the first time since I had known him, he brought down a photo album. That was the first time he had shown me pictures of his siblings. He told me where they all got sent. I think it was a very tough day for him. Very, very tough day.

I do not know how you cope with that sort of experience. He was ringing because he knew I was there in Canberra, things were going on, and I think it was probably to ask me what was happening. He did not want to go but he wanted to know what was happening. He was clearly going through a pretty stressful time. And of course I think, and I might be wrong, I got the impression he was still shitty. There was this great celebration about the Apology but there was all this work still to be done that no one was paying attention to. He told me that on the day that the Apology occurred, the Northern Territory Government had restructured the councils [on Aboriginal communities] and really marginalised Indigenous voices in local government. That was one of the impacts of it. He was just going, *Well! Isn't that typical?* So I think he was torn about the day.

There is no doubt there is a point to most of his stories. Basically a lot of his stories might be amusing and funny, but they were often funny stories about badly-designed government policies that would lead to ridiculous processes or outcomes, or the incompetence of people involved in Indigenous affairs. These might be amusing stories, but they would also be about his experience of being an Indigenous person growing up in this country. Because he was a storyteller, you wanted to listen to him. I do not think you realised how much knowledge he was actually imparting to you about his experience, and about experiences he had lived through.

Again, I do not think you can ask people to be patient when they have spent decades banging their head against a wall seeing some of the things that he had seen, that should not have occurred, or things that should occur that did not occur. I do not know how people cope with dealing with some of the issues he did, day in and day out, without completely dropping the bundle, or being so bitter about it, and the lack of progress. I mean with the housing program [in the Northern Territory under the Intervention], I was there when he told people that the housing program would be delayed, it would not happen, it was too slow. At the end of the day he just could not get people to do it. They were not interested. Just following things that have failed before, you have to think it is amazing the mindset where you keep repeating actions which have led to shit results. You think, *How can that keep occurring?* The housing stuff for instance, it took fourteen months or something before they built one house. Something ridiculous.

He had heaps of stories. I used to take his stories and tell them myself, not as well as he could, but I have had tables in stitches with some of the stories he had told me; the ones about his mate Bluey. I think Bluey is a crocodile farmer, and there was one about the guy going to get croc eggs with two young fellas. One has the paddle and one's got the gun and the croc turns up and the guy drops the paddle and runs off, and the other one jumps on Bluey's shoulders and shits himself. Shit was running down Bluey's neck and he could not see the croc because the kid, the young fella's got his hands over Bluey's eyes, and he's feeling the hot shit coming out. Oh! He just had people rolling around laughing so hard they had tears coming out of their eyes.

And then there was the one he told about when Bluey was being lowered by the helicopter on a rope and he was being lowered down into [a croc's nest], and there was a big female croc there with her jaws wide open. Bluey got on the two-way radio but the helicopter pilot could not hear him, so he starts to swing. He is swinging himself to and fro trying to get through on the radio and he can't. He pulls a gun, and he's swinging and he ends up shooting the top of his foot off. Those stories.

The ones from when Tracker was very young and living in Darwin, when him and his mate were doing a bit of redistribution of wealth from house to house, and they go to this house – it had been cased – *this is a good house to go to*. They go and get in and they are creeping around the house. It is empty. And then eventually Tracker, he has the torch and he looks, and there are these photos on the table and he looks at the photos, he looks at his mate and he looks at the photos and he looks at his mate, and he goes, *That's you in the photo*. It was his house. I just could not believe that one. I think it was the police force or something in Darwin where the car used to break down all the time and they used to come out and push it. The wagon with the copper, and they could have all run off but they didn't. They had to push. There were some funny stories there.

Of course he had some good stories too about all the different pollies he knew. He got me a couple of beauties. We were at the United Nations Climate Change Conference, at the union caucus which was about a hundred and thirty people, and we had to all go around and introduce ourselves, and say who we were, and where we come from. Tracker got up before me. I did not know what to do. Now what did he say? He said, *Yes, I'm Tracker Tilmouth. I'm from Australia and the whitefellas stole my country*. He looked down at me and gave me a big wink. What was I supposed to say after that? *Yeah! I stole it*. It was stuff like that.

And then someone said to him – there were all these Yanks coming up, and because when we were over there the film *Australia* came out with Nicole Kidman, they said, have you seen the film *Australia*?

He goes, *Seen it, see the little kid?* They go, *Yeah, yeah.* And he goes, *That's fucking me, except I was better looking.* They did not know whether to believe him or not. It was quite funny. His funny side you would not believe. He was so witty.

We were in the union caucus and he started talking to the leader of the union, the international trade union, and he goes, *What's the Indigenous group doing?* And I said, *I don't know.* And I was saying I could not believe this because there was an Indigenous caucus as well at the UN Climate Change Conference. And they go, *We don't know. Hang on why don't we have a discussion with the Indigenous group?* We had a copy of their agendas and things and it was about land rights. Anyway we got the job, Tracker and I got the job to go scout them out and find out what was going on. Everybody had their little secretariat, their own little room, like the business people did, environmental groups and whatever, so there was this small room there for the Indigenous caucus. And so I went there with Tracker and we stuck our heads in and there was a guy, and if he was an inch, I reckoned he was about six foot ten. He was six foot ten, he was huge, fifteen or sixteen stone, six ten, from North America. He had the headband, the long hair, the jeans with belt buckles, the lot, right, and he was typing away at the smallest laptop I have ever seen in my life. Tracker sticks his head in and goes, *Hey big chief, little laptop, how ya going?* And Tracker looks at me and goes, *Don't you try that.* I could not believe it.

It was funny, *big chief, little laptop*. I will take that to my grave, that one. But it was truly amazing how he cut through a whole range of stuff there. He could do the UN process pretty well. He knew how things operated. He could read the play because he had been involved with a lot of the UN processes to do with land rights and the rights of Indigenous people. So he was going full on and he was basically saying, *I know how it works, this is what will happen here, this is what is going on here, this is how they will play the game here.* He just knew it. He was like an antenna.

Nathan Miller

I do not think the way I knew Tracker that storytelling was the issue. I think everyone saw Tracker in different situations and different ways but I did not see him from a storytelling point of view. I saw him from a vision point of view. I saw him from an objectives point of view, enthusiasm point of view, and ideas. Those are the four things that I actually saw more than the others. His strategy would be communication, humour and just making you follow him, or at least walk beside him if not following him, whether you liked it or not. I had asked Tracker, *What do you want me to say?* He said to me, *You could always say I'm a gentleman.* I said to him, *I'm not going to lie, and I don't associate myself with gentlemen.* I think that was one of his main qualities, he was a gentleman and he had a soft heart, and a good heart, but the coat he was wearing was not that of a gentleman, just one fastened like a traveller.

I reckon if I can give it a title, Tracker was a traveller of ideas. He was very good with identifying and seeing opportunities. Some were realistic, and some of them were not. The problem was, he did not take the unrealistic ones away, he used them all. And the thing was, he would use a shotgun, shoot out ten ideas, and maybe if one would catch that would have been enough. You understand what I am saying? He was taking all the opportunities, realistic or not realistic, hoping that the unrealistic maybe would become realistic in one way or another, and with him saying, *I will try them all and if I get one of them I am okay.*

I also think one of the things that helped him, was a lot of white Australians like to be associated with Aboriginals because it makes them feel good. He had well-educated white people, especially within the circles that he was messing around with, who could speak with him and feel comfortable with him from an educational point of view and make themselves feel good because, *I have got an Aboriginal friend.*

I think it is true. I did not research it but the fact is that a lot of white people understand that Aboriginals have been done wrong in this country and want to feel good somehow. By having an Aboriginal friend they feel good, but on the other hand, let's say the majority of Aboriginals living in the country or even in the poor suburbs of the big cities, they are not the Aboriginal people that white people usually associate with. But the minute they have an educated Aboriginal who can speak with anyone else, it makes them feel very good. I think so, I do not know. That is my observation. I might be wrong. I think

Tracker utilised this. For him it was another vehicle. On the other hand people eventually forgot the idea that he was an Aboriginal and just enjoyed him as a person. He managed to do it. I think with Tracker, although he was working for the Aboriginal people, they associated with him at the end of the day, divorced themselves from the fact that he was Aboriginal and just looked at him as another mate. At least I did. I did not care if he was Aboriginal or not. Every circle he walked into he enriched it. I worked with and met him a lot, but Lindsay [my wife] met him once, and the day she met him she fell in love with him. I am serious. I do not know why and I am not asking.

His stories and sayings were like so many grains, where you are unable to pick up a grain or even remember it. You take a patch of land, it is millions of grains, you cannot pick up the grains, but you remember the land. If you look at a painting, you can go very close and you see a lot of little strokes but you will not remember them, and when you walk back you will see the full picture, which all of the strokes brought together to form the picture. So, little sayings! I cannot remember, but at the end of the day his character came out of these sayings. I can identify the character but I cannot identify the little sayings. Everything with me is art and easy for me to explain like that.

I liked being associated with Tracker. I liked to talk with him. I liked to phone him. I liked just to talk nonsense with him. I liked him as a friend. Because at the end of the day I know a lot of people. I have travelled the world, I have lived in at least three countries in my life, and I can tell you I have never met another person like Tracker. Not as a personality. With all the good and bad, I am not trying to say that Tracker was a perfect person, he was the epitome of good friendship, and a good person to be in contact with. I do not know if he held grudges or not, I did not know him from that point of view. With me, my relationship with him was always digging each other, he would laugh at me, or tease me, or whatever, and I would do the same to him.

For instance he would phone me and come up with some ideas or whatever it was, and I would say to him, *Tracker, next time you phone me ask yourself, am I going to talk crap or not, and then make a decision if you want to phone me.* And he did not get upset about it. He would expect me to say it. And the same would be vice versa. How many people can you say something like that to? He would not even listen to what I said. He would just brush it off. I could say, *Tracker, you know you're talking nonsense so why are you talking about it?* He just switched to another idea very quickly.

He was a casual person, and he liked people. He looked at people as resources. He would use people but not in a bad way, you understand. He would use them for objectives but at the end of the day they are good objectives. So if he used me, it was not that I did not know he was using me. I knew, but I knew what he was using me for and I was happy to be used for it. Even if he thought he was actually tricking me. I hope he liked me. I definitely liked him.

The success of Tracker's stories was that he managed to make me a groupie. Groupie is a bit of a strong word but I had a lot of time for Tracker. But the stories, what I laugh at all the time, was the way he would call me out of the blue and say nothing, just phone me out of the blue, then all of sudden bombard me and expect me to raise fifty million dollars – like within three days, when I do not have fifty dollars in my pocket. He would say, *We've got that, that, that, we need – we will put in the infrastructure – and you, et cetera – twenty million dollars.* He was funny, he was really funny.

Hello Natives, How Are You?

Sean Bowden

I nearly drove off the road one time when we were driving out to Wadeye. We didn't only fly, we would drive. We did this journey a lot and we would camp out, spend three or four days working there. Tracker gave me his tuckerbox at one point and I still have it. I use it all the time. He brought it over and said, *Here Bowds, I'm giving this to you.* He does not give many things away, Tracker. A ceremonial thing almost, handing this thing to me. It is a great tuckerbox. We had done all these trips and I did not have a tuckerbox, and he produced it and then when we had finished the trip, he said *you keep it.*

Incredible things have happened along the way. We would catch fish. We would stop, and there was an abattoir there at a place called Palumpa which was about an hour from Wadeye in those days, and he would just walk into the fridge and cut the best meat himself off a hanging beast because he was a butcher and he knew where the best piece was.

First he would go in and say, *What have you got for sale?* There was a whitefella there usually and he would produce this crappy blade beef or something – mince, but Tracker, he would just walk into the fridge and say, *Oh! You blokes give me a knife.* He would walk in and cut the rib eye off the bone, off the carcass. And it was beautiful, the best meat you have ever eaten.

Then he got worked up one day after we had stopped in to buy some meat at Palumpa because he had been done over by a non-Aboriginal consultant that got in his way at a meeting – nothing he hated more. He tolerated us non-Aboriginal players until we got in his way, then he would get vicious and I have been on the end of that. I've got three or four stories that are horrible, things that he has done to me, where his temper had flared to the point where I threatened to come around and fight him one night. I was that angry. I was so furious with what he had done.

Although the next morning I was full of remorse. I rang him and apologised. *Bowds, you don't have to apologise, you're my mate.* Which just floored me. I had said terrible things to him. I had said, *Look, if I was there now I'd punch your head in, I would not be able to control myself. I'm so angry at you. You are low, what you've done.* He told a story about me that was not true and he told it to a very important mutual friend of ours, it was a lie. He knew it was a lie but he did it to hurt me. It did hurt me and it caused me trouble.

Anyway, we were driving along and he starts parrot-talking in this high-pitched nasal voice, like he was Queen Elizabeth, about how that day this guy spoke to the meeting in pidgin English, and did not want Tracker in the meeting, because this guy only wanted to speak to the traditional landowners. Tracks was infuriated by this and created a narrative of what he would do the next time he was in a meeting with this bloke. He said, *I've had it with these guys speaking pidgin English, I've had it.* He said, *The next time I have a meeting, and there's another one speaking pidgin English, I'm going to get them to carry me into the meeting on one of those pontoons that the Queen sits on, and I'm going to wear my long socks and I'm going to address the meeting. I'm then going to have these whitefellas sit down in front of me, and I will say* – adopting Queen Elizabeth's voice – *Hello natives, how are you? I am here, to teach you to speak in the Queen's English and then after you have learnt to speak properly, you will carry me further on high, and we will meet the Aboriginal owners of this land and you and we will both speak to them in the Queen's English.* He just went on and on with this story to the point that I was laughing so much, I nearly drove off the road.

Greg Crough

I think if you look at a lot of Aboriginal people in the bush, even generally, but particularly concerning the remote areas, the white people they are often dealing with are what I think Tracker would call *white trash* a lot of the time. And I think there was a perception among Aboriginal people that this is what all white people are like. The people who work in community stores or Aboriginal organisations, in government agencies out in those communities, I do not want to stereotype them, but they are very similar in some respects to each other. That is not the way the rest of society is like, it is much more complex, you are dealing with much more sophisticated structures and systems. He thought that people needed to understand that the person they were dealing with is not necessarily the way this society operates. You need to get behind them and understand the relationships, in the same way that he always said, *They do not understand the relationships between Aboriginal people either.*

The ways that you all relate to each other, the families and the structures in Aboriginal society, and the organisations, not just the personal relationships, are very complex. White society is the same, and you need to move beyond just that person you see in the community store, or the ATSIC person, or the DAA person who comes out every now and again. You need to understand the complexities of it because otherwise you're not going to be able to deal with it properly. And to deal with it you need to get yourselves organised as well. From his own perspective I think he felt he had enough strength and enough nous to understand and deal with these things, but he realised that a lot of people were not sophisticated enough to deal with white society on the terms that he could because they did not fully understand it. So I think he always saw: *I need to tell you how it works so you can work out how to deal with it.* He was telling stories about this is how the government works, this is how funding of Aboriginal programs works. This is how companies operate. You need to understand this and work it out, otherwise you are just going to be a passive recipient of whatever happens to you.

One of the things I noticed he did is if he took some people to a meeting, he would explain to the other people there, the business people or whatever, who these people were that they were dealing with. I did not feel that he ever got up front and had the black faces behind him, and just spoke on their behalf. It was, *This is who you are dealing with, this is such and such, this is how they're are relating to each other. You need as white people to understand how these people work together.*

I'm not just here to talk on their behalf, just bring them along to show you we have Aboriginal people behind us. I always thought he tried to do that. He was not always successful but he would try to get people to speak, to understand what was going on, and get the non-Aboriginal people there to better understand what they were dealing with as well. He would definitely try to get people involved: *I'm not here to speak on your behalf, you need to speak and you need to tell these people what your perspective on this is.* I saw him a number of times do exactly that. *There is no point you being here if you don't participate.*

One advantage Tracker obviously had was that he found out where he came from after he was taken away. He re-established many of those connections with people and the communities where he came from, and he understood that he was able to have a deeper understanding of something that he lost when he was taken away. Whether you consider that traditional storytelling or whatever it is, he did understand where he came from, where people related to each other, where the traditional stories were and why they were important. And to use that in various circumstances. He was very much a transitional figure. Maybe that is not the right word but he had enough understanding of the way white society operated, and he had enough understanding of his own community, to bridge the gap between them better than many other people at the time.

I would say he was very iconoclastic in the sense that nothing was sacred. I know this is out of the Aboriginal context, but nothing was sacred to him. He would say things and put his point of view to the Prime Minister right down to somebody in a community of ten people out in the middle of Central Australia. I have never really fully understood whether part of the way he spoke and his humour and some of the things he said was because there was an underlying lack of confidence in himself. You know I never saw him as a big-noting, completely overconfident sort of person, and at times you felt he was trying to get through as best he could with the skill base that he had. I don't want to say it was a lack of confidence, but he was always held back a bit by that, and he dealt with it by saying things that at times maybe he should not have said. He was not the sophisticated, urbane, vain sort of person that glided through things, and he was very rough around the edges, but he also had a very sophisticated understanding of what he was trying to do and how to do it, even if those rough edges came through a lot of the time.

Nicole Courtman

Another thing I had seen Tracker do, was to talk about the loss of language and culture with mining companies, or to a related industry person, or a contractor to mining. In this case it was a white fellow who was from England, and Tracker was trying to get his head around the context that Aboriginal people are in, trying to teach him a bit about culture and words, and those sorts of things. And having this captive audience, where here was this English guy sitting there and not knowing much about Aboriginal people; well not knowing anything really about Aboriginal Australia at all, and probably the first time he had sat around with a group of Aboriginal people; and Tracker was capturing his imagination and telling him a little bit about culture and helping to facilitate the group to do that, to talk about language and art, and music, and those sorts of cultural things.

Once he had the person captured he was then able to draw attention to the fact that so much of that had been lost because of the impact of invasion, however you want to refer to it. And you could really see that by doing the storytelling what he was doing, rather than give someone a history book to read or any of those things, he had the man sitting there with people who were capturing his attention and engaging with him, and then Tracker would say – *Hang on, this has happened to these people and they are real.* And to see the shift in thinking by that executive was just incredible.

But it was done so subtly, and with humour. One minute laughing, and then adding a little line that went, *Oh! You were laughing but it was not funny.* We were all laughing, sometimes you laugh because there is nothing else that you can do, and that is something in our work. All the time there will be situations where you have a laugh. It was not so much because it was a funny situation, it was more like an emotional release. In terms of storytelling, I guess the impact is the key thing that a lot of non-Aboriginal people do not understand. Most people are interested in learning about the culture and about Aboriginal people, but the reality of the impact of invasion on people is a hard topic to broach and learning ways to do that is really important.

I agree that Aboriginal storytelling has a distinctive character. In the situation I was describing, Tracker actually talked about the landscape of an area in north-west Queensland. He had a lot of knowledge of that area because his wife is from around there, but he was there with traditional owners. My understanding is that you do not talk about a country unless you are from there, or you have permission to talk about it. He was there with the traditional owners of that land, with their permission to talk about it. He was talking about stories for explaining that natural environment, the hills in that area, and the storytelling that surrounds the environment there, and he was doing that to capture the imagination of the executive from corporate Australia, and he was very clever at how he captured his imagination. He told the story and then brought humour to make the point that so much of this has been lost. We have still got people, obviously, with connection to country, and the culture has not died, but there has been an impact on it. So he was translating traditional storytelling into a language that a non-Aboriginal person could understand. And the traditional storytelling always has something like a moral element to it, and he was adapting that for the particular purposes of a practical negotiation at the same time.

Toly Sawenko

The thing about traditional societies was that a lot of the communication was oral, it was spoken, it was people. A lot of the communication was face-to-face, oral communication. It was people in groups talking about issues. It was people passing on information and knowledge. That, I think, is still a favoured way of doing business among Aboriginal communities. People do not like to rely on bits of paper floating around. Quite often the task of having a meeting at a community on Land Council business which Tracker was involved with, or any other member of the Land Council was involved with, was breaking down what was written on a piece of paper from government or business or mining, and actually converting it into a story that people could understand, and to communicate verbally and orally in language that made sense to people. There is a link between that favoured way of communicating and Tracker always preferring to deal with people conversationally and face to face. Or when it was over the phone, the million mobile phone calls, or else in a meeting or a gathering, he did not rely on written communication very much. He did not rely on words on paper. He took that key element from traditional Aboriginal methods of communication and he used it in different platforms. He used it in official meetings for work and all the rest of it, but he also used it in his dealing with people.

He understood the ideas and metaphors, if you like, that people relate to. In rural bush communities there are certain things that everyone is familiar with. People are familiar with fences. They are familiar with roads. They are familiar with gates. They are familiar with a whole bunch of ideas and images from that world. And he would use those in his language to express ideas. So if he wanted to talk about the role of the Land Council, he would say that the Land Council was like a protective fence around an area of land, which is what matters to people. In that land is the culture and the way of life, and people making decisions for themselves. He used the analogy of the fenced area as a way of showing what the Land Council did, and the Land Council were the people who controlled the gate, who could come in and what they could do there. But also, to make sure that they left and the gate was closed so that people were not disturbed or interfered with, and that they dealt with people outside their world on their own terms. He was very good at using analogies like that, that people could understand to express what would otherwise be a fairly complicated idea.

He understood what people cared about and he was very mindful of how he could relate to that. He operated in a number of worlds. He operated in the traditional world of people living their life on the land. He operated in the world of bureaucracies and he operated in the world of politics. He operated in the world of business. He was comfortable in all those places and could operate effectively in them. It was just something that he regarded as essential to what he wanted to do.

Geoffrey Bagshaw

A characteristic of Tracker was a profound optimism that things would work out. That does not mean to say that there was not a lot of hard work, and a lot of pain and anguish and so on to be gone through, but in the end, things would work out if one applied oneself to them. The flip side of that coin was that he was not disenchanted. A lot of people have become that. They have burnt out.

A really important thing about Tracker was the way he engaged people and that allowed him to tell his story and the story of people, particularly in Central Australia. In the traditional context, humour is pretty much number one. It infuses most aspects of social relations. I have been in some very funny situations, in all contexts, in funerals and so on. Humour I think has a universal human effect of relieving tension, relaxing people, allowing them to focus on the relationship between individuals rather than the relationship between individuals and abstract ideas. I suspect it was for that reason that Tracker had been so successful in Central Australia, precisely because of the humour.

Maybe Tracker just had that natural inclination towards humour but I think he was aware too that humour was an important dimension of interpersonal relations in a traditional context. I last saw Tracker probably in 2010 or 2011, and I was walking down Mitchell Street in Darwin, and I get this call from across the other side of the road. Who is it? It was Tracker. It struck me that although he was really grounded in Central Australia, he operated comfortably and familiarly in the Top End as well, and I think the whole Croker Island experience had a lot to do with that. Often I have seen the opposite was the case, where Aboriginal people felt, *Oh! God no, I'm petrified because it's somebody else's country and I can't talk. I've just got to sit quietly.* He was not like that. He would engage people across the board.

One thing that I think was probably true of Tracker, and in my experience is true of Aboriginal storytelling generally, is that of always contextualising in terms of personal relationships. It is not just saying *I met a bloke who told me this*, but *I met so and so, who is so and so's cousin, who told me this in relation to a third party's brother.* It is locating the story and probably yourself as the narrator within that field of interpersonal relations. Traditionally kinship is the idiom of social relatedness, but I think more broadly today it is all about: *Well! You can't tell a story without saying how the actors are related to each other and ideally what your relationship is with them.* I think that is almost a diagnostic aspect of Aboriginal storytelling that there is nothing in the abstract. It is not just telling a story for a story's sake, or to say the abstract principal or the moral of the story stands on its own. No it doesn't. It only stands, it only has meaning, in relation to the actors involved and their relationships.

Also, one of the aspects of storytelling is that there is a lot of recourse to the authority, the imputed authority of people who have gone before, old people. Now, if you look at things like genealogies and oral histories, old people were not doing things much differently to anybody else. There was not a pure, theoretically correct cultural world at all, with a lot of the things going down, but nonetheless because these stories have been passed on or refer to people who are no longer around, they have an authority. Tracker, too, had an awareness of the views of the old people, and that is an important thing about his approach, and also Rossy's. They are aware of what the old guys said. They knew the people who were around at the time, of what Wenten Rubuntja said, or whoever, and who now have the lineament of myth almost. They were old people who were important. Tracker was aware of that, and he was also aware that things change, that there is a dynamic aspect to social, political and economic relations, and he was not burdened by the past, but not uninformed about it either, and brought with him a sense of the past, the importance of what old people were saying, to his involvement with any particular issue.

Richie Howitt

It does seem to me that one of the hallmarks of the storytelling tradition is that the story is always contextual and so when it gets repeated, you will end up with the story being told by a good storyteller in a way that responds to the circumstances of the listeners. In that sense, understanding the story and the telling as the means of a transformational moment, where you shift people into a new understanding of context, that is actually storytelling at its best, and Tracker's storytelling did reflect a lot of that. He was perhaps a little less sensitive to context sometimes, because it was such a good story, but he would tell it again and again as it worked in other contexts. At his best he tuned into exactly what would shift his audience into thinking about something differently, and I have seen him do that. It was that ability to bring together people, his listeners, in that immediate context, and link that to the bigger strategic context, the bigger political context, that was where his storytelling, his approach to leadership, really paid dividends in so many ways.

I think one of the things that happened was that Tracker's combination of a sense of humour and his raconteur style meant that some people would assume he did not know what he was talking about. You know, the way that he would joke about, how he tried people out – and sometimes he went over the line, sometimes his judgement calls were a bit too far across the boundary, and they would cause problems and a bit of friction. His gender politics would sometimes get in the way of some potentially useful contributions. I am trying to be diplomatic here.

He once told me a fantastic story about doing some interviews for people for a job at the Land Council. One of his interview questions was, *Hey! Do you like dogs?* If you did not understand where that question was coming from, you would think this guy was an idiot. Why would you ask this at a job interview? And yet if you were terrified of dogs you could not do the work. There was this jump to the core issue without necessarily putting it in an intellectual way, that was so much a part of Tracker's style. I think another of his interview questions was, *What sort of country music do you like?* It was exactly those sorts of questions which showed his willingness to step outside and just prod people. And given how much prodding you experience in this work, how far people are tested in this work, seeing how someone responds to provocation in an interview is not a bad idea.

The way I understood Tracker's way of working was that he liked to challenge people. He liked to shit-stir, and in the process to give people's thinking a jolt. As a teacher, my sense of one of our responsibilities is that we have to give people's thinking a jolt. If you are going to think through the solutions to problems and circumstances that nobody has actually thought of yet, then you have to think differently. That will be uncomfortable in all sorts of situations. And Tracker's approach was to try and grapple with that discomfort with humour.

There was Tracker's memorable chairing of a session at the twentieth anniversary of the Land Rights Act Conference, when he mentioned how much the audience might miss Paul Keating, but in introducing the minister, John Herron, he asked for a drink of water and some Herron paracetamol. It was a classic Tracker moment, when Herron was really pushing practical reconciliation, and they were not interested in symbolism and all that crap, it was just this beautifully gentle and hilarious gibe. It was also part of the moment when he talked about how they had been through the three Gerrys, they had Gerrymander in Queensland, then they had Gerry Hand as Minister for Aboriginal Affairs, then Jerry Lewis [Robert Tickner], and now they had a geriatric. It was that ability to nail some really funny lines, diffuse the serious tension and try and move to do something about the issues, that I think was one of the hallmarks of Tracker's approach. It did not change John Herron's approach to anything, but it made it possible to have a different sort of conversation around elements of that conference.

Allan Cooney

Ultimately what Tracker wanted was not a great highfaluting principle, he wanted equality for everyone. He wanted everyone to have an opportunity, not just Aboriginal people, as he felt everybody occupied the same plane. He had a lot of palaver that he put out in front of himself but if you dug behind it, it was about equality and it probably came from his earlier years when he felt he did not have that. He was not inclined to fight against the world, all he wanted was genuine equality where people did not have to go through what he went through at a young age.

He also did some funny and interesting things. He got in a lift one day in Adelaide when we were heading down to have breakfast in the hotel where we stayed. Two people got in the lift in their gym gear, in lycra, and they got down to the second floor or wherever the gym was, and got out. The doors closed and Tracker looked at me and said, *I don't know why white people just can't grow old gracefully.*

I think the thing that most people missed with Tracker and certainly it did not appear in his public persona, was the really deep love that he had for his daughters, his family, his closest friends. None of that was visible from the outside looking in. It was a very private thing for him, but people that he loved, he loved pretty much unconditionally. People outside saw the tough facade that he needed to survive. Behind all of that, when you got in behind it all, there was an absolute sweetheart. I know what he said and felt particularly about his daughters, and I think that is a real measure of anyone, and certainly a measure of Tracker in my eyes. I have heard some pretty harsh stuff said about Tracker but absolutely nobody knew that side of the bloke in the public arena. I loved the bloke, and would feel my life was very much the poorer if I had not been in contact with him. He was a force of nature but we cannot have fine weather all the time.

From the point of view of a working relationship with Tracker, he knew everyone, he took an intense interest in national affairs and what goes on in the country, and he knew people. If he did not know someone he made himself known to them, and he opened all the doors that allowed this to happen. I could ring Tracker and say we need to talk to x, and Tracker would ring me back the next day and say *book us on a plane on Tuesday, we are off to Canberra.* We would go to Canberra, the doors would open in front of us and I did not have to go through a long process of creating relationships or any of those sorts of things.

He was really interesting to travel with. We would get on a plane together and sit down shoulder to shoulder and we would have a bit of a chat, then Tracker would look around and he would say to me, *I wonder if there's anyone interesting on this plane.* He would stand up and walk up and down the plane until he found somebody interesting to talk to, and then he would engage in a conversation. I do not know how many times I saw him sitting on the arm of an aisle seat with an audience of about twenty people, telling a yarn in a 737 flying across from Alice Springs to Melbourne, or wherever we were going.

I said to him one day, there is an economic project in Tassie called Southwood. Basically, Forestry Tasmania had developed a new way of processing timber. They had set up in a really depressed rural area in Tasmania, and kicked off a whole new economy there. There were shops opening, people moving to the town. It was up in the Huon Valley. I said to Tracker, *We need to go and have a look at this and see if we can get an understanding of what these guys have done.*

He rang me two days later and said it was all organised, Forestry Tasmania was going to put us up in some big hotel in Hobart, and they would fly us up and show us the setup. Yeah! I do not know how he did that. They met us, they paid for our flight, they put us up and took us for a tour. We spent a couple of days there. They stuck us in a helicopter with a helicopter pilot and flew us up over the forestry projects. I would never have been able to do that in a million years. I would not have been able to open those doors. I know who he spoke to and how he did it but even so, it takes a huge skill and ability, and personal charisma, to pull that off.

Patrick Tilmouth

Tracker and I went to the hospital in Darwin for his checkup and he would stop along the way to talk to everybody. He would have to talk to the cleaner, he knew everybody, everybody in the hospital. You would go to Casuarina [shopping plaza] with him and he knew everybody there. Here [in Alice Springs] you could not walk through the shopping centre because it would take you an hour to go from one end to the other with him, because everyone pulled him up to have a yarn, and he had a yarn to them. And the same in Darwin. I got a surprise even in the hospital. He goes up to the hospital and he reckoned, *Oh! Where's my favourite vampire? Where's my favourite vampire. Come and get some blood.* In the meantime we talked to everybody right through the hospital. He knew everyone.

Feeding Cream to Pigs

Forrest Holder

The one and only time I ever saw Tracker on the piss was in Darwin. He burst into my room at three o'clock in the morning and asked me if I was from Langley, and if I was CIA. The story went on from there, but the source was a young Sioux woman who when I was driving her and Tracker around earlier had heard my accent. Later on she asked Tracker, *Where is he from? He sounds like he's from Virginia.* She reckoned I was CIA, that I came out of Langley. Anyway, that got it into Tracker's head. I just said, *Go to bed Tracker.* This is three o'clock in the morning. *Leave me alone Tracker, I'm tired, go to bed.*

There was a time during the Century zinc negotiations and they were at a pivotal stage. I cannot remember why I needed to talk to Tracker, but I was stuck in Alice Springs and he was in Brisbane and he was in the Department of Premier and Cabinet at a really high-powered meeting. I got hold of the telephone number of the head of Premier and Cabinet, the senior bureaucrat, his private mobile, and I rang it and it was switched on. So he answered the phone and I said, *It's Forrest here, I'd like to talk to Tracker please.* He handed the phone over to Tracker and I had my conversation with him, whatever it was about I cannot remember, and Tracker hung up and he gave the phone back to this bloke. The bloke said to him, *How did he get my number?* Tracker said to him, *That's Forrest. He's from Langley, He's CIA. He knows all the numbers in your black books and he knows the doors you knock on at three o'clock in the morning, you'd better watch out.*

You know the people who work for Aboriginal people in Australia, the first thing they should do is decolonise their minds. If your mind is not decolonised, then how can you work for Aboriginal people? You have got to not come in with your cultural, social, political and economic chauvinisms about what the cute little fuzzy wuzzies are doing and think, *Oh! If they could only just be like us everything would be right.* Regrettably, time and time again the terms of engagement between government and Aboriginal people, or their representatives, are not set and defined by them. This happened with the negotiations with the Commonwealth following the Mabo decision.

One of the great strengths that came from the Kalkaringi Convention in 1998 was that the terms were set by them via the Combined Aboriginal Nations of Central Australia, not by government. It was not just their stories, I mean the stories are the basis from which they were coming from, it was their strength, it was from the platform of their law that they were laying their claim as sovereign peoples. Regretfully, all of the negotiations I went to for the National Indigenous Working Group on Native Title for Mabo and following Wik, the entire set of discussions was set by government. They did not come from the stories where people's rights were defined, where their strength was, where their culture was, where their language was, where their law was, it did not come from that, it came from government. Everything that Aboriginal people would have had on the table got pushed aside and the government said, *Here, we'll talk about this.* Tracker was really good on that. He was one of those on the A Team that really got up people's noses because he was telling them where they were heading.

When Tracker and Jack Crosby [Central Land Council senior policy officer] and I were having an argument at the Land Council over the native title package that was being offered by Keating, Crosby's position was, *Oh! Look this is a gem of a package, this is a land fund and the Indigenous Land Corporation to administer it, and native title legislation, social justice package. The Indigenous Land Fund, that's forever. Three hundred years and Aboriginal people can buy the place back.* I just stopped him and I said, *Look, this bill and the land fund itself is just thirty pieces of silver mate. It will be a big mistake if the legal rights discovered by the Mabo decision are traded off for statutory rights.* Tracker took that thirty pieces of silver expression and used it at a meeting in Canberra and really put peoples' noses out of joint. But the A Team followed the advice from eminent senior legal counsel and went down the path set by Keating.

Humour was a shield for Tracker. He did not show it, but he was really fragile. He did not show it because being stolen and everything, his showing signs of being hurt would have been a sign of weakness. Also, he did not get close to people really.

He also just could not fucking sit still. You could try to have a conversation with him and he would just walk off. That did not work with me because I just followed him around the bloody Land Council building, even into the toilets. He was on the toilet one day trying to have a shit and he was crying out, begging me to go away, but I didn't, I had his captive attention.

The Aboriginal leadership from around Australia and the Torres Strait mob went to Canberra when Howard got elected in 1996 and he had his Ten Point fucking Plan. All the Aboriginal leadership and their assistants or advisers were assembled in a large meeting room in Parliament House, and they were waiting for Beazley to come and talk to them. There must have been eighty or a hundred people in the room and it was not crowded, that is how big the room was. Beazley was a big man with a big presence so when he bustled in from the far end of the room the room went quiet. Quick as a flash Tracker, who was way up the other end, called out in a stentorian voice, *All stand!* like you hear in court when the judge comes in. And by the way, some people started to. Of course everybody erupted in laughter. It broke the ice. At the very start of the meeting Tracker did that – broke the ice, and it made everybody feel comfortable and the meeting progressed from there. He had a gift as far as that was concerned.

Chris Athanasiou

Tracker was charismatic. He was a person who could get away with anything. He would be standing at one end of the corridor of Parliament House and down the other end was the leader of the Democrats, Cheryl Kernot and her deputy, Natasha Stott Despoja, both blondes, and I am standing beside Tracker, and at the top of his voice he yells, *Hey! Big blondie and little blondie.* I was looking for a hole in the floor to swallow me up and thought, *Holy shit, did he say that?* And of course they all blushingly came down, *Oh! Tracker, how are you?* On he goes at his irreverent best. In our quieter moments I said, *You know Tracks, I reckon the world has lost. The fact that you haven't done it, you should have gone and been a bloody standup comic because I reckon the world has lost one of its best by you not doing it.* He was quick and he was funny, and he was charismatic, and people just liked him.

We are all flawed. I am not saying he was perfect but he had amazing charisma and you wanted to like him, wanted to listen to his stories. He would be telling us stories about the time he went to the United Nations. He had all these little barbs at the end of it, but they were engaging stories. You could see that he had been to these places, he had done all these things, and he had brought all these stories back and tied them up. He nailed the characters, the main players in it all.

Some of his sayings were sexist, but the one that resonates loudly with me was, every time I was trying to lift the bar, or get things right, or explain things so that everyone understood, he would turn to me and say, *Christo, stop feeding cream to pigs.* Isn't it a great one? And he was always talking about the corn-feds on the verandah, just to put down those who wanted to jump the fence.

He used stories to get the Indigenous position across: the disadvantage and the social position in a way that people [were likely to accept]. It was quick, easy, succinct and digestible. He would have people thinking about issues but not crying about them. He did not see that as a useful thing. He did not necessarily like the black armband approach. He just wanted that to be in people's minds so that it would drive them on, but he did not want it to be completely covered in negativity. A lot of his storytelling was political, more Machiavellian sort of storytelling, where he would have a story that was going to make somebody he wanted to make look silly, look really, really silly. He would have the room falling around laughing.

Tracker would never offer up at first blush the deeply cultural, significant stories and information, but because we did not just work at a national or territory level, there were a number of times where I would be involved in something and he would be explaining to me how it really worked. He knew what was going on. He just did not wander around spouting it very much, from what I could see, but when he saw that someone needed to have more insight into something, absolutely.

He also was so imbued with the historical narrative of, let's say, the land rights struggle from the 1970s, he had narratives about all of that, and for me they were deeply Indigenous stories, the people, the players, the places, the things. He had a story about them all, something he had done with them, or where he had been. A lot of it, again, would end in humour. It was not as if he had just bobbed up in the 90s, he had been around and that came through in his storytelling.

Phillip Toyne

His jokes were often amazingly offensive. They were often racist. Not just racist about whitefellas, I mean he was racist about blackfellas as well. And it may well have been that he copped backhanders from Aboriginal people about not being dark enough. I know certainly that the Luritja mob I worked with and the Pitjantjatjara mob could be quite cruel about people like him, whom they would call *yella fellas*. And that was pretty offensive. But he seemed to be able to turn back people having a go at him by just making a joke at them and again, it was this whole issue of being a sort of buffoon but with a really sharp edge to it. So I never felt that he came out second best.

I was not a witness to it, but one thing I remember was something that happened to Rick Farley [former head of the National Farmers Federation] when they went out to this Aboriginal meeting at one of the station homesteads out Yuendumu somewhere, when they arrived late at night and had to walk into the homestead in the dark. So Tracker yelled out to all the people sleeping in their swags on the floor, *Smile you blokes so we can see where you are.* And that was the sort of thing that he was famous for doing, making an unbelievable joke about blackfellas being blackfellas.

I remember him describing having Christmas with his in-laws when he was first going out with his wife, and he had us in hysterics describing how the Woods family were less than impressed with the daughter bringing home a blackfella. And of course he played it up, and made it sound like he was a bush myall or something, when in fact he was a really personable bloke. He could have played that really, really well and impressed the family, or he could have taken the piss out of them. His version of it of course was that they were absolutely horrified and he took the piss out of them.

When we were out bush he would rush around the place and bring people up to talk to me. There was none of this lazy, take-it-easy sort of stuff that I was used to with the field officers. He was a hustler and he would get people together, and he was pretty blunt about their need to get themselves organised to talk to a lawyer for Legal Aid time in the bush courts.

We would get out there the day before the magistrate arrived and he would try and find the defendants on the list, and I would be exposed for the first time to the offences they had committed or were charged with, and he would have to go out and find them. One thing he was not particularly good at was interpreting of course. So we would have to find somebody else to interpret for most stuff because Legal Aid only did bush court in the north-east and north-west of Alice Springs. They did not go to Pitjantjatjara land or other places where he might have been better set up with speaking the language.

Ross Ainsworth

Probably you would not be able to put it in the book but his favourite statement about somebody, primarily a bureaucrat who had just messed everything up, would be, *That bloke would fuck up Christmas Day.*

There were so many people in the system who were trying to stop things going forward rather than helping them go forward. He constantly came up against these people trying to stop what he was doing.

All these issues were around ownership and the rights and responsibilities of ownership. The rights and responsibilities of ownership in the traditional Aboriginal context are totally different than they are in current Australian rules, regulations, law, politics, so to explain what your rights and responsibilities are in reality, as opposed to what they might have been in the Aboriginal system, that is the hard part. Tracker had a grip on that, and was as good as anyone in explaining why and how but it is still for me, the biggest disconnect. People primarily want to get their land back because they think then they will get their rights and responsibilities back, but they don't. They get a modified set of rights and responsibilities which are a mixture of their Indigenous rights and responsibilities, and their Australian citizen rights and responsibilities, and it is a very hard mix to put together and make it work. Most of the time it does not mix, it is bloody oil and water. You constantly get this disconnect, this conflict. He was pretty good at trying to explain and take the edge off that conflict.

Tracker might have been the director of the Central Land Council at the time when they were negotiating for the railway line to go through the Devil's Marbles. It was a really big issue obviously, and the train had to go around one side or the other side because the original line, the line on the map, went straight through the middle. They had a huge meeting and lawyers, the courts and everyone was there, a huge number of people, negotiating for days and days about where the alternative route should be, and what was satisfactory and what was not satisfactory. Anyway, they finally agreed to the route, and the next morning was the final sort of sign-up and confirmation, the whitefella commercial legal signing. In the morning whoever the senior bloke was, he came up to Tracker, as the TO [traditional landowner] to the CLC boss, and he said, *Tracker we don't want that railway.* Tracker had gone, *Fucking what? We've been sitting here for days talking about this fucking railway and everyone's agreed. Now you're telling me this, what the hell are you talking about?* The old fella said, *No Tracker, we only want that train.* And Tracker said well, for four or five days they'd been sitting there talking about trains and railways and they didn't know what the difference was between the railway and the train. Or at least the senior TO! Tracker said, *You stupid bastard, the railway is the train.*

Oh! Is that right? I didn't know, the train or the railway.

And somebody like Tracker was sitting next to this bloke for five days and did not work out they did not know the difference between a railway and a train. So how was a judge, a land court judge, or some barrister or somebody else going to figure it out? Or some low-level dickhead bureaucrat in the ILC, how are they going to communicate with this person? You have to go to extraordinary lengths to get across, about something as simple as what is the difference between a railway and a train, when you are talking about the rights and responsibilities of the traditional landowners. A land claim or management of a proprietary limited company, a mining agreement with God knows how many ins and outs – we assume our logic and our sort of deductive processes will be the same for everyone, and it is just the language that is different. Well! That is bullshit. The whole process is different.

One story about Tracker that stands out was when he was trying one day to sort out a pastoral issue, and the traditional owners wanted to take charge, and they wanted everyone else to clear off out of the way. I remember him saying, *Righto! You blokes, imagine that you just inherited Qantas. So Qantas is your traditional country and it's an airline, you own it. So, righto, you Jacko and you Bernie, you're the pilots because you used to work for Qantas as baggage handlers. So you get in the pilot's seat and then the rest of you mob, you have to get in the seats, load up and then these two are going to fly you to Sydney.* One of them said, *Bullshit! They can't fly this plane.* And he said, *That's exactly it.*

Yes, they used to work for the station but they don't know how to fly it. You cannot start flying this plane until you've actually learnt how to fly it. Just because you worked for Qantas doesn't mean you can fly a plane. So I reckoned that was probably the simplest and clearest explanation, and they all went, *Yeah! Well! I certainly wouldn't get in with that bastard flying the plane.* So they all got that real clear.

James Nugent

There were so many times that Tracker would make you laugh or would shock you. Clearly that facility to do that, to disarm people and to just bring it to a very human level was absolutely critical. In Indigenous affairs, there is so much grief and so much pain and sorrow, but no one has a sense of humour like Aboriginal people down on the ground, that ability to gently poke fun at people – not to bring them down, but to bring everyone together. It is very important. I guess for politicians meeting Tracker too, it was nice not to have your head bitten off, or to be boxed into a corner instantly. You were engaged because he was a very personable guy and his ability to crack a joke and have the one-liners coming out set the tone. Of course, then you were boxed up and put into a difficult position.

He had a good turn of phrase, not necessarily when talking about the pastoral issue when negotiating, but he used to say, *We don't want to scare the horses yet. You don't go in all guns blazing. We won't scare them off yet.*

In a large and diverse group of people there are loads of different modes of Aboriginal storytelling, and you hear a lot of different ones at Land Council meetings when delegates from various areas stand up to say what they have got to say or put their point of view across. Often they are quite oblique, or the point is necessarily made by analogy, and I think Tracker had all those elements, and his larrikinism was unthreatening because often it seemed to be quite out there. It was like he was just having a laugh. But he had thought the issues though, and once you got beyond the disarming of what appeared to be throwaway lines, there was actually a very insightful and incisive point that he was driving at.

He also had piercing green eyes, and he was not one to back away. He was not the sort to say, *Well! I'll see you outside.* He was always going to be able to talk someone around, or at least talk them down off the ledge. Which was not confronting, he was not a confronting sort of negotiator. He was much more about getting people in a situation where they were willing to listen, or where they were not being defensive so that he could actually get his point across. In a sense he was much more attuned to a business or to a commercial world where people actually have a mutual stake in something, and it is to their benefit to work together to get that done.

Geoff Clark

In the early 1980s we continued holding Federation of Land Council meetings all across the Territory, Darwin, Hatches Creek, or Katherine, Tennant Creek. There were certainly lots of meetings in Sydney in those early days with Kevin Cook and Kevin Tory with the coalition. [Jack] Ah Kit was involved, Galarrwuy, the Dodsons, Mansell, the [Paul and Isabel] Coes of the world. When you reflect back on the gatherings of Aboriginal leadership in those early days, before people came to prominence, we had some very deep and meaningful discussions about the future of Aboriginal affairs and the current play, and sent lots of delegations to Geneva and those places, and Tracker was certainly very much a part of all those things. Another story that became very prominent was the Stolen Generation. I remember at Basso's Farm, where we would sit around with people singing and telling jokes, sitting around the camp fire, where a lot of the content of what we did was discussed, and where there used to be meetings if there was a political development or crisis or something to do with land rights, or native title, or Stolen Generation.

And we were all sitting around and feeling pretty mortified about the stories of the Stolen Generation that were coming out, and becoming prominent. Tracker pipes up and says, *It's a bit different for me, my fucking grannies tried to give me away.* The complete reverse. Gerry Hand or someone had turned up and said we are very sorry about the Stolen Generation, and Tracker made this joke, that his grannies could not wait to give him away because he was such a bastard of a kid. Those sorts of situations happened on a regular basis, and there was always somebody trying to outdo Tracker with their jokes, so even though there were very serious talks throughout all the 80s and 90s, it was entertaining and quite hilarious at times, and usually led by Tracker.

He seemed to have had access to alternative motives or rumours that were circulating around. He must have had a very good network, Tracker, and he always seemed to come up with the alternative views that were being circulated in the corridors [of parliament], or when somebody would say something. He was a wealth of information in matters of tactics.

Some of our ideas and strategies were difficult to accomplish, while we were in Geneva for instance, where we were covering all those principles that are now contained in the Declaration of Indigenous People's Rights, so you can imagine the debate and the stories. Throughout that process in the UN it became very prominent that people needed to understand the information, to be given the information, before they would be able to give consent. There was a lot of misrepresentation in those early days of people saying – the community advisors, ultimately white people – *Oh! No! This mob don't do this, or that mob don't agree with that,* when in fact, when you sat down with the mob, you found out it was the complete opposite. Tracker was very aware of that and you could attribute a lot of the informed-consent stuff to people like Tracker.

You never knew when you were going to be the brunt or subject of Tracker's jokes, because they would always be directed at somebody, and lots of times it could very well have been yourself. But it was done in such a pleasant manner I suppose that it was not offensive. Lots of times there would be tension about whatever we were debating. You would have bureaucrats in front of you, and the humour was told to deliver a message, that was one method. Another way was to diffuse the tension. Lots of times things were extremely tense, and a bit of humour would often give you that sort of space to sit back a little bit and reflect, and lose the aggression of the argument in the debate. I think it is a very important part of Aboriginal debating, a sense of humour and a good belly laugh was always helpful too.

Just going to the last few meetings, messing around and telling jokes with blackfellas for three or four hours, we were rolling around on the ground. It is people outdoing one another. Some people would not engage much in the debate of the day, or sit with their enemies if you like, but usually the sessions in the evenings would draw everybody in. Nobody was excluded from the laughter, because the sense of humour would be such an inclusive process, and if you were not laughing you had to be deaf, dumb or stupid, or all of the above.

So that was a lot of the 1980s and 1990s stuff, where people would sing, tell jokes, and had a real sort of caring and inclusive nature in the way in which they sat around and talked about some very serious issues, treaty, Barunga, land rights, the native title debate, the setting up of ATSIC, a whole range of milestone discussions. There were big minds involved in the federation of land rights.

And you had the constant threat of mining, for example Noonkanbah in Western Australia, and serious delegations coming to national meetings with real issues on their hands, people under threat of being removed from their lands. How we managed that was through our sense of humour, and laughter overcame some of the pain and the agony of those very serious matters.

I think that some of our problem, in losing our ability to keep our story straight, or to be able to tell the story of ourselves anymore, goes back to the traditional people who were good storytellers, and there used to be an obligation under the traditional system where you would have to go and spend two or three months on the trail talking to people and carrying the message. And the message could not be delivered off key, or inaccurately, and that was a rule. That ability was certainly there in the 1980s or 1990s. I think people have lost that capacity to sit around and meet because we just do not have the resources anymore.

The world has become so fast. There is too much information and you get the armchair experts sitting back now on social media or Facebook, and not being confronted with the emotions of decision-making. You know when you deliver a harsh message or a sad message, the sharing of that emotion is important too. I do not think we have the eye-to-eye stuff. We do not have the rallies like 1988 and 1985 on the steps of Parliament House, and Sydney and elsewhere, when people actually made an effort to get to a common place for a common purpose and a common message. In the old days the world was not going as fast, and we could sit around and spend more time yarning and really understanding each other's concepts. Today there is misinterpretation about who we are and what we represent.

One thing that me and Mansell are doing now is that we are going around, talking about a seventh state, a Federation of First Nations type of thing. We are sitting around, just having cups of coffee with people and having dinners. It is not the town halls where you are going to get five hundred people anymore, I think it is the five or ten people that you sit around and have these conversations with. That may build into hundreds of people, hundreds of thousands of people one day.

The Greatest Footballer That Ever Played

Danny Schwartz

Tracker was one of the most charismatic people I know. He could get a whole table laughing, and he could get the whole table on his side. He was a people's man, a man of the people, a man who could relate to people, a man who people liked and enjoyed and would laugh with, that was his strategy, and he was loveable, likeable and naughty. He was the sort of guy that would be sitting at a table and he would say, *A flat white for the round black.* And I would say, *A short black for the tall white.*

The first time I was up north, Tracker in describing Kakadu said, *This is Jurassic Park.* I will never forget driving with him on quite a wide road and there was a crocodile ahead and he said, *Watch that crocodile cross the road.* As it was crossing the road he said, *You see how his nose is over one edge and the tail is over the other edge* – and it was true, at that very moment I felt like I was in Jurassic Park, with that croc which would have been eight metres in length.

In every single moment you spent with Tracker in the country, he had stories about the country, he had stories about where he was taking me, and once when we sat down at a lake he said, *Danny, with the depth of our culture, we just have to look at that lily in the water. We have stories about the petals above, about the stems, about the roots, we have different stories about each different part of that lily, not just the lily, but every part of that lily we've got different stories about it. That's how deep our understanding and our knowledge of the country is.*

It is those sort of stories that Tracker had imparted to me, that made me understand the depth. There are people in the Aboriginal community who are some of my closest friends now, but it was Tracker who made me understand the lay of the land. He said to me, *Danny, this is like Bosnia Herzegovina two hundred years ago. This is like Bosnia*

Herzegovina. I said, *Really?* He said, *Yeah! We're all tiny little communities, all fighting each other. There is no love between us, we are all fighting.*

He said, *Now we consider we're all one Aboriginal people, well we're not, we were Bosnia Herzegovina, we were different communities, together, living on this land. But we were all fighting each other, we all hate each other. Now we've got to love each other. Now we're all Aboriginal under one flag and we're all one, well bullshit. We're not all one. We're different. We are different in the way we look, we're different in our cultures, we are different in so many things. And we would have to kill for our wives over there. We hated each other. We all hated each other. But now we've got to be seen as being in love with one another. In Europe it's understood they all hated each other and there it was. It's only in the last hundred years that we've now seen ourselves all as one, cause we've had to. But we're not, we're different.*

He was the first one to show me that tremendous map with the different [Aboriginal] languages. It was sitting on the wall in his office. All the places that he had been to, and all the places where he grew up, he would show me on the map, and how the different people worked. I once said to him I had some mates, and they were telling me these great stories how they had spent some time in Aboriginal communities and they had got a skin name, and Tracker looked at me and goes, *You get a bloody skin name and I'll never be a friend of yours ever, ever, I'll never talk to you again. That's my story. You've got your story. You're Jewish, you've got your community. I'm black and I've got my community. They're wankers, don't worry about them.*

And the mutual respect we had for each other showed me that all those friends of mine who said, *Oh! I've got a skin name, and I've become part of the community,* they were the wallies and that the relationship I had with Tracker was a true relationship, respecting the diversity and the differences and respecting each other for who we were. It was those things that really made me understand and also, to be able to develop the true friendships that I have now with the communities that I have. Respecting their differences, them respecting my differences, me being proud of me, them being proud of themselves.

The reality is that, at least for someone like me, I did not have to stay in contact with Tracker because he stayed in contact with me all the time. He was constantly calling with another idea. The frustrating thing about it was that every single time he had an idea, it was a great idea, but it was just so hard to implement because it involved so much detail to do it. The last three projects I have talked about with him were all potentially exceedingly successful, but they involved so much work. The culling of camels and the camel trade, the abattoirs in the Northern Territory, the whole notion of the Northern Territory being a food bowl, he talks about that all the time and I wished I had the time and energy to get involved.

The energy deal he was talking about was just incredible. I do not have the capacity to do that. It was basically powering the whole of the Northern Territory and Darwin out of the gas, and having a share in that. The difficulty was that Tracker's ideas were so grand, they involved so much money that only people like Noel Pearson can get. You know if those tens upon tens of millions of dollars that Noel has got up north in Cape York were given to Tracker, Tracker would have had an economic plan for the Northern Territory that would be employing hundreds, that would be educating hundreds, and benefitting thousands. I just think he did not have the capacity to do the things he wanted to do, and I kept saying, *But you need the equity, you need the money to do it.*

To my mind Noel has been able to get the whitefellas on side because he seems to be saying his fellow blackfellas are drunks and uneducated and they cannot look after themselves. He provides a very missionary style of argument to try and get them back on the front foot. Tracker comes from the angle that we are not to be blamed and we are the victims, we need to be provided with the independence to be able to get ourselves to move forward. I think the politicians like Noel's notion of the downtrodden black and the requirement of a missionary person to come along and provide for them.

A normal Trackerism was: *They like to give us the fish, they don't want to teach us how to fish.* And: *We've got to go out and teach ourselves how to fish. We don't just want to get the fish.* And that was the difference. Noel says what the whitefellas want to hear, but Tracker did not. Tracker talked about empowerment. Tracker talked about land rights, as opposed to native title. Noel had no problem talking about native title, and not land rights. The whole notion of land rights is very, very different to native title, and so Tracker talked about freehold. Tracker talked about the value of the land and what people could do with the land. He understood that value. Noel on the other hand is very happy to talk about native title. He does not have the foundation that Tracker had. Tracker did not sit on the same platform. His was a whole different platform of empowerment, of self-growth, of give us the land and we will do.

He did not schmooze enough but he was a good schmoozer, a great schmoozer who could talk to anyone from the Prime Minister down, but he did not say what they wanted to hear. Whereas Noel says what they want to hear.

Bob Beadman

If you pared away all of the theatre, you would find that the views that Tracker held and those of Noel Pearson were very, very closely aligned, and I think Noel has been able to get there by his legal training, and the forums that that has opened up for him and the flourishes that he can bring to his rhetoric. He is a very, very captivating man when he gets up there in front of an audience, a white audience. But I do not think he is so successful in front of an Aboriginal audience. I think he has left them behind. And if I am correct in the way that I read some responses from Aboriginal Australia to him, they think he has left them behind too.

Whereas on the other hand, Tracker did not have that flourish up in front of the TV cameras or an audience, or that seriousness, and focus and intensiveness about him, but he did not leave the Aboriginal audience behind. He was still tuned in there and he was bringing them along. I have admired them both. I think that Noel's been absolutely pioneering in the way that he has taken some of this debate, and very brave in the way he has done it because he has not had this Aboriginal backing. I think they have slowly joined on to his wagon, Marcia [Langton] and Galarrwuy [Yunupingu] and the like, but by the same token, Tracker worked to another level with different audiences and he managed to engage with local audiences very, very well. As I say, throw away the theatre, and I think their views were very closely aligned. But maybe they would be horrified at that assessment.

Doug Turner

Noel [Pearson] has been more successful in the way he puts the story across because he plays the game. He is playing a different game, and the way that Noel does it is he puts it out there for everybody to see what he is doing, he is not hiding anything, he is open and he plays on the conscience of white Australia basically, and white Australia sees all his moves. Noel has got the whole community looking at what he is doing, and saying, that is a bloody good idea. He is open about things, he is transparent, and so the government cannot come back at him and say, *no you are doing the wrong thing*. They cannot pull the rug out from under his feet because it will backfire on the government. It is all about politics basically, to show that you are open and transparent, you are trying to bring about a positive change, and you bring the government with you so you make them look good as well, talking about the level of alcoholism in communities and how we are not in conflict with the government, we are running some positive programs and we are getting support for those programs with taxpayer funds.

White Australia can see those things happening, it sympathises with those sorts of programs trying to support the communities and trying to make them work. The government wants to be looked upon as doing positive things, and this is what they are doing with Noel Pearson up in Cape York. That is how you play the game, basically.

Noel is still only speaking for his local area, and he cannot speak for other areas like Alice Springs, because it is a different community and Noel needs to build respect in those other communities. But Noel is not about building respect in those communities because he is going flat out with his own community. Tracker had been out there doing things like that as well but he was a little bit subtler. People saw Tracker in a different light to Noel, who is more the diplomat. Tracker is more go in boots and all to try to make things happen, and drag bits and pieces together to make it work. That was how he used to operate, and he was very quiet about not letting anybody know what he was thinking, and what he was trying to pull together to make things happen. We just listened to him, the way he was talking, because he was talking in a roundabout fashion so people could not understand clearly where he was coming from, that was the rule with Tracker. But he still achieved the things that he attempted to make happen.

Murrandoo Yanner

Tracker deflated egos, people who rightfully need to be brought to ground a bit, he did not stroke their ego. When Noelie gave this big speech at the first Alice Springs native title conference – which I missed, but I heard about it from dozens of people, including my older brother Bull who I sent down on my behalf – right at the end of the speech, Tracker got up and there were hundreds of people sitting there looking towards the podium and about to ask Noel some questions about his speech, and Tracker walked halfway down the aisle so all eyes were on him and he looked up at Pearson, and Pearson had just spouted a whole hour of what he knows about native title, and Tracker summed it up, *And what would you know about native title Pearson?* Then he turned his back and walked out.

It was a phenomenal moment, and I thought it was good, because Noelie thinks he knows more than he probably really knows. He is an extremely intelligent man but it is easy to be popular if you're spouting shit that whitefellas love to hear: *Oh! Blackfellas just need a house and job and they'll be right. Get them off of this and that.* Any of us from the extreme left, or hardcore Murris, could be the right-wing pin-up boy tomorrow if we spouted the same shit. But that is the easy road in life I think, not the hard road. The hard road is where Tracker continued to work and spend his whole life working towards the struggle for our mob.

Tracker was trying to make a difference. That is a bullshit flowery term at times, but if it takes on a true physical form anywhere, it would be with him. Not just to be personally remembered, but it was important to him to make a difference and change the world, at least parts of it, change Australia, or change significant parts of Australia through legislation, and I think even through people. I know there are half-mad rednecks that he has converted. People saw Aboriginal people through him and eventually got a good opinion of us, whereas before, whatever they heard turned them off. I think history will judge him correctly.

During the Century mine negotiations, the mining manager Ian Williams and his people came to a meeting with the traditional landholders in Burketown with a big fish tank, and a little barge, and a little cup of lead and zinc which they poured in the fish tank and said, *Look! If it {the barge} has a spillage or that sort of thing,* there would be this and that, and: *the lead and zinc won't hurt you.* And Tracker whispered to one of the old fellas from Mornington [Island], *Listen! Say this.*

The old fella sticks his hand up and Ian Williams' mob look around from the front of the hall of two hundred people where he's giving his presentation to the traditional landowners, and says, *Hey mate if that stuff's harmless, that cup you just poured in, why don't you drink that cup of lead and zinc then if it's harmless?* And Ian Williams wouldn't, obviously. It really impressed people, *Oh yeah, can't trust these bastards, lying bastards.* Even when Tracker was facilitating or being the moderator up there, he would slip in and plant the seeds amongst the mob if he thought they were being a bit slack and not firing up.

Sean Bowden

I spent hours enthralled, listening to him, and every story had a rationale and a meaning, and often disguised a deep-seated anger, or frustration, or bitterness that Tracker had either experienced himself or had seen experienced by others. Sometimes, because of that, his humour was a bit hard to take, and would be taken the wrong way.

He would often use imagery as a traditional Aboriginal man would use imagery, and he would often act in the style of Ganbulapula, a classic Yolngu hero-ancestor from north-east Arnhem. Ganbulapula was a very prominent leader in the Yirritja moiety, and a powerful ancestor of the Gumatj clan. In the story, he was leading a ceremony and he wanted to change things a bit, he wanted to modernise the way things were done and other people would not agree with him. So he ran amok a bit, and then he got a coffin, a log coffin that he was in control of and instead of putting it in the right place, he threw it, he threw it away into the distance. He threw it into the sea from the ceremony ground at Gulkula because he was saying to all these people, *You are not listening to me,* and so he did something that caught their attention and from chaos he created order. The log coffin with its sacred insignia and messages floated off on the tide taking its knowledge to people as it travelled around the coastal areas. Off the back of that story and its imagery, the Gumatj have this concept of looking up to the future, because Ganbulapula threw the coffin through some wild honey bees, and the bees were in the sky, and this insignia is used by all the senior young men, the Yunupingu men, and it has been a motif for them in embracing the future. Very potent imagery. *Look up to the future.*

I think Tracker was often trying to use similar imagery in a contemporary way. In this way another of his storytelling methods was to shock people. I remember him being interviewed by Lindsay Murdoch of *The Age*, and Lindsay asked him to describe what was going on at Wadeye. Tracker said it was 'nigger farming'. Lindsay dropped his pen and just looked at him and started shuffling and sweating. He just could not grasp that language. What Tracker was saying was that all these Aboriginal people at Wadeye are in a pen and are being used by outsiders, by governments and service providers, to make money. Sometimes he was a little bit too irreverent and maybe he should have gone further with Lindsay Murdoch and properly articulated the case, but he was doing what a lot of those senior guys do, and he was, as they say in Arnhem Land, flying a flag, putting the flag up and allowing the next person to come along and explain it a bit better. He did a lot of that, and then he would withdraw and allow someone else to continue.

He did it with Galarrwuy Yunupingu once, when Galarrwuy was very frustrated in 2005, 2006, when he was looking for his next move. Tracker said, *Listen, Bapatji. You should get that Barunga Statement and you should roll it up and get rid of it. Put it in a log coffin or something.*[83] It went straight to Galarrwuy's mind and Galarrwuy later came out and made a statement saying, *I am so frustrated I'd like the Barunga statement back. I'm going to get it and I'm going to put it in a log coffin and I'm going to bury it.*

---

83. The Barunga Statement was a declaration of Aboriginal rights presented to Prime Minister Bob Hawke by Galarrwuy Yunupingu in 1988. The statement, framed by bark paintings, called for the recognition of a wide range of Indigenous rights including a negotiated treaty. The statement hangs in Parliament House, but there has never been a treaty. Bapatji is an affectionate nickname for Galarrwuy Yunupingu.

I did not know about the Ganbulapula story then, but Galarrwuy said, *I'll wait until someone can read it {the Barunga Statement} properly.* Tracker must have known that, must have matched those stories up somehow in the deep recesses of his brain and so he was able to speak straight to Galarrwuy's mind. It was front page of *The Age* or *Sydney Morning Herald*. It caused all sorts of ructions, but there was Tracker doing what he did best, prompting the Indigenous leaders, the traditional leadership.

Still, it was not always his strongest suit dealing with those guys. I think deep down he felt his own loss in that field. That he was not like them. There were these awful trade-offs that Aboriginal people had to deal with — the men and women that were not taken away, that stayed *in situ*, they suffered for that in different ways. But they were able to maintain the great gift of a classical, traditional culture. I think Tracker felt that a bit, felt it acutely sometimes around guys like Galarrwuy and others, that he did not have all of that traditional culture at his disposal. Yet he had much more of it than he ever let on.

And like the traditional Aboriginal men could, he would be using you in his strategic game, and not necessarily telling you that he was, because those old fellas didn't tell you either if they had a purpose for you. You just obey and do. I think there was a bit of that in my relationship with Tracker. Sometimes I wanted to know what the hell he was on about, and he would not say. He kept to himself. He was almost playing this game in his own head that was very Galarrwuy-esque. Galarrwuy sometimes said to me, *I live in my own head and I don't talk to anyone else. I only think of my father.* So who Tracker was thinking of I do not know, but he was thinking of something along those lines, because it was that unfathomable aspect of him, and you could get caught up in the irreverent Tracker, the myth of the CLC director and all that, but there was something else going on.

I am expressing some frustration here because he was inexplicable, and he was irreverent and mercurial. It was like the great footballer, Gary Ablett. No one knew what was going on in his head. No one knew if he was going to kick nine goals on a given day, or not even turn up. Sometimes he wouldn't play. Or he wouldn't contribute. But he was the greatest footballer that ever played.

Travelling with the Ancients

Tracker Tilmouth

Alexis Wright: You were talking the other day about all that travelling around you did with the old men, you called them the ancients. What did you learn?

You got a feeling for the country. What did I learn from them? I learnt everything. If I talk about those trips I cannot say the names of the places because they were sacred sites, and people would get very upset if they knew I saw that. And what were those old blokes like? I learnt that you have got to put everything into perspective. Why rush? Why run up and down the fence like a friggin mad dog? Relax. Nothing is going to change. Sit back under the gum tree, have a sleep. Because nothing is changing. It is going to take a long time to change. These old blokes were just so calm and collected. I would be racing around making cups of tea and cooking damper for them like a blue-arse fly, but they would say, *No. Sit down, sit down.*

They do not change, so why should the country change? So just relax. This is what we forget. This is why I would give an arm and a leg to go camping down at Coolibah Station in the bush on the edge of the Vic, at Bluey's [Bluey Pugh], because you can lay back and have the absolutely magnificent ranges looking at you, with the Victoria River running through it. And Bluey is an absolute brilliant bloke.

But they were very powerful men [in the Western Desert]. Extremely powerful men. They have all passed away now but I can remember them. I can see them now. Old Tjutjuna, Mick Miama, Kenny Kulitja, Lesley Munamatji, Tony Tjama, Harry Tjutjuna, and all those blokes. Kutikajarra, and all those places we went. Kutikajarra is two boomerang. That is down near Pipalyatjara. Big boss, really big bosses. Brilliant people, absolutely brilliant. You would sit down and I could talk Pitjantjatjara, Yankunytjatjara, and they would say *grandson*, they called me grandson.

Peace. That is what I learnt from them. Peace of mind. They always thought I was half mad. People still think I am half mad. But Rossy said, *While you're laughing at him, he's robbing you.* He said, *Be careful of Tracks.* Because he would say, *Do you want to talk to me or Tracker?* They would say, *Oh! We'll talk to you, Tracker's mad.* Rossy would say, *Yeah I know.* He used to say that. That is the way we played it. We played it for years.

But they give you peace. They give you peace of mind. You have got to have peace inside. If you have peace inside, that means you are happy who you are and what you are, and what you are doing, you have got enjoyment. That is the problem we have got. We have got no method philosophically. We have got no ability to create peace within ourselves. As Aboriginal people we take it on board, we take all the problems on board, we end up on grog, we end up on drugs, we end up on everything. We carry the burden of dispossession, of dislocation, of identity. So much weight is put on identity now and you know [we are questioning ourselves]: *Am I a certain person from this tribe?* Then you get the title running out before that person even speaks.

Look mate! We know you're from the country, you don't have to tell us. We can tell your flat nose, the forehead on you like Mount Gillick, we can see it a mile away. You don't need to say I'm from this tribe Yorta Yorta, or this, that, or whatever, whatever. You have seen the line-up of titles waiting for the white bloke to tick you off. *Oh! I've got in?* Yes. He is in the box. He is a blackfella. We have got this identity crisis. We bring it on ourselves, an identity crisis. There is no need to let someone else certify you and codify you.

Then they want the professorship to go with it. Dr whoever, whoever, for imparting knowledge on white people. That is like paying the pig feeders, to feed the cream to the pigs, the pig feeders. So you know you are dealing with people who have really got an identity crisis. These old blokes out bush got me away from that identity position. I did not have to find myself, and I was comfortable with what I was and I still am comfortable with what I am. I was glad in a way that I did not go to the Alcoota handback of land to us because we paid five million dollars for a block of land that my family owned for forty thousand years. It was stolen from them in the first place. We paid money for it. Then we got blessed and they said, *Here is your title*. We have already got the title, brother. We do not need this. We do not need to be part of it. And they put so much store in the Land Rights Act. To some people that is a good thing, for some people who think further than that it is not necessary. It just makes a lot of white people feel really good.

Alexis Wright: *Your position of being at peace with yourself, inner peace, is a position of strength too. Would you say you have learnt this from those old men?*

Well! Eight years of cancer, nearly eight years of cancer. It was 2008 when they diagnosed me. I have beaten it every time. *It is a hard road.* Oh! Look, it is your journey, and you can go out and throw yourself around the room and carry on like a pork chop, or get on with it.

Alexis Wright: *Would you link the mental toughness and kind of person you are now back to some of those old men, of what they have imparted to you?*

Yes. They said peace is the argument; that is what they taught you. They had no problems. *Oh! The car broke down, so what? Oh! We've got this, so what? What, me worry?* And you had people running all over them, whitefellas: make sure you're this, that. It is like when you go to those meetings down south and they have people from the bush country turn up. The white blokes are all over them, making sure they are set properly and they have got food, and cups of tea all round. These [bush] people are looking at you sideways with a big grin. You know they are laughing at these white blokes running around for them. But they see it all. Magnificent…*These are my people, I have been adopted.* How many white academics have said that? *I am adopted into this tribe or I am adopted into that. I have got this skin and I've got*…Hang on a minute, who said?

So you have this ongoing thing and that is reflected by Aboriginal people the other way around too. *I'm this so I need to be accepted by the white society as being different. I go to the barbecue and I am not Johnny Come Lately from over here, I'm Yorta Yorta* or something like that, or whatever the name is they give, *I'm from this mob, that mob.* Yes, wonderful. Uwa! Do you need to tell me that? I thought you are an Aboriginal person and would know that Aboriginal culture extends no matter where you are. You are accepted as who you are, not from what you are or your language. You do not have to prove it and that is the problem. We spend too much time proving who we aren't, rather than who we are. That is what happened to a certain extent to the Waanyi argument where there were degrees of Waanyi-ness which is bullshit, absolute bullshit.[84]

I said to Bradley Foster [Waanyi native title holder] on a few occasions, *You want to get away from the skull measuring because that will fuck you quicker than anything else.* And it did, it buggered them. You had degrees of Waanyi-ness and then this also happened with Yanner with the Gangalidda/Gawara native title claim, also in the Gulf of Carpentaria in Queensland and Northern Territory. He has got a big argument with, what's his name? Clarence Waldron. They are related and they are arguing about how much of a Gangalidda/Gawara person they are. It is not an argument worth having. It is wasting your energy and Clarry is not a well man. He is very sick. And I have got a lot of respect for Clarry.

But you just waste your time arguing about things that really it is not worth having an argument about. It is like trying to work with the Kalkadoon mob. Degrees of scientificity.[85] So you have got these sorts of arguments that are always arising and falling, on degrees of the inner search for peace. That is what it is, an inner search. How do I feel comfortable, because I am not comfortable where I am. We are shuffling each other around and around the top rail.

The trouble with Aboriginal society is that we have gone from an Aboriginal society to a quasi-North American society. We have got a council of chiefs, we have got elders, we have got this, we have got

---

84. Tracker is referring to the disagreements over identity that occurred, and the reliance on and disagreement over non-Aboriginal professional historical and anthropological advice in the Waanyi native title claim in the Gulf of Carpentaria in Queensland.

85. Referring to the internal arguments that take place among Aboriginal people who have been placed into the position of having to work together, often with very few resources, on major issues affecting their future, such as native title negotiations with mining development on the resource-rich Kalkadoon land in North West Queensland, near Mount Isa.

that, like the American Indians. An Aboriginal society did not have that, and we should still not have that. As they said to me, Conrad Ratara [Arrernte leader] and a couple of blokes from Hermannsburg the last time I was in Alice. They all come up and gave me a big hug and said, *Brother, you're still going.* I said, *Yeah.* And Ratara said to me, *You know the rules, brother.* I said, *Yeah.* He said, *The heart stop, you stop.* I said, *Yep.* He said, *You're going to remember that. That's the law.* I said, *I've never forgotten.* Just to make sure I was comfortable. He was not being frivolous, he was making sure I was comfortable within myself, big hug, big brother. *You've got to remember,* he said, *when the heart stop you stop.* Because he knows that I am thinking all the time. We go way back. So him and Jakamarra Nelson – we were talking at the airport [in Alice Springs], he could see I was not feeling well. But what he said was inside. He gave me a big hug, *Your heart stop, you stop. Remember that. That's the law.* So a quiet word like that, you know he is thinking about you. Me and him have been mates for years.

But that is the sort of little comment you get. Now you only get that off a blackfella, you will not get that off a white bloke. They know you know a little bit about the law and that. So comments like that, that is what the old blacks bring to you, the bush people bring to you. So you say righto, that is noted. Peace. They tell you to just find peace.

Noel Leslie and some whose names I cannot mention. Tjutjuna, I can mention his name and Hairy Big Foot, Harry Brumby, all those blokes. I used to drive Nosepeg [Tjupurrula] around. Big boss. Big, big bloke and big boss Aboriginal way, big law man. But all my old grannies too, like old Dinny Nolan Tjampitjinpa and those blokes, Tilmouth Well mob. Blokes there that were just as strong, old grandfather old Kaapa Tjampinjinpa. Mr Lynch – Johnny Lynch [Tjapanangka]. We are Yirampa [Honey Ant] Dreaming coming into Papunya that way, from the east side. Right through Mount Allan there, there is a big honey ant man travelling through Tilmouth Well, all the Granites right to Namakurlangu, that is Anmatyerre. That belongs to our mob. Comes right across. I am just saying Anmatyerre, Eastern Arrernte, Alyawarre are all joined. So knowing all that sort of stuff helps.

List of People, Places and Organisations

Tony Abbott Liberal Party politician and former Prime Minister (2013–2015).
Aboriginals Benefit Account (ABA) Formerly Aboriginals Benefit Trust Account. Account established under federal law to receive and distribute royalty-equivalent monies from mining on Aboriginal land in the Northern Territory.
Aboriginal Carbon Fund A national not-for-profit company building wealth for Aboriginal traditional owners through the ethical trade of carbon credits.
Aboriginal Development Commission (ADC) Government body established in 1980 to further the economic and social development of Aboriginal and Torres Strait Islander people by establishing a capital account to promote development, self-management and self-sufficiency. The ADC was absorbed into the Aboriginal and Torres Strait Islander Commission in 1990.
Aboriginal Provisional Government (APG) Aboriginal independence movement, set up in 1990. Its aim is not to govern Aboriginal people but to be a political vehicle for self-determination.
Aboriginal and Torres Strait Islander Commission (ATSIC) Government body established in 1990 through which Aboriginal people and Torres Strait Islanders were formally involved in the processes of government affecting their lives. The agency was dismantled in 2005 in the aftermath of corruption allegations and litigation.
Adelaide Bore Aboriginal community approximately 230 km north of Alice Springs.
Adels Grove Property in Lawn Hill, Queensland, approximately 250 km north of Mount Isa.
John (Jack) Ah Kit Important Aboriginal leader and a former director of the Northern Land Council (1984–1990). He was Labor member for Arnhem in the Northern Territory from 1995–2005.
Richie Ahmat Born on Thursday Island in the Torres Strait. Richie's parents are Wuthathi and Yupungathi descendants from the east and west coasts of Cape York. Richie was involved in some of the meetings during the negotiations over the Century Agreement, through his involvement with the CFMEU.

Aileron Station Cattle property located in Anmatyerre country, 130 km north of Alice Springs.

Alcoota Station Cattle property approximately 110 km north-east of Alice Springs in the Northern Territory. Alcoota was one of the Northern Territory's longest and most litigated land claims. A pastoralist lease in the Central Land Council region of Central Australia, it was acquired for the traditional landowners to convert to Aboriginal land under claim through the Aboriginal Land Rights (Northern Territory) Act 1976. The pastoral lease, covering 2,970 square km, was lodged almost immediately after it was purchased for the Engawala community in 1993 by the Alcoota Aboriginal Corporation, with funds from ATSIC. It cost Northern Territory taxpayers more than $2 million in legal costs to contest the claim, and the case was eventually thrown out by the Supreme Court in 2002. Although the land claim hearing began in 1996, it was adjourned due to politically motivated litigation intended to prevent it going ahead. The land claim hearing was finally completed in 2004, and recommendation for grant in 2007. The handback of title was finally made in July 2012. More traditional landowners have returned to live on their country, while the cattle property is managed on behalf of the traditional landowners. It is the traditional country of the Alyawarre to the north and Anmatyerre to the west, as well as the Central and Eastern Arrernte. It is Tracker Tilmouth's traditional country.

Ali Curung (Alekarenge) Aboriginal community of about 960 people located 150 km south of Tennant Creek, in the Northern Territory. Alekarenge is a Kaytetye word meaning 'Country of Dogs' or 'Dog Dreaming'.

Jon Altman Social scientist with a disciplinary focus on anthropology and economics, the founding director of the Centre for Aboriginal Economic Policy Research (CAEPR) at the Australian National University.

Alyawarre Language group of the traditional Aboriginal landowners of Alyawarre lands, east of Alice Springs.

Ammaroo Cattle station in the Sandover region of the Northern Territory, approximately 255 km north-east of Alice Springs.

Amata Aboriginal community in the APY Lands in South Australia, comprising one of their six main communities. It sits at the base of the Musgrave Ranges, approximately 95 km south of Uluru, or about 390 km south-west of Alice Springs.

Amoonguna (Imengkwerne) Aboriginal community on the Ross River Highway, approximately 10 km south of Alice Springs in the Northern Territory.

Ampilatwatye Aboriginal community in Alyawarre country, 250 km south-east of Tennant Creek and 265 km north-east of Alice Springs in the Northern Territory.

Alison Nampitjinpa Anderson Australian politician in the Northern Territory Legislative Assembly since 2005, representing the electorates of MacDonnell and

LIST OF PEOPLE, PLACES AND ORGANISATIONS

Namatjira. She has been an elected member representing the Australian Labor Party, and then the CLP as a government minister. She became the leader of the Palmer United Party in the Northern Territory in 2014, but resigned to sit as an independent from 2014–2016. In 2016 she announced her retirement from politics.

Angas Downs Aboriginal-owned pastoral lease within Macdonnell Shire, situated 220 km south-west of Alice Springs. It belonged to Arthur and Bess Liddle when Tracker worked there. The 320,500 hectare lease was purchased in 1994 by the Imanpa Development Association, which includes Matuntara descendents (the original occupiers of the Angas Downs region, Yankunytjatjara and Pitjantjatjara people). It was formally recognised as an Indigenous Protected Area in 2009.

Anindilyakwa Land Council (ALC) Established in 1991 for the traditional landowners of the Groote Eylandt archipelago.

Anmatjere Community Government Council Located in the town of Ti Tree. The region covered by the Anmatjere Council was merged into the Central Desert Shire, and Anmatjere Council no longer exists. Anmatjere is an another spelling of Anmatyerre.

Anmatyerre Aboriginal people whose traditional lands north of Alice Springs comprise communities and outstations including Aileron, Napperby, Alcoota, and the town of Ti Tree.

Aputula Also known as Finke, Aboriginal community 220 km south of Alice Springs – but approximately 460 km by road as it lies 159 km east of the Stuart Highway.

APY Lands Traditional lands of the Anangu Pitjantjatjara, Ngaanyatjarra and Yankunytjatjara peoples, covering a vast area including the remote north-west corner of South Australia, south-west corner of the Northern Territory, and across the border in the east of Western Australia.

Areyonga Aboriginal community in the western region of Central Australia, 170 km west of Alice Springs.

Armour Energy Corporation involved in the discovery and development of gas and associated liquid resources in Australia.

Arnhem Land Area of approximately 34,000 square kilometres in the north-east corner of the Northern Territory.

Arrernte Language group of the traditional Aboriginal landowners of Arrernte lands in the Central Australia region of the Northern Territory.

Atula Cattle station now called Apiwentye, it has been owned and operated by Aboriginal people since 1989 and was handed back to the traditional owners, Eastern Arrernte people, in 1994. It is located on the Plenty River Western Channel in the Northern Territory, approximately 250 km from Alice Springs.

Australian Conservation Foundation (ACF) National environmental conservation body set up in the mid-1960s.

David Avery Former principal lawyer, Central Land Council.

Faith Bandler AC (1918–2015) Campaigned for the successful 1967 amendment to the Australian Constitution, which gave the Commonwealth the power to legislate for Aboriginal people living in a state as well as those living in a Federal territory.

Frank Baarda Long-term resident of Yuendumu who works for the Yuendumu Mining Company.

Richard Bartlett Director of the Centre for Mining, Energy and Natural Resources Law in the Faculty of Law, University of Western Australia, and has appeared as counsel in native title litigation before the High Court of Australia.

Basso's Farm Aboriginal town camp on the northern outskirts of Alice Springs.

Kim Beazley AC Former Australian diplomat and Labor Party politician who served as Labor leader, Deputy Prime Minister, and leader of the Labor Opposition from 1996 to 2001. He was a minister under governments led by both Bob Hawke and Paul Keating, and deputy Prime Minister under Keating from 1995 to 1996.

Dickie Bedford A member of the Bunuba people of the Fitzroy Crossing region of the Western Kimberley, in Western Australia.

Wayne Bergmann Former director of the Kimberley Land Council.

Berrimah Eastern suburb of Darwin.

Bronwyn Bishop Former Liberal Party politician.

Johannes 'Joh' Bjelke-Petersen Former Australian politician, he was the longest-lived and longest-serving Premier of Queensland (1968–1987.).

Allen Blanchard Former Australian politician, Labor Member for Moore in the Northern Territory from 1983 to 1990.

Bond Springs Cattle station 20 km north of Alice Springs in the MacDonnell Ranges.

Boodjamulla National Park Formerly known as Lawn Hill National Park, it is south of the Gulf of Carpentaria in North West Queensland. Covering 2,280 km, its southern most point lies approximately 180 km north of Mount Isa.

Bootu Creek Manganese Mine Located 110 km north of Tennant Creek in the Northern Territory, on Banka Banka pastoral lease, the custodial land of the Kumapla (Dingo) clan of the Warumungu people.

Borroloola Town in the Northern Territory located on the MacArthur River, approximately 50 km upstream from the Gulf of Carpentaria and 710 km south-east of Darwin, population approximately 900.

LIST OF PEOPLE, PLACES AND ORGANISATIONS

Mike Bowden Former AFL player for the Richmond Football Club and teacher, who has lived and worked for Aboriginal communities and organisations for many years in the Northern Territory.

Bruce Breaden Senior Luritja man from west of Alice Springs and a former Chairman of the Central Land Council.

Bulman Cattle station in Central Arnhem Land 400 km south-east of Darwin.

The Bungalow Government institution and school for Aboriginal children of mixed descent who had been removed from their families. Established in Alice Springs, it was relocated to Jay Creek in 1928, 45 km west of Alice Springs. It was relocated a second time to the old Alice Springs Telegraph Station in 1932. It closed in 1942. In Jay Creek the Bungalow suffered terribly from insalubrious conditions including overcrowding, an insufficient water supply and lack of fruit and vegetables.

Denis Burke Country Liberal Party Chief Minister of the Northern Territory, 1999–2001.

Burketown Small town in the north-west of Queensland with a population of approximately 200 people, located 30 km south of the Gulf of Carpentaria and 320 km north of Mount Isa.

Chris Burns Labor member of the Northern Territory Legislative Assembly, who held the seat of Johnston from its creation in 2001 until his retirement in 2012.

Bushy Park Station Cattle station 85 km north of Alice Springs.

Canning Stock Route Track that runs 1,850 km through the Great Sandy Desert from Halls Creek in the north (in the Kimberley region of Western Australia) to Wiluna in the south (in the Mid West region of Western Australia.).

Calton Hills Cattle station in North West Queensland, 65 km north of Mount Isa. Tracker Tilmouth was instrumental in negotiating its acquisition on behalf of the Kalkadoon traditional landowners.

Carpentaria Land Council The largest and most eminent corporate entity representing the interests of traditional landowners in the southern Gulf of Carpentaria, with membership representing nine Aboriginal language groups whose traditional lands and waters are located in the Gulf. It was first established in 1982.

Ian Cawood Former senior ranger at Ayers Rock (now Uluru–Kata Tjuta National Park). He compiled the book, *Uluru (Ayers Rock – Mount Olga) National Park Reptiles* for the Territory Parks and Wildlife Commission, 1978.

Central Australian Aboriginal Congress Aboriginal Corporation ('Congress') The largest Aboriginal medical service in the Northern Territory. Based in Alice Springs, it provides health services to people throughout Central Australia. Tracker Tilmouth was involved in the establishment of the service in 1973.

Central Land Council (CLC) Aboriginal land council that represents 18,000 Aboriginal people from the fifteen language groups of the southern half of the Northern Territory, an area that covers 771,747 square km of land in Central Australia.
Centrecorp Foundation Investment corporation established by the Central Land Council in Central Australia in the 1980s to allow Aboriginal people to participate commercially in the Northern Territory economy, rather than simply having development take place around them.
Centrefarm Aboriginal Horticulture Limited Aboriginal-owned not-for-profit Australian company, originally established in 2002 by Aboriginal landowners in Central Australia to drive the economic development of Aboriginal land for the benefit of the traditional landowners.
Century Mine Large open-cut zinc, lead and silver mine that began production in 1999, located on the traditional land of the Waanyi nation at Lawn Hill in the highlands south of the Gulf of Carpentaria, 240 km north of Mount Isa. It is Australia's largest open-pit zinc mine. Mining ended in 2016.
Christine Christopherson Traditional landowner in Arnhem Land. She is an activist for local and national Indigenous issues, and an artist.
Cloncurry Town and locality in North West Queensland, 105 km east of Mount Isa.
Clontarf Foundation Established in 2000 to improve the education, life skills and employment prospects of young Aboriginal men.
Paul Coe Wiradjuri man, an important activist and lawyer born at Erambie Mission in Cowra, NSW.
Robert Lindsay 'Bob' Collins (1946–2007) Former federal senator for the Northern Territory from 1987 to 1998. He was charged with child sex offences but committed suicide before facing court. He was replaced in the Senate by Trish Crossin.
Combined Aboriginal Nations of Central Australia (CANCA) Established by meetings requested by senior traditional men to the Central Land Council when Tracker was the director. CANCA hosted the Kalkaringi Convention in Kalkaringi in 1998, which produced the Kalkaringi Statement advocating for an Aboriginal future for Central Australia, including Aboriginal self-government. This model of Aboriginal self-determination was seen as threatening familiar power structures, and was ignored and not supported by the 'status quo' administration of Aboriginal welfare-orientated policies throughout the Northern Territory. CANCA directed and collaborated with other interest groups in the Northern Territory such as the conservative pastoral landholders who were also dissatisfied with the direction of the Northern Territory Government's statehood campaign, and successfully defeated the referendum for Northern Territory statehood in 1998.

Combined Aboriginal Organisations of Central Australia (CAO) Collective of the major Aboriginal organisations in Alice Springs. It was established in the 1980s and plays a key policy and advocacy role and platform for Aboriginal organisations in Central Australia.

Community Development Employment Program (CDEP) An initiative of the Australian Government for Aboriginal and Torres Strait Islander people in remote areas to work for their unemployment entitlements. The scheme was abolished in July 2007 and replaced by Job Services Australia in 2009.

Congress See **Central Australian Aboriginal Congress**

Construction, Forestry, Mining and Energy Union (CFMEU) The main trade union in construction, forestry and furnishing products, mining and energy production for over 100,000 workers in Australia.

Coolibah Station Cattle station that covers 85 hectares of escarpment and river country close to Judbarra / Gregory National Park in the Top End of the Northern Territory, approximately 345 km south of Darwin. Much of the film *Jedda* was filmed on this property.

H.C. 'Nugget' Coombs (1906–97) Economist, public servant, and supporter of Aboriginal people. Chairperson of the Council for Aboriginal Affairs, which was set up after the 1967 referendum to advise the government on Aboriginal matters.

Peter Costello AC Former Liberal politician who served as Treasurer in the Howard Liberal government, 1996–2007.

Barbara Cox Former Eastern Central Australia regional manager, Central Land Council.

Josie Crawshaw Aboriginal activist who lives in Darwin. Former CEO of Strong Aboriginal Families, Together (SAF,T), the Northern Territory's peak body for Aboriginal children and families.

Simon Crean Former Labor politician, who was Leader of the Opposition and a cabinet minister. He was president of the Australian Council of Trade Unions before entering federal politics.

Croker Island Island in the Arafura Sea off the coast of Arnhem Land in the Northern Territory, 230 km north-east of Darwin. It is the traditional land of the Yarmirr people. In 1941 the Methodist Overseas Mission established an Aboriginal children's home on the island, for children removed from their families and homes under government policy. The Croker Island Mission accommodated Aboriginal children from Darwin and Alice Springs in temporary cottages until the children were evacuated to institutions in NSW because of WWII. The mission began operating again in 1946, housing the children in eight new cottages. It was at this time that Tracker and his brothers William and Patrick were removed from their family in Alice Springs (Mbantua) and brought to live at the mission. The mission's aims were: 'To build up the half-castes committed to our care by the Government into a Christian community at Croker Island…where the people shall be settled on the land in pastoral and agricultural pursuits…foster the development of personality both individual and social, and to give to each a sense of his or her own worth, to the local community, to Australia as a whole, and especially in the sight of God…educate the people to European standards of life, so that they may be entitled to citizenship status, and may be able to take their place in, and be ultimately assimilated in the general life of the Commonwealth. (Review Report, Croker Island Institution, from Establishment to 31st December, 1949, F.H. Moy, Director of Native Affairs) The mission was closed in 1968. See **Minjilang** for the community on Croker Island.

Patricia 'Trish' Crossin Former Labor senator for the Northern Territory from 1998 to 2013.

Dr Trevor Cutter (1945–1990) Pioneer of Aboriginal health provision. In 1974 he visited Alice Springs to assess conditions and stayed to work with Central Australian Aboriginal Congress to provide the area's first Aboriginal medical health service.

Daguragu Aboriginal community 365 km south-west of Katherine in the Northern Territory.

Daly River Called Nauiyu by the Malak Malak people, Daly River is an Aboriginal community of approximately 500 people. It is 140 km south from Darwin and 140 km north-east of Wadeye.

Danila Dilba Health Service Aboriginal community-controlled organisation based in Alice Springs, initially set up in 1973. It provides culturally appropriate comprehensive primary health care and community services to Biluru (Aboriginal and Torres Strait Islander) people in the Yilli Rreung (greater Darwin) region.

Patricia D'Arango Former manager, Native Title Unit, Central Land Council.

Deloitte Access Economics Australian economics advisory practice.

Desert Knowledge Australia Statutory corporation of the Northern Territory Government with a national and international mandate to bring about change to sustain and enhance the lives and livelihoods of Australia's desert peoples.

Michael C. Dillon Worked in key positions influencing policy for decades in Indigenous public sector management. A former advisor to Jenny Macklin as Minister for Aboriginal Affairs, he was until recently CEO of the Indigenous Land Corporation.

Gatjil Djerrkura OAM (1949–2004) Aboriginal leader in the Northern Territory and Australia. He was a senior elder of the Wangurri Aboriginal clan of the Yolngu people in Arnhem Land, and served as a chairman of the Aboriginal and Torres Strait Islander Commission from 1996–2000.

LIST OF PEOPLE, PLACES AND ORGANISATIONS

Docker River (Kaltukatjara) Aboriginal community 505 km west of Alice Springs, near the Western Australia border. It is home to approximately 300 Aboriginal people.

Michael 'Mick' Dodson AM Indigenous Australian barrister, academic, and member of the Yawuru peoples of the Broome area of the southern Kimberley region. Dodson became director of the Northern Land Council in 1990. He is chairperson of the Australian Institute of Aboriginal and Torres Strait Islander Studies, director of the National Centre for Indigenous Studies at Australian National University and is currently Professor of Law, ANU. His brother is Patrick Dodson.

Patrick Dodson Yawuru man from Broome, Western Australia. He is a former director of the Central Land Council, former chairman of the Council for Aboriginal Reconciliation, a former Commissioner into Aboriginal Deaths in Custody and former Roman Catholic priest. Dodson is widely regarded as the father of reconciliation, and involved in the movement for constitutional recognition of Indigenous people. He became a Labor senator for Western Australia in 2016.

Doomadgee Aboriginal community located in North West Queensland, south of the Gulf of Carpentaria and 515 km north of Mount Isa in Queensland. At the 2011 census it had a population of 1,258 people. Originally known as Dumaji, it was previously an Aboriginal mission established in 1936 by Exclusive Plymouth Brethern.

Douglas–Daly River Region Region located 125 km north-west of Katherine.

Jim Downing Uniting Church Minister who helped establish the Institute for Aboriginal Development in Alice Springs during the late 1960s, which established courses in interpreting and translation and in various Central Australian languages including Pitjantjatjara, Pintupi, Warlpiri and Arrernte. He passed away in 2009.

Elliott Small town in the middle of the Northern Territory, 760 km north of Alice Springs and 635 km south of Darwin.

Energy Resources of Australia Ltd (ERA) Australia's longest continually operating uranium producer which has operated the Ranger mine for more than three decades. The mine is located eight kilometres east of Jabiru and 260 kilometres south-east of Darwin. The mine is surrounded by but separate from the World Heritage–listed Kakadu National Park.

Ernabella (Pukatja) Anangu community of approximately 600 people on APY Lands in the north west of South Australia in the Musgrave Ranges, approximately 335 km south-west of Alice Springs.

Essington House Darwin home for adolescent boys who were awaiting a court appearance or placement in foster or institutional care. It later became an assessment and training centre for girls and boys. It was opened by the government in 1963 and closed in 1974.

Paul Everingham Member of the Country Liberal Party, the head of government of the Northern Territory from 1977, and Chief Minister when the Territory was granted self-government in 1978. He served as the second and last Majority Leader and the first Chief Minister of the Northern Territory to 1984. Everingham used his powers to oppose and contest Aboriginal land rights in the Northern Territory through the Aboriginal Land Rights Act.

John Faulkner Former Australian Labor politician who was a minister in the Keating Labor government (1993–96).

Finke see **Aputula**.

Tim Fischer AC Australian politician and former Deputy Prime Minister in the Howard Government, 1996–1999. He retired from parliament in 2001.

Gary Foley Well-known Aboriginal activist and academic in Melbourne.

Barney Foran Adjunct Research Fellow, Institute for Land, Water and Society at Charles Sturt University. He led research teams in the CSIRO's Resource Futures group, which produced long-range analyses of Australia's physical economy, focusing on population, fisheries, land and water.

Norman Fry Former Director, Northern Land Council, after Jack Ah Kit.

Noel Fullerton Noted camel man in Alice Springs for many years, and one of the founders of the Alice Springs Camel Cup.

Harold Furber Arrernte man, born in Alice Springs to Emily Furber, daughter to Mrs Rita Furber (formerly Rice) and Mr Frank Furber, both senior Arrernte lawkeepers of the Alice Springs area. He spent most of his childhood on Croker Island Mission, and he and Tracker both left the island together at age twelve when they were sent to Darwin by the mission to attend high school. They were accommodated at Essington House, of which Harold said, *'It was like a receiving home for kids, they also heard children's court there.'* ('The Day I Left Croker Island', in *Take Power*, ed. Alexis Wright, IAD Press, Alice Springs, 1998, p. 124). Harold has worked for Aboriginal organisations in Central Australia for many years, including as deputy director of the Central Land Council, and is a strong advocate for the Stolen Generations. He is the chairman of the Desert Peoples Centre, Alice Springs.

The Gap The Heavitree Gap is a water gap in the MacDonnell Ranges, located at the southern entrance to Alice Springs. An important sacred site for the Arrernte people and home to many Aboriginal families.

Garma Festival Annual festival of traditional culture held at Gulkula in North East Arnhem Land, organised by the Yothu Yindi Foundation. Its aims are reconciliation, education and understanding through sharing of culture, and the creation of economic opportunities beneficial to North East Arnhem Land. The festival is promoted as

LIST OF PEOPLE, PLACES AND ORGANISATIONS

Australia's leading Indigenous cultural exchange event and a hub for major discussion forums, often attracting high-profile federal politicians and other leaders.

Gascoyne Region in the north-west of Western Australia.

Geraldton City located on the Mid West coast of Western Australia, 370 km north of Perth.

Rev Dr Djiniyini Gondarra Prominent Aboriginal leader and spokesperson, born in Milingimbi in East Arnhem Land.

Adam Goodes Former champion Australian rules footballer who played for the Sydney Swans team in the Australian Football League. He was named the Australian of the Year in 2014 for his community work and advocacy against racism.

Goofy Bore On Mount Skinner near Utopia on the Sandover River, approximately 170 km north of Alice Springs.

The Gorge Katherine Gorge in the Nitmiluk National Park, which is owned by the Jawoyn people, located 30 km north-east of Katherine.

Wayne Goss (1951–2014) Australian politician, Labor Premier of Queensland 1989–1996.

Gove Peninsula Vast tract of Aboriginal-owned land in Arnhem Land, on the west coast of the Gulf of Carpentaria. The Gove Operations Bauxite Mine Alumina Refinery is located here. Rio Tinto, the operator of the mine, undertook a phased suspension of alumina production in 2014 while continuing to focus on its bauxite operations. In 2011, a historic agreement was signed with Rirratjingu, Gumatj and Galpu landowners, the Northern Land Council, and Rio Tinto Alcan, formally acknowledging traditional landowners for the first time in the operation's history. See also **Nhulunbuy** and **Yirrkala**.

The Granites Gold mine on Warlpiri land in the Tanami region, approximately 500 km north-west of Alice Springs in the Northern Territory. It falls within the boundaries of the Central Land Council.

Granites Mine Affected Areas Aboriginal Corporation (GMAAAC) Aboriginal body representing nine communities affected by the Granites gold mine on Warlpiri land that plans and implements community projects from royalty monies.

Groote Eylandt Island in the Gulf of Carpentaria that belongs to the Warnindhilyagwa people.

Gundjeihmi Aboriginal Corporation Founded in 1995 to manage the collection, disbursement and investment of funds derived from the Ranger uranium mine on behalf of the stakeholders, the Mirarr clan.

Mr Gunner Important Urapuntja community leader and traditional landowner of the Alyawarre and Anmatyerre people from Utopia. He is remembered for his work as a CANCA leader for Aboriginal rights including Aboriginal self-government in the Northern Territory, compensation for the stolen generations, and former executive member of the Central Land Council.

Haasts Bluff (Ikuntji) Aboriginal community 205 km west of Alice Springs.

Brian Harradine (1935–2014) Independent federal Tasmanian senator, 1975–2005.

Harts Range (Atitjere) Cattle property in the Sandover region, approximately 135 km north-east of Alice Springs in the Northern Territory.

Hatches Creek Aboriginal community approximately 180 km south-east of Tennant Creek and 335 km north of Alice Springs in the Northern Territory.

Olga Havnen Well-known Aboriginal leader and scholar in the Northern Territory.

Bob Hawke AC Former Australian Labor Prime Minister (1983–1991).

Hermannsburg Known in Western Arrernte as Ntaria. Aboriginal community in Ljirapinta Ward of the MacDonnell Shire in the Northern Territory, 130 km west of Alice Springs. The community has a population of about 600 people, and was originally established as an Aboriginal mission in 1877 by Lutheran missionaries.

John Herron AO Minister for Aboriginal Affairs (1991–2001) in the conservative Coalition government of Prime Minister John Howard. In April 2000 he tabled a report in the Australian Parliament which questioned whether or not there was ever a Stolen Generation, on the basis that only ten per cent of Aboriginal children had been removed, so they could not constitute an entire 'generation'.

Kim Hill Former director of the Northern Land Council.

Robert Hill Former senior Liberal senator and Minister for Defence (2001–2006).

John Howard Former conservative Liberal Prime Minister (1996–2007).

Huckitta Cattle station 185 km north-east of Alice Springs.

Imanpa Aboriginal community originally established on a 1,628 ha excision from Mount Ebenezer station in 1978. The purpose was to relocate a drinker's camp from the Mount Ebenezer Road house (which the Imanpa community now own and run), and establish a centre for displaced stockmen from several pastoral properties in that region. Families are now drawn from Areyonga, Aputula, Kaltukatjara, Mutitjulu and Alice Springs. Located 155 km east of Uluru and 210 km south-west of Alice Springs.

Indigenous Business Australia (IBA) Established in 1990 following the proclamation of the *Aboriginal and Torres Strait Islander Commission (ATSIC) Act 1989*, it was originally the Aboriginal and Torres Strait Islander Commercial Development Corporation (CDC). A commercially focused organisation that encourages economic independence for Aboriginal and Torres Strait Islander peoples.

Indigenous Land Corporation (ILC) Australian Commonwealth statutory authority established in 1995, with national responsibilities to assist Aboriginal and Torres Strait Islander people to acquire land and to manage assets.

LIST OF PEOPLE, PLACES AND ORGANISATIONS

Institute for Aboriginal Development (IAD) Aboriginal corporation based in Alice Springs, established by the Uniting Church in 1969 to provide adult training programs for Aboriginal people.

Inpex Japanese worldwide oil and gas exploration and production company, which with French partner Total operates the Ichthys gas project in Darwin, and off the coast of Western Australia.

Inverway Station Cattle station 615 km south of Darwin in the Northern Territory.

Irrmarne Aboriginal community 350 km north-east of Alice Springs on the Sandover Highway.

Ja Ja Community in the Northern Territory, approximately 215 km east of Darwin and 18 km from Jabiru.

Jabiluka Pair of uranium deposits 225 km east of Darwin, surrounded by, but not part of, the World Heritage–listed Kakadu National Park, on land belonging to the Mirarr people. Mine development was to have been built on the land, but Mirarr leaders Jacqui Katona and Yvonne Margarula organised an eight-month blockade in the 1990s to stop the mine going ahead. The ERA mining company built surface infrastructure and the decline down to the ore body, but falling uranium prices and ongoing protest about the use of land resulted in the Jabiluka Long-Term Care and Maintenance Agreement signed in February 2005, which gives the traditional owners veto rights over future development in Jabiluka. Rehabilitation works commenced on the site in 2003, after the Mirarr agitated to have Rio Tinto clean up the site. Jacqui Katona and Yvonne Margarula won the 1999 US Goldman Environmental Prize in recognition of their efforts to protect their country and culture against uranium mining.

Jabiru Town with a population of about 1,100, mostly mining administered. It was originally built in 1982 to house the community living at Jabiru East near the Ranger Uranium Mine eight kilometres away. The mine and town are completely surrounded by the Kakadu National Park. Jabiru is situated about 215 km east of Darwin.

Jawoyn Region of traditional Aboriginal land in the Northern Territory that includes the Katherine region, western Arnhem Land and the southern area of Kakadu National Park. It is approximately 50,000 square km.

Jawoyn Association Aboriginal Corporation Representative body for the Jawoyn Aboriginal traditional land owners in the Katherine region of the Northern Territory, established in 1985.

Jay Creek Town 45 km west of Alice Springs. See **The Bungalow**.

Joint Council on Aboriginal Land and Mining (JCALM) Council that included Tracker Tilmouth (Central Land Council), Peter Yu (Kimberley Land Council), Murrandoo Yanner (Carpentaria Land Council), Noel Pearson (Cape York Land Council) and Galarrwuy Yunupingu (Northern Land Council). Robert De Crespigny

(Normandy Mining Limited) and Paul Wand (Conzinc Riotinto of Australia Limited) represented mining interests, and others also represented mining companies.

Neville Jones Arrived in the Northern Territory to train as a patrol officer in 1970. The former superintendent of Docker River, he became a senior bureaucrat in the Department of Aboriginal Affairs.

Barnaby Joyce Federal politician, currently Deputy Prime Minister and leader of the National Party.

Kakadu National Park UNESCO World Heritage Site and Australia's largest national park, at nearly 20,000 square km. It is located in the Top End, the northernmost region of the Northern Territory.

Kalkadoon Lands of the Kalkadoon people located in the Mount Isa region.

Kalkaringi Township 365 km south-west of Katherine in the Northern Territory. Site for the Kalkaringi Convention and Kalkaringi Statement; see **Combined Aboriginal Nations of Central Australia**.

Karlantijpa North Aboriginal Land Trust Aboriginal land trust located in the Central Land Council area of the Northern Territory, approximately 90 km north-west of Tennant Creek.

Katherine The third largest town in the Northern Territory. It lies on the Katherine River 270 km south-east of Darwin on the Stuart Highway.

Francis Jupurrurla Kelly Warlpiri man living at Yuendumu, and long-term member and chairman of the Central Land Council.

Kimberley Land Council (KLC) Peak Aboriginal body in the Kimberley region of northern Western Australia covering approximately 423,000 square km. Formed in 1978, the land council works with Aboriginal people to secure native title recognition, conservation and land management, and cultural business enterprises.

Kintore Known locally as Walungurru, an Aboriginal community 460 km west of Alice Springs in the Northern Territory, near the Western Australia border.

Alec Kruger Published his biography *Alone on the Soaks: The Life and Times of Alec Kruger*, with Gerard Waterford in 2007 with IAD Press, Alice Springs.

Kulgera Locality in the Northern Territory 20 km north of the border with South Australia, 240 km south of Alice Springs and 245 km south-east of Uluru.

Kununurra Town in far northern Western Australia in the east of the Kimberley region, 250 km south-west of Katherine.

Francis Xavier Kurrupuwu Member of the Northern Territory Legislative Assembly from 2012 to 2016.

Lajamanu Aboriginal community located 560 km south of Katherine, and approximately 650 km from Darwin in the Northern Territory.

LIST OF PEOPLE, PLACES AND ORGANISATIONS

Marcia Langton AM One of Australia's leading Aboriginal scholars, and a descendant of the Yiman and Bidjara nations, she holds the Foundation Chair in Australian Indigenous Studies at the University of Melbourne. She has previously worked as an anthropologist for the Central Land Council, the Queensland Government, and the Cape York Land Council, and also on the 1989 Royal Commission into Aboriginal Deaths in Custody, and authored the report 'Too Much Sorry Business'. In recent years she has supported the Northern Territory National Emergency Response.

Laramba Community in Anmatyerre country 170 km north-west of Alice Springs.

Larrimah Small hamlet on the Stuart Highway 430 km south-east from Darwin.

Lawn Hill Boodjamulla National Park in North West Queensland, 255 km north of Mount Isa, was formerly known as Lawn Hill National Park.

Janet Layton Aboriginal elder and political leader.

Larisa Lee Former CLP and independent Member for Arnhem in the Northern Territory Legislative Assembly (2014–2016).

Lhere Artepe Central Arrernte native title representative body in Alice Springs. It was formed in 2002 following the Federal Court decision that native title was recognised to exist within the municipality of Alice Springs. The organisation helps the native title holders to care for their country and strengthen their culture.

Arthur Liddle (1918–1997) Important Arrernte man who was the former owner of Angas Downs Station in Central Australia.

Bess Liddle Important Luritja woman and elder.

Little Sisters (Inarlenge) One of the eighteen Aboriginal town camps in Alice Springs.

Loves Creek Station at the eastern end of the MacDonnell Ranges, 70 km east of Alice Springs. In the 1970s the Eastern Arrernte traditional landowners lobbied for living space on the property, and the Central Land Council helped them to purchase it in 1993 using funds from the ABTA. A land claim was lodged in 1994, and in 2012 the pastoral lease was handed back to its traditional owners as inalienable Aboriginal freehold land under the Land Rights Act. The property is well managed and the numbers of cattle have increased from 8,000 head at the time of purchase to 23,000.

Mabo *Mabo v Queensland (1989)*, commonly referred to as Mabo after its key plaintiff, Eddie Koiki Mabo, was a landmark High Court of Australia decision in 1992 that for the first time recognised native title in Australia. The High Court rejected the doctrine of *terra nullius* in favour of the common law doctrine of Aboriginal title, and overruled *Milirrpum v Nabalco Pty Ltd (1971)*, a decision of the Supreme Court of the Northern Territory.

MacArthur River Mine One of the world's largest zinc, lead and silver mines, it is located in the north-western Northern Territory approximately 90 km south-west of the Gulf of Carpentaria and 720 km south-east of Darwin.

MacDonald Downs Cattle station approximately 280 km north-east of Alice Springs.

MacDonnell Ranges 644 km-long series of mountains in Central Australia, 55 km west of Alice Springs.

Jenny Macklin Former Labor Minister for Aboriginal Affairs in the Rudd and Gillard governments (2007–2013).

John Macumba Born with cerebral palsy in the remote central desert of the Pitjantjatjara Lands, he is considered one of the pioneers of Indigenous media in Australia, including setting up CAAMA (Central Australia Aboriginal Media Association) radio in Central Australia. The John Macumba Media and Training Centre in Alice Springs is named after him.

Maningrida Large Aboriginal community in Central Arnhem Land on the coast of the Arafura Sea. It is located 370 km east of Darwin, and with a population of approximately 2,000.

Yvonne Margarula Led the Mirarr people's campaign, along with Jacqui Katona, to stop the Jabiluka uranium mine in the Northern Territory.

Clare Martin ALP Chief Minister of the Northern Territory, 2005–2007.

Mataranka Community 365 km south-east of Darwin in the Top End region of the Northern Territory.

Leon Melpi Wadeye Aboriginal elder.

Mereenie Oil and Gas Field Located in the Amadeus Basin 210 km west of Alice Springs on the traditional lands of the Arrernte, Luritja and Yankunytjatjara peoples.

Mick Miller (1937–1998) Waanyi and Kuku Yalanji man, an important Queensland Aboriginal statesman.

Mimili Aboriginal community in the Everard Ranges on the APY Lands in the north-west of South Australia, 385 km south of Alice Springs, with a population of around 300.

Minjilang Formerly Mission Bay, a West Arnhem Land Aboriginal community on Croker Island, 235 km east-north-east of Darwin. Minjilang was home to the Croker Island Mission where Tracker Tilmouth and his brothers William and Patrick grew up. See **Croker Island**.

Mistake Creek Aboriginal-owned and operated cattle station acquired for its traditional landowners, the Tjupanyin people, in the early 1990s with the help of the Central Land Council under claim through the Land Rights Act. The property now runs about 23,000 head of cattle. It is located approximately 1,000 km south-south-west of Darwin on the border with Western Australia.

Morr Morr Pastoral Company The largest Aboriginal-owned pastoral group in Australia, based in Normanton, Queensland.

Mount Allan Aboriginal-owned and operated cattle station approximately 245 km north-west of Alice Springs. Acquired with the help of the Central Land Council for the traditional landowners to convert to Aboriginal land under claim through the Land Rights Act.

Mount Ebenezer Cattle station 200 km south-west of Alice Springs. It shares a boundary with Angas Downs Station to the west. Mount Ebenezer Roadhouse is owned and run by the Impana community and connects to Yulara, Kata Tjuta and Uluru east to the Stuart Highway about 200 km south-west of Alice Springs.

Mount Isa Major mining town in the Gulf Country region of North West Queensland. It has a population of approximately 33,000.

Mount Liebig (Watiyawanu) Aboriginal community 360 km west of Alice Springs in the Northern Territory, on the western edge of the Greater MacDonnell Ranges.

Mount Riddock Pastoral lease of 2,635 km square on the Plenty Highway, 110 km north-east of Alice Springs.

Mount Skinner Cattle station 170 km north of Alice Springs.

Mount Swan Cattle station 150 km north-east of Alice Springs.

Mount Wedge Pastoral lease approximately 200 km north-west of Alice Springs, owned by the Ngarlatji Aboriginal Land Corporation, acquired with help of the Central Land Council under the Land Rights Act.

Muckaty Station (Warlmanpa), 2,380 km square Aboriginal freehold landholding in the Northern Territory, approximately 110 km north of Tennant Creek.

Warren Mundine Bundjalung Aboriginal leader, businessman, and former national president of the Australian Labor Party. He held the position of chairman of the Australian Government's Indigenous Advisory Council until it was dissolved in 2017.

Mutitjulu Aboriginal community at the eastern end of Uluru in the Northern Territory, 340 km south-west of Alice Springs and 25 km south of Yulara. It is home of the Anangu Pitjantjatjara people with associations also to Yankunytjatjara, Luritja, and Yangkunytjatjara language groups.

Namakurlangu Also known as Coniston, cattle station 220 km north-west of Alice Springs.

Napperby Pastoral property 175 km north-west of Alice Springs.

Napperby Creek Waterway 165 km north-west of Alice Springs, and to the south of Napperby Station.

National Federation of Land Councils Collective of Aboriginal Land Councils.

Native Title Representative Bodies (NTRB) Appointed under the Native Title Act to represent native title holders and claimants in native title–related proceedings, appearing in court on behalf of native title claimants, responding to applications such as proposed mining on native title land or land subject to a claim. The bodies assist claimants to prepare anthropological and historical evidence in support of their native title applications and act as mediators between claimants and government.

Big Bill Neidjie (c.1920–2002) Senior elder of Kakadu National Park and a traditional owner of the Bunitj estate in northern Kakadu. His book *Story About Feeling*, edited by Keith Taylor, was published by Magabala Books in 1989.

Harry Jakamarra Nelson Senior Warlpiri traditional landowner, leader and educator from Yuendumu.

Neutral Junction Pastoral lease in Barrow Creek in the Northern Territory, 210 km south of Tennant Creek and 245 km north of Alice Springs.

Tobias Nganbe Aboriginal leader and educator from Wadeye.

Ngukurr Aboriginal community on the Roper River in southern Arnhem Land, Northern Territory, 490 km south-east of Darwin and 265 km east of Katherine.

Nhulunbuy Also referred to as Gove, mining township located on the Gove Peninsula in North East Arnhem Land on Yolngu land. It is 550 km north-east of Katherine. It was established when Rio Tinto opened an alumina mine and refinery nearby. It had a population of 3,933 at the 2011 census, but the closure in 2014 of the refinery has seen a significant drop in population. See also **Gove** and **Yirrkala**.

Noonamah Suburban area of Darwin located 45 km south-east of Darwin CBD.

Normanton Cattle town in North West Queensland, south of the Gulf of Carpentaria and 380 km north of Mount Isa.

North Australian Indigenous Land and Sea Management Alliance Ltd (NAILSMA) Leader in finding solutions to support Aboriginal people to manage their country sustainably.

North Australia Research Unit (NARU) Established in 1973 in Darwin to support research into northern Australia, and to provide support for Canberra-based members of Australian National University and members of other institutions undertaking research.

Northern Land Council (NLC) Independent statutory authority of the Commonwealth responsible for assisting 30,000 Aboriginal peoples living in the Top End of the Northern Territory to acquire and manage their traditional lands and seas.

Nullawil Small rural town in Victoria, 270 km north-west of Melbourne.

Number Five Bore In the eastern Alyawarre region of Central Australia.

Oak Valley Aboriginal community in Maralinga 750 km south of Alice Springs in South Australia.

Lois (Lowitja) O'Donoghue Aboriginal former public administrator and inaugural chairperson of the now-dissolved Aboriginal and Torres Strait Islander Commission.

Orange Creek Cattle station 85 km north-west of Alice Springs in the Northern Territory.

Papunya Aboriginal community 210 km west of Alice Springs.

LIST OF PEOPLE, PLACES AND ORGANISATIONS

Marnie Parkinson Principal legal officer, Carpentaria Land Council.

Fred Pascoe Mayor of the Carpentaria Shire Council in North West Queensland, Aboriginal community leader, and CEO of the Bynoe Community Advancement Co-Operative Society Ltd.

Darryl Pearce Arrernte man and former Director of Lhere Artepe Aboriginal Corporation.

Noel Pearson Member of the Bagaarrmugu and Kuku Yalanji peoples of Cape York, an Aboriginal leader, lawyer, academic, and founder of the Cape York Institute for Policy and Leadership, an organisation promoting the economic and social development of Cape York.

Nova Peris Former athlete and politician, and ALP senator for the Northern Territory (2013–2016).

Charles Nelson (Charlie) Perkins AO (1936–2000) Arrernte/Kalkadoon man, a highly respected Aboriginal leader, activist and administrator. He was one of the key members of the Freedom Ride in NSW against racism towards Aboriginal people in small town Australia. He achieved much to support Aboriginal people during his lifetime.

Neville Perkins OAM Important politician, and a descendant of the Eastern and Central Arrernte peoples from Mbantua (Alice Springs). He was an Australian Labor Party member of the Northern Territory Legislative Assembly from 1977 to 1981, representing the electorate of MacDonnell. He was the first Aboriginal person in Australia to hold a shadow ministry in an Australian parliament, and subsequently became the party's deputy leader.

Marshall Perron Country Liberal Party Chief Minister of the Northern Territory, 1988–1995.

Tony Petrick Senior elder of the Atitjere community of the Harts Range area.

Stuart Phillpot Economist and expert in rural industries who worked in Central Australia for many years.

Pigeon Hole Aboriginal outstation community in the Kalkaringi region in the Victoria River district of the Northern Territory, 280 km south-south-west of Katherine.

Pine Creek Small town 85 km north-east of Katherine in the Northern Territory.

Pine Hill Anmatyerre traditional country in Central Australia.

Pine Hill Station Cattle station 50 km south-east of Ti Tree and about 170 km north-east of Alice Springs.

Olive Pink (1884–1975) Australian botanical illustrator, anthropologist, gardener, and activist for Aboriginal people in Central Australia.

Pipalyatjara Aboriginal community in the Anangu Pitjantjatjara Yankunytjatjara Lands in South Australia, 550 km south-west of Alice Springs and 25 km from the junction of South Australia, Western Australia and the Northern Territory.

Pitjantjatjara Lands 102,360 km square of traditional lands in the far north-west of South Australia. Part of the Anangu Pitjantjatjara Yankunytjatjara (APY) Aboriginal local government area.

Port Keats See **Wadeye**.

Bess Nungarrayi Price Politician and Country Liberal Party Member for Stuart in the Northern Territory Legislative Assembly (2012–2016), where she was Minister for Community Services.

Richard Priest Long-term Northern Territory public servant, specialising in Aboriginal Affairs.

Bill Pritchard Professor in Human Geography specialising in agriculture, food and rural places, at the University of Sydney.

Blue Pugh Operates a large crocodile farm with his wife Janelle on their property Coolibah Station in the Top End of the Northern Territory. Their story is told in the chapter 'Pumping the Adrenalin', in Sue Williams, *Outback Heroines* (Penguin, 2013). He was Tracker's good friend and a business partner.

Tjuki Tjukanku Pumpjack Born sometime around 1926–1928 in Apara in the Musgrave Ranges and was a *wati papa* (dingo man).

Bob Randall (1929–2015) Yankunytjatjara elder and member of the Stolen Generations. He was a well-known songwriter and musician, famous for the song *My Brown Skin Baby They Take Him Away*.

Ranger Uranium Mine Mine surrounded by but not included in Kakadu National Park, 225 km from Darwin. It is located on the traditional lands of the Mirarr people.

Retta Dixon Home Notorious Darwin institution set up in the post-war period where 'half-caste' Aboriginal children of the Stolen Generation were housed and trained under government policies aimed at assimilating these children into white Australia. The home, on Bagot Road, was established in 1946 and closed in 1982. At age three Tracker spent about a year and a half at Retta Dixon Home with his brothers William and Patrick, after they were removed from their father and aunty's family home in Alice Springs by the authorities when their mother died, and before they were sent to Croker Island.

Henry Reynolds Historian whose research has focused on the history of colonial frontier conflict and Indigenous dispossession in Australia.

Robert (Rob) Riley (1954–1996) Aboriginal activist advancing Indigenous issues in Australia, former chairman of the National Aboriginal Conference, and part of the negotiating team on the Native Title Act.

Rio Tinto Australian–British multinational, one of the world's largest metals and mining corporations.

Andrew Robb AO Former Minister for Trade and Investment in the Tony Abbott federal government (2013–2016).

Sugar Ray Robinson Former deputy chairperson of ATSIC (1996–2003).

Joseph 'Joe' Roe Senior Goolarabooloo law man whose grandfather was Paddy Roe.

Wenten Rubuntja AM (c. 1923–2005) Former chairman of the Central Land Council and senior traditional Arrernte law boss across Central Australia. He was one of the most important and significant land rights leaders, an important person in the movement for the protection of Aboriginal sacred sites in the Northern Territory, and organised the formation of organisations in Alice Springs over many decades. He was also well known as a painter.

Philip Ruddock Liberal Party politician who was Minister for Immigration and Multicultural and Indigenous Affairs, 1996–2003.

Maurie Japarta Ryan Member of the Gurindji nation, established the First Nations Political Party, and was appointed chairperson of the Central Land Council in 2013. In 2014 he was stood down after his area withdrew his position as their delegate to the full land council.

Santa Teresa (Ltyentye Apurte) Aboriginal community 85 km east of Alice Springs, in Arrernte country. There are about 550 people living in the community, which was originally established in 1953. The Catholic Marist Brothers have been working there mainly in education since 1977.

Marion Scrymgour Former Labor Party member of the Northern Territory Legislative Assembly (2001–2012), representing the electorate of Arafura.

Nigel Scullion Federal Minister for Indigenous Affairs in the Abbott and then Turnbull federal governments since 2013. Country Liberal Party member of the Australian Senate for the Northern Territory since November 2001.

Geoffrey Shaw Former managing director, Tangentyere Council, and important Aboriginal leader in Central Australia.

John Sheldon Former employee and acting CEO of the Northern Land Council.

Warren Snowdon Labor member of the Australian House of Representatives, representing the Division of the Northern Territory from 1987 to 1996 and from 1998 to 2001. Since November 2001 he has represented the Division of Lingiari for the Northern Territory.

Monty Soilleux Former Central Land Council employee in computer system management.

Peter ('Stracky') Strachan Worked on innovative programs for many years with Commonwealth employment, education and training in Melbourne, before going to live and work in Central Australia to use his expertise to implement employment, education and training programs for Aboriginal people through organisations such as Tangentyere Council and the Central Land Council.

Maxie Stuart ('Kwementyaye') (c. 1932–2014) Important Arrernte elder and a former chairman of the Central Land Council. He spent time in Yatala gaol after being convicted of murder in 1959. His conviction was seen as suspect by many and subject to several appeals to higher courts, the Judicial Committee of the Privy Council, and a royal commission.

John Taylor Emeritus professor at the Centre for Aboriginal Economic Policy Research, ANU, with a disciplinary background in geography and population studies.

Tanami Desert Desert in the Northern Territory and Western Australia that is Kukatja and Warlpiri country, and home to many of Australia's rare and endangered species. It is traversed by the Tanami Track.

Tangentyere Council Major service delivery agency for the eighteen Aboriginal Housing Associations known as 'town camps' in Alice Springs. It began operating in the early 1970s.

Tempe Downs Aboriginal pastoral lease on Luritja country, 166 km west of Alice Springs.

Ten Point Plan See **Wik**.

Tennant Creek Remote town in the Northern Territory, 500 km north of Alice Springs.

Thamarrurr Development Corporation Organisation based in Wadeye and owned by the twenty clan groups of the Thamarrurr region. The governing body of the corporation is made up of twelve board directors representing the three ceremony groups and twenty clan groups of the region.

Ti Tree Small town on Anmatyerre land 180 km north of Alice Springs and 285 km south of Tennant Creek, on the Stuart Highway. It is a horticultural centre for commercially grown fresh vegetables and fruit for Territory markets.

Robert 'Bobby' Tickner Former Labor Minister for Aboriginal Affairs (1990–1996).

Tilmouth Well Located on the southern end of Napperby Station, on Anmatyerre and Arrernte country, about 165 km north-west of Alice Springs.

Tipperary Station Cattle station located about 35 km east of Daly River and 140 km south of Darwin, in the north-west of the Northern Territory's Top End.

Tiwi Islands Islands of the Northern Territory in the Arafura and Timor seas, 80 km north of Darwin.

Dinny Nolan Tjampitjinpa (c. 1922–2006) Senior lawman from the Warlpiri/Anmatyerre language group and leader for rainmaking and Water Dreaming ceremonies. He was born in Yuendumu but settled in Papunya in the 1970s.

LIST OF PEOPLE, PLACES AND ORGANISATIONS

Kaapa Mbitjana Tjampitjinpa (c.1920–1989) A senior Aboriginal man born on Napperby Station. Of Anmatyerre, Warlpiri and Arrernte heritage, he had ritual responsibility for a site known as Warlugulong which he often painted. He was one of the earliest and most significant artists at Papunya and is a pivotal figure in the establishment of contemporary Indigenous Australian art.

Johnny Lynch Tjapanangka (1920–1981) Artist and former leading stockman at Narwietooma station. He painted events along the Honey Ant Dreaming trail, which ends at Woodgreen Station.

Tjukurla Community on the edge of Lake Hopkins in Western Australia, halfway between Warakurna (WA) and Kintore (Walungurru, NT), 540 km west of Alice Springs.

Tjunkata 'Nosepeg' Tjupurrula OAM (1914–1993) From the Western Desert area of Central Australia, born in Pintupi/Wenampa country. A consummate politician and a senior elder in his community, he was a driving force in the outstation movement in the 1960s to the 1980s. His paintings are held in collections across the world.

Patricia Turner AM Distinguished Arrernte/Gurdanji woman who served in senior positions of government, was a former CEO of ATSIC, and the inaugural CEO of National Indigenous Television, and is the CEO of the National Aboriginal Community Controlled Health Organisation (NACCHO).

Undoolya Station The oldest working cattle station in the Northern Territory, operating as a pastoral lease since 1872 when the pastoral lease was granted to Edward Bagot. Fifteen minutes drive east of Alice Springs.

Urapuntja Medical Service Provides health services to the homelands and outstations in the Utopia region of the Northern Territory.

Utopia Aboriginal homeland formed in 1978 on the traditional lands of the Alyawarre and Anmatyerre people. It combines the former Utopia pastoral lease with a tract of unalienated land to its north to cover an area of 3,500 km square. It comprises sixteen communities and is home to approximately 1,000 people. Alparra, the largest and most central community, is 200 km north-east of Alice Springs and 275 south of Tennant Creek.

Victoria River Waterway in the Northern Territory that runs 560 km from its source at the northern edge of the Tanami Desert to the Timor Sea. The Victoria River Crossing or Roadhouse is a settlement 225 km south of Katherine.

Wadeye Formerly a Catholic mission known as Port Keats, Wadeye is an Aboriginal town in the Northern Territory, and had a population of about 1,627 people in the 2006 census. It is located on the north-west coast of the Northern Territory, 245 km south-west of Darwin (400 km by road).

Wallara Located 190 km south-west of Alice Springs, and includes Kings Canyon in Watarrka National Park. Wallara Ranch was set up in the north-west corner of Angas Downs on a property originally leased from Arthur Liddle by Jack Cotterill in 1960 to establish the ranch, for the purpose of opening up Kings Canyon to tourism.

Warakurna Large community located in the Goldfields-Esperance Region of Western Australia, 70 km west of the border with the Northern Territory and 585 km west of Alice Springs.

Warburton (Milyirrtjarra) Aboriginal community in the Ngaanyatjarra Lands in the Gibson Desert. Located 785 km west of Alice Springs, in Western Australia.

Tom Webb Former owner of the Alcoota pastoral lease.

Neil D. Westbury Key advisor in Indigenous affairs policy and public sector management with over forty years of experience working at a senior level.

Westmoreland Coal The sixth-largest North American coal producer.

Gough Whitlam Leader of the Labor Party from 1967–1977, and Prime Minister of Australia from 1972–1975.

Wik The Wik peoples are not a single tribe, but rather a group of tribes on lands in the central west of Cape York Peninsula in Queensland. On 30 June 1993 the Wik peoples made a claim in the Federal Court of Australia for native title. The land claimed included two pastoral leases that had been issued by the Queensland government. On 23 December 1996 a majority in the High Court held that the issuing of two pastoral leases under consideration in the case *Wik Peoples v The State of Queensland* did not necessarily extinguish native title. The decision provoked significant debate in Australian politics, including intense discussions on the validity of land holdings in Australia. In 1998, the mining industry publicly campaigned for the Senate to pass the government's Wik bill, with the president of the Minerals Council of Australia, Nick Stump, telling a Parliament House press conference that the 1993 Native Title Act could not deliver 'workable' results for 'time-sensitive' mineral investments. The Howard government formulated a 'ten point plan', the *Native Title Amendment Act 1998 (Cth)*, to bring certainty to land ownership in Australia. The legislation, opposed by the Australian Labor Party and the Australian Democrats, was passed with amendments to gain the support of independent senator Brian Harradine.

Willowra Formerly a pastoral lease but now a community under the Wirliyatjarra Land Trust, situated approximately 300 km north of Alice Springs.

Woodapulli Outstation in the Victoria Daly Shire located in the Katherine region of the Northern Territory.

Woodgreen Station 150 km north-north-east of Alice Springs in Anmatyerre country.

Wurli Wurlinjang Health Service Aboriginal-run health service based in Katherine.

Yarrabah Aboriginal community 10 km (50 km by road) east of Cairns.

Yirrkala Aboriginal community on the Gove Peninsula in Arnhem Land, located 15 km from the town of Nhulunbuy and 655 km (over 1,000 km by road) from Darwin.

Peter Yu Yawuru man from Broome, Western Australia, and former executive director of the Kimberley Land Council.

Yuendumu Large remote community in Central Australia situated 260 km north-west of Alice Springs.

Yulara Town in the MacDonnell region of the Northern Territory, 20 km north of Uluru and 220 km west of Alice Springs.

Galarrwuy Yunupingu AM Gumatj clan leader, Indigenous leader and former chairman of the Northern Land Council who has been involved in the fight for land rights throughout his career.

Smithy Zimran ('Kumantjayi') Great Pintupi leader from Kintore in the Western Desert of Central Australia. Initial chairman of the Combined Aboriginal Nations of Central Australia, former executive member of the Central Land Council, campaigner for Aboriginal rights, and fundraiser for much-needed Aboriginal-controlled dialysis treatment in Central Australia.

Contributor Biographies

Ross Ainsworth is a veterinarian with forty years of experience in the Australian and Southeast Asian cattle industry. His experience ranges from government and private veterinary practice and cattle station management, to CEO of the Northern Territory Livestock Exporters Association. He currently lives in Indonesia with bases in Jakarta and the province of Lampung (South Sumatra).

Lesley Alford is an environmental consultant who worked for the Central Land Council for seven years, and has spent the last few decades working for land management in the Top End of the Northern Territory, and is actively involved in the Rapid Creek Land Care Group.

Chris Athanasiou is a barrister who has represented many Aboriginal groups on Native Title issues and developing agreements, and was a former manager and principal legal officer of the Central Land Council's Native Title Unit.

Geoffrey Bagshaw is an anthropologist who has for many years worked for Aboriginal land councils on Aboriginal land and native title claims across Australia.

Rodger Barnes worked as the mining manager in the Central Land Council for more than twenty years, where he was responsible for obtaining informed group decisions of traditional Aboriginal landowners over exploration and mining proposals as well as ensuring fair and reasonable agreements over land access under the Aboriginal Land Rights Act and Native Title Act. He has completed a Masters of Philosophy, developed projects with the Centre of Social Responsibility in Mining, University of Queensland, and is now based in Ethiopia where he works in capacity building and advisory roles on social performance in the extractives sector.

Lois Bartram worked as a nursing sister and house mother on Croker Island Mission, and then during the late 1960s and early 1970s for the internal refugees of Laos during the Secret War of widespread American bombing of that country and removal of people in the years of the Vietnam War.

Bob Beadman lives in Darwin, and is a veteran of Aboriginal affairs in Australia, and in the Northern Territory. He was the Northern Territory Government's inaugural co-ordinator general for remote services, and has worked, written and spoken extensively on the issues of Aboriginal affairs policy of over more than fifty years.

Nick Bolkus is a former Australian Labor Party politician. He was a senator from 1981 to 2005 representing the state of South Australia, a member of Cabinet, and held several ministerial positions.

Sean Bowden is a Darwin lawyer. Over his career he has been involved in many of the larger projects and regional development initiatives in the Northern Territory and nationally. He has advised a range of interest groups and stakeholders including peak Aboriginal groups and representatives, major mining companies and government. He has been involved at a grassroots level on behalf of representative Indigenous organisations in the development of remote Aboriginal communities, with a particular emphasis on economic development.

Lloyd 'Lyodie' Bray was a strong Arrernte man, leader, and legend in Alice Springs AFL football.

Laurie Brereton (Laurence John) is a former Australian politician who was a state minister, a federal member of Cabinet, and Labor member of the Australian House of Representatives from 1990 to 2004 representing the Division of Kingsford Smith, New South Wales.

Andrew Chalk is a Brisbane barrister who has represented many Aboriginal nations of the Gulf of Carpentaria in their native title claims, and has advised Aboriginal land councils and representative bodies throughout Australia over many years.

Geoff Clark is a Kirrae Whurrong man, an Australian Aboriginal politician, and has been an activist on human rights for most of his life. He was part of the Aboriginal working group into the development of the United Nations Declaration on the Rights of Indigenous Peoples, and previously led the Aboriginal and Torres Strait Islander Commission (ATSIC) from 1999 until 2004. He is a member of the working party established with the 2017 Uluru Statement from the Heart.

Owen Cole has family ties with the Warumungu and Luritja peoples of Central Australia. He is an economist and the managing director of the Yeperenye Shopping Centre, and had also worked with the Aboriginal Development Commission, ATSIC and the Central Land Council.

Allan Cooney is a rural industries developer specialising in business development and management, executive management and leadership in large scale agriculture. He was the first general manager of Centrefarm Aboriginal Horticulture Limited. In 2013 he led the Australian Antarctic Division's Casey station. He is the chief executive officer of the Livestock and Property Marketing network TopX Australia.

CONTRIBUTOR BIOGRAPHIES

Nicole Courtman is the Registrar of the Aboriginal Land Rights Act 1983 in NSW, and deputy CEO of the National Centre of Indigenous Excellence (NCIE), University of Sydney.

Greg Crough is an executive director at Ernst Young based in New York. He had previously worked as the chief economist in the International Tax Division of the Australian Taxation Office, and had also worked for Aboriginal people in the Northern Territory.

Steve Ellis has worked for the Central Land Council's regional services for many years. He has specialist knowledge and experience in land management and the cattle industry in Northern Australia.

Martin Ferguson (Martin John) AM is an Australian politician, and an Australian Labor Party member of the Australian House of Representatives from 1996 to 2013 representing the Division of Batman, Victoria.

Vincent Forrester is a member of the Luritja and Arrernte language groups of Central Australia. He is prominent political activist, artist and community leader, and founding member of a number of Aboriginal organisations in Central Australia, and was the Northern Territory Chairman of the National Aboriginal Conference. He lived at Mutitjulu where he was the chairman of the community council and developed a cultural tourism venture. He continues to campaign against the Intervention, and he is a member of the working party established with the 2017 Uluru Statement from the Heart.

Gerry Hand (Gerard Leslie) is a former Australian politician and Labor member of the Australian House of Representatives, representing the seat of Melbourne. He was the Minister for Aboriginal Affairs in the third Hawke ministry, and then Minister for Immigration, Local Government and Ethnic Affairs in the fourth Hawke ministry and first Keating ministry.

Peter Hansen was born at Yuendumu, and has family ties with the Warlpiri people of Central Australia. When he was a child he was taken away from his family in Central Australia, and grew up on Croker Island Mission. He continues to live and work in Jabiru where he has lived for many years.

Bill Heffernan (William Daniel) is a former federal Australian politician, who was a Liberal Party member of the Senate, representing the state of New South Wales from 1996 to 2016.

Forrest Holder was a senior project officer working on land acquisition and resource agreements in the Policy Directorate of the Central Land Council. He studied economics and had previously worked underground in mines. He now lives on Kangaroo Island.

Richie Howitt is a professor in the Department of Geography and Planning, Macquarie University. His research focuses on Indigenous rights and the interface between Indigenous communities, natural resource development, governments and corporations. He has worked for Aboriginal people across Australia for many years.

Jacqui Katona is a member of the Djok clan located within Kakadu National Park. She received the Australian Conservation Foundation's 1997 Peter Rawlinson Environmental Award, and with senior traditional owner of the Mirarr people Yvonne Margarula, she is the recipient of the 1999 Godman Prize for their campaign against mining in the fragile landscape of Jabiluka. Jacqui is an honorary postdoctoral associate in Human Geography with Macquarie University, and is studying law at the University of Melbourne.

Bob Katter (Robert Carl Jnr) is an Australian federal politician, a member of the Australian House of Representatives since 1993 for the Division of Kennedy, and the leader of the Katter's Australian Party. Prior to his election to federal politics he was a member of the Legislative Assembly of Queensland from 1974–1992 for the National Party, and held various ministerial portfolios between 1983–1989.

Tim 'Snowy' Lander lives and works in Central Australia. He has specialist knowledge and experience in land management and the cattle industry in Northern Australia. He ran a remote conservation property about 400 kilometres south-west of Alice Springs and had reintroduced emus to this land to help with the quandong crop, and he was involved in creating opportunities for young people to work out bush.

John Liddle is a member of the Arrernte and Pertame language groups in Central Australia and has been involved in improving Indigenous health for thirty-six years. He was the director of the Central Australian Aboriginal Congress for many years, and established the Ingkintja Male Health services to Aboriginal males through Central Australia, and was instrumental in facilitating Male Health Summits in 2008 and 2010, and continues to lobby for better health services for Indigenous men.

Lawrie Liddle is a member of the Arrernte and Pertame language groups in Central Australia, educated in Victoria, and worked in the cattle industry for his family and contract mustering. He worked for the Central Land Council for many years as a co-ordinator for the Anmatyerre region in the mid-north of Central Australia.

Ian Manning is the Deputy Executive Director of National Economics, National Institute of Economic and Industry Research based in Melbourne.

Michael Mansell is a Palawa, Trawlwoolway, and Pinterrairer man from Tasmania. He is an Aboriginal political leader and lawyer who has worked continuously for social, political and legal changes for Aboriginal people. He and others set up the Tasmanian Aboriginal Centre in the 1970s which he was the chairman and legal manager throughout most of its history, and he is the long standing secretary of the Aboriginal Provisional Government. He is providing legal advice to Aboriginal people across Australia on treaties, and his latest book is *Treaty and Statehood: Aboriginal Self-determination*.

Tony McGrady (Anthony) was an Australian politician for the Australian Labor Party, as the Member for Mount Isa to the Legislative Assembly of Queensland, and held the Ministry for Mines and Energy 1998–2001, and Police and Corrective Services 2001, State Development and Innovation 2004, and Speaker of the Legislative Assembly 2005–6. He was a longstanding mayor of Mount Isa and is now retired.

Daryl Melham AM, a barrister and solicitor, is a former Australian politician and Labor member of the Australian House of Representatives representing the Division of Banks in New South Wales from 1990 to 2013, and a former Shadow Minister for Aboriginal and Torres Strait Islander Affairs.

Sam Miles is an agronomist with more than forty years of experience in community development, regional, business and strategic planning in the Northern Territory. He is a key strategist in Centrefarm Aboriginal Horticulture Limited since his engagement by the Central Land Council in 1999–2000 to undertake an economic development consultancy.

Chippy Miller (Louis) is an Arrernte man who was born in Alice Springs and a first cousin to Tracker Tilmouth, a former member of the board of directors of the Central Australia Aboriginal Congress, the former regionalization co-ordinator at AMSANT (Aboriginal Medical Services Alliance Northern Territory) in the Northern Territory.

Nathan Miller is a Melbourne documentary photographer originally from Tel Aviv, Israel, and was the marketing manager of Netafim in Australia. He is originally from Israel and immigrated to Australia with his family in 1989.

Dave Murray managed the Amoonguna Aboriginal community abattoir, and with Tracker Tilmouth co-developed and instigated a vertically integrated program to supply meat from Aboriginal pastoral lands to communities in Central Australia.

James Nugent is the principal legal officer in the Central Land Council and has lived in Alice Springs for many years.

Michael O'Connor is the National Secretary of the CFMEU (Construction, Forestry, Mining and Energy Union).

David Ross has family ties to the Kaytetye people of Central Australia. He joined the Central Land Council in 1979, and has been its director since 2000. He was a Commissioner of ATSIC for two years from 1994, the chairman of the Indigenous Land Corporation from 1995 to 1999, and has held a number of key positions, including as chairman of the board of management of the Centre for Indigenous Natural and Cultural Resource Management at the Northern Territory University, and is a member of the South Australian Museum Board Aboriginal Advisory Group.

Toly Sawenko worked in Central Australia for many years in fields of education, health, research and community development. He helped to establish the Urapuntja Aboriginal Health Service in the Utopia homelands region. He also worked for the Central Land Council in a number of roles including land claim research, regional office management, and economic development, notably the creation of Centrefarm Aboriginal Horticulture Limited.

Danny Schwartz is a long-time property developer from Melbourne, and businessman who has some involvement with Aboriginal people and leadership across Australia.

Julie-Anne Stoll had experience from apricot cutting and grape picking in the Barossa, to nursing. A geology degree and Master in Environmental Studies led to a move to the Northern Territory and the Central Land Council in 1990, starting as environmental officer, then mining officer and senior mining officer, then manager of mining. She went for a three-year stint, and stayed twenty-seven years – an exciting job, interesting people, unique cultural setting, special relationships, stunning country, good rocks.

Ellen Stubbens has family ties with the Arrernte people from Central Australia, and worked for many years with the Central Land Council and the Central Australian Aboriginal Congress.

William and Patrick (Michael) Tilmouth are the brothers of Tracker Tilmouth. Patrick was a great family man who worked as a painter across the Northern Territory. Sadly Patrick passed away in 2016. William was the executive director of Tangentyere Council from 1988 to 2010, and the regional chair of the Central Australian ATSIC. He is the founding chair of Children's Ground, and has been the president of the Central Australia Aboriginal Congress since 2012.

Phillip Toyne AO was an Australian environmental and Indigenous rights activist, lawyer, author, and founder of Landcare Australia. He was the head of the Australian Conservation Foundation from 1986 to 1992, and negotiated the Pitjatjantjara Land Rights Act, and the successful land rights claim of the traditional owners of Uluru in 1983.

Doug Turner is from the Nukunu community of the southern Flinders Ranges of South Australia and is Kokatha on his father's side, and connected to Yankunytjatjara, Pitjantjatjara, Arrernte and Warlpiri language groups. He has lived and worked in Central Australia for many years and travelled all over the remote communities. He is a natural resource scientist, holds a MA in teaching, and now works as a lecturer with the College of Medicine at Flinders University.

Gordon Williams is from the Djugun tribe of Broome in Western Australia. As a five-year-old he was taken away from his mother and sent to Beagle Bay Mission.

He worked as ringer, crocodile hunter, truck driver, and as a labourer. In 1970, he started working for the Department of Aboriginal Affairs in Docker River, and through to Tennant Creek, Batchelor, and Alice Springs, then the ADC. He worked for the Central Land Council for many years based at Mutitjulu. In retirement, Gordon is a gold hunter with a metal detector.

Murrandoo Yanner is the chairperson of the Gangalidda and Garawa Native Title Aboriginal Corporation (CGNTAC), director of the Carpentaria Land Council, and the director of the Gulf Region Aboriginal Corporation (GRAC) in the Gulf of Carpentaria.

Acknowledgements

Tracker was the one who made us look more, and work harder. Our special friend always. Strong in my heart is his great gift of giving precious time to me in his last years to work on this book.

I would like to especially acknowledge and say thank you to all of the contributors for their generosity in helping to weave this monumental tribute to Tracker with the rich threads of their stories, memories and insights.

The journey of this book begun when my publisher and mentor Ivor Indyk persuaded me to focus in, by reminding me of the writing that I had always wanted to do with Tracker, and to make this book become a reality. What a waste it would have been if this time had been lost.

The Writing and Society Research Centre at Western Sydney University always gave this work enormous support, especially Anthony Uhlmann, Suzanne Gapps, and our dean, Peter Hutchings. Thank you for your kindness and generosity of spirit.

The Australia Research Council's support made such a large project possible, and I thank you for sharing the vision of this important man's contribution to the life of this country.

Thank you Jenni Whyte for your prompt transcriptions of hours of recordings, and for your patience to find the words caught in the wind, and other noisy background interference.

There were many, many people who helped with queries, gave correct spelling of language words, helped locate people from one end of the country to the other, and answered many other questions. Thank you for sharing your great wealth of knowledge. It is as always an honour and privilege to know you.

A special thank you to Cathryn Tilmouth for helping enormously with research work, locating information and for gathering family photos. Thank you to all the Tilmouth family, Lois Bartram, the Central Land Council, Neva Collings, Emily Hansen, Maggie Urban and Lesley Alford for contributing photos from their collections.

Holly Gallagher and Sophia Barnes, thank you for providing support for the final production of the book. And thank you to Ben Juers for the beautiful illustration of Tracker's Akubra.

The beauty of this book is the masterful work of Ivor Indyk, Nick Tapper and Harry Williamson. Thank you.

This book would not have been possible without the generous support of Kathy, Shaneen, Cathryn, and Amanda, and the Tilmouth family's guidance and courage. Thank you.

Thank you Toly for sharing the journey of memories and stories of our great friend. And special appreciation to my daughters Tate and Lily.

The holes in this book are the missing stories of hundreds of people who knew Tracker. You can go anywhere in this country and there will always be someone with a great story to tell about Tracker, of something he said or did. Keep sharing those stories. Embellish them. Make his stories your own story. Most of all, be the story. That is what he would have wanted.

Tracker's story is like the country itself. Far bigger than one book, and as he would have said, *We are only getting started here Wrighty.*

The research undertaken for this project was funded by the Australian Government through the Australian Research Council.

The publication of this project has been assisted by the Commonwealth Government through the Australia Council, its arts funding and advisory body.

The Giramondo Publishing Company is grateful for the support given to its publishing program by Western Sydney University.

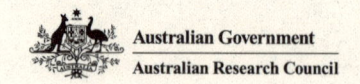